Drugs and Society:

A Critical Reader
Second Edition

Maureen E. Kelleher

Bruce K. Mac Murray

Thomas M. Shapiro

Northeastern University

KENDALL/HUNT PUBLISHING COMPANY

2460 Kerper Boulevard   P.O. Box 539   Dubuque, Iowa 52004-0539

to Bert,
to Barbara, Nicholas and Benjamin
to Joe and Adelle

Contents

Preface

The Second Edition of *Drugs and Society: A Critical Reader* explores the sociological issues revolving around American drug use and abuse. The readings are selected because of the range of issues they cover and their theoretical orientation. We emphasize the idea that labeling, power and conflict play important roles in the assessment of drug behavior.

A number of basic sociological themes are presented in the text. Included among these themes are: the role of societal definitions and social responses to drugs, cultural and subcultural issues, and the development of deviant classes of users. The material used to illustrate such topics ranges from socio-historical research and sociological theory and research to current popular media presentations.

The first section of the book lays the sociological groundwork. From this foundation, the reader explores a wide scope of issues either unique to particular drugs or that crossover into numerous drug domains. Alcohol, tobacco, marijuana, heroin, cocaine, amphetamines and psychedelics are all discussed at length. In addition, selections about the drug industry—legal and illegal—and treatment issues are included in the text.

The book attempts to come to grips with a gamut of drugs. The sociological orientation does not emphasize individual pharmacological effects, but rather broader issues about drugs that affect the everyday social life of us all.

We would like to thank members of the Department of Sociology and Anthropology, Northeastern University, for their support and interest while this project was underway.

We would in particular like to thank Kevin Mulvey and Claudia Toole for bibliographic and research assistance. The typing assistance of Kathryn Owen and Trude Lawrence is also greatly appreciated.

Introduction

A Sociological Perspective on Drugs

This book, *Drugs and Society: A Critical Reader,* examines drugs and their place in contemporary American society. As sociologists, we focus our interests less on the pharmacological effects of drugs and more on the process of defining what role particular drugs play in our own individual behavior as well as broader social life. From this perspective, emphasis is placed upon the role of power in the development of both individual attitudes and a national posture toward particular drugs. The focus of this reader, therefore, highlights a very explicit set of concerns including: 1) societal definitions and responses to drugs, 2) how political and ideological climates affect the availability of certain drugs and social policies developed to deal with them, 3) the processes of prohibition, legalization and decriminalization for drugs and their use, 4) cultural and subcultural aspects of drug use, 5) the legitimate and illegitimate business of buying and selling drugs, and 6) the creation of deviant and criminal classes of drug users.

Defining Drug Effects and Drug Problems

Drugs in contemporary American society serve as a lightning rod for both public opinion and political posturing. To be against drug abuse, in this sense, is to take a stand upholding America's traditional standards of morality. But what is drug abuse and what is the nature of America's drug problem today?

One approach to this issue suggests that drug problems exist when users become addicted or dependent upon particular substances. There are several logical inconsistencies with the application of this position in practice, however. First, although some illegal drugs do produce clearcut physiologically based tolerance and addiction (for example, heroin and the other opiates), other illicit substances, such as marijuana and the psychedelics, do not. Second, several of the legal drugs also produce physical addiction with long term use (e.g., alcohol and tobacco). Third, some medical prescription drugs are addictive (for example, the barbiturates and minor tranquilizers), yet they also remain legal. Furthermore, addiction to these various substances also results in quite different societal responses depending upon the social definition of the drug: for example, a criminal justice response in the case of the illegal drugs, a treatment response for the legal drugs and a supply solution for the prescriptive drugs.

A somewhat different approach emphasizes a concern not with the question of whether or not a given drug is addictive, but with the long-term, negative consequences that result from a user's involvement with drugs. In this view, such concerns as the damaging health effects of tobacco and alcohol, the potentially negative psychological repercussions from the continual use of such drugs as cocaine and the amphetamines, and the social consequences of involvement with the criminal drug world related to heroin, marijuana and the psychedelics must all be taken into account.

The problem with both of these approaches lies in their implications for legislation and social policy for drugs. On the one hand, because all drugs are potentially addictive or dependence-producing on some level (physiological, psychological or social) and because no drug is totally safe without any possible side effects and risks, one can make an argument for the criminalization and banning of any given drug. Of course, such a proposal is not even seriously considered in the United

States today. On the other hand, based upon this same information, one could also propose that particular drug users be targeted and screened as most susceptible to negative drug consequences, for example individuals with convictions for driving while intoxicated, those with particular mental health problems, individuals with a history of family violence or interpersonal abuse, and transportation workers.

Obviously, America's drug problem is not simply an issue of criminal drug abuse. Rather, our drug problem also has a deeper and more hidden dimension involving the abuse of legal and medicinal drugs such as alcohol, tobacco, prescription tranquilizers and diet stimulants. Nor is this country's drug problem limited to any one age group, gender, social class, racial or ethnic group any more than it is restricted to any one drug or category of substances. The problem is that we have become a "drugged society" in which much of our everyday behavior, lifestyle and social activities are oriented around the use of drugs. We learn to believe and act upon a view that drugs can help us face contemporary life. In this way, our very ability to have good times and enjoy ourselves, to work long and hard at a job and to successfully cope with daily stresses and strains, is seen as inextricably intertwined with the use of drugs. Given this situation and knowing that no drug produces *only* positive effects, we should expect and not be surprised that our society has problems with drugs.

Despite this reality, the United States throughout its historical experience with drugs has chosen an approach which seeks to define particular substances as "good" or "bad" (or more or less harmful) in their consequences for individuals and the society generally. The key to this view is the belief that the use of some drugs leads to major social problems, while the use of others is less socially threatening.

The Creation of Drugs as a Social Problem

From a sociological viewpoint, the construction of social drug problems is seen as significantly influenced by collective group behavior and social movements. According to this form of analysis, the process of problem formation is a matter of socially creating a definition of behavior as deviant or societally problematic and then mobilizing political forces to produce some action to resolve the problem.

The emergence of a social problem, however, is seen not as an automatic process, but rather as one which involves the active selection of some particular area of social behavior and the definition of this behavior as troublesome. For America's modern experience with cocaine, for example, early evidence of an increased use of the drug and related increases in cocaine's illegal imports in the 1970's did not touch off a quick response within the legal, medical or social arenas. Rather, the definition of cocaine as a problem drug took place primarily during the 1980's as media exposés began focusing on the phenomenon of "crack" and the experiences of a number of sports and entertainment celebrities (such as John DeLorean, Len Bias, Richard Pryor and John Belushi) and as community leaders, law enforcement personnel, and politicians all pointed to cocaine and its harmful consequences as an important issue for national concern. This "political drug cycle" became further evident in the 1986 Congressional election campaigns. At this time, tremendous attention and rhetoric in Washington focused on new legislation and greater Federal funding to get tough on drugs; after the elections, however, the Administration imposed large budget cuts upon programs specifically devoted to drug enforcement, education and treatment, with no resulting furor either on Capitol Hill or in the media.

The Formulation of Social Policy for Drugs

Once a social situation has become defined and legitimated as a problem demanding public attention, collective concern turns to finding the appropriate means of mobilizing action to deal with the problem. In the case of cocaine, such an approach has come primarily in terms of three loosely related activities which form the core of drug policy in the United States: (1) a visible and professedly aggressive criminal drug enforcement initiative, which aims to increase pressure both on those who deal in coke domestically as well as through efforts to help curb supplies of the drug coming into the U.S. via international trafficking; (2) campaigns designed at various levels to better inform and educate the general public about the effects and dangers of cocaine use; and (3) public service advertising efforts to get help for users through the establishment of cocaine hot lines and via referrals to appropriate treatment clinics.

Although there is a clarion call of consensus about the dangers of cocaine and evidence that these efforts may have been somewhat successful in reducing the usage patterns for cocaine, at least for youths (Johnston, et. al., 1988), the case of cocaine is also instructive in another sense. For at precisely the same time that social policy efforts have been ongoing to control and deter illegal cocaine imports and domestic distribution and use of the drug, the Federal government has also been very divided over the foreign policy issue of international drug trafficking. Indeed, the administration has been quite reluctant to expose or take any other action regarding the involvement of top Latin American officials in the cocaine trade, allegedly because of national security interests.

Recent Drug Usage Patterns in America

In 1983, when we put together the first edition of this book, we noted the upward trend in the use of many licit and illicit drugs during the decade of the 1970's by America's young people (those under the age of 25). Since that time, research conducted at the University of Michigan (Johnston, et. al., 1988) indicates that drug use among this population has generally stabilized and in some cases even declined somewhat. Declines in drug use were specifically observed for marijuana, the stimulants, sedatives and methaqualone. The drop in current drug use for both cocaine and marijuana has apparently occurred in conjunction with a related increase in the perceived harmfulness and potential dangerousness of these drugs. In addition, however, little change has taken place in the use of LSD as well as for heroin and other opiates, with some suggestion of an increase in the use of inhalants.

At the same time, the usage patterns for such licit drugs as alcohol and tobacco also remain stable for this population. Particularly disturbing in this regard is the finding that young people report usage rates for these drugs which are very similar to those found for adults. For example in the case of alcohol, the Johnston, et. al. research (1988) reports that the vast majority of high school seniors have had some experience with alcohol and two-thirds have used alcohol within the past month. Further, approximately 5% of this youth population are daily drinkers with over one-third reporting one or more heavy drinking episodes (consisting of the consumption of five or more drinks in a row) within the past two weeks. For cigarettes, nearly a fifth of all high school seniors are already daily smokers, the majority of whom began smoking by the age of 13.[1]

Thus, although the usage patterns among young people for some selected drugs is on the decline, the pattern for other drugs is stable, often at relatively high usage levels. Overall, the majority of high school seniors have tried an illicit drug at some point in their life, with over a third having used an illegal drug other than marijuana and almost one-half having used such a substance in the past year. As the University of Michigan researchers note, these rates are clearly the highest of any country in the industrialized world. There is some cause for cautious optimism about the recent declining trend in the use of illicit drugs by American youth. However, this view must be tempered with the recognition that the usage patterns for both licit and illicit drugs still remain quite high and that America, as a "drugged society," is currently raising a new generation of drug users.

This book examines a number of different themes and issues related to the American experience with drugs. The first chapter lays out a sociological perspective on drugs. These readings present a range of theoretical views, all of which emphasize the importance of social factors and consequences in understanding drug effects and social policy, above and beyond strictly pharmacological concerns. Chapter 2 focuses on the business of drugs. The articles in this chapter suggest the "good guy/bad guy" dichotomy typically associated with the distinction between illicit versus licit and prescription drug transactions is overly simplistic. Instead, a view which takes note of the particular social costs involved in the legal business of selling and dispensing drugs as well as the problems associated with the "black market" for illegal drugs is offered. The third chapter takes up the specific user group of women, their status as a target group for legal and medicinal drugs in particular and the consequent situation by which women form a major victim group for drug related problems. Chapters 4 through 8 present a discussion of the specific drugs categories of alcohol, tobacco, marijuana and the psychedelics, heroin, cocaine and the amphetamines. The final chapter examines issues related to the treatment and social policy of drug problems and some of the differing approaches available which attempt to deal with drug problems.

In closing, let us restate that this reader endorses a particular interpretation of the various roles that drugs serve in American society. In line with this position, we are hopeful that this selection of articles helps promote a better awareness of the many dimensions to our country's current drug situation and furthers the critical examination of the sources and potential solutions to these drug problems.

Notes

1. Lloyd D. Johnston, Patrick M. O'Malley and Jerald G. Bachman, "Illicit Drug Use, Smoking, and Drinking by America's High School Students, College Students, and Young Adults, 1975–1987." National Institute on Drug Abuse (forthcoming).

Chapter I
The Sociology of Drugs

The first chapter of this reader offers an introduction to the sociological perspective on drugs and their relationship to human social behavior. Crucial to this sociological view is a concern with the social context of drugs, their social definition, and related cultural attitudes, laws and social policies about the appropriate role of drugs in society. This chapter begins to frame the discussion of these issues by examining the important role that social factors play in the definition of problems related to the use of drugs and how society responds to such problems through the creation and modification of laws and attitudes regulating drug use.

The first article by David Musto illustrates that the controversy about drugs and their social use is by no means a strictly contemporary phenomenon. Musto's analysis indicates that concern about questions of health, as well as moral and legal issues related to drugs, have been discussed for over a century in American society. Indeed, as Musto notes, the original "discovery" of U.S. drug problems and early efforts to cope with these problems are in many ways similar to the present day situation.

Gusfield's article examines social aspects of the criminalization of drugs, focusing on what he terms the "symbolic crusade" in the development of prohibition against alcohol. A key component to understanding this social movement in Gusfield's view is the particular value orientation and interests of social groups concerning the morality of alcohol, those who consume it, and its proper place (or lack thereof) in respectable American society. The Galliher, McCartney and Baum article, in contrast, provides a more contemporary example taking up the decriminalization of marijuana penalties during the 1970's. Using the case of Nebraska as an illustrative example, these authors discuss the many different agendae and political factors that play a part in formulating and revising criminal drug legislation.

The article by Zinberg and Harding addresses the important concepts of "set" and "setting" for drug use and emphasizes the flexibility and diversity that characterizes the drug effects experienced by human beings. According to these authors, providing a full understanding and explanation of drug behavior requires going beyond a sole focus on the pharmacology and biology of a drug and its user to a view which includes the social situation, expectations and supporting definitions for drugs and their use. The concluding piece by Jock Young suggests that much of what we as citizens commonly perceive and take for granted as drug problems today are the result of a process of problem creation framed by the media's coverage of drug issues. Young argues that the risk in adopting such a view is that it suffers from biases which serve to misdirect attention toward individual, high profile cases and away from the larger reality of a society's drug problems.

This beginning chapter introduces the reader to a sociological perspective on drugs through a consideration of how social factors serve to define the expectations and effects of drugs for users, create societal awareness of problems related to drug use and shape public policy designed to help prevent and cope with these drug problems.

1. The American Disease: Narcotics in Nineteenth-Century America

David F. Musto

Before 1800, opium was available in America in its crude form as an ingredient of multidrug prescriptions, or in such extracts as laudanum, containing alcohol, or "black drop," containing no alcohol. Valued for its calming and soporific effects, opium was also a specific against symptoms of gastrointestinal illnesses such as cholera, food poisoning, and parasites. Its relatively mild psychological effect when taken by mouth or as part of a more complex prescription was enhanced by frequent use, and the drug was supplied freely by physicians. In addition, self-dosing with patent medicines and the ministrations of quacks contributed to narcotic intake. The medical profession's need for something that worked in a world of mysterious mortal diseases and infections cannot be overlooked as a major stimulus for the growth of the opium market. A drug that calmed was especially appealing since physicians could at least treat the patient's anxiety.

Technological advances in organic chemistry during the early nineteenth century led to plentiful supplies of potent habit-forming drugs. Alkaloids in crude opium were separated and crystallized to isolate active principles that give opium its physiological and psychic effects. Analysis of the coca leaf occurred in mid-century, and cocaine was finally isolated.[1]

Opium and Its Derivatives

Morphine grew in popularity as its great power over pain became better appreciated. It was cheap, compact, and had a standard strength—unlike tinctures of other forms of opium extracted from the crude plant. When the hypodermic needle became popular in the middle of the century it permitted direct injection into the body of a powerful, purified substance. Of the many substances injected experimentally, morphine was found to be exceptionally effective as a pain-killer and calming agent, and it came into medical practice after the Civil War. Writers have remarked on the coincidence to explain the apparent frequency of addiction in the United States in the latter half of the century.[2] Of course, this line of reasoning does not explain the relatively few addicts proportionally or absolutely in such nations as France, Germany, Great Britain, Russia, and Italy, which also fought wars during the latter half of the nineteenth century and also used morphine as an analgesic.

Whatever the cause, a relatively high level of opium consumption was established in the United States during the nineteenth century. This appetite for narcotics calls for some examination if only because opiate addiction has been described in the United States as "un-American" and "non-Western."[3]

Because opium has not been commercially grown to any great extent in America, the national supply was imported. Before 1915 (1909 for smoking opium) no restriction other than a tariff was placed upon importation, and except for opium for smoking, these tariffs were modest. Tariff records reveal the demand for opium and opiates during most of the nineteenth and early twentieth centuries. It is reasonable to assume that smuggling did not severely modify the overall trends of opium importation, because the period of free entry (1890–96) did not dramatically alter the importation curve. The imported opium was mostly crude, although it did include opium prepared for smoking. The United States exported almost no manufactured opiates before World War I because European drugs undersold them on the world market.[4]

Crude opium contained an estimated 9 percent morphine content extractable by American pharmaceutical concerns. One of the largest morphine-producing firms in the nineteenth century, Rosengarten and Company of Philadelphia (later merged into what is now Merck, Sharpe and Dohme), began manufacturing morphine salts in 1832. The first statistics on the importation of opium date from 1840 and reveal a continual increase in consumption during the rest of the century. The per capita importation of crude opium reached its peak in 1896. The Civil War, far from initiating opiate use on a large scale in the United States, hardly makes a ripple in its constantly expanding consumption, but addicted Civil War veterans, a group of unknown size, may have spread addiction by recruiting other users. Although there is some reduction in crude opium imports during 1861–65, presumably due to the blockade of the South, the amounts imported within a few years before and after the war are very similar. The rapid rise in crude opium did not begin until the 1870s; then it quickly outstripped the annual increase in population. Morphine did not begin to be imported in great amounts until the late 1870s.[5] Another cause of increased consumption was the widespread use of opiates by physicians and manufacturers of patent medicines during a period when there was little fear of their use. The unregulated patent medicine craze in the United States hit its peak in the late nineteenth century—a time when the opiate content in those medicines was probably also at its highest.

The characteristics of opium and its derivatives were ideal for the patent medicine manufacturers. There was no requirement that patent medicines containing opiates be so labeled in interstate commerce until the Pure Food and Drug Act of 1906. Many proprietary medicines that could be bought at any store or by mail order contained morphine, cocaine, laudanum, or (after 1898) heroin. Attempts at state regulation of sales were not successful during the last century.[6] Even "cures" for the opium habit frequently contained large amounts of opiates. Hay fever remedies commonly contained cocaine as their active ingredient, Coca-Cola, until 1903, contained cocaine (and since then caffeine).[7] Opiates and cocaine became popular—if unrecognized—items in the everyday life of Americans. The manufacturers were remarkably effective during the nineteenth century in preventing any congressional action to require even the disclosure of dangerous drugs in commercial preparations.[8]

After 1896, the per capita importation of crude opium gradually began to decline and, just before prohibitive laws rendered the importation statistics valueless, had fallen to the level of the 1880s. That level was not low, but consumption did drop as agitation mounted for strict controls. One traditional opium import which did not decline after 1900 was smoking opium, in spite of its holding no special interest for prescribing physicians, patent medicine manufacturers, or wounded Civil War veterans. Smoking opium, solely a pastime, lacked any of the elaborate advertising campaigns which boosted morphine and cocaine preparations; it had had a slow but steady rise in per capita consumption since import statistics began in 1860.[9] Suddenly in 1909 smoking opium was excluded from the United States. Weighing heavily against it was its symbolic association since mid-century with the Chinese, who were actively persecuted, especially on the West Coast. By then they were almost totally excluded from immigrating into the United States.

The prohibition of smoking opium also served notice to other nations that America was determined to rid itself of the evils of addiction. In 1909 the United States convened the first international meeting to consider opium traffic between nations, specifically that traffic into China which was so unwelcome to the Chinese government. Although motivation for American initiative in the Chinese problem was a mixture of moral leadership, protection of U.S. domestic welfare, and a desire to soften up Chinese resistance to American financial investments, the United States was also led by the nature of the narcotic trade to seek control of international shipments of crude narcotics to manufacturing countries and thence to markets. But the United States, on the eve of entering an international conference it had called to help China with its opium problem, discovered it had no national opium restrictions. To save face, it quickly enacted one. American prejudice against the Chinese, and the association of smoking opium with aliens, was in effect an immense aid in securing legislation in the program to help China. Indeed, a prime reason for calling the International Opium Commission was to mollify China's resentment of treatment of Chinese in the United States.

What might explain the pattern of decline of opium importation for consumption in the United States before the Harrison Act in 1914? First would be a growing fear of opiates and especially of morphine addiction, which was marked by the quick spread of antimorphine laws in various states in the 1890s.[10] That opium addiction was undesirable had long been common opinion in the United States. Oliver Wendell Holmes, Sr., in an address delivered just before the Civil War, blamed its prevalence on the ignorance of physicians. Holmes, then dean of Harvard Medical School, reported that in the western United States "the constant prescription of opiates by certain physicians . . . has rendered the habitual use of that drug in that region very prevalent. . . . A frightful endemic demoralization betrays itself in the frequency with which the haggard features and drooping shoulders of the opium drunkards are met with in the street."

As the century progressed and the hypodermic injection of opiates increased their physiological effect, the danger of morphine addiction was more widely broadcast. For this reason patent medicine makers resisted attempts to require the listing of ingredients on labels. The knowledge that such substances were in baby soothing syrups and other compounds would hurt sales. Nevertheless growing publicity disclosing the contents of patent medicines, early regulatory laws in the states, and public opinion all worked together as forces to curb this use of opiates and cocaine.

Another possible explanation, although untestable, is that the opiates had nearly saturated the market for such drugs: that is, those who were environmentally or biochemically disposed to opiates had been fairly well located by the marketers and the consumption curve leveled off as the demand was met. Such reasoning could apply also to a product like cigarettes, the use of which grew at a fantastic rate with the beginning of World War I but eventually leveled off in per capita consumption: although they are easily available not everyone desires to smoke them.

The numbers of those overusing opiates must have increased during the nineteenth century as the per capita importation of crude opium increased from less than 12 grains annually in the 1840s to more than 52 grains in the 1890s.[11] Eventually the medical consensus was that morphine had been overused by the physician, addiction was a substantial possibility, and addition of narcotics to patent medicines should be minimized or stopped. There is reason to emphasize the gradual development of this medical opinion since physicians, as well as everyone else, had what now seems a very delayed realization that dangerously addicting substances were distributed with little worry for their effect. Cocaine and heroin were both introduced from excellent laboratories by men with considerable clinical experience who judged them to be relatively harmless, in fact, to be possible cures for morphine and alcohol addiction.[12]

By 1900, America had developed a comparatively large addict population, perhaps 250,000, along with a fear of addiction and addicting drugs.[13] This fear had certain elements which have been powerful enough to permit the most profoundly punitive methods to be employed in the fight against addicts and suppliers. For at least seventy years purveyors of these drugs for nonmedical uses have been branded "worse than murderers," in that destroying the personality is worse than simply killing the body. What is most human is what is destroyed in the drug habitués, the opponents of narcotics argued.

In the nineteenth century addicts were identified with foreign groups and internal minorities who were already actively feared and the objects of elaborate and massive social and legal restraints. Two repressed groups which were associated with the use of certain drugs were the Chinese and the Negroes. The Chinese and their custom of opium smoking were closely watched after their entry into the United States about 1870. At first, the Chinese represented only one more group brought in to help build railroads, but, particularly after economic depression made them a labor surplus and a threat to American citizens, many forms of antagonism arose to drive them out or at least to isolate them. Along with this prejudice came a fear of opium smoking as one of the ways in which the Chinese were supposed to undermine American society.[14]

Cocaine was especially feared in the South by 1900 because of its euphoric and stimulating properties. The South feared that Negro cocaine users might become oblivious of their prescribed bounds and attack white society.[15] Morphine did not become so closely associated with an ethnic minority, perhaps because from its inception it was considered a simple substitute for medicinal opium and suitable for all classes. When opiates began to be feared for their addictive properties, morphine was most closely attached to the "lower classes" or the "underworld," but without greater specificity.[16]

The crusade for alcohol prohibition which culminated in the adoption of the 18th Amendment started in the South and West early in this century. Intrastate Prohibition weighed most heavily on the poor since, until the Webb-Kenyon Act of 1913, it was quite legal to purchase liquor in bulk from wet states for shipment into dry states. When poor southerners, and particularly Negroes, were alleged to turn to cola drinks laced with cocaine or to cocaine itself for excitement as a result of liquor scarcity, more laws against cocaine quickly followed. Here, however, the South was at a loss for comprehensive legal control since the goal was to prohibit interstate as well as intrastate shipment. This could be done only with a federal statute which would threaten the states' police and commerce powers. Consequently, the story of the Harrison Act's passage contains many examples of the South's fear of the Negro as a ground for permitting a deviation from strict interpretation of the Constitution.

Cocaine

Cocaine is a good example of a drug whose dangers became widely accepted although at first it was immensely popular. It was pure, cheap, and widely distributed; its advocates distrusted not only the opinions of their opponents but also their motivation. Cocaine users were so impressed by its euphoric properties that they were unable to evalue the drug objectively.

Cocaine achieved popularity in the United States as a general tonic, for sinusitis and hay fever, and as a cure for the opium, morphine, and alcohol habits. Learned journals published accounts which just avoided advising unlimited intake of cocaine.[17] Medical entrepreneurs such as the neurologist William Hammond, former surgeon general of the army, swore by it and took a wineglass of it with each meal. He was also proud to announce cocaine as the official remedy of the Hay

Fever Association, a solid endorsement for anyone. . . . Sigmund Freud is perhaps the best-remembered proponent of cocaine as a general tonic and an addiction cure. He wrote several articles in the European medical press on the wonderful substance to which his attention had been drawn by American medical journals.[18]

In the United States the exhilarating properties of cocaine made it a favorite ingredient of medicine, soda pop, wines, and so on. The Parke Davis Company, an exceptionally enthusiastic producer of cocaine, even sold coca-leaf cigarettes and coca cheroots to accompany their other products, which provided cocaine in a variety of media and routes such as a liqueurlike alcohol mixture called Coca Cordial, tablets, hypodermic injections, ointments, and sprays.

If cocaine was a spur to violence against whites in the South, as was generally believed by whites, then reaction against its users made sense. The fear of the cocainized black coincided with the peak of lynchings, legal segregation, and voting laws all designed to remove political and social power from him. Fear of cocaine might have contributed to the dread that the black would rise above "his place," as well as reflecting the extent to which cocaine may have released defiance and retribution. So far, evidence does not suggest that cocaine caused a crime wave but rather that anticipation of black rebellion inspired white alarm. Anecdotes often told of superhuman strength, cunning, and efficiency resulting from cocaine. One of the most terrifying beliefs about cocaine was that it actually improved pistol marksmanship. Another myth, that cocaine made blacks almost unaffected by mere .32 caliber bullets, is said to have caused southern police departments to switch to .38 caliber revolvers. These fantasies characterized white fear, not the reality of cocaine's effects, and gave one more reason for the repression of blacks.[19]

The claim of widespread use of cocaine by Negroes is called into question by the report in 1914 of 2,100 consecutive Negro admissions to a Georgia asylum over the previous five years. The medical director acknowledged the newspaper reports of "cocainomania" among Negroes but was surprised to discover that only two cocaine users—and these incidental to the admitting diagnosis—were hospitalized between 1909 and 1914. He offered an explanation for cocaine disuse among Negroes—that poverty prevented a drug problem equal to that among whites.[20]

The most accepted medical use of cocaine was as a surface anesthetic, for example, on the eye to permit surgery on a conscious patient, or as an injection near a nerve to stop conduction of pain stimuli. When sniffed, cocaine crystals shrink mucous membranes and drain sinuses. Along with sinus drainage, the patient gets a "high." Eventually such substitutes or modifications of cocaine were developed as benzocaine and procaine, which do not have such euphoric effects but are still capable of preventing nerve conduction.

Since cocaine was by no means limited to physicians' prescriptions, the "lower classes," particularly in "dry" states, found they could get a jolt which took the place of hard liquor. Bars began putting a pinch of cocaine in a shot of whiskey and cocaine was peddled door to door. By 1900, state laws and municipal ordinances were being rapidly enacted against these activities. But law-abiding middle and upper-class employers also found practical uses for cocaine; it was reportedly distributed to construction and mine workers to keep them going at a high pitch and with little food.[21] This value of cocaine had been first discovered by the Spanish in sixteenth-century Peru and was put to work among the native slaves who mined silver. Cocaine thus was economically valuable, but the fear of its overstimulating powers among social subgroups predominated, in the United States, and its provision to laborers waned.

State Laws

State laws designed to curb the abuse of morphine and cocaine came mostly in the last decade of the nineteenth century. The realization of "abuse" and its seriousness gradually undermined confidence in simple regulatory laws and led to a determination that decisive action must be taken. Addiction became a challenge to medical and legal institutions. State and municipal laws generally required cocaine or morphine to be ordered on a physician's prescription, which then had to be retained for perhaps a year for inspection. The laws had one great loophole: the patent medicine manufacturers repeatedly obtained exemptions for certain quantities of narcotics in proprietary medicines. These loopholes permitted the narcotized patent medicines to be sold, but the laws lulled the public into believing that this abuse of narcotics was under control. To some extent these lacunary antinarcotic laws did alert the more wary, and manufacturers began to be cautious. But as curbs on the sale of narcotics for nonmedicinal use, the laws were not effective; they were not well enforced because, among other factors, the states did not have sufficient manpower to maintain surveillance.

Although a state might enact an antinarcotic law and even enforce it, bordering states without such laws often provided drugs for users and sellers. New York State reformers bitterly criticized New Jersey's lax narcotic regulations, which vitiated enforcement of New York's carefully framed legislation.[22] Furthermore, although the law-abiding physician had more paper work, unethical physicians could circumvent state and local laws and the consequent paper work in various ways. The "dope doctors" could simply purchase drugs by mail from another state and then dispense them to their "patients," thereby bypassing laws which relied on prescriptions and pharmacies to monitor drug use. Generally, physicians resented the legal advantage of patent medicines which, by means of statutory exemptions, contained narcotic dosages capable of producing addiction. These evasions were in painful contradiction to the intent of legislation and a distinct reminder of the political influence of those profiting from narcotic sales.

Federal control over narcotic use and the prescription practices of the medical profession were thought in 1900 to be unconstitutional. Gradually, federal commerce and tax powers were broadened by Supreme Court decisions, notably those upholding a federal tax on colored oleomargarine, federal prohibition against transportation of women across state lines for immoral purposes, the interstate transportation of lottery tickets, and carrying liquor into a state that prohibited liquor imports. But that congressional activity was still circumscribed by the Constitution was reflected in the Supreme Court ruling in *Hammer v. Dagenhart* (1918) wherein the court declared that congress could not regulate the interstate shipment of goods produced by child labor.[23] The ruling clearly indicated that federal police powers under the guise of tax or interstate commerce powers had narrow application.

As a result of constitutional uncertainty over legislation enabling federal law to prevail in an area of morals, there was little effort until after 1900 to enact a federal law to control the sale and prescription of narcotics. After the passage of the Pure Food and Drug Act (1906), some elements of the pharmacy trade supported a regulatory antinarcotic law based on the interstate commerce clause, a movement seconded by Dr. Harvey Wiley of the Agriculture Department.[24] Finally, by 1912, when the State Department's campaign for a federal antinarcotic law was making substantial progress, proponents opted for basing it on government's revenue powers. Thus the framing of an antinarcotic law paralleled the widening possibilities open to Congress in the area of policing morals. Even so, the Harrison Act of 1914 had to survive a number of unfavorable or close court decisions until its broad police powers were upheld in 1919. And as late as 1937 the Marihuana Tax Act was carefully kept separate from the Harrison Act in order to discourage more court attacks.[25] The Drug Abuse Act of 1970 scrapped the Harrison Act's foundation on revenue powers and rests on the interstate commerce powers of Congress, returning to the basis proposed more than sixty years before. In the last half century, the interstate commerce clause has been substantially broadened so that its powers can sustain strict regulation of drug use without the need to portray a police function as a revenue measure.[26]

Reformers

Lay reformers took a vigorous and uncomplicated stand on narcotics. In general, two problems enflamed them: corporate disregard of public welfare and individual immorality. This dichotomy is artificial but it helps to identify the objects of the reformers' zeal and it made a difference in the kinds of laws proposed. Reformers like Samuel Hopkins Adams, whose "Great American Fraud" series in *Collier's* in 1905–07 revealed the danger of patent medicines, were of course concerned over the damage done to unsuspecting victims of such medicines. Adams directed his attack against pharmaceutical manufacturers whose expensive and inaccurate advertising promotions sold harmful nostrums to the public. In keeping with his exposés of crooked politicians and corporations, Adams argued that regulatory laws should be aimed at the suppliers.[27] For other reformers, though, the addict evoked fears; their agitation resulted in legislation directed more at the user, who might be sent to jail for possession, than at the manufacturer who produced barrels of morphine and heroin. The Southerner's fear of the Negro and the Westerner's fear of the Chinese predominated in this approach to the drug problem. The origin of concern thus affected the aim and quality of the laws. Both classes of reformers looked to federal legislation as the most effective weapon, and both tended to mesaure progress in the reform campaign by the amount of legislation enacted.

The reformers can also be examined from another viewpoint. One group thought in moral abstractions while another was interested in a practical solution. The Right Reverend Charles Brent, who played an important role in the movement for narcotic control, was an abstract reformer who saw the narcotics problem, like any other social problem, to be a question which required first of all a moral approach to the decision.[28] Did narcotics have a value other than as a medicine? No: unlike alcohol they had no beverage or caloric value. Should such substances be permitted for casual use? No: there was no justification, since there was the possibility only of danger in narcotics for nonmedicinal uses. Therefore recreational use of narcotics should be prohibited, their traffic curtailed on a world scale, and a scourge eliminated from the earth. To compromise, to permit some (for instance the Chinese) to use narcotics would be inconsistent with morality, and therefore not permissible. Reformers like Brent were charitable but unwilling to compromise.

Other reformers sought a practical and partial solution which edged toward total narcotic restriction but was modified to allow for the cravings of addicts. These compromises often came from political divisions smaller than the federal government. In contrast to Bishop Brent's proposals, the compromise programs were based on the assumption that the supply of and the desire for narcotics could not be eliminated, and therefore any attempt at total prohibition would be a failure.[29]

Narcotics, however, constituted only a small part of the American reform movement at the turn of the century. In the last decade of the nineteenth century, rising public interest in protecting the environment and health was evident in exposés, public education and reform proposals in Congress for such things as a pure food law, but not until the presidential years of Theodore Roosevelt was this interest translated into substantial national legislation. Roosevelt's advocacy of ecology and conservation followed a popular revulsion against the excessive concentration of wealth and the manner in which it was amassed, and the disregard of general welfare by powerful private interest.

Upton Sinclair's bitterness led to *The Jungle*, in which the young Socialist portrayed the slaughterhouse owner's utter disregard for employee welfare. Often credited with giving the final push toward enactment of the Meat Inspection Act in 1906, Sinclair soon became disillusioned with his efforts at substantial reform through idealistic principles: the big meat packers benefited from the reforms enacted by Congress since small business firms could not afford the new inspection requirements nor meet the standards of foreign nations which had criticized the purity of American meat exports.

But if some reforms were actually in assistance to institutions reformers hated, other reforms were the nuisance of corrective their advocates desired. An aggressive administrator of the new regulations restricting environmental and physiological damage was Dr. Harvey Washington Wiley, who developed the Agriculture Department's Bureau of Chemistry into an avid detector of unsavory manufacturing practices.[30] He was condemned by industry because his criticisms and regulations often appeared to go beyond all reasonable limits. For example, he wanted to prohibit caffeine-containing drinks such as Coca-Cola as well as patent medicines containing narcotics. His particular attention to unlabeled additives resulted in an indictment of the Coca-Cola Company and the holding up of shipments of French wines not labeled to show sulfur dioxide as a preservative. These disputes required the attention of the President, the Supreme Court, or a Cabinet officer. Theodore Roosevelt's support of Wiley waned in 1908 as the criticisms grew, and he felt some personal evaluation was necessary. He called Wiley to the White House to confront industrial spokesmen. All went well until the conversation turned to the President's treasured sugar substitute, saccharin. Wiley at once declared saccharin a threat to health which should be prohibited in foods. Roosevelt angrily reacted: "Anybody who says saccharin is injurious is an idiot. Dr. Rixey gives it to me every day!" His doubt about Wiley strengthened by this encounter, Roosevelt established the Referee Board of Consulting Scientific Experts. By 1912 Wiley had been forced out of government service because of his aggressive and, some thought, unreasonable antagonism to food and drug impurities and false claims.[31]

The Health Professions and Narcotics

Medicine and pharmacy were in active stages of professional organization when they became involved with the issue of narcotic control. The status of both pharmacists and physicians was less than desirable, and both suffered from weak licensing laws, meager training requirements, and a surplus of practitioners. Their intense battles for professional advancement and unification had an effect on the progress and final form of antinarcotic legislation.

9

Although the state of medicine in the nineteenth century was improving, its only tangible progress lay in some ability to contain a few communicable diseases. Yet, if the physician could not effect cure, he could assuage pain and apprehension: opiates were preeminent for these functions and were apparently used with great frequency. Drugs are still overused in this casual, convenient way—penicillin, the sulfas, tetracycline, barbiturates, and so on—they carry a message of effective treatment to the patient, fulfilling his emotional needs even if sometimes risky and superfluous from an objective viewpoint.

The American Medical Association (founded in 1847), which now appears monolithic and powerful, was a weak institution at the close of the last century. The vast majority of doctors refrained from membership. The AMA's battle for higher standards of training, licensure, and practice was threatening to many within the profession and seemed to the public to be but a covert plea for special preferment by one of several schools of medical practice.[32] While one may admit that the AMA reform program improved the political, economic, and social status of the medical profession, the public welfare was also to be improved. The Flexner Report, with its independent and corroborating analysis of the profession's weaknesses, was accepted by impartial critics.[33] Meanwhile, however, the low standards of the nineteenth century predominated and were consistent with the great reliance on such symptomatic relief agents as the opiates.

Although the drive to organize pharmacy was contemporary with the AMA's efforts, it was not so successful. However fragmented medicine might appear, pharmacy was far more fundamentally split into special-interest groups, often divided on questions of legislation, ethics, and professional standards. The druggist operated a competitive retail business to which his prescription service usually contributed only a fraction of his profits. He had some difficulty adhering to the strict professional standards enunciated by the American Pharmaceutical Association (1852)—stressing the ancient science of pharmacy—as the highest priority in his business. He found an ideal relationship with the physician was particularly difficult to attain since the oversupply of doctors led many of them to do their own dispensing. Similarly, pharmaceutical manufacturers, importers, exporters, and wholesalers were also engaged in businesses far removed from the archetypal pharmacist dispensing an intricate prescription. The various professional components often felt that their particular interests could not be adequately served by an association in which all elements of pharmacy had an equal voice. Dissatisfaction with the APhA led to many trade associations with specific membership criteria.[34]

Physicians and pharmacists were vocal and effective in their lobbying efforts. Each saw that in addition to aiding the public welfare, strict narcotic laws could be a distinct advantage for institutional development if great care was exercised in their framing. Knowledge of this rivalry and ambition clarifies legislative history; it also reminds us that in the competition to find a convenient law it as rather easy to lose sight of the victim of drug abuse. The public's fear of addicts and minority-group drug users might supply the powerful motive force for legislation, but the law's final form would await the approval of the institutional interests affected.

Notes

1. I am greatly indebted to Glenn Sonnedecker's "Emergence of the Concept of Opiate Addiction," *J. Mondial Pharmacie*, Sept.–Dec. 1962, pp. 275–90; Jan.–Mar. 1963, pp. 27–34. Another article of relevance is D. I. Macht, "The History of Opium and Some of Its Preparations and Alkaloids," JAMA 64 : 477–81 (1915). . . . *The Opium Problem*, by Charles E. Terry and Mildred Pellens (New York: Bureau of Social Hygiene, 1928; reprint ed., Montclair, N.J.: Patterson Smith, 1970), is a very useful anthology of articles published up to the mid-1920s.

2. Norman Howard-Jones, "A Critical Study of the Origins and Early Development of Hypodermic Medication," *J. Hist. Med.* 2 : 201–49 (1947). . . . The lack of statistics on the number of Civil War veterans who became addicts in the service suggests that the war was a convenient event to blame for late 19th-century addiction. According to a recent study, morphine was usually dusted or rubbed into wounds and only sometimes injected (Stewart Brooks, *Civil War Medicine* [Springfield, Ill.: Thomas, 1966], pp. 65, 88). An extensive report on rising opium consumption in the U.S. published only seven years after the war makes no mention of the recent conflict as the cause of addiction, but rather places its beginnings in the rising teetotalism of the 1840s and 1850s (F. E. Oliver, "The Use and Abuse of Opium," Third Report of the Massachusetts Board of Health, 1872, pp. 162–77). . . .

3. Excessive opiate use in the 19th century was not considered "un-American" but "peculiarly American" (Harvey Washington Wiley, "An Opium Bonfire," *Good Housekeeping*, August 1912, p. 252). An anonymous writer in 1861 bemoaned, "in no country in the world is quackery carried on to so enormous extent as it is in the United States" ("Quackery and the Quacked," *Nat. Quart. Rev. 2* : 354 [1861]). George Beard, a leadin neurologist and psychiatrist of the latter half of the century, associated narcotic use with the frailty of advanced civilization and predicted a great increase in the 20th century (*American Nervousness: Its Causes and Consequences* [New York: Putnam, 1881], p. 64). . . .

4. Some opium was grown in the U.S. during the 19th century and perhaps later (Terry and Pellens, *The Opium Problem*, p. 7). During the blockade the Confederacy attempted to grow opium to replenish its supplies but found smuggling to be more certain (Norman H. Frank, *Pharmaceutical Conditions and Drug Supply in the Confederacy* [Madison, Wis.: Institute of the History of Pharmacy, 1955]; *Memoranda on the Manufacture of and Traffic in Morphine in the U.S. . . . in Continuation of Senate Doc. 377*, 61st Cong., 2nd Sess., 31 Oct. 1911, prepared for the Secretary of State by Hamilton Wright; for cocaine exports see p. 12; for morphine, p. 14).

5. Statistics on opium and morphine importation until the Harrison Act (in effect after 1 March 1915) are among the best available for estimating the use of narcotics in the United States. . . . A convenient source of these figures for 1850–1926 is Terry and Pellen's *The Opium Problem* (pp. 50–51) where the important distinction is made between total imports and that portion of imports "entered for consumption." Hamilton Wright provided statistics which extend the record back to 1840 (ibid., "Report," Appendix IV, pp. 81–83).

6. M. I. Wilbert, "Sale and Use of Cocaine and Narcotics," *Publ. Health Rep. 29* : 3180–83 (1914); *Registration of Producers and Importers of Opium, etc.*, Committee on Ways and Means, H. Rept. no. 23, 63rd Cong., 2nd Sess., 24 June 1913, p. 3.

7. L. F. Kebler, *Habit Forming Agents: Their Indiscriminate Sale and Use, a Menace to the Public Welfare*, Agriculture Dept., Farmer's Bulletin no. 393 (April 1910), pp. 8–12, 15–18. William Hammond, "Dr. Hammond's Remarks on Coca," *Trans. Med. Soc. Virginia*, 1887, pp. 213–26, esp. p. 226 for hay fever. Oscar E. Anderson, *The Health of a Nation: Harvey W. Wiley and the Fight for Pure Food* (Chicago: Univ. of Chicago Press, 1958), p. 315.

8. To protect their formulas they did not patent their products; only the names were legally protected by trademarks. But by 1905 the Proprietary Association of America had endorsed a law to exempt small amounts of narcotics, similar to Section 6 of the future Harrison Act. . . . Manufacturers whose medicines continued to contain excessive narcotics (e.g. Dr. Tucker's Asthma Specific, which contained cocaine) were not permitted to join the PAA. See J. H. Young, *The Toadstool Millionaires* (Princeton Univ. Press, 1961), pp. 237 ff., and idem, *The Medical Messiahs* (Princeton Univ. Press, 1967), p. 34; typed transcript of proceedings of 31st Annual Meeting of the PAA, 20–22 May 1913, Washington, D.C., pp. 14–15; editorial, *Amer. Druggist Pharmaceut. Rec. 57* ; 126 (1910). The model law prepared in 1905 by representatives of the PAA, NARD, NWDA, and the APhA is found in "Sale of Narcotics and Proprietary Medicines Containing Alcohol," *Am. J. Pharm.* 78 : 145–48 (1906).

9. See above (ch. 1, n. 5), for source of statistics. Wright's "Report" describes manipulation of duty in an attempt to reduce the importation of smoking opium in the late 19th century (Hamilton Wright, "Report on the International Opium Commission and on the Opium Problem as Seen within the United States and Its Possessions," contained in *Opium Problem: Message from the President of the United States,* Sen. Doc. no. 377, 61st Cong., 2nd Sess., 21 Feb. 1910).

10. See, e.g., *General Laws of Texas,* 1905, ch. 35, sect. 2.

11. "Address before the Massachusetts Medical Society, 30 May 1860," in *The Works of Oliver Wendell Holmes* (Boston: Houghton Mifflin, 1892), 9 : 200–01.

12. See F. X. Dercum, "Relative Infrequency of the Drug Habit among the Middle and Upper Classes," *Penn. Med. J. 20* : 362–64, n. 22 (1917). Some physicians did begin to sense the danger: in 1900 Dr. John Witherspoon, who was to become AMA president in 1913, delivered his "Oration on Medicine, A Protest against Some of the Evils in the Profession of Medicine" (*JAMA 34* : 1591 [1900]). . . .

See also T. D. Crothers, "New Phase of Criminal Morphinomania," *J. Inebriety 21* : 41–51 (1899).

13. The number of narcotic addicts in the U.S. is a very difficult figure to arrive at. One problem is in the definition of an addict, for there are at least two major categories among those who use narcotics in a regular fashion, the hard-core addict who requires daily opiates to hold off abstinence symptoms, and occasional users who can stop without any significant symptoms. There is another category of "addict," composed of individuals who are not taking enough opiates to create the possibility of an abstinence syndrome but who believe they are. These individuals are dependent on addict life style or even simple needle injections, although physiologically they could not be classified as addicts.

Given these qualifications, most authors who have closely studied the question of the addict-population in the past (Wilbert, Terry, Pelleus, Kolb, DuMez, Lindesmith) tend to agree that there was a peak in addiction around 1900 and that in the teens of this century this number began to decrease and reached a relatively small number (about 100,000) in the 1920s. The peak might be 200,000 to 400,000 in 1900. A peak of drug use in 1919 reported by New York City and Federal officials which estimated the total in the U.S. at about one million seems highly unlikely. It seems reasonable to maintain that the decline in opiate use after 1900 probably continued. What actually increased was the fear directed at addiction by officials and the public. By 1930 only the most irresponsible spokesmen argued that addiction had not reached a low figure and was represented chiefly in the largest urban centers. In general, exaggerated figures of the number of narcotics addicts have reflected public concern rather than actual numbers. Nevertheless, the number in the U.S. seems to have exceeded in the 20th century the per capita rate in other Western nations and without question was so perceived by the federal government until the 1920s, when the admission became an embarrassment.

14. E. C. Sandmeyer, *The Anti-Chinese Movement in California* (Urbana: Univ. of Illinois Press, 1939). . . . Anti-Chinese feeling was not confined to the West Coast; see E.G. John W. Foster, "The Chinese Boycott" (*Atlantic Monthly,* January 1906, pp. 118–27), for extralegal methods directed at Chinese, particularly in Boston; and Jacob Riis, *How the Other Half Lives* (New York: C. Scribner's Sons, 1890) for his prejudicial remarks about New York's Chinatown.

15. The association of cocaine with the southern Negro became a cliché a decade or more before the Harrison Act. See W. Scheppegrell, "The Abuse and Dangers of Cocaine," *Med. News 73* : 417–22 (1898), esp. p. 421. In June 1900 the *JAMA* (34 : 1637) editorially reported that "the Negroes in some parts of the South are reported as being addicted to a new form of vice—that of 'cocaine sniffing' or the 'coke habit.'" In February 1901 the *JAMA* (36 : 330) called attention again to this new vice. See also in the New York *Tribune,* 21 June 1903, an extended statement by Col. J. W. Watson of Georgia on how cocaine sniffing "threatens to depopulate the Southern States of their colored population." Atlanta seemed particularly affected, and legal action was urged against the sale "of a soda fountain drink manufactured in Atlanta and known as Coca-Cola." The Colonel was satisfied that "many of the horrible crimes committed in the Southern States by the colored people can be traced directly to the cocaine habit," and that the habit was also present among young whites. Examination of the Atlanta *Constitution* (27 Dec. 1914) also reveals a frequently claimed association between cocaine use and the Negro; by 1914 the Atlanta police chief was blaming "70% of the crimes" on drug use. . . . In the District of Columbia the police chief considered cocaine the greatest menace of any drug. There it was peddled from door to door (*Report of the President's Homes Commission,* S. Doc. no. 644, 60th Cong., 2nd Sess., 8 Jan. 1909 (GPO, 1909), pp. 254–55. . . . The leader of a drive against cocaine, Dr. Christopher Koch, of the State Pharmacy

Board, testified before Congress on behalf of federal antinarcotic laws and drew attention to the dangers of the cocaine-crazed southern Negro. In 1914 Dr. Koch was quoted as asserting, "Most of the attacks upon white women of the South are the direct result of a cocaine-crazed Negro brain" (*Literary Digest,* 28 March, 1914, p. 687). Dr. E. H. Williams portrayed in the *N.Y. Times* (8 Feb. 1914) a lurid and fearful picture of "the Negro cocaine fiends" who terrorized the South. Dr. Williams published a similar study, but with more statistics, in the *Medical Record* (85 : 247–49 [1914], "The Drug Habit Menace in the South"). There Dr. Williams attempted to answer a study from the Georgia State Asylum (see ch. 1, no. 20 below) which reported almost no Negro cocaine takers admitted in the years 1909–14. In his *Opiate Addiction: Its Handling and Treatment* (New York: Macmillan, 1922), Dr. Williams attributed popular agitation for antinarcotic laws to spectacular crimes, especially in the South. Also in 1914 Dr. Harvey Wiley referred to "old colored men" hiding cocaine under their pushcart wares and spreading the drugs throughout America's cities (H. W. Wiley and A. L. Pierce, "The Cocaine Crime," *Good Housekeeping,* March 1914, pp. 393–98). Thus the problem of cocaine proceeded from an association with Negroes in about 1900, when a massive repression and disenfranchisement were under way in the South, to a convenient explanation for crime waves, and eventually Northerners used it as an argument against Southern fear of infringement of states' rights. For example, Wright wrote the editor of the Louisville *Journal Courier* that "a strong editorial from you on the abuse of cocaine in the South would do a great deal of good [but] do not quote me or the Department of State" (16 April 1910, WP, entry 36). . . .

16. Perhaps it is impossible to describe accurately the distribution of morphine addiction or nonmedical use in the 19th century among the various social groups. It is reasonable, however, to assume that morphine's introduction as a replacement for opium meant a wide distribution among the middle class, which enjoyed professional medical care. But as fear of morphine grew, and the need for symptomatic relief declined, the middle class may have used morphine less often. (See F. X. Dercum, "Relative Infrequency of Drug Habit . . . ," *Penna. Med. J.20* : 362–64 [1917].)

17. G. Archie Stockwell, "Erythoxylon Coca," *Boston Med. Surg. J. 96* : 402 (1877).

18. Freud's first and most comprehensive study, "Uber Coca," was abstracted in the *St. Louis Med. Surg. J. 47* : 502–05 (1884), the year of its publication in Vienna. . . . The second paper, "Beitrag zur Kenntniss der Cocawirkung" (1885), continued the optimistic tone which was much muted in his last paper, "Bemerkungen über Cocainsucht und Cocaïnfurcht" (1887), a response to an attack on cocaine therapy by Erlenmeyer. The three papers are translated in S. A. Edminster et al., trans., *The Cocaine Papers* (Vienna: Dunquin Press, 1963). Two substantial and illuminating studies of Freud's interest in cocaine are Siegfried Bernfeld, "Freud's Studies on Cocaine, 1884–1887, *Yearbook of Psychoanalysis 10* : 9–38 (1954–55); and Hortense Koller Becker, "Carl Koller and Cocaine," *Psychoan. Quart. 32* : 309–73 (1963). Karl Koller, Freud's colleague, received from Freud the whimsical nickname Coca Koller.

19. N.Y. *Times,* 8 Feb. 1914; *Med. Record 85* : 247–49 (1914).

20. E. M. Green, "Psychoses Among Negroes: A Comparative Study," *J. Nerv. Ment. Dis. 41* : 697–708 (1914). Dr. E. H. Williams's reply that the cocainized Negroes were in jails and not insane asylums is found in the *Medical Record* (85 : 247–49 [1914]), and also in *Everybody's Magazine* (August 1914, pp. 276–77). . . .

21. Hamilton Wright, "Report International Opium," *Opium Problem: Message,* p. 49.

22. M. I. Wilbert, "Sale and Use of Cocaine," *Publ. Health Rep. 29,* 3180–83 (1914).

23. 247 U.S. 251 (1918). For discussions of the complicated byways of the federal police powers involved in such attempts at federal regulation see B. F. Wright, *The Growth of American Constitutional Law* (New York: Holt, Rinehart and Winston, 1942).

24. According to a memorandum by Dr. Reid Hunt of the Public Health Service, Wiley and the drug trades—the retail interests especially (represented by the National Association of Retail Druggists)—cooperated to perfect an antinarcotic law based on the interstate commerce powers of the Constitution after it became apparent that pure food advocates feared any tampering with the Pure Food and Drug Act through amendment (*PHSR,* 2 Nov. 1908).

25. See statement of C. M. Hester, Assistant General Counsel of the Treasury Department, in *Taxation of Marihuana, Hearings before the Committee on Ways and Means of the House of Representatives on Hr 6385,* 27–30 April and 4 May 1937, 75th Cong., 1st Sess. (GPO, 1937), pp. 7–13. . . .

26. For recent comment on the interest commerce powers and the resting of national restrictive drug laws on these powers, see M. P. Rosenthal, "Proposals for Dangerous Drug Legislation," in Appendix B of *Narcotics and Drug Abuse,* Presidential Commission on Law Enforcement and the Administration of Justice (GPO, 1967), pp. 80–134, esp. p. 129 and n. 484.

27. Reprinted in book form by the AMA particularly for the reception rooms of physicians. Similar exposés of proprietary medicines made by the AMA appeared in three volumes, *Nostrums and Quackery,* in 1911, 1921, and 1936, the last entitled *Nostrums and Quackery and Pseudo Medicine.* Adams attacked such well-known proprietaries as Pe-ru-na which contained more than 25% alcohol, and Hostetter's Stomach Bitters which contained more than 40%; and those containing unlabeled narcotics, acetanalid, and other dangerous substances. . . .

28. C. H. Brent to James F. Smith, Commissioner of Education, Manila, 6 July 1903 (BP, container 6).

29. Beal's model law and the New York State Whitney Acts (1917 and 1918) avoided prohibition but attempted to prevent new addicts and did permit maintenance of confirmed habitúes.

30. The standard biography of Wiley is Anderson's *The Health of a Nation.*

31. Ibid., pp. 210, 243 ff. Dr. Presley M. Rixey (1852–1928), Surgeon General of the Navy, was the President's official physician. . . .

32. The history of the pharmaceutical profession and drug trades in America is outlined in *Kremer's and Urdang's History of Pharmacy,* 3rd edition, revised by Glenn Sonnedecker (Philadelphia: Lippincott, 1963), pp. 133–296. For the history of medicine in America see R. Shryock, *The Development of Modern Medicine* (Philadelphia: Univ. of Pa. Press, 1947); M. Fishbein, *A History of the American Medical Association, 1847–1947* (Philadelphia: Saunders, 1947); R. Stevens, *American Medicine and the Public Interest* (New Haven: Yale University Press, 1971). J. M. Burrow, *AMA: Voice of American Medicine* (Baltimore: Johns Hopkins Press, 1963), describes the weakness of the AMA before World War I (see pp. 27 ff. and his ch. 3, pp. 5 ff.).

33. The Flexner Report recommended closure of substandard medical schools in the United States and pointed to Johns Hopkins as the model for a modern medical school. (A. Flexner, *Medical Education in the United States and Canada,* Carnegie Foundation for the Advancement of Teaching, Bull, no. 4, New York, 1910.)

34. On the founding of the APhA see Glenn Sonnedecker, *History of Pharmacy,* 3rd ed. (Philadelphia: J. B. Lippincott Co., 1963), pp. 181 ff. Some of the important national drug trade organizations and their dates of founding are: Proprietary Association of America (PAA), 1881, composed of manufacturers of "patent medicines," and over-the-counter proprietaries; National Wholesale Druggists Association (NWDA), 1876, and National Association of Retail Druggists (NARD), 1898, for owners of pharmacies; American Pharmaceutical Manufacturers Association, 1908. The National Association of Manufacturers of Medicinal Products (1912), makers of prescription drugs, merged in 1958 with the PMA. See Sonnedecker, *History of Pharmacy,* pp. 188 ff.

2. Symbolic Crusade: Status Politics and the American Temperance Movement

Joseph R. Gusfield

For many observers of American life the Temperance movement is evidence for an excessive moral perfectionism and an overly legalistic bent to American culture. It seems the action of devoted sectarians who are unable to compromise with human impulse. The legal measures taken to enforce abstinence display the reputed American faith in the power of Law to correct all evils. This moralism and utopianism bring smiles to the cynical and fear to the sinners. Such a movement seems at once naive, intolerant, saintly, and silly.

Although controversies of morality, religion, and culture have been recognized as endemic elements of American politics, they have generally been viewed as minor themes in the interplay of economic and class conflicts. Only in recent years have American historians and social scientists de-emphasized economic issues as the major points of dissension in American society.[1] We share this newer point of view, especially in its insistence on the significant role of cultural conflicts in American politics. Our social system has not experienced the sharp class organization and class conflict which have been so salient in European history. Under continuous conditions of relative affluence and without a feudal resistance to nineteenth-century commercialism and industry, American society has possessed a comparatively high degree of consensus on economic matters. In its bland attitude toward class issues, political controversy in the United States has given only a limited role to strong economic antagonisms. Controversies of personality, cultural difference, and the nuances of style and morality have occupied part of the political stage. Consensus about fundamentals of governmental form, free enterprise economy, and church power has left a political vacuum which moral issues have partially filled. Differences between ethnic groups, cultures, and religious organizations have been able to assume a greater importance than has been true of societies marked by deeper economic divisions. ". . . agreement on fundamentals will permit almost every kind of social conflict, tension and difference to find political expression."[2]

It is within an analytical context of concern with noneconomic issues that we have studied the Temperance movement. This is a study of moral reform as a political and social issue. We have chosen the Temperance movement because of its persistence and power in the history of the United States. Typical of moral reform efforts, Temperance has usually been the attempt of the moral people, in this case the abstainers, to correct the behavior of the immoral people, in this case the drinkers. The issue has appeared as a moral one, divorced from any direct economic interests in abstinence or indulgence. This quality of "disinterested reform" is the analytical focus of our study.

• • •

The sociologist picks up where the historian closes. Put in another way, he delves into the assumptions with which the historian begins. . . . The amount written about Temperance is monumentally staggering to someone who tries to read it all. Claims, counterclaims, factual histories, and proceedings of organizations overwhelm us in their immensity. Despite this plethora of documents and analyses, we are left with either partisan writings, histories which preach, or analyses which fail to go beyond general remarks about moral perfectionism, rural-urban conflict, or the Protestant envy of the sinner.[3] It is here, in the analysis of the process, that the sociologist focuses his interest. He studies just that which is so often *ad hoc* to the interpretation of the historian.

We will describe the relation between Temperance attitudes, the organized Temperance movement, and the conflicts between divergent subcultures in American society. Issues of moral reform are analyzed as one way through which a cultural group acts to preserve, defend, or enhance the dominance and prestige of its own style of living within the total society. In the set of religious, ethnic, and cultural communities that have made up American society, drinking (and abstinence) has been one of the significant consumption habits distinguishing one subculture from another. It has been one of the major characteristics through which Americans have defined their own cultural commitments. The "drunken bum," "the sophisticated gourmet," or the "blue-nosed teetotaler" are all terms by which we express our approval or disapproval of cultures by reference to the moral position they accord drinking. Horace Greeley recognized this cultural base to political loyalties and animosities in the 1844 elections in New York state: "Upon those Working Men who stick to their business, hope to improve their circumstances by honest industry and *go on Sundays to church rather than to the grog-shop* [italics added] the appeals of Loco-Focoism fell comparatively harmless; while the opposite class were rallied with unprecedented unanimity against us."[4]

Precisely because drinking and nondrinking have been ways to identify the members of a subculture, drinking and abstinence became symbols of social status, identifying social levels of the society whose styles of life separated them culturally. They indicated to what culture the actor was committed and hence what social groups he took as his models of imitation and avoidance and his points of positive and negative reference for judging his behavior. The rural, native American Protestant of the nineteenth century respected Temperance ideals. He adhered to a culture in which self-control, industriousness, and impulse renunciation were both praised and made necessary. Any lapse was a serious threat to his system of respect. Sobriety was virtuous and, in a community dominated by middle-class Protestants, necessary to social acceptance and to self-esteem. In the twentieth century this is less often true. As Americans are less work-minded, more urban, and less theological, the same behavior which once brought rewards and self-assurance to the abstainer today more often brings contempt and rejection. The demands for self-control and individual industry count for less in an atmosphere of teamwork where tolerance, good interpersonal relations, and the ability to relax oneself and others are greatly prized. Abstinence has lost much of its utility to confer prestige and esteem.

Our attention to the significance of drink and abstinence as symbols of membership in status groups does not imply that religious and moral beliefs have not been important in the Temperance movement. We are not reducing moral reform to something else. Instead, we are adding something. Religious motives and moral fervor do not happen *in vacuo,* apart from a specific setting. We have examined the social conditions which made the facts of other people's drinking especially galling to the abstainer and the need for reformist action acutely pressing to him. These conditions are found in the development of threats to the socially dominant position of the Temperance adherent by those whose style of life differs from his. As his own claim to social respect and honor are diminished, the sober, abstaining citizen seeks for public acts through which he may reaffirm the dominance and prestige of his style of life. Converting the sinner to virtue is one way; law is another. Even if the law is not enforced or enforceable, the symbolic import of its passage is important to the reformer. It settles the controversies between those who represent clashing cultures. The public support of one conception of morality at the expense of another enhances the prestige and self-esteem of the victors and degrades the culture of the losers.

16

In its earliest development, Temperance[5] was one way in which a declining social elite tried to retain some of its social power and leadership. The New England Federalist "aristocracy" was alarmed by the political defeats of the early nineteenth century and by the decreased deference shown their clergy. The rural farmer, the evangelical Protestant, and the uneducated middle class appeared as a rising social group who rejected the social status, as well as political power, of the Federalist leadership. In the first quarter of the nineteenth century, the moral supremacy of the educated was under attack by the frontiersman, the artisan, and the independent farmer. The Federalist saw his own declining status in the increased power of the drinker, the ignorant, the secularist, and the religious revivalist. During the 1820's, the men who founded the Temperance movement sought to make Americans into a clean, sober, godly, and decorous people whose aspirations and style of living would reflect the moral leadership of New England Federalism. If they could not control the politics of the country, they reasoned that they might at least control its morals.

Spurred by religious revivalism, Temperance became more ultraist than its founders had intended. The settling of frontiers and the influx of non-Protestant cultures increased the symbolic importance of morality and religious behavior in distinguishing between the reputable and the disreputable. During the 1830's and 1840's, it became a large and influential movement, composed of several major organizations. Religious dedication and a sober life were becoming touchstones of middle-class respectability. Large numbers of men were attracted to Temperance organizations as a means of self-help. In the interests of social and economic mobility, they sought to preserve their abstinence or reform their own drinking habits. Abstinence was becoming a symbol of middle-class membership and a necessity for ambitious and aspiring young men. It was one of the ways society could distinguish the industrious from the ne'er-do-well; the steady worker from the unreliable drifter; the good credit risk from the bad gamble; the native American from the immigrant. In this process the movement lost its association with New England upper classes and became democratized.

The political role of Temperance emerged in the 1840's in its use as a symbol of native and immigrant, Protestant and Catholic tensions. The "disinterested reformer" of the 1840's was likely to see the curtailment of alcohol sales as a way of solving the problems presented by an immigrant, urban poor whose culture clashed with American Protestantism. He sensed the rising power of these strange, alien peoples and used Temperance legislation as one means of impressing upon the immigrant the central power and dominance of native American Protestant morality. Along with Abolition and Nativism, Temperance formed one of a trio of major movements during the 1840's and 1850's.

Throughout its history, Temperance has revealed two diverse types of disinterested reform. By the last quarter of the nineteenth century, these had become clear and somewhat distinct elements within the movement. One was an *assimilative reform.* Here the reformer was sympathetic to the plight of the urban poor and critical of the conditions produced by industry and the factory system. This urban, progressivist impulse in Temperance reflected the fears of an older, established social group at the sight of rising industrialism. While commercial and professional men saw America changing from a country of small towns to one of cities, they were still socially dominant. The norm of abstinence had become the public morality after the Civil War. In the doctrines of abstinence they could still offer the poor and the immigrants a way of living which had the sanction of respect and success attached to it. Through reform of the drinker, the middle-class professional and businessman coped with urban problems in a way which affirmed his sense of cultural dominance. He could feel his own social position affirmed by a Temperance argument that invited the drinker (whom he largely identified with the poor, the alien, and the downtrodden) to follow the reformer's habits and lift himself to middle-class respect and income. He was even able to denounce the rich for their sumptuary sophistication. He could do this because he felt secure that abstinence was still the public morality. It was not yet somebody else's America.

A more hostile attitude to reform is found when the object of the reformer's efforts is no longer someone he can pity or help. *Coercive reform* emerges when the object of reform is seen as an intractable defender of another culture, someone who rejects the reformer's values and really doesn't want to change. The champion of assimilative reform viewed the drinker as part of a social system in which the reformer's culture was dominant. On this assumption, his invitation to the drinker to reform made sense. The champion of coercive reform cannot make this assumption. He sees the object of reform as someone who rejects the social dominance of the reformer and denies the legitimacy of his life style. Since the dominance of his culture and the social status of his group are denied, the coercive reformer turns to law and force as ways to affirm it.

In the last quarter of the nineteenth century, coercive reform was most evident in the Populist wing of the Temperance movement. As a phase of the rural distrust of the city, it was allied to an agrarian radicalism which fought the power of industrial and urban political and economic forces. Already convinced that the old, rural middle class was losing out in the sweep of history, the Populist as Temperance adherent could not assume that his way of life was still dominant in America. He had to fight it out by political action which would coerce the public definition of what is moral and respectable. He had to shore up his waning self-esteem by inflicting his morality on everybody.

As America became more urban, more secular, and more Catholic, the sense of declining status intensified the coercive, Populist elements in the Temperance movement. The political defeat of Populism in both North and South heightened the decline, so evident in the drama of William Jennings Bryan. With the development of the Anti-Saloon League in 1896, the Temperance movement began to separate itself from a complex of economic and social reforms and concentrate on the cultural struggle of the traditional rural Protestant society against the developing urban and industrial social system. Coercive reform became the dominating theme of Temperance. It culminated in the drive for national Prohibition. The Eighteenth Amendment was the high point of the struggle to assert the public dominance of old middle-class values. It established the victory of Protestant over Catholic, rural over urban, tradition over modernity, the middle class over both the lower and the upper strata.

The significance of Prohibition is in the fact that it happened. The establishment of Prohibition laws was a battle in the struggle for status between two divergent styles of life. It marked the public affirmation of the abstemious, ascetic qualities of American Protestantism. In this sense, it was an act of ceremonial deference toward old middle-class culture. If the law was often disobeyed and not enforced, the respectability of its adherents was honored in the breach. After all, it was *their* law that drinkers had to avoid.

If Prohibition was the high point of old middle-class defense, Repeal was the nadir. As the Prohibition period lengthened and resistance solidified, Temperance forces grew more hostile, coercive, and nativist. The more assimilative, progressivist adherents were alienated from a movement of such soured Populism. In 1928, anti-Catholic and anti-urban forces led the movement with a "knockout punch" thrown at Al Smith in an open ring. By 1933, they had lost their power and their fight. In the Great Depression both the old order of nineteenth-century economics and the culture of the Temperance ethic were cruelly discredited.

The repeal of the Eighteenth Amendment gave the final push to the decline of old middle-class values in American culture. Since 1933, the Temperance movement has seen itself fighting a losing battle against old enemies and new ones. In contemporary American society, even in his own local communities, it is the total abstainer who is the despised nonconformist. The Protestant churches and the public schools are no longer his allies. The respectable, upper middle-class citizen can no longer be safely counted upon to support abstinence.

What underlies the tragic dilemmas of the Temperance movement are basic changes in the American social system and culture during the past half-century. As we have changed from a commercial society to an industrial one, we have developed a new set of values in which self-control, impulse renunciation, discipline, and sobriety are no longer such hallowed virtues. Thorstein Veblen, himself the epitome of the rural, middle-class Protestant, saw the new society of consumers coming into being. In his satirical fashion, he depicted a society in which leisure and consumption fixed men's status and took precedence over the work-mindedness and efficiency concerns of his own Swedish-American farm communities. More recently, David Riesman has brilliantly depicted the major outlines of this society by pointing to the intensity with which modern Americans are replacing an interest in work and morality with an interest in interpersonal relations and styles of consuming leisure.

For the "other-directed" man neither the intolerance nor the seriousness of the abstainer is acceptable. Nor is the intense rebelliousness and social isolation of the hard drinker acceptable. Analysis of American alcohol consumption is consistent with this. The contemporary American is less likely than his nineteenth-century ancestor to be either a total abstainer or a hard drinker. Moderation is his drinking watchword. One must get along with others and liquor has proven to be a necessary and effective facilitator to sociability. It relaxes reserve and permits fellowship at the same time that it displays the drinker's tolerance for some moral lapse in himself and others.

For those who have grown up to believe in the validity of the Temperance ethic, American culture today seems a strange system in which Truth is condemned as Falsehood and Vice as Virtue. The total abstainer finds himself the exponent of a point of view which is rejected in the centers of urban and national society and among their followers at all levels of American communities. Self-control and foresight made sense in a scarcity, production-minded economy. In an easygoing, affluent society, the credit mechanism has made the Ant a fool and the Grasshopper a hero of the counter-cyclical maintenance of consumer demand. In a consumption-centered society, people must learn to have fun and be good mixers if they are to achieve respect. Not Horatio Alger but *Playboy* magazine is the instructor of the college boy who wants to learn the skills of social ascent. Though they have their noses to the grindstone, their feet must tap to the sound of the dance.

It is at this point that the study of Temperance assumes significance for a general understanding of contemporary American politics and social tensions. Social systems and cultures die slowly, leaving their rear guards behind to fight delaying action. Even after they have ceased to be relevant economic groups, the old middle classes of America are still searching for some way to restore a sense of lost respect. The dishonoring of their values is a part of the process of cultural and social change. A heightened stress on the importance of tradition is a major response of such "doomed classes."

This fundamentalist defense is a primary motif in the current phase of Temperance. To different degrees and within different areas, the contemporary Temperance adherent is part of the rear guard with which small-town America and commercial capitalism fight their losing battle against a nationalized culture and an industrial economy of mass organizations. Increasingly, he fights alone. Churches, schools, and public officials are disdainful of "rigid" attitudes and doctrines. Within the American middle class, in almost all communities, there is a sharp split between two stylistic components. In one the abstainer can feel at home. Here the local community of neighbors and townsmen is the point of reference for behavior. In the other, the more cosmopolitan centers of urban institutions are mediated to the town through national institutions, communications media, and the two-way geographical mobility which brings in newcomers and sends out college students for training elsewhere. The clash between the drinker and the abstainer reflects these diverse references. The localistic culture clings to the traditional while the easier, relaxed, modern ways are the province of the national culture. It is this national culture which becomes the more prestigeful and powerful as America becomes more homogeneous.

The anger and bitterness of the "doomed class" is by no means an "irrational" reaction. There *has* been a decline in the social status of the old middle class and in the dominance of his values. This sense of anger at the loss of status and bitterness about lowered self-esteem pervades the entire Temperance movement today. It takes a number of forms. At one extreme and within certain Temperance elements, it is expressed as a general, diffuse criticism of modern political and social doctrines and a defense of tradition in almost all areas of American life. At the other extreme, within other parts of the Temperance movement, it is part of the intense nationalism, economic conservatism, and social stagnation of the radical right. (This latter is especially true of the Prohibition Party.)

The study of the American Temperance movement is a phase of the process by which, as Richard Hofstadter expressed it, "a large part of the Populist-Progressive tradition has turned sour, become ill-liberal and ill-tempered."[6] The values and the economic position of the native American Protestant, old middle class of individual enterprisers have been losing out in the shuffle of time and social change. The efforts of the old middle class and of those who have built their self-conceptions on their values to defend and restore their lost prestige have taken a number of forms. In fluoridation, domestic Communism, school curricula, and the United Nations, they have found issues which range tradition against modernity. Temperance has been one of the classic issues on which divergent cultures have faced each other in America. Such issues of style have been significant because they have been ways through which groups have tried to handle the problems which have been important to them.

It is this conception of political acts as symbolic acts that is, for us, the most significant fruit of studying Temperance. We consider Temperance as one form which the politics of status goals has taken in the United States. Far from being a pointless interruption of the American political system, it has exemplified one of its characteristic processes. Since governmental actions symbolize the position of groups in the status structure, seemingly ceremonial or ritual acts of government are often of great importance to many social groups. Issues which seem foolish or impractical items are often important for what they symbolize about the style or culture which is being recognized or derogated. Being acts of deference or degradation, the individual finds in governmental action that his own perceptions of his status in the society are confirmed or rejected.

These considerations take us a long way toward understanding why and how social status has been a provocative and frequent source of political tensions in the United States. Issues like fluoridation or domestic Communism or Temperance may seem to generate "irrational" emotions and excessive zeal if we fail to recognize them as symbolic rather than instrumental, pragmatic issues. If we conceive of status as somehow an unfit issue for political controversy, we are simply ignoring a clash of interests which generate a high order of emotion and political action in the United States. When a society experiences profound changes, the fortunes and the respect of people undergo loss or gain. We have always understood the desire to defend respect. It is less clear because it is symbolic in nature but it is not less significant.

• • •

Notes

1. For manifestations of this viewpoint in American history see Lee Benson, *The Concept of Jacksonian Democracy* (Princeton, N.J.: Princeton University Press, 1961), and Louis Hartz, *The Liberal Tradition in America* (New York: Harcourt, Brace and Co., 1955). These trends in historiography are discussed in John Higham (ed.), *The Reconstruction of American History* (New York: Harper Torch Books, 1962).
2. Benson, *op. cit.,* p. 275.
3. A major exception to this is John A. Krout, *The Origins of Prohibition* (New York: A. A. Knopf, 1925). Even Peter Odegard's otherwise excellent work on *Pressure Politics* (New York: Columbia University Press, 1928) is marred by his utter lack of sympathy with Temperance goals. The same moralistic condemnation of moralism limits the utility of the very recent work of Andrew Sinclair, *Prohibition* (Boston: Little, Brown and Co., 1962).
4. Quoted in Benson, *op. cit.,* p. 199.
5. The term "Temperance" is an inadequate name for a movement which preaches total abstinence rather than "temperate" use of alcohol. The word was affixed to the movement in its early years (1820's) when its doctrine was not yet as extreme as it later came to be.
6. Richard Hofstadter, *The Age of Reform* (New York: A. A. Knopf, 1955), pp. 19–20.

3. Nebraska's Marijuana Law: A Case of Unexpected Legislative Innovation

John F. Galliher, James L. McCartney, and Barbara E. Baum

The social processes involved in the development of criminal laws have been studied by several scholars (Jeffery, 1957; Hall, 1952; Chambliss, 1964; Lindesmith, 1965; Sutherland, 1950; Becker, 1963). Generally, two major perspectives have guided these studies. One orientation has been the functionalist perspective (Pound, 1922, 1942; Durkheim, 1964) which stresses the emergence of moral consensus and the functional interdependence of the law with other institutions. Dicey (1920) suggests that public consensus is preceded by the origination of such ideas among elites, and is only later accepted by the mass of citizens. Such consensus, he claims, supplies the foundation for eventual legal change. An alternative view is the conflict orientation (Quinney, 1970; Vold, 1958: 203–219; Engels, 1972; Laski, 1935) which views law as the instrument through which one interest group dominates another. In the development of workman's compensation laws, Friedman and Ladinsky (1967) trace the history of conflict and eventual accommodation between workers and factory owners.

Both the functionalist and conflict orientations either explicitly or implicitly assume that people typically make rational decisions to maximize what they imagine will be their material gains. However, Edelman (1964) suggests that this assumption may not be correct, and that the political behavior of citizens often is determined not on the basis of their real or material interests, but on whether or not a given piece of legislation symbolically reassures them.

Within the sociology of law there have been more studies directed to the development of radically new legislation than to adjustments in existing statues. Perhaps these latter instances are less dramatic, or it may be that they seem to be less clearly instances supporting the major theoretical perspectives. We have chosen to focus on the process of legal change as represented by the widespread phenomenon of alteration of drug laws controlling the possession of marijuana.

Becker (1963: 121–146) and Dickson (1968: 143–156) have written about the early history of marijuana control legislation, and have shown how the Federal Bureau of Narcotics successfully lobbied during the 1930s for the passage of legislation that would eliminate what it claimed to be the marijuana "drug problem." Although drug use appears to have been viewed earlier as an evil affecting the lower classes (Clausen, 1961: 189–196), by the late 1960s, marijuana use had become fashionable among many middle and upper class college youths (Goode, 1970: 35–40; 1972: 36–37). With this new class of law violators, including the children of senators, judges, and other prominent citizens, the conditions were set for a reconsideration of the existing laws.

From: John F. Galliher, James L. McCartney and Barbara E. Baum, NEBRASKA'S MARIJUANA LAW: A CASE OF UNEXPECTED LEGISLATIVE INNOVATION, *Law and Society Review,* Vol. 8, pages 441–455. Copyright © 1974 by Executive Office, Law and Society Association. Reprinted by permission of the Law and Society Association.

Authors' note: This investigation was supported by Biomedical Sciences Support Grant FR-07053 from the General Research Support Branch, Division of Research Resources, Bureau of Health Professions Education and Manpower Training, National Institutes of Health. We are grateful for the helpful criticism and guidance of Alfred R. Lindesmith, Nicholas Babchuk, Malcolm Spector, and Edward Hunvald. An earlier version of this paper was presented at the annual meetings of the American Sociological Association, New York City, 1973. Readers will note that the anonymity of sources has been preserved throughout the article.

Late in 1968 and early in 1969, ten states changed their narcotics control laws to make the maximum penalty for possession of marijuana as a misdemeanor, punishable by less than one year of confinement.[1] Nebraska was one of these first states to pass such legislation and, moreover, it established the lowest maximum penalty among these states. In fact, the maximum penalty of seven days, which was prescribed in Nebraska's law, was much lower than that stipulated in the bills of most other states which later passed similar legislation (National Organization for the Reform of Marijuana Laws, 1971).

Earlier, the accepted model for controlling drug usage had been one of increasing prescribed penalties (see Lindesmith, 1965: 80–82; Clausen, 1961: 215–217). Becker (1963: 136) suggests that these attempts to suppress drug use are legitimized by the Protestant Ethic which proscribes loss of self-control, by traditional American values that disapprove of any action taken solely to produce a state of ecstasy, and by the humanitarian belief that all drugs enslave the user. The question that stimulated our research was why a traditionally conservative state such as Nebraska, which, we suspected, might reflect the values discussed by Becker, would be a leader in passing legislation reducing penalties for vice such as marijuana use. Using either the consensus model, which views law as the product of compromise and shared values, or the conflict models, which sees law as the outcome of struggles between the interests of differing groups, one would not predict this development in Nebraska. We would not have predicted early consensus on such a radical departure in social control in this tradition-oriented state, nor would we have predicted that the proponents of reduced penalties would be strong enough to overcome a more conservative orientation in the control of drugs.

Prelude to the New Law

Before 1969, the penalties in Nebraska for possession or sale of marijuana consisted of a two- to five-year sentence in prison and a fine. Marijuana was classed along with opium derivatives and other narcotic drugs in legislation, modeled after the federal Harrison Act of 1914 (38 Stat. 785 *as amended*), and passed in 1943 (Rev. Stat. of Neb. ch. 28, §§451–470).[2] Drug abuse was a minor problem in Nebraska prior to the late 1960s. Newpaper reports in the state capital, a city of more than 100,000 population, list one case per year between 1950 and 1967 (*Lincoln Star,* 1950–1967). The Nebraska State Patrol (1970: 3) recorded an average of 15 cases per year for the entire state between 1950 and 1967.

Late in 1967, numerous incidents of marijuana possession were recorded in the press, many of them involving college students. One prominent state senator (hereafter referred to as Senator C) spoke out publicly on the topic. His district, although primarily rural, had the third highest number of cases reported in the late 1960s (Nebraska State Patrol, 1970: 14). He spoke at the state university in November 1967 and was rebuked by a group of students when he proposed spending money for undercover agents to deal with the "definite problem" of marijuana use on campus (DeFrain, 1967: 5). Earlier in 1967, Senator C had been the sponsor of a law which expanded the 1943 drug laws to include depressant, stimulant, and hallucinogenic drugs, and established a narcotics control division in the state highway patrol (Legislative Bill 876, Ch. 161 at 460, June 7, 1967; henceforth LB 876).

In 1968, drug arrests in Nebraska increased sevenfold over the number in 1967 (Nebraska State Patrol, 1970: 3). Many of the arrests involved students; but in the western, more rural part of the state, several out-of-state persons were arrested with substantial harvests of marijuana in the hundreds of pounds. Marijuana had grown abundantly in the state since World War I, when

23

it was commercially harvested to produce rope fiber. One knowledgeable official at the Nebraska State Patrol estimated that there were 115,000 acres of marijuana growing wild in the state as late as 1969 (Thomas, 1969).

Response to the increasing number of arrests consisted primarily of statements of concern by some public officials and occasional newspaper editorials. Senator C felt that administrators at the state university were not taking the problem seriously (Senate Debate on LB 876, May 2, 1967). There was also mention of legislation to declare marijuana a noxious weed and to provide penalties for farmers who did not eradicate it on their property. Farmers vigorously opposed this, maintaining that such weed control was costly, time-consuming, and ultimately impossible (Wall, 1968: 14). The issue was not raised again.

In 1969, Senator C introduced legislation (LB 8, 1969) that would permanently expel from college any student convicted of marijuana possession. It was amended to provide for a 30-day suspension from college, but, although it passed the legislature, it was vetoed by the governor. The veto prompted a public expression of outrage by the senator and an unsuccessful attempt to overturn the veto (*Lincoln Journal,* February 25, 1969).

One day after introducing the suspension bill, Senator C had introduced another bill (LB 2, April 11, 1969) which would have reduced the penalty for possession of marijuana to a misdemeanor; and as amended, it provided for a maximum seven-day sentence for first possession, and a mandatory drug education course. It is this innovative bill that we focus on this paper.

Public Response to LB 2

LB 2 was assigned to the Committee on Public Health and Welfare and the first hearings were held on January 28, 1969. We reviewed newspapers from the two urban areas of the state, Omaha and Lincoln, the state capital, from January 1969 to June 1969. This included the period immediately preceding the bill's introduction, during its consideration by the legislature, and after its passage. We wanted to see what publicly identifiable groups were lobbying for or against the legislation and what the public reaction was to its passage. We expected that most of the interest in drugs and related legislation would be concentrated in these two cities since they had recorded the greatest increase in drug arrests, and since both had several colleges in addition to a university.

We found no debate about the bill in the press either by politicians or citizens. The newspapers merely noted that the bill was being considered. It quickly passed the unicameral legislature without a dissenting vote, and was signed into law by the governor with little commentary thereafter. A total of three short articles appeared within six months of the bill's passage, all supporting the educational provision of the legislation. We also reviewed the newspaper from January to June 1969 in the small town where Senator C lived, to see the reaction of his constituents. As with the urban newspapers, the local paper simply noted the bill, but made no editorial comment.

Legislative Hearings

Another reflection of lack of concern with this legislation is that only one witness came to the public hearings. A county attorney argued in favor of the new law as more reasonable and humane than treating "experimenting" with drugs by young people as a felony (Public Hearings on LB 2, January 28, 1969: 4).[3]

The sponsor of the bill, Senator C, was from a rural area of the state and was well-known for being one of the most conservative members of a very conservative legislature. Considering his previous record for introducing tough drug bills (LB 876 and LB 8), he hardly seemed the type of person to introduce such lenient legislation. Nevertheless, the records of public hearings, legislative debate, and our personal interviews with Senator C revealed quite clearly that his motivation for introducing the bill was punitive and not humanitarian. His argument to the senate, supported indirectly by the prosecutor at the public hearings, was that too many people had been getting away without being punished for possession of marijuana. Prosecutors and judges did not favor convicting young people under a law requiring what these officials considered to be much too severe a punishment.

> We have found the penalties were too severe . . . to the point where we nullified what we are trying to do because the courts in many cases would not enforce the penalties (Public Hearings on LB 2, January 28, 1969: 1).
> The County Attorneys of this state and the courts that would hear these charges feel that the felony charge in the case of possession for the first time is too strong and irregardless [sic] of the evidence, generally speaking, they will not enforce it (Senate Debate on LB 8, February 21, 1969: 350).
> The penalty of a felony was so great, it was the belief of the County Attorneys that they wasted their time trying to enforce it, because the judges would not apply the felony penalty (Senate Debate on LB 2, March 18, 1969: 744).

To ensure that those found in possession of marijuana would receive some punishment, Senator C advocated a reduction in the penalty to a point that he felt would seem reasonable to those enforcing the law.

> With the 7 day penalty for the possession of a nominal amount, the courts will rather promiscuously [sic] based on the evidence, apply these penalties (Senate Debate on LB 2, March 18, 1969: 744).

While the sponsor's motivation was clear, it still was not evident why Nebraska was one of the first states to pass this type of legislation, why it was supported by other legislators, and why no public opposition emerged to this legislation.

Critical Events

To further our understanding of the events involved in the bill's passage, the two senior authors interviewed key informants, including several other members of Nebraska's unicameral legislature, newsmen covering the legislature for both local newspapers, and a legislative reporter for a local radio station. Selected civil servants were also interviewed, including several county attorneys, the head of the state police narcotics division, and the head of the legislative drafting group, an agency of the state legislature which assists elected representatives in writing bills. A professor from the University of Nebraska Law School who specializes in criminal law and two defense attorneys in narcotics cases were also interviewed, as well as the ex-governor under whose administration the bill was passed. We also interviewed several of the former administrative aides to the ex-governor.[4]

The law professor recalled that a few months before the legislation had passed, a county attorney's son had been arrested for possession of marijuana. He felt this might have had some influence on the bill's success. Checking out his lead through back issues of the newspapers in the state capital, we found that, indeed, in August 1968, six months before the new marijuana control bill passed, the son of an outstate county attorney was arrested in the state capital where he was a student at the state university, and charged with possession of marijuana. The county attorney resigned his office to serve as his son's defense attorney, and in a press release he vowed to fight to change what he considered a harmful and unjust law (*Lincoln Journal,* August 13, 1968). Another university student arrested with the county attorney's boy was the son of a university professor. The county attorney's son was represented at first by his father, but soon his father hired a prominent Democratic lawyer who was later to become president of the Nebraska Bar Association. The university professor's son was represented by a popular Republic ex-governor who had declined to run for re-election. According to the outstate county attorney, these lawyers were intentionally selected as the most politically powerful bipartisan team of attorneys in the state. With regard to using this influence, the ex-governor said, "We recognized the case on our clients was air-tight so [we] figured it was best to attack the law." He wrote a draft of a first-offense marijuana possession misdemeanor law, and, after discussing the issue with the county attorney who was prosecuting the two boys, sent him the proposal.

This county attorney said that during the fall of 1968 he felt compelled to prosecute his colleague's son in part because, in his judgment, the boys had quite a large amount (one ounce) of marijuana in their possession. He claimed to have had no enthusiasm for his task, yet he indicated that he never considered not enforcing the law. Undoubtedly, the unusual publicity created by this case narrowed his options. The notion of a marijuana misdemeanor law provided him with an option in handling his colleague's son's case, and he said that, more importantly, it provided an avenue for getting more convictions in other drug cases. He said that, in enforcing the felony law, "We felt compelled to reduce charges to all sorts of ridiculous things such as disturbing the peace." Reducing the penalty to a misdemeanor would result in more convictions on appropriate charges since judges and juries would be more willing to convict if penalties were lowered. He said that the County Attorneys Association unofficially endorsed the idea because the prosecutors from Lincoln and Omaha had experienced special difficulties in getting convictions in drug cases. Since large quantities of drugs had not yet penetrated the other areas of the state, the other county attorneys were not as concerned. The Association, therefore, did not go on record in favor of such legislation for fear of appearing to take a promarijuana position. Nevertheless, the county attorneys said, they were all concerned about the potential of a felony conviction for "college kids just experimenting with marijuana"—a concern reflected in the testimony of the county attorney who testified at the public hearings. In short, the county attorneys wanted a more nearly just and enforceable law, one that both should be and could be enforced. The county attorney in Lincoln sent a tentative version of the bill to the state legislative drafting group and contacted a friend in the legislature, Senator C, asking him to sponsor the bill. In making this request, he argued that, if penalties were reduced, it would help get more convictions. Senator C agreed to sponsor the bill.

Just prior to introducing the misdemeanor marijuana bill, Senator C introduced another bill (Public Hearings on LB 8, January 27, 1969) which would have suspended college students for life from any Nebraska college or university, state or private, upon conviction of possession of marijuana.[5] The day after the school suspension bill was introduced, Senator C introduced the county attorney's misdemeanor bill. No one except a TV newsman (Terry, 1969) characterized this legislator's proposal as being soft on drug offenses; certainly none of his colleagues in the legislature did. To think of this man introducing a permissive piece of drug legislation was beyond credibility, given his general conservatism and longstanding and well-known hostility toward drug use. Not only had he introduced anti-LSD legislation and the punitive college suspension bill, but he also had argued that the misdemeanor legislation would make it harder on drug users.[6] With these strong credentials, he hardly could be accused of being permissive on the drug issue.

Yet, even the punishment-oriented sponsor of the bill recognized the wisdom of leniency for at least some of the middle and upper classes. During the public hearings on the college suspension bill, a member of the firm of the ex-governor representing the professor's son spoke against the suspension bill and in support of the misdemeanor bill which the legislator had publicly promised to introduce. Senator C was unusually courteous and respectful of him and publicly volunteered to make the misdemeanor bill retroactive to cover the ex-governor's client (Public Hearings on LB 8, January 27, 1969: 12), which he later did (Senate Debate on LB 2, March 18, 1969: 745).

Conclusion

Nebraska was one of the first states to reduce first-offense possession of marijuana to a misdemeanor, and several events and conditions seem to explain its early lead. The timing of the county attorney's son's arrest was important, of course, as a triggering event. This case assumed special significance because of the prestige of the defense attorneys. The speed with which the unicameral legislature can respond to such incidents is also an essential element in this explanation. A unicameral legislature avoids the usual conflict between the two houses, which often delays and sometimes kills prospective legislation. Moreover, several informants mentioned that in Nebraska there was perhaps special reluctance to punish young people for using marijuana because it commonly grows wild in the state. Reflecting this attitude was an editorial in one of the Lincoln newspapers (Dobler, 1968: 4), appearing approximately two months after the arrest of the outstate prosecutor's son, which discussed the long history of marijuana in the state. The editorial observed that the state had long endured the presence of large amounts of marijuana without serious disruption.

One of the most striking features in Nebraska's early lead, paradoxically, was the absence of any organized support for or opposition to this legislation. The only organization known to have supported this bill was the County Attorneys Association, and this support was unofficial, or at least not publicly announced. From newspaper reports it was clear that at least some students favored reducing or eliminating penalties for marijuana use, but we could find no evidence of any active support by students.[7] The bill quickly passed with *no* opposition. It could not have been predicted that a radically different and apparently lenient piece of drug legislation would go unnoticed in a state supposed to be very much influenced by the fundamentalist sentiments which justify punitive reactions to drug use (cf. Becker, 1963: 136).

One explanation for both the absence of organized support as well as the unexpected lack of opposition may be that the felony marijuana law which had previously been used only on the lower classes was threatening to middle class families. Whether or not middle class parents continued to perceive marijuana as a harmful drug, the threat of a felony charge and a prison term for their children clearly was perceived as more harmful—a theme that emerged often in our interviews. This threat is clearly illustrated in the case of the prosecutor's son. In the search for support for the bill this type of interest is not visible as are organized groups, yet its influence in forestalling opposition may be no less real.

Both moral conservatives and liberals, for different reasons of course, supported the bill. The more liberal members of the state government, including the governor, backed the legislation as a remedy against sending "decent" college kids to the penitentiary for a "minor mistake." This opposition to severe punishment for marijuana possession reflects a widespread feeling, according to Lindesmith (letter in possession of authors), that victimless crime or morality legislation arbitrarily creates "criminals" who not only do not view themselves as such; but, more importantly, are not so viewed by much of the public because of the absence of external social harm.

Apparently the moral conservatives in the state legislature did not oppose this bill because its sponsor justified it as a vehicle for insuring a greater likelihood of punishment since the felony possession law was not being enforced. Hall (1952) suggests that in a similar fashion at the end of the Middle Ages in England, merchants lobbied for the elimination of the death penalty for property crimes since severe penalties, out of line with public sentiment, allowed property offenders to escape any punishment under the law. In drug cases, Lindesmith (1965: 80–82) has also observed that, since felony convictions take more time in courts than do misdemeanors and are more difficult to get because of "technicalities," police will make fewer felony arrests and instead reduce charges to loitering or vagrancy. Also, with high minimum penalties, judges and prosecutors are likely to collaborate in avoiding imposition of the severe penalties by accepting guilty pleas to lesser charges. All of these things, apparently, were happening in Nebraska.

The issue of the seriousness of marijuana possession laws only developed with visible and seemingly widespread marijuana use among the middle and upper classes. As long as marijuana use appeared only among the poor, the problem of drug convictions didn't emerge for either conservatives or liberals. Only when confronting an increasing number of cases of middle class defendants did judges and juries begin to balk. While conservatives became angry with the leniency of the courts toward affluent defendants, liberals became worried and disgusted by the law's potential results, which included sending middle class defendants to prison.

Both moral conservatives and liberals recognized, for differing reasons, that severe penalties for possession of marijuana were not appropriate when the defendants were the children of middle class, affluent parents. Borrowing from the *consensus* and *conflict* models of legal change, we see that both conservatives and liberals *agreed* on the specific law although they fundamentally *disagreed* on the basic issue covered by the law. Perhaps most significantly, this consensus among diverse groups may offer some clues to understanding why a number of states in rapid succession passed similar legislation even though these laws represented a radical departure in controlling marijuana use.[8] Yet, contrary to the conflict orientation, no organized interest groups are in evidence in this case; and, unlike the functionalist perspective, there is no evidence of a massive opinion shift involved in this legislative change. For a complete understanding of these events, we must turn, as Edelman (1964) advises, to the symbolic properties of political events.

We see some parallels in our data with the argument by Warriner (1958) about the symbolic functions of preserving official morality. In a small Kansas community he found inconsistencies between citizens' public expressions and private behavior regarding alcohol consumption. Publicly, they were uniformly opposed to drinking, yet most drank within the privacy of their homes. Irrespective of their behavior, citizens felt that it was important to give symbolic support to the community's normative structure. Public support for national prohibition, according to Gusfield (1963: 1967), was also mainly a result of an effort to give symbolic support to the values prescribing total abstinence. Gusfield distinguishes this *symbolic* function of the law from its *instrumental* or actual enforcement or control function. Edelman (1964) observes that often citizens are satisfied that their interests are being protected once relevant legislation is passed, even if it is not enforced. The mere passage of the law symbolizes to them that their values are being supported. This, apparently, was the case with national prohibition (Gusfield, 1963).

This distinction between the instrumental and symbolic functions of law seems ideally suited for an analysis of Nebraska's marijuana law. Using this distinction, it becomes clear that the senate sponsor of the misdemeanor marijuana bill essentially argued that it would be an improvement because of its instrumental features, i.e., its ability to control. One unspoken, but no less real cost of this legislation was a certain loss of symbolic support for norms prohibiting drug use. Marijuana possession was still punishable under criminal law but the punishment was so light as to imply the offense was trivial. Those less condemning of marijuana use, on the other hand, gained some symbolic support for their position, and in fact made some instrumental gains as well because, while the probability of conviction might increase, the punishment was minimal. The basis for consensus on the legislation becomes clear: both moral conservatives and liberals gained something from this legal change.

Ironically, the pressure to enforce the law rather than to ignore it, as Edelman says so often occurs, was the result of the dramatic opposition to the law by the county attorney whose son was arrested. Because he was a prosecutor, he was in a special position to call public attention to his son's arrest. Moreover, his son was arrested in the state capital where state government and the mass media were centralized, which further served to publicize the case. Therefore, the other county attorney could not use the technique of ignoring the law to suit these specific interests. His options seemed limited by the publicity. The only course of action seemed to be a direct effort to change the relevant law.

It would appear that Senator C was taking a considerable chance of being labeled permissive regarding drug usage by introducing such legislation. He might have been protected from such criticism, however, by introducing the college suspension bill the day before. This emphasized his position on drugs, and, given the suspension bill's extreme provisions, absorbed most of the public and media attention. Like the county prosecutors, the senator made no statements to the press on behalf of the misdemeanor bill. Perhaps both the prosecutors and the senator were afraid of or at least uncertain of possible public reaction. However, the senator did have considerable commentary regarding the suspension bill and its ultimate veto. (See footnote 5.)

One possible interpretation of these events is that the senator intentionally introduced the suspension bill immediately prior to the misdemeanor bill in an attempt to distract the public and the media. Indeed, several respondents mentioned that the senator typically supports both extremes on an issue in an effort to protect himself from criticism. Another (not mutually exclusive) possibility is that those in the mass media felt that the bill was reasonable and they did not wish to arouse public indignation. Cooperation between the media and political officials is not uncommon, as Ross and Staines (1972) have concluded.

While the full impact of the legislation is not possible to assess so soon after its passage, some subsequent developments relevant to the legal change are apparent. In Omaha, which accounts for almost 50 percent of all drug offenses in Nebraska (Nebraska State Patrol, 1970: 14), a city ordinance allowed cases involving possession of marijuana to be prosecuted in city courts as misdemeanors or, alternatively, under state laws as felonies. Under the new state law county attorneys now have no option and must handle possession of marijuana as a misdemeanor. In Lincoln, where nearly one-fourth of all state narcotics cases are processed (Nebraska State Patrol, 1970: 14), the prosecutor claimed that all marijuana possession cases are now prosecuted as such, while under the previous felony law guilty pleas were often accepted to lesser non-narcotic offenses such as peace disturbance.

During the first full year this law was in effect, arrests involving marijuana possession nearly doubled (Nebraska State Patrol, 1970: 9). Even though arrests have rapidly escalated, a review of Omaha and Lincoln newspapers since the bill's passage indicates that neither student nor other groups have publicly protested, and there is no public argument that the law is oppressive. A maximum sentence of seven days is apparently acceptable, or at least tolerable. On the other hand, the bill's senate sponsor feels that most law-abiding citizens recognize that the increased arrests vividly demonstrate that the legislation which he introduced was badly needed. The lack of conflict regarding the consequences of the bill offers testimony to the symbolic and instrumental utility of the law. Moral conservatives may indeed feel, as Senator C speculates, that the new law offers more control as evidenced by increased convictions; those more tolerant of marijuana use may well regard the law as an instrumental and certainly a symbolic victory.

• • •

Notes

1. The first states to pass such drug legislation were Alaska, August 4, 1968; Wyoming, March 7, 1969; New Mexico, April 2, 1969; Utah, May 13, 1969; Washington, May 23, 1969; North Carolina, June 23, 1969; Connecticut, July 1, 1969; Iowa, July 1, 1969; and Illinois, July 18, 1969 (see Rosenthal, 1969; Arnold, 1969: 1, 60). The date of Nebraska's legislation, April 11, 1969, is missing from both of the above accounts.
2. The penalty prescribed under the 1943 Nebraska drug legislation was a fine of up to $3,000 and two to five years in prison.
3. Prosecuting attorneys are called county attorneys in Nebraska.
4. Perhaps because of pride in their state's trend-setting legislation, all respondents seemed eager to be interviewed and readily made their files available. Moreover, we found that each respondent volunteered the names of other people who might have some information relevant to our questions, and these other respondents volunteered yet another set of names. In this serial sample selection, we eventually found that no new names were being mentioned and felt we had contacted all knowledgeable respondents.
5. The suspension period was amended to 30 days (Public Hearings LB 8, January 27, 1969: 12), and was passed, aided by what was often characterized as Senator C's aggressive, overwhelming style (Senate Debate LB 8, February 4, 1969: 105–08; February 21, 1969: 345–51). The bill, however, was vetoed by the governor, and the outraged sponsor was only a few votes short of overriding the veto (Senate Debate LB 8, February 27, 1969: 454–66).
6. Two years before, in 1967, this legislator had introduced a bill creating penalties for possession of LSD and establishing a narcotics control division in the state highway patrol (LB 876, effective June 7, 1967). He justified this legislation in punitive and control terms (Public Hearings on LB 876, April 18, 1967; Senate Debate on LB 876, May 2, 1967).
   "As far as I am concerned, nothing can be too harsh for those people who pervade [sic] this step, because I can think of nothing more horrible, than to have a son or daughter of mine become afflicted with this habit . . . [and] . . . be unable to break themselves or himself of the habit" (Public Hearings on LB 876, April 18, 1967: 3).
   "Are you going to wait until it happens in your family, to your son or daughter becomes contaminated [sic] or maybe your grandchild or the kid next door. [sic] Are you going to wait till you have to have a vivid explanation of this thing or are you going to do something about it? I think drugs is [sic] the most terrible thing that can happen to the human mind. And I am not willing to sit still and not attempt to do something about it" (Senate Debate on LB 876, May 2, 1967: 1913).
7. Because of his strong position on drugs and from other university-baiting positions, Senator C was not a popular figure on the state university campus. Perhaps this accounts for lack of student enthusiasm for his bill, or perhaps more likely, students might have viewed it as still too punitive to merit active support.

8. It is interesting to observe that most of the states that were in the initial group making a first offense of marijuana possession punishable only as a misdemeanor or at least giving this option to the court were in the west or western plains. Besides Nebraska, these states include Alaska, California, Iowa, Montana, New Mexico, North Dakota, South Dakota, Utah, Washington, and Wyoming. Only Connecticut, Illinois, and North Carolina are early passage states clearly not in this region. Aside from mere geographical proximity which makes the spread of ideas easily understandable, the agricultural and cultural characteristics of Nebraska undoubtedly exist to a degree in many of these other western states. Large quantities of open land where marijuana grows wild is one similarity. Since many of these states are predominantly rural in character, the concern with sending local (often country) boys to the penitentiary may have been widespread. Finally, many of these states are also predominantly rural Protestant so that punitive and repressive arguments in favor of reduction of penalties were likely to have been used.

References

Arnold Martin. 1969 "Varied Drug Laws Raising U.S. Fears," *New York Times* (August 17).

Becker, Howard S. 1963 *Outsiders*. New York: Free Press of Glencoe.

Chambliss, William J. 1964 "A Sociological Analysis of the Law of Vagrancy," 12 *Social Problems* 67.

Clausen, J. A. 1961 "Drug Addiction," in Robert K. Merton and Robert A. Nisbet (eds.), *Contemporary Social Problems*. New York: Harcourt, Brace and World.

De Frain, John. 1967 "Students Clash over Narcotics." *Lincoln Journal* (November 21).

Dicey, A. V. 1920 *Lectures on the Relation between Law and Public Opinion in England during the Nineteenth Century*. London: Macmillan.

Dickson, Donald T. 1968 "Bureaucracy and Morality: An Organizational Perspective on a Moral Crusade," 16 *Social Problems* 143.

Dobler, William O. 1968 "In Perspective," *Lincoln Star* (October 9).

Durkheim, Emile. 1964 *The Division of Labor in Society*. New York: Free Press of Glencoe.

Edelman, Murray. 1964 *The Symbolic Uses of Politics*. Urbana: University of Illinois Press.

Engels, Frederick. 1972 *The Origin of the Family, Private Property, and the State*. New York: International Publishers.

Friedman, Lawrence M. and Jack Ladinsky. 1967 "Social Change and the Law of Industrial Accidents," 67 *Columbia Law Review* 50.

Goode, Erich. 1970 *The Marijuana Smokers*. New York: Basic Books. 1972 *Drugs in American Society*. New York: Alfred A. Knopf.

Gusfield, J. R. 1963 *Symbolic Crusade: Status Politics and the American Temperance Movement*. Urbana: University of Illinois Press. 1967 "Moral Passage: The Symbolic Process in Public Designations of Deviance," 15 *Social Problems* 175.

Hall, Jerome. 1952 *Theft, Law, and Society*. Indianapolis: Bobbs-Merrill.

Jeffery, C. R. 1957 "The Development of Crime in Early English Society," 47 *Journal of Criminal Law, Criminology, and Police Science* 647.

Laski, Harold J. 1935 *The State in Theory and Practice*. New York: Viking Press.

Lindesmith, Alfred R. 1965 *The Addict and the Law*. Bloomington: Indiana University Press.

National Organization for the Reform of Marijuana Laws. 1971 "The Criminal Penalties under the Current Marijuana Laws." Washington: National Organization for the Reform of Marijuana Laws.

Nebraska State Patrol, Division of Drug Control. 1970 *Activity Summary: Drug and Narcotic Cases*. Lincoln: Nebraska State Patrol.

Pound, Roscoe. 1922 *An Introduction to the Philosophy of Law*. New Haven: Yale University Press. 1942 *Social Control through Law*. New Haven: Yale University Press.

Quinney, Richard. 1970 *The Social Reality of Crime*. Boston: Little, Brown and Co.

Rosenthal, M. P. 1969 "A Plea for Amelioration of the Marijuana Laws," 47 *Texas Law Review* 1359.

Ross, Robert and Graham L. Staines. 1972 "The Politics of Social Problems," 20 *Social Problems* 18.

Sutherland, E. H. 1950 "The Diffusion of Sexual Psychopath Laws," 56 *American Journal of Sociology* 142.

Terry, Lee. 1969 KETV, Channel 7 News Observation, Omaha (February 27).

Thomas, Fred. 1969 "Puffers Find Pot of Gold under Nebraska Rainbow," *Omaha World Herald* (August 31).

Vold, George B. 1958 *Theoretical Criminology.* New York: Oxford University Press.

Wall, Millan. 1968 "Farmers Oppose Declaring Marijuana a Noxious Weed," *Lincoln Star* (February 15).

Warriner, C. K. 1958 "The Nature and Functions of Official Morality," 64 *American Journal of Sociology* 165.

---

4. Control and Intoxicant Use: A Theoretical and Practical Overview

Norman E. Zinberg and Wayne M. Harding

The Social Setting and Control

In the last decade it has become increasingly commonplace for investigators to divide the variables that are presumed to influence drug-taking behavior into three groups: (1) drug variables (the pharmacological properties of the drug being used); (2) set variables (the attitudes and personality of the user); and (3) setting variables (the social and physical environment in which use occurs). Underlying this model—which corresponds to the public-health model of agent, host, and environment—is the premise that at any one time variables from each of the three groups interact in complex ways to determine who uses an intoxicant, how it is used, and what its effects are.

Our primary theoretical and research interest has been the impact of setting variables on control. We will begin by defining the two aspects of setting with which we are most concerned, rituals and social sanctions. Next, the importance of setting variables will be illustrated by considering how control over alcohol use has developed in American culture and how it operates today, and then by describing how today's social setting is influencing the development of control over illicit drug use. Finally, examples will be given of the interaction of the drug, set, and setting variables in shaping the use of illicit drugs.

Rituals and Social Sanctions

As used here, the term rituals refers to the stylized, prescribed behavior patterns surrounding the use of a drug. This behavior may include methods of procuring and administering the drug, selection of a physical and social setting for use, activities undertaken after the drug has been administered, and methods of preventing untoward drug effects. For example, two familiar alcohol-using rituals are having cocktails before dinner and drinking beer at ball games.

Social sanctions are the norms regarding whether and how a particular drug should be used. They include both the informal (and often unspoken) values and rules of conduct shared by a group and the formal laws and policies regulating drug use. Two of the informal sanctions or basic rules of conduct that regulate the use of alcohol are "Know your limit" and "Don't drive when you're drunk." Although laws and regulations are clearly social sanctions we will emphasize informal social sanctions, which frequently are internalized and actually may exert greater influence over use than do formal rules. For instance, most Americans avoid drunkenness more because they feel it is unseemly—and drunken driving more because they have learned it is unsafe—than because of the possible legal consequences (Zinberg *et al.*, 1977).

Rituals and social sanctions operate in different social contexts that range all the way from small discrete clusters of users (drinks at a weekly poker game with friends) through larger collections of people (cocktail parties, or drugs at rock concerts) to entire classes or segments of society (morning coffee, or wine with meals in Italian households). Different segments of society may develop complementary, or even opposing, rituals and social sanctions, and usually each segment is cognizant of the alternatives and to some degree is influenced by them. Rituals and social sanctions can operate either for or against control. Drinking muscatel from a bag-wrapped bottle while squatting in a doorway is not a controlling ritual nor is the soliciting of psychedelics from strangers on the street. According positive status to the ability to withstand extraordinarily high doses of LSD or to the sizableness of one's heroin habit is not a controlling sanction. We are chiefly concerned with the rituals and sanctions that promote moderate use, as exemplified by the evolution of control over alcohol consumption.

Social Setting and Alcohol Use

The history of alcohol consumption in America reveals striking variations in patterns of use from one era to another. Sometimes a period of control, or lack of control, has coincided with a major historical epoch. The following five social prescriptions defining controlled or moderate use of alcohol, which have been derived from studies of use in many different cultures, will serve as a standard for assessing control in the major periods of American history:

(1) Group drinking is clearly differentiated from drunkenness and is associated with ritualistic or religious celebrations.
(2) Drinking is associated with eating or ritualistic feasting.
(3) Both sexes, as well as two or more generations, are included in the drinking situation, whether they drink or not.
(4) Drinking is divorced from the individual effort to escape personal anxiety or difficult (even intolerable) social situations. Further, alcohol is not considered medicinally valuable.
(5) Inappropriate behavior when drinking (violence, aggression, overt sexuality) is absolutely disapproved, and protection against such behavior is offered by the sober or the less intoxicated. This general acceptance of a concept of restraint usually indicates that drinking is only one of many activities and thus carries a low level of emotionalism. It also shows that drinking is not associated with a male or female rite of passage or sense of superiority.

The importance of these social prescriptions in controlling alcohol use is evident in the changing patterns of consumption through the colonial period, the Revolutionary War and nineteenth century, the Prohibition era, and the period that has followed repeal of the Volstead Act.

Pre-Revolutionary America (1620–1775), though veritably steeped in alcohol, strongly and effectively prohibited drunkenness. Families drank and ate together in taverns, and drinking was associated with celebrations and rituals. Tavern-keepers were people of status; keeping the peace and preventing excesses stemming from drunkenness were grave duties. Manliness or strength was not measured by the extent of consumption or by violent acts resulting from it. Pre-Revolutionary society, however, did not abide by all the prescriptions, for certain alcoholic beverages were viewed as medicines. For example, "groaning beer," a very potent alcoholic beverage, was consumed in large quantities by pregnant and lactating women. Even though alcohol was viewed as medicinally valuable, alcohol-related problems remained at a low level, due in part to the strict standards that limited consumption and dictated deportment when drinking.

Beginning with the Revolutionary War and continuing with the Industrial Revolution and expansion of the frontier through the nineteenth century, an era of excess dawned. Men were separated from their families, which left them to drink together and with prostitutes. Alcohol was served without food and was not limited to special occasions. Violence resulting from drunkenness became more common. In the face of increasing drunkenness and alcoholism, people began to believe (as in the case with some illicit drugs today) that it was the powerful pharmacological properties of the intoxicant itself that made more controlled use difficult or impossible. By the latter part of the nineteenth century the West was won, and the family and personal disruptions brought on by the Industrial Revolution were moderated. In both the West and the East, families became more closely integrated. There was a change in the character of the neighborhood saloon or bar. Customers partook of free lunches with their beverages and tended once again to represent a mix of generations and sexes who frowned on violence, overt sexuality, and excessive consumption of alcoholic beverages. This moderation, however, was interrupted in the early twentieth century by the passage of the Volstead Act, which ushered in another era of excess. In the speakeasy ambience of the Prohibition era, men again drank together and with prostitutes, food was replaced by alcohol, and the drinking experience was colored with illicitness and potential violence.

Although Repeal provided relief from excessive and unpopular legal control, years passed before regular but moderate alcohol use emerged as normative behavior. Today, however, the vast majority of drinkers manage to control their use. Of an estimated 105 million drinkers fewer than eight million are alcoholics (Harding and Zinberg, 1977). While alcoholism is still a major public health problem, the extent of noncompulsive use of such a powerful, addictive, and easily available intoxicant is remarkable. This can only be fully understood in terms of the rituals and sanctions that pattern the way alcohol is used.

Alcohol-using rituals define appropriate use and limit consumption to specific occasions: a drink with a business luncheon, wine with dinner, or perhaps beer with the boys. Positive social sanctions permit and even encourage alcohol use, but there are also negative sanctions that condemn promiscuous use and drunkenness; for example, "Don't mix drinks," "Don't drink before sundown," and "Know your limit." This is not to say that users never break these rules, but when they do they are aware of making a special exception. They know, for instance, that having a Bloody Mary with breakfast is acceptable behavior for an occasional Sunday brunch, but that drinking vodka with breakfast every morning would violate accepted social standards.

The internalization of rituals and social sanctions begins in early childhood. Children see their parents and other adults drink. They are exposed to acceptable and unacceptable models of alcohol use in magazines and movies and on television. Some may sip their parent's drink or be served wine with meals or on religious occasions. So, by the time they reach adolescence they have already absorbed an enormous amount of information about how to drink. When the adolescent tests—as most do—the limits he has learned and gets drunk and nauseated, there is little need to fear that this excess will become habitual. As he matures the adolescent has numerous examples of adult use at hand and can easily find friends who share both his interest in drinking and his commitment to becoming a controlled drinker. Support for control continues throughout adult life.

Obviously the influence of social learning on the alcohol user is not always so straightforward. Social sanctions and rituals promoting control are not uniformly distributed throughout the culture. Some ethnic groups, such as the Irish, lack strong sanctions against drunkenness and have a correspondingly higher rate of alcoholism. Alcohol socialization within the family may break down as a result of divorce, death, or some other disruptive event. In some instances the influence of other variables—personality, genetic differences, as well as other setting variables—may outweigh the influence of social learning. Nonetheless, controlling rituals and social sanctions exert a crucial and distinct influence on the way most Americans use alcohol (Harding and Zinberg, 1977).

Social Setting and Illicit Drug Use

In contrast to the situation with alcohol, the opportunities for learning how to control illicit drug consumption, although changing, are still extremely limited. Neither the family nor the culture regularly provides long-term education or models of use. The worst propaganda of the 1960s against illicit drug use has faded, but the chief educational message from media and the schools is still that reasonable, controlled use of illicit drugs is impossible. Certainly, no official advice is given on how to use these drugs safely. Compounding these disadvantages are the possible problems of variable dosage and purity of drugs on the black market, and the very real threat of arrest and incarceration. Ironically, the efforts to eliminate any and all use of illicit drugs work against the development of control by those who decide to use drugs anyway.

Despite these difficulties, our DAC and NIDA studies and the work of other investigators have shown that it is possible to attain a high level of control over illicit drugs. Furthermore, there is some indication that occasional rather than intensive patterns of consumption predominate in the use of most if not all illicit drugs. Our research comparing controlled and compulsive users of marihuana, psychedelics, and opiates suggests that rituals and social sanctions promote this control in four basic and overlapping ways:

(1) Sanctions define moderate use and condemn compulsive use. Controlled opiate users have sanctions limiting frequency of use to levels far below that required for addiction. Many have special sanctions, such as "Don't use every day." A complementary ritual would be to restrict the use of an opiate to weekends.

(2) Sanctions limit use to physical and social settings that are conducive to a positive or "safe" drug experience. The maxim for psychedelics is "Use in a good place at a good time with good people." Rituals consonant with such sanctions are the selection of a pleasant rural setting for psychedelic use, or the timing of use to avoid driving while "tripping."

(3) Sanctions identify potentially untoward drug effects. Rituals embody the relevant precautions to be taken before and during use. Opiate users may minimize the risk of overdose by using only a portion of the drug and waiting to gauge its effect before using more. Marihuana users similarly titrate their dosage to avoid becoming too high (dysphoric).

(4) Sanctions and rituals operate to compartmentalize drug use and support the users' non-drug-related obligations and relationships. Users may budget the amount of money they spend on drugs, as they do for entertainment. Drugs may be used only in the evenings and on weekends to avoid interfering with work performance.

The process by which controlling rituals and sanctions are acquired varies from subject to subject. Most individuals come by them gradually during the course of their drug-using careers. But the most important source of precepts and practices for control seems to be peer using groups. Virtually all of our subjects required the assistance of other noncompulsive users to construct appropriate rituals and sanctions out of the folklore and practices circulating in the diverse drug-using subcultures. The peer group provides instruction in and reinforces proper use; despite the popular image of peer pressure as a corrupting force pushing weak individuals toward drug misuse, many segments of the drug subculture stand firmly against misuse of drugs.

This does not imply that all illicit drug use, even among controlled users, is altogether safe or decorous. As with alcohol consumption, there are occasions when less than decorous behavior occurs. Obviously the only way to completely eliminate the attendant risks is to remain abstinent. We should never condone excessive use of any intoxicant, but we must recognize that if occasional lapses of control occur, they do not signify a breakdown of overall control. Drunkenness at a wedding reception is not a reliable indicator of alcoholism. Unfortunately, occasions of impropriety following the use of illicit drugs are likely to be taken (by abstainers, usually) as proof of the prevailing mythology that with these drugs the only possibilities are abstinence or compulsive use.

Despite occasional lapses by some subjects, the bulk of the controlled users we have studied demonstrate as much responsibility, caution, and control over their illicit drug use as does the average social drinker.

Interactions among Drug, Set, and Setting

As stated earlier, in order to understand drug use, drug, set, and setting variables must all be taken into account. The use of opiates during the Vietnam War and psychedelic use during the past decade and a half illustrate how these variables can interact and also how control of an illicit drug can evolve.

Recent estimates indicate that during the Vietnam War as many as 35 percent of enlisted men used heroin. Of these, 54 percent became addicted to it, and 73 percent of all those who used at least five times became addicted (Robins *et al.,* 1977). When the extent of heroin use in Vietnam was first realized, officials of the armed forces and government assumed that the commonly believed maxim, "Once an addict always an addict," would operate, and that returning veterans would contribute to a major heroin epidemic in the United States. Treatment and rehabilitation centers were set up in Vietnam, and the Army's claim that heroin addiction stopped "at the shore of the South China Sea" was heard everywhere. As virtually all observers agreed, however, those programs were largely failures. Often people in the rehabilitation centers used more heroin than when they were on active duty, and recidivism rates in Vietnam approached 90 percent (Zinberg 1972).

Although pessimism was warranted at the time, most addiction did indeed stop at the South China Sea. As Lee Robins has shown, only 50 percent of the men who had been addicted in Vietnam used heroin at all after their return to the United States; and, what is more surprising, only 12 percent became readdicted (Robins *et al.,* 1977). In order to account for the fact that so many veterans used heroin in Vietnam and that their rate of addiction dropped dramatically after they returned to the United States, set, drug, and particularly setting variables must be considered.

Undoubtedly some personality configurations are such that dependence on almost any available intoxicating substance is likely. But even the most generous estimate of the number of such individuals is not large enough to explain the extraordinarily high rate of use in Vietnam. And since the military screens out the worst psychological problems at enlistment, the number of addiction-prone personalities might even have been lower than in a normal population. Robins found that a youthful liability scale correlated well with heroin use in Vietnam. The scale included some items that could be indicative of personality difficulties (truancy, dropout or explusion from school, fighting, arrests, and so on), but it also included many non-personality-related items, such as race or living in the inner city. And it accounted for only a portion of the variance in heroin use.

It should be noted here that the bulk of research evidence linking personality with drug use has been riddled with serious methodological problems. Perhaps the most frequent problem in attempting to assess the importance of the user's personality is the difficulty of drawing sound conclusions when interviewing those who have become dependent on intoxicating substances. In the American cultural setting these users tend to sound and look like a group that is extremely vulnerable to dependence, and in a retrospective study it is easy to make a case for their original vulnerability. Until recently, studies of drug consumption have reinforced this tendency by centering on the most severe cases of misuse (Zinberg, 1975).

Another reasonable explanation for the high rate of heroin use and of addiction in Vietnam might be the availability of the drug. Robins notes that 85 percent of veterans had been offered heroin in Vietnam, and that it was remarkably inexpensive (Robins *et al.,* 1977). Another drug variable, the route of administration, must also have contributed to widespread use in Vietnam. Heroin was so potent and inexpensive that smoking was an effective and economic method of use, and this no doubt made it more attractive than if injection had been the primary mode of administration. These two drug variables also seem to explain the decrease in heroin use and addiction among veterans following their return to the United States. The decreased availability of heroin in the United States (reflected in high price) and its decreased potency (which made smoking it wholly impractical) made it more difficult for the returning veterans to continue to use the drug as they had in Vietnam.

In the case of Vietnam, the drug variable may carry more explanatory power than the various personality variables, but like them it has limits. Ready availability of heroin seems to account for the high prevalence of use, but it alone does not explain why some individuals became addicted and others did not, any more than availability of alcohol is sufficient to explain the difference between the alcoholic and the social drinker. (Our current NIDA study, too, indicates that opiates are just as available to controlled users as to compulsive users.) Availability is inextricably intertwined with the social and psychological factors that create demand for an intoxicant. Once a reasonably large number of users decide that a substance is attractive and desirable, it is surprising how quickly that substance can become more plentiful. (Cocaine is a current example.) When the morale of U.S. troops in Germany declined in 1972, large quantities of various drugs, including heroin, became much more available than they had been before, even though Germany is much farther from opium-growing areas than Vietnam.

The social setting of Vietnam was both alien and extremely stressful. This abhorrent environment must have been a significant factor, if not the primary factor, in leading men who ordinarily would not have considered using heroin to use it and sometimes to become addicted. Their low rate of addiction after returning home suggests that the veterans themselves associated heroin use with Vietnam, much as hospital patients who are receiving large amounts of opiates for a painful medical condition associate the drug with the condition and do not crave it after they have left the hospital.

The importance of the three variables—drug, set, and setting—becomes even clearer when we attempt to account for the changes in psychedelic use that have taken place during the last ten or fifteen years. Whereas the Vietnam data primarily illustrate how the prevalence of use is affected by these variables, psychedelic use illustrates how a more specific aspect of control—control over adverse effects—is influenced by drug, set, and setting.

About 1963, the use of psychedelics became a subject of national hysteria—the so-called "drug revolution"—epitomized by Timothy Leary's "Tune In, Turn On, and Drop Out" slogan. These drugs, known then as psychotomimetics (imitators of psychosis), were widely believed to cause psychosis, suicide, and even murder. Equally well publicized were the contentions that they could bring about spiritual rebirth or a sense of mystical oneness with the universe. Certainly there were numerous cases of not merely transient but prolonged psychosis following the use of psychedelics. In the mid-1960s such psychiatric hospitals as the Massachusetts Mental Health Center and

Bellevue were reporting that as many as one-third of their emergency admissions resulted from the ingestion of these drugs. By the late 60s, however, the rate of admissions had dropped dramatically (Zinberg *et al.,* 1977). Initially, many observers concluded that this drop was due to a decline in use brought about by fear tactics—the warnings about various health hazards, the chromosome breaks and birth defects, reported in the newspapers. In fact, although psychedelic use continued to be the fastest growing drug use in America through 1973, the dysfunctional sequelae virtually disappeared. What then had changed?

Neither the drugs themselves nor the personalities of the users were the major factor in cases of psychotic reactions to psychedelics. A retrospective study of the way such drugs had been used before the early 60s has revealed that although responses to the drugs varied widely, they included few of the horrible, highly publicized consequences of the mid-60s (McGlothlin and Arnold, 1971). In another study conducted before the drug revolution, typologies of response to the drugs were found, but not a one-to-one relationship between untoward reactions and emotional disturbance (Barr *et al.,* 1972). It appears therefore that the hysteria and conflict over psychedelic use that characterized the mid-60s created a climate in which bad trips occurred more often than they had before. Becker in his prophetic article of 1967 compared the then current anxiety about psychedelics to anxiety about marihuana in the late 1920s when several psychoses had been reported (Becker, 1967). He hypothesized that the psychoses of the 1920s had come not from reactions to the drug itself but from the secondary anxiety generated by the media, which had exaggerated the drug's effects. Suggesting that such unpleasant reactions had disappeared later because the actual effects of marihuana use had become more widely known, he correctly predicted that the same thing would happen in relation to the psychedelics.

Social learning about psychedelics also brought a change in the reactions of those who had expected to gain insight and enlightenment from their use. Interviews have shown that the user of the early 1960s who hoped for heaven, feared hell, and was unfamiliar with drug effects had a far more extreme experience than the user of the 1970s, who had been exposed to a decade of publicity about psychedelic colors, music, and sensations (Zinberg, 1974). The later user had been thoroughly prepared, albeit largely unconsciously, for the experience, and therefore his response was far less extreme.

Increased control over the psychedelics seems to be attributable to the subcultural development of controlling sanctions and rituals very like those regarding alcohol use in the larger culture. The rule "Use the first time only with a guru" counseled neophytes to team up with experienced users who could reduce their secondary anxiety about what was happening by interpreting it as a drug effect. "Only use at a good time, in a good place, with good people" gave users sound advice about taking drugs that would make them intensely sensitive to their inner and outer surroundings. In addition, it conveyed the message that the drug experience could be merely a pleasant consciousness change rather than a visit to the extreme of heaven or hell. The specific rituals that developed to express these sanctions—as to just when it was best to take the drug, how it was best to come down, and so on—varied from group to group, though some that were particularly effective spread from one group to another. Today (1979), controlling rituals and sanctions are widely available to those who use psychedelics.

The psychedelics also provide a good example of the role that pharamacology plays with regard to control of use. Since they produce a long period of well-defined consciousness change, they are more easily controlled than other drugs. The length of intoxication and its intensity make the psychedelics special-occasion drugs, requiring users to set aside a considerable period of time in which to deal with drug effects. And the process of defining a special occasion brings in a variety of controlling factors, including the development of sanctions and rituals. Although at the height of the drug revolution some users took psychedelics several times a week, reports from the Haight Ashbury Free Medical Clinic and from our own study show that no case of such use lasted longer than a year or two at the most (Zinberg *et al.*, 1977). While that was, of course, a long time in which to make frequent use of such powerful substances, and the resulting psychological damage cannot be assessed, it is still hard to imagine anyone becoming habituated to the psychedelics. So, though the social setting variable explains the reduction and virtual elimination of severe emotional reactions to psychedelic drugs, the drug variable is most important in accounting for the low rate of dependence.

References

Barr, H. L., Langs, R. J. Holt, R. R. *et al.*, *LSD: Personality and Experience,* Wiley Interscience, New York, 1972.

Becker, H. S., History, culture and subjective experience: an exploration of the social bases of drug-induced experiences, *Journal of Health and Social Behavior* 8:163–176, 1967.

Dole, V. P. and Nyswander, M., Heroin addiction—a metabolic disease, *Archives of Internal Medicine* 120:19–24, 1967.

Dole, V. P. and Nyswander, M., Methadone maintenance treatment: a ten-year perspective, JAMA 235:2117–2119, 1976.

Harding, W. M. and Zinberg, N. E., The effectiveness of the subculture in developing rituals and social sanctions for controlled use, *Drugs, Rituals and Altered States of Consciousness* (Ed. B. M. du Toit). A. A. Balkema, Rotterdam, Netherlands, 1977.

Heller, M., *The Sources of Drug Abuse,* Addiction Services Agency Report, New York, June, 1972.

Josephson, E., Trends in adolescent marihuana use, *Drug Use: Epidemiological and Sociological Approaches* (Eds. E. Josephson and E. E. Carroll). Hemisphere Publishing Corporation, Washington, D.C., 1974.

McGlothlin, W. H. and Arnold, D. O., LSD revisited—a ten-year followup of medical LSD use, *Archives of General Psychiatry* 24:35–49, 1971.

National Institute on Drug Abuse, *Marihuana and Health,* Sixth Annual Report to the U.S. Congress from the Secretary of Health, Education and Welfare, 1976.

Robins, L. N., Helzer, J. E., Hesselbrock, M. *et al.* Vietnam veterans three years after Vietnam: how our study changed our view of heroin, Problems of Drug Dependence, Proceedings of the Thirty-ninth Annual Scientific Meeting, Committee on Problems of Drug Dependence, Boston, Massachusetts, 1977.

Szasz, T., *Ceremonial Chemistry: The Ritual Persecution of Drugs, Addicts and Pushers,* Anchor Press/Doubleday, Garden City, New York, 1975.

Young, J., *The Drugtakers: The Social Meaning of Drug Use,* MacGibbon and Kee, Ltd., London, 1971.

Zinberg, N. E., Heroin use in Vietnam and the United States, *Archives of General Psychiatry* 26:486–488, 1972.

Zinberg, N. E., *"High" States: A Beginning Study.* Drug Abuse Council Special Studies Series SS-3, Washington, D.C., 1974.

Zinberg, N.E., Addiction and ego function, *Psychoanal. St. Ch.* 30:567–588, 1975.

Zinberg, N. E. and Fraser, K. M., The role of the social setting in the prevention and treatment of alcoholism, *The Diagnosis and Treatment of Alcoholism* (Ed. J. H. Mendelson), in press, 1979.

Zinberg, N. E., Harding, W. M., and Apsler, R., What is drug abuse? *Journal of Drug Issues* 8:9–35, 1978a.

Zinberg, N. E., Harding, W. M., Stelmack, S. *et al.,* Patterns of heroin use, *Recent Developments in Chemotherapy of Narcotic Addiction, Annals of the New York Academy of Sciences* 311:10–24, 1978b.

Zinberg, N. E., Harding, W. M., and Winkeller, M., A study of social regulatory mechanisms in controlled illicit drug users, *Social Meanings of Drugs: Principles of Social Pharmacology* (Ed. K. Blum, S. J. Feinglass, and A. H. Briggs), Basic Books, New York, in press; and *Journal of Drug Issues* 7:117–133, 1977.

5. The Myth of the Drug Taker in the Mass Media

Jock Young

The most amazing quality of mass media reporting of the drug problem is their ability to get the wrong end of the stick. Indeed in *The drugtakers* I formulated, with tongue in cheek, Young's Law of Information on Drugs. Namely, that the *greater* the public health risk (measured in number of mortalities) of a psychotropic substance, the *less* the amount of information (including advertising) critical of its effects. Tobacco, alcohol, the barbiturates, amphetamines, heroin, LSD and marihuana (listed in declining public health risk) would all seem to fit this proposition—apart from those exceptional and short-lived occasions when lung cancer scares occur. It is the explanation of the social basis of this 'Law' with which this article is concerned.

We live in a world which is extremely socially segregated: direct experience of individuals with behaviour different from our own conventions and values is rare. It is in just such a world that we come to rely on the mass media for a sizeable proportion of our information as to the goings on of outsiders to our small discrete social worlds. Criticism of the mass media has centered round the notion that journalists are biased, misinformed or just plain deceitful. The impression is given that if the profession were to revamp its ethics and remove its bias, the body of responsible journalism would be uncovered and the population receive from then on the simple facts of the matter, to interpret as they please. Minor adjustments have to be made to the set after which the picture will focus and the facts be held objectively. I wish to suggest, to the contrary, that 'facts' do not speak for themselves, that they are only given meaning in terms of the frame of reference provided. Further, that the mass media offer an amazingly systematic frame of reference. It is not random bias but a consistent world view which is purveyed. The model of society held by the mass media, and implicit in their reporting of both deviant and normal, I will term consensualist. Its constitution is simplicity itself: namely, that the vast majority of people in society share a common definition of reality—agree as to what activities are praiseworthy and what are condemnable. That this consensus is functional to an organic system which they envisage as society. That behaviour outside this reality is a product of irrationality or sickness, that it is in itself meaningless activity which leads nowhere and is, most importantly, behaviour which has direct and unpleasant consequences for the small minority who are impelled to act this way. The model carries with it a notion of merited rewards and just punishments. It argues for the equitable nature of the *status quo* and draws the parameters of happiness and experience. Specifically, it defines material rewards as the payment for hard work, sexual pleasure as the concomitant of supporting the nuclear family, and religious or mystical experience as not an alternative interpretation of reality but as an activity acceptable only in a disenchanted form which solemnizes (their word) the family and bulwarks the *status quo*. The illicit drug taker is, I want to suggest, the deviant *par excellence*. For his culture disdains work and revels in hedonism, his sexual relations are reputedly licentious and promiscuous, and the psychedelics promise a re-enchantment of the world—a subversive take-on reality.

It is not drugs *per se* which are designated—for our culture is historically normal in that drug use is ubiquitous. Rather it is drugs taken for hedonistic reasons. The social drinker who is relaxing between his work bouts, the middle-aged barbiturate addict who needs drugs in order to sleep, the tranquillizer habitué who takes drugs in order to ease his work or marital tensions—or even the physician morphine addict who uses the drug to keep him working under pain or stress: all of these individuals are ignored or treated lightly. It is when drug use is seen as unrelated to productivity, when it leads to 'undeserved' pleasures, when it gives rise to experiences which question the taken-for-granted 'reality', that the forces of condemnation are bought into play.

The mass media carries a mythology of the average man and the deviant—within which Mr. Average is seen to prosper and be content in his universe of hard work and industrious consumption and the deviant is portrayed as being beset by forces which lead to ineluctable misfortune. But the real world outside this spectacle differs radically from this. For often the worker doubts the fairness of his rewards, the middle-class housewife surveys her Ideal Home with ambivalance, the husband eyes his secretary and then goes back to his wife, the adolescent Seeker looks at the Established Church and cannot for the life of him see how it refers to the same reality as that of the Christian mystics. For popular consciousness is a collage of contradictions: it is both sceptical and complacent, satisfied and discontented, rational and superstitious, conservative and downright subversive. It is on this base that the mass media acts. For there exists widespread suspicion that the sacrifices made are not worth the rewards received. This is the basis for what Albert Cohen calls moral indignation. Thus he writes:

> . . . the dedicated pursuit of culturally approved goals, the adherence to normatively sanctioned means—these imply a certain self restraint, effort, discipline, inhibition. What is the effect of others who, though their activities do not manifestly damage our own interests are morally undisciplined, who give themselves up to idleness, self indulgence, or forbidden vices? What effect does the propinquity of the wicked have upon the peace of mind of the virtuous?[1]

What Cohen is arguing is that deviant activities, even although they may have no direct effect on the interests of those who observe them, may be condemned because they represent concrete examples of individuals who are, so to speak, dodging the rules. For if a person lives by a code of conduct which forbids certain pleasures, which involves the deferring of gratification in certain areas, it is hardly surprising that he will react strongly against those whom he sees to be taking short cuts. This is a partial explanation of the vigorous repression against what Edwin Schur calls 'crimes without victims': homosexuality, prostitution, abortion and drug taking.

The mass media have discovered that people read avidly news which titillates their sensibilities and confirms their prejudices. The ethos of 'give the public what it wants' involves a constant play on the normative worries of large segments of the population; it utilizes outgroups as living Rorschach blots on to which collective fears and doubts are projected. Moral indignation, if first galvanized by the newspapers and then resolved in a *just* fashion, makes a fine basis for newspaper readership. To this extent then newspaper men are accurate when they suggest that they are just giving the public what it wants, only what this represents is reinforcing the consensual part of the popular consciousness and denigrating any subversive notions.

The widespread appeal of the mass media rests, therefore, on its ability to fascinate and titillate its audience and then reassure by finally condemning. This is a propaganda of a very sophisticated sort, playing on widespread discontent and insecurities and little resembling the crude manipulative model of the mass media commonly held in liberal and left circles.

Illicit drug use is custom built for this sort of treatment. A characteristic reaction to drug use is that of ambivalence for, as with so many social relationships between 'normal' and 'deviant', the normal person simultaneously both covets and castigates the deviant action. This after all is the basis of moral indignation, namely that the wicked are undeservedly realizing the covert desires of the virtuous. Richard Blum captured well this fascination-repulsion relationship to drug use when he wrote:

> Pharmaceutical materials do not dispense themselves and the illicit drugs are rarely given away, let alone forced on people. Consequently, the menace lies within the person, for there would be no drug threat without a drug attraction. The amount of public interest in stories about druggies suggests the same drug attraction and repulsion in ordinary citizens. 'Fascination' is the better term since it implies witchcraft and enchantment. People are fascinated with drugs—because they are attracted by the states and conditions drugs are said to produce. That is another side to the fear of being disrupted; it is the desire for release, for escape, for magic, and for ecstatic joys. That is the derivation of the menace in drugs—their representation as keys to forbidden kingdoms inside ourselves. The *dreadful* in the drug is the *dreadful* in ourselves.[2]

This is an explanation of the hostility and attraction which drugs evoke. It makes understandable the findings in opinion polls on both sides of the Atlantic which show the drug pusher to be evaluated a higher community menace than the property criminal. It is rooted in moral indignation. Alasdair MacIntyre captured the attitude well when he wrote:

> Most of the hostility that I have met with comes from people who have never examined the facts at all. I suspect that what makes them dislike cannabis is not the belief that the effects of taking it are harmful but rather a horrifying suspicion that here is a source of pure pleasure which is available to those who have not *earned* it, who do not deserve it.[3]

I want to suggest that the media unwittingly have set themselves up as the guardians of consensus; that as major providers of information about actions, events, groups and ideas they forge this information in a closed consensual image. Further I want to suggest that the myths generated and carried by the media although based on ignorance are not of a random nature. The myths are grounded in a particular view of society which throws up certain contradictions which they attempt to solve. They contain certain simple structures irrespective of whether one considers the myth of the prostitute, the criminal, the striker, the pornographer, the delinquent, or the drug taker.

The mass media is committed, on one hand, to reporting that which is newsworthy and, on the other, to interpreting it within a consensual frame of reference. This leads to the first major contradiction that the media must face: for it is precisely alternative deviant realities such as the world of the illicit drug user which are simultaneously highly newsworthy and, because they are alternative realities, violations of the consensual image of society. For if different realms of meaning exist, and illicit pleasure is in fact pleasurable then the mass media world of the happy worker and joyful consumer is threatened. The contradiction is resolved by a skillful defusing of deviant action. Namely, that much drug taking is a product of personality disorders and is, moreover, unpleasurable. Illicit pleasure, the tinder of moral indignation, is accentuated in reporting in order to maximize its news value. The forbidden is thus potentially all the more tempting. To circumvent this the myth contains the notion of in-built justice mechanisms. Atypical pleasure leads to atypical pain. Thus premarital sexual intercourse gives rise to V.D., LSD to madness and marihuana to pitiful degeneracy. Whatever the outcome the message is the same: *deviance is unpleasurable.*

No one would voluntarily choose to be a drug user of this sort, because of the sticky fate that awaits him. Only the sick person, impelled by forces beyond his control, would find himself involved in such an activity. Thus initially there is a bifurcation of the world and human nature into:

(a) the normal rational average citizen who lives in well normed communities, shares common values, and displays a well-deserved happiness—he is the vast majority;
(b) the tiny majority of psychologically sick whose actions are determined by their affliction and are probably a product of social disorganization. Moreover, their deviancy has an in-built punishment. They are unhappy because of their deviancy. Normality is seen to be rewarded and deviance punished. The underlying message is simple: the rational is the pleasurable is the handsomely rewarded is the freely chosen is the meaningful is the non-deviant; the irrational is the painful is the punished is the determined is the meaningless is the deviant. See top diagram opposite.

The overtypical 'man in the street' makes free choices to work hard, marry and consume regularly. He relaxes at the right time and place with beer and cigarettes which give him 'luxury' and 'deep pleasure' but do not threaten either the ethos of productivity or the mundane world of taken for granted experience.

Every day attempts are made in the newspapers to lay the ghost of deviation. Every day the same message is repeated, the same morality play enacted, the same parameters drawn, the same doubts and fears dispelled. But the simple bifurcation model comes in certain instances to face further contradictions which must also be met.

Now and then large numbers of individuals engage in activities which are palpably deviant, e.g., strikes, rioting and marihuana smoking. The simple consensual model would not seem to fit this. For the 'normal' young person, the 'normal' working-class individual, the 'normal' woman, etc., much of necessity embrace the consensus. A significant elaboration of the consensual myth is necessary in order to deal with large-scale deviation. Namely that there exists a body of innocents within society who are corrupted by normal people who are wicked, who seek to gain from their fellows' weakness. Thus we have the following two media descriptions:

> The docks, the car industry, mines, major airports, electricity, the building trade, and the students have all been steadily infiltrated in one guise or another until the militants can disrupt the national life at will.[4]

Drugs: The Real Criminals

> The drug pusher—the contemptible creature who peddles poison for profit—deserves no mercy from the law. The criminal who sets out to hook young people on drugs deserves far more implacable retribution than the victims of the evil.[5]

N.B. The simple bifurcation of the social universe becomes now a fourfold split:

(a) sick (who can't help it)
(b) innocent (who are corrupted)
(c) wicked (who are corrupt) and a reduced number of
(d) the normal

Thus we have the sick who must be treated and cured, the innocent who must be saved, the wicked who must be punished and the normal who must be congratulated and rewarded.

Deviance then does not ever occur out of volition (for after all it is essentially unpleasurable), it either occurs out of sickness or corruption. Indeed for every example of widespread deviance it is possible to detect the intervention of a corruption. Thus:

strikers	agitators
student sit-ins	foreign agitators
prostitutes	pimps
spiritualists	con-men
illegal immigrants	immigrant runners
marihuana smokers	pushers
junkies	junkie doctors

But the mass media sometimes find themselves in a position where a growing body of opinion insists that certain illicit activities are both pleasurable and harmless. As in the case of marihuana, a crisis of confidence occurs. This is solved by what I shall term the nemesis effect. Namely that those individiuals who violate the natural law of happiness and productivity ineluctably suffer in the *long run*. Thus in the long run deviancy must be seen to be unpleasurable. In this mould the stereotype of marihuana has changed. Initially it reflected the exaggerated ambivalence of the mass media towards drugs. Thus, it held promise of uninhibited pleasure, yet plummeted the taker into unmitigated misery. So we had a distorted spectrum ranging from extreme sexuality, through aggressive criminality, to wildly psychotic episodes. The informed journalist, more recently, however, found this model difficult to affix to marihuana usage. He, therefore, switched gear and indicated how the innocuous pleasures of smoking are paid for by the sacrificial few who mysteriously escalate to the nightmares of heroin addiction. Similarly, the American journalist William Braden[6] notes how the press reporting of LSD went through three stages:

1. *Favourable reporting:* in the early 1960s LSD was seen as a therapeutic aid to the mentally ill and the addicted. That is, as a vehicle back to a normality it was in accord with consensual values.

2. *Initial negative reporting:* LSD was simultaneously identified with an ineffable mystical experience and as a cause of suicide, violence and madness. This was concomitant with the movement of LSD out of the hands of the therapists into the psychedelic subculture centering around Timothy Leary.

3. *Secondary negative reporting:* The discovery that LSD *might* result in abnormal chromosome breakage obviated both the sticky problems of mysticism that the psychedelics were giving rise to plus finally providing tangible evidence that LSD was really dangerous after all. As *Chicago's American* put it: LSD: THE 'FLY NOW, DIE LATER' DRUG (the best epithet for the nemesis effect that I've come across). Thus the press found itself armed with a hard 'incontrovertible' fact to use against the growing subculture of pro-LSD advocates.

Every now and then an initially legitimate body of experts will come up with evidence which grossly violates the stereotype. The reception the mass media gave the Wootton Report is fascinating in that we have a government setting up an Advisory Committee to try and elucidate the 'objective' facts about the drug problem which came up with results which violated the political canons that implicitly circumscribed the possible answers that could be accepted as 'objective'! This violation of the consensual myth was dealt with by a flood of invective from the mass media. It:

(a) reaffirmed that corruption was the reason for marihuana smoking—that innocent youngsters had been corrupted by evil pushers:

(b) (most remarkable) suggested that an innocent (ivory-towered) Wootton Committee had been corrupted by a pro-pot lobby.

The corrupter-corrupted imagery was thus used against both the marihuana smoker *and* the Committee that suggested amelioration of their suggestion. As Lady Wootton noted later in the House of Lords:

> The causes of the [hysteria] are familiar to students of social psychology. They occur in other connections as well particularly in relation to sexual crimes, and they are always liable to recur when the public senses that some critical and objective study threatens to block an outlet for indulgence in the pleasures of moral indignation.

To conclude, the mass media portrayal of the drug taker is not a function of random ignorance but a coherent part of a consensual mythology. The mass media are a double-coated pill, for if on the outside they titillate a taste for illicit delights, on the inside, they contain a palliative. They stimulate interest and bromide desire. The myth of the drug user is rooted in moral indignation; it bulwarks the hypothetical world of the normal citizen, it blinkers its audience to deviant realities outside the consensus, it spells out justice for the righteous and punishment for the wicked. Although much of its world view is fantasy, its effects are real enough. For by fanning up moral panics over drug use, it contributes enormously to public hostility to the drug taker and precludes any rational approach to the problem. It also provides a bevy of convenient scapegoats on to which real material and moral discontent can be directed and significant structural changes averted.

References

1. A. K. Cohen, 'The sociology of the deviant act', *American Sociological Review* 30 (1965), pp. 5–14.
2. R. Blum, *Society and drugs* (San Francisco: Jossey-Bass Inc., 1969), p. 335.
3. A. MacIntyre, 'The cannabis taboo', *New Society* (5 December 1968), p. 848.
4. *Daily Express,* 9 December 1970.
5. *Daily Mirror,* 12 March 1970.
6. See W. Braden, 'LSD and the press', reproduced in this Reader.

Chapter II
The Business of Drugs

The pharmaceutical drug industry has helped to wipe out once-fearsome plagues, produced treatments for once-untreatable diseases, found cures and palliatives for all sorts of ailments, and helped to prolong life. Innovative product development and a virtual technological revolution in drugs have made these accomplishments possible. These contributions have been significant.

Serious problems, however, persist in a profit-making industry responsible for such a large part of our nation's health care. The sociological perspective examines the broad outlines of the drug industry's power within the American economic and political system. This power is expressed in many ways: the role of drug companies in shaping legislation and regulations regarding their products, the role of drugs in everyday American life, and the values that are created around the use of drugs. Understanding the legal side of the industry is a necessary prerequisite to understanding the sociology of drug use, both licit and illicit. The distinctions between acceptable and unacceptable drug use are fine lines that have shifted historically in the American experience. A key case illustrating this is that values about the use of licit drug use may stretch over to the use of illicit drugs as well.

The first article by Silverman, Lee, and Lydecker furnishes a framework for looking at the pharmaceutical industry. It is big business, in fact, one of the most profitable in America. The authors explore how the industry's profit-making goal may conflict with the nation's health. This issue is raised by looking at the political economy of the drug industry, that is, its ability to define whether or not a drug gets on the market, the restrictions placed on a drug's use, and the industry's ability through promotions to determine the range and extent of a drug's use.

A critical sociological approach does not take for granted, or as permanent or natural, current legal and social definitions about drugs. The selection by Conrad illustrates how drug companies can expand and even create a market for their product. He presents a case study of how the drug companies expanded the definition of what a hyperactive child is to include a medical (drug) solution. The article by Davis presents a case history of how one "wonder drug", DMSO, previously used as an industrial solvent, became approved by the Food and Drug Administration. Davis underlines the importance of historical, political, and media influences on the drug approval process. Taken together, these two articles illustrate that not all "legal" drugs gain approval and are used simply because of their medical utility and effectiveness.

Pollack reports on the current status of drugs produced by high-tech biotechnology. The promise is bright and exciting. However, the cost of these new miracle drugs is out of the reach of many patients for whom they are a matter of life and death. Pollack's article raises the issue of whether drugs should be marketed only if they make a profit.

The last article in this chapter by Ball, et al. offers a glimpse of the other side of the drug business, the black market for heroin. Illegal drugs have a very different market, where the risks are far greater and the profits are tremendous. The authors examine how addicts support their drug use and detail the heroin-crime connection. The astonishing figures cited by Ball and his colleagues should prompt a serious reconsideration of alternative approaches to heroin addiction in the United States.

6. Drugs and the Drug Industry

Milton Silverman, Philip R. Lee, and Mia Lydecker

Since the end of World War II in 1945, and certainly since 1955, there has been growing evidence that appropriate treatment with drugs represents probably the most widely applied and most cost-effective form of medical treatment. There has been mounting proof that drugs can control most bacterial infections and now some viral infections, speed recovery, minimize crippling and other disabilities, make feasible surgical feats that were once impractical or impossible, and reduce the financial burdens of illness on society. Such developments as the introduction of sulfa drugs in the 1930s, penicillin and the other antibiotics beginning in the 1940s, the antihypertension drugs, the diuretics, the major tranquilizers, and cortisone and its relatives in the 1950s, the drugs against depression in the 1960s, and the beta-blockers for use against hypertension, heart arrhythmias, and angina, and the histamine-blockers against duodenal ulcer in the 1970s have come close to revolutionizing the practice of medicine.

Much of the credit clearly belongs to the drug industry in general and the American drug industry in particular. During the past decade, pharmaceutical firms have continued to produce drug products of remarkably high quality—though not of invariably perfect quality. They have introduced a myriad of drugs, all of them by definition new and some of them important. They have raised their prices, but these raises must be considered modest in comparison with the astronomical increases in physician fees and hospital bills. Some of the companies have continued to rail at the Food and Drug Administration, and especially at FDA's enforcement of the 1962 Kefauver-Harris Amendments. These amendments stipulated for the first time that a new drug could not win FDA approval without substantial scientific evidence of not only its relative safety but also its efficacy. Nevertheless, most industry leaders who once denounced Kefauver-Harris as an unmitigated disaster have found that they can live with the law in reasonable comfort. And profitably.

Much credit, too, belongs to physicians who prescribe or administer drugs. There appears to be a growing awareness among them that practically no drug is absolutely safe; any drug product sufficiently potent to alleviate a symptom or control a disease is also able under some conditions to cause injury, tissue damage, or even death. Fewer physicians seem to accept the rationalization that "the prescription may not help but it won't hurt."

Credit for a portion of the new attitudes toward drugs must go to clinical pharmacists, who are probably more knowledgeable about drugs than are most physicians. Once a diagnosis has been reached, physicians are increasingly turning to clinically trained pharmacists to suggest which drug and which form of that drug might be most useful for a particular patient.

As remarkable as this drug revolution may be, it has one distressing flaw: *many patients cannot afford to pay for the drugs they need.*

As remarkable as this drug revolution may be, it has one distressing flaw: *many patients cannot afford to pay for the drugs they need.*

• • •

Under the present system of health care delivery in the United States, there is no national program to cover drug costs under a national health insurance plan. This country is probably the last industrialized nation in the world without such a program.

There are, of course, some groups who have more or less adequate protection against drug costs. Drug coverage is provided under the Veterans Administration (VA) medical care program for veterans with service-connected disabilities, and by the Department of Defense for military personnel and their dependents. Similar benefits are furnished under many union health programs and some private insurance plans. There are, however, three groups whose protection is glaringly deficient:

Under Medicare, the elderly—those aged 65 or more—have most of their prescription drug expenses covered, but only when they are hospitalized; to purchase drugs from a community pharmacy, they must pay out of pocket or purchase supplemental private insurance, which few of them can afford. Among the elderly, pockets are notoriously empty. They represent only about 11 percent of the population, but they account for 25 percent of all out-of-hospital prescription drug expenditures.

For the medically indigent and those on welfare, drug coverage is provided in nearly all states under a Medicaid program for both in-hospital and out-of-hospital drug costs, but unfortunately only as an optional benefit. Coverage is usually determined by state formularies specifying those drug products for which reimbursement is allowed. In twenty-one states, only the medically indigent are covered; in most others, the medically indigent and the medically needy are beneficiaries; and in three, there is no Medicaid drug coverage at all. In many states with drug programs, shrinking budgets have reduced such coverage to distressingly low levels. Like the elderly, the poor suffer from an inordinately high amount of sickness.

Finally, there are those persons of any age who are victims of serious, chronic, disabling diseases and who could benefit greatly from drug treatment. Many of these patients have no job, no insurance protection, no membership in any health plan, and rapidly dwindling assets. As a group, they have no strong voice to speak for them in the halls of Congress.

To some people, the very idea of setting up a government program to deliver adequate help to these groups, and perhaps others, is anathema. They have reacted by using bumper strips and other signs asking, "Do you want health care controlled by the people who gave you the Postal Service?"

This is an intriguing question. It might be countered by such equally simplistic queries as "Do you want health care controlled by the people in the private sector who gave you polluted air, soil, rivers, and lakes? Or who were responsible for destructive oil spills? Or who marketed poisonous soups and drugs whose toxic properties were long concealed? Or who produced flammable nightwear for children? Or whose automobiles had to be recalled as defective by the tens or hundreds of thousands? Or who have been largely responsible for the rapid increase in the cost of health care during the last fifteen years?"

All of these questions—and the list could be expanded many times—must be dismissed as irrelevant. The vital problems concern how to devise the best possible system, with the maximum benefits, the minimum defects, and the greatest help for those who desperately need it.

Intimately related here is the issue of what is termed distributive justice. Unless the coverage is provided on all drugs for all people—an approach that seems totally impossible for the foreseeable future because of unacceptably high costs—the benefits must necessarily be rationed. But in what way? Should the program be designed to help primarily those who have paid their taxes and thus *earned* the coverage? Or those who have been economically and culturally deprived and may be thought to *deserve* it? Or those who are seriously ill and *need* it?

Modern Drug Use

Any rational decisions in this complex and often emotion-charged field must be based on reasonably complete knowledge of the clinical and economic facts involved. Unfortunately, this knowledge is not readily available. Many of the so-called facts are based on data that are often outdated, incomplete, and of questionable reliability.

There is, for example, no agreement on how to answer what should be the simplest of questions: What is the current prescription drug bill at the retail level? At a 1977 conference, it was stated that recent estimates ranged from $10 billion a year or less to $14 billion or more.[1] Using the latest available information on sales at the manufacturers' level[2] together with an old and possibly useful rule of thumb that total retail drug sales are roughly double total manufacturers' sales, it may be suggested that the nation's prescription drug bill was in the neighborhood of $18 billion in 1978 and $20 billion in 1979.

Included in these figures are prescription drugs dispensed not only by independent and chain pharmacies in the community but also by mail-order pharmacies, dispensing physicians, discount pharmacies, nursing homes, hospital pharmacies serving both inpatients and outpatients, and governmental institutions.

These figures may appear large, but they represent only a small fraction of the nation's bill for all health care services and supplies: $163 billion in fiscal 1977, and $200 billion in fiscal 1979.

Roughly 35 percent of hospital drugs and 9 percent of prescription drugs dispensed outside of hospitals are paid for under the Medicare and Medicaid programs.[3] Paying for drugs in such quantities makes the United States government one of the largest single drug purchasers in the world. For that reason, if for no other, the government now has a more-than-passing interest in drug prices.

There is similar confusion over the matter of total numbers of prescriptions dispensed each year. One reason for this is the fact that a prescription filled for a hospitalized patient may be substantially different in nature, size, and cost from one filled in a neighborhood pharmacy. Another reason is that the figures obtained by various marketing survey groups are derived by different methods for different purposes, and their various findings are not readily comparable.

According to one survey, the number of prescriptions dispensed annually by retail pharmacies rose steadily to a peak of 1.52 billion in 1973 and then dropped slowly each year thereafter: 1.50 billion in 1974, 1.49 billion in 1975, 1.46 billion in 1976, 1.41 billion in 1977, 1.40 billion in 1978 and 1.37 billion in 1979.[4] One proposed explanation for this decrease, especially in the face of steadily rising total annual expenditures, is that, since 1973, American physicians have been writing fewer prescriptions but each prescription calls for a larger quantity of the drug product. Other explanations include the possibility that, during the recent recession, some patients postponed obtaining refills. Recent regulations of the Drug Enforcement Administration (DEA) make it somewhat more difficult to obtain refills of certain classes of drugs—for example, barbiturates and other sedatives—and hospital pharmacies rather than community pharmacies are filling more prescriptions for outpatients. Perhaps some physicians are responding to pressures to cut down on their prescribing.

Among these billions of prescriptions, drug experts are struck—and some of them seriously alarmed—by the continuing high proportions represented by two classes of drugs: antibiotics and other antibacterial agents on the one hand, and such psychoactive drugs as stimulants, sedatives, and tranquilizers on the other.

Antibiotics and other anti-infectives account for about 14 percent of all prescriptions and for 15 to 20 percent of those dispensed to hospitalized patients.[5] Many of these drugs are ordered for the treatment of the common cold, the "flu," and other upper-respiratory viral infections for which there is no evidence that they possess any value. Often, especially for patients about to undergo surgery, these drugs are ordered as prophylactics to prevent postsurgical infection, but in situations or in amounts which are open to question.

In the case of psychoactive drugs, there has been much controversy. They account for about 12 percent of all prescriptions. Their use more than doubled between 1958 and 1973, soaring from roughly 90 million to 223 million prescriptions annually.[6] Studies have shown that 67 percent of all psychoactive drugs, 74 percent of antidepressants, and 82 percent of stimulants were prescribed for women. Women between the ages of 40 and 59 were the largest consumers.

• • •

A recent report[7] also shows the following:

- The average price of a retail pharmacy prescription rose from $2.00 in 1950 to $3.62 in 1960, $3.72 in 1970, $5.60 in 1976, $5.98 in 1977, $6.44 in 1978, and $7.03 in 1979. In 1979, the average price for a prescription calling for a brand-name product was $7.35, while one calling for a generic-name product was $5.03.
- At least some physicians are more inclined to prescribe generically, allowing a pharmacist to dispense a low-cost product instead of a more costly brand-name version. Generic prescribing, at least as seen in retail pharmacy records, increased from 6.4 percent of all new prescriptions in 1966 to 14.1 percent in 1979.
- The average number of retail store prescriptions dispensed per capita, which had risen steadily from about 2.4 annually in 1950 to 3.6 in 1960, 5.4 in 1970, and 7.3 in 1973, dropped to 6.5 by 1977 and to 6.2 by 1979.

"The word is getting through," says one of our clinical colleagues. "We've been prescribing too much. We've been prescribing when a drug wasn't really needed for medical reasons. And we've been prescribing needlessly expensive products. We hear it from drug experts. We hear it from our professional colleagues. We hear it from the insurance companies, and the people at Medicare and Medicaid. Hell, we're even hearing it now from patients."

Whether this downward trend is a reflection of changing patterns of prescribing, better patient information about drugs—especially about their potential risks—or economic conditions remains to be seen.

In general, it may be expected that either drug use or drug expenditures or both will grow for many years to come. This will be due to a number of factors:

- The slowing but still continuing growth of the total population.
- The increasing proportion of elderly people in the population. (The elderly on the average use three times as many prescriptions as do those aged up to 65.)[8]
- The increasing proportion of women in the population. (Women use about 50 percent more drugs than do men.)[9]

- The increasing number of people with health insurance and the related increase in the number of physician visits. (Recent studies have indicated that almost two-thirds of all physician visits result in the prescription or recommendation of a drug. The number of prescriptions written averages about 1.7 per visit.)[10]
- The growing use of hospitalization. (On the average, one new prescription is written for each day in a hospital, or roughly eight prescriptions for a typical hospital stay.[11] On the other hand, present efforts to contain hospital costs may eventually result in less or shorter hospitalization.)
- The possible or probable introduction of new, innovative, "breakthrough" drugs that can be used to control conditions that cannot be controlled by any drugs now available.
- With the implementation of national health insurance, it is our estimate that drug use, especially out of hospitals, would increase by about 10 to 15 percent the first year, with small annual increments thereafter, for the particular population group covered. Some observers predict that the increase would be only 5 percent, while others put the figure closer to 25 percent.[12]

Finally, it must be noted, the approximately 1.4 billion community pharmacy prescriptions, carrying a retail price tag of roughly $9.8 billion, do not give the total drug bill for the United States. We estimate that there should be added about 0.3 billion prescriptions filled by discount stores and other miscellaneous outlets and by dispensing physicians, 1.2 billion filled for nongovernmental hospital inpatients and outpatients, and 0.1 billion dispensed by VA hospitals and pharmacies and other governmental institutions. That gives a total of about 3.0 billion prescriptions and a total annual expenditure of $18.0 billion. There may also be added nearly $5.0 billion for over-the-counter products.

Who pays this drug bill? The public does, through out-of-pocket expenditures, taxes, insurance premiums, and increased prices of all kinds of goods—from automobiles and canned foods to television sets and paper clips—produced by companies that pay health insurance premiums for their employees.

It all comes out of the public purse.

So far as prescription drug expenditures are concerned, at least as of 1978, only about 14 percent of the costs outside of hospitals were covered by any form of insurance. In striking contrast, insurance covered 66 percent of physicians' services and 90 percent of hospital care costs.[13]

The Drug Industry

Five years ago, we portrayed the drug industry—the American drug industry in particular—as big, profitable, and powerful. It seemed to be remarkably productive—far more so that some of its critics proclaimed, but perhaps less so than some industry spokesmen declared.[14] Its innovative discoveries of important new products had contributed significantly to the control of disease.

Since that time, even during the recession of the mid-1970s, the American drug industry has continued to be big, profitable, powerful, and productive.

Ironically, starting as far back as the early 1900s, the industry has often greeted proposed changes with a the-sky-is-falling attitude. Each time a governmental law or regulation was proposed to improve the safety, efficacy, and even cleanliness of drug products, or to limit drug expenditures, many industry representatives warned that the proposed controls would inevitably force them to curtail their vital research designed to develop better drugs for the future. Yet, although new controls were put into effect, the industry has continued to remain productive and to prosper. (It is conceivable, of course, that some future action by the government may actually bring the sky tumbling down upon the drug companies. That would not only be sad for the companies but an absolute disaster for patients.)

There are several yardsticks by which to measure the productivity of the American drug industry. From 1940 to 1975, of the 971 new single drug entities introduced (not counting new combination products or new dosage forms), 662, or 64 percent, were developed in the United States.[15] U.S. sources—mainly industrial but also university and governmental—developed approximately twice as many new products as the rest of the world combined.

Drug sales in this country have continued to mount year after year. As shown in Table 1, domestic sales in actual dollars rose fivefold from $1.9 billion to an estimated $10.1 billion between 1961 and 1979.[16] Much of the increase during the past decade was the result of inflation, but the figures given in constant 1967 dollars, to account for inflation, show a fourfold rise from about $1.8 billion in 1961 to $7.2 billion in 1979.

Table 1. The American Drug Industry: Worldwide and U.S. Sales.

Year	Worldwide (actual dollars, in millions)	U.S. (actual dollars, in millions)	U.S. (constant dollars, in millions)	Deflator Index
1961	2,685	1,934	1,787	1.082
1962	2,932	2,199	2,082	1.056
1963	3,152	2,317	2,224	1.042
1964	3,405	2,479	2,386	1.039
1965	3,841	2,779	2,693	1.032
1966	4,256	3,011	2,935	1.026
1967	4,707	3,226	3,226	1.000
1968	5,280	3,655	3,692	0.990
1969	5,832	4,008	4,028	0.995
1970	6,442	4,322	4,352	0.993
1971	7,020	4,667	4,714	0.990
1972	7,827	5,018	5,023	0.991
1973	8,755	5,507	5,513	0.999
1974	10,120	6,083	5,838	1.042
1975	11,543	6,895	6,091	1.132
1976	12,832	7,669	6,375	1.203
1977	13,896	8,233	6,565	1.254
1978	16,840	9,156	6,542	1.319
1979 (est.)	n.a.	10,154	7,191	1.412

Source: Pharmaceutical Manufacturers Association, *Annual Survey Reports,* Washington, D.C.

Worldwide Sales: Data shown for human and veterinary products, dosage forms only.

U.S. Sales: Data shown for human products, dosage forms only. Constant Dollars: 1967 = 100.

Table 2. Net Drug Industry Profits After Taxes,
as Based on Percentage of Investment.

Year	All Manufacturing Industries (%)	Drug Industry (%)
1964	11.6	18.2
1965	13.0	20.3
1966	13.5	20.3
1967	11.7	18.7
1968	12.1	18.3
1969	11.5	18.3
1970	9.3	17.6
1971	9.7	17.9
1972	10.6	18.6
1973	13.1	19.2
1974	14.9	18.8
1975	11.5	17.5
1976	13.9	18.0
1977	14.2	18.2
1978	15.0	18.8
1979	16.5	19.5

Source: Federal Trade Commission, *Quarterly Financial Reports*, various issues.

Many industry spokesmen have long warned about the riskiness of the drug business. There is no question that the discovery of an unanticipated side effect may demolish the prospects of a new drug which took many years and many millions of dollars to develop, but the drug industry remains one of the most profitable of all manufacturing industries in the country. As indicated in Table 2, net profits after taxes, as based on equity or investment, have continued to be remarkably steady and high.

In other nations, notably West Germany and Great Britain, drug profits have been considered to be so high that the governments felt obliged to take corrective action. In Great Britain, for example, an agreement was hammered out between the industry and the Department of Health and Social Security to reduce profits after taxes as based on investment from 21 percent in 1969 to 15 percent in 1975.[17]

Some economists, both in and out of the industry, have charged that the accounting system on which such profits are calculated is unfair. The present system treats the industry's substantial investment in research as an ordinary business expense for salaries, supplies, and rent. Instead, it has been held, research expenditures should be treated as if they were a capital investment. Such an approach would reduce the industry's net profit rate but that rate would still be significantly above average.

Beyond any doubt, the annual research investment of the American drug industry has been substantial, rising from $245 million in 1961 to $1.4 billion in 1978 and an estimated $1.6 billion in 1978 (see Table 3). These amounts, given in actual dollars, cover all research conducted world-wide on both human and veterinary products by U.S. firms and all research conducted in the U.S.

Table 3. The American Drug Industry:
Worldwide Sales and Research
(in millions of dollars).

Year	Sales	Research	Percentage (Research/Sales)
1961	2,685	245	9.1
1962	2,932	259	8.8
1963	3,152	292	9.3
1964	3,405	310	9.1
1965	3,841	365	9.5
1966	4,256	416	9.8
1967	4,707	461	9.8
1968	5,280	495	9.4
1969	5,832	550	9.4
1970	6,442	619	9.6
1971	7,020	684	9.7
1972	7,827	726	9.3
1973	8,755	825	9.4
1974	10,120	942	9.3
1975	11,543	1,062	9.2
1976	12,832	1,164	9.1
1977	13,896	1,266	9.1
1978	16,840	1,397	8.2
1979 (est.)	n.a.	1,593	–

Source: Pharmaceutical Manufacturers Association, *Annual Survey Reports,* Washington D.C.

by U.S.-based subsidiaries of foreign-owned companies. In practically every year, research expenditures have represented between 9.1 and 9.8 percent of sales. It is not known what portion of these sums actually covers physician education, promotional activities, and the like.

Increasingly, especially in the last decade, American firms are moving the scene of much of their research to foreign countries—not to escape high labor costs but because competent investigators are available in many foreign medical centers and can work under somewhat less rigid controls than those enforced by the U.S. Food and Drug Administration. Such a step has clearly helped U.S. firms to get their products on the market quickly in such countries as Great Britain, France, and West Germany, and in scores of Third World nations. It has not, however, enhanced the firms' chances of winning approval in the U.S. At least until recently, FDA—quite probably reflecting the views in Congress—has been singularly unimpressed by the results of foreign drug testing; but in recent years, overseas studies conducted in accordance with modern testing standards have been increasingly acceptable to FDA.

Although the American companies have been appropriately and openly proud of some of their research accomplishments, they have often shown equal pride in what are commonly called "me-too" drugs. These are products that are essentially minor modifications of an important, innovative drug which is still under patent. The me-too versions by definition have no advantages in safety, efficacy, or economy. They can be sold only by means of massive promotional campaigns. The me-too products merely pollute the pharmaceutical atmosphere.

The matter of drug promotion is still sensitive in drug company circles.[18] Company spokesmen show no eagerness to discuss it, and promotion expenditures are rarely if ever revealed in reports to stockholders. In the past fifteen years, or especially since the forceful application of the Kefauver-Harris Amendments, FDA has prodded most American drug companies to improve the quality of their printed advertisements in medical journals. Advertisements so biased, incomplete, or actually inaccurate that they disgust many physicians, and even many company researchers, are now uncommon. Seldom is a company forced to make a public retraction of its claims.

Journal advertising, however, represents only a minor portion of drug promotion. Most promotion—perhaps two-thirds or more—is accomplished by drug detailers or sales representatives who call on physicians and pharmacists. Their presentations are mostly oral, and it is difficult to prove or disprove any accusation that they may occasionally stray from the truth. It is our impression, and that of many of our clinical colleagues, that the quality of detailing has improved. This may be due in part to attempts by some firms to set higher standards in hiring detailers, and to train and retrain them to stick to the facts. Some improvement may also be due to the growing skepticism of the medical profession—especially the young members—and to the increasing willingness of many physicians to depend on specially trained clinical pharmacists to recommend which drug product should be prescribed.

What remains virtually unchanged is the staggering amount of all this promotion. It is our estimate that all forms of drug promotion represent roughly 20 percent *and possibly more* of sales at the manufacturers' level. This would come to about $1.8 billion in 1978 and an estimated $2.0 billion in 1979. Such expenditures are significantly larger than the industry's total investment in research. They are also larger than the total spent on all educational activities conducted by all the medical schools in the United States to train medical students.[19] This detailing and advertising avalanche is the most intense promotion that physicians will face during their entire professional lifetimes. Too often, drug promotion in its sheer volume is more confusing than educational. Too often, it leads a physician to prescribe a drug when no prescription is medically needed.

Some U.S. firms have insisted for many years that the FDA's regulation of promotion is needlessly harsh. "We recognize our social responsibilities now," one official said to us. "Whether the FDA was around or not, we would tell physicians the truth, the whole truth, and nothing but the truth."

A few years ago, it became possible for us to learn how American and other multinational pharmaceutical firms comport themselves when there *is* no FDA around. We compared what a company said about one of its products to physicians in the United States and to physicians in about a dozen countries in Latin America. In the United States, with the FDA watching, the company invariably told the truth: it gave a limited number of indications and disclosed in great detail the warnings, contraindications, and potential adverse reactions. In Latin America, most (although not all) companies grossly exaggerated their claims for efficacy and minimized, glossed over, or completely omitted any mention of hazards.[20] During the past few years, their activities in East African countries have been shown to be at least equally revolting.[21] Since these findings were made public, many American multi-national firms (although not all of them) have dramatically improved their promotion in foreign countries. In general, they have found that they can tell the truth and still make a profit.

In Great Britain, officials of the National Health Service recently took steps to reduce somewhat the flood of drug promotion, at least in Britain. In its agreement with the Association of the British Pharmaceutical Industry, the government announced, the industry would reduce its promotion of products purchased by the National Health Service from 14 percent of sales to 12 percent in 1977 and 10 percent in 1979. "This will release 13 million pounds a year for patient care in 1979," stated David Ennals, the Secretary of State for Social Services. "Of course the industry can spend as much as it likes on promotion—but not at the expense of the NHS."[22]

As part of the British understanding, the industry agreed that each advertisement must contain not only essential information on efficacy, side effects, precautions, and contraindications, but also on cost. In addition, Ennals said, he would soon introduce regulations to prohibit misleading graphs and tables and "to stop misuse of words like 'safe.' "

In the United States, the drug industry consists of about 750 companies in interstate commerce (nobody seems to know the exact number) and an unknown number in intrastate commerce. Generally they are grouped into the PMA (for Pharmaceutical Manufacturers Association) companies and the non-PMA companies. As of the end of 1979, PMA had 143 members, all either U.S. firms or U.S. subsidiaries of foreign companies. They accounted for some 90 percent of all prescription drug sales, drug profits, and drug research, and close to 100 percent of all drug promotion. They controlled about 90 percent or more of all drug patents.

At one time, it was customary to describe the PMA members as brand-name companies, while the non-PMA firms supposedly sold mainly generic-name products. Such a grouping is no longer valid. Many PMA companies have gone into the generic-name business, and one—Eli Lilly—is reputedly the largest manufacturer of generics in the world. Furthermore, some generic firms market their products under new brand names.

For many years, strong bonds linked PMA with the American Medical Association. The reasons seemed obvious: PMA needed expert medical witnesses to testify on its behalf before the hearings chaired particularly by Senators Estes Kefauver and Gaylord Nelson, while the AMA needed the revenues from drug advertising in its journals to finance its disastrous attempt to block the Medicare program. Where other groups and agencies were concerned—industry critics, consumer groups, the American Pharmaceutical Association, the American Public Health Association, and FDA—there appeared to be within PMA a state of multiple industrial paranoia. As one industry witness put it after a congressional hearing, "It's them against us."

"Anything we propose is always wrong," a PMA official complained to us. "And anything we oppose is always right."

During the last several years, and for reasons which are not exactly clear, the situation has perceptibly changed. FDA officials, industry leaders, pharmacy leaders, and consumer advocates can gather amicably around the same table.

"In the old days," one of our associates recalls, "practically every meeting ended with table-pounding, profanity, denunciations, and everybody walking out of the room furious. Now we still have disagreements, but at the end of the meeting we all go out and have dinner together. And nobody accuses anybody else of selling out."

Another industry critic put it this way: "I'll be damned, but an industry vice-president turns out to be one of my best and most trusted friends!"

Perhaps our most cherished reaction came from a PMA official after we had commented—somewhat unfavorably—on certain drug company promotional activities. "How in hell can we argue with you," he wrote, "when you insist on being accurate and fair?"

Total peace in this arena has not yet broken out, but the new level of discussion has proved to be a pleasant relief to many of us. And also productive.

Drug Names, Drug Approval, and the "Drug Lag"

Practically never does a patient swallow a pure drug. What is actually used is a drug product: a mixture of the active ingredient (the actual drug) plus a combination of binders, buffers, flavors, colors, and perhaps other ingredients. Such an agent usually carries three names:

- The *chemical* name, generally long, complex, and decipherable only by chemists. It gives the molecular structure of the drug and may suggest its probable action on the body.
- The public, established, or *generic* name, usually simpler but often impossible for a prescribing physician to remember.
- The trademark or *brand* name, short, simple, and easy to write on a prescription pad. In most instances, the brand name is monopolized forever by one company.

One drug product, for example, has the chemical name of 10-(3-dimethylaminopropyl)-2-chlorphenothiazine—the "phenothiazine" will suggest to a drug expert that the chemical will act as a tranquilizer—the generic name of chlorpromazine, and the brand name in the United States of Thorazine. It was, in fact, the first major tranquilizer to be synthesized.

Under the patent system in the United States, the creator or discoverer of a new patented product has the exclusive right to market it for the life of the patent. That patent life is seventeen years in this country. For many inventions—a new kind of light bulb, for example, or a new spot remover—the manufacturer may be able to get his product on the market in a year or less, and then have sixteen years of full protection. With a new drug, however, the situation is far different. Before it can be marketed, it must be approved for relative safety and efficacy by the Food and Drug Administration. This is not so simple.

FDA's New Drug Application (NDA) process[23] usually requires years of testing on animals and then on human subjects—first on normal, healthy volunteers, then on several hundred patients being treated by experts in special clinical facilities, and finally on several thousand patients treated by specialists or other physicians. Along the way, many proposed products drop out; their efficacy is not substantial, or the subjects may suffer unanticipated and undesirable side effects. Before a new product wins FDA's stamp of approval, five to ten years have elapsed, and the company may have invested as much as fifty or sixty million dollars. A new study based on 1976 data from fourteen companies puts the average figure at $54 million.[24] Meanwhile, the life of the patent has been steadily ticking away, and the company has on the average only nine years or so remaining to recoup its investment.[25]

This situation, which developed largely since passage of the Kefauver-Harris Amendments in 1962 and their implementation a few years later, has been understandably galling to the drug industry. Leaders of the industry charge that the NDA procedure is needlessly complex and that FDA makes unrealistic demands to get what it feels is essential evidence, while most other countries seemingly get along comfortably with a more relaxed and far more speedy system. FDA's defenders say that the American system undoubtedly saved this country from having a thalidomide disaster, a rash of cancer cases caused by supposedly safe heart disease remedies, and an epidemic of deaths caused by a superpotent anti-asthma drug. They also note that the American drug industry has not been too badly damaged financially. "The average new drug commercialized by the pharmaceutical industry today," a drug security analyst said recently, "will generate approximately $50 million in sales worldwide in its fifth year on the market."[26]

Nevertheless, it is evident that the problem of delays is being partially alleviated. FDA is moving more rapidly. Top priority is being given to the review of breakthrough drugs urgently needed to control a hitherto uncontrollable disease, while unimportant me-too drugs are put on a slower track and given less prompt study.[27] As further improvements, it is being suggested now that the rules be changed so that the manufacturer is given a guaranteed ten years of patent protection after marketing begins, or that the patent protection should start only at the moment FDA approval is received.

In proposed legislation introduced in 1978,[28] Congressman Paul Rogers and Senator Edward Kennedy called for a change in the law so that FDA could approve a new drug after trials on a few hundred patients and officially recognize human trials in certain foreign countries. This kind of approval would presumably be restricted to urgently needed breakthrough drugs. It would not be applied in the case of one more antihistamine or another antibiotic no better than penicillin or tetracycline. Furthermore, it could and probably would be conditioned on the willingness of the company to maintain postmarketing surveillance and check on any unexpected adverse reactions that did not appear in the early trials. The proposed legislation was passed by the Senate but did not get out of committee in the House in 1978. It was reintroduced by Senator Kennedy and Representative Henry Waxman with significant modifications in 1979.[29] By late 1980, the bill had not yet been considered by the House.

On the other hand, some critics insisted that FDA cannot solve the problem of delayed drug approval because FDA *is* the problem and should be abolished. Moreover, there are some critics who declare that FDA is moving too fast and approving drugs without adequate trials. One problem that has been recognized only recently is that some adverse reactions may not be detectable until patients have used a drug for twenty years or so, while other reactions may not be detected until they affect the next generation. For example, diethylstilbestrol (DES), a hormone-like product used many years ago in an attempt to prevent an impending miscarriage, was found to cause cancer of the vagina in the daughters of some of the treated women—and, in fact, to be worthless in the prevention of miscarriage.

Regardless of the propriety of FDA's operations, it is obvious that the introduction of new drugs each year in the United States has dropped markedly since passage of the Kefauver Amendments. For this reason, there have been increasing demands that the law be scrapped and that the companies themselves be allowed to decide on their own whether or not to put a new drug on the market.[30] Such a proposal is truly frightening; we believe some companies could be trusted to behave responsibly, but others—on their past record—could not. In the past, the latter have marketed drugs that were unsafe or ineffective and whose promotion was inaccurate, biased, or false.[31]

In any consideration of the drop in the number of new drugs introduced annually, three facts have often been ignored:

- The same or a similar drop has occurred at about the same time in other countries.
- In the United States, the drop began in 1959, three years before the Kefauver Amendments were passed and about five years before they were put into effect.
- The number of new drugs introduced annually—that is, new single drug entities and not merely new dosage forms or new combinations of old drugs—tells only part of the story. Many drug experts have indicated that only a very few of these products, perhaps half a dozen per year, represent *important* new therapeutic advances.[32] Most of the others provide little or no therapeutic gain; in short, they are only me-too drugs.

Related in some way to this delay in getting approval of new drugs in the United States, and perhaps to the fact that research in this field is becoming more difficult, is what has been termed the "drug lag." Regrettably, there is no agreement on how to define the drug lag or on how to measure it. There is, in fact, no agreement on whether it has been a good thing or a bad thing for the health of Americans. On the one hand, it has been likened to a disaster ranking with bubonic plague and used to bludgeon the FDA into speeding the approval of new drugs;[33] on the other, some concerned individuals have insisted that the drug lag is not big enough.[34]

In a general way, the drug lag refers to the fact that some newly discovered drugs—including a number discovered by American drug companies—are marketed in other countries months or years before they are approved for marketing in this country. Some may never reach the market in the United States. The existence of the American drug lag can scarcely be denied.[35]

It is vital to note, however, that the lag is not found only in the United States. There are some drugs, for example, that were available in West Germany before they were available in Switzerland, some that were available in Switzerland before they were available in Sweden, some that were available in Sweden before they were available in the United States, and some that were available in the United States before they were available in Norway.

What has been unclear is whether these various lags represent a threat mostly to the health of the people in the countries involved or mostly to the sales of the companies whose products are concerned. According to European experts, there are far fewer prescription drugs on the market in the Netherlands, Denmark, and Sweden than there are in such nations as France, Italy, West Germany, and Great Britain.[36] From such information, it might be concluded that the Dutch and the Scandinavians cannot be treated as well as the French, the Italians, the West Germans, and the British. It is our opinion, however, that the health care—including drug therapy—available in the Netherlands and Scandinavia ranks among the best in Europe.

Some European physicians—mostly those in general practice but also including some specialists—have expressed their dismay that products which they were accustomed to using in their own countries were not available in the United States or, for that matter, in Canada.

Many foreign physicians seem to be unaware that most drugs not approved—or not approved quickly—by FDA were blocked on the grounds that the manufacturer had failed to submit adequate data to prove objectively that the product was safe and effective. Many foreign physicians also seem unaware that some drugs they use customarily in Europe have been taken off the U.S. market as unsafe. It is likewise not appreciated by many physicians, American and foreign alike, that most FDA decisions are based on the advice of its advisory committees, which include some of the most knowledgeable drug experts in the nation.

The impact of the drug lag in the United States is difficult to assess. The three-year delay in gaining FDA approval of the Italian anti-tuberculosis drug rifampin was probably a disservice to some American patients. An even more glaring case involves the so-called beta-blockers, some of which have been widely accepted for the treatment of hypertension, cardiac arrhythmias, and angina. For roughly a decade, against the advice of leading nongovernmental drug authorities, and for reasons which we find difficult to comprehend, the FDA adamantly refused to approve any beta-blocker. Yet, it has turned out that FDA's actions were not irrational: some members of this drug group—including the first one to be approved in Great Britain—were later found to be associated with the development of malignant or nonmalignant tumors in experimental animals, and one had to be taken off the market in Europe because of its probable relation to eye damage.[37]

FDA's decision not to approve thalidomide, later disclosed to be a cause of fetal deformities, was a blessing for Americans.[38] So were FDA's actions to remove from the market such headache remedies as aminopyrine and the dipyrones, still commonly used in many countries but now held responsible for serious or fatal blood diseases. Particular abuse was heaped on FDA for holding up a new anti-epilepsy drug, sodium valproate, indicated particularly for the treatment of a form of the disorder known as "absence seizures." Approved in France in 1967, the drug was not cleared by the FDA until 1978. The 11-year delay, it was charged, has "cruelly" prevented patients from getting desperately needed help. This was a low blow, for it was, in fact, the company which had lagged in requesting approval, and which had even had to be urged by FDA to put in an application for approval.[39] Furthermore, it now appears that sodium valproate is not an unmixed blessing: its use has recently been associated with rare but serious and sometimes fatal liver destruction.[40]

Another curious aspect of the drug lag controversy has involved a drug known as clioquinol or Enterovioform, marketed for decades by Ciba or Ciba-Geigy and now also by other companies for the prevention and treatment of diarrhea and amoebic dysentery. Although it is still widely available—in some countries, without a prescription—it was removed from the market in the United States in 1961 and in Japan in 1970. After prolonged lawsuits, the Japanese courts ruled that the drug was responsible for an epidemic of drug-induced paralysis, visual defects or blindness, and even death in some 10,000 patients—a situation that was termed the worst drug disaster in history. Victims were reported not only in Japan but also in a number of countries. Significantly, the disease virtually disappeared in Japan when clioquinol was banned.[41]

The drug lag in the United States has been blamed both on the policies of FDA and the provisions of the 1962 Kefauver Amendments. One of the most thorough studies in this hotly disputed field was that undertaken by the Department of Health, Education, and Welfare's Review Panel on New Drugs, under the chairmanship of law professor Norman Dorsen of New York University. In May 1977, the panel concluded in its report to the Secretary of HEW that

> the available evidence does not justify a departure from the system of regulation instituted by the 1962 Amendments. While in the last decade there has been an increase in the cost of drug development and a decline in the average number of new chemical entities approved annually by FDA, the studies to date do not show persuasively that these trends are principally attributable to the 1962 Amendments. . . . Although drug approvals declined after 1962, data indicate that decline began earlier. Furthermore, the 1962 Amendments were implemented gradually, and their full impact was not felt until the 1970s.[42]

A revealing analysis in this field was carried out by Paul de Haen, generally regarded as the foremost authority on the subject of which drugs were introduced in which countries and in which year. For this study, he surveyed twenty-nine drugs in fourteen major therapeutic classes marketed between roughly 1967 and 1976 in England, France, West Germany, and Italy.[43] He found that (1) during that decade, only 24 percent of the drugs reached all four countries; and (2) the time to achieve marketing in all four, where this actually occurred, ranged from one to thirteen years.

There were no clinical or scientific explanations for these lags—for example, why one new anti-arthritic was marketed in England in 1962 but not in Italy until 1974; or, for that matter, why the widely used sedative flurazepam (Dalmane) was introduced in the United States in 1970 but had still to be marketed in France by 1979.

One explanation, de Haen said, may rest on industry management decisions. "In some instances, there may be commercial and competitive reasons why it is not practical to offer a drug in a given country."

He observed that the costly delays in winning approval of a new drug are not limited to the United States. "Progress in science and the requirement of extended pharmacologic and therapeutic evaluations have placed a heavy burden on innovating manufacturers in all countries, for which the patient has to pay eventually. However, he may be rewarded with greater therapeutic efficacy and reliability."

The drug lag is therefore not unique to the United States. What seems to be unique is the fuss that has been made about it in this country.

"In spite of the fact that there are many drugs that have only been introduced in a limited number of European countries, and that there has been a considerable delay in the transfer of others from one country to another," de Haen said, "no complaints about this subject have been expressed in the European literature."

More important than further fruitless and sometimes paranoid debate about the nature of the drug lag in the United States and who or what is responsible, it seems to us, is determining what should be done about it. What should be done to help the patients—usually few in number—who, in the clinical judgment of competent physicians and drug experts, may be helped by a drug not yet approved in this country but on the market elsewhere?

Erasing the 1962 Amendments or demolishing FDA do not seem to us to offer attractive solutions. One possible technique might be to enable FDA, under existing or new law, to provide for such patients by setting up a simple "compassionate approval" procedure, allowing a company to furnish supplies to a limited number of physicians, possibly on the condition that each physician be required to make a complete report to FDA on the outcome of treatment, until such time as the drug is finally approved or rejected.

A number of European countries have established mechanisms whereby a drug not available in one country can be specially imported from another, provided that the physician will simply say to his own government, "I need this drug for the best care of this particular patient." Once such a provision is on the law books, European drug officials say, it is practically never used. It has, however, convinced these officials and the physicians in those countries that the drug lag problem is no problem.

Such solutions as these may be strongly opposed by some drug companies and by some consumer groups. They may be viewed with suspicion by American physicians who, unlike their colleagues in foreign countries, are more likely to be sued for malpractice if something goes wrong, although this risk might be minimized by obtaining in advance the informed consent of the patient. On the other hand, these approaches might conceivably mark the end for too many years of noisy, wasteful rhetoric. And they could, in probably a limited number of cases, improve the quality of health care.

Thus, it may be concluded that the drug lag—which probably never was and certainly is not now a significant problem in most other nations—will continue to exist in the United States. It will probably do this at least as long as the attack on it is financially fueled by those drug companies which believe, at least in the short run, that they have most to gain from a quick and easy drug approval process in this country. Our own drug lag may have inconvenienced or, more infrequently, harmed some American patients, but it has probably safeguarded the health and even the lives of many more Americans.

As Mark Twain once said of the music of Richard Wagner, the drug lag may not be as bad as it sounds.

Notes

1. Milton Silverman, "Drug Insurance: Who Needs It?" in *National Drug Insurance Conference,* p. 8.
2. *Annual Survey Report* (Washington, D.C.: Pharmaceutical Manufacturers Association, various years).
3. Vincent Gardner (Health Care Financing Administration and National Association of Chain Drug Stores) and Thomas Fulda (Health Care Financing Administration), personal communications, 1979 and 1980.
4. "The Top 200 Drugs," *Pharmacy Times* 46:31 (April 1980).
5. H. E. Simmons and Paul D. Stolley, "This Is Medical Progress? Trends and Consequences of Antibiotic Use in the United States." *Journal of the American Medical Association* 227:1023 (March 4, 1974).
6. Michael B. Balter and J. Levine, "The Nature and Extent of Psychotropic Drug Usage in the United States," *Psychopharmacology Bulletin* 5:3 (July 1969).
7. "The Top 200 Drugs."
8. RxTF, *Drug Users,* p. 21.
9. Ibid.
10. U.S. Department of Health, Education, and Welfare, National Center for Health Statistics, *The National Ambulatory Medical Care Survey,* 1975 Summary, Series 13, No. 33, 1978.
11. *Pills, Profits, and Politics,* p. 19.
12. RxTF, *Insurance Design,* p. 77.
13. Robert M. Gibson, "National Health Expenditures, 1978," *Health Care Financing Review* 1:1 (Summer 1979).
14. *Pills, Profits, and Politics,* Chapter 2.
15. Paul de Haen, "Compilation of New Drugs, 1940 Through 1975," *Pharmacy Times* 42:40 (March 1976).
16. Pharmaceutical Manufacturers Association, *Annual Survey Report,* various years.
17. David Ennals, "Address to Parliament," London, April 28, 1977.
18. *Pills, Profits, and Politics,* Chapter 3.
19. "Undergraduate Medical Education," *Journal of the American Medical Association* 243:849 (March 7, 1980).
20. *Drugging of the Americas.*
21. John S. Yudkin, "Provision of Medicines in a Developing Country," *Lancet* 1:810 (April 15, 1978).
22. Ennals, "Address to Parliament."
23. *Pills, Profits, and Politics,* p. 35.
24. Ronald W. Hansen, "The Pharmaceutical Development Process: Estimates of Development Costs and Times and the Effects of Proposed Regulatory Changes," in Robert I. Chien, ed., *Issues in Pharmaceutical Economics* (Lexington, Mass.: D. C. Heath, 1979).
25. C. Joseph Stetler, paper presented before a meeting of the Food and Drug Law Institute, Washington, D.C., May 21, 1979.
26. Richard Emmitt, quoted in *F-D-C Reports,* March 13, 1978, p. 13.
27. "FDA Hastens Approval of 'Important' New Drugs," *American Pharmacist* NS19:182 (April 1979).
28. Drug Regulation Reform Act of 1978, S. 2755, H.R. 11611.
29. Drug Regulation Reform Act of 1979, S. 1075, H.R. 7035.
30. Sam Peltzman, *Regulation of Pharmaceutical Regulation* (Washington, D.C.: American Enterprise Institute for Public Policy Research, 1974); and "Frustrating Drug Advancement," *Newsweek,* January 8, 1973, p. 49.
31. *Pills, Profits, and Politics,* Chapters 4 and 5; *Drugging of the Americas;* Richard J. Barnet and Ronald Müller, *Global Reach: The Power of the Multinational Corporations* (New York: Simon and Schuster, 1974); Robert J. Ledogar, *Hungry for Profits* (New York: IDOC/North America, 1975); Yudkin, "Provision of Medicines"; Joseph A. Roman, "Mefenamic Acid—Classic Case of Misinformation," *American Pharmacist* NS19:48 (April 1979); Charles Medawar, *Insult or Injury* (London: Social Audit, 1979), pp. 111–124.
32. U.S. Department of Health, Education, and Welfare, Food and Drug Administration, *New Drug Evaluation Briefing Book* (Washington, D.C., various years).
33. William M. Wardell, "The Drug Lag Revisited: Comparison by Therapeutic Area of Patterns of Drugs Marketed in the United States and Great Britain from 1972 through 1976," *Clinical Pharmacology and Therapeutics* 24:499 (November 1978); and William M. Wardell, statement in U.S. House of Representatives, *FDA's Process,* pp. 79–91.

34. Barbara Moulton, statement in U.S. House of Representatives, *FDA's Process*, pp. 399–406.
35. *Pills, Profits, and Politics*, pp. 243–248; William M. Wardell, "A Close Inspection of the 'Calm Look,' " *Journal of the American Medical Association* 239:2004 (May 12, 1978); and Gregory J. Ahart, statement in U.S. House of Representatives, *FDA's Process*, pp. 29, 30, and 35.
36. M. N. Graham Dukes and Inge Lunde, personal communications, 1979 and 1980.
37. Donald Kennedy, statement in U.S. House of Representatives, *FDA's Process*, p. 154.
38. *Sunday Times of London*, Insight Team, *Suffer the Children: The Story of Thalidomide* (New York: Viking Press, 1979).
39. Donald Kennedy, statement in U.S. House of Representatives, *FDA's Process*, pp. 187, 188, and 201.
40. Frederick Suchy et al., "Acute Hepatic Failure Associated with the Use of Sodium Valproate," *New England Journal of Medicine* 300:962 (April 26, 1979).
41. Olle Hansson, *Arzneimittel-Multis und der SMON-Skandal* (Berlin: Arzneimittel-Informations-Dienst GmbH, 1979); and T. Soda, ed., *Drug-Induced Sufferings—Medical, Pharmaceutical and Legal Aspects* (Proceedings of the Kyoto International Conference Against Drug-Induced Sufferings, Kyoto, Japan, April 14–18, 1979) (Amsterdam-Oxford-Princeton: Excerpta Medica; New York: Elsevier North-Holland, 1980).
42. Review Panel on New Drug Regulation, *Final Report* ("The Dorsen Report") (Washington, D.C.: U.S. Department of Health, Education, and Welfare, May 1977), pp. 28 and 29.
43. Paul de Haen, "Is There a Drug Lag in Europe?" *Medical Marketing and Media* 14:15 (July 1979).

7. An Incipient "Wonder Drug" Movement: DMSO and the Food and Drug Administration

Phillip W. Davis

• • •

Most applications to the U.S. Food and Drug Administration (FDA) for permission to market new drugs go unnoticed by the public. Applications are either approved or returned to the applicant for more testing, with little or no controversy. But the struggle to legalize dimethyl sulfoxide (DMSO) as a prescription painkiller in the United States has been dramatic and well-publicized. A fledgling advocacy movement, visible in the mid-1960s and then again in the early 1980s, has embraced both experts and the thousands of lay persons who have been treating themselves with DMSO at home. Yet the movement never quite got on its feet, and by 1984 DMSO was still "banned" by the FDA as a general painkiller. This paper reviews the history of DMSO in the United States in an attempt to understand why the movement has so far failed.

DMSO is a clear, colorless liquid with a pungent odor. It was first isolated in 1867 by Dr. Alexander Saytzeff, a Russian chemist. A byproduct of the wood and paper processing industries, DMSO is extracted from lignins, a natural substance which bonds wood fibers together in trees. It is also easily manufactured in the laboratory from organic chemicals. In the United States DMSO has been widely used in industry as a solvent for such substances as polymers, resins, and plastics. It can be easily bought over the counter in hardware stores as a solvent. Many people also claim the substance has medicinal uses as well. Though its safety and effectiveness are still the subject of debate, DMSO is known to relieve pain, act as a diuretic, penetrate membranes such as the human skin, and transport some substances with it as it penetrates. These properties have encouraged countless persons to use industrial DMSO as a home remedy for such medical problems as arthritis, bursitis, and assorted athletic injuries.

Applied to the skin, DMSO quickly enters the blood stream, giving the user a characteristic "garlic breath" and leaving an onion-like aftertaste. In higher concentrations, DMSO can produce nausea, diarrhea, drowsiness, and skin rash at the point of application. A few cases of extreme allergic reaction have been reported. DMSO has been taken orally and intravenously, although most people have simply dabbed it on the skin over the troublesome area, consuming an ounce or two a month with a few applications a week.

This discussion of an "incipent" (Jackson *et al,* 1960) movement is divided into eight parts.[1] I begin by discussing the data. Second, I examine the historical context of the relevant drug controls, and the thalidomide controversy. Third, I look at the emergence of the DMSO movement. Fourth, I outline the FDA's reactions to advocates' claims. Fifth, I discuss the rediscovery of DMSO by the media. Sixth, I examine the conflicts over definitions between lay and scientific advocates. Seventh, I discuss DMSO's "black market." Lastly, I note the newer discoveries and sanctions in the "wonder drug's" career.

From Philip W. Davis, AN INCIPIENT "WONDER DRUG" MOVEMENT: DSMO AND THE FOOD AND DRUG ADMINISTRATION. Copyright © 1984 by the Society for the Study of Social Problems. Reprinted from *Social Problems,* Vol. 32, No. 2, December, 1984, pp. 197–212, by permission.

The Data

This paper uses three sources of data: (1) the testimony, documentation, and conclusions of official reports of medical conferences, and two Congressional hearings on DMSO (U.S. Congress: House, 1980a; U.S. Congress: Senate, 1980a); (2) the media coverage of DMSO from 1964 to 1966, and from 1980 to 1982, including three trade books on DMSO (Bristol, 1982; McGrady, 1979; Tarshis, 1981); and (3) semi-structured interviews. In 1981 I interviewed 50 users of DMSO and eight DMSO distributors. The users responded to ads I placed in newspapers. Most of this self-selecting, accidentally sampled group were over 55 and had some college education. Three of the distributors were legally selling DMSO on a full-time basis, having formed their own companies which bottled, labeled, and retailed DMSO. The others were selling DMSO from their apartments and homes without business licenses. All quotes in this paper are from my interviews, unless otherwise attributed.

Historical Context of U.S. Controls

The controversy surrounding DMSO must be seen against the socio-political background of developing federal controls and changes in the drug approval process. These changes involve increasingly specific definitions of safety, effectiveness, and approval. The first major attempt by the federal government to ensure the safety of food and drugs in the United States was the Food and Drug Act of 1906. In part, the act was a response to public clamor over unhygienic conditions in the food processing industry. The act prohibited food adulteration and false or misleading labels on pharmaceuticals (Silverman and Lee, 1974; Wardell and Lasagna, 1975). In 1938, largely as a response to 107 deaths due to a poisonous elixir, the Food, Drug, and Cosmetic Act was passed, requiring that drugs meet certain safety criteria before they could be transported across state lines for commercial purposes. A new drug was "approved" if the government did not take action against it within 60 days of an application for approval (Wardell and Lasagna, 1975). New drugs at this point still did not have to be effective.

Senator Estes Kefauver (Democrat-Tennessee), Chair of the Senate Judiciary Antitrust and Monopoly Subcommittee, began an investigation of the drug industry late in 1958. He wrote a bill to protect the consumer against continuing abuses in drug labeling and advertising and introduced it in the Senate in April, 1961 (*Congressional Quarterly Almanac,* 1962:200; Harris, 1964). In November, 1961, West German pediatricians learned that a current outbreak of phocomelia—flipper-like limbs in newborn infants—was due to thalidomide, a sedative being marketed under the name Contergan by Chemie Grunenthal Company (Taussig, 19662). The press in the United States largely overlooked the story. *Time* medicine editor Gilbert Cant, for example, knew that a new drug called Kevadon was being sold in Canada and had been submitted for approval in the United States in 1960 by the William S. Merrell Company of Cincinnati, but he did not discover that Kevadon was thalidomide until months after the news in Germany (Mintz, 1965). Kefauver heard about Kevadon and had a Senate aide pass a memo on to *Washington Post* reporter Morton Mintz in June, 1962 (Roberts, 1977; *Congressional Quarterly Almanac,* 1962). On July 15, Mintz reported that Kevadon would probably have passed the existing drug laws if a single person, FDA medical officer Frances Kelsey, had not intuitively felt Merrell should submit more test data (Mintz, 1962). By 1963, more than 10,000 "thalidomide babies" had been born worldwide. There were at least 10 deformed babies born in the United States to mothers who took Kevadon samples in the critical first trimester of pregnancy when the fetus is most vulnerable to thalidomide's mutagenic effects (Lear, 1962; Mintz, 1965; Teff and Munro, 1976).

The outcry worldwide over thalidomide led to overwhelming support for Kefauver's bill. Incorporating some revisions by Representative Oren Harris (Democrat-Arkansas) which would delay drug approval, the Drug Amendments of 1962 became law on October 10. Federal law now required "substantial evidence" of a new drug's safety *and* effectiveness before approval. "Substantial evidence" was defined as "evidence consisting of adequate and well-controlled investigations, including clinical investigations by experts qualified by scientific training and experience to evaluate effectiveness of the drug involved" (*Congressional Quarterly Almanac,* 1962:199). "Approval" meant a written statement explicitly indicating approval, rather than automatic approval if the FDA did not act. Before a drug company could test a new drug on humans, it first had to establish the drug's toxicity on laboratory animals. These data were to be submitted to the FDA, which could then issue a Notice of a Claimed Investigational Exemption for a New Drug (IND), permitting the company to conduct restricted tests on humans. With test results in hand, the drug company was to submit a New Drug Application (NDA). The FDA either approved the application—thereby allowing the drug to be marketed—or demanded further tests (Wardell and Lasagna, 1975).[2]

The Emergence of DMSO

As the new provisions of the Kefauver-Harris amendment were being developed, an industrial solvent was being scientifically, socially, and economically redefined in Oregon as a unique drug. Officials at the Crown Zellerbach Company asked staff chemist Robert Herschler to investigate the commercial uses of DMSO. As a paper goods manufacturer, Crown had an abundant supply of the chemical waste. Herschler found that DMSO dissolved polymers, resins, and pesticides, and it could clean plastics-processing equipment (Sullivan, 1963). Herschler was especially interested in DMSO's apparent ability to penetrate plant leaves, thinking DMSO might carry nutrients and fungicides into diseased trees. Other research was going on as well. British researchers noted the "cryoprotective" ability of DMSO to act as an antifreeze in safely storing blood cells (Lovelock and Bishop, 1959). Stanley Jacob, Assistant Professor of Surgery at the University of Oregon Medical Center, was seeking better ways to preserve animal tissue at freezing temperatures for transplantation (McGrady, 1979). He read the British report on DMSO and approached Crown officials, who referred him to Herschler late in 1962 (Jacob, 1980; McGrady, 1979; Sullivan, 1963).

Following his meeting with Herschler, Jacob applied DMSO in large doses to laboratory animals under a variety of conditions. He noticed that scalded rats seemed to be tranquilized by DMSO, indicating an analgesic—pain-killing—action. He decided that it was relatively safe and is said to have applied it to himself and co-workers. Herschler is said to have applied it to his assistant's recently sprained ankle, with a decrease in the pain and swelling (McGrady, 1979; Tarshis, 1981). Jacob and Herschler both noticed DMSO seemed to penetrate the skin because, within minutes of getting DMSO on their hands, they experienced a strong garlic-like taste and odor. While these early "tests" were uncontrolled, Herschler and Jacob believed DMSO might be used to treat arthritis or carry therapeutic drugs to the brain in treating mental retardation and mental illness (Tarshis, 1981).

Jacob's preliminary tests attracted the interest of the local press. The idea of a cheap and common chemical accidentally discovered to have medical promise made good copy. An article in *The Oregonian* on December 11, 1963 (Sullivan, 1963) described Jacob's tests on a few patients with colds, arthritis, burn wounds, and headaches. The story was picked up by the *New York Times* (Plumb, 1963) and given front-page treatment on December 18. The article referred to

DMSO's "remarkable" qualities of penetration, pain relief, and transportation of other substances. On the day the story was published, Crown stock soared from $4.50 to $60.25 a share; in the next three weeks the stock climbed five points. It dropped back to its starting level, however, after company officials announced that DMSO would have little effect on Crown's overall sales (McGrady, 1979; *Newsweek,* 1963). Within months, the story of the "discovery of DMSO" was carried in *Newsweek* (1963), *U.S. News and World Report* (1963), *Life* (1964), and the *Saturday Evening Post* (Davidson, 1964).

The wave of popular publicity—which had begun to tout DMSO as a "wonder drug"—scooped professional reporting of the news about DMSO. Jacob, Herschler, and Margaret Bischel, a medical student and assistant, did not publish in professional journals until 1964 (Jacob *et al.,* 1964a, b). They reported seven "biological actions" of DMSO, claiming that it penetrated membranes, decreased inflammation, relieved pain, inhibited the growth of bacteria, increased urine production, increased the effectiveness of other drugs, and relaxed muscles. Jacob's colleagues were leary of the publicity, his growing popularity among patients at the medical center's clinic, and the unusually long list of properties (McGrady, 1979).

FDA Reactions

Amid considerable clamor in the press, the small group of medical and business "enthusiasts" approached the FDA, which by then was operating under the 1962 provisions. Their data demonstrated low toxicity in animals. Crown received a Claimed Investigational Exemption—IND #1310—and was approached by more than 30 pharmaceutical companies hoping to test and eventually market the drug (Tarshis, 1981). Crown issued research licenses in 1964 to six of the largest—Merck and Company, Geigy Pharmaceuticals, American Home Products Corporation, Syntex Corporation, the U.S. branch of Schering Corporation in West Germany, and the Squibb and Sons division of Olin Mathieson Chemical Corporation. These drug houses financed research over the next year to study DMSO's safety and efficacy in humans (Martin and Hauthal, 1975).

The research seemed to support the statements in the press and an editorial in the *New York Times* (1965) called DMSO "the closest thing to a wonder drug produced in the 1960s." DMSO's reported side effects were temporary itching, flaking, and burning where it had been rubbed on the skin, along with some drowsiness, nausea, and a characteristic garlic breath. DMSO appeared to reduce pain and inflammation in musculo-skeletal disorders such as arthritis and bursitis. While Merck, Squibb, and Syntex submitted New Drug Applications to the FDA and NDA's in the United States, Schering of West Berlin received approval to market DMSO in Germany under the name of Dolicur in August, 1965 (Jacob, 1980; Martin and Hauthal, 1975).

Among the data submitted by Merch with its NDA was a report by Lionel Rubin from the University of Pennsylvania's school of Veterinary Medicine. He had continued the animal toxicity research and found DMSO caused abnormal changes in the eyes of laboratory animals (Gordon, 1967). The reports did not unduly alarm Jacob and other researchers since no study had shown eye damage in humans. On September 9, 1965, the *Wall Street Journal* reported that a woman in Ireland died after three days of DMSO treatments for a sprained wrist. Squibb representatives speculated that the woman died of an allergic reaction, although no autopsy was performed (Carley, 1965).

The reports of nearsighted laboratory animals and the woman's death were the first indications that DMSO might have dangerous side effects. On September 22, the FDA not only denied the NDA's but cancelled Crown's IND. The FDA followed this up on November 10 by sending telegrams to the World Health Organization, U.S. embassies, and all doctors testing DMSO in the

United States to warn them of the hazard of possible eye toxicity and to recall all unused DMSO. On November 11, new reports of eye damage to laboratory dogs, rabbits, and pigs came from the Huntingdon Research Centre in Great Britain (Kleberger, 1967). On November 15, the German drug houses voluntarily decided to stop marketing their DMSO products, and on November 19, FDA Commissioner George P. Larrick officially prohibited all tests of DMSO on humans (*Federal Register,* 1965).

The FDA's "ban" created a focus for the growing number of advocates: a pro-DMSO movement was becoming visible. More than 100,000 patients had been treated with the drug (*FDA Drug Bulletin,* 1980). An unknown number of people were using industrial DMSO as a home remedy for the pain of arthritis, sprains, and minor burns. Jacob advised some of his patients to write their congressmen to complain, if they wanted to "do something." Crown asked him to stop the petitions and, according to one advocate historian, he did try to stop his patients from writing (McGrady, 1979). However, the flow of letters was to continue, on and off, for another 20 years. A few congressmen complained to the FDA that DMSO was a "persecuted drug." Medical investigators claimed that the FDA had overreacted and had no evidence of eye damage in humans (*Time,* 1967).

The FDA's action in 1965 did not put an end to claims about DMSO. The New York Academy of Sciences held a symposium on DMSO in March, 1966. While there was further confirmation of eye damage to animals caused by DMSO (Rubin and Barnett, 1967), conference organizers made a point of announcing that no evidence of eye damage in humans had been reported at the symposium (Leake *et al.,* 1967). In response to numerous complaints and the absence of eye damage in humans, the FDA decided in December, 1966, to allow DMSO to be tested on humans. It could only be applied externally for conditions for which there was no existing effective treatment, and the test patients had to receive eye examinations every three months (*Federal Register,* 1966). Only Squibb pursued the matter and, in 1967, sponsored a study of 67 prisoners at the California Medical Facility at Vacaville who were treated with a DMSO gel for two weeks. Another 60 inmates were then tested over two months. No evidence of eye damage was found and the researchers concluded that DMSO did not produce any "serious" toxic effects (Brobyn, 1975).

Relations between researchers and the FDA were tense but, in light of the study on prisoners, the FDA allowed DMSO to be tested for no more than 14 days in acute "soft-tissue" injuries such as sprains and tendonitis. The FDA also approved a 90 percent solution of DMSO in 1978 to be used, only with a veterinarian's prescription, for topical use on dogs and horses to reduce swelling from injuries (*FDA Drug Bulletin,* 1980). Veterinary DMSO was marketed in a gel as Domoso by Diamond Laboratories of Des Moines, Iowa.

When researchers and patients complained that test restrictions were unwarranted, the FDA turned to the National Academy of Sciences in 1971 to review the safety and effectiveness of DMSO. Citing the absence of well-controlled studies, the committee concluded that there was inadequate evidence of effectiveness in any disease and that the toxicity potential was sufficient to warrant DMSO remaining an investigational drug (Goyan, 1980; Harter, 1983; National Academy of Sciences, 1973). In the same year, Pat McGrady Sr. published an elaborate advocate's account of DMSO called *The Persecuted Drug: The Story of DMSO* (1979) which went into six printings (Mutter, 1981).

With the FDA receiving support from a prestigious group of scientists, researchers decided to seek approval for the treatment of some rare condition (Bristol, 1982). In 1974, the FDA allowed Jacob to monitor studies under two IND's sponsored by Research Industries Corporation (RIC) of Salt Lake City, Utah. The INDs were to test DMSO's effectiveness in treating interstitial cystitis, a rare and painful urinary bladder infection, and scleroderma, a painful hardening and ulceration of the skin (Moyle, 1980). On May 4, 1977, Arthur Scherbel of the Cleveland Clinic wrote to RIC president Henry Moyle stating that four of the 11 scleroderma patients in this study of orally administered DMSO developed progressive myopia during the treatments. On May 16, Moyle and Jacob met with Dr. Kaniambakam Chakra Pani, the FDA medical officer in charge of reviewing all DMSO studies submitted to the FDA (U.S. Congress: Senate, 1980a). Moyle and Jacob later claimed that they showed Scherbel's letter to Pani, but Pani consistently denied having been notified of reports of eye toxicity. Whether the report of eye damage had been "submitted" to the FDA was to become the basis of conspiracy charges against Jacob and Pani in 1981.

Unaware of Scherbel's letter at the time, the FDA nonetheless turned down RIC's NDA for scleroderma in 1978, citing the lack of controls such as "double-blind" tests. Researchers were frustrated because the garlic odor and taste associated with DMSO made it easy for both researchers and subjects to tell which subjects in the experimental group were receiving DMSO rather than a placebo. On the other hand, the FDA approved RIC's NDA for cystitus in 1978, largely upon Pani's recommendation. RIC was authorized to market Rimso-50, a 50 percent solution of medical-grade DMSO for direct "instillation" into the bladder to cystitis patients. Researchers, physicians, and patients agreed that a 50 percent solution was too weak to help arthritic pain (*American Medical News*, 1981a; *FDA Drug Bulletin*, 1980).

The Rediscovery of DMSO

The general public was not aware of these complex administrative and scientific issues because the media generally neglected DMSO after the wave of publicity between 1963 and 1965 concerning the discovery and "ban" of DMSO. The press did not cover the unsuccessful federal legislation late in 1979 which would "bypass" FDA restrictions on DMSO (*FDA Consumer*, 1980). The wife of Representative Steven Symms (Republican-Idaho) had scleroderma, and Representative Robert Duncan (Democrat-Oregon) was an outspoken supporter of DMSO. They introduced three bills in the House of Representatives which were referred to the House Committee on Interstate and Foreign Commerce. The bills sought congressional approval of DMSO for use in the treatment of scleroderma, acute brain and spinal cord injuries, and the inflammation of arthritis, bursitis, rheumatism, and "other disorders of the musculo-skeletal system" (U.S. Congress: House, 1979a,b). The bills did not leave the committee.

DMSO was "rediscovered" by the press and public in 1980. Representative Claude Pepper (Democrat-Florida) planned a one-day hearing on DMSO and arthritis before the House Select Committee on Aging. Pepper had a longstanding interest in arthritis and had followed DMSO's growing controversy (Pepper, 1980). Having learned of the scheduled hearing, CBS television broadcast a feature program on March 23 called "The Riddle of DMSO" as part of its highly rated Sunday night show "Sixty Minutes." During the program, CBS news correspondent Mike Wallace interviewed Jacob, several enthusiastic users of DMSO, and Dr. Richard Crout, director of the FDA's Bureau of Drugs. The program put the FDA on the defensive. Wallace put several pro-DMSO research reports in front of Crout and said ". . . it's not as though this is some quack remedy that a few people have used and swear by." Crout responded, "It's a relatively safe drug, as drugs go," but there were some "key holes" in the evidence, namely, the absence of controlled trials (U.S. Congress: House, 1980a:131). An estimated 37 million viewers saw the program, and

Jacob reported receiving up to 10,000 letters and phone inquiries in the following week (Bergreen, 1980). The day after the program, Pepper's committee heard testimony from Jacob, other physicians, several congressmen, and Crout of the FDA, essentially repeating the televised debate.

With Pepper's support, Representative Larry Hopkins (Republican-Kentucky) introduced a bill which would require a federal study of the efficacy of DMSO for treating arthritis. It was referred to the House Committee on Interstate and Foreign Commerce on April 2, 1980 (U.S. Congress: House 1980b). On May 16, 1980, Senator James McClure (Republican-Idaho) introduced three bills which were referred to the Senate Committee on Labor and Human Resources. They were identical to those introduced by Symms in the House of Representatives concerning the use of DMSO for scleroderma, brain injury, and arthritis. None of the bills left committee but Hopkin's request for a federal DMSO study was added to another bill which, after revisions, became law as the Health Programs Extension Act in December, 1980. The controversial DMSO provision had been deleted (*Congressional Quarterly Almanac,* 1980; U.S. Congress: Senate, 1980b).

On July 31, following a rebroadcast of the "Sixty Minutes" program on DMSO earlier in the month, Senator Edward Kennedy (Democrat-Massachusetts) chaired a Senate Subcommittee on Health and Scientific Research hearing on DMSO. The hearing stemmed from Kennedy's long interest in U.S. health care reforms and his contention that both the drug industry and the FDA had mishandled DMSO (U.S. Congress: Senate, 1980:2). As the recognized advocate of DMSO, Jacob was again asked to testify. The FDA was represented this time by Commissioner Jere Goyan who defended the FDA's policies and warned of the risk run by home users. Goyan also alluded to pending investigations of researchers and said there might be difficulties ahead for Pani because of "possible improprieties in his interactions with Research Industries Corporation" (Goyan, 1980:36). The nature of the alleged improprieties was to become public more than a year later in a criminal court.

By late 1980, the media's interest in DMSO was as great as it had been in 1964 and 1965. A second major wave of articles on DMSO appeared in popular magazines and newspapers, including *Better Homes and Gardens* (1981), *Fate* (Fuller, 1981), *McCalls* (Chan, 1981), *Newsweek* (Clark, 1980), *People* (Wilhelm, 1981), *Runner's World* (Kissin, 1981; Wischnia, 1980), *Sports Illustrated* (Reed, 1981), *Time* (1980), *Vogue* (Weber, 1981), and the *Wall Street Journal* (1981). The articles neglected the political activity in congress and focused upon arthritis sufferers who were turning to DMSO with miraculous results. The public read about the use of DMSO by such famous people as George Wallace, the former governor of Alabama who had been paralyzed by gunshot wounds and treated by Jacob in Oregon for two weeks. One article quoted Jacob as saying he had continued to use DMSO personally since 1963 in order to catch any new side effects (Wilhelm, 1981).

Conflicts over Definitions

Scientists and lay advocates had different experiences with DMSO and different relationships with the approving agency. Both groups claimed the FDA's restrictions were unwarranted, but scientists and lay advocates constructed and promoted different definitions of the statutory standards, the FDA, and DMSO itself.

Definitions of Statutory Standards

Scientific advocates of DMSO espoused a technical definition of the statutory standards. They claimed that DMSO's effectiveness had already been scientifically proven for simple pain, scleroderma, and arthritis. Jacob told Pepper's House committee in 1980:

> There are literally thousands of scientific articles. I think it can be stated without qualification that this is safe and effective for many diseases for which we do not have other treatments and for many diseases for which we do have other treatments (U.S. Congress: House, 1980a:20).

Lay advocates applied personal definitions to the FDA's statutory standards of safety and efficacy, pleading for the "legalization" of DMSO on the basis of their personal experience with the substance. According to these claims, personal biological reality superceded both scientific and bureaucratic definitions of safety and efficacy. Lay advocates argued that DMSO should be approved for pain relief and other conditions because it "worked" better and quicker than other treatments. One advocate wrote to the House Committee:

> **I DRANK SIX TABLESPOONS OF DMSO DAILY FOR TWO MONTHS!** I might add at this point that I was doubtful that anything could help my pain trauma. The first week I did not notice an appreciable difference, but with each day of the second week, my pain lessens. I sing its praises (U.S. Congress: House, 1980a:144; emphasis in original).

Not all lay advocates "sang the praises" of DMSO, but many believed that DMSO met subjective, common-sense criteria of effectiveness, namely, pain relief and speedy recovery. Lay advocates defined DMSO as safe because they personally experienced DMSO's side effects to be minor:

> I walk into work after using it and people at work say, "Who is using DMSO?" There's kind of a garlic smell but it's not really offensive.

If home users were aware of the FDA's fear of eye toxicity, they tended to be suspicious:

> They talk like it causes cataracts. You know they probably have those rats bathing in it.

One lay advocate claimed she had experienced a desirable side effect: her straight grey hair started to turn red and curly after a year of using DMSO.

Definitions of the FDA

Lay advocates had greater latitude than the experts in denouncing the FDA. While scientific advocates said the FDA "overreacted" (Herschler and Jacob, 1980), lay advocates resorted to name calling" (Lee and Lee, 1939), often depicting the FDA as "stupid," "uncaring," and "malicious":

> There are literally millions of our citizens who are being denied access to this marvelous substance because of the stupid, negligent, malicious, or worse conduct within the FDA towards DMSO (U.S. Congress: House, 1980a:144).

Some advocates claimed that the FDA was engaged in a conspiracy with the pharmaceutical companies and the American Medical Association (AMA) to protect profits from drugs which had already been approved. Others questioned the administrative autonomy of the agency:

> You see, I don't have much faith in the FDA. First of all, its staffed by men from the AMA.

From the lay perspective, the hypothesized conspiracy was a reasonable way of explaining the FDA's actions.

Both lay and scientific advocates claimed that the FDA's actions were motivated by the need to save face. They said the agency recognized its "error" but was refusing to own up to it. According to Jacob:

> So here you have a government agency whose job is to evaluate test data, going out and spending millions of dollars of tax money in order to *find* something negative about a drug—simply to back up a decision that they shouldn't have made in the first place (quoted in Tarshis, 1981:175; emphasis in original).

Definitions of DMSO

Scientific and lay advocates developed quite different definitions of DMSO itself. Medical researchers usually used the cautious rhetoric of the scientific world. Jacob, for example, defined DMSO as a new "therapeutic principle" rather than a drug (Jacob, 1980). While Jacob said, "DMSO is not a miracle panacea" (quoted in Tarshis, 1981:122), lay advocates were free to define DMSO as a pain-relieving "wonder drug." Some lay advocates defined DMSO in explicity metaphysical terms:

> I noticed I was able to move my neck so much more freely. Cause when I'd go out and drive, instead of turning my head I'd have to go like that [turns from waist]. And now I can turn my head, you know? To me it was a miracle.

Scientific advocates blamed the FDA's continued rejection of DMSO partially on lay definitions. In a summary of the New York Academy of Sciences' conference in 1974, Arthur Scherbel, medical researcher at the Cleveland Clinic, noted:

> The DMSO controversy persisted because of widespread lay publicity which demanded the return of DMSO. During this time, certain well-meaning lay group organizations sent hundreds of letters to members of Congress, demanding that DMSO again be made available. . . . Pressure tactics by well-meaning lay groups should be discontinued (Scherbel, 1975:508).

Scientific advocates worked to demystify the drug in the eyes of the FDA, but distributors and many law advocates continued to define DMSO in personal and metaphysical terms.

The DMSO "Black Market"

Many DMSO users crossed into Mexico for injections of sterilized DMSO at arthritis clinics in border towns such as Tecate, Nogales, and Juarez (Moyle, 1980). Most home users, however, purchased unsterilized DMSO on a "black market" which was more evasive than illegal. By 1981, industrial DMSO was being sold in hobby shops, carpet stores, ice cream parlors, dry cleaners, hardware stores, health food stores, garden and plant shops, shoe stores, and drug stores. Some individuals peddled the solvent from houses, apartments, health spa lockers, and car trunks. On a larger scale, some distributors established mail order businesses and opened stores selling DMSO exclusively. These distribution channels were technically legal so long as the distributors and retailers had business licenses and did not make medical claims about impure, industrial DMSO. Home users also tried, with some success, to obtain DMSO gel from veterinarians by claiming they needed it to treat their pets. Speculative distributors purchased DMSO solvent in 55-gallon drums and then bottled and labeled it for sale in four-, six-, eight-, and 16-ounce containers. DMSO cost about $4 a gallon to manufacture, and distributors paid about $1 per pint for bulk DMSO (at 1982 prices). After bottling and labeling the solvent, distributors charged retailers about $10 a pint. Consumer's paid between $20 and $30 a pint (Bristol, 1982; Schlaadt and Shannon, 1982).

From the distributors' perspective, the FDA's rules could justifiably be broken or evaded. To avoid conflict with the FDA's regulations, distributors clearly labeled the bottles as containing a solvent. A few distributors did not label rebottled DMSO at all. One distributor said:

> I don't label the bottles. If they don't want to buy it without a label, they don't have to. They can buy it somewhere else.

Others printed labels which specified the "technical applications" of DMSO and issued various disclaimers. One label stated:

> Note: This product is intended to be used as a technical solvent only. The choice of process is the sole responsibility of the customer. **CAUTION: ABSORBED THROUGH THE SKIN.**

Most distributors shared the attitude of one young entrepreneur, who said:

> We're walking a fine line right now as far as legality. But so long as we sell it as a solvent, we're OK.

To avoid practicing unlicensed medicine by telling buyers how to use DMSO, most distributors mailed or handed out photocopies of popular magazine articles which described DMSO's application techniques. Distributors helped to promote the "wonder drug" image as "under the counter advertisers" (Silverman and Lee, 1974) by leaving anonymously published brochures and pamphlets with clerks in health food stores and hobby shops. The carefully worded brochures strongly implied that effectiveness had been established for conditions which had only, in fact, been investigated.

The issue of DMSO's legality was complicated by differences in the reactions of individual state governments. By 1981, Florida, Louisiana, Montana, Oklahoma, Oregon, Texas, and Washington State had interpreted the FDA's rules to allow physicians to prescribe medical-grade DMSO for conditions other than cystitis. Many states passed pro-Laetril legislation in the 1970s (Markle and Petersen, 1980), and DMSO seemed to be a less stigmatized drug. Washington legislators went so far as to declare DMSO an over-the-counter drug but required all DMSO to be manufactured within the state (Bristol, 1982). Without this kind of provision, the other states were risking a greater conflict with federal law (Garmon, 1982).

Tougher Sanctions and Newer Discoveries

Seizures of Solvent

The FDA had no authority over the sale and marketing of industrial DMSO provided the labels and advertisements did not define it as a "drug" and include medical claims. The FDA's most common tactics were to remain visible, monitor shipments (Harter, 1983), and ask distributors for lists of customers to keep them on their toes.

While rumors of frequent FDA seizures of DMSO solvent were widespread among distributors, the FDA was very selective in deciding who to raid since months of investigation went into each case. In February, 1981, for example, FDA agents went to DMSO, Incorporated in Buffalo,

New York, in response to complaints by the health department that company president Michael Grassia was advertising the solvent as a medicine. Grassia removed his storefront sign which read "Arthritis Backache?" but was visited again in May by an FDA investigator posing as a customer. The investigator bought a copy of McGrady's book, some solvent, and distilled water being sold as a package for home users. In July, Grassia's store was "raided" by an FDA investigator and a U.S. Marshal who seized 366 bottles of DMSO, 75 copies of McGrady's book, and three 55-gallon drums of solvent. The FDA claimed the seized DMSO was being sold as a drug, despite the fact that it was labeled as a solvent, and that the book was an illegal "label" because it was being sold "in proximity" to the DMSO (Ballentine, 1983; Mutter, 1981; Tell, 1981).[3]

Prosecution of Jacob

Although the eye damage reported in Scherbel's 1977 letter was never directly traced to DMSO, the FDA suspected that the information and the letter had been "concealed." Goyan personally re-examined the scleroderma research sponsored by RIC and found it of such poor quality that the cystitis reports were re-examined as well. After Goyan testified at Kennedy's hearing, Jacob, RIC, and Pani were investigated and their records audited. Federal prosecutors discovered Jacob had given $36,500 to Pani during the time Pani was reviewing all NDAs for DMSO, including the approved NDA for cystitis. Jacob was charged with four counts of conspiracy to conceal information on DMSO's toxicity and one count of giving an "illegal gratuity" to a federal official. Pani was charged with conspiracy and receiving the gratuity (Engel, 1981; Goyan, 1980; Meyer, 1981; Mintz, 1980).

Both Jacob and Pani pleaded not guilty. Their trial began on May 6, 1982. The prosecution said Jacob had made 24 payments in checks written to Pani between December 1, 1975, and January 6, 1979. Pani told the jury in Baltimore—the site of Pani's office—that he and Jacob had become friends over the years and that the money from Jacob was a loan to help pay his wife's medical bills, who was dying of diabetes (Meyer, 1982a). Jacob said the "personal loan" was a mistake but he refuted Assistant U.S. Attorney Richard Dunn's allegation that he "wanted to buy a friend" at the FDA (Meyer, 1982b). On May 14, the judge declared a mistrial because of a hung jury. Pani, 64 years old and already on suspension from the FDA, retired from his federal position after the trial.

On May 19, 1982, prosecutors announced they were taking Pani and Jacob to trial a second time. Pani pleaded guilty to a lesser charge of receiving an outside supplement to his salary for performing official services (Valentine, 1982a). He was sentenced to one year of unsupervised probation and 200 hours of community service (Garmon, 1982). Jacob pleaded not guilty and his trial began on October 25, 1982. In a surprising turn of events, federal prosecutors dropped all charges against Jacob, who read a statement to the court in which the acknowledged that he had created a "conflict of interest" by giving Pani the money. Jacob's defense attorney, Bernard Fensterwald, told the press that the prosecution decided to drop charges if Jacob would read the statement because it did not want to risk a likely acquittal (Valentine, 1982b). Jacob was given a warm reception in Oregon after the trial, and there were no signs of a loss in his status among DMSO advocates.

Medical Research Continues

In 1981 and 1982, as the FDA was applying criminal definitions to Jacob's behavior, researchers were examining DMSO's possible effectiveness in treating stroke, head injuries, bursitis, breast and prostate cancer, spinal cord injury, herpes, retinitis pigmentosa, and arthritis (*American*

Medical News, 1981a; Garmon, 1982). Jack de la Torre of Northwestern University Medical School in Chicago concluded that DMSO helped treat stroke-related brain injuries in monkeys because it dilated blood vessels, thus improving the delivery of oxygen to the brain. Another researcher, however, repeated de la Torre's experiment with a larger animal population and found DMSO ineffective in treating strokes (Garmon, 1982). A few of the newer studies warned of previously unrecognized hazards. DMSO inhibited the metabolism of sulindac, a widely used arthritis drug, and caused damage to the chromosomes in hamster ovary cells (*American Medical News,* 1981a; Garmon, 1982). Cancer researchers found that DMSO stimulated "inappropriate cellular proliferation" in laboratory rats and warned that "long-term toxicity might result" (Rubin and Earp, 1983:62).

On September 15, 1982, the New York Academy of Sciences hosted its third conference on DMSO with Jacob—still facing his second trial at that point—one of the key speakers. Lionel Rubin, one of the first to warn of eye damage in animals, told the academy that most studies showed DMSO was not mutagenic, although a few showed DMSO caused DNA damage in yeast and might "disrupt the integrity of rat chromosome structure" (Rubin, 1983:9). He noted that in the 17 years since the FDA "ban," there was no clear evidence of eye damage in humans, although one study reported DMSO caused eye damage in rhesus monkeys (Rubin, 1983). John Harter, one of the FDA's two new reviewers of DMSO studies, told the academy that claims of an FDA conspiracy were "ludicrous." Arthur Scherbel replied that the FDA's "resistance" to approving DMSO and the resulting home trials by millions of Americans had "become one of the great tragedies of American medicine in the twentieth century" (Scherbel, 1983:316). Jacob and Herschler (1983:xiii) told the academy, "Unfortunately, medical science is still confronting political barriers blocking availability of DMSO as a safe and effective prescription drug."

In early 1984, DMSO was still available by prescription in the United States only for interstitial cystitis. Several new states had passed legislation protecting the prescription of DMSO, bringing the total number of states to 13 (Brody, 1983). In 45 other countries—including Austria, Canada, Ireland, Germany, Great Britain, and Switzerland—DSMO was available by prescription for skin conditions such as shingles and scleroderma (Gillespie, 1983; Jacob, 1980; U.S. Congress: House, 1980a). Working on more than 30 INDs, researchers were still trying to establish DMSO's safety and efficacy for a host of conditions and uses. And home users were still buying DMSO solvent on the "black market," with no sign that it was to become an approved pain reliever.

Discussion

This analysis of the DMSO controversy in the United States raises four points: First, the FDA's criteria were in flux. DMSO came along just as the federal government was clarifying the concepts of new drug "safety," "effectiveness," and "approval," largely in response to the thalidomide tragedy. The FDA was on guard for new drugs which might slip past its medical reviewers. When criteria change, agencies require time and interaction with applicants to establish what the working rules and guidelines will be and to interpret the new critiera. The FDA's standards are shaped by external events, and the federal requirement that new drugs be effective as well as safe was an attempt to increase the FDA's power and to lengthen the time required for new drug approval. The FDA does not test new drugs and must wait for applications to evaluate them according to evolving criteria. This fact has fueled the perception of advocates that the FDA has been "stalling" over DMSO.

Second, "wonder drug" is a suspicious term, especially in administrative and scientific worlds which might be blamed for lax restrictions and unrecognized hazards. Yet, the belief that a new discovery is at hand can mobilize people with incurable medical conditions into positions of advocacy and protest when the new drug meets with resistance. Both DMSO and Laetrile advocates idolized "discoverers," issued cries of conspiracy, and relied heavily upon testimonials to mobilize support. The pro-Laetrile movement however, was far more organized and even held national lay conferences (Markle and Petersen, 1980). The medical claims about DMSO tended to remove it from the realm of what critics called "fruit-pit" pharmacology (Sanders, 1982). While DMSO advocates did not suffer from "huckster" and "dupe" labels, it was difficult for scientific advocates and the agency to ignore the "wonder drug" image.

Third, the media helped to generate the DMSO movement's two periods of peak activity. The media capitalized on the idea that a cheap, chemical waste might also be a drug with unusual properties, including pain relief for incurable inflammatory diseases. While the press was the first to announce DMSO's "remarkable properties," a highly rated CBS television program mobilized the largest number of lay advocates and a black market to supply them. The press usually publicizes unusual side effects after drugs are approved. In the case of DMSO, it popularized a new drug before it was approved.

Fourth, while scientific advocates tended to conform to professional and administrative restrictions, lay advocates were free to define DMSO in dramatic or even mystical ways. Scientific advocates were concerned with the degree of "fit" between their research and agency requirements. Lay advocates and home users were primarily concerned with DMSO's availability. Both groups sought the medical and administrative approval for DMSO and were alarmed over the FDA's restrictions. They had different definitions of DMSO, the FDA, and the rules. They also had different relationships with the FDA.

Notes

1. Jackson *et al.* (1960:35) described the internal conditions which maintain movement incipience. They suggest that in incipient movements, communication linking "like-minded" people over an extended area into one group is ineffective. In this paper, I describe external as well as internal conditions.
2. The tighter controls in the 1962 amendment have resulted in what critics call a "drug lag." The rate of new drug approval in the United States since 1962 fell below that of many countries in western Europe (Wardell and Lasagna, 1975).
3. The action was contested by the New York Civil Liberties Union (NYCLU) on behalf of McGrady's widow. The NYCLU filed a motion for the federal government to return the books to Grassia, claiming that there was no precedent for construing literature as a label. Without a court order, the FDA released the books from seizure, but Grassia did not claim them and they were donated to the Erie County Public Library. The FDA agreed to make no further seizures of the book and the court ruled the DMSO *was* improperly labeled as an unapproved drug (Ballentine, 1983; Mutter, 1981).

References

American Medical News. 1981a "New DMSO studies being reviewed by FDA." American Medical News 24(32):49.
————. 1981b "DMSO interaction found to inhibit arthritis drug." American Medical News 24(33):32.
Ballentine, Carol. 1983 "When a book is a label." FDA Consumer 17(8):34–35.
Bergreen, Laurence. 1980 "How a '60 Minutes' report on the 'wonder drug' called DMSO created an avalanche of mail—and a national controversy." TV Guide, July 26:3–6.
Better Homes and Gardens. 1981 "DMSO: A wonder drug?" Better Homes and Gardens 59 (June):99.
Bristol, Thomas. 1982 DMSO: The Responsible User's Guide. Portland, OR: DMSO News Service.

Brobyn, Richard. 1975 "The human toxicology of dimethyl sulfoxide." Annals of the New York Academy of Sciences 243(1):500–509.

Brody, Jane. 1983 "Debate rages on DMSO despite its users' claims." The New York Times, May 18:Cl.

Carley, William. 1965 "DMSO may have caused death of woman, makers of 'wonder' drug warns doctors." *Wall Street Journal,* September 9:6.

Chan, Janet. 1981 "A perplexing new painkiller called DMSO." McCall's 108 (February):37–39.

Clark, Matt. 1980 "DMSO: A miracle or dangerous drug?" Newsweek 96 (7):56.

Congressional Quarterly Almanac. 1962 "Congress tightens drug regulations." Congressional Quarterly Almanac 18:197–210.

————. 1980 "Health Research." Congressional Quarterly Almanac 36:463–466.

Davidson, Bill. 1964 "Great DMSO mystery." Saturday Evening Post 237 (July 25):72.

Engel, Margaret. 1981 "FDA medical officer indicted." The Washington Post, December 19:1.

FDA Consumer. 1980 "DMSO: No proof of 'miracles.' " FDA Consumer 14(7):28–29.

FDA Drug Bulletin. 1980 "Users of DMSO for unapproved indications." FDA Drug Bulletin 10(3):20–21.

Federal Register. 1965 "Dimethyl sulfoxide (DMSO) preparations: Termination of clinical testing and investigational use." Federal Register 30(228):14639.

————. 1966 "Dimethyl Sulfoxide (DMSO) preparations: Clinical testing and investigational use." Federal Register 31(248):16403–16404.

Fuller, Curtis. 1981 "The DMSO story." Fate 34(1):15–22.

Garmon, Linda. 1982 "Judging DMSO: There's the rub." Science News 122(23):398–408.

Gillespie, Judy. 1983 "DMSO: An Oregon doctor fights to legitimize the so-called wonder drug." *US,* January 31:34–35.

Gordon, Dan. 1967 "Dimethyl sulfoxide in ophthamology, with special reference to possible toxic effects." Annals of the New York Academy of Sciences 141(1):392–401.

Goyan, Jere. 1980 Testimony before the Senate Labor and Human Resources Subcommittee on Health and Scientific Research, July 31. Pp. 23–42 of U.S. Congress: Senate, Preclinical and Clinical Testing by the Pharmaceutical Industry, 1980-DMSO Hearings, 96th Congress, 2nd session. Washington DC: U.S. Government Printing Office.

Harris, Richard. 1964 The Real Voice. New York: Collier-Macmillian.

Harter, John. 1983 "The status of dimethyl sulfoxide from the perspective of the Food and Drug Administration." Annals of the New York Academy of Sciences 411 (1):1–5.

Herschler, Robert J., and Stanley W. Jacob. 1980 "The case of dimethyl sulfoxide." Pp. 519–529 in Louis Lasagna, (ed.), Controversies in Therapeutics. Philadelphia: W. B. Saunders.

Jackson, Maurice, Eleanora Petersen, James Bull, Sverre Monsen, and Patricia Richmond. 1960 "The failure of an incipient social movement." Pacific Sociological Review 3(1):35–40.

Jacob, Stanley W. 1980 Testimony before the House Select Committee on Aging, March 24. Pp. 19–25 of U.S. Congress: House, DMSO: New Hope for Arthritis? Hearings, 96th Congress, 2nd session. Washington, DC: U.S. Government Printing Office.

Jacob, Stanley W., and Robert J. Herschler. 1983 "Introductory remarks: Dimethyl sulfoxide after twenty years." Annals of the New York Academy of Sciences 411(1):xiii–xvii.

Jacob, Stanley W., Margaret Bischel, and Robert J. Herschler. 1964a "Dimethyl sulfoxide (DMSO): A new concept in pharmacotherapy." Current Therapeutic Research 6(2):134–135.

————. 1964b "Dimethyl Sulfoxide: Effects on the permeability of biologic membranes (Preliminary report)." Current Therapeutic Research 6(3):193–198.

Kissin, Ray. 1981 "FDA two, B-15 and DMSO, nothing." Runner's World 16(2):11.

Kleberger, Kurt-Eberhard. 1967 "An opthalmological evaluation of DMSO." Annals of the New York Academy of Sciences 141(1):381–385.

Leake, Chauncey. 1967 "Introductory remarks to the Conference on Biological Actions of Dimethyl Sulfoxide." Annals of the New York Academy of Sciences 141(1):1–3.

Leake, Chauncey, Edward Rosenbaum, and Stanley W. Jacob. 1967 "Summary of the New York Academy of Sciences Symposium on the Biological Actions of Dimethyl Sulfoxide'." Annals of the New York Academy of Sciences 14(1):670–671.

Lear, John. 1962 "The unfinished story of thalidomide." Saturday Review 45(35):35–40.

Lee, Alfred McClung, and Elizabeth Bryant Lee (eds.). 1939 The Fine Art of Propaganda. New York: Harcourt, Brace, and Janovich.

Leonard, C. D. 1967 "Use of dimethyl sulfoxide as a carrier for iron in nutritional foliar sprays applied to citrus." Annals of the New York Academy of Sciences 141(1):148–158.

Life. 1964 "New wonder drug: DMSO." Life 57 (July 10):37.

Lovelock, J. E., and M. W. H. Bishop. 1959 "Prevention of freezing damage to living cells by dimethyl sulfoxide." Nature 183(4672):1394–1395.

McGrady, Pat, Sr. 1979 The Persecuted Drug: The Story of DMSO. New York: Grosset and Dunlap Company.

Markel, Gerald E., and James Petersen. 1980 "Social context of the Laetrile phenomenon." Pp. 151–173 in Gerald E. Markle and James Petersen (eds.), Politics, Science, and Cancer: The Laetrile Phenomenon. Boulder, CO: Westview Press.

Martin, Dieter, and Hermann Hauthal. 1975 Dimethyl Sulphoxide. Translated by E. S. Halberstadt. New York: John Wiley and Sons.

Meyer, Eugene. 1981 "Official pleads not guilty of DMSO payoffs." The Washington Post, December 24: Sec. B, p. 2.

———. 1982a "Trial told doctor traveled with advocate of DMSO chemical." The Washington Post, May 7: sec. B, p. 9.

———. 1982b "DMSO conspiracy trial ends with a hung jury." The Washington Post, May 15: sec. A, p. 6.

Mintz, Morton. 1962 "Heroine of FDA keeps bad drug off market." The Washington Post, July 15:1.

———. 1965 The Therapeutic Nightmare. Boston: Houghton Mifflin.

———. 1980 "FDA aides probed in testing of DMSO." The Washington Post, August 1:sec. A, p. 2.

Moyle, Henry. 1980 Testimony before the Senate Labor and Human Resources Subcommittee on Health and Scientific Research, July 31. Pp. 82–95 of U.S. Congress: Senate, Preclinical and Clinical Testing by the Pharmaceutical Industry, 1980-DMSO Hearings, 96th Congress, 2nd session. Washington, DC: U.S. Government Printing Office.

Mutter, John. 1981 "Late author's family fights FDA seizure of DMSO book." Publisher's Weekly 220(19):12–13.

National Academy of Sciences. 1973 Dimethyl Sulfoxide as a Therapeutic Agent. Report of the Ad Hoc Committee, Prepared for the Food and Drug Administration. Distributed by National Technical Information Service, US Department of Commerce, PB-224 574.

Newsweek. 1963 "Sweet taste of DMSO." Newsweek 62(26):68.

———. 1967 "Bringing back DMSO." Newsweek 69(2):48.

New York Times. 1965 "DMSO—promise and danger." The New York Times, April 3:28.

Pepper, Claude. 1980 Statement before the House Select Committee on Aging, March 24. Pp. 1–3 of U.S. Congress: House, DMSO: New Hope for Arthritis? Hearing, 96th Congress, 2nd session. Washington, DC: U.S. Government Printing Office.

Plumb, Robert K. 1963 "Multipurpose drug reported on coast." The New York Times, December 18:31.

Reed, J. D. 1981 "A miracle! Or is it a mirage?" Sports Illustrated 54 (April 20):71–74.

Roberts, Chalmers. 1977 The Washington Post: The First 100 Years. Boston: Houghton Mifflin.

Rubin, Lionel. 1983 "Toxicologic update of dimethyl sulfoxide." Annals of the New York Academy of Sciences 411(1):6–10.

Rubin, Lionel, and K. C. Barnett. 1967 "Occular effects of oral and dermal application of dimethyl sulfoxide in animals." Annals of the New York Academy of Sciences 141(1):333–345.

Rubin, Richard, and H. Shelton Earp. 1983 "Dimethyl sulfoxide stimulates tryosine residue phosphorylation of rat liver epidermal growth factor receptor." Science 219(7):60–63.

Sanders, Lisa. 1982 "Biogenosis, DMSO, and starch blockers." Health 14(9):28–30.

Scherbel, Arthur L. 1975 "Summary of the dimethyl sulfoxide conference." Annals of the New York Academy of Sciences 243(1):507–508.

———. 1983 "Summary." Annals of the New York Academy of Sciences 411(1):316–317.

Schlaadt, Richard G., and Peter T. Shannon. 1982 Drugs of Choice: Current Perspectives on Drug Use. Englewood Cliffs, NJ: Prentice-Hall.

Silverman, Milton, and Philip Lee. 1974 Pills, Profits, and Policy. Berkeley: University of California Press.

Sullivan, Ann. 1963 "New Zellerbach 'forest drug' may open up doors." The Oregonian (Portland), December 11:1.

Tarshis, Barry. 1981 DMSO: The True Story of A Remarkable Pain-Killing Drug (From the Exclusive Files of Dr. Stanley Jacob and Robert Herschler). New York: William Morrow and Company.

Taussig, Helen. 1962 "The thalidomide syndrome." Scientific American 207(2):29–35.

Teff, Harvey, and Colin Munro. 1976 Thalidomide: The Legal Aftermath. Westmead, England: Saxon House.

Tell, Larry. 1981 "FDA seizes DMSO book: NYCLU defends writer." National Law Journal 3 (August 31):4.

Time. 1967 "Blackout on DMSO." Time 89(18):70–72.

———. 1980 "DMSO Dustup." Time 115(17):52.

U.S. Congress: House. 1979a "Dimethyl sulfoxide." Congressional Record, 96th Congress, 1st session, October 29, 125:29857.

———. 1979b "DMSO." Congressional Record, 96th Congress, 1st session, November 8, 125:31565.

———. 1980a DMSO: New Hope for Arthritis? Hearings. Select Committee on Aging, 96th Congress, 2nd Session, March 24. Washington DC: U.S. Government Printing Office.

———. 1980b "Hope on the horizon for arthritis sufferers." Congressional Record, 96th Congress, 2nd session, July 2, 126:18625.

U.S. Congress: Senate. 1980a Preclinical and Clinical Testing by the Pharmaceutical Industry, 1980-DMSO Hearings. Committee on Labor and Human Resources, Subcommittee on Health and Scientific Research, 96th Congress, 2nd Session, July 31. Washington DC: U.S. Government Printing Office.

———. 1980b "Statements on introduced bills and joint resolutions." Congressional Record, 96th Congress, 2nd Session, May 16, 126:11578–11579.

U.S. News and World Report. 1963 "A drug to replace hypodermic needles?" U.S. News and World Report 55(27):7.

Valentine, Paul. 1982a "New trial starts for Oregon doctor accused of conspiracy in DMSO case." The Washington Post, October 26: sec. C, p. 5.

———. 1982b "Federal prosecutors drop charges against surgeon in DMSO case." The Washington Post, October 30: sec. B, p. 5.

Wall Street Journal. 1981 "Cheap as solvent, expensive as cure-all, DMSO makes comeback among believers." The Wall Street Journal, January 9:21.

Wardell, William, and Louis Lasagna. 1975 Regulation and Drug Development. Washington, DC: American Enterprise Institute for Public Policy Research.

Weber, Melva. 1981 "Possible cure calls for absolute caution." Vogue 171 (June):103.

Wilhelm, Maria. 1981 "The balm was banned in '65, but now 'wonder drug' DMSO stirs a booming black market." People 15(3):16–19.

Wischnia, Bob. 1980 "DMSO: Is it the magic formula or the perfect chemical hoax?" Runner's World 15(11):62–65.

8. The Discovery of Hyperkinesis: Notes on the Medicalization of Deviant Behavior

Peter Conrad

Introduction

The increasing medicalization of deviant behavior and the medical institution's role as an agent of social control has gained considerable notice (Friedson, 1970; Pitts, 1971; Kitterie, 1971; Zola, 1972). By medicalization we mean defining behavior as a medical problem or illness and mandating or licensing the medical profession to provide some type of treatment for it. Examples include alcoholism, drug addiction and treating violence as a genetic or brain disorder. This re-definition is not a new function of the medical institution; psychiatry and public health have always been concerned with social behavior and have traditionally functioned as agents of social control (Foucault, 1965; Szasz, 1970; Rosen, 1972). . . .

This paper describes how certain forms of behavior in children have become defined as a medical problem and how medicine has become a major agent for their social control since the discovery of hyperkinesis. By discovery we mean both origin of the diagnosis and treatment for this disorder; and discovery of children who exhibit this behavior. The first section analyzes the discovery of hyperkinesis and why it suddenly became popular in the 1960's. The second section will discuss the medicalization of deviant behavior and its ramifications.

The Medical Diagnosis of Hyperkinesis

Hyperkinesis is a relatively recent phenomenon as a medical diagnostic category. Only in the past two decades has it been available as a recognized diagnostic category and only in the last decade has it received widespread notice and medical popularity. However, the roots of the diagnosis and treatment of this clinical entity are found earlier.

Hyperkinesis is also known as Minimal Brain Dysfunction, Hyperactive Syndrome, Hyperkinetic Disorder of Childhood, and by several other diagnostic categories. Although the symptoms and the presumed etiology vary, in general the behaviors are quite similar and greatly overlap.[1] Typical symptom patterns for diagnosing the disorder include: extreme excess of motor activity (hyperactivity); very short attention span (the child flits from activity to activity); restlessness, fidgetiness; often wildly oscillating mood swings (he's fine one day, a terror the next); clumsiness; aggressive-like behavior; impulsivity; in school he cannot sit still, cannot comply with rules, has low frustration level; frequently there may be sleeping problems and acquisition of speech may be delayed (Stewart, 1966, 1970; Wender, 1971). Most of the symptoms for the disorder are deviant behaviors.[2] It is six times as prevalent among boys as among girls. We use the term hyperkinesis to represent all the diagnostic categories of this disorder.

The Discovery of Hyperkinesis

It is useful to divide the analysis into what might be considered *clinical factors* directly related to the diagnosis and treatment of hyperkinesis and *social factors* that set the context for the emergence of the new diagnostic category.

Clinical Factors

Bradley (1937) observed that amphetamine drugs has a spectacular effect in altering the behavior of school children who exhibited behavior disorders of learning disabilities. Fifteen of the thirty children he treated actually became more subdued in their behavior. Bradley termed the effect of this medication paradoxical, since he expected that amphetamines would stimulate children as they stimulated adults. After the medication was discontinued the children's behavior returned to premedication level.

A scattering of reports in the medical literature on the utility of stimulant medications for "childhood behavior disorders" appeared in the next two decades. The next significant contribution was the work of Strauss and his associates (Strauss and Lehtinen, 1947) who found certain behavior (including hyperkinesis behaviors) in postencephaletic children suffering from what they called minimal brain injury (damage). This was the first time these behaviors were attributed to the new organic distinction of minimal brain damage.

This disorder still remained unnamed or else it was called a variety of names (usually just "childhood behavior disorder"). It did not appear as a specific diagnostic category until Laufer, et al. (1957) described it as the "hyperkinetic impulse disorder" in 1957. Upon finding "the salient characteristics of the behavior pattern . . . are strikingly similar to those with clear cut organic causation" these researchers described a disorder with no clear-cut history of evidence for organicity (Laufer, et al., 1957).

In 1966 a task force sponsored by the U.S. Public Health Service and the National Association for Crippled Children and Adults attempted to clarify the ambiguity and confusion in terminology and symptomology in diagnosing children's behavior and learning disorders. From over three dozen diagnoses, they agreed on the term "minimal brain dysfunction" as an overriding diagnosis that would include hyperkinesis and other disorders (Clements, 1966). Since this time M.B.D. has been the primary formal diagnosis or label.

In the middle 1950's a new drug, Ritalin, was synthesized, that has many qualities of amphetamines without some of their more undesirable side effects. In 1961 this drug was approved by the F.D.A. for use with children. Since this time there has been much research published on the use of Ritalin in the treatment of childhood behavior disorders. This medication became the "treatment of choice" for treating children with hyperkinesis.

Since the early sixties, more research appeared on the etiology, diagnosis and treatment of hyperkinesis (cf. DeLong, 1972; Grinspoon and Singer, 1973; Cole, 1975)—as much as three-quarters concerned with drug treatment of the disorder. There had been increasing publicity of the disorder in the mass media as well. The *Reader's Guide to Periodical Literature* had no articles on hyperkinesis before 1967, one each in 1968 and 1969 and a total of forty for 1970 through 1974 (a mean of eight per year).

Now hyperkinesis has become the most common child psychiatric problem (Gross and Wilson, 1974: 142); special pediatric clinics have been established to treat hyperkinetic children, and substantial federal funds have been invested in etiological and treatment research. Outside the medical profession, teachers have developed a working clinical knowledge of hyperkinesis' symptoms and treatment (cf. Robin and Bosco, 1973); articles appear regularly in mass circulation magazines and newspapers so that parents often come to clinics with knowledge of this diagnosis. Hyperkinesis is no longer the relatively esoteric diagnostic category it may have been twenty years ago, it is now a well-known clinical disorder.

Social Factors

The social factors affecting the discovery of hyperkinesis can be divided into two areas: (1) The Pharmaceutical Revolution; (2) Government Action.

(1) *The Pharmaceutical Revolution.* Since the 1930's the pharmaceutical industry has been synthesizing and manufacturing a large number of psychoactive drugs, contributing to a virtual revolution in drug making and drug taking in America (Silverman and Lee, 1974).

Psychoactive drugs are agents that affect the central nervous system. Benzedrine, Ritalin, and Dexedrine are all synthesized psychoactive stimulants which were indicated for narcolepsy, appetite control (as "diet pills"), mild depression, fatigue, and more recently hyperkinetic children.

Until the early sixties there was little or no promotion and advertisement of any of these medications for use with childhood disorders.[3] Then two major pharmaceutical firms (Smith, Kline and French, manufacturer of Dexedrine and CIBA, manufacturer of Ritalin) began to advertise in medical journals and through direct mailing and efforts of the "detail men." Most of this advertising of the pharmaceutical treatment of hyperkinesis was directed to the medical sphere; but some of the promotion was targeted for the educational sector also (Hentoff, 1972). This promotion was probably significant in disseminating information concerning the diagnosis and treatment of this newly discovered disorder.[4] Since 1955 the use of psychoactive medications (especially phenothiazines) for the treatment of persons who are mentally ill, along with the concurrent dramatic decline in inpatient populations, has made psychopharmacology an integral part of treatment for mental disorders. It has also undoubtedly increased the confidence in the medical profession for the pharmaceutical approach to mental and behavioral problems.

(2) *Government Action.* Since the publication of the U.S.P.H.S. report on M.B.D. there have been at least two significant governmental reports on treating school children with stimulant medications for behavior disorders. Both of these came as a response to the national publicity created by the *Washington Post* report (1970) that five to ten percent of the 62,000 grammar school children in Omaha, Nebraska were being treated with "behavior modification drugs to improve deportment and increase learning potential" (quoted in Grinspoon and Singer, 1973). Although the figures were later found to be a little exaggerated, it nevertheless spurred a Congressional investigation (U.S. Government Printing Office, 1970) and a conference sponsored by the Office of Child Development (1971) on the use of stimulant drugs in the treatment of behaviorally disturbed school children.

The Congressional Subcommittee on Privacy chaired by Congressman Cornelius E. Gallagher held hearings on the issue of prescribing drugs for hyperactive school children. In general, the committee showed great concern over the facility in which the medication was prescribed; more specifically that some children at least were receiving drugs from general practitioners whose primary diagnosis was based on teachers' and parents' reports that the child was doing poorly in school. There was also a concern with the absence of follow-up studies on the long-term effects of treatment.

The H.E.W. committee was a rather hastily convened group of professionals (a majority were M.D.'s) many of whom already had commitments to drug treatment for children's behavior problems. They recommended that only M.D.'s make the diagnosis and prescribe treatment, that the pharmaceutical companies promote the treatment of the disorder only through medical channels, that parents should not be coerced to accept any particular treatment and that long-term follow-up research should be done. This report served as blue ribbon approval for treating hyperkinesis with psychoactive medications.

Discussion

We will focus discussion on three issues: How children's deviant behavior became conceptualized as a medical problem; why this occurred when it did; and what are some of the implications of the medicalization of deviant behavior.

How does deviant behavior become conceptualized as a medical problem? We assume that before the discovery of hyperkinesis this type of deviance was seen as disruptive, disobedient, rebellious, anti-social or deviant behavior. Perhaps the label "emotionally disturbed" was sometimes used, when it was in vogue in the early sixties, and the child was usually managed in the context of the family or the school or in extreme cases, the child guidance clinic. How then did this constellation of deviant behaviors become a medical disorder?

The treatment was available long before the disorder treated was clearly conceptualized. It was twenty years after Bradley's discovery of the "paradoxical effect" of stimulants on certain deviant children that Laufer named the disorder and described its characteristic symptoms. Only in the late fifties were both the diagnostic label and the pharmaceutical treatment available. The pharmaceutical revolution in mental health and the increased interest in child psychiatry provided a favorable background for the dissemination of knowledge about this new disorder. The latter probably made the medical profession more likely to consider behavior problems in children as within their clinical jurisdiction.

There were agents outside the medical profession itself that were significant in "promoting" hyperkinesis as a disorder within the medical framework. These agents might be conceptualized in Becker's terms as "moral entrepreneurs," those who crusade for creation and enforcement of the rules (Becker, 1963).[5] In this case the moral entrepreneurs were the pharmaceutical companies and the Association for Children with Learning Disabilities.

The pharmaceutical companies spent considerable time and money promoting stimulant medications for this new disorder. From the middle 1960's on, medical journals and the free "throwaway" magazines contained elaborate advertising for Ritalin and Dexedrine. These ads explained the utility of treating hyperkinesis and urged the physician to diagnose and treat hyperkinetic children. The ads run from one to six pages. For example, a two-page ad in 1971 stated:

MBD . . . MEDICAL MYTH OR DIAGNOSABLE DISEASE ENTITY What medical practitioner has not, at one time or another, been called upon to examine an impulsive, excitable hyperkinetic child? A child with difficulty in concentrating. Easily frustrated. Unusually aggressive. A classroom rebel. In the absence of any organic pathology, the conduct of such children was, until a few short years ago, usually dismissed as . . . spunkiness, or evidence of youthful vitality. But it is now evident that in many of these children the hyperkinetic syndrome exists as a distinct medical entity. This syndrome is readily diagnosed through patient histories, neurologic signs, and psychometric testing—has been classified by an expert panel convened by the United States Department of Health, Education and Welfare as Minimal Brain Dysfunction, MBD.

The pharmaceutical firms also supplied sophisticated packets of "diagnostic and treatment" information on hyperkinesis to physicians, paid for professional conferences on the subject, and supported research in the identification and treatment of the disorder. Clearly these corporations had a vested interest in the labeling and treatment of hyperkinesis; CIBA had $13 million profit from Ritalin alone in 1971, which was 15 percent of the total gross profits (Charles, 1971; Hentoff, 1972).

The other moral entrepreneur, less powerful than the pharmaceutical companies, but nevertheless influential, is the Association for Children with Learning Disabilities. Although their focus is not specifically on hyperkinetic children, they do include it in their conception of Learning Disabilities along with aphasia, reading problems like dyslexia and perceptual motor problems. Founded in the early 1950's by parents and professionals, it has functioned much as the National Association for Mental Health does for mental illness: promoting conferences, sponsoring legislation, providing social support. One of the main functions has been to disseminate information concerning this relatively new area in education, Learning Disabilities. While the organization does have a more educational than medical perspective, most of the literature indicates that for hyperkinesis members have adopted the medical model and the medical approach to the problem. They have sensitized teachers and schools to the conception of hyperkinesis as a medical problem.

The medical model of hyperactive behavior has become very well accepted in our society. Physicians find treatment relatively simple and the results sometimes spectacular. Hyperkinesis minimizes parents' guilt by emphasizing "it's not their fault, it's an organic problem" and allows for nonpunitive management or control of deviance. Medication often makes a child less disruptive in the classroom and sometimes aids a child in learning. Children often like their "magic pills" which make their behavior more socially acceptable and they probably benefit from a reduced stigma also. There are, however, some other, perhaps more subtle ramifications of the medicalization of deviant behavior.

The Medicalization of Deviant Behavior

Pitts has commented that "medicalization is one of the most effective means of social control and that it is destined to become the main mode of *formal* social control" (1971:391). Kitterie (1971) has termed it "the coming of the therapeutic state."

Medicalization of mental illness dates at least from the seventeenth century (Foucault, 1965; Szasz, 1970). Even slaves who ran away were once considered to be suffering from the disease *drapedomania* (Chorover, 1973). In recent years alcoholism, violence, and drug addiction as well as hyperactive behavior in children have all become defined as medical problems, both in etiology or explanation of the behavior and the means of social control or treatment.

There are many reasons why this medicalization has occurred. Much scientific research, especially in pharmacology and genetics, has become technologically more sophisticated, and found more subtle correlates with human behavior. Sometimes these findings (as in the case of XYY chromosomes and violence) become etiological explanations for deviance. Pharmacological technology that makes new discoveries affecting behavior (e.g., antibuse, methadone and stimulants) are used as treatment for deviance. In part this application is encouraged by the prestige of the medical profession and its attachment to science. As Freidson notes, the medical profession has first claim to jurisdiction over anything that deals with the functioning of the body and especially anything that can be labeled illness (1970:251). Advances in genetics, pharmacology and "psychosurgery" also may advance medicine's jurisdiction over deviant behavior.

Second, the application of pharmacological technology is related to the humanitarian trend in the conception and control of deviant behavior. Alcoholism is no longer sin or even moral weakness, it is now a disease. Alcoholics are no longer arrested in many places for "public drunkenness," they are now somehow "treated," even if it is only to be dried out. Hyperactive children are now considered to have an illness rather than to be disruptive, disobedient, overactive problem children. They are not as likely to be the "bad boy" of the classroom; they are children with a medical disorder. Clearly there are some real humanitarian benefits to be gained by such a medical conceptualization of deviant behavior. There is less condemnation of the deviants (they have an illness, it is not their fault) and perhaps less social stigma. In some cases, even the medical treatment itself is more humanitarian social control than the criminal justice system.

There is, however, another side to the medicalization of deviant behavior. The four aspects of this side of the issue include (1) the problem of expert control; (2) medical social control; (3) the individualization of social problems; and (4) the "depoliticization" of deviant behavior.

1. *The problem of expert control.* The medical profession is a profession of experts; they have a monopoly on anything that can be conceptualized as illness. Because of the way the medical profession is organized and the mandate it has from society, decisions related to medical diagnoses and treatment are virtually controlled by medical professionals.

Some conditions that enter the medical domain are not *ipso facto* medical problems, especially deviant behavior, whether alcoholism, hyperactivity or drug addiction. By defining a problem as medical it is removed from the public realm where there can be discussion by ordinary people and put on a plane where only medical people can discuss it. As Reynolds states,

> The increasing acceptance, especially among the more educated segments of our populace, of technical solutions—solutions administered by disinterested politically and morally neutral experts—results in the withdrawal of more and more areas of human experience from the realm of public discussion. For when drunkenness, juvenile delinquency, sub par performance and extreme political beliefs are seen as symptoms of an underlying illness or biological defect the merits and drawbacks of such behavior or beliefs need not be evaluated (1973:200–221).

The public may have their own conceptualizations of deviant behavior but that of the experts is usually dominant.

2. *Medical social control.* Defining deviant behavior as a medical problem allows certain things to be done that could not otherwise be considered; for example, the body may be cut open or psychoactive medications may be given. This treatment can be a form of social control.

In regard to drug treatment Lennard points out: "Psychoactive drugs, especially those legally prescribed, tend to restrain individuals from behavior and experience that are not complementary to the requirements of the dominant value system" (1971:57). These forms of medical social control presume a prior definition of deviance as a medical problem. Psychosurgery on an individual prone to violent outbursts requires a diagnosis that there was something wrong with his brain or nervous system. Similarly, prescribing drugs to restless, overactive and disruptive school children requires a diagnosis of hyperkinesis. These forms of social control, what Chorover (1973) has called "psychotechnology," are very powerful and often very efficient means of controlling deviance. These relatively new and increasingly popular forms of social control could not be utilized without the medicalization of deviant behavior. As is suggested from the discovery of hyperkinesis, if a mechanism of medical social control seems useful, then the deviant behavior it modifies will develop a medical label or diagnosis. No overt malevolence on the part of the medical profession is implied: rather it is part of a complex process, of which the medical profession is only a part. The larger process might be called the individualization of social problems.

3. *The individualization of social problems.* The medicalization of deviant behavior is part of a larger phenomenon that is prevalent in our society, the individualization of social problems. We tend to look for causes and solutions to complex social problems in the individual rather than in the social system. This view resembles Ryan's (1971) notion of "blaming the victim;" seeing the causes of the problem in individuals rather than in the society where they live. We then seek to change the "victim" rather than the society. The medical perspective of diagnosing an illness in an individual lends itself to the individualization of social problems. Rather than seeing certain deviant behaviors as symptomatic of problems in the social system, the medical perspective focuses on the individual diagnosing and treating the illness, generally ignoring the social situation.

Hyperkinesis serves as a good example. Both the school and the parents are concerned with the child's behavior; the child is very difficult at home and disruptive in school. No punishments or rewards seem consistently to work in modifying the behavior; and both parents and school are at their wits' end. A medical evaluation is suggested. The diagnoses of hyperkinetic behavior leads to prescribing stimulant medications. The child's behavior seems to become more socially acceptable, reducing problems in school and at home.

But there is an alternate perspective. By focusing on the symptoms and defining them as hyperkinesis we ignore the possibility that behavior is not an illness but an adaptation to a social situation. It diverts our attention from the family or school and from seriously entertaining the idea that the "problem" could be in the structure of the social system. And by giving medications we are essentially supporting the existing systems and do not allow this behavior to be a factor of change in the system.

4. *The depoliticization of deviant behavior.* Depoliticization of deviant behavior is a result of both the process of medicalization and individualization of social problems. To our western world, probably one of the clearest examples of such a depoliticization of deviant behavior occurred when political dissenters in the Soviet Union were declared mentally ill and confined in mental hospitals (cf. Conrad, 1972). This strategy served to neutralize the meaning of political protest and dissent, rendering it the ravings of mad persons.

The medicalization of deviant behavior depoliticizes deviance in the same manner. By defining the overactive, restless and disruptive child as hyperkinetic we ignore the meaning of behavior in the context of the social system. If we focused our analysis on the school system we might see the child's behavior as symptomatic of some "disorder" in the school or classroom situation, rather than symptomatic of an individual neurological disorder.

Conclusion

I have discussed the social ramifications of the medicalization of deviant behavior, using hyperkinesis as the example. A number of consequences of this medicalization have been outlined, including the depoliticization of deviant behavior, decision-making power of experts, and the role of medicine as an agent of social control. In the last analysis medical social control may be the central issue, as in this role medicine becomes a *de facto* agent of the *status quo*. The medical profession may not have entirely sought this role, but its members have been, in general, disturbingly unconcerned and unquestioning in their acceptance of it. With the increasing medical knowledge and technology it is likely that more deviant behavior will be medicalized and medicine's social control function will expand.

Notes

1. The U.S.P.H.S. report (Clements, 1966) included 38 terms that were used to describe or distinguish the conditions that it labeled Minimal Brain Dysfunction. Although the literature attempts to differentiate M.B.D., hyperkinesis, hyperactive syndrome, and several other diagnostic labels, it is our belief that in practice they are almost interchangeable.
2. For a fuller discussion of the construction of the diagnosis of hyperkinesis, see Conrad (forthcoming), especially Chapter 6.
3. The American Medical Association's change in policy in accepting more pharmaceutical advertising in the late fifties may have been important. Probably the F.D.A. approval of the use of Ritalin for children in 1961 was more significant. Until 1970, Ritalin was advertising for treatment of "functional behavior problems in children." Since then, because of an F.D.A. order, it has only been promoted for treatment of M.B.D.
4. The drug industry spends fully 25 percent of its budget on promotion and advertising. See Coleman et al. (1966) for the role of the detail men and how physicians rely upon them for information.
5. Freidson also notes the medical professional role as moral entrepreneur in this process also:

   The profession does treat the illness laymen take to it, but it also seeks to discover illness of which the laymen may not even be aware. One of the greatest ambitions of the physician is to discover and describe a "new" disease or syndrome . . . (1970:252).

References

Becker, Howard S. (1963). *Outsiders*. New York: Free Press.
Bradley, Charles (1937). "The behavior of children receiving Benzedrine." *American Journal of Psychiatry* 94 (March): 577–585.
Charles, Alan (1971). "The case of Ritalin." *New Republic* 23 (October): 17–19.
Chorover, Stephen L. (1973). "Big brother and psychotechnology." *Psychology Today* (October): 43–54.
Clements, Samuel D. (1966). "Task force I: Minimal brain dysfunction in children." National Institute of Neurological Diseases and Blindness, Monograph no. 3. Washington, D.C.: U.S. Department of Health, Education, and Welfare.
Cole, Sherwood (1975). "Hyperactive children: The use of stimulant drugs evaluated." *American Journal of Orthopsychiatry* 45 (January): 28–37.
Coleman, James, Elihu Katz, and Herbert Menzel (1966). *Medical Innovation*. Indianapolis: Bobbs-Merrill.
Conrad, Peter (1972). "Ideological deviance: An analysis of the Soviet use of mental hospitals for political dissenters." Unpublished manuscript.
——— Forthcoming. "Identifying hyperactive children: A study in the medicalization of deviant behavior." Unpublished Ph.D. dissertation. Boston University.
DeLong, Arthur R. (1972). "What have we learned from psychoactive drugs research with hyperactives?" *American Journal of Diseases in Children* 123 (February): 177–180.
Foucault, Michel (1965). *Madness and Civilization*. New York: Pantheon.
Grinspoon, Lester and Susan Singer (1973). "Amphetamines in the treatment of hyperactive children." *Harvard Educational Review* 43 (November): 515–555.
Gross, Mortimer B. and William E. Wilson (1974). *Minimal Brain Dysfunction*. New York: Brunner Mazel.
Hentoff, Nat (1972). "Drug pushing in the schools: The professionals." *The Village Voice* 22 (May): 21–23.
Kitterie, Nicholas (1971). *The Right to Be Different*. Baltimore: Johns Hopkins Press.
Laufer, M. W., Denhoff, E., and Solomons, G. (1975). "Hyperkinetic impulse disorder in children's behavior problems." *Psychosomatic Medicine* 19 (January): 38–49.
Lennard, Henry L. and Associates (1971). *Mystification and Drug Misuse*. New York: Harper and Row.
Office of Child Development (1971). "Report of the conference on the use of stimulant drugs in treatment of behaviorally disturbed children." Washington, D.C.: Office of Child Development, Department of Health, Education and Welfare, January 11–12.
Pitts, Jesse (1968). "Social control: The concept." In David Sills (ed.), *International Encyclopedia of the Social Sciences*. Volume 14. New York: Macmillan.
Reynolds, Janice M. (1973). "The medical institution." pp. 198–324 in Larry T. Reynolds and James M. Henslin, *American Society: A Critical Analysis*. New York: David McKay.

Robin, Stanley S. and James J. Bosco (1973). "Ritalin for school children: The teacher's perspective." *Journal of School Health* 47 (December): 624–628.

Rosen, George (1972). "The evolution of social medicine." Pp. 30–60 in Howard E. Freeman, Sol Levine, and Leo Reeder, *Handbook of Medical Sociology*. Englewood Cliffs, N.J.: Prentice-Hall.

Ryan, William (1970). *Blaming the Victim*. New York: Vintage.

Silverman, Milton and Philip R. Lee (1974). *Pills, Profits and Politics*. Berkeley: University of California Press.

Sroufe, L. Alan and Mark Stewart (1973). "Treating problem children with stimulant drugs." *New England Journal of Medicine* 289 (August 23): 407–421.

Stewart, Mark A. (1970). "Hyperactive Children." *Scientific American* 222 (April): 794–798.

Stewart, Mark A., A. Ferris, N. P. Pitts and A. G. Craig (1966). "The hyperactive child syndrome." *American Journal of Orthopsychiatry* 36 (October): 861–867.

Strauss, A. A. and L. E. Lehtinen (1974). *Psychopathology and Education of the Brain-Injured Child*. Vol. 1. New York: Grune and Stratton.

U.S. Government Printing Office (1970). "Federal involvement in the use of behavior modification drugs on grammar school children of the right to privacy inquiry: Hearing before a subcommittee of the committee on government operations." Washington, D.C.: 91st Congress, 2nd session (September 29).

Wender, Paul (1971). *Minimal Brain Dysfunction in Children*. New York: John Wiley and Sons.

Zola, Irving (1972). "Medicine as an institution of social control." *Sociological Review* 20 (November): 487–504.

---

9. High Cost of High-Tech Drugs Is Protested

Andrew Pollack

The Armour Pharmaceutical Company introduced a major drug last October—the first blood-clotting factor for hemophiliacs made using the tools of biotechnology. This purer version of Factor VIII virtually eliminated any chance that hemophiliacs would contract AIDS, hepatitis or other diseases from treatment.

There was one catch: This high-tech version costs five to eight times as much as older versions, bringing the cost of a year's supply to more than $25,000 and potentially putting the drug out of the reach of patients for whom it is a matter of life and death.

In the last year or two, a number of new drugs have appeared that are selling for virtually unprecedented prices. These include TPA, for heart attacks; AZT for AIDS, and human growth hormone, for dwarfism.

Like the new Factor VIII, the drugs unarguably represent substantial medical advances. But their prices are arousing protests from hospitals and patient groups, and are raising demands for balancing the drug industry's need for profits with the medical needs of patients.

"Where it used to be hundreds of dollars now it's tens of thousands of dollars" for the most expensive drugs, said Arthur M. Zoloth, director of pharmacy services at the Virginia Mason Medical Center in Seattle. "There's no question these are significant advances, but the health care system's not really developed to handle the major impact" of these prices on patients and hospitals, he said.

Pharmaceutical companies say their research and development costs have increased and the prices are necessary to maintain the flow of innovative products. "We're taking the revenues that come from product sales and funneling them in a major way into research," said Robert A. Swanson, Genetech's president. The investment will lead to "new products that can treat diseases that heretofore haven't been tackled," he said.

Nevertheless, some critics say the industry is taking advantage of consumers who have no alternatives. "The drug companies evidently feel that they can get away with whatever the market will bear," said Representative Henry A. Waxman, the California Democrat who is chairman of the House health and environment subcommittee. Because new drugs could mean life or death, "the people have no choice but to pay," Mr. Waxman said.

Determining whether prices are excessive is difficult because drug companies do not release information on their costs and because the definition of an excessive profit is open to debate. But analysts say the new drugs are clearly generating or will generate substantial profits for their producers, which are already among the most profitable manufacturers in the nation.

Congress Is Asked to Ease the Pressure

The high prices are increasing pressure on Congress to help keep drugs affordable—either by regulating prices or by helping consumers to pay for them. A special Federal appropriation has already been made to help some people pay for AZT, an antiviral drug that has been shown to prolong life in some AIDS patients. A health insurance bill for catastrophic illness, awaiting passage in Congress, would extend Medicare coverage to drugs for the first time.

Also disturbing to some medical authorities is that many of the very expensive drugs are the products of new biotechnology. Genetic engineering and other tools of biotechnology are expected to result in some astounding drugs in the next decade. But the handful that have reached the market suggest that the prices will be equally astounding.

Tissue plasminogen activator, or TPA, a genetically engineered drug made by Genentech Inc. for the treatment of heart attacks, cost $2,200 a dose, 10 times as much as a competitive product not made with the new technology. Human growth hormone, another genetically engineered drug for children who are dwarfs that is made by Genentech and Eli Lilly & Company, can cost $8,000 to more than $30,000 a year. And Merck & Company's hepatitis B vaccine, the first vaccine made by genetic engineering, sells for $120 a treatment, higher than most vaccines and out of the reach of developing nations, where the disease is prevalent.

Some others are not biotechnology products. The Burroughs Wellcome Company's AZT costs $8,000 a year. Some advanced antibiotics cost three times as much as older products. Merck's new cholesterol-reducing drug called lovastatin can cost $600 a year and up to $3,000 in severe cases.

Sharp Price Increases in This Decade

The emergence of the new superexpensive drugs comes at a time when drug prices in general have been rising extremely fast. From 1981 through 1986, prescription drug prices rose 79 percent, while the Consumer Price Index advanced only 28 percent, according to a 1987 study by the House subcommittee on health and the environment. In 1987, drug costs rose 8 percent, general medical expenses 5.8 percent and overall prices 4.4 percent, according to the Bureau of Labor Statistics.

"In the last two to three years, during a period in which many major medical components had zero or small price increases, drug prices became the fastest-growing component," said Willis B. Goldbeck, president of the Washington Business Group on Health, which represents large corporations with employee health care plans.

Pharmaceutical companies say drugs constitute less than 10 percent of total health care expenditures and provide tremendous benefits. Moreover, John Doorley, a Merck spokesman, noted that even expensive drugs can save money over all by keeping people out of the hospital or making surgery unnecessary.

Nonetheless, concern over price is deepening. "In some cases, we're closing out people from the only drug that is available," said Richard Kessel, executive director of the New York State Consumer Protection Board, which has been investigating the price of AZT.

Hospitals are also being squeezed. They can lose money by using the new drugs, because insurance reimbursements do not keep pace with the higher costs.

"It can't continue to go on like it's been going on here for the last few years," said Michael G. Cunningham, assistant director of pharmaceutical services at the University of California Medical Center in San Francisco.

When So Much Is Spent on So Few

The center's drug budget has quadrupled since 1982, to about $10 million. That pays for more than 1,200 drugs, used to treat thousands of patients. But a third of the funds goes to a handful of drugs used to treat relatively few patients—$1.2 million for growth hormone for 40 children, $700,000 for Factor VIII for 40 hemophiliacs, $1 million for AZT for 100 to 150 AIDS patients and $500,000 for drugs used in 150 organ transplants.

Hospitals are beginning to argue that the pressure to cut health care costs has fallen largely on them, while drug companies have been able to continue to earn relatively high profits—about 13 cents per dollar of sales in recent years, or three times the average for manufacturing corporations in general. The industry's return on equity in 1986, the last full year for which data are available, was 22.9 percent versus 9.6 percent for all manufacturers.

The drug companies say the prices are needed to finance research and development. Those costs for the major drug houses have increased to 15 percent of sales from less than 12 percent in 1980, according to the Pharmaceutical Manufacturers Association, a trade group.

The Focus Shifts to Chronic Diseases

A study commissioned by the group last year found that the cost of bringing a drug to market more than doubled in the last decade, to $65 million. It can take 10 years from the start of development to marketing, with two or three of those years spent merely waiting for the Food and Drug Administration's approval.

A major reason for the cost increases, according to the study, is that companies are now working more on chronic diseases, such as cancer and heart disease, rather than on infectious diseases. "Drugs designed for such diseases generally require more extensive development and testing," said the study, which was conducted by Steven N. Wiggins, a professor of economics at Texas A & M University.

To these factors can now be added the costs of biotechnology. Armour, a division of the Rorer Group, says its new Factor VIII, which it calls Monoclate, is so expensive because it is purified using highly specific antibodies, one of the main tools of biotechnology.

Some say that biotechnology per se should not necessarily result in high-priced drugs. Indeed, one of the great promises of genetic engineering, a key biotechnology tool, was that it would result in lower prices by allowing genetically modified bacteria to produce substances that were hard to produce otherwise.

Human growth hormone, for instance, was once extracted from cadavers and was in such short supply that thousands of children were unable to obtain it. Now, because of genetic engineering, it is abundant—and the product is safer. The same is true of hepatitis B vaccine, which was previously extracted from blood serum.

Still, the promise of low prices has not been realized. In some cases, like TPA, the product is too complex for bacteria to make, requiring the use of far more expensive animal cells. Even with hepatitis B vaccine, made by yeast, and growth hormone, which is produced by bacteria, prices have not dropped.

"The product wound up being much more expensive than any of us expected," said Carl Coussan, executive director of the Parent Council for Growth Normality, a group of parents whose children require the hormone.

Drug Given to Some Who Couldn't Pay

The new growth hormone sells for less per milligram than the substance extracted from cadavers, but the recommended dose is larger. Moreover, in most cases, the Federal Government gave the older product away.

Still, Mr. Coussan said parents were grateful that the drug was available. Genentech, he said, has aggressively arranged for insurance companies to cover the costs. The company has also given away the drug to children who could not pay for it.

Critics of the drug industry say research and development expenditures cannot possibly account for the entire rise in prices.

Analysts say other factors are at work, the main one being that companies base prices on the value of the drug to consumers and not the cost. The rapid advance of technology is also spurring companies to try to recover their costs faster, analysts say.

"Science is advancing so rapidly that product life cycles are shrinking," said Viren Mehta, an analyst at S. G. Warburg & Company, an investment firm. "Any company that is fortunate enough to come up with an innovative product has to make the most of it for as long as it can."

'83 Act Encourages Research, and Profits

Yet another factor is that the manufacturers of some of the more expensive drugs have been granted monopolies for seven years under the Orphan Drug Act, a 1983 law designed to encourage companies to develop treatments for relatively rare diseases. Lawmakers little envisioned, however, that drugs would fetch such high prices, making them extremely profitable even with relatively few customers.

Genentech and Eli Lilly were granted such "orphan drug status" for different versions of human growth hormone. The price has not gone down since Genentech won approval for the product in 1985, despite increasing production volumes and Lilly's entry into the market.

"To grant orphan drug status and allow them to charge $10,000 to $20,000 is not fair to the consuming public," said Sim Fass, president of the Biotechnology General Corporation, which is being kept out of the market by the 1983 law.

M. Kathleen Behrens, biotechnology analyst for Robertson, Colman & Stephens, an investment banker in San Francisco, estimates Genentech's gross margin on the drug, the amount by which the price exceeds the manufacturing cost, is 90 to 95 percent, higher than the 85 percent for most drugs. Mr. Swanson questioned that figure but declined to say what the gross margin is.

Genentech recorded $86 million in growth hormone sales in 1987. Lilly's sales are estimated at $10 million. Only about 35 drugs in the pharmaceutical industry have yearly sales higher than that.

The Controversy Over Pentamidine

Another orphan drug surrounded by controversy is pentamidine, an antibiotic used to treat a form of pneumonia that affects many people with AIDS. Since Lyphomed Inc. received the F.D.A.'s permission in 1984 to market the drug, the Rosemont, Ill., company has quadrupled the price, to $100 a vial. A British company sells the drug for about $18 a vial.

Lyphomed did not invent the drug (which it calls Pentam), and San Francisco General Hospital did the research showing that an aerosol version could be safer and more effective than the intravenous form.

But Brian Tambi, a Lyphomed vice president, said once the company found that the aerosol version might be more effective, it had to begin clinical trials, which are expected to cost up to $10 million. Moreover, he said, Lyphomed, which normally sells to distributors, found that it had to sell Pentam directly to physicians, requiring a sales force of 25.

"The money we are earning from Pentam is going to the expenses for Pentam," Mr. Tambi said.

A New Hunt for Ways to Reduce the Costs

Robert Goldman, an analyst for William Blair & Company in Chicago, said, "You can justify the price hikes, but it looks bad."

With drug prices rising, hospitals and health insurers are seeking new ways to cut costs. Some corporate health plans are beginning to buy drugs in bulk for employees. Hospitals are trying to limit the most expensive drugs to cases of real need.

Still, once an improved drug appears, the forces propelling its usage can become overwhelming. Doctors like to use the best treatment available, and they risk lawsuits if they do not.

Publicity surrounding a new drug can also lead patients to demand it. Hemophiliacs are demanding the new form of Factor VIII, even though there might not be much medical benefit for those who have been taking the older form of the drug, said Dr. Craig Kessler, associate medical director of the National Hemophilia Foundation.

Moreover, he said, two of the three manufacturers of the older version have stopped selling their products, afraid of being sued if they continued to market the old products when a safer one was available.

Congress might eventually pass laws to restrain prices. Representative Waxman has proposed changing the Orphan Drug Act to allow more competition for certain orphan drugs.

There currently does not appear to be much sentiment in Washington for regulation of drug prices, something that is done in many other countries. Still, analysts say, if the Government begins paying for drugs through Medicare, it will begin putting pressure on drug companies to lower prices. That would be the first step toward price controls.

The High Price of New Drugs

Drug	Manufacturer		Price*
TPA	Genetech	Dissolves Blood Clots	$2,200
Factor VIII	Armour	Speeds Blood Clotting	25,000
Lovastatin	Merck	Lowers Cholesterol	600–3,000
AZT	Burroughs Welcome	Treats AIDS	$8,000
Growth Hormone	Genetech/Eli Lilly	Stimulates Growth	8,000–30,000
Cyclosporine	Sandoz	Suppresses rejection of new organs	5,000–7,000

*All per year except TPA, which requires only a single dose.
Source: Company Reports

10. Lifetime Criminality of Heroin Addicts in the United States

John C. Ball, Lawrence Rosen, John A. Flueck, and David N. Nurco

There has been a long and continuing controversy about the relationship of crime and opiate addiction in the United States (Terry and Pellens, 1928; Lindesmith, 1968; Musto, 1973; Inciardi, 1981). This controversy has involved disagreement about the etiology of the problem, the extent of crime committed by addicts, the seriousness of their crimes, the prevalence of violent crimes, the effect of control legislation, the efficacy of treatment, and similar issues. Although this controversy is unlikely to end in the near future (because it is fueled by diverse theoretical and political viewpoints as well as by competing vested institutional interests), it is important to divorce the scientific aspects of the problem from other considerations so that research can address and resolve specific questions. In the present study, research attention is focused upon the extent and characteristics of crimes committed by heroin addicts.

In pursuing the research problem of determining the annual and lifetime extent of criminality among heroin addicts, a series of methodological issues were addressed. First, it was decided to utilize a probability based sample of a well-defined Baltimore addict population in the study because of the availability of comprehensive follow-up data on this representative sample of 243 male addicts. Second, the extent of crimes committed by the addict sample was analyzed by means of a new measure of criminal behavior: crime-days per year at risk. Third, the results of interview data were supplemented by use of official records pertaining to arrests and periods of incarceration. Fourth, the validity of the interview data was intensively reviewed and subjected to separate investigation. Fifth, it proved to be feasible to analyze the entire time span from onset of opiate addiction to time of interview for each addict in the sample. Sixth, important within group differences in criminality, addiction and incarceration were observed for the sample and analyzed. And seventh, an initial national estimate of the extent of criminality among heroin addicts was derived.

Before proceeding to discuss the data collection procedures and research findings, it is pertinent to comment upon the scope of this study. We have directed our research attention and analysis to the extent of criminality among opiate addicts. We have *not* considered the issue of etiology, nor have we investigated those factors which might lead to a cessation of crime or addiction, nor have we addressed policy questions concerning prevention, control and treatment. We recognize that these and other issues are important but we believe that they can best be considered after the question of the extent of on-going criminality within the addict population has been delineated and analyzed.

The Sample and Follow-up Interview Procedure

This paper is based on interview data and collateral records pertaining to 243 Baltimore opiate addicts (most were heroin addicts). The 243 male addicts were a random sample selected from a population of 4,069 known opiate users arrested (or identified) by the Baltimore Police Department between 1952 and 1971. The sample was unselected for criminality, but stratified by race and year of police contact. Of the 243 subjects, 109 were white and 134 were black.

• • •

A New Measure of Criminal Behavior: Crime-Days Per Year at Risk

In the present paper, a new measure of criminal behavior is employed: Crime-Days Per Year at Risk. A *crime-day* is a 24-hour period in which an individual commits one or more crimes. The number of *crime-days per year at risk* refers to the number of days per year that an individual has committed crimes from 0 to 365.

This new measure, Crime-Days Per Year at Risk, was found to have unique analytical powers as it permits the calculation of uniform crime rates by years at risk and it is not confounded by multiple crimes committed on a given day. Furthermore, the term Crime-Days Per Year at Risk appears to be an effective procedure for explaining the extent of continual criminal behavior because it relates the number of crimes committed by individuals to a common frame of reference— times per year. The relevant terms have been defined as follows:

Crime-Day. A crime-day is defined as a 24-hour period during which one or more crimes is committed by a given individual. Each day of the year, then, is either a crime-day or a non-crime day.

Heroin Addiction. This term refers to the daily use of opiates. (Daily use is defined as use during at least four days per week for a month, or longer.)

Average Crime-Days per Year. This measure is defined as the average number of Crime-Days per Year at Risk for a given individual. The range is from 0 to 365. Thus, an individual with 1,489 crime-days during a seven year risk period has an average Crime-Days Per Year at Risk of 213. (Actual computation is by days at risk and number of crime-days.)

Years at Risk. Years at risk is the number of years an individual is "on the street" or not incarcerated. It is calculated on a cumulative basis by subtracting jail, prison, and hospital time from the years since onset of regular opiate use to time of interview.

Principal Type of Crime. This is the predominate type of crime engaged in by a given individual during his years at risk, as theft (boosting, burglary, etc.), con games, robbery, gambling, drug sales, etc. This principal type of criminal behavior is the most common offense committed from a crime-day viewpoint.

Criminal Career. This is the criminal behavior pattern which an individual has followed while at risk. The two main elements in determining the crime pattern are (a) type of crime and (b) frequency of crime. Examples of crime patterns are: daily theft, daily con games, weekly robbery, weekly forgery, infrequent assault, and so forth. In each case, the crime pattern, or career, is the most common, or usual, offense committed during the subject's years at risk and the frequency of commission.

In order to obtain answers to the criminological questions advanced, the study was organized according to the following procedures: (1) A sample of 243 male opiate addicts was selected for study, (2) Periods of addiction and periods of abstinence from opiate dependence were enumerated, (3) The number of crime-days per year at risk was determined for each member of the sample, (4) The addicts were classified by principal type of criminal career pursued from onset of regular opiate use to interview, (5) The extent of crimes committed were analyzed by criminal career types, (6) The sample was separated into thirds on the basis of crime-days and criminality related to arrest and periods of incarceration; and (7) Annual and lifetime estimates of criminality among heroin addicts in the United States were calculated.

Lifetime Criminality Since Onset of Opiate Addiction

The total number of crime-days accumulated by each of the 243 addicts during his years at risk is tabulated in Table 1. Almost two-thirds of the sample had more than 1,000 crime-days per individual; almost one-quarter (23 percent) had more than 3,000 crime-days per individual. The mean number of crime-days for the 237 addicts who had at least one crime-day was 1,999. This addict sample, then, averaged some 2,000 crime-days during an 11 year risk period.

The total amount of days during which crime was commited by these 243 addicts during their years at risk was 473,738. This total of almost one-half million crime-days is clearly an under-enumeration of their offenses as multiple crimes during a crime-day were common. It is also pertinent to note that drug use or possession were not classified as crimes in this study.

In estimating the lifetime criminality of these 243 male addicts, one could project additional crime-days from the time of interview to old age or death. If this were done, several hundred thousand additional crime-days would be added to the present figure (i.e., 473,738) to account for crime committed in future years. Inasmuch as the addicts of the sample had a mean age of only 36 years and were still active in their criminality, it is evident that the future extent of their criminality would be considerable.

Table 1. Total Crime-Days Amassed By 243 Male Addicts During Years at Risk.

Crime Days	Number of Addicts	Percent of Addicts
0(None)	6	2.5
1–99	20	8.2
100–499	31	12.8
500–999	31	12.8
1,000–1,999	54	22.2
2,000–2,999	46	18.9
3,000–3,999	27	11.1
4,000–4,999	12	4.9
5,000–5,999	10	4.1
6,000–9,450	6	2.5
Total	243	100.0

Total Crime-days since onset of addiction: 473,738
Mean Crime-days per addict: 1,998.9

Nonetheless, we have decided not to project the future criminality of this sample in our analysis. Although such a projection would provide a more realistic (and higher) total of the lifetime extent of crimes committed by these addicts, it seems more prudent to restrict our analysis to the years at risk during which we have adequate data. Therefore, we are defining "lifetime criminality" for purposes of this study as crimes committed from onset of opiate use to time of interview; this is an average 11 year risk period during which the addicts were "on the street."

The total enumeration of crime-days presented in Table 1 is based upon different risk periods for the 243 addicts. This is because each addict's risk period, or years "on the street," was determined by his age at onset, amount of time incarcerated (which was subtracted) and age at interview. Consequently, although most of the sample had 10 or more years of "street" time (N = 198), there were 37 who had from 5 to 9 risk years and 8 who had from 2 to 4 risk years.

Annual Extent of Criminality for the 243 Addicts

The extent of criminality within this sample of 243 addicts on an annual basis is presented in Table 2. The measure of criminality employed is the number of crime-days accumulated by each addict per year at risk. This measure—crime-days per year at risk—controls for the differential risk periods and, therefore, provides a yearly *rate* of criminality for this sample.

Most of the addicts were continually engaged in a high level of crime during their years at risk. Thus, two-thirds of the 243 addicts committed over 100 crimes every year they were on the "streets." And one-fifth committed over 300 crimes every year since they became addictd. The mean number of crime-days per year at risk for this sample was 178. That is, the average addict in this sample amassed 178 crime-days every year while at risk.

There were, however, important variations in crime rates within this sample (Table 2). Thus, in addition to the high crime rate subjects who had 100, 200 or 300 crime-days per year, there was a smaller group who were not so involved in crime. Seventy-eight (one third) of the sample had less than 100 crime-days per year and 17 of these had either no crime-days or less than one a year. These differences in criminality within the sample will be analyzed further below.

Table 2. Crime-Days Per Year At Risk For 243 Male Addicts

Crime-Days Per Year at Risk	Number of Addicts	Percent of Addicts
No Crime-Days	6	2.5
Less than 1 per yr.	11	4.5
1–49	35	14.4
50–99	26	10.7
100–149	31	12.8
150–199	32	13.2
200–249	25	10.3
250–299	26	10.7
300–349	28	11.5
350–365	23	9.5
Total:	243	1000

Mean Crime-Days Per year at risk: 178.5

Table 3. Crime-Days Per Year At Risk By Type of Criminal Career And Addiction Status

Crime Career Type	Number of Addicts	Crime-Days Per Year At Risk	Crime-Days Per Year At Risk:	
			addicted	abstinent
1. Theft-daily	41	330.3	347.7	109.7
2. Sale of Drugs-daily	13	328.0	353.2	88.3
3. Other Crimes-daily	7	319.4	341.4	151.0
4. Weekly Theft	58	189.6	280.9	23.3
5. Weekly Sale of Drugs	18	181.1	284.0	27.6
6. Weekly, Other Crimes	7	201.9	297.0	70.1
7. Infrequent Theft	57	72.4	140.7	7.4
8. Infrequent Sales	14	102.4	260.9	10.5
9. Infrequent, Other Crimes	22	46.8	108.2	2.3
— No Crime	6	—	—	—
Total:	243	178.5	248.0	40.8

Criminal Careers of the 243 Addicts

Each of the 243 addicts were classified as to the common criminal career which he had followed since onset of regular opiate use. These criminal career types were determined on the basis of the principal, or most common, type of crime committed, and secondly, on the frequency of commission—whether daily, weekly or less often. Six of the 243 addicts had committed no crimes during their risk periods.

It was found that the 237 addicts who had committed crimes could be classified into nine types of criminal careers. These nine were: daily theft, daily drug sales, other daily crime; weekly theft, weekly drug sales, weekly other crimes; infrequent theft, infrequent sales and infrequent other crimes. (Table 3). Some two-thirds of the 237 addicts had theft as their principal type of crime. Of these 156 who were career thieves, 41 engaged in daily theft during their years at risk, 58 engaged in weekly theft and 57 in infrequent theft.

The selling of drugs was the second most favored type of crime committed by these addicts; 45 were principally engaged in selling drugs, or "dealing." Of the 45 dealers, 13 pursued this crime on a daily basis, 18 on a weekly basis and 14 on an infrequent basis.

The remainder of the sample were engaged in committing other types of crimes on a daily, weekly or infrequent basis. Of these 36, only 7 were engaged in daily crime, 7 in weekly crime and 22 in infrequent crimes. Confidence games, forgery, gambling and procuring (pimping) were the principal types of crime committed by these 36 addicts.

The classification of the sample into nine criminal career types somewhat obscures the fact that many addicts engaged in more than one type of crime during their years at risk. This situation is especially notable with regard to the 61 addicts who were daily criminals. Thus, 55 of the 61 had engaged in theft during their years at risk and 43 had engaged in some dealing, although only 13 had this as their principal daily criminal activity. In addition to theft and dealing—the two most common types of crime—33 of the 61 had engaged in other crimes, such as forgery, gambling, confidence games, robbery and pimping. The complete list of all crimes reported by these 61 daily criminals during their years on the street is: theft (this includes shoplifting: "cracking shorts," burglary and other forms of stealing), dealing, forgery, gambling, confidence games (flim-flam, etc.), pimping, abortionist, assault, mugging, robbery, and armed robbery.

The Impact of Addiction Upon Criminal Careers

The extent of criminality among all nine career types was affected by their addiction status. Thus, there was an overall six-fold increase in the number of crime-days per year at risk during addiction as contrasted with the abstinent periods (Table 3). When addicted, the 237 male addicts committed one or more crimes during 248 days per year; when not addicted, they had only 41 crime-days per year (for a detailed analysis of this relationship, see Ball et al., 1981). Although the extent of criminality within this addict sample was notably increased when the subjects were addicted to opiate drugs, the non-addicted crime rate was still quite high. As might be expected, the highest crime rates when not addicted were found among the three criminal career types who had the highest crime rate when addicted (daily theft, daily sales and daily other crimes). In these three career types, the addicts committed crimes from one to three days per week when not addicted (for these three groups, the rates per year at risk were 109.7, 88.3 and 151.0). In considering the rates of criminality for the nine career types when abstinent from opiates, it seems significant that these nine rates vary more (from 2.3 to 151.0) than do the rates when these same subjects are addicted. In a sense, then, one effect of opiate addiction is to raise the number of crimes committed to a threshold, or support, level, and this occurs for all nine career types. Thus, when addicted, 7 of the 9 career types commit more than 260 crimes per year and none of the nine career groups fall below 100 crime-days per year at risk.

Lifetime Arrests and Incarceration of the 237 Addicts

In order to ascertain the likelihood of arrest and incarceration for these Baltimore addicts and to relate these events to the extent of their criminality, the sample was separated into three equal groups on the basis of crime-days per year at risk. Group A, of 79 addicts, was the highest in criminality; their crime-days per year at risk was from 241 to 365. Group B, also of 79 addicts, was the middle classification with respect to criminality; their crime-days per year at risk were from 113 to 240. Group C was lower in criminality; their crime-days per year at risk was from 1 to 112. The six addicts without crime-days were excluded from this analysis.

With respect to age at interview and years of risk, the three groups were quite similar. Thus, Groups A, B and C were not significantly different in these regards (Table 4). With regard to age at onset, however, both Group A and B had an earlier age at onset than Group C. Thus, there is an association between early onset and increased criminality within this sample. In addition, the higher crime groups had a smaller white representation.

Most of the 237 addicts had been arrested several times and the likelihood of arrest differed by their involvement in crime. But the association is complex and liable to misinterpretation, as will be seen.

First, with respect to their total arrests for whatever offense, there were significant differences among the three groups. Group A had the highest number of arrests (mean = 14.4), Group B had the second highest (mean = 12.8) and Group C the lowest (mean = 9.1). But total arrests include both drug possession arrests as well as others, so further analysis is indicated.

Although drug possession arrests were not the principal type of arrest for the sample, such arrests were common with most of the addicts having some 3 or 4 drug arrests. The likelihood of such arrests, however, did not differ significantly among the three groups.

Table 4. Lifetime Arrest and Incarceration of the 237 Addicts

| Variables | Classified by Crime-Days Per year At Risk | | | | |
	A. Highest Third (241–365)	B. Middle Third (113–240)	C. Lowest Third (1–112)	Total (N=237) (1–365)	P-Values* (Dif. in Groups)
I. Age, Risk Years and Race:					
1. Age at onset (mean)	18.6	18.9	20.8	19.4	(.00)
2. Age at interview (mean)	35.0	35.1	37.4	35.8	(.31)
3. Years at risk (mean)	11.0	10.4	12.2	11.2	(.13)
4. White (percent)	26.6	46.8	58.2	43.9	(.00)
II. Arrests:					
5. Total arrests	14.4	12.8	9.1	12.1	(.00)
6. Drug Pos. Arrests (mean)	3.4	3.6	4.2	3.7	(.66)
7. Non-Drug Arrest (mean)	11.0	9.2	6.0	8.7	(.00)
8. Violent Crime Arrests, (mean)	2.0	1.4	1.0	1.5	(.01)
III. Incarceration:					
9. Hospital Periods (mean)	0.2	0.2	0.2	0.2	(.51)
10. Prison Periods (mean)	3.9	2.9	2.0	2.9	(.00)

*P-Values of differences among the three groups are based on the Kruskal-Wallis Test.

The three groups did differ significantly with respect to arrests for non-drug offenses and violent crime offenses. The non-drug arrests (i.e., mostly theft) were almost twice as frequent among Group A as among Group C (11.0 vs. 6.0); Group B was intermediate with respect to the number of non-drug arrests (mean = 9.2).

A similar association between arrests and the extent of criminality was found with respect to arrests for violent crime. Group A was highest with a mean of two such arrests per addict; Group B was intermediate with 1.4 arrests per addict; and Group C was lowest with a mean of one arrest for violent crime per addict. These group differences were statistically significant.

During the years from onset of opiate use to time of interview (an average period of 15.4 years) few of the addicts had been hospitalized for their drug abuse but most had spent considerable time in prison. With respect to hospitalization, only 16 percent had such hospital periods and the frequency of these periods did not differ among the three groups. With respect to prison periods, 88.8 percent of the 237 addicts had one or more such periods and the frequency of imprisonment was related to criminality. Thus, Group A had almost twice as many prison periods as Group C and Group B was intermediate in the number of imprisonments (A = 3.9, B = 2.9, C = 2.0). These differences were significant.

Two further observations about arrests within these three groups are relevant. The first refers to the probability of arrest and the second concerns arrests for violent crimes.

The probability of arrest for the entire sample was low as less than one percent of their crime-days were marked by arrest. To be exact, the 237 addicts had 2,869 arrests and 473,738 crime-days (i.e., probability = .0061). But even this low overall probability of arrest was influenced by the extent of criminality; arrests were less likely (per 100 crime-days) as the number of crimes increased. Thus, the probability of arrest for Group A, the high crime group, was .0041 while that of Group B was .0070 and that of Group C was .0176 percent. The likelihood of arrest, then, was over four times as great (per 100 crime-days) among those addicts in Group C than in Group A.

Estimating the Annual and Lifetime Criminality of Heroin Addicts in the United States

The research findings concerning the criminality of a representative sample of Baltimore addicts provides a means for estimating the extent of crimes committed by addicts throughout the United States. Before proceeding to this estimation procedure, however, several introductory comments are warranted.

First, we take the position that it is worthwhile to provide an initial estimate of the extent of criminality within this population once adequate data is available. It is worthwhile both with respect to furthering our understanding of crime and drug addiction as national problems and with respect to developing our research methodology for such measurement. In this latter regard, we hold that it is desirable to advance an estimate as soon as feasible.

Secondly, it is pertinent to comment upon the representativeness of the Baltimore sample with respect to the U.S. population of opiate addicts. Although one could prepare a treatise on this topic (and we are quite aware that the population of opiate addicts is not homogeneous and not unchanging, see Ball and Chambers, 1970), there is reason to maintain that this Baltimore sample is generally similar to the U.S. addict population insofar as most relevant variables are concerned. For example, in a criminological study (Ball, Levine, Demaree & Neman, 1975) of 42,293 drug abuse patients throughout the United States, it was found that 86.3 of the males had been arrested one or more times, that 50.4 percent had been arrested four or more times, that 18.2 percent had over 10 arrests; that 54.3 percent had been in jail or prison, that 32.5 percent had been incarcerated for more than a year, and that 19.6 percent had been incarcerated for more than three years prior to treatment. These arrest and incarceration figures are comparable to those of the Baltimore sample, especially when it is recognized that the national data refer to a younger population.

In developing our estimate of the extent of criminality among heroin addicts in the United States, we are referring to a population of 450,000 addicts. This figure was derived by The Strategy Council on Drug Abuse and published in the *1979 Federal Strategy for Drug Abuse and Drug Traffic Prevention*. This figure can, of course, be updated without effecting the other parts of the crime estimation procedure.

Estimation of Annual Criminality, Male

The factors involved in this calculation are:

A. That male opiate addicts commit at least one crime on 178 days per year at risk (i.e., crime-days per year at risk = 178.5).
B. That these addicts are not at risk 32 percent of their careers (i.e., incarceration time = 31.7 percent).
C. That there are approximately 450,000 addicts in the United States; that 76.7 percent of these are male and 23.3 percent female. (the proportions by sex are from Ball et al., 1975).
 # Then, using a simple multiplicative estimation approach, Crime-Days for males = 178.5 × .683 × 345,150 = 42,080,688 crime-days per calendar year.

Although female addict criminality can not be derived from the Baltimore data directly, a rough estimate of this lower rate is that it is 50 percent less than for men (based on lower arrest rates) and also some 50 percent less incarceration time (see Tables IV & VI in Ball et al., 1975). Based on these considerations, the number of crime-days per year for the 104,850 U.S. female addicts correspondingly is: $89.25 \times .842 \times 104,850 = 7,879,477$ crime-days per calendar year.

Lifetime Criminality of U.S. Heroin Addicts

This estimation involves the following:

A. That male opiate addicts commit crimes on 178 days per year at risk (i.e., 178.5 crime-days per year at risk).
B. That these addicts have an active average lifetime of 16.4 years from onset of opiate addiction to time of interview (this period is defined as their lifetime for purposes of calculation); that of these 16.4 years, 11.2 years are "street" time and 5.2 years are prison time (or 31.7%).
C. That there are approximately 450,000 addicts in the United States; that 76.7 percent of these are male and 23.3 percent female.

\# Then, lifetime crimes for addicts = $178.5 \times 11.2 \times 345,150 = 689,954,850$ total crime-days.

Based on our research findings of the extent of crime committed by Baltimore heroin addicts, we have derived an estimate of the crimes committed by the 450,000 heroin addicts in the United States. It is estimated that the 345,000 male addicts commit 42 million crimes per year. The smaller population of female addicts commit almost 8 million crimes per calendar year.

On a lifetime basis—conservatively calculated as lasting only 16 years from onset of addiction—it is estimated this male population of 345,000 addicts commits crimes on over 689,000,000 days. We regard these estimates as a lower bound because of the shortened risk period and the fact that multiple offenses per day are frequent but not counted in the crime-day measurement.

The estimation of the lifetime criminality of female addicts follows the same procedure as for males, except that their crime rate is lower and they have less time incarcerated (and hence more years at risk). Again, calculating their crime-days at 50 percent of the male rate (or 89.25 crime-days per year at risk) and their incarceration time as 50 percent less (or only 2.6 years of the 16.4 years), then: Female Lifetime Criminality = 89.25×13.8 (years) $\times 104,850 = 129,913,850$ total crime-days.

The lifetime criminality for the 450,000 heroin addicts in the United States is, then, the sum of the total crime-days for the 345,150 males and the 104,850 females, or 819,868,700 crime-days.

Conclusion

This study has established that most heroin addicts are deeply enmeshed in a criminal lifestyle which involves the commission of thousands of offenses per individual after the onset of their opiate use. The extent of criminality within the addict population of the United States is staggering. Our estimation is that the 450,000 heroin addicts commit over 50 million crimes per year. And furthermore, that during an 11 year risk period, while they are on "the street," these male addicts are responsible for committing some 700 million crimes.

These estimates are based on a long-term follow-up study of a probability-based sample of Baltimore opiate addicts. In this study each of the addicts was interviewed with respect to his criminality and collateral information was obtained from official records. The extent of criminal behavior was determined by means of a new measure: crime-days per year at risk. Use of this measure has made it possible to derive national estimates of criminality. We believe that our estimates of criminality are conservative.

In addition to finding that two-thirds of our addicts were rather continuously involved in criminal behavior (i.e., committing offenses from 113 to 365 days per year at risk), it was observed that their offenses included both crimes against property and violent crimes. Most of the sample were repeatedly involved in both property offenses and violent offenses. Thus, 86 percent had been arrested one or more times for theft and 60 percent had been arrested one or more times for crimes of violence. (These arrest figures, of course, grossly underestimate the extent of these two types of criminality as the probability of arrest was exceedingly low.) These findings are of particular significance inasmuch as there has been a growing concern about violent crime, and especially "street" crime, in the United States. In this regard, our results indicate that it may be unrealistic to attack violent crime as an entity, for to a large extent it overlaps with other types of criminal behavior.

Lastly, with respect to the research findings, it should be noted that most of the addicts followed over the years in our study had been arrested numerous times and had spent considerable time in prison. But their frequent arrests (12 per addict) and periods of incarceration (3 per addict) had little noticeable effect on their criminal careers. For most continued their high level of criminality year after year despite arrests and incarceration; in fact, the number of arrests and periods of incarceration was directly related to the extent of their criminality. Indeed, the continuity and persistency of the addicts' criminal behavior stands out as a major conclusion of the study. In this regard, one is inclined to agree with a statement by Frank Tannenbaum in his Foreward to *New Horizons in Criminology:* "What to do with the professional criminals is a problem sufficient to tax the best thought of the community."

What to do. First and foremost, it is time to face the reality of the problem. For the fact is that heroin addicts are responsible for the commission of millions of crimes per year in the United States and many of these offenses are of a serious nature. Given these realities, it seems strange indeed to find that a fundamental controversy about the criminality of addicts continues. In this regard, a recent author has taken the position that nothing can be done about this problem because our knowledge is incomplete. Thus, Silberman states that neither drug abuse nor crime can be reduced because "we simply do not know how large that contribution [of heroin to crime] is, or what the processes are through which drug abuse contributes to crime."

Without commenting upon the inadequacy of particular arguments about what can not be done about crime, and without reviewing the significant advances which have been made in criminology research concerning crime rates (e.g., Fienberg and Reiss, 1980; Hindelang, 1981), let it suffice to say that there is a pressing need to address the problem by informing the public and its leaders about the extent and continuity of crime among heroin addicts. For no significant action can occur until the public recognizes the problem for what it is. And this is not to deny that other problems in society exist. Quite the contrary. For it may well be that control and reduction of the crime-drug problem is a prerequisite for addressing many other social issues.

References

Ball, J. C. and C. D. Chambers (eds.), *The Epidemiology of Opiate Addiction in the United States.* Springfield, Ill.: Charles C Thomas, 1970.

Ball, J. C., B. K. Levine, R. G. Demaree and J. G. Neman, "Pretreatment Criminality of Male and Female Drug Abuse Patients in the United States." *Addictive Diseases* 1(4):481–489, 1975.

Ball, J. C., L. Rosen, J. A. Flueck and D. N. Nurco, "The Criminality of Heroin Addicts when Addicted and when Off Opiates." in J. A. Inciardi, Ed., *The Drugs-Crime Connection.* Beverly Hills: Sage. Chapter 2, 1981.

Bonito, A. J., D. N. Nurco and J. W. Shaffer, "The Veridicality of Addicts' Self-Reports in Social Research." *International Journal of the Addictions* 11(5):719–724, 1976.

Chambers, C. D., "Narcotic Addiction and Crime: An Empirical Review," in J. A. Inciardi and C. D. Chambers, Eds., *Drugs and the Criminal Justice System.* Beverly Hills: Sage. Chapter 5, 1974.

Fienberg, S. E. and A. J. Reiss, Jr. (eds.), *Indicators of Crime and Criminal Justice: Quantitative Studies.* Washington: U.S. Dept of Justice, 1980.

Hindelang, M. J., "Variations in Sex-Age-Race-Specific Incidence Rates of Offending," *American Sociological Review* 46(4):461–474, 1981.

Johnston, L. D., D. N. Nurco and L. N. Robins (eds.), *Conducting Follow-up Research on Drug Treatment Programs.* Washington: DHEW Publication No. (ADM) 77–487. Treatment Program Monograph Series. No. 2, 1977.

Lindesmith, A. R., *Addiction and Opiates.* Chicago: Aldine, 1968.

Musto, D. F., *The American Disease.* New Haven: Yale University Press, 1973.

Nurco, D. N. and R. L. DuPont, "A Preliminary Report on Crime and Addiction Within a Community-Wide Population of Narcotic Addicts." *Drug and Alcohol Dependence* 2:109–121, 1977.

Silberman, C. E., *Criminal Violence, Criminal Justice.* New York: Random House, 1978.

The Strategy Council on Drug Abuse, *Federal Strategy for Drug Abuse and Drug Traffic Prevention.* Washington: U.S. Government Printing Office, 1979.

Tannenbaum, F., "Foreward," in H. E. Barnes and N. K. Teeters, *New Horizons in Criminology.* New York: Prentice-Hall, 1945.

Terry, C. E. and M. Pellens, *The Opium Problem.* New York: Bureau of Social Hygiene. Reprinted by Patterson Smith, 1970, 1928.

Chapter III
Women, Drugs and Reproduction

Chapter 3 focuses on the impact of drug use and abuse by women. In many ways women are a unique cohort of drug users. They are conspicuous consumers of prescribed medications and often become invisible abusers of those very prescribed medications. In 1972 Phyllis Chesler wrote the pathbreaking *Women in Madness* which tracks one such road to drug dependence. Chesler argued that the psychiatric profession aids and abets this dependence through the prescription of tranquilizers and anti-depressants in a response to "women's problems" such as depression.

The medical establishment's response to these problems today is not so unique. The profile of the typical 19th century drug addict was a middle-aged, middle class woman who usually started her use of "medicine", often patent drugs, under some type of medical supervision. These women relied upon such medications as Lydia E. Pinkham's Vegetable Compound, the most popular elixir for "female complaints" at the turn of century, which had about an 18% alcohol content.

The consumers of Pinkham's elixer who used it to *excess* were trapped by Victorian expectations for female behavior. These expectations grossly restricted a woman's life to the small circle of hearth and home and the alcohol in Pinkham's medicine was an escape hatch. These women were the precursors to today's mostly invisible female alcoholic population. While this invisibility is likely to diminish as women participate more and more in the workforce, it is not clear that real changes in the expectations for a woman's role in American society will occur to help negate a need for the use of an "escape" drug.

"Women's complaints" and the need to escape them are not always easily faulted as some type of nameless malaise. Many concerns of women revolve around very specific issues related to fertility. Trying to become pregnant as well as trying to prevent pregnancy has often involved the use of drugs, the most infamous being "the pill".

This chapter helps the reader begin exploring some of the issues surrounding female drug use. The chapter starts with a selection by Gomberg which lays out a brief discussion of the historical role of women in American society and the relationship between this role and the abuse of alcohol and other drugs among today's female population. Nellis follows with insight into how legal drugs are promoted, especially the use of tranquilizers for women.

Seaman and Seaman explore the use of DES, "the grandmother product of all synthetic estrogens". This product originally touted to prevent miscarriages and later used more indiscriminately for many women with no history of pregnancy loss has become a time-bomb drug. The children of DES users have been linked to rare forms of cancer. Drug companies, the medical profession and the FDA were slow to respond to research making this link.

Minkin points out that cancer has also been linked to Depo-Provera, an injectable contraceptive used internationally for family planning and banned in the United States by the FDA as a contraceptive. The attempt to suppress findings linking Depo with cancer takes on almost conspiratorial overtones as Minkin tracks the history of this drug's use.

Finally, The Boston Women's Health Collective, the authors of *Our Bodies Ourselves,* lay out the very technical effects of using the birth control pill reminding the reader that it is women who "see the doctor, get examined, remember to take the pill, feel the effects and run the risks". We hope that these selections help illustrate the range of drug risks for women in today's society.

11. Women: Alcohol and Other Drugs

Edith S. Lisansky Gomberg

Introduction

The use and abuse of chemical substances has intermittently been an issue of concern in Western societies. Attitudes toward different drugs have varied over time: when tobacco was introduced in Europe in the 16th century, it evoked strong opposition from the authorities who tried to prohibit its use. When coffee was introduced in the next century, its use was also disapproved. The use of tobacco and coffee became widespread and attempts to prohibit or control the usage gradually diminished.

Although both sexes drank, smoke, and used other drugs, social concerns have traditionally focused on the effects of drugs on male behavior and functioning, and scientific research has had the same foci. Occasional voices may have spoken out about the impairment of women's mothering (e.g., during the Gin Epidemic) but women have been viewed as using drug substances medicinally and social concerns were minimal.

In American history, concern about various drug substances has focused on different ethnic and racial groups. Substance abuse has been linked to newly arrived immigrant groups, to aborigines, Orientals and Blacks. The urban working class saloon, frequented by industrial workers, primarily foreign-born men, came under attack (Kingsdale, 1980). Chinese immigrants were perceived as a threat because of opium use. It was widely believed that cocaine was frequently used by Southern Blacks, and this was not called into question until publication of a report in 1914 of Black admissions to mental hospitals in Georgia (Musto, 1973). In 1901, the United States Senate adopted a resolution forbidding the sale of opium and alcohol, ". . . to aboriginal tribes and uncivilized races . . . (including) Indians, Alaskans, the inhabitants of Hawaii, railroad workers, and immigrants at ports of entry" (Sinclair, 1962). There are, to this day, widely held, stereotypical views about the linkage between illegal drugs and different racial and ethnic groups.

Interestingly enough, although there is no evidence of expressed concern about *women and drugs,* anti-drug writings in the 19th and early 20th century make occasional reference to the danger of various drugs present to "youth." Contemporary concern about adolescent drug use has a history a century old: "temperance education" goes back a century. But even the Women's Christian Temperance Union, which was genuinely concerned with many women's issues, concentrated its efforts on male drunkenness and the effects of male alcoholism on the family. Perhaps ignoring women's use of drugs and alcohol was related to the middle class image of women as models of virtue, gentility and self-control.

From Elizabeth S. Lisansky Gomberg, WOMEN: ALCOHOL AND OTHER DRUGS, which originally appeared in *Drugs and Society,* Vol. 1, No. 1, pp. 75–109 (as edited), Fall, 1986. Copyright © 1986 The Haworth Press. Reprinted by permission.

The purpose of this paper is to provide a review of some of the historical and contemporary events related to problems of women and drugs. It is intended to raise issues that need study and to contribute to a heightened consciousness about women, medication and drugs, still in need of being addressed. The conclusion of this article will be a presentation of research issues and questions arising from the review of the problem of women and substance use and abuse.

The 20th Century

From the viewpoint of women's history, this century may be divided into two periods, pre-World War II and post-World War II. The first decade of the 20th century was the end of the Victorian period, and the first two decades were the peak and the tapering off of the European migrations to the United States. The 1920s, presumably the decade of the "flapper," seemed to be a period of increasing freedoms for women, e.g., smoking in public became more socially acceptable. The large majority of poor, working class and lower-middle class women were largely unaffected by "the flapper age." The either-or choice, job *or* marriage, continued for all women. In 1920, only 12 percent of all professional women in the United States were married. In 1924, 75 percent of women earning a Ph.D degree were single (Berkin, 1979). One has only to look at the plays (Moss Hart's "Lady in the Dark") or movies of the 1920s and 1930s, to see the theme of the achieving woman who gives up here career and finds fulfillment in marriage. Some of the films of Spencer Tracy and Katherine Hepburn stand out as exceptions, however, suggesting the possibility that women could express their work talent and have a loving relationship at the same time.

The Depression of the 1930s re-evoked the argument that women worked for "pin money," and in 26 states bills were introduced to prohibit married women from working outside the home. This came about although women's jobs were largely domestic, menial, and not competitive with men's work.

World War II created an unprecedented demand for women's labor. A decade earlier it had been her patriotic duty to leave jobs for men to do; now it was her patriotic duty to work at such jobs. From 1940 to 1945, the proportion of women in the work force rose from 25 percent to 36 percent. Furthermore, among the six million women working outside the home for the first time, many were engaged in skilled jobs in heavy industry (e.g., "Rosie the Riveter"). When the war ended, dismissal and pressure to resign reduced the percentage of women in the workplace, but not without resistance. Not only were societal demands shifting, the workplace itself was changing and labor needs pulled women toward "pink collar" work, i.e., toward clerical and service jobs. During the 1950s, the pressure on women to leave the workplace and return to full-time house-wifery and mothering was reflected in much of the social sciences: a number of social problems such as juvenile delinquency and emotional disorders of young people was attributed to mothers in the workplace. Nonetheless, there was resistance against being displaced and an interesting contradiction: in the 1950s, white middle-class women were marrying at an earlier age than their grandmothers had done, but at the same time there were more women working outside the home than ever before. These were not often women with young children at home; the movement of these young women toward the workplace began a decade later.

It is not necessary to reiterate the statistics about the evermounting proportion of the American labor force that is female. The increasing presence of women in the workplace, the astronomical rise in divorce rates, the increase in single, female-headed households and one-parent families, have been well documented. Moynihan's description of the female-headed households among Blacks created a storm of controversy (Rainwater & Yancy, 1967), but it is as appropriate today as it was when written. The sexual revolution has created freedoms, but men as well as women are "liberated," and one interpretation of male liberation is abdication of the traditional male role of economic responsibility for children of divorce.

Almost parallel with these developments has been a sharp increase in societal concern over women's alcohol and drug usage. The concern comes in part from the feminist movement, which emphasizes the papering over and neglect of women's problems in this area. Feminists have also called attention to issues related to women's use of prescribed and psychoactive drugs. But, societal concern is primarily with abusive use of alcohol and illicit drugs.

Why the Current Concern about Women and Drug Abuse?

As noted above, pressure was exerted on women in the workplace when World War II ended to return to their traditional homemaker roles. Although women had demonstrated their competence in wartime industry the old issue of *lesser ability* arose again. Review of research on male/female comparisons on a variety of performance tasks led to the conclusion, as early as 1946, that the differences were exaggerated:

> Scientific evidence available . . . fails to indicate differences attributable to such membership that would justify casting men and women in different social roles. (Seward, 1946, p. 245)

Although men and women tend to differ in patterns of abilities such as girls manifesting greater verbal ability, and boys excelling in visual-spatial and mathematical ability, the overlap is enormous, and the conclusion that women are less trainable, less competent, less talented than men is unwarranted. The sexes do differ in patterns of ability, but differences in achievement appear to be much more related to socialization, drive to achieve, and access to the opportunity structure.

In the same post-World War II period, the social science/psychoanalytical literature about the consequences of inadequate mothering burgeoned. Mothers working outside the home, it was argued, are inadequate nurturers and the resultant deprivation contributes importantly to juvenile delinquency, behavior disorders, neuroses, alcoholism and schizophrenia, among other unhappy conditions. As summarized by Hays (1964):

> Women have been admitted into industry and white-collar work in large numbers. . . . Nevertheless, the controversy still goes on as to whether the working mother can be a successful housewife, whether her children suffer from this situation, whether her abilities are inferior to those of men, in short men are simply not happy about her economic freedom. (p. 270)

The first heralds of the new feminism were Friedan's book, *The Feminine Mystique* (1963), and Rossi's (1964) essay on equality between the sexes. Rossi's essay is a critique of the psychoanalytically-influenced social scientists who promoted the image of the "healthy" woman adult as one *exclusively* devoted to marriage and parenthood. So a new feminism was born, generated partly by the rebellious challenge to conventional ways and norms and by the civil rights movement of the 1960s.

In the twenty years which have passed, progress has been made in women's economic status. Women are more visibly present in some professions. More women are in the workplace (albeit in low-level and dead-end jobs). Affirmative Action programs exist. A woman has also been nominated by the Democratic Party for Vice President in the 1984 election campaign. Progress may be slow, but it is visible. Parallel with this progress has been a mounting public, governmental, and media concern about female substance abuse. It is true that insofar as alcoholic beverages are concerned, the percentage of American women who drink (in any quantity) has risen from mid-century to the 1970s (Gomberg, 1974). But, that percentage has levelled off and a survey conducted in 1981 found no evidence of any major increase in women's drinking over the time period 1970 to 1981 (Wilsnack, Wilsnack, & Klassen, 1984). It is difficult to judge whether there has been an increase in women's use of narcotics or other illegal drugs because the number of such drug abusers which appear in the literature are, admittedly, estimates. Use is made of medically-prescribed mood-modifying drugs by both sexes; but from the inception of their use women have been the larger users. Public and governmental concern does not seem to extend to women's use of prescribed psychoactive drugs, e.g., minor tranquilizers. Concern has focused on women's drinking and women's use of illicit drugs.

The current concern about women's substance abuse seems to be linked to several different phenomena. *First,* it should be pointed out that concern has grown almost proportionately with female progress in the workplace, and this suggests that economic competition may be one important factor promoting concern. *Second,* a growth industry of substance abuse treatment facilities, professionals and paraprofessionals has developed, and while much of the concern about female substance abuse is genuine, it is also good for business. *Third,* the federal government has created two federal agencies to deal with problems related to alcohol and drugs, and again, mixed with genuine concern is the necessity for a bureaucracy to justify its existence and Congressional committees to justify their expenditures. And finally, there has been a long history of association between female intoxication and immorality, and a longstanding belief that the woman alcoholic is "sexually promiscuous." When alcohol is involved in a rape, there is considerable difference in social attitudes depending on whether the rapist or the victim has been drinking: it appears to be more forgivable when the rapist has been drinking (loss of control!) and less forgivable when the victim has been drinking (Marolla & Scully, 1979).

It appears that the present high degree of concern about women's drinking and use of illicit drugs may also be linked to societal hostility and to backlash, relating to rapid change and shifts in sex roles. Such a linkage is hypothetical and difficult to document. Marris (1974), however, has described "the conservative impulse"—the sense of loss which accompanies swift and marked social change and the deep need to maintain continuity in goals and relationships. It is a tenable hypothesis that the feminist movement and the visible and rapid changes in sex roles have produced a sense of loss in many men and women. Coexisting with change in sex roles are shifts that have occurred in family structure, in sexual permissiveness, and in adolescent freedoms—all sources of societal concern. Changes in female sex roles may indeed have produced a backlash in which the challenge to the traditional female role is seen as producing a host of familial and social problems, including substance abuse among women.

Deeply-rooted anxieties and ambivalence about women's behavior is not new, but the increased competition with men for economic benefits and for power appears to have intensified this anxiety and ambivalence. The presence in the workplace of married women with children still creates controversy, yet the statistics show an increasing proportion of women returning to or entering the workplace while their children are still very young. The disturbance this evokes appears to manifest itself in a counterattack: breaking out of the traditional role of housewife/wife/mother produces not only delinquency and emotional disorder in children and adolescents, it produces the drinking and drug abuse which are destructive to the fetus in utero. There is less attention and handwringing about the misery of the woman substance abuser than there is about "addicted babies" and fetal alcohol effects. A disproportionate number of research dollars have gone into fetal effects, leaving other research areas relatively neglected. Granted the toxic effect of heavy drinking and narcotic, sedative and stimulant abuse on the fetus, it still needs to be pointed out that negative effects of prescribed medication (thalidomide?) have come in for less concern and attention. And, if it is the health of infants which touches deeply into public concern, the relatively high rates of infant mortality among non-white groups in the United States should cause a great outcry, but they do not.

Current Status: Women's Use of Substances

Since patterns of usage vary with different substances which may be more or less socially acceptable, use of substances in five different categories will be summarized (a) prescribed medication in general, (b) prescribed psychoactive drugs, (c) over-the-counter (OTC) medication, (d) the "social" drugs: tobacco and alcohol, and (e) illegal or "street" drugs. Comparisons of men's and women's use of substances indicate that women consume more prescribed and psychoactive medications than do men, and that women consume less of the "social" drugs and the "street" drugs. There are some age variations which relate to different stages of the life span and to cohort/generational differences, and there are social class and regional differences as well. What follows is a brief review of some of these issues.

Prescribed Medication

Several reports have dealt with the relationship between the physician and the female patient (e.g., Corea, 1977). A recent study compared male physician response to five medical complaints made by men and women patients in their forties: back pain, headache, dizziness, chest pain, and fatigue. With an equal number of physician visits, "men received more extensive workups than women in all five of the complaints" (Armitage et al., 1979, p. 2187). The authors suggest that the physicians may be responding to "current stereotypes" in which the male is "typically stoic" and the female "typically hypochondriacal."

Are prescriptions more readily written for the female patient? Is it that women make more physician/clinic/hospital/office visits, and therefore, are more likely to receive a prescription? Are women patients more likely to want, and communicate that wanting, of medication to the physician? While the reasons are difficult to establish, it is clear that women use more prescription drugs than men, and this is true in spite of the fact that women have more adverse drug reactions even when controlling for dose and number of drugs prescribed (Simpson et al., 1978; Hamilton & Parry, 1983).

Verbrugge's (1982) report, that women use more legal drugs of all types than men do, is primarily linked to morbidity and age. "Personal characteristics" also contribute to the sex difference in the amount of drug use. Such "personal characteristics" of the women include: being slightly older than the men in the study, having less active social roles, experiencing more disruptive events and more morbidity, considering their health to be worse, feeling more helpless about life, and, being unable to ignore symptoms as easily.

Prescribed Psychoactive Drugs

One of the best documented facts in the study of women and drug use is the relatively large number of mood-modifying, psychoactive drugs prescribed for women. The national survey conducted by Parry et al. (1973), indicated that 13 percent of the men and 29 percent of the women had reported using "psychotherapeutic" prescription drugs during the past year. Many studies have reported responses of women and men in the United States and Canada, but the greater female use of psychoactive drugs is by no means confined to these two countries. Cooperstock (1971) indicated higher prevalence of use by women in the United Kingdom as well as in the United States and Canada. Balter, Levine, and Manheimer (1974) surveyed the use of "anti-anxiety/sedative" drugs in nine European countries and reported the percentage of women who had used psychoactive drugs during the past year as approximately twice the percentage of men.

Even with this impressive consistency of results, there are questions. Cooperstock (1975) raised the question of under-reporting in survey response as well as the question of "hidden" psychotropic drugs, i.e., mixed drug preparations containing a psychotropic agent as well as a substance intended for some somatic condition. Clearly, however, women receive more prescriptions for mood-modifying drugs. There is no decisive answer whether this is due to more physician visits by women patients, to physicians' stereotypes and attitudes toward their male and female patients, or to women patients' greater desire and demand for medication. Perhaps all of these combine to produce the male-female ratio of use of psychoactive drugs.

Over-the-Counter (OTC) Drugs

The use of patent medicines is very difficult to document and researchers may have to rely on more drug company records than user information. Prescription drugs are usually a matter of record and prescription statistics have been used in research. Prescriptions involve writing by the physician and producing the medication by the pharmacist. OTC drugs, however, are sold in drug stores, supermarkets, general stores, department stores, etc. From the information which is available, there may be more use by women than by men, particularly in the age group 15 to 44 (Bush & Rabin, 1976). Young men appear to purchase a relatively large amount of stimulant OTC drugs. Among people over 60, there appears to be small gender difference in purchase and use.

Some reports suggest that although there are no overall sex differences in use of mood-modifying OTC drugs (Burt, Glynn, & Sowder, 1979), some variations may occur. Men, for example, are more likely to purchase drugs like Nodoz, whereas women are more likely to be using prescription stimulant drugs (amphetamines). It will probably be evident that the male-female ratio will vary with particular classes of OTC drugs: antacids, analgesics, antihistamines, vitamins, etc. If the incidence of colds or respiratory illnesses in general is examined up to age 3, boys have more; from that age on, women always have more colds or respiratory illnesses (Monto & Ullman, 1974). One of the most popular self-medications is NyQuil, which commands 25 percent of the market (Ray, 1983). This OTC remedy, which contains 25 percent alcohol, may represent an updated equivalent of the 19th century tonics for women.

The "Social" Drugs: Tobacco and Alcohol

1. Tobacco

Men and women have both shared in the ritual use, and later the secular use, of tobacco in almost all cultures, especially in Western societies. In industrialized nations, women are fast approaching men in the rate of initiation and prevalence of tobacco use. This trend began in the 1920s in the United States (Nuehring & Markle, 1974).

Among adolescents in general, initiation into smoking during preteen or teenage years is chiefly social in origin. More smoking occurs among lower income and low-achieving students, and among those who are more likely to drink alcoholic beverages. From the mid-1960s to the mid-1970s little change occurred in the pattern of boys' initiation into and maintenance of smoking. The overall change in adolescent regular smoking, which went from 4 percent in 1968 to 32 percent in 1974, was "almost entirely due to increased smoking among teenage girls" (Gritz, 1980). In addition, there has been a sharp increment in the proportion of *heavy* smokers among females age 13 to 35. Among adults, there has been a gradual decline during the 1960s and 1970s in the percentage of males who smoke, but there has been very little change among women (Schuman, 1978). The following is of some demographic interest: women's smoking is more prevalent among higher income groups, while men show the opposite trend. Among young women 18 to 35 years of age, housewives smoke more heavily than employed women. While there is still a higher percentage of smokers among men, the gender differences are small: for the 12 to 17 year olds, 12 percent of the girls and 13 percent of the boys use cigarettes; for the 18 to 25 year old age group, the percentages are 40 percent for women and 45 percent for men, and for adults 26 years of age and older, 33 percent of the women and 41 percent of the men smoke cigarettes (Fishburne, Abelson, & Cisin, 1979).

2. Alcohol

One must distinguish between drinking per se and problems created by drinking alcoholic beverages. For temperance believers, *any* drinking is harmful and sinful: "total abstinence is the only safe way to avoid the evils which alcohol engenders" (Fundamental Facts Concerning Beverage Alcohol, 1956, p. 8).

Surveys of American drinking practices (Cahalan, Cisin, & Crossley, 1969: Clark & Midanik, 1982) indicate that about two-thirds of Americans 18 years of age and older drink and that most of them consume alcoholic beverages in small and moderate quantities which do not cause problems for themselves or others. Epidemiologists and other social scientists have distinguished such drinkers from "heavy drinkers" and from "problem drinkers."

Now, when we look at women's use of alcohol, are we talking about infrequent and moderate drinking or about alcoholism? It is true that the percentage of American women who drink has risen from midcentury up to the 1970s when the percentage leveled off (Leland, 1982). Evidence about a rising prevalence of heavy, alcoholic drinking, however, is more equivocal.

It is not always clear whether the handwringing and the viewing with alarm has to do with women's drinking per se or with heavy drinking, intoxication and alcoholism. Certainly problem drinking is just that: a problem which is devastating for both women and men and their families. But are we speaking of excessive use or any use at all? Most ascetic religious groups frown upon drinking by either sex. But other, more permissive groups, seem to be reasonably accepting of women's drinking *in limited quantity*. The Talmud states this quite clearly:

One cup of wine is good for a woman;
Two are degrading;
Three induce her to act like an immoral woman;
And four cause her to lose all self-respect and sense
of shame. (The Talmud [The Study of the Mishna])[1]

When we examine prevalence of problem drinking and alcoholism among women, the numbers are estimates. It is true that more women have entered rehabilitation facilities and Alcoholics Anonymous during the last decade than they did before that, but readiness to seek treatment does not necessarily mean an increase in prevalence. Some surveys have reported a relatively high percentage of heavy/frequent drinkers among women in the workplace (Johnson, 1982), but the relationship between employment outside the home, part-time work, unemployment, housewife status, and drinking, is not really clear. What is clear is the ominous note sounded in Fillmore's (1984) statement that,

> heavy-frequent drinking is more common in the younger age groups as compared to older cohorts measured at the same age . . . the youngest cohort, who in 1979 were ages 21–29, seem to show a much higher rate of heavy-frequent drinking than past cohorts measured at the same age, particularly among the employed. (pp. 29, 31)

Coupled with these epidemiological findings is the observation of an increasing proportion of young women who appear in substance abuse treatment facilities. It appears that in those facilities to which women come for help, the mean age is no longer in the forties—as it was a generation ago.

Is it possible that the proportion of American women who drink (as compared with the proportion who are abstinent) remains constant while the proportion who drink problematically rises in the young adult age group? What are the consequences? Will these young women go on to become middle-aged alcoholics? Will treatment head off the progression of alcoholism, begun relatively early in life? Will the youngsters who are now 10 to 19 years of age maintain the same "much higher rate of heavy-frequent drinking" as the current group of women who are now in their twenties, or will they show even higher or perhaps lower rates of heavy-frequent drinking? These questions certainly suggest that we turn our attention and effort toward *prevention*.

There have been many reviews of the literature on female alcoholism (e.g., Lindbeck, 1972; Gomberg, 1974; Shaw, 1980; Ferrence, 1980).

Illegal or "Street" Drugs

Prior to the passage of the Harrison Act in 1914, there were apparently more, perhaps twice as many, women who used narcotics heavily (Martin & Martin, 1980). The typical "opiate addict" in the 19th century and up to 1914 was

> a 30 to 50 year old white woman who functioned well. . . . She bought opium or morphine legally at the local store, used it orally, and caused few, if any, social problems. She may have ordered her "family remedy" through the mail from Sears Roebuck—two ounces of laudanum for 18 cents. (Ray, 1983, p. 334)

At the present time it is estimated, admittedly a guess, that women comprise about 20 to 25 percent of the addict population, numbering more than 100,000 women. The percentage of persons over 18 using heroin is calculated at 1.8 percent of men and 0.6 percent of women (Burt, Glynn, & Sowder, 1979). In 1969, the gender ratio of males to females for those entering treatment for narcotics addiction was four to one; by 1980, it had become three to one. The image of the typical heroin addict as a young adult Black male is apparently changing: in 1969, admissions to treatment facilities consisted of 55 percent Blacks and 30 percent Whites; by 1980, this had become 30 percent Blacks and 58 percent Whites. The age of addicts, at least those in treatment facilities, has also shifted downward: in 1969, adolescents under 18 constituted 6 percent of admissions to treatment programs, young adults 18 to 25 constituted 37 percent of admissions. In 1980, the proportion of adolescents admitted to treatment programs had gone up to 13 percent and the proportion of young adults down to 30 percent.

The male-female ratios of "lifetime users" (ever used) of cocaine, hallucinogens, inhalants, marijuana, and hashish show a larger percentage of boys than girls among adolescents 12 to 17 years of age. Among adults, males also show a higher prevalence of use. Although "lifetime use" of these drugs is higher for men, sex differences with respect to *current* usage are small (except for marijuana). Thus, it appears that a higher proportion of women who try these drugs continue to use them after they are first tried. Male users, however, use larger quantities than female users. In summary, more men have tried illicit drugs and take larger doses of drugs, but many claim that, ". . . The sexes are involved with them in equal percentages at present" (Fidell, 1982).

The current situation relating to the use of *cocaine* has developed so rapidly, there is little reliable information about the usage by men or women. There is no question about the rapid escalation of its use. During the 1970s, the "ever used" incidence appeared to have tripled in all age groups. By 1980, estimates were that 28 percent of young adults between 18 and 25 had used cocaine, a third of them within the previous month. Cocaine overdose deaths have multiplied within recent years: between 1980 and 1983, San Francisco reported a 300 percent increase in cocaine overdose (Smith, 1984). Several patterns of use have been identified: experimental use, recreational use, situational use, intensified drug use and compulsive drug use (Siegel, 1977). High school seniors who reported ever having experimented with cocaine increased from 9 percent in 1975 to 17 percent in 1981, and Ray (1983) believes that use by adolescents and young adults will continue to increase. Available information indicates that cocaine, like other illegal drugs, has more male users than female users. Concern has been expressed by health authorities about increasing use of cocaine by women.

The male-female ratio of *"designer drug" use* is not known; such drugs having appeared so recently as drugs of abuse that statistics about prevalence have not been obtained. It is to be expected that more males will be experimenting with these new drugs as they appear, although some women, probably heroin addicts, will be experimenting with them as well.

What is Drug Abuse?

Drug abuse is usually defined in terms of heavy alcohol consumption and/or use of illicit drugs—and the consequences of such use. Drug abuse is deviant behavior and, as Gusfield (1967) points out:

> Deviant designations have histories; the public definition of behavior as deviant is itself changeable. It is open to reversals of political power, twists of public opinion, and the development of social movements and moral crusades. What is attacked as criminal today may be seen as sick next year and fought over as possibly legitimate by the next generation. (p. 187)

A 19th century woman might have ordered laudanum from a Sears & Roebuck catalogue, but a 1985 woman probably has a supply of minor tranquilizers, sedatives, and stimulants ordered by prescription from a pharmacist. Marijuana has gone from "Reefer Madness," cause of depravation and insanity, to very widespread use and acceptance; it may be legalized before the century is out. Alcoholics have gone from being viewed as weak-willed and immoral sinners to being accepted as people with a "disease." In Los Angeles, it is positively stylish, if you are well-to-do and abusing alcohol or cocaine, to go to the Betty Ford Center for rehabilitation (Corkery, 1985).

A differentiation needs to be made between the *therapeutic* and the *recreational* uses of drugs. (There is also a religious use made of drugs like peyote by the Native American Church, but few Indians or non-Indians use alcohol, cocaine, tranquilizers, etc., for religious purposes.) This differentiation between the therapeutic and recreational use has not changed over time: when women used opiate-laced tonics as medication for a variety of disorders, there was no outcry. Nor is there a current outcry about relatively heavy female use of psychoactive drugs. Feminists may protest that women are overmedicated, but it is really not considered a social problem. Nor is it viewed as a medical problem; women are at higher risk for adverse drug effects, e.g., tardive dyskinesia (Simpson et al., 1978) and negative drug interaction effects, but that has little apparent effect on the number of prescriptions written.

In terms of defining women problem drug users, consider Woman "A", for example, who is a regular user of minor tranquilizers and sedatives or who is taking prescribed antidepressant drugs, and Woman "B" who smokes two packs of cigarettes a day. By current standards, neither presents drug problems. However, Woman "C" who drinks frequently and heavily, and Woman "D" who is a user of cocaine or heroin, *are* considered problem users. Women "C" and "D" are, in fact, considered "sicker" and more deviant than their male counterparts (Karpman, 1948; Gomberg, 1974; Rosenfield, 1982).

The fact that women are viewed differently than male drug abusers raises the question whether a substance is being used for medicinal or recreational purposes. Women may be stigmatized for their apparent hedonism but the fact is that women appear to use virtually all drug substances in more or less medicinal ways. Kolb (1938) commented fifty years ago that women used opiates to relieve, ". . . mental and physical distress," whereas men were more likely to use opiates recreationally, i.e., for the pleasure involved. There is, of course, a component of relief-of-distress in men's use of substances just as there is pleasure-seeking in women's use. But our hypothesis remains: *women tend more frequently to use substances in medicinal, therapeutic ways than do men,* and they tend to do this because of patterns of social approval and disapproval. Gender socialization orients women and men toward different patterns of drug use and even toward different substances. Women, generally being more law-abiding than men, gravitate toward more legally acceptable, socially-acceptable substances such as cigarettes, alcohol, and use of prescriptive drugs.

To sum up, women are users of prescription drugs, psychoactive drugs and patent medicines to a greater extent than men, but this is not viewed as drug abuse; it is medication. The heavy use of alcohol and/or illicit drugs is disapproved whether it occurs among women or among men— that *is* drug abuse. And a widely-held view is that such drug abuse, i.e., heavy use of alcohol and/ or illicit drugs, is *more* disapproved by society for women than for men (Lisansky, 1957; Gomberg, 1974; Fillmore, 1984).

What follows is a discussion of some of the issues and questions linked to the problem of greater female than male use of medication and psychoactive drugs. Then I will present some of the viewpoints and explanations that have been offered about the problematic use of alcohol and illicit drugs by women. Finally, I will raise a number of research questions dealing with women and drug substances, questions which I believe need to be answered.

Women and Medication

The Physiological Events in Women's Lives

It is a fact of life that the biological stages of the life span are more clearly marked for women than for men. Men's biosexual lives are also phased, but the phases are not as clearly defined as the menstrual cycle, pregnancy, childbirth and lactation, and menopause. These are not only *biological* events, they are events surrounded by folk beliefs, myths, and attitudes. In many cultures the menstruating woman is perceived as "unclean," and is often isolated during her period or required to cleanse herself ritualistically at its termination. At the end of the last century Havelock Ellis observed that it was still believed that menstruating women would despoil religious rites, sour milk, spoil the wine fermentation, and cause plants to die (Hays, 1964). Research attempts to pin down the relationship between stages of the menstrual cycle and efficiency of performance, moodiness, depression, psychiatric symptoms, and suicide attempts, have produced ambiguous results at best. There have been some interesting attempts to link stages of the menstrual cycle to psychoanalytical dream interpretation, to suicide, and to blood alcohol concentration (Benedek & Rubinstein, 1939; Wetzel & McClure, 1972; Jones & Jones, 1976).

There are several levels on which this linkage between women's physiological cyclical life events and the prescription of medication may be approached. There are women's own perceptions of these events, and there are the perceptions of others, including the perceptions of physicians or other health caretakers. Many women turn to analgesics, diuretics, and tranquilizers at stages of the menstrual cycle. It is women who take "the pill" to avoid contraception and other pills to stimulate fertility. It is women for whom estrogen and similar substances have been prescribed in menopause. Yet reliable information about the effects of various prescribed drugs on hormonal or behavioral responses is minimal (Halbreich et al., 1984). Women themselves share in the social attitudes and mythology about menstruation, and while some women do indeed experience pain and discomfort, menstruation, pregnancy and menopause are, for most women, normal biological events that do not necessarily require psychoactive medication. I have argued that substance use for pleasure, for erotic enhancement, or for "highs" has not been sanctioned for women, but medicine is always permitted. It is difficult to decide whether educational campaigns directed toward lessened use of psychoactive medication for normal physiological cycles should first target the women themselves or the caregivers in order to reduce the misuse of psychoactive substances. Physicians, however, will continue to prescribe tranquilizers as long as women wish to use them. Perhaps increasing economic independence will produce a recognition of the physiological events in women's lives as normal, healthy events for most women, which will not require self-medication or excessive reliance on physician's prescription pads.

The Relative Health Status of Men and Women

Women experience more acute illness, and men have more serious chronic conditions and more injuries during their lifetimes. The data on chronic medical conditions present a mixed picture: women after age 45 have more chronic illness than do men. Men, however, have higher prevalence rate for "killer" conditions, i.e., major causes of death (Verbrugge, 1981).

Gender-defined social roles lead to health risks, including hazards, lifestyle behaviors, and role-linked stresses. Such roles also define health attitudes and the availability of medical/health care. Verbrugge (1982) has included both "real morbidity" and "perceived morbidity" as producing differences in the sexes' use of medications. There are sex differences in exposure to hazards, in lifestyle behaviors, in role-linked stresses, in health attitudes, and in use of the health care systems. Probably the most significant difference lies in *health attitudes:* in general, women seem more concerned about health problems, and their socially-defined role behaviors do not encourage the kind of stoicism (and denial of symptoms) which is part of men's "macho" behavior. Women consistently report worse health status than men do. Women use more outpatient health services, make more visits to a physician per year, are more likely to have a regular source of medical care, and are more likely to seek psychiatric help. The importance of visits to physicians as related to use of prescribed medication has been demonstrated (Bush & Osterweis, 1978). The differences of physicians' attitudes toward medical complaints by men and by women has also been demonstrated (Armitage, Schneiderman, & Bass, 1979).

It would appear that gender differences in "real morbidity," perceived health status, use of physicians' services, and attitudes of physicians all play a role in producing the gender differential in prescription practices. Questions have been raised: since women use health services more, is the difference in prescription and medication based primarily on the greater frequency of visits? Cooperstock (1976) has pointed out that:

> recent statistics in Ontario indicate that greater use of physicians' services by women is an inadequate explanation of the higher rate of prescribing psychotropic drugs. (p. 760)

Another question is, do women request drugs more often than do men? Again, data are scarce, but one report does suggest that women patients *sought* and received more drugs than male patients (Winstead et al., 1974).

The issue of relative health status of the two sexes is further complicated by other demographic variables, such as age, education, employment status, and marital status.

Mental Health Issues

It is hardly necessary to reiterate the consistent finding of higher prevalence of depression in women or to review the epidemiology of suicide. Women make more suicide attempts than men, but men are more often suicide completers than are women. There is disagreement as to whether women have higher rates of mental disorder than men. Gove and Tudor (1977) concluded that rates were higher for women, but Dohrenwend and Dohrenwend (1977) have concluded that sex differences in *overall* rates of mental illness are nonexistent. The issues seem to revolve around the question of whether investigators include "personality disorders" or not. Rates are higher for women when they are excluded from mental illness counts.

Although there are many works about gender and mental health issues (e.g., Gomberg & Franks, 1979), it is necessary to distinguish between disordered, diagnosable, symptomatic behaviors on the one hand, and "psychological distress" on the other. *Diagnosable mental disorders* may occur with approximately equal frequency in both sexes, although particular disorders will vary in prevalence by gender. But there is a great deal of evidence that *psychological distress* occurs more frequently among women than among men (Selected Symptoms, 1970). The question is whether the prescription of psychoactive drugs, minor tranquilizers, sedatives, stimulants, antidepressants, etc., is really warranted as medication for psychological distress. The highest risk candidates for depression among women are young poor women with young children at home, unemployed, and often with very little emotional or any other kind of support (Brown & Harris, 1978). Are these problems solved with medication, with tranquilizers? Even if a biological/genetic vulnerability to mild depression is demonstrated, are tranquilizers the solution?

Sex Roles, Health, and Medication

The physiological events in women's lives and their physical, mental, and economic health are all part of a socially-assigned role, i.e., the responsibilities and the rights, privileges and immunities assigned to each of the sexes. In a way, it is ironic to describe housewives and homemakers as living a "traditional role," because women have always worked outside the home, on farms, in factories, or as slave labor, and inside the home as immigrant home industry workers. It is a recent historical development that defines the feminine role as exclusively homemaker. The rise of a large middle class in the affluent, industrialized countries produced that definition.

Insofar as use of substances is concerned, it appears that use of medication and very moderate use of intoxicants by women are acceptable in Western societies. Intoxication, pleasure seeking, and heavier use of substances is not acceptable. If a pregnant woman ingests a prescribed substance which does fetal damage (thalidomide), society reacts with sympathy, but no blame is attached to the woman or the physician. If, however, she uses heroin or drinks heavily during a pregnancy, she has voluntarily chosen this course and therefore carries societal censure. Fetal impairment, whether transient, moderate or severe, is attributable to her lack of control and self-indulgence.

Even single episodes of intoxication may be taboo, counter to assigned female role. In a cross-cultural comparison of sex roles, Child, Barry, and Bacon (1965) commented,

> It seems reasonable to expect that most societies would limit drinking and drunkenness in women more than in men. Under the general prevailing conditions of human life, temporary incapacity of a woman is more threatening than is temporary incapacity of a man. For example, care of a field can be postponed for a day, but care of a child cannot. The general social role of the sexes makes drunkeness more threatening in women than in men. (p. 60)

Certainly for the helpless infant nurturant care may not be postponed. But intoxication threatens many different kinds of behaviors: indeed the care of a crop or a hunt may be postponed, but if it threatens the food supply of a community, it is no small matter.

Another aspect of assigned female role is that of caretaker of the sick and the old, but the relationship between this and female medication use has not been worked out. Szasz (1974) wryly comments on the fantasy of, "male parthenogenesis . . . of the birth of medicine," and adds that, "although the noble priest-physicians of antiquity are no doubt the far-distant ancestors of the modern medical scientist, his next of kin is his mother—the medieval white witch" (p. 62). Whether woman's role in a society is shaman/healer/white witch or caretaker, there would appear to be a link between these roles and women's attitudes and practices surrounding medication (Gomberg, 1982).

How does the nurturer obtain nurturance? How do women satisfy their needs for nurturance? A cross-cultural survey of sex differences in socialization (Barry, Bacon, & Child, 1957) reports that of the 110 cultures studied, in 82 percent of the cultures, socialization for "nurturance" is greater for girls. In no culture was socialization pressure toward "nurturance" found to be greater for boys than for girls. "Responsibility" training in socialization was greater for girls in 61 percent of the cultures studied; for boys, in 11 percent. Current studies indicate that the average working woman spends more time at work and works harder than does the average working man (ISR Newsletter, 1977). For married women in the workplace, there are dual work role responsibilities—in both Marxist and capitalist societies.

It is suggested that one way of obtaining nurturance in a legitimate, socially-acceptable way, is through perceived illness and resulting health care and medication. A socially-permissible way for the woman nurturer to be taken care of is to be sick, to seek health care, to seek and take medication. Perhaps there is a symbolism in the drugs women are prescribed.

Women and Drug/Alcohol Abuse

Before discussing some of the explanations of women's substance abuse, it is worth empha- sizing the "invisibility" of women's problems. This would appear to contradict the assertion that the last decade has witnessed a mounting concern about women's substance abuse (the concern mixed with blame and attributions to emancipation). Women's problems are invisible in the sense that the focus, concern, and research are almost always on the male; the female counterpart has until recently been ignored. Thus, in 1957 when I published some findings about women (Lisansky, 1958), there were only four research reports about the woman alcoholic and, years later, when Sandmaier titled her book on female alcohol abuse, *The Invisible Alcoholics* (1980), it was still an appropriate adjective. The sex bias in alcoholism research has been pointed out many times and the relatively fewer facilities available to women alcoholics and drug abusers has also been pointed out.

This is not unique to substance abuse. A book about "shopping bag ladies" (Rousseau, 1981) comments about the invisibility of homeless women. A recent review of the literature on alcohol and sexuality (Gomberg, in press) revealed a paucity of research literature about alcoholism and homosexual men, but virtually nothing on the alcoholism of lesbian women. Nor is "invisibility" confined to women with problems. A recent letter from a woman business executive which ap- peared in *Working Woman* magazine (March, 1985) describes the behavior of a male visitor to the company laboratory: "it was as though I did not exist" (p. 33). Women, a Simone de Beauvoir (1953) and others have pointed out, constitute "the second sex."

There is relatively little research literature on women substance abusers compared to male substance abusers, but speculation and theorizing about why some women abuse drugs and alcohol do exist. Some of these explanations are biological, some psychodynamic, others sociocultural, and probably the most useful of all are those explanations which integrate these viewpoints. The origins of behavior, acceptable and unacceptable, are more complex and multilayered than can be ex- plained by any one discipline.

Biological Explanations

More work has been done on the genetic predisposition toward female alcoholism, perhaps because there are more women with alcohol problems than with narcotics dependence. Two reports about genetics and female alcohol abuse have appeared (Goodwin et al., 1977; Bohman et al., 1981). There is general agreement that for both men and women "there is a hereditary factor in alcoholism" (Holden, 1985). While a hereditary factor has not been specifically elucidated for women narcotics addicts, it is likely, at a time when studies are regularly reporting genetic factors in criminality, smoking, food likes and dislikes, etc., that a genetic factor will also be discovered to explain women's narcotic addiction.

There have also been explanations of alcoholism in terms of nutritional, vitamin or enzymatic deficiencies, or in terms of body build. A study which appeared 30 years ago (Fleetwood, 1955) reported the existence of a "resentment substance" in the blood which diminished in alcoholics when they drank. More recent work on the metabolism of alcohol and biochemical effects is summarized by Roach (1982), Majchrowicz (1982), and Lieber (1982). It would appear that the biochemical response to alcohol and to drug substances may be different among high-risk and low-risk people. This is work in progress.

Psychodynamic or Psychological Explanations

Although *psychoanalysis* offered an explanation of male alcoholism in terms of "early oral fixation," there was no theory to account for female alcohol/drug problems. As with psychoanalytic theory in general, the reasoning was that if it explained the male, it explained the female. Explanation was rooted in distortion of the early mother-child relationship. If female development is described in terms of passivity and masochism (Shainess, 1984; Caplan, 1985), do these constructs underlie substance abuse? Perhaps Menninger (1938) offered a theoretical construct relevant to female alcoholism in his description of alcoholism as self-destructive behavior. Suicide attempts are frequent among women substance abusers and their low self-evaluation often appears clinically in self-abasing behaviors.

Learning theory and social learning theorists have focused on the role of alcohol as a tension reducer, in minimizing anxiety, fear, and conflicting feelings. Drinking behavior and alcoholic behavior are learned because they are reinforced. In later stages of problem drinking one reward of alcohol lies in postponing the unpleasant effects of withdrawal. Social learning theory also deals with the social environment, i.e., the cultural norms with which a person grows up and the stresses which are experienced. Learning theory is presumably equally applicable to both men and women.

A promising current line of explanation deals with *stress and coping mechanisms*. It is now understood that the term *"stress"* is too broad, and that distinguishing between different kinds and amounts may be useful. One classification is of stress as chronic, acute and "daily hassle" stress, while another is of stress as physical interpersonal, internal, or environmental. We are coming to understand that a stressful *event* by itself explains little; the meaning and significance of stress is in the *response* to the event, the *experience* of stress, i.e., in distress. A useful model of stress and coping has been drawn by Maracek (1978). An event not experienced as stressful does not necessitate coping, but if the event *is* experienced as distress the question then is whether the individual can cope successfully. Those who are poor copers with minimally-effective defenses against stressful experience are at higher risk for the development of psychological disorders, including substance abuse. Ongoing research with women alcoholics in treatment facilities and a group of control women suggests that there are significant differences between the two groups in the experience of stress and in the repertoire of responses for coping with stress (Gomberg, in press).

One category of stresses which has recently had some attention is sexual trauma. Whether men and women are more likely to become drug abusers when there is a history of sexual abuse and whether this is more relevant as an explanation of female alcoholism than of male alcoholism, are questions.

Related to explanations dealing with stress and coping mechanisms are concepts dealing with social supports and social networks. The application of these concepts to explanations of female substance abuse should be productive.

One explanation of substance abuse is the existence of particular *personality traits* manifested by individuals who became substance abusers. This explanation assumes that the traits preexist the substance abuse and indeed are part of the etiology. A review of this literature indicates that the characteristics identified so far are impulsivity, nonconformity, gregariousness, and poor self-concept (Barnes, 1979). Supporting evidence is uneven, but the behaviors involved in impulsivity and poor impulse control as related to the development of drinking problems do seem to have sound data support. Studies of adolescent substance use have noted the relevance of impulsivity (Honzik, 1984), and studies of adolescent substance abuse have stressed the importance of impulsive personality style (Zucker, 1979). Impulsivity and antisocial behavior have been compared among adolescent girls and adolescent boys (Zucker & DeVoe, 1975). One of the few longitudinal studies of women raises the question of impulsivity and impulse control (Jones, 1971). Ongoing research studies of women alcoholics in treatment facilities show an early history of difficulties in impulse control. Compared with nonalcoholic women, the alcoholic women have run away from home more often, dropped out of school earlier, made significantly more suicide attempts, etc. (Gomberg, in press).

As an explanation of female substance abuse problems, *gender role* and problems generated by sexually-assigned role have come in for a good deal of recent attention. Sex role explanations have varied widely: drug abuse among women has been attributed to overidentification with the *traditional* role ("hyperfemininity"), to adoption of a nontraditional *"emancipated"* role with its freedoms and responsibilities, to *conflict* over traditional versus nontraditional sex role styles, and to *dual role burdens* usually borne by married women working outside the home who work a regular workday and then come home to domestic responsibilities. Female substance abuse has also been linked to the low level, low status, unstimulating occupations in which a very large percentage of women work.

One direction of sex role explanations has been the equation of stereotypes of women's behavior with characteristics of depression. Whether sex role socialization is linked to women's depression is a question. There is no question about the linkage of depression and substance abuse. Depression runs through the literature on female alcoholism, and depressed mood is apparently characteristic of women narcotics addicts as well. Since mild depression characteristically occurs more often among women than among men, the question is why does depression sometimes lead to greater substance abuse among women? Another question is, why does depression occur more frequently among women?

It should be noted that many behaviors repeatedly reported in the literature of female substance abuse are included in the psychological explanations: feelings of distress and depression, inadequate coping mechanisms, low self-esteem, impulsivity and difficulties related to sex role. It is not always clear whether they are antecedent to or a consequence of substance abuse.

Sociological Explanations

People grow up and mature within a family, a primary group with particular characteristics and particular interactions. This is the family-of-origin, early social environment. *Socialization* is a developmental process in which attitudes, beliefs, and behaviors relating to drug substances, as well as to all other aspects of life, are learned from others. Nor is the process restricted to the family. Early on, the child begins to learn from his/her peers, and pressures to drink or to experiment with drugs often come from peers. Coping mechanisms are also learned during this process of socialization. Although there are similarities, the processes and goals of socialization differ for the two sexes; clearly, this is how sex roles are learned. Socialization theories probably are most closely linked to sex role, stress, coping, and are consistent with social learning theory explanations of substance use and abuse by women.

Sociocultural theories are based on the literature of ethnic and religious group differences in drinking. Demographic (gender, age, education, etc.) and anthropological studies of various subgroups within the United States (Irish, Italians, Jews, Chinese, etc.) have produced consistent results over time. Sociocultural theory goes back to Bales' (1946) exposition of three factors which he believes determine a group or society's use of alcohol and drugs: the level of tension within the group, the norms relating to substance use, and the degree to which the group offers alternatives to deal with stress. This view would link to sex role and social learning theories in a psychosocial, integrated theory seeking to explain substance use and abuse.

Social deviance theory has viewed deviant behavior such as substance abuse as socially-defined bahavior, i.e., "conduct which is generally thought to require the attention of social control agencies" (Erikson, 1964). Deviance is not intrinsic to the behavior, but is a property conferred on the behavior by society. Persons who are labeled "delinquent" or "alcoholic" continue to engage in those roles. Since deviance is defined by the social group in any given time and place, it is interesting to note the different directions such labeling may take. When a society defines alcoholism as a "disease," that society has determined that alcoholic persons have an "illness" and are therefore entitled to a "sick" role.

It seems to be true that female deviants are considered less worthy than male deviants, and there is literature on "stigma" which supports that view. Generally, men and women receive more severe societal reactions when the deviant behavior is inconsistent with traditional sex role norms: men, for example, are more likely to be hospitalized for depression, women for substance abuse (Rosenfield, 1982). One form of deviance theory speaks of "blaming the victim," and interprets disordered or deviant behavior as a response to oppressive conditions. Cloward and Piven (1979), for example, explain female deviant behavior as "hidden protests . . . and resistance" (p. 651).

When one considers biological, psychological, and sociological explanations of substance abuse, it is clear that each set of theories has only limited applicability. The most productive course of action is to integrate explanations in a theory which will explain vulnerability to substance abuse problems in terms of a person's biological, psychological, and social history and characteristics (Gomberg & Lisansky, 1984).

Research Questions

Having reviewed some of the available information about women's use and abuse of various substances and having stated some of the explanations offered to explain the origins of substance abuse among women, I would recommend priority status for several research questions.

1. Definition and elaboration is needed in the distinction between *medicinal and recreational use of drug substances.* When does a social use of a substance shift to use of the same substance to reduce tension, ease psychic pain, or heighten emotions? Does addiction carry with it the component of medicinal use to diminish the painful withdrawal from the drug? Is the context in which a drug is used critical in determination of whether it is used medicinally or recreationally? Perhaps motivation theories are relevant, but will one set of motivations explain the socially-acceptable use of a substance like alcohol and the deviant, excessive, problematic use of it as well?

2. Since we have a fair amount of evidence that, at particular stages of a pregnancy, heavy drinking or heroin-addictive behavior produce *teratogenic risks,* the research question becomes one of determining the effects of prescribed medications, sedatives, stimulants, psychoactive drugs, and even patent medicines, on fetal development (e.g., Cooper, 1978, Chasnoff et al., 1983). Considering the number of women involved, it is important to know about the effects of mood-

modifying drugs and other medications on fetal development. And still considering teratogenic risks, an important research question is: What is the effect of the father's heavy alcohol or drug use on the fetus?

3. Epidemiologists have given as data about *gender differences in psychotropic drug use.* Further questions include: When men and women show the same symptomatic behaviors, are chemotherapeutic drugs prescribed equally or differently for the two sexes? To what extent are mood-modifying drugs being prescribed for insomnia, anxiety, boredom, loneliness, loss, stress, i.e., for the human condition? Do prescribing practices show gender differences among younger people, young adults, the middle aged and the elderly? Are medical practitioners, who prescribe psychoactive drugs more frequently than other physicians, more likely to hold stereotypical views of male and female character? What is the relationship between development of a new psychoactive drug by a drug company, the advertising, the activity of the "detail persons," and the extent to which physicians write prescriptions for the new drug?

4. *Changes in the workplace:* probably the single most important change in female role has been the increasing presence of women in the workplace. This has had positive effects for women, yet it has also been reported that problem drinking has significantly higher rates among employed married women than among single working women or housewives (Johnson, 1982). Recent work contradicts the latter finding, reporting "no evidence of unusually-heavy drinking among working wives" (Wilsnack, Wilsnack, & Klassen, 1984). It would seem to be a good time to begin clarifying the issues involved in women's working outside the home and women's use of alcohol and drugs. In which occupational classifications is "role overload" most likely to occur? Is substance abuse more likely to appear more frequently in those occupations with least prestige, low wages, little power? Are women in higher prestige managerial positions likely to respond to heightened pressure and drive for achievement with more drinking and/or drug use? What is the relationship between employment, use of medical care resources, and the use of drug substances?

5. *Psychological theory clarification:* although the terms are widely used, there is need for definition and classification of stresses, of coping mechanisms, of social supports. How do these phenomena interact?

6. *Prevention efforts* are called for, particularly for adolescents and young adults. To what extent may we utilize the current trends toward health promotion and the current interest in fitness, diet and exercise to combat drug abuse? Can we design programs that will be effective in lowering the number of cigarette smokers among young women, as well as moderating their drinking? Can we design programs targeted to persons at high risk for alcohol and other substance abuse problems?

These questions represent only a few of the many research problems that need to be addressed. The tasks are enormous. Are we up to the challenge?

Notes

1. I am indebted to Mark Keller, Editor Emeritus of the *Journal of Studies on Alcohol,* for the Talmudic reference.

References

Armitage, K. J., Schneiderman, L. J., & Bass, R. A. (1979). Response of physicians to medical complaints in men and women. *Journal of the American Medical Association, 241,* 2186–2187.

Bales, R. F. (1946). Cultural differences in rates of alcoholism. *Quarterly Journal of Studies on Alcohol, 6,* 480–499.

Balter, M. B., Levine, J., & Manheimer, D. I. (1974). Cross-national study of the extent of antianxiety/ sedative drug use. *New England Journal of Medicine, 290,* 769–774.

Barnes, G. E. (1979). The alcoholic personality: a reanalysis of the literature. *Journal of Studies on Alcohol, 40,* 571–634.

Barry, H., Bacon, M. K., & Child, I. L. (1957). A cross-cultural survey of some sex differences in socialization. *The Journal of Abnormal and Social Psychology, 55,* 327–332.

Benedek, T. & Rubinstein, B. B. (1939). Ovarian activity and psychodynamic processes. *Psychosomatic Medicine, 1.*

Berkin, C. R., & Norton, M. B. (Eds.). (1979). *Women of America: a history.* Boston: Houghton Mifflin.

Bohman, M., Sigvardsson, S., & Cloninger, C. R. (1981). Maternal inheritance of alcohol abuse: cross-fostering analysis of adopted women. *Archives of General Psychiatry, 38,* 965–969.

Boulding, E. (1976). Familial constraints on women's work roles. In N. Blaxall & B. Regan (Eds.), *Women and the workplace* (pp. 95–117). Chicago: University of Chicago Press.

Brown, G. W. & Harris, T. (1978). *Social origins of depression, a study of psychiatric disorder in women.* New York: The Free Press.

Burt, M. R., Glynn, T. J., & Sowder, B. J. (1979). *Psychosocial characteristics of drug-abusing women.* DHEW publication No. ADM 80-917. Rockville, MD: National Institute on Drug Abuse.

Bush, P. J., & Osterweis, M. (1978). Pathways to medicine use. *Journal of Health and Social Behavior, 19,* 179–189.

Bush, P. J., & Rabin, D. L. (1976). Who's using nonprescribed medicines? *Medical Care, XIV,* 1014–1023.

Cahalan, D., Cisin, I. H., & Crossley, H. M. (1969). *American drinking practices: a national study of drinking behavior and attitudes.* New Haven: College and University Press.

Caplan, P. J. (1985). *The myth of women's masochism.* New York: Dutton.

Child, I. L., Barry, H., & Bacon, M. K. (1965). Sex differences in a cross-cultural study of drinking. *Quarterly Journal of Studies on Alcohol,* Supplement No. 3, 49–61.

Chasnoff, I. J., Burns, W. J., & Schnoll, S. H. (1984). Perinatal addiction: the effects of maternal narcotic and nonnarcotic substance abuse on the fetus and neonate. *45th Annual Meeting of the Committee on Problems of Drug Dependence. N.I.D.A. Research Monograph No. 49,* 220–226.

Clark, W. B., & Midanik, L. (1982). Alcohol use and alcohol problems among U.S. adults: results of the 1979 national survey. In *Alcohol consumption and related problems.* NIAAA Alcohol and Health Monograph No. 1. Publication No. ADM 82-1190, Washington, D.C.

Cloward, R. A., & Piven, F. F. (1979). Hidden protest: the channeling of female innovation and resistance. *Signs: Journal of Women in Culture and Society, 4,* 651–669.

Cooper, S. J. (1978). Psychotropic drugs in pregnancy: morphological and psychological adverse effects on offspring. *Journal of Biosocial Science, 10,* 321–334.

Cooperstock, R. (1971). Sex differences in the use of mood-modifying drugs: an explanatory model. *Journal of Health and Social Behavior, 12,* 238–244.

Cooperstock, R. (1975). A critical examination of two studies of psychotropic drug consumption. *Addiction Res. Foundation Substudy 716.*

Cooperstock, R. (1976). Psychtropic drug use among women. *Canadian Medical Association Journal, 115,* 760–763.

Corea, G. (1977). The hidden malpractice: how American medicine treats women as patients and professionals. New York: William Morrow and Co., Inc.

Corkery, P. J. (1985). Addiction a L.A. mode. *The New Republic,* July 8, 1985, 18–21.

De Beauvoir, S. (1953). *The Second Sex.* New York: Knopf.

Dohrenwend, B. P., & Dohrenwend, B. S. (1977). Reply to Gove and Tudor's comment on 'Sex differences in psychiatric disorders'. *American Journal of Sociology, 82,* 1336–1345.

Erikson, K. T. (1964). Notes on the sociology of deviance. In H. S. Becker (Ed.), *Perspectives on Deviance: The other side.* New York: Free Press.

Ferrence, R. G. (1980). Sex differences in the prevalence of problem drinking. In O. J. Kalant (Ed.), *Alcohol and Drug Problems in Women.* (pp. 69–124). New York: Plenum.

Fidell, L. S. (1982). Gender and drug use and abuse. In I. Al-Issa (Ed.), *Gender and psychopathology.* (pp. 221–236). New York: Academic Press.

Fillmore, K. M. (1984). "When angels fall": women's drinking as cultural preoccupation and as reality. In S. C. Wilsnack & L. J. Beckman (Eds.), *Alcohol problems in women* (pp. 7–36). New York: Guilford Press.

127

Fishburne, P. M., Abelson, H. I., & Cisin, I. (1979). *National survey on drug abuse: main findings,* 1979, Rockville, MD: National Institute on Drug Abuse.

Fleetwood, M. F. (1955). Biochemical experimental investigations of emotions and chronic alcoholism. In O. Diethelm (Ed.), *Etiology of chronic alcoholism* (pp. 43–109). Springfield, IL: Charles C. Thomas.

Friedan, B. (1963). *The feminine mystique.* New York: Norton.

Fundamental facts concerning beverage alcohol. (1956). Columbus, OH: Lewis C. Berger.

Gomberg, E. S. (1974). Women and alcoholism. In V. Franks & V. Burtle (Eds.), *Women in Therapy* (pp. 169–190). New York: Brunner/Mazel.

Gomberg, E. S. L. (1982). Historical and political perspective: women and drug use. *Journal of Social Issues. 38,* 9–24.

Gomberg, E. S. L. (forthcoming). Alcohol, gender and sexual problems: an interface. In W. M. Cox (Ed.), *Treatment and prevention of alcohol problems: a resource manual.* New York: Academic Press.

Gomberg, E. S. L. (in press). Women and alcoholism: psychosocial issues. In *Proceedings of the National Research Conference on Women and Alcohol,* Seattle, Washington, May, 1984.

Gomberg, E. S. & Franks, V. (1979). (Eds.), *Gender and disordered behavior,* New York: Brunner/Mazel.

Gomberg, E. S. L. & Lisansky, J. M. (1984). Antecedents of alcohol problems in women. In S. C. Wilsnack & L. J. Beckman (Eds.), *Alcohol problems in women* (pp. 233–259). New York: The Guilford Press.

Goodwin, D. W., Schulsinger, F., Knop, J., Mednick, S., & Guze, S. B. (1977). Psychopathology in adopted and nonadopted daughters of alcoholics. *Archives of General Psychiatry, 34,* 1005–1009.

Gove, W. R., & Tudor, J. F. (1977). Sex differences in mental illness: a comment on Dohrenwend and Dohrenwend. *American Journal of Sociology, 82,* 1327–1336.

Gritz, E. R. (1980). Problems related to the use of tobacco by women. In O. J. Kalant (Ed.), *Alcohol and Drug Problems in Women* (pp. 487–543). New York: Plenum.

Gusfield, J. R. (1967). Moral passage: the symbolic process in public designations of deviance. *Social Problems, 15,* 175–188.

Halbreich, U., Asnis, G., Goldstein, S., Nathan, R. S., Zander, K. & Herne, J. V. (1984). Sex differences in response to psychopharmacological intervention in humans. *Psychopharmacology Bulletin, 20,* 526–530.

Hamilton, J. A., & Parry, B. (1983). Sex-related differences in clinical drug response: implications for women's health. *Journal of the American Medical Women's Association, 38,* 126–132.

Hartman, H. (1976). Capitalism, patriarchy and job segregation by sex. In N. Blaxall & B. Regan (Eds.), *Women and the workplace.* Chicago: University of Chicago Press.

Hays, H. R. (1964). *The dangerous sex: the myth of feminine evil.* New York: G. P. Putnam's Sons.

Holden, C. (1985). The neglected disease in medical education. *Science, 229,* 23 August, 1985, 741–742.

Honzik, M. P. (1984). Life span development. In M. R. Rosenzweig & L. W. Porter (Eds.), *Annual review of psychology* (35) (pp. 309–331). Palo Alto: Annual Reviews, Inc.

Johnson, P. B. (1982). Sex differences, women's roles and alcohol use: preliminary national data. *Journal of Social Issues, 38,* 93–116.

Jones, M. C. (1971). Personality antecedents and correlates of drinking patterns in women. *Journal of Consulting and Clinical Psychology, 36,* 61–69.

Jones, B. M. & Jones, M. K. (1976). Alcohol effects on women during the menstrual cycle. *Annals of the New York Academy of Sciences, 273,* 576–587.

Karpman, B. (1948). *The alcoholic woman.* Washington, D.C.: Linacre Press.

Leland, J. (1982). Gender, drinking, and alcohol abuse. In I. Al-Issa (Ed.), *Gender and psychopathology,* (pp. 201–236). New York: Academic Press.

Lieber, C. S. (1982). Medical issues; the disease of alcoholism. In E. L. Gomberg, H. R. White, & J. A. Carpenter (Eds.), *Alcohol, science and society revisited* (pp. 233–261). Ann Arbor: University of Michigan Press.

Lindbeck, V. L. (1972). The woman alcoholic: a review of the literature. *The International Journal of the Addictions, 7,* 567–580.

Lisansky, E. S. (1958). The woman alcoholic. *Annals of the American Academy of Political and Social Science, 351,* 73–82.

Majchrowicz, E. (1982). The role of blood in alcohol intoxication and addiction. In E. L. Gomberg, H. R. White, & J. A. Carpenter (Eds.), *Alcohol, science and society revisited* (pp. 171–185). Ann Arbor, MI: University of Michigan Press.

Maracek, J. (1978). Psychological disorders in women: indices of role strain. In I. H. Frieze, J. E. Parsons, P. B. Johnson, D. N. Ruble, & G. L. Zellman (Eds.), *Women and sex roles: a social psychological perspective* (pp. 255–276). New York: W. W. Norton & Co.

Marolla, J. A. & Scully, D. H. (1979). Rape and psychiatric vocabularies of motive. In E. S. Gomberg & V. Franks (Eds.), *Gender and disordered behavior: sex differences in psychopathology* (pp. 301–318). New York: Brunner/Mazel.

Marris, P. (1974). *Loss and change.* New York: Pantheon Books.

Martin, C. A., & Martin, W. R. (1980). Opiate dependence in women. In O. J. Kalant (Ed.), *Alcohol and drug problems in women* (pp. 465–485). New York: Plenum.

Menninger, K. (1938). *Man against himself.* New York: Harcourt, Brace & Co.

Monto, A. S., & Ullman, B. M. (1974). Acute respiratory illness in an American community. *Journal of the American Medical Association, 227,* 164–169.

Musto, D. F. (1973). *The American disease: origins of narcotic control.* New Haven: Yale University Press.

Nuehring, E. & Markle, G. E. (1974). Nicotine and norms: the reemergence of a deviant behavior. *Social Problems, 21,* 513–526.

Parry, H. J., Balter, M. B., Mellinger, G. D., Cisin, I. H., & Manheimer, D. I. (1973). National patterns of psychotherapeutic drug use. *Archives of General Psychiatry, 28,* 769–783.

Rainwater, L., & Yancey, W. L. (1967). *The Moynihan report and the politics of controversy.* Cambridge, MA: The M.I.T. Press.

Ray, O. (1983). *Drugs, society and human behavior.* St. Louis: Mosby.

Roach, M. K. (1982). The biochemical and physiological effects of alcohol. In E. L. Gomberg, H. R. White, & J. A. Carpenter (Eds.), *Alcohol, science and society revisited* (pp. 17–37). Ann Arbor: University of Michigan Press.

Rorabaugh, W. J. (1979). *The alcoholic republic: an American tradition.* New York: Oxford University Press.

Rosaldo, M. Z., & Lamphere, L. (Eds.) (1974). *Women, culture and society.* Stanford, CA: Stanford University Press.

Rosenfield, S. (1982). Sex roles and societal reactions to mental illnesses: the labeling of "deviant" deviance. *Journal of Health and Social Behavior, 23,* 18–24.

Rossi, A. S. (1964). Equality between the sexes: an immodest proposal. *Daedalus, 93,* 607–652.

Rousseau, A. M. (1981). *Shopping Bag Ladies.* New York: Pilgrim Press.

Sandmaier, M. (1980). *The invisible alcoholics: women and alcohol abuse in America.* New York: McGraw Hill Book Company.

Schuman, L. M. (1978). Patterns of smoking behavior. In M. E. Jarvik, J. W. Cullen, E. R. Gritz, T. N. Vogt, & L. J. West (Eds.), *Research on smoking behavior.* NIDA Monograph No. 17. Washington, D.C.

Selected symptoms of psychological distress. (1970). National Center for Health Statistics Series 11, No. 37. Rockville, MD: HEW.

Seward, G. H. (1946). *Sex and the social order.* New York: McGraw-Hill Book Co.

Shaw, S. (1980). The causes of increasing drinking problems amongst women: a general etiological theory. In *Camberwell Council on Alcoholism: Women and alcohol* (pp. 1–40). London: Tavistock.

Shainess, N. (1984). *Sweet suffering: woman as victim.* Indianapolis: Bobbs-Merrill.

Siegel, R. K. (1977). Cocaine: recreational use and intoxication. National Institute on Drug Abuse Research Monograph Series: *Cocaine.* Rockville, MD: DHEW 119–133.

Simpson, G. M., Varga, E., Lee, J. H., and Zoubok, B. (1978). Tardive dyskinesia and psychotropic drug history. *Psychopharmacology, 58,* 117–124.

Sinclair, A. (1962). *Prohibition, the era of excess.* Boston: Little, Brown.

Smith, D. E. (1984). Diagnostic, treatment and aftercare approaches to cocaine abuse. *Journal of Substance Abuse Treatment, 1,* 5–9.

Szasz, T. (1974). *Ceremonial chemistry. The ritual persecution of drugs, addicts and pushers.* New York: Anchor Press/Doubleday.

The Talmud (The Study of the Mishna) in Hebrew and Aramaic, Babylonian. I. Epstein (Ed.). London: Soncino Press.

Verbrugge, L. (1981). Sex differentials in health and mortality. In A. H. Stromberg (Ed.), *Women, health and medicine.* Palo Alto, CA: Mayfield Publishing Co.

Verbrugge, L. M. (1982). Sex differences in legal drug use. *Journal of Social Issues, 38,* 59–76.

Weitzman, L. J. (1985). *The divorce revolution: the unexpected social and economic consequences for women and children in America.* New York: The Free Press.

Wetzel, R. D. & McClure, J. N. (1972). Suicide and the menstrual cycle: a review. *Comprehensive Psychiatry, 13,* 369–374.

Who works at work? (1977). *ISR Newsletter, 5,* No. 3.

Wilsnack, R. W., Wilsnack, S. C., & Klassen, A. D. (1984). Women's drinking and drinking problems: patterns from a 1981 national survey. *American Journal of Public Health, 74,* 1231–1238.

Winstead, D., Blackwell, B., Anderson, A., & Ellers, M. K. (1974). Diazepam on demand: drug seeking behavior in anxious in-patients. *Archives of General Psychiatry, 30,* 349–351.

Working Woman magazine, March 1985, 33–34.

Zucker, R. A. (1979). Developmental aspects of drinking through the young adult years. In H. T. Blane & M. E. Chafetz (Eds.), *Youth, alcohol and social policy* (pp. 91–146). New York: Plenum.

Zucker, R. A., & Devoe, C. I. (1975). Life history characteristics associated with problem drinking and antisocial behavior in adolescent girls: a comparison with male findings. In R. D. Wirt, G. Winokur, & M. Roff (Eds.). *Life history research in psychopathology* (Vol. 4). Minneapolis: University of Minnesota Press.

12. The Unadmitted Problem

Muriel Nellis

For too long, the lonely anguish of women's drug and alcohol habits has been the subject of whispered confidences, gossip-column innuendoes, and hushed family embarrassment. For too long, this anguish has been viewed as an individual fall from grace. Admittedly, every situation is distinguished, in some way, from any other. These differences confirm the uniqueness of human experience, but they do not change a universal fact: an insidious epidemic has been raging among the women of this nation—addiction to drugs. All kinds of drugs, in tablets, capsules, and liquids—tranquilizers, sleeping pills, diet pills, pain killers, alcohol—over-the-counter and prescribed. And all of them legal. The combinations are literally mind boggling.

In 1978, the acting director of the National Institute on Drug Abuse told the House Select Committee on Narcotics Abuse and Control that, in the past year, 36 million women had used tranquilizers; 16 million used sedatives (sleeping pills); 12 million used stimulants primarily in the form of diet pills; and almost 12 million women received prescriptions for these drugs from doctors for the first time. Those numbers do not include whole classes of prescribed pain killers, all of which are mood altering and addictive. Nor do they include the billions of doses dispensed to patients directly, without a prescription, in doctors' offices, in military, public, or private hospitals, and in clinics or nursing homes. Nor do these statistics tell us how many of these women used combinations of prescription drugs or combined them with the most widely used depressant, alcohol. According to recent figures, at least half of the probably 10 million alcoholics in the country are women.

Social Stigma

For women, legal drug and alcohol abuse has become a common hazard that threatens one out of every four of us. The least suspecting among us is the most vulnerable. Elaine, like many other women, spent years trying to deny that she was dependent on drugs. She explained:

> It's hell for a woman to admit a drug habit. It's frightening too. I think most women on drugs or alcohol bear a heavier load of guilt and anger than men. A man on drugs may not get respect, but he can usually find some lady to care for him. We don't even have that to count on. A woman with a drug need is the lowest; she has not one single attribute that society values. And we feel so personally guilty. We blame ourselves; our men also blame us. And when we look outside for help, most professionals blame us too.

Since the social stigma associated with alcohol or drug use is particularly severe for women, it is all the more difficult for millions of women to confront this agonizing fact of life, even though it is a poorly kept secret. Writing about women and alcoholism, Joseph Hirsh offered the following insight on the cultural underpinnings of the existing social stigma:

> Women represent important social and moral symbols that are the bedrock of society. And when angels fall, they fall disturbingly far. We would rather have them in their place; which is another way of saying that they define and make our own place possible and even more comfortable.

We learn and are reminded that, as females, our actions affect the social, moral, and inspirational symbols of civilized behavior. We are our great-grandmothers' posterity. The responsibilities of tradition either invade or enrich our inner and outer lives, depending on whether or not meeting those expectations is perceived as oppressive or fulfilling.

It would follow that an imperfect cornerstone in the structure of our society is uncomfortable, even threatening. Generally, and individually, there has been a disinclination to consider, let alone accept, the existence of women addicts. Even now, that turn-away mentality persists.

• • •

The Pattern of Prescription-Drug Use

While it is now clear that women as well as men are pursuing dangerous drug-using paths, health specialists and official regulators continue to focus on a male drug culture. This presumably benign oversight has permitted a malignant growth to go unchecked. But neither ignorance nor denial will alter the facts.

Statistics attesting to the enormity of the patterns of prescription-drug use by women are shocking. Of the 160 million prescriptions written last year for tranquilizers, sedatives, and stimulants, only about 10 percent were authorized by psychiatrists, the one group of doctors whose training emphasizes the effects of psychoactive therapeutics. The largest percentage of these prescriptions was written by general practitioners, internists, and obstetricians-gynecologists. Depending on the drug classification—tranquilizer, sedative, or stimulant—60 to 80 percent of all the drugs prescribed were for female patients.

During each of the past several years, 90 percent of the women in hospitals for drug-related emergencies used legal, prescribed drugs; and the greatest number of drug-related deaths were the result of a combination of drugs plus alcohol.

Mental health experts estimate that about 10 percent of our population suffers from some serious mental disease, but that almost three-quarters of the nation is affected by disabling anxiety, insecurity, tension—the totality of the pressures of living. They further speculate that 70 to 80 percent of the symptoms of illness told to physicians, from sleeplessness to stomach aches, are but the open wounds of hidden life strains—an acceptable way to present pleas for relief.

This national malaise has particular significance for women, as the following facts indicate:

- At every age over 15, more women than men receive treatment for mental health problems. Except in the 25 to 34-year range, the institutional diagnosis of "depression" is far greater for women than men. (This greater female proportion, seen at hospitals and clinics, does not include those who are similarly treated by general practitioners, private mental-health therapists, religious counselors, self-help groups, or those troubled but untreated.)
- Women make the majority of visits to doctors. They have higher rates of admission to general hospitals and report more physical ailments.
- In addition, women enter and return to private psychiatric therapy in and outside of hospitals more often than men.
- Minimally, women are prescribed *more than twice* the amount of drugs than are men, *for the same psychological symptoms.*
- Although women of almost every description are represented in this emotionally distressed group, single women present the fewest symptoms of mental disorder; married women with families, the greatest number.

- A sizable percentage of women who finally seek help for emotional problems have already turned to alcohol or mood-affecting drugs for stress therapy.
- In the past ten years, the number of women who voluntarily sought help for alcoholism has doubled, though still not approaching the 5 million females presumed to be alcoholic. The number of deaths from cirrhosis of the liver is rapidly increasing among women.

Although there is a tendency within the health bureaucracy—and therefore the literature—to define dependence on mood-altering drugs separately from dependence on drugs prescribed for a specific physical symptom, questions are being raised increasingly about the validity of this distinction. What may begin as a purely medical therapy too often becomes an addictive problem.

Another traditional distinction without a difference between drugs and medications bears some comment. To differentiate between the so-called hard and soft drugs, implying degrees of change, it has become professionally fashionable to refer to physical and psychological addictions as dissimilar. Those women who have suffered stomach cramps, nervous perspiration, or irritability at either the thought, or the absence, of their customary drink or dose, strongly disagree with these arbitrary variations. A more realistic definition of addiction presumes that all function is intertwined.

Even to distinguish between addictive drugs by using the words *hard* and *soft*—like *major* and *minor*—promote the drawing of improper inferences regarding their destructive potential. Children born to mothers addicted to opiates frequently suffer immediate trauma that may cause long-term consequences. Likewise, the growing population of limbless, brain-damaged, facially disfigured, or motor-impaired children is evidence of the inherent dangers associated with maternal use of tranquilizers, sedatives, and alcohol.

At the Conference of Pain, Discomfort, and Humanitarian Care, recently held at the National Institutes of Health, many speakers concluded that the management of chronic pain has become a major problem, affecting as much as 40 percent of all Americans. Such common diseases as arthritis, gout, back pains, headaches, and rheumatism are costing sufferers not only pain, but billions of dollars each year, largely for ineffective treatment, much of it in the form of addictive drugs.

It appears that too many doctors are responding to, "It doesn't matter what's causing it, just help." They are helping by prescribing more drugs and, in some cases, causing new problems. Specialists in pain clinics are openly concerned by the apparent absence of understanding among general practitioners of the peculiar and unpleasant interactions between different pain relievers. Similarly, among behavioral specialists there is great consternation over the simultaneous prescription of sedatives with pain drugs, which often promote serious physical and emotional depression.

Sadly, the history of progress in drug development is spotty and repetitious. Too often a new discovery is no more than a variation on an older, troublesome theme. Just as heroin was perceived as an alternative treatment for morphine addiction, now methadone is the (addictive) substitute for heroin. The "major" tranquilizers, correctly hailed as reducing the use of electroconvulsive shock treatments or brain surgery in severe psychotic disturbance, are now overprescribed for traumas and neurotic conditions that would never have required or been treated by the earlier, dramatic procedures. In the same continuum of reduced risk, barbiturates and other heavy sedatives were replaced by the so-called minor tranquilizers. But this breakthrough foisted more of these drugs on larger populations—for a wider variety of milder nondisease conditions.

Once again, new research, new remedies. New choices, new consequences. Increasing combinations are increasingly harmful. Some are lethal. The most serious problem we confront is not so much with any one drug, which, when taken wisely and prescribed carefully, may be very helpful, but rather with the growing numbers of compounds and variations of the same chemical classes, and the range of professionals empowered to dispense them.

"Minor" Tranquilizers—Major Hazard

To many physicians and patients, with little or no understanding of severe brain or mental disorders, "minor" tranquilizers are equated with mild ones, and *mild* sounds safe. Safe tranquilizers? Not on your life. True, there is virtually no drug that is completely safe, and certainly not for everyone. But this class of drugs, which comes in so many colors, bearing so many names, so freely prescribed for so many types and degrees of misery, is full of guile and without innocence.

Recently, Dr. David Smith, Director of the Haight-Ashbury Clinic in San Francisco, noted that withdrawal symptoms occurred in people who had taken only low, therapeutic doses of Valium for more than a year. (Valium is the single most prescribed drug in the United States.) Although former alcoholics seemed especially predisposed to this withdrawal reaction, persons without a history of alcoholism were also affected. Doris had such an experience.

> For five years after my first introduction to tranquilizers I used them daily. Not in large amounts, but regularly. First I took one for a way to sleep—when my head was so full of problems, and the noise of thinking kept me awake. After that, I took them to prevent anything from "getting to me." When my fourteen-year-old daughter asked me for one before a big test, I decided to get rid of the pills. I was miserable, my nerves were shot, and I felt like I had a virus—exhausted, then aching and tense. It took between two and three months before I felt normal.

As drugs proliferate and medical care becomes increasingly fragmented, overprescription becomes commonplace—and too easy to blame on the other guy. In surveys taken among doctors about overprescribing patterns, the respondents overwhelmingly indicate concern about "other doctors" who engage in the practice, but deny subscribing to that behavior themselves. As one doctor told me, "There are bad apples in any profession. The rest of us aren't responsible for them. That's a job for the authorities; it has nothing to do with me. I seldom use more than a couple dozen medications in my practice. I'm a specialist, and the hundreds of other compounds don't mean much to me."

Alas, they often mean *too* much to the patient who consults more than one specialist, including my good friend Kathy.

Just prior to starting a new job, Kathy went to her internist for a routine physical. She mentioned that she had heard that her new boss had a reputation as a perfectionist, and she admitted feeling some anxiety about it. Her doctor prescribed a mild, low-dose tranquilizer, just to get her "over the hump."

During her first week at work, Kathy strained a muscle in her neck. Since it was quite painful, an office mate sent Kathy to her own neurologist, who prescribed a "muscle relaxant." A week or so later, a totally unrelated condition, some ovary spasms, led Kathy to her gynecologist, who prescribed a third medication.

What Kathy didn't know until the reaction set in was that all three prescriptions contained different amounts of the same kind of tranquilizer.

They all looked different. They each had separate instructions. Each doctor was satisfied that I was healthy, except for some minor discomfort. Aside from asking about any allergies or family history of major diseases, they never questioned me about drugs.

Fortunately, Kathy's reaction to these drugs was paradoxical. Instead of becoming overly tranquilized, her behavior reversed, and her otherwise pleasant and friendly disposition turned curt and short-tempered. Out of common concern over this disquieting, uncharacteristic behavior, a group of long-time friends gathered to find out what was troubling her and to offer their help. She was astonished. She had no idea that her personality had been so affected. Together, Kathy and her friends traced the events that seemed to coincide with her erratic moods, and only then did the pattern of drug use emerge. It soon became clear that there was a relationship between her behavior and her visits to doctors, each followed by a new prescription.

Kathy did not know the active ingredients of the drugs prescribed, so she and a friend drove to the pharmacy that had sold her all three. They requested copies of the manufacturers' description circulars that accompany the drugs supplied to the pharmacists. Since there were no instructions from the doctors to withhold such information, surrendering the inserts was only a minor inconvenience to the druggist. Although the language of the pamphlets seemed undecipherable at first, it soon made her puzzling behavior clear. Somewhere in the small print Kathy found her own symptoms.

The circulars warned that "careful consideration should be given to the pharmacology of other psychotropics employed, which may potentiate the action of Valium." There might be "adverse reactions": "headaches," "constipation," "tremors." She had experienced them all. The pamphlets had a name for other behaviors she had shown: "paradoxical reactions." Examples of these included "acute hyperexcited states," "anxiety," "insomnia," and "rage." Kathy had mistakenly attributed her symptoms to her job and some physical demons.

Even if many physicians sincerely believe that the drugs they prescribe are not toxic, one cannot attribute similar naiveté to the industry that produced them and markets them, through the doctor, to the patient-consumer. I actually heard the head of a major medical advertising company describe how his company, through artful language and marketing campaigns, has helped "enlarge the whole concept of illness" in order to accommodate the classes of mood-altering drugs.

Target: The Female Consumer

Although they like to be thought of as public service institutions, the self-described ethical pharmaceutical manufacturers are among the most profit-minded industries in the world, and the most profitable pharmaceutical companies are those whose major sales are psychoactive drugs. It is estimated that this industry spends three or four times as much on advertising, sales, and promotion techniques as it does on research. In the case of mood-altering drugs, the promotional push has been particularly cost effective. Growth, both in production percentages and in gross profit per product, is greatest for those fortunate companies that have succeeded best in designing disease states—in enlarging the whole concept of illness—and thus designating the need for these broad-application, symptomatic "happiness" pills.

135

At a congressional hearing before the House Select Committee on Narcotics Abuse and Control in 1978, a representative of the Pharmaceutical Manufacturers Association (the lobbyists for the industry) was questioned by the chief counsel about the dismal, unattractive women seen repeatedly in medical journal ads. The unabashed response was:

> Illustrations in medical ads, are designed to attract the attention of the reader. They typically depict individuals whom the physician will relate to his own practice—people like those he's seen in his own office.

Let's look at how the pharmaceutical companies depict those people that *he* sees in *his* office. Using quasi-medical jargon to describe very real problems, the ads in medical journals aim to trigger responses in physicians' recognition of the stressful experiences of many of the women who populate their waiting rooms. Through this language, over the years, pharmaceutical companies have defined certain "diseases" as "environmental depression" and "empty-nest syndrome" and then come to the rescue with first one chemical cure, then another, and yet another. Many of the drugs with different patent names are, in fact, copycat drugs or combinations of drugs, all in the classification known as benzo-diazepine, better known and loved by too many as Valium, Librium, Librax, Dalmane, and others. These are the second generation of the "mild" tranquilizers sired by the meprobamates Miltown and Equanil.

Typically, in the single, double, or four-page ads that fill the pages (and the coffers) of the medical journals, one-half to two-thirds of the layout is pictorial. The visual impact is heightened by a phrase connoting a diagnosis. To the busy professional reader, the female-patient message is clear, regardless of the compressed small type that fulfills Federal Food and Drug Administration (FDA) requirements for indications of use, problems, and drug composition.

Thus, under the headline EMPTY-NEST SYNDROME, a full-page picture allows us to look inside five unpeopled rooms in what was clearly once a busy home. The dining room is empty of all but furniture. The bedrooms, with toys still in place, make it clear that once there were children. The attic is filled with remnants of a lifetime passed and stored away. At the bottom of the page, sitting all alone in the living room, is an attractive, middle-aged woman. The companion page urges in large bold type: TRIAVIL FOR DEPRESSION WITH MODERATE ANXIETY. And in just a bit smaller type: "In Many Cases a Result of the 'Empty-Nest Syndome.' " In the text, the ad described the "midlife crisis" as a critical crossroad during which depression and anxiety are common. To treat it (only its symptoms, of course!), this coping compound will provide simultaneous antidepressant and tranquilizing therapy.

There are many physicians, it should be noted, who feel that such combination of drugs is irrational. Furthermore, experts in pharmacology urge physicians to be wary of providing tranquilizers to those who in fact may be suffering a truly medical depression—an illness caused by physiological imbalances—because such treatments could actually heighten the depression, not help it. Even the ad for Triavil notes at the very bottom of the page that "suicide is a possibility in any depressive illness. The patient should not have access to large quantities of the drug." It also says that anyone suspected of an overdose should quickly be hospitalized. Having shown this woman to be all alone, how specious it is to suggest quick treatment for an overdose. Who will see her in time?

Medical Advertising and the Elderly

In the August 1977 issue of the *Journal of the American Medical Association,* a grateful-looking elderly lady is pictured accepting a tablet from a clearly caring, young female nurse. In the center of this full-page ad are a few simple paragraphs under the headline TRANZENE HELPS YOU RELIEVE INSTITUTIONAL ANXIETY. The first paragraph describes "institutional anxiety" as distress related not only to health but to *the nursing home or the institution itself.* The second paragraph tells the doctor that the drug is efficacious and equivalent to the diazepams. This reference is designed to make prescribing more comfortable, since diazepams are part of a family of drugs that most general practitioners have learned to dispense freely to women of all ages. Finally, the doctor is told why this old therapy in a new home is more appropriate: It permits once-a-day dosage; it is easier to administer and costs less to provide, saving the institution staff many hours of dispensing medication (but depriving the patient of a few minutes of human contact).

Almost without exception, medical journal advertising designed to promote medication for the elderly depicts women almost surrealistically as shrinking, wizened little people, or as the unseen problem element in a tense family scene. The theme of the ads is that patients are troublesome and cause problems when they are awake, and are thus clearly less stress-producing if they are less aware, less active, asleep, or at any rate, controlled. These drugs are always suggested as management tools, sparing institutions or family members the inconvenience of the elderly female's sleepless nights or upsetting confusion. There is rarely even a cynical attempt to pretend that the patient's well-being is the primary reason to prescribe the medication.

The life crises go on, and no female is too young to be helped. The pharmaceutical company Pfizer advised doctors that Vistaril can reduce childhood anxieties. Accompanying the portrait of a tearful little girl are the words: "School, the Dark, Separation, Dental Visits, Monsters." On the next page the physician is urged to help when "the everyday anxieties of children sometimes get out of hand."

For the older (female) student, Librium may help her get "back on her feet" when "afflicted by a sense of lost identity in a strange environment, . . . concerned over competition, apprehensive about national and world conditions, and confronted by the possible consequences of her 'new freedom' [which] may provoke acute feelings of insecurity."

Chemical solutions for other everyday human problems:

- "For anxiety that comes from not fitting in." Serentil.
- "You can't set her free. But you can help her feel less anxious. Beset by the seemingly insurmountable problems of raising a young family and confined to the home most of the time, her symptoms reflect a sense of inadequacy and isolation." Serax.
- "M A. (Fine Arts) . . . P.T.A. (President-elect) . . . with too little time to pursue a vocation for which she has spent many years in training . . . a situation that may bespeak continuous frustration and stress." Valium.

Finally, Abbott Laboratories' "me too" tranquilizer, Tranxene, has been promoted in the form of a cynical ode to "what she doesn't know won't hurt her":

- "A different tranquilizer. Times change . . .—A change of look . . . is a physically distinctive change of therapy. It's very different in form and appearance from any other tranquilizer your patients have previously received or seen.—Yet the same effectiveness . . . clinically equivalent to diazepam in treating anxiety."

Occasionally, disaffection with particular promotional devices has caused certain alterations or corrections in advertising, although changing very little in the prescribing habits of already captured doctors. Seduced by the industrial helpmates, doctors have unwittingly been reduced to the status of handmaidens to the new high priests of our medical culture—pills.

Senator Gaylord Nelson of Wisconsin, former Chairman of the Senate Subcommittee on Antitrust and Monopoly, who has been outspoken in his concern about the unhealthy practices of the drug industry, has said:

> The companies make claims through heavy promotional campaigns they know very well are not justified from a medical standpoint. They convince doctors to prescribe these drugs for purposes for which they shouldn't be prescribed. In my judgment, the present situation is intolerable. I do not believe that any doctor should base his drug prescribing on information received from advertising and promotion. . . . The whole field of prescription and over-the-counter drug use is simply out of control. I think that the drug industry has outwitted, outspent, outinfluenced, pressured, successfully cajoled the medical profession, particularly the AMA, the Food and Drug Administration, the public, and the government.

The Role of a Pharmacist

There was a time when the neighborhood druggist was called "Doc." He knew everyone in the community and played an important, comforting role in health care. That local professional was respected for his concern and advice. He was reliable, available, and was the front-line intermediary between the physician and his customer. Now, the few pharmacists who own their establishments are mostly discount tradesmen or franchised dealers for distributors of house brands of packaged drugs. They manage a business, leaving others to deal with the public and the cash register. In most communities, chain-store outlets—primarily convenience one-stop shops—hire and fire their highly trained pharmacists in much the same way as they do other clerks. The major distinction is the placement of these specialists in an isolated, protected space, connected to humanity by a phone, with only occasional personal contact.

Just recently, waiting my turn at the cashier's line in such a market, I was witness to the following scene:

A clerk called over the loft barrier to the druggist: "Joe, that saleswoman from Sandoz (a manufacturer) wants to see you."

Locking the door behind him, the pharmacist emerged and greeted his visitor, who said, "I know you're busy and I promise not to keep you long. But you know I've just been working this territory for a few months and I need your help with some of our mutual clients. Okay?"

"Sure. No problem. How can I help?"

"Well, can you give me some idea which local docs are writing 'scrips'?"

"Well, Brown and Gordon are good. Barry, just fair . . ."

Looking at her clipboard, the saleswoman asked, "How about Thomas? Springer? Johnson?"

"Springer, yes. Thomas, poor, Johnson is getting better."

"How about my products? Who's writing? Young?"

"No, sorry, Young never does. Barry is coming on, but Healy is really big for you."

"None from Young? Whew, better do something about that. I've got my work cut out for me. You've really been a big help. I'll be back in a month, and by then you'll see some changes. Meantime—think oral. And oh, this is for you." The saleswoman handed him a small package, book size.

He smiled and said, "That's really nice. Thanks a lot and good luck." As the saleswoman left, the clerk and the druggist agreed, "She's cute and on the ball. She'll do fine."

Juxtapose that event with one other. Both happened within one week, in the same place. Again, I was in the store. A major news story had hit the nation. Dr. Peter Bourne, Special Assistant to the President for Health, had issued a questionable prescription for Quaaludes, a sedative-hypnotic tranquilizer. The networks and local media were all scurrying for a different handle on the incident. A camera crew from a nearby network affiliate was engaged in debate over company policy with the pharmacist. I overheard a cameraman say, "But, sir, all we want to do is film the pills, or whatever it is, so viewers can identify the stuff." The pharmacist was adamant, insisting that "no pictures of any products can be taken without the approval from the main office."

The television crew spokesman tried to convince the druggist that their request was in the interest of providing good graphic information, that they would limit their shots and would not compromise security or the name of the store, and that they would take into account any other logical consideration that might cause concern.

Nothing would do. The pharmacist insisted: "Ethics and privacy rules are involved here, and it's my job to protect them."

Incredulous, I wondered how this retail pharmacist could interpret those lofty measures so differently for public information purposes than he did for the manufacturer's representatives.

A Detail Man's Story

I have, of course, no way of knowing whether that "on-the-ball" manufacturer's representative, with her list of neighborhood doctors and their inclinations to prescribe her company's products, will "do fine," as the pharmacist predicted. From time to time, though, I have met people in the business of promoting and selling "health" who have had to come to grips with their personal integrity and conscience. This story, told me by one disillusioned pharmaceutical detail man, is worth relating at some length:

> I was always interested in chemistry, even as a kid. I really wanted to do something to help people feel well and stay healthy. I couldn't go to medical school—the war got in the way, and I suppose a bunch of other things did as well. But I did graduate from college with a degree in chemistry. I had a driving wish to help, a degree to make it possible, and I was very ambitious. Becoming a salesman for a pharmaceutical manufacturer seemed a pretty good thing to do.
>
> I'm not sure whether everyone is naive, but I was—even about what drug companies' intentions really were. For the first several years, I really buried myself in all the papers and all the courses I could take, on the chemistry of the drugs I was promoting. I worked with a good bunch of guys, and I learned as quickly as I could from them until the cracks started to open up. I saw my friends fall into them.
>
> The company pressure to sell more and more, especially tranquilizers, where they made their greatest profit, was tremendous. You get so caught up in the system. Your salary increases and bonuses depend on meeting sales figures, you've got a mortgage to meet and a family to take care of—all of these things are pretty distracting. For a while you really don't think about what you're selling so much as how much you're selling.
>
> There is so much fancy footwork. After a group hearings before Senator [Edward] Kennedy's health subcommittee, we were no longer able to use words like "samples" or sales "quotas." Mr. Clark, the company president went before the committee at the time they were describing free samples as "payola" to doctors and pharmacists. Clark assured the Senators that *his company* did not give "samples" and did not use "quotas." He did not say that our samples are known as "clinical trial supplies" and "starter" packages!

In fact, all we had done was change the words. We were probably sending out more free goods than we had ever done when we called them "samples."

There is always somebody from the company negotiating with the folks at the Food and Drug Administration. Every so often they make a breakthrough. They convince somebody over there that our drug is safe for some other use beyond the original purpose. As soon as they get clearance, we have a new sales pitch to make. For a while, I used to look forward to some new uses or new research, because it would give me a chance to change my pitch to the same group of doctors and pharmacists that I had to see over and over and who had heard my old sales stuff about my tranquilizers for a couple of years.

We had pretty good classes in ways to impress even old clients with familiar drugs. Hell, half the time the doctors didn't even realize how we maneuvered them into purchasing more or prescribing more.

One of the sales tools we used is a question chart. It's offered to doctors as a way to find out what they *don't* need any more information about, regarding a particular drug that our company really wants to sell more of. We tell the doctors that we don't want to bother them by repeating information that they already know. We get them to fill out this form, which tells us exactly how often they use a particular drug, for what diagnosis, who they largely give it to. Of course, the company's real purpose is to find out where they *haven't* yet applied its use. They use this information to shift advertising directions or in the next discussion with the FDA.

Let me give you an example. Dr. A, thinking he's going to be spared the same old sales pitch on the usefulness of our tranquilizer, writes that he prescribes this drug to a particular age group for just one or two syndromes. When that pattern comes up in several regions, the company knows that it's time to shift gears. The next campaign, then, instead of focusing on anxiety for a particular middle-aged female group, might talk about muscle strain or stomach aches brought on by a family crisis or new-town stresses. Then we have new material.

When we started to find out something about the half-life of a drug, where it worked on the brain, and how long it would stay in the body even after a person had stopped taking the medication, some doctors were interested, but most I spoke to weren't. All they wanted to know was how much does it cost and are there any bad side effects. They really didn't care what happened to the whole body. Let's face it, if I referred to the hippocampus or the medulla and they didn't respond with interest, it wasn't going to help my sales or friendship with them to continue, so I just stopped. Sales were the bottom line for the company, and, of course, for me.

You get on to a terrible treadmill. It's something that I didn't understand for several years, that tricky business of trying to balance original ideals— "do something well and do some good"— against the backdrop of a design to only make money. I had a strong sense of being a professional, not a used car salesman or a life insurance salesman. The job pressure by division managers is pretty intense. You walk the fine edge of a double-edged sword. It's hard to live with yourself. If you have the responsibility of a wife and kids you know that you can get fired any time, or not get an increased salary, you're really stuck in the middle. The company benefits. One day you wonder about who is being hurt in all of this and decide that it's everyone—you, your family, your health, and everyone else you've done business with. And you wake up to what you've been doing all those years.

It hit me the day I was standing in a pharmacy which was one of my better outlets. I watched a dozen women get their prescriptions of one hundred tranquilizers each, and I knew in my heart-of-hearts that not all of those women needed one hundred tablets of tranquilizers. I had done my job too well.

I had to get out of it. So did many of my friends—the ones who were still alive. But they are not alive to tell about it.

The company makes you sign all kinds of papers guarding them against the possibility of any of us talking publicly about the tactics used. Frankly, most of us are scared, and so what we know is not understood by people who need to know.

---

13. The Amazing Story of DES

Barbara Seaman and Gideon Seaman, M.D.

One day, a Virginia woman named Grace M. was reading the newspaper when she noticed an article concerning a drug called DES—diethylstilbestrol, often called simply stilbestrol. The article pointed out a newly discovered danger associated with this drug: The daughters of some of the women who had taken it during their pregnancies had developed vaginal cancer as a result, said the author of the report, Dr. Arthur Herbst.

"I became alarmed and called my doctor immediately," recalls Mrs. M. "I had first taken DES in 1949 when I was pregnant with one daughter, and again in 1955 before the birth of another. So I took my daughters to the doctor, and from the examinations, Marilyn, the 14-year-old, was found to have cancer of the vagina.

"Three weeks later, she had vaginal surgery in New York City. She was four weeks in the hospital. The doctors told me they had gotten all of it, there was no problem, everything was taken care of, this type of cancer rarely ever spread beyond the female organs.

"And so, reassured, we went back to Virginia. A year later, Marilyn developed cancer of the lung and also three tumors on her trachea and her bronchial tubes. The doctors operated and removed the lung and the tumors.

"About four months later, Marilyn started having severe head pains. The cancer had spread into her head. She had whole-head radiation, and her hip started to hurt, and she had hip radiation and from hip radiation she went on to the arms and legs, and eventually she went blind and died, two and half years after we had discovered the cancer. It is a horrible, terrible thing to watch your child suffer, and eventually, when she dies, you think it is a blessing—the death is far easier to accept than the actual suffering."

Today, Mrs. M.'s other daughter, Patty, who is in her twenties, is under constant care. She is checked every three months because she has adenosis, an abnormal condition in her vaginal tract associated with prenatal exposure to DES and thought to be a possible precursor of cancer of the vagina.

On December 16, 1975, a 21-year-old woman named Sherry L. spoke on the steps of the Food and Drug Administration in Rockville, Maryland, at a National Women's Health Network memorial service that was held for all the women who have died from unnecessary estrogen products. Sherry herself is a "DES daughter"—like Marilyn M., *and an estimated 1.5 million other young United States women*. She has cervical abnormalities that were discovered in a routine checkup at a women's health center and in tests at Massachusetts General Hospital's DES screening program. She has to undergo continual monitoring. Sherry is anxious about the outcome of her life. "I relieve a lot of my anxiety by working on DES projects, but it's still hard to live with," she says.

Mothers suffer equally. On Long Island, New York, many are active in an organization called DES-Action. This is a group of mothers and daughters who were exposed to the drug and who have banded together for mutual support, advice, and possible action. Similar activist groups are organizing in other areas. DES women in California have prodded the state health department to publish material alerting women and doctors to the dangers of DES, and to offer doctors one-day courses in the use of the colposcope, an instrument that aids in the discovery of vaginal abnormalities. Other women exposed to DES have themselves filed suits against the drug companies who make it—or have joined in filing class-action suits.

Why are these tragedies, connected to a relatively small group of people, receiving so much attention? In terms of the population as a whole, the cause of a group of mothers and daughters who, over a thirty-year span, were given a drug that proved dangerous to many does not seem of imminent concern to the rest of us.

But these women are not the only ones at risk. Abnormalities are now beginning to show up in some of the sons of women who were given DES during pregnancy. And in spite of the alarming track record of this synthetic hormone in after-the-fact testing, *DES is still being given today in the form of the morning-after pill, a favorite contraceptive handed out at many university health services. It is also being given as a milk suppressant to new mothers* who do not wish to nurse their babies.

And on top of all that, this known carcinogen *is in the meat we eat.* The fact is that today— man, woman, or child—*we are all chemically medicated to some degree with DES, without our permission and usually without our knowledge.*

• • •

DES is the grandmother product of all synthetic estrogens, as well as being the loss leader. (Leader to the pharmaceutical industry, loss to the women who have taken it.)

Synthesized by Sir Charles Dodds in England in 1938, it was the first hormone product that was both cheap to manufacture and effective to take by mouth. DES has been defined by Dr. Robert H. Furman, vice-president of Eli Lilly, as "a synthetic compound capable of producing feminizing effects similar to those of the naturally occurring feminizing hormone estrogen." *Similar to,* but not identical with, as Dodds himself points out.

Nearly thirty years later, in 1965, Sir Charles made this comment about his brainchild: "It is interesting . . . to speculate on the difference in attitude toward new drugs thirty years ago and today. Within a few months of the first publication of the synthesis of stilbestrol, the substance was being marketed throughout the world. No long-term toxicity tests on animals such as dogs were ever done with stilbestrol. . . . It is really surprising that we escaped major pharmacological diasters until a few years ago."

According to Dr. Furman, the following are the four medical conditions for which DES is presently most often prescribed:

- as replacement therapy for women in menopause, or whose ovaries have been removed or never developed
- for the prevention of post-partum breast engorgement in mothers who decline to breast feed
- to treat certain cases of cancer of the prostate
- to treat certain breast cancers

DES is commercially in hale and hearty shape. But many women who have been exposed to it are not so hale—and some are dead.

The Boston Disease: Its Origins

Paul Rheingold is an attorney specializing in malpractice and drug-liability cases. Rheingold's office, in New York's skyscraper Pan Am building, affords sweeping views of the city. But the visitor's eye is riveted to an enormous picture on the wall—a blown-up x-ray of a human patient with a surgical retractor visible in his abdomen. The picture graphically illustrates Rheingold's type of practice.

Rheingold is planning a class-action suit against the drug companies to pay for the health care of the daughters of women who were given DES while they were pregnant. He also handles individual DES lawsuits. "You know," he mused when we interviewed him in 1976, "it's almost like a Boston disease. The closer you get to Boston, the more DES daughters you find, and the farther away you get, the fewer."

He could have said Harvard because, in point of fact, the tragic story of DES begins at Harvard University. The first promoters of DES as a therapy for pregnant women were Dr. George Van Siclen Smith, head of Harvard's gynecology department from 1942 to 1967 and now professor emeritus, and his wife, biochemist Dr. Olive Watkins Smith.

George and Olive Smith married in 1930, when he was a Fellow in gynecology at Harvard Medical School, and she was a young Ph.D. out of Radcliffe. Today they are a handsome enough couple to star in a leisure village advertisement, except that leisure is the one thing they don't have. He is still in private practice, and she performs research—seventy hours a week—at the Fearing Research Laboratory of the Free Hospital for Women in Brookline.

They are tall, the two of them, and blue-eyed. Dr. George's hair is faded brown and parted in the middle, 1920s fashion. He wears austere clothes and highly polished shoes. Dr. Olive wore her usual lab coat and sneakers when we interviewed them. Her abundant white hair was brushed back from her face. They chuckle a lot together, and they are proud of their grown daughter and son. They also adopt a parental attitude toward the doctors they trained— "our boys"—including some who will appear later in this story, such as DES investigators Arthur Herbst, Philip Corfman, and John Lewis.

Philip Corfman, of the National Institutes of Health's Division of Child Health and Human Development, has given grants for several studies on the aftermath of DES. Dr. George said of Corfman, "He's too young to be an administrator. He was a good resident. We wanted to keep him here."

George and Olive Smith "started right in on the ovary" in 1928, and have been working on it ever since. As Dr. George puts it, "We have just *lived* ovarian hormones—pituitary and placental—for years and years." The Smiths were among the first to demonstrate how pituitary and ovarian hormones function over the course of the normal menstrual cycle, and, with the help of a tip from their friend Dr. Gregory Pincus, inventor of the birth control pill, were the first to demonstrate estradiol as one of the naturally occurring forms of estrogen.

The First DES Study

The Smiths' natural conservatism made them cautious about treatments such as radical mastectomy, so their espousal of DES is all the more poignant.

From the mid-1930s on, Dr. George and Dr. Olive, together and separately, published many important papers on estrogen excretion in normal pregnancy. It was in 1941, based on their observation of low hormone levels in mothers spontaneously aborting, that they conceived the idea of using the newly developed DES to help pregnancies that seemed threatened by miscarriage. Dr. Olive stated in her landmark report, published in the *American Journal of Obstetrics and Gynecology* in November 1948, "It was found . . . that diethylstilbestrol . . . might theoretically . . . provide an ideal agent for progesterone deficiency in pregnancy."

The report described a study of 632 DES-treated pregnancies, which dated back to 1943. The earliest DES mothers were not all Bostonians, for 117 obstetricians from 48 cities and towns in New York, New Jersey, Pennsylvania, the District of Columbia, Illinois, North Carolina, Virginia, Texas, New Mexico, California, and all of the New England states cooperated in the study by following the Smiths' regimen and sending them a record of each treated case. Presumably the cooperating doctors gave the pills to the pregnant patients who seemed in danger of miscarrying, although possibly some gave them to women who merely had had problems with previous pregnancies.

The obstetricians supplied the records, and E. R. Squibb & Sons supplied the DES pills, which were given in the following dosages: "Five milligrams daily by mouth, starting during the sixth or seventh week (counting from the start of the last menstrual period). The daily dosage is increased by 5 milligrams at two-week intervals to the fifteenth week, when 25 milligrams daily are being taken. Thereafter, the daily dosage is increased by 5 mg at weekly intervals. Administration is discontinued at the end of the thirty-fifth week, since a drop in estrogen and progesterone normally precedes the onset of labor."

By 1948 the Smiths were convinced that DES could be effective against many complications of pregnancy, including threatened miscarriage and diabetes. In addition, the babies of DES-treated mothers were said to be unusually rugged; the placentas were found to be "grossly more healthy-looking."

The Big Boston Success

The following year the Smiths completed their second major study at Boston Lying-In—then, as now, one of the world's most prestigious maternity hospitals. This study, which had begun in April 1947, included 387 women who received DES throughout pregnancy, compared to 550 who did not. All of these women—the stilbestrol mothers as well as the unmedicated—were observed to be having *normal first pregnancies*. Those who did not receive DES got no special treatment, or even a placebo. Only 28 of the 387 treated patients dropped out of the study. Possibly the high level of cooperation could be accounted for by the fact that the women taking DES were given extra attention and encouragement. Women with known illnesses such as diabetes or hypertension were excluded from the study, in spite of the Smith's claims that DES had proved effective in pregnancies threatened by diabetes. Those in the study were all normal and healthy first-time mothers. What was the reason for giving them a powerful drug, except in the name of research?

Yet the women who were given DES were never informed that they were part of a highly controversial experiment. Some DES mothers now recall that they were told the pills were "vitamins."

"The babies of treated mothers," wrote the Smiths, "gave evidence of having been in a better maternal environment. . . . The explanation appears to be that the drug stimulated better placental function and hence bigger and healthier babies. . . . Although stilbestrol was expected to keep more gestations normal . . . we did not anticipate that it could render normal gestation 'more normal,' as it were."

The Smiths had a dream—a dream of helping women with problem pregnancies achieve motherhood, and then, as their experiment unfolded, a yet more daring dream of making normal pregnancies more normal! There was understandable excitement and controversy when they reported their Boston Lying-In study at the Seventy-second Annual Meeting of the American Gynecological Society in Hot Springs, Virginia.

Not only was the research not conclusive—by today's standards it wasn't even good. The untreated group was simply that—an untreated group. On the other hand, the DES mothers had been given that extra attention and support.

Nowadays a well-designed drug study must handle both treated and untreated patients in exactly the same way. The untreated patients are given placebos and the same kind of care as the treated. Codes are kept secret so that the doctors and staff (as well as the patients) never know who has received the real medication until it's all over.

The first discussant, Dr. Ernest W. Page of San Francisco, reacted skeptically. "Dr. Olive Smith and Dr. George Smith have been among the most astute and assiduous observers in this field for over fifteen years, [but] it is difficult to believe that such a potent drug as stilbestrol will prove to be like an essential vitamin—necessary for the most successful outcome of normal pregnancies."

Dr. Willard M. Allen of St. Louis, an authority on ovulation in rabbits, was puzzled. He pointed out that, in rabbits at least, "the administration of estrogen is very deleterious to the fetus. In early pregnancy estrogen will *prevent implantation or produce abortion,* and during the later stages it leads to death of the fetus."

(Dr. Allen was on to something. Humans may have turned out to be more like rabbits than the Smiths expected, and the use of DES today as a morning-after contraceptive makes up for some of the loss the drug industry must have suffered when its popularity as a miscarriage preventive fell off. But we're getting ahead of our story.)

The regional battle lines concerning DES were drawn on that day in 1949 in Hot Springs, Virginia. In general, the New Englanders supported the Smiths—and Harvard—while the midwesterners did not. Dr. William J. Dieckmann of the University of Chicago and Chicago Lying-In Hospital pointed out that the untreated control group in the Smiths' study *was not given a placebo,* which he considered essential for scientific accuracy. He proposed a plan for testing DES at Chicago Living-In, using a placebo as a control, and recommended that other obstetricians who had large clinic services do the same.

Troublesome News from New Orleans and Chicago

Dr. Dieckmann was as good as his word, and he began a DES study. Before his work was completed, a New Orleans obstetrician, Dr. John Henry Ferguson of Charity Hospital and Tulane University, also attempted to replicate the Harvard DES work. Like Dieckmann, Ferguson believed that the Smiths had erred in not giving their control patients an inert pill. Alternate pregnant patients at Charity Hospital were given tablets called "white stilbestrol" and "yellow stilbestrol," but only the whites ones contained the real stuff.

Close to half of the women dropped out of Ferguson's study. Luckily for them (and their fetuses!), 46 of the "real" stilbestrol mothers missed their appointments, 35 disappeared, 41 would not cooperate, and 33 provided inadequate data or delivered at home. Ferguson was left with only 184 obedient DES mothers, and 198 controls. Nonetheless, his study was important, for it was the first to show stilbestrol had no more effect than the placebo. In fact, more DES patients than placebo patients had miscarriages and premature births, while the control group babies (and placentas) were slightly bigger and healthier. The only diabetic patient in the study, a DES mother, lost her baby! Dr. Ferguson had, in the words of one admiring contemporary, "driven a very large nail into the coffin that we will use someday to bury some of the extremely outsized claims for the beneficial effects of stilbestrol."

The Dieckmann Chicago study was begun on September 29, 1950. This time Eli Lilly & Company had provided the carefully prepared DES pills and placebos, while we, out of our tax dollars, provided the money, for the study was sponsored by our National Institutes of Health. All 2,162 Chicago Lying-In clinic patients were included—first-time mothers and experienced ones, the healthy and the sick women who had miscarried previously and those who had not. Every patient was offered a box of tablets, without charge, and was told that "the tablets were of value in preventing some of the complications of pregnancy and would cause no harm to [the patient] or the fetus." Coding was properly kept top secret. Most of the staff didn't know what drug was being studied, and none knew which patients got DES and which a placebo. Five hundred sixteen women dropped out of the study, leaving 840 DES mothers and 806 in the placebo group.

The Dieckmann Chicago study was completed on November 20, 1952, and reported at Lake Placid, New York, in 1953, at the annual meeting of American gynecologists. The DES babies in this study did not do better in any respect. To the contrary: Twice as many of the DES mothers had miscarriages; they had more hypertension (high blood pressure) and smaller babies than the mothers on placebos. Dr. Dieckmann and his associates concluded that DES *actually favors premature labor,* as in rabbits. "We think that the number of patients studied and the methods used showed that stilbestrol has no therapeutic value in pregnancy," they announced firmly.

It was now fifteen years after Charles Dodds perfected the first oral estrogen in London, and twelve years after the Smiths of Boston started to treat pregnant women with it. The Chicago and even the New Orleans studies were scientifically more valid than the study performed at Boston Lying-In. In both later studies, DES was shown to be not helpful, and possibly deleterious.

But even more serious in its implications was the testing of DES for carcinogenicity by animal researchers. At the National Cancer Institute, for example, Michael B. Shimkin and Hugh C. Grady dissolved the new DES in sesame oil and fed it to male mice. These mice were of a strain called C_3H, which is so highly susceptible to cancer that most of the virgin females develop cancer spontaneously, though males do not.

The DES-fed males *did.* They also developed serious abnormalities of the spleen and sex organs. By 1940, when the Smiths were conceiving their human experiments, DES had already been proven carcinogenic in mice.

The Smiths were aware of this research, for as Dr. Olive told us in 1976, "Before we even started any clinical work at all, we went through all the literature."

"However," said her husband, "you can do all kinds of things to rats and mice by giving them overdoses."

The New Orleans and Chicago reports, if not the mouse studies, must have convinced many obstetricians that there was no value in using DES, though apparently not some of the sons of Harvard. In 1953, when the bad news from Chicago was brought to the Lake Placid meeting, one doctor was quick to quip: "As a former Bostonian, I would be entirely lacking in . . . loyalty if I had not used stilbestrol in my private practice."

• • •

The Herbst Report

Back in Boston, while the Lake Placid meeting was taking place, a young New Yorker named Arthur Herbst was graduating cum laude from Harvard College, class of '53. After serving as a line officer in the navy, Herbst got his M.D. from Harvard Medical School in 1959, trained in obstetrics and gynecology, and became one of George Smith's "boys." In 1966, at Massachusetts General Hospital, a 15-year-old girl with clear-cell adenocarcinoma of the vagina came to his attention. It was the first time that this type of cancer had ever been seen at Massachusetts General Hospital in any woman under twenty-five.

(Adenocarcinoma is cancer that occurs in *glandular tissue.* In normal women, the vaginal lining has no such tissue, but we now know that the vaginas of most daughters of women who took DES while pregnant, including those who are thus far free from cancer, have many tiny glands. We have learned only after thirty years of widespread use in humans that DES interferes with the formation of normal genital tissue at a critical time in the early development of the fetus.)

Within the next three years, 6 similar cases of clear-cell adenocarcinoma in young women turned up at Massachusetts General Hospital. The youngest patient was 15, the oldest 22. These 7 cases were more than had been reported in such young women *in all of the world's medical literature.* Arthur Herbst and his colleague Howard Ulfelder, in a study designed by David C. Poskanzer, began a careful search for the source of this mysterious cancer. The patients and their mothers all were questioned about possible causes, such as douches, tampons, birth control pills, and sexual activity. "Finally," says Herbst, *"one of the mothers made an intuitive guess that the cause might be the DES she was given in pregnancy."* The researchers then added prenatal hormones to their list of questions.

And that was the connection. The mothers of the young women with adenocarcinoma all had taken DES while pregnant.

Today George Smith says sadly, "We've been in on that from the beginning because we're close friends with Dr. Herbst. Of course he felt terrible about it, but a lot is being learned as the result of it, and who could predict thirty years ago that anything like this would develop? I mean, regardless of the rat and mouse work."

Herbst's relationship with the Smiths did not prevent him from publishing his findings in the *New England Journal of Medicine* on April 22, 1971, in an article co-authored with Drs. Ulfelder and Poskanzer. At this point Herbst had examined 8 cases of adenocarcinoma in young women. All but one were DES daughters.

The frightening implications of these findings go far beyond DES because, for the first time, Herbst showed that estrogen products can be cancer-producing in humans. It had been known since 1896, when surgeons started removing the ovaries of breast-cancer patients, that hormones—even the hormones produced by a woman's own body—could *speed* up the growth of an existing malignancy.

It had been known since 1932 that breast cancer could be produced in *male* mice by giving them estrogen injections, that sex hormones could *produce* cancer in laboratory animals, serving as "seed" as well as "fertilizer" in *susceptible* strains.

Like our distant mouse relative, we humans vary in our cancer thresholds, but unlike mice, we haven't been bred for susceptibility or resistance. We just have to take pot luck with our own genes, and we never know where we stand personally. Then too, we don't live in cages in a scientifically controlled experiment, so we may be randomly exposed to a great many carcinogens we're unaware of. Finally, a cancer that takes four or five months to develop in a mouse takes years or decades to develop in a human being. In terms of the human cancer span, most estrogen products have not been in widespread use long enough for us to chart all the returns.

DES was the first hormone product to be named a human carcinogen. Young women exposed in the womb to DES in the 1940s and 1950s developed cancer in the 1960s and 1970s. The work of Herbst and his colleagues was a crucial "missing link" concerning estrogens and the *initiation* of cancer in humans, for all estrogens have a similar way of behaving biologically. Mice who get cancer from DES *also get it from other estrogen products.* In 1971, the millions of hormone-using women all over the world should have been warned of the significance of Herbst's DES findings. They should have been warned that a scientist had found that estrogens *cause* cancer as well as *help it grow.*

They were not. Only in 1975, when additional hormone products, such as Premarin and the sequential pill, were also linked to cancer, did the U.S. Food and Drug Administration start to acknowledge that estrogen products must be viewed as a group. There *are* differences among them, but it isn't clear what all of them are. The risks established for any one product must be assumed to apply to the others.

Herbst himself—and the editors of the *New England Journal of Medicine*—understood the sweeping implications of his 1971 report concerning the DES link among the young women with cancer. In March, several weeks before publication, Dr. Franz Ingelfinger, then editor of the *New England Journal of Medicine,* sent galleys of Herbst's article to the FDA. On April 14, Herbst also shipped the FDA his raw data sheets. Then he waited . . . and waited.

• • •

Our FDA commissioner, who testified that he felt Dr. Ingraham's warning letter to physicians was "premature," should have restricted DES for use in pregnancy cases (indeed, his predecessors would have!)—even though it was not yet known to be lethal—simply because it didn't work. Under the circumstances, with the proof of the drug's effectiveness three and a half years overdue, it is astonishing the FDA did not take action the moment that the Herbst galleys were received.

Let us examine the results of the FDA's inaction: During the 1940s and especially the early 1950s (after the Boston studies had been published, but before they were challenged in Chicago and New Orleans), DES was enormously popular as a pregnancy treatment. It has been estimated that estrogens were prescribed for nearly 6 million pregnant women between 1943 and 1959, resulting in the birth of at least 3 million children who had been exposed *in utero* to estrogens. Use of stilbestrol in pregnancy declined by the 1960s (probably because doctors became aware that it didn't work). On the basis of research that has been done on pharmacy records from 1960 to 1970, let's assume that some 30,000 unborn females were exposed to DES in 1971, an average of 2,500 a month. Had the FDA acted decisively upon receiving the Herbst galleys in March, instead of waiting until November, when Congressman Fountain forced their hand, more than 20,000 young women who are now in danger of developing adenocarcinoma could have been spared. Four out of every thousand, or a total of 80, may be diagnosed as having vaginal or cervical cancer before the age of 30. How many will develop cancer in later years is anybody's guess.

Peter Greenwald has stated: "Four per 1,000 is . . . 44 times higher than the annual incidence for leukemia, and considerably higher than the annual incidences of breast cancer and colon cancer. . . . If this rate is unimportant, then I think a number of researchers should seek other occupations."

Two DES Women Speak

If cancer happens to *you,* the rate seems like 100 percent. Here are two women who have been affected by DES. Their stories bring the statistics into perspective. Janice L. is a young bride who lost her womb to DES; Helen G. lost her daughter.

Janice L. of Los Angeles, whose mother was treated with DES:

"I went to a gynecologist for what I supposed was a routine exam. At that time he told me that he had found what he described as an irritation, and made another appointment for me to come back. So I did.

"I was operated on last August. The repercussions of this operation are still strong in my life. . . . Assuming that I will live a long, full life, there is always the chance that the cancer will appear again, and meanwhile I have to live with the fact that it has rendered me sterile. Family life is very important to me. The fact that I can never have a child matters terribly. . . .

"I have talked to many other women who have had hysterectomies, and I understand it is common knowledge that you go through a transition period where you feel like you are not a woman. I am still trying to adjust.

"And added to this is the constant fear hanging over my head—the suspicion that the cancer will crop up again.

"Not only has it affected me, but naturally it has affected my family—especially my mother. Sometimes I can just cry when I see her. She feels so guilty."

About one-quarter of the young women who have developed DES cancer have died. One of them was 18-year-old Susan G.

Helen G. of Glen Cove, Long Island:

"My daughter was born on February 9, 1951, and she was fine until she was 15. Then one day she hemorrhaged, and the doctors told me she had a very rare form of cancer.

"In Glen Cove, no one had ever treated it, no one had ever even seen it. They recommended a doctor in New York City, which is about twenty-five miles away. The doctor who treated Susan there was wonderful to her. He was treating one other case like hers, from California.

"She was fine for a while, and then the cancer spread. She died when she was 18, in March 1969.

"About two years later, I received a call from a Dr. Herbst, I think it was, asking about Susan, and telling me there was some connection between diethylstilbestrol, DES, and my daughter's vaginal cancer. I could not believe that something with any inherent danger would be given out as indiscriminately as that drug was given out in the 1950s.

"The other thing that bothers me is that many friends contacted me when this became publicly known and said they had taken it, and asked me what I would suggest they do. I suggested . . . they take their daughters and have them checked immediately. And many of them were told by gynecologists, 'Oh, do not worry. The chances of your daughter developing cancer—well, you can get hit by an automobile faster.'

"That bothered me, the attitude of the doctors.

"You know, statistics are meaningless, unless one of the statistics is one of your own children."

Don Harper Mills, a physician and lawyer who serves as a medico-legal expert on the editorial board of the *Journal of the American Medical Association (JAMA),* advises all physicians who have ever used DES in pregnancy to search their records and send a notice to all such patients at their last known address. Few physicians are complying. Janice L's condition was spotted by *her own* gynecologist; the doctor her mother had used denied, at first, that he had given her DES. Grace M. took her daughters in for a checkup after reading a newspaper article. Helen G.'s daughter died before the connection between DES and cancer was established.

We have not yet located one DES mother whose prescribing physician has complied with the Mills recommendation published by the AMA on July 22, 1974. Still earlier, in May 1973, the American College of Obstetricians and Gynecologists (ACOG) issued a technical bulletin to its members, with an editorial that emphasized the need for early examination of girls at risk. All ACOG members were urged to "notify patients who have been treated with stilbestrol during pregnancy so that their daughters can be examined."

Paul Rheingold, the attorney, has not heard of many doctors who have complied either. He guesses there are three reasons for this lack of cooperation: fear of lawsuits, laziness, and sloppy record-keeping. In Rheingold's experience, many doctors do not begin to keep the kinds of records they should.

• • •

Neither the drug companies, nor the government, nor professional medical societies such as the AMA or ACOG have offered to finance the search for and treatment of DES daughters. Who will?

14. This is Science?

Steve Minkin

It is late autumn 1978. A green-and-white bus wends its way through the paddies and outlying villages beyond Chiang Mai, a provincial capital in northern Thailand. The countryside is lush with tropical fruits and flowers; ear-splitting Suzuki motorcycles scream past ancient Buddhist shrines and ornate temples with curved orange roofs.

As the hot sun rises, a small group of Thai women moves slowly on the trails winding beneath a moist canopy of trees. Along the way they meet other women wearing worn workshirts, sarongs and brightly colored headcloths. Four hours later they arrive at a roadside village where hundreds of other women are already gathered around the bus, waiting for a medical team to set up shop and inject them with Depo-Provera.

Depo-Provera, a long-lasting injectable contraceptive, is rapidly surpassing the pill in popularity with family-planning programs around the world. An estimated ten million women have already used "the shot," which causes sterility for from three to six months depending on the dose. In 1978, the United States Food and Drug Administration (FDA) refused to approve Depo-Provera for use as a contraceptive primarily because in laboratory tests it caused malignant breast nodules on beagle dogs.

In addition to cancer, the FDA was also troubled by the risk of side effects to children born to women inadvertently injected with Depo while they were pregnant. Such side effects may include congenital heart defects, abnormal development of the penis or vagina and the possibility of genital cancers later in life. Users themselves frequently suffered irregular menstrual bleeding disturbances, sometimes referred to in medical journals as "menstrual chaos."

But American population-control zealots at home and abroad claim Depo-Provera is safe—even ideal for use by breast-feeding mothers.

Through elaborate export arrangements, public and private population-control organizations manage to deliver Depo to clinics in more than 80 countries around the world, despite the fact that the FDA forbids U.S. pharmaceutical companies from exporting products banned for domestic consumption. Depo-Provera is a product of the Upjohn company of Kalamazoo, Michigan, which manufactures the drug in Canada and Belgium to avoid the export ban (see "The Corporate Crime of the Century," *MJ,* Nov. '79).

Controversy has swirled around Depo-Provera since its contraceptive properties were discovered in the early 1960s (it was originally developed and is still effective as a palliative for uterine cancer).

As side effects appeared and animal tests produced alarming results—first on beagle dogs and later on rhesus monkeys—the opposition of Depo-Provera escalated. Congressional hearings have been held, suits have been filed and the FDA has issued its ban against Depo's use as a contraceptive, which Upjohn and domestic population controllers continue to challenge.

From Stephen Minkin, THIS IS SCIENCE?, which originally appeared in *Mother Jones,* Vol. VI, No. IX, November, 1981, pp. 34–39; 50–54, as edited. Copyright © Foundation for National Progress 1981. Reprinted with permission.

This, then, is the latest chapter in a 20-year struggle over whether or not Depo-Provera should be used *anywhere* as a contraceptive. It is more precisely the story of how two avid supporters of Depo-Provera attempt to validate a highly controversial birth-control technique by producing a clearly unscientific study on women in Thailand.

On command, the Thai women, who are regular users of Depo-Provera, roll up their sleeves and tighten their expressions. Shots are dispensed rapidly—about one a minute—and women are sent home to their families barren for three to six months.

Women who have not yet begun receiving the shot are hustled into a semi-circle for a short lecture on Depo-Provera, according to health worker Mingfong Ho. Most of it concerns the cost of the contraceptive, its three-month cycle and its effectiveness. Little is said about possible side effects. Weight gain and hair loss are mentioned in passing.

What about the possibility of cervical, uterine or breast cancer, Mingfong quietly asks the nurse. Does she ever mention that? The nurse lifts one eyebrow. "Cervical cancer? Most of these women will die of malaria, cholera, dysentery or even in childbirth long before they get cervical cancer." She smiles at Mingfong before turning back to her injections. "This is not America, you know."

Meanwhile in America

In Chapel Hill, North Carolina, not too many weeks after the Thai women received their injections, Dr. Malcolm Potts signs a document entitled "Depo-Provera and Cancer of the Human Endometrium." Potts is concerned about reports of new experimental findings that could doom Depo-Provera, a contraceptive he has championed for a decade.

Malcolm Potts, the father of three children, is a Cambridge-educated scientist who has written more than a hundred technical papers and four books about reproduction, birth control and family planning. By some he is considered brilliant. Others find him one of the most obsessed supporters of population control. As medical director of the International Planned Parenthood Federation (IPPF) between 1969 and 1978, he was responsible for the distribution of millions of shots of Depo-Provera to nations such as Thailand, Kenya, Sri Lanka, Botswana, Tanzania, Zaire and Jamaica. Now he is the executive director of the International Fertility Research Program (IFRP) and is leading the worldwide crusade to save Depo-Provera.

The IFRP has come to represent the union between U.S. foreign policy objectives and the corporate drive to expand contraceptive markets overseas. Successive administrations have identified overpopulation as a serious threat to U.S. security and commercial interests and to the maintaining of our supply of critical raw materials. A recent State Department white paper blames overpopulation for the social unrest in countries as disparate as Vietnam and Iran. The paper concludes: "Our interests in many of these countries include—in addition to our traditional concern for human welfare and dignity—such geopolitical factors as strategic location, provision of military basis of support and supply of oil and other critical materials."

By some government and IFRP officials, population control is seen almost as a weapon. For example, Dr. Stephen Mumford, the head of IFRP's "Voluntary Sterilization Program," insists in his book *Population Growth Control* that the U.S. Department of Defense is the only American or world organization capable of intervening to control world population.

During the past ten years the IFRP has become increasingly involved in finding experimental test subjects overseas. According to Potts, the IFRP "is funded by U.S. AID [Agency for International Development] and is devoted to shortening the time between the development of new fertility-control technology and its use in family planning." In addition to the $31 million the IFRP has received from AID and other government agencies to date, it is also generously supported by private population-control organizations like the International Planned Parenthood Federation and contraceptive manufacturers, including the Upjohn company.

What Malcolm Potts learned in December 1978 was the alarming results of autopsies on two rhesus monkeys that had been injected with Depo-Provera. The autopsies revealed endometrial carcinoma—cancer of the uterine lining. The monkeys, two out of ten in the study, had routinely been sacrificed at the end of FDA-required animal safety tests. Reportedly, not a single case of endometrial cancer had ever been found in rhesus monkeys prior to these experiments, despite the large number of these animals that have been used in medical experiments.

Malcolm Potts knew bad news when he heard it, but he was not about to abandon his support for Depo-Provera. The report he signed contained the plan for counteracting the negative impact of the primate cancers.

Less than a year earlier, the FDA had viewed Depo-Provera as "posing a substantial threat to potential users" because beagle dogs treated with the hormone showed an "increased incidence of mammary carcinoma." The decision to test Depo on monkeys resulted from the established toxicological principle that drugs must be tested on two or more species. Determination of safety was to be based on "the least favorable result in any one of the species." Now that a second species—and more importantly, a primate—had shown cancer, it seemed obvious that Depo-Provera could be a serious threat to women.

Potts is unconvinced by these studies. He insists that Depo must be given to millions of women over the course of decades before its carcinogenic effects can be judged. "We are not going to know whether Depo-Provera is safe," he explains, "until a large number of women use it for a very long time. . . . You cannot prove a drug is safe until you use it." When asked for how long, Potts replied, "I would say at least two decades. You could even make the argument that it would be two generations, as in the case of cancer of the vagina, which appears to develop in female babies born to women who had hormones in pregnancy. We are not going to be totally confident about the equation of risks and benefits for about 30 years. It is really that sort of time scale."

Despite his insistence on the primacy of massive human experimentation, Potts had nonetheless claimed, before the monkey experiments showed signs of cancers, "that the absence of tumors in monkeys is comforting." However, when the malignant tumors appeared, Potts' comfort and composure disappeared. He must have known that once the news of monkey cancers reached the public, an anti-Depo avalanche could crush the program.

He as almost right. The family-planning world was stunned by the news. Philippine representatives, for example, informed the United Nations Fund for Population Activities that their government intended to stop its Depo program completely. In Washington, D.C., the final report from the House Committee on Population called the findings "disturbing."

As concern mounted in Washington and New York and in Third World capitals, population-control specialists at the U.N. World Health Organization (WHO) attempted to smother the doubts about Depo. Potts was aware of these efforts and wrote in an unpublished report, "WHO seems to be accumulating arguments rather similar to those that were used in the case of the beagles, that the monkeys data should not be applied to women."

While less-imaginative colleagues at the World Health Organization and elsewhere searched for ways to dismiss the validity of the new findings, Potts veered off in a more creative direction. He understood the reasoning behind giving high doses of a drug to a few monkeys: such a technique highlights a lower risk that might apply to very large numbers of women. To trump those studies, a study on women would have to be produced. The document he signed outlined both his reasoning and his plan.

Missionary Trail

Dr. Edwin McDaniel springs from a tradition of medical missionaries. Born in Michigan, he moved to Thailand as a child with his missionary parents. His son is a medical missionary. Ed McDaniel has spent 33 years "trying my best to save the lives of these people, whom I have come to know and love since childhood."

He has much compassion for Thai women and is articulate about it. "If one has never seen a pale, attractive young woman, crazed with high fever and septicemia, rapidly fade away and die before one's very eyes, as I have, because of a botched up criminal abortion, or if one has never seen a mother of five, purple and gasping her last, in the throes of air hunger, because a few hours earlier a granny midwife had stomped on her pregnant uterus until the thin wall of the uterus burst open; and the woman, now hemorrhaging from the ruptured uterus, has been brought to the hospital too late—all because the mental, emotional, physical and economic burden of adding yet *another* baby to the family has simply been just too much for her and her day-laborer husband to face up to. If one has not personally seen piteous cases like these (and suicides due to the shame or economic crisis of an unwanted pregnancy), then one has not seen *life as it really is* for most of the world's poor."

For the first 15 years of his practice at the McCormick Hospital in Chiang Mai, McDaniel concentrated on "curing disease, with a minor 'sideline' of certain public health measures." These included malaria prevention and immunization against diphtheria, whooping cough, tetanus, typhoid and polio.

Later he took over the Department of Obstetrics and Midwifery, because "no other doctor wanted it." McDaniel recognized that to see women safely through their pregnancies and deliveries was not enough. "I came to realize that to give complete obstetrical care (and, indirectly, whole-family welfare) to our women, we had to *also* help them to have children *when* and *in the numbers* that they really wanted!"

According to McDaniel, the birth-control methods available at the time were unsuitable for the area. His patients considered diaphragms clumsy and were embarrassed to be fitted by a male doctor. Condoms proved expensive and were associated with prostitution. A month's supply of contraceptive pills cost the equivalent of a week's wages for a local day-laborer.

In the summer of 1963, on home leave in the United States, McDaniel learned about the IUD. He viewed the new contraceptive as "a possible panacea." The initial response in Thailand to the IUD was phenomenal. But soon the well-known IUD-associated complications appeared—expulsions, pelvic pain, infections, uterine perforations and septic abortions.

Faced with an overwhelming problem but inadequate tools, McDaniel was in search of a technical breakthrough. In April 1965, three years before the dog and monkey experiments began, a friend gave him a small supply of Depo-Provera. McDaniel was so impressed that by the end of the year he made Depo a standard family-planning option for women in Thailand.

Now, more than 15 years and nearly one million injections later, despite the formation of tumors in dogs and monkeys and an FDA ban on Depo as a contraceptive, the missionary doctor has no regrets. He believes Depo-Provera is "one of the safest and most remarkable drugs to come upon the world scene in recent years."

Missing Cases

Malcolm Potts knew and admired Ed McDaniel. He was particulary pleased with McDaniel's enthusiasm for Depo. Furthermore, he felt that Chiang Mai, where 100,000 women (more than half of the female population) had used Depo-Provera, was an ideal place to perform a human epidemiological study—a study that would, he believed, confirm Depo's safety once and for all.

IFRP documents show that Potts anticipated from the start that a human study performed in Chiang Mai would show no link between Depo-Provera and endometrial cancer. But he also knew that, at best, the findings "would only provide a weak assurance that Depo-Provera was not the cause of carcinoma of the endometrium." Nonetheless, it appears Potts felt the research was justified on the grounds that it could be used "by those in favor of continued use of Depo" to show that the monkey cancers were "not relevant to the human situation."

With this in mind, Potts traveled to Chiang Mai on February 17, 1979, to confer with McDaniel about setting up the study. Prior to his journey, Potts had received figures showing that 60 Thai women had been hospitalized in Chiang Mai with endometrial cancer between 1973 and 1978. In a telegram to McDaniel sent on January 4, 1979, Potts inquired about the women's ages. He knew that endometrial cancer primarily strikes older women and he thought that the cases would probably follow this statistical pattern. If the women were too old to have used Depo-Provera, they would not be good subjects for the study. Potts wrote, "The usefulness of sixty cases is assessed in the table appended, although it is suspected that many (perhaps most) of the women are beyond reproductive years."

Contrary to this reasonable expectation, Potts and McDaniel learned that most of the cancer victims were young enough to have been injected. An IFRP report prepared upon Potts' return says that "the number of relatively young women with the disease is notable, and the IFRP and colleagues in Chiang Mai feel there is an obligation to check whether women with the disease have used Depo-Provera. This should be done without delay."

Considering their admitted obligation, their sense of urgency and their solvency, it is difficult to understand why Potts and McDaniel never did determine how many of the original 60 cancer patients had used Depo-Provera. This was acknowledged to be a simple task. An unpublished IFRP report even states that "at a minimum, it is both necessary and relatively easy to check how many, if any, women in the group have had Depo-Provera."

But the study *never* determined how many of the women were injected; and the alarming information about the young age of many of the cancer victims was not revealed.

Ostensibly, the study was a survey of *all* hospital admissions for proven endometrial cancer in Chiang Mai and neighboring Lumpoon provinces over a five-year period. However, Potts and McDaniel examined only a carefully selected fraction of the diagnosed cases.

Here is how they systematically disqualified the cases they chose not to examine.

First, 11 of the 60 cases simply disappeared. Only 49 cases of endometrial cancer occurred in the area between 1974 and 1978 according to the study, despite initial reports.

Minus 11 cases.

Potts and McDaniel then eliminated 12 subjects with so-called presumptive diagnoses, whose hospital records indicated treatment for endometrial cancer but for whom no pathology reports were obtained.

Minus 23 cases.

Another ten cases were discarded as "disproven by negative pathology reports." A careful reading of the text shows that rather than being disproven, these pathology reports simply had not arrived at the medical record room in time for the study. (If the researchers had waited to obtain these records, it would have more than doubled the number of subjects ultimately studied.)

Minus 33 cases.

Next removed were 11 cases involving women who came from other provinces to be treated for cancer in the Chiang Mai-area hospitals. The rationale for dropping these cases was that Depo had not been used widely in other Thai provinces. The doctors provided no information about these women, who may have been migrant workers or may have lived in Chiang Mai. In either case they might have been exposed to Depo.

Minus 44 cases.

Of the 16 remaining subjects, four were eliminated because they were over 60 and were therefore too old to have used Depo-Provera; another because she had never married or borne children and was therefore unlikely to have practiced birth control; a sixth because she had given a false address; and a final one because she had moved far away from her original home. The reasons seem fairly legitimate for eliminating these seven cases from the study.

Minus 51 cases.

Of the cases of endometrial cancer originally reported, only nine were scrutinized. Of these nine cases, Potts and McDaniel found that none had used Depo-Provera. They obtained this information through nurse interviews or by registered mail. Only four of the nine were still alive, and family members provided information on the five dead subjects.

From this sample of nine Thai women came a conclusion that has had an impact on the lives of millions of women throughout the world. "Widespread and long-term use of DMPA [Depo-Provera] can and should be continued." In addition, the study concluded that "the data on monkeys given very large doses of Depo-Provera for ten years should not apply to women given normal doses of DMPA for prolonged periods."

Depo Abuse

The Chiang Mai study, or at least the conclusion of the study, cleared the way for expanded Depo-Provera use. Indonesia, Thailand and other Third World nations confidently stepped up their programs. And privately population-control groups like the International Planned Parenthood Federation and the population council continued their worldwide promotion and use of the Depo-Provera injection as the preferred birth-control method.

Accompanying the expanded use of Depo since the Potts-McDaniel study—and perhaps more significant than it—has been the torrent of abuse surrounding the distribution of Depo. At a Cambodian refugee camp in Khao I Dang, Thailand, for example, women who agreed to take the drug were given a chicken—a powerful inducement in a camp where refugees are fed about four ounces of meat a week. And the International Committee of the Red Cross (ICRC) reported that at the Kamput refugee camp the injections were simply compulsory. According to Dr. N. J. Willmott, medical coordinator at Kamput for the ICRC, in a letter dated February 14, 1980, "Depo-Provera is given to women intending marriage as a prerequisite to marriage."

Women in many Third World countries are reluctant to complain about contraceptive side effects. Prior to Depo-Provera use, when the intrauterine device was the contraceptive of choice, the Indonesian army would force women to submit to IUD insertions by male doctors, despite the women's religious and personal objections. An AID evaluation report comments, "Government is feared and obeyed, but not resisted—not even in the subtle form of complaints of physical discomfort that might be expected from IUD acceptors."

In Bangladesh an army officer quoted in the English language *Bangladesh Observer* stated that "legal and other measures for fertility control must be preimposed to coerce [villagers] to take involuntary birth-control measures." One of the most prevalent forms of coercion is to dangle food in front of women whose families are desperately hungry.

British journalist Joseph Hanlon gave the following eyewitness account from Bangladesh: "The big AID sponsors, especially the World Bank, are putting considerable pressure on Bangladesh to show quick results in its family-planning program. In practice, that means sterilization and injection, which can be done with little involvement of the women themselves and without setting up a proper family-planning and maternal health service.

"Women are under pressure to participate. For example, in many areas of Bangladesh, those who are sterilized or on injectables receive six kilograms of wheat a month, plus oil, powdered milk and fish meal. These 'rewards' are taken from the U.N. World Food Program's 'Vulnerable Group Feeding Program,' which is supposed to go to mothers of small children without condition. But part of the international cooperation at a local level is that somehow no one ever officially tells World Food Program Headquarters in Rome that the rules are being bent."

The reader should not be left with the impression that women accept Depo-Provera only under coercion. Many welcome it as a highly effective birth-control method, which it is. Long before Depo, the demand existed for contraception by poverty-stricken women who sought greater control of their maternal destinies. The Depo program is objectionable because women are told that the injection is safe—despite the evidence to the contrary.

Nor should the impression be left that everyone in the family-planning movement accepts the Potts-McDaniel conclusion and remains loyal to Depo-Provera. Dr. Colin McCord, for example, while he was a U.N. technical advisor, informed the Bangladesh government that the current Depo campaign could be disastrous in more ways than one. "I know that Depo-Provera is popular and effective," he says, "but the dropout rates are high, and I don't think the small increment in fertility control that will result from the use of this drug justifies the possibility that we might be responsible for an epidemic of uterine cancer 10 to 20 years from now. Such an epidemic would be a disaster, not only for the women involved, but also for the credibility of population-control programs."

But perhaps the most devastating news to Depo enthusiasts was contained in a "confidential" WHO report released *after* the Potts-McDaniel study. The report says that "there has been a marked increase in admissions for cancer of the cervix and breast" in Chiang Mai. WHO officials, grasping for an explanation that defends Depo, attribute the escalation to increased hospital utilization and cancer screening. The report does not say how many of the cancer victims had used Depo-Provera. It seems obvious, though, that if cervical and breast cancer are increasing in an area where 56 percent of the women are using or have used Depo, the drug is not yet above suspicion.

The Newest Technique

The Depo-Provera controversy is only one of many issues in a much larger crisis facing women, whose bodies have become the battleground in the war against population explosion.

Today Depo-Provera is the focal point because it is, for population-control practitioners, the simplest, most effective technology—one shot every three to six months brings almost 100-percent results.

But Depo is only a single step in the modern development of increasingly bizarre birth-control technologies. What's next?

The latest development is called "Silastic implantation." A Silastic implant is a solid time-release substance placed under the skin by a large-gauge needle. The implant gradually releases synthetic progesterone into a woman's bloodstream and can effectively create infertility for from three to five years.

There have been no long-term animal studies on this new device. In the summer of 1980, the WHO became involved in experiments testing Silastic implants—on the women of Chiang Mai province, Thailand.

---

15. Birth Control Pills

The Boston Women's Health Book Collective

The Food and Drug Administration approved the Pill for marketing in 1960 without adequate testing or study. A synthetic pill almost 100 percent effective in preventing pregnancy when taken daily, it created tremendous excitement among the medical, scientific, pharmaceutical and population-control communities. Very few professionals cautioned against using it too widely or too quickly; to do so meant fighting against the prevailing ideology which supported rapid development and distribution of new drugs generally and risking the charge of holding back progress. To women, it seemed like a wonderful alternative to the methods then available.

The Pill became a gigantic experiment: within two years about 1.2 million American women used it, and by 1973 the number rose to an estimated 10 million. Though the increase in its use has ended, the Pill is still the most widely used reversible contraceptive both in the U.S. and worldwide.

Many women first heard about its dangers not from physicians but when they read Barbara Seaman's book, *The Doctor's Case Against the Pill,* published in 1969 and again, updated, in 1979, and elected to stop taking the Pill or to find another alternative. Although medical literature confirmed the dangers of the Pill as early as 1962, it was not until 1970 that the FDA issued package warnings, which one FDA official now admits "didn't say much of anything important." Since 1978 the FDA has required physicians and pharmacists to hand out comprehensive information sheets on its possible negative effects and complications.

In late 1980, the drug company G. D. Searle financed a publicity campaign to falsely reassure women about the Pill's safety. Searle misrepresented the findings of a ten-year government-funded project carried out in Walnut Creek, California, one of three major studies begun in 1968. (The other two were done in England.) New information about the Pill is emerging all the time—in fact, it is now the most widely researched drug on the market. We need to evaluate carefully both the methods and purposes of this research.

How They Work

• • •

The Pill interrupts your menstrual cycle by introducing synthetic versions of the female hormones. Combination birth control pills prevent pregnancy primarily by inhibiting the development of the egg in the ovary. During your period, the low estrogen level normally indirectly triggers your pituitary gland to send out FSH, a hormone that starts an egg developing to maturity in one of your ovaries. The Pill gives you just enough synthetic estrogen to raise your estrogen level high enough to keep FSH from being released. So during a month on the Pill, your ovaries remain relatively inactive and there is no egg to be fertilized by sperm. This is the same principle by which a woman's body checks ovulation when she is pregnant: the corpus luteum and placenta put estrogen into her blood, thereby inhibiting FSH. So in a way, using much lower levels of hormones, the Pill simulates pregnancy, and some of the Pill's negative effects are like those of early pregnancy. If ovulation occurs, it is because your body needed a higher dose of estrogen than your Pill gave you to inhibit FSH, or because you have missed one or more pills.

Synthetic progesterone, called progestin, is used differently in different varieties of the Pill. The *combination pill* combines estrogen and progestin for the entire twenty or twenty-one days. Progestin provides two important extra contraceptive effects: increased thickness of cervical mucus and incomplete development of the uterine lining. The *progestin-only pills* depend on these two effects and do not inhibit ovulation. They are therefore not quite as effective in preventing pregnancy. The *sequential pill* uses estrogen alone for several days and then a combination of estrogen and progestin. Less effective than combination pills, and with more dangerous effects than the other two, sequentials were taken off the market by the FDA in 1976.*

Effectiveness

The combination pills have the very low theoretical pregnancy rate of 0.5 percent, but in actual use, they show a failure rate of 2 percent. Pregnancy can occur if you forget to take you pill for two or more days, if you don't use a backup method of birth control for your first packet of pills or while taking antibiotics for an acute infection, and occasionally when you change from one brand of pill to another. (In this case, use an extra method for two weeks to be safe.)

• • •

Reversibility

If you want to become pregnant, stop taking pills at the end of a packet. It may be several months before your ovaries are functioning regularly, and your first non-Pill periods may be a week or two late or missed completely. It is a good idea to use another method of birth control for three to six months after you go off the Pill to allow your body to return to normal before you try to get pregnant.

It is unclear at present whether women who have taken the Pill have a higher rate of temporary or permanent infertility or a higher number of miscarriages. Most women do have successful pregnancies after they go off the Pill. However, some women, especially those who menstruated irregularly before taking the Pill, have difficulty conceiving after they stop taking it. If you have not started to ovulate within one year after going off the Pill, you can request treatment with clomiphene citrate.

Safety

Many of us are uneasy about taking a medication which affects almost every organ in our bodies each day for months and years, since its effects have not been conclusively tested and it has been in wide use for only twenty years. Yet some of us choose to take whatever risks are involved because we falsely believe we are getting 100 percent effectiveness and absolutely don't want to become pregnant. What price do we pay for this alleged perfect protection?

---

*Some pharmacies still have them in stock and physicians may be prescribing them. If you are using Oracon, NorQuen, Ortho-Novum SQ or other sequentials, get your prescription changed to a combination or progestin-only pill or use another form of birth control.

A great deal of information exists on the adverse effects of the Pill, as the following pages demonstrate. In most cases of Pill-related injury or death, women had not been examined carefully enough by the doctor who prescribed the Pill for them, had not had checkups while taking the Pill, or had not been told that there was some risk involved in taking it. Some women ignored pains that were, in fact, warning signals, and sought help too late. Some of the Pill-related deaths were unpredictable and unpreventable.

How Long to Take the Pill

If you are not now experiencing problems, you may want to enjoy the freedom of the Pill indefinitely. Yet if you take the Pill for many years at a time, you are in a sense part of a huge experiment on the long-term effects of daily hormone ingestion in healthy women. Researchers disagree on how long a woman should stay on the Pill. Some suggest two- or three-year intervals with three-month breaks in between; others say in some cases it is safe to take it for ten years without stopping. If you want to have a baby at some point later on, you may choose not to stay on the Pill for more than two to four years at a time. Once you pass forty, you are at higher risk of Pill-related death. Some researchers believe that complication and problems increase the longer you take the Pill, and you may continue to have problems for years after you stop taking it.

Going Off the Pill

It is a sad fact that many women get pregnant in the first few months after going off the Pill because they feel awkward using another method of birth control, especially one of the safer barrier methods. We need discussion, information and support in making the switch to another method. It helps to have a partner or partners who understand and appreciate our desire to change to a safer form of contraception.

Warning Signals

Any problem lasting more than two or three cycles should be reported to a physician or medical facility. The following are symptoms of serious problems: severe pain or swelling in the legs (thigh or calf), bad headache, blurred vision (or loss of sight), chest pain or shortness of breath, abdominal pain. *Report these immediately,* for they are signs of heart attack, stroke or liver tumors and mean you should stop taking the Pill. (*Note on leg pain:* Some leg cramps may be caused by fluid retention induced by the estrogen in the Pill. Don't confuse this with severe leg pain, but also don't hesitate to call a medical practitioner if your leg cramps become painful.)

Who Should Absolutely Not Use the Pill

The Pill is dangerous for certain women. The FDA requires drug companies to publish a list of contraindications and conditions that prohibit the use of the Pill and include the list with your package of pills. Do not use the Pill if you have:

Any disease or condition associated with poor blood circulation or excess blood clotting: Bad varicose veins, thrombophlebitis (clots in veins, frequently in the leg), pulmonary embolism (blood clot which has traveled to the lung, usually from the leg), stroke, heart disease or defect, coronary artery disease.

Hepatitis or other liver diseases. As it is the liver which metabolizes sex steroids (progesterone and estrogen), no one with liver disease should take the Pill until the disease is cleared up. Use a good alternative method of contraception, because pregnancy can be a great strain on the liver. A woman who tends to get jaundice during pregnancy should not use the Pill.

Liver tumors; undiagnosed abnormal genital bleeding; cancer of the breast or of the reproductive organs; pregnancy.

Who Is Strongly Advised Not to Use the Pill

Women with the following conditions are strongly advised not to use the Pill:

Migraine headaches.*

Hypertension. A woman with high blood pressure (hypertension) or mild varicose veins must take the Pill with caution.*

Diabetes,* prediabetes or a strong family history of diabetes. Sugar metabolism is extensively altered in women on the Pill. The progestin tends to bind the body's insulin and keep it out of circulation, which increases a diabetic woman's insulin requirement. If you are a diabetic, or if close relatives are diabetic, you should have regular periodic blood tests if you go on the Pill. Many doctors do put diabetic women on the Pill because pregnancy is especially hazardous to a diabetic.

Gallbladder disease.*

Cholecystitis during previous pregnancy, congenital hyperbilirubinemia (Gilbert's Disease).

Mononucleosis in the acute phase.

Sickle cell anemia or trait. Black women planning to go on the Pill should have a sickle cell test. If it is positive, you should discuss the hazards of going on the Pill, which include an increased risk of intravascular blood clotting.*

Elective surgery planned in the next four weeks.

Major surgery requiring immobilization.*

Long leg casts or major injury to the lower leg.

Impaired liver function in the past year.

Women over forty run a statistically higher risk of thromboembolism and other complications when taking the Pill. Since such risks also increase during pregnancy, women over forty should consider a barrier method or sterilization—tubal ligation for you or vasectomy for your partner.

Smokers, especially women who smoke fifteen or more cigarettes a day, run a statistically higher risk of stroke and heart attack on the Pill.

Who Should Probably Not Use the Pill

Women with the following situations or conditions should probably not use the Pill:

Lactation. The Pill may dry up the mother's supply of milk, especially if administered soon after she gives birth. Even if it does not dry it up, the Pill decreases the amounts of protein, fat and calcium in the milk. Some estrogen will also come through in the milk. At present this is a controversial subject, since no one knows the long-term effects of this substance on children.

---

*Starred conditions are contraindications to combination pills and may not be contraindications to progestin-only pills.

Pregnancy ended within the past ten to fourteen days.*

Weight gain of ten pounds or more while taking the Pill.*

Women who don't have regular periods (at least ten periods a year). This includes women who are just beginning to menstruate and women whose menstrual cycles suggest that they aren't ovulating or that they might have infertility problems.*

Cardiac or renal disease or a history of these diseases.*

Conditions likely to make a woman unreliable at following Pill instructions: major psychiatric problems, alcoholism, mental retardation.

It may not be wise for women with the following conditions to take the Pill: **depression,* chloasma, or hair loss related to pregnancy or a history of such;* asthma;* epilepsy;* uterine fibromyomata;* acne; varicose veins, history of hepatitis but normal liver function tests for at least one year; a woman who is a DES daughter.**

Complications and Negative Effects

The Pill enters our bloodstream, travels through the body and affects many tissues and organs, just as natural estrogens and progesterone do. However, the hormones in the Pill are synthetic and have exaggerated effects on some women.

Even though there is an FDA-required package insert, health workers and doctors must clearly explain the risks we take in choosing the Pill. Unfortunately, they don't always know themselves. Also, they sometimes believe that effects are psychosomatic and that telling us what might happen will influence our perceptions. This attitude is insulting and dangerous. Find out what the risks are before you get a prescription for the Pill.

Many of us experience none or only a few effects from using the Pill. Some women have pregnancy-like symptoms during the first three months, but after that they don't notice anything. Also, many women choose to put up with mild effects in exchange for the Pill's convenience and effectiveness. If you want to use it, try it for a few months to see how your body responds.

The Pill and Circulatory Disease: Heart Attack and Stroke

In general, the risk of death due to circulatory disease (heart attacks, strokes, pulmonary embolism, other clotting disorders) is much higher in women who use or have used the Pill than among women who have never used it. (This may be related to higher triglyceride [blood fat] and cholesterol levels in Pill users.)[1] This risk probably increases the longer you take the Pill, and persists even when you stop if you have taken it for at least five years.[2] Cardiovascular disease is responsible for most Pill-related deaths. If you are a smoker and use the Pill, your chance of death due to a circulatory disease is ten times that of nonsmokers who have never used it. Women between thirty-five and forty-four on the Pill have a five times' greater death rate due to circulatory disease.* See above for warning signals.

---

*Starred conditions are contraindications to combination pills and may not be contraindications to progestin-only pills.
*In other words, the risk of circulatory disease is low for nonsmokers who are healthy and younger than thirty-five, even if they take the Pill. (*Contraceptive Technology 1982–1983*, p. 49)

The Pill and High Blood Pressure

Between 5 and 7 percent of women on the Pill will develop hypertension (abnormally high blood pressure) and will be at greater risk for heart attack and stroke. Women who develop hypertension should go off the Pill. Women with a family history of hyptertension or who already have high blood pressure are strongly advised by practitioners to choose some other form of birth control.

It is not yet clear whether the effects of hypertension created by the Pill continue even after you stop taking it. Some studies indicate that certain effects persist. Also, the incidence of high blood pressure tends to increase with increased duration of Pill use and with age. Low-dose pills cause fewer problems, but are not quite as effective in preventing pregnancy.

The Pill and Cancer

A study done in 1968 showed that cervical cancer was about three to five times more common in women who had used oral contraceptives for at least four years than among women who had never used the Pill. This study scared many of us unnecessarily, because when the statistics were examined more closely, it became apparent that the deciding factor was not Pill use but the frequency of sexual intercourse and, in particular, the number of sexual partners. The Pill is implicated here only in that it allows some of us to feel freer to have sexual experience, since it provides constant protection against pregnancy.

Recently, however, more studies are showing that there may be particular connections between the Pill and certain forms of cancer. For example, if a woman has cervical dysplasia (abnormal cells in the cervix), the Pill may cause that dysplasia to become cancerous.[3]

There may be a relationship between skin cancer and the Pill, although researchers disagree and are currently studying this.[4]

Researchers disagree about the relationship between the Pill and breast cancer. The most recent research indicates that there is no relationship between the Pill and breast cancer.[5] However, some unanswered questions still remain about the long-term effects of using the Pill, especially its use before a woman's first full-term pregnancy.

The sequential pill (which has been removed from the market) has been linked to cancer of the uterus. Several recent studies show that the combination pill may *protect* women from endometrial and ovarian cancer. However, one of these studies, in which age was considered as a factor, found no protection from ovarian cancer for women under forty years of age. Theoretically, the progesterone in the combination pill balances the estrogen. It's not yet known how long after women stop taking the Pill that this possible protection lasts.

The Pill and Your Present or Future Children

Birth defects (sex malformation or cardiac defects) have been reported in increased incidence among babies of mothers who were taking the Pill while pregnant, who took hormones to prevent miscarriages, who were given progesterone as a pregnancy test or who became pregnant within three months of stopping the Pill.

There may be a higher rate of jaundice among infants whose mothers took the Pill before pregnancy.

Don't use the Pill while breastfeeding.

Children who find pills and eat them may become nauseated. We do not know what harm this may cause. You should go to or call a medical facility if your child swallows more than a few pills.

• • •

164

Other Effects

In some women, other effects of the Pill include: migraines or other frequent headaches, diabetes, depression, change in intensity of sexual desire and response, nausea, fatigue, vaginitis and vaginal discharge, urinary tract infection, changes in menstrual flow, vaginal bleeding or staining between periods, breast changes, skin problems, gum inflammation, liver and gallbladder disease, aggravate epilepsy and asthma, virus infections, and cervical dysplasia.

• • •

Beneficial Effects

Besides greater freedom from pregnancy, the Pill has a number of beneficial effects. Women taking it have shorter menstrual periods with less bleeding and cramping. Premenstrual tension tends to decrease. Iron deficiency anemia is less likely, probably because of decreased menstrual flow. Benign breast growths are less frequent. The Pill also protects against pelvic inflammatory disease (PID), and may protect against ovarian and endometrial cancer, functional ovarian cysts and rheumatoid arthritis.

Nutrition and the Pill

The Pill alters the nutritional requirements of women who take it, which may contribute to some of the complications and negative effects. Pill use has been linked to increased requirements for Vitamins C, B_2 (riboflavin), B_{12} and especially B_6 (pyridoxine) and folic acid* (folate or folacin). Women who face the greatest nutritional risks are teenagers, poor women, women recovering from a recent illness or surgery or who have just given birth, women who have taken the Pill for two years or more who take brands with moderate to high estrogen levels. Since metabolic changes occur within the first few months after beginning the Pill, it is a good idea to have a physical exam and blood tests after you have used the Pill for six months to see if you are suffering from any particular deficiencies.

Studies show that women on the Pill have impaired glucose tolerance tests. This means that their carbohydrate metabolism is adversely affected, resulting in weight gain and/or elevated glucose and insulin levels (ranging from mild to diabetic). These alterations are most often seen when women take combination pills, especially those containing seventy-five micrograms or more of estrogen. Trying a different brand and eating wholesome foods may help to decrease glucose and insulin levels.[6]

While on the Pill, try to maintain a healthy nutritional balance: 1. by eating wholesome foods—especially those containing complex carbohydrates; 2. by reducing sugar intake; and 3. by taking vitamins, especially B-complex, C supplements and folic acid. Doing the same thing for a few months after you stop taking the Pill is also a good idea, especially if you plan to become pregnant. A higher than average number of women who conceived within four months after discontinuing the Pill develop folic acid and B_6 deficiencies during pregnancy.[7]

---

*Up to 20 percent of women taking the Pill will show abnormal Pap smears, which may be caused by folic acid deficiencies. The Pill seems to impair our ability to absorb the type of folic acid found in food, but does not do so when the folic acid is already broken down in a vitamin pill. Some nonprescription vitamins contain 400 micrograms of folic acid, the Recommended Daily Allowance (RDA).

Water Metabolism and Weight Gain

The Pill alters water metabolism. Estrogenic pills (Enovid, Ovulen) can cause fluid retention because of increased sodium, a temporary and usually cyclic effect. You may experience swollen ankles, breast tenderness, discomfort with contact lenses or a weight gain of up to five pounds. Changing your brand of Pill, reducing your salt intake moderately or taking a diuretic drug are all ways of controlling water retention. (Diuretics have their own risks, such as robbing your body of potassium, so use them sparingly if at all and only with a health practitioner's advice.)

Progestin-dominant pills (Ortho-Novum, Norlestrin, Ovral) can cause appetite increase and permanent weight gain because of the buildup of protein in muscular tissue. If you want to gain weight, this is helpful. Pill-related depression may also lead to increased appetite and weight gain.

How to Get Pills

As we have seen, certain physical conditions make taking birth control pills very dangerous, *so it is in your vital interest to have a careful exam before taking pills.* Don't borrow them from a friend. Be sure a health practitioner gives you an internal pelvic exam, breast exam, eye exam, Pap smear and blood-pressure, blood and urine tests. The interview should include questions about you and your family's medical history of breast cancer, blood clots, diabetes, migraines and so on. If you were born between 1945 and 1970, find out if your mother took DES while she was pregnant. If so, you should have a colposcopy test, as you might have adenosis, a condition that the Pill can aggravate. *Too many people prescribe and use birth control pills hurriedly; make sure you are carefully checked for each one of the contraindications.* When you are on the Pill, you should have an exam every six months to a year.

How to Use Pills

Combination pills come in packets of twenty-one or twenty-eight pills. With twenty-one-day pills, you take one pill every day for twenty-one days and then stop for seven days, during which time you will menstruate. With twenty-eight-day pills, which give you twenty-one hormone pills followed by seven different-colored placebos (without drugs), you take one pill a day with no pause between packets. You will have your period during the time that you are taking the seven different-colored pills. The twenty-eight-day pill is good if you feel you would have trouble remembering the on-and-off schedule of the twenty-one-day pill. There is no medical difference between them.

Most pill regimens start the first pill on the fifth day after your period starts, counting the day you start your period as day one. (Some pills start on the first Sunday after your period comes or on the first day your period begins.) Take one pill at approximately the same time each day. If you feel nausea, take the pill with a meal or after a snack at bedtime. Here is an almost foolproof schedule: take a pill at bedtime, check the packet each morning to make sure you've taken a pill the night before, and carry a spare packet of pills with you in case you get caught away from home or lose pills. *Read the directions carefully.*

If You Forget a Pill

Take the forgotten pill as soon as you remember it, and take the next pill at its appointed time, even if this means taking two pills in one day. If you forget two pills, take two pills as soon as you remember, then take two pills the next day to catch up and use an additional method of contraception (foam, condoms) for the rest of that cycle. You may have some spotting. If you forget three pills or more, withdrawal bleeding will probably begin, so act as though you are at the end of a cycle. Don't make up the missed pills; stop taking your pills and start using a second method of birth control immediately. Start a new package of pills the Sunday after you realized your missed three or more pills, even if you are bleeding. Use an extra method of birth control from the day you realize you forgot the pills through two weeks of the next cycle. If you miss a pill or two and skip a period, start using another method of birth control and get a pregnancy test. If you've been taking your pills correctly and you skip a period, it is unlikely that you are pregnant, but you may need a different brand of pill.

Protection

Your first packet of pills may not protect you completely, as an egg may have started to develop before you take the first pill. To be safe, use another method of birth control for the first month. After this, you will be protected against pregnancy all month long, even during the days between packets. Recent evidence suggests that if you are taking antibiotics for an acute infection, or if you get sick and have several days of vomiting or diarrhea, you should use another method of birth control for the rest of the cycle to be safe.

Responsibility

Birth control pills are primarily the woman's responsibility. You see the doctor, get examined, remember to take the pill, feel the effects and run the risks.

Advantages

Almost complete protection against unwanted pregnancy.
Regularity of menstrual cycles—a period every twenty-eight days.
Lighter flow during periods. This effect pleases most women, bothers some.
Relief of premenstrual tension.
Fewer menstrual cramps or none at all.
An estrogenic pill will clear up acne for some women.
You may enjoy sex more because the fear of pregnancy is gone.
Taking the Pill has no immediate physical relationship to lovemaking, which is especially relaxing if you are just starting to have intercourse and have a lot to learn about your body and a man's. Later on, when you are more comfortable with sex and more able to communicate openly with your partner(s), the interruptions involved in using a diaphragm or foam and condoms may not seem so prohibitive.

Disadvantages

Most of the disadvantages have been described under the section on effects. The only one to add is that you do have to remember to take a pill every day. Some women are forgetful, or live lives that are too chaotic for them to remember to do so. Younger women who live at home and feel a need to hide their pills from their parents sometimes leave them behind or are unable to take them on time.

• • •

Notes

1. J. Schwartz, et al. *Connections: Nutrition, Contraception, Women, Eating.* Boston, MA: Boston Family Planning Project, 1982.
2. D. Slone, et al. "Risk of Myocardial Infarction in Relation to Current and Discontinued Use of Oral Contraceptives," *New England Journal of Medicine* 305:8 (1981), pp. 420–24.
3. E. Stern, et al. "Steroid Contraceptive Use and Cervical Dysplasia: Increase in the Risk of Progression," *Science* 196 (1977), p. 1460.
4. C. Bain, et al. "Oral Contraceptive Use and Malignant Melanoma," *Journal of the National Cancer Institute* 68 (1982), pp. 537–39; E. A. Holly, et al, "Cutaneous Melanoma in Relation to Exogenous Hormones and Reproductive Factors," *Journal of the National Cancer Institute* 70 (1983).
5. The Centers for Disease Control. "Long-Term Oral Contraceptive Use and the Risk of Breast Cancer; The Centers for Disease Control Cancer and Steroid Hormone Study," *Journal of the American Medical Association* 249 (1983), pp. 1591–95.
6. J. Schwartz, et al. *Connections: Nutrition, Contraception, Women, Eating.* Boston, MA: Boston Family Planning Project, 1982; Kay Behall, "Oral Contraceptives and Nutrition: A Report on Research in Progress," U.S. Department of Agriculture (undated).
7. Kay Behall. "Oral Contraceptives and Nutrition: A Report on Research in Progress," U.S. Department of Agriculture (undated), p. 2.

Chapter IV
Alcohol

Chapter 4 introduces one of the most commonly used and abused drugs in the United States—alcohol (only caffeine is used more frequently). In our lifetime, most of us will use alcohol, some of us will abuse alcohol and many of us who abuse alcohol will become alcoholics.

Why? Part of the answer to the pervasive use of this drug in America is based on alcohol's acceptability. Alcohol is legal and viewed as a legitimate social lubricant. As a result, we have few highly visible societal restrictions for alcohol, mainly use of the drug by people under a certain age (usually 21), some setting restrictions, and the use of a motor vehicle by individuals who are intoxicated. These few restrictions, combined with an almost caricature imagery of alcoholics which ranges from the stereotype skid row alcoholic to the "harmless drunk" with a lampshade on his head at the office party allow most of us to ignore the potential for harm caused by this drug.

Those who do become dependent on alcohol will experience a variety of physiological effects such as withdrawal symptoms when the drug is stopped, tolerance to the drug and "blackout" periods. Medical effects include hepatitis, cirrhosis, gastritis, and cerebral degeneration to name a few. Alcohol effects also include behavioral, psychological and attitudinal responses such as drinking despite understanding the serious medical consequences of abuse, drinking despite the loss of a job, the disruption of a marriage, and arrest for drunkenness or driving while intoxicated.

For those who admit to a problem with alcohol, the most visible and respected treatment program is Alcoholics Anonymous which defines alcoholism as a disease of the body characterized by an inherited predisposition or changed physiological response to alcohol; and, a disease of the mind, characterized by an obsession with alcohol. In the first selection in this chapter, Schneider traces the changes in American society which have shifted the view of alcoholism as a sin or a crime to a perception of alcoholism as a disease. He argues that three critical events (including the founding of A. A.), none of which were medical or scientific breakthroughs, precipitated this shift in definitions.

A U.S. Department of Health and Human Services report on the social consequences of alcohol use focuses on a series of social problems that emerge with abuse for the individual and the impact of that abuse on others. Included in this article is a discussion of differences between specific ethnic groups, sexes, and age groups. Economic costs like job absenteeism and accidents, as well as social costs like violent crime can all be traced to alcohol abuse.

Two groups have been recently targeted for legislative intervention for alcohol use: teenagers and inebriated drivers. Chauncey argues that teenage drinking is a created social problem that emerged in the 1970's in part as a result of advocacy work by the National Institute on Alcohol Abuse and Alcoholism.

Berg follows up with a general discussion of drunk driving and in particular the social movements that have emerged to respond to this problem including RID (Remove Intoxicated Drivers), MADD (Mothers Against Drunk Driving) and SADD (Students Against Drunk Driving). Berg traces the emergence of these groups and their public policy impact.

There is no one treatment, public policy or preventative intervention that will easily resolve the issue of how alcohol is used in society. However, what we hope is that this chapter will begin to establish a clearer understanding of the dimension and consequences of alcohol abuse.

16. Deviant Drinking as Disease: Alcoholism as a Social Accomplishment

Joseph W. Schneider

• • •

This paper presents a brief social history of the idea that certain kinds of deviant drinking behavior should be identified by the label "disease." The historical location is the United States since roughly the end of the eighteenth century. I define the claim that such behavior is a disease, is a social and political construction, warranting study in its own right (Berger and Luckmann, 1966; MacAndrew, 1969; Mulford, 1969; Freidson, 1970; Spector and Kitsuse, 1977). Whether such drinking "really" is a disease and, as such, what its causes might be, are not at issue. The analysis will trace the connection between ideas and social structures which appear to support or "own" them (Gusfield, 1975). This study is an investigation of the social bases of an assertion about a drinking behavior. More generally, this discussion is a case example of the medicalization of deviance and social control (Pitts, 1968, Szasz, 1970; Freidson, 1970: 244–277; Kittrie, 1971; Zola, 1972; Conrad, 1976) wherein a form of non-normative behavior is labelled first a "sin," then a "crime," and finally a "sickness."[1]

Clarification of the Problem

To those who treat problems caused by alcohol, debates about the definition of alcoholism as a disease are tedious and academic. After all, if one is employed in a hospital clinic treating alcoholics, then alcoholism must be a disease. However, whether something is a disease depends on significant portions of the medical community accepting the definition or not opposing its use by those in other fields. Because physicians represent the dominant healing profession in most industrialized societies, they have control over the use of the labels "sickness," "illness," and "disease," even if they are sometimes unable to treat those conditions effectively (Freidson, 1970:251). As such, these designations become political rather than scientific achievements (Spector and Kitsuse, 1977). Zola (1972) captures the expansive quality of medical jurisdiction clearly:

> My contention is that if anything can be shown in some way to effect the inner workings of the body and to a lesser extent the mind, then it can be labelled an "illness" or jurisdictionally a "medical problem."

This becomes particularly likely when the effects Zola describes are defined as negative rather than positive. The label "sick," although free from the opprobrium and implied culpability of "criminal," nevertheless involves a clearly disvalued moral condition, a deviation from "health," and a threat to the on-going network of interaction (Parsons, 1951). This common moral dimension provides the foundation for the historical shift from one system of social control (the church and state) increasingly to another (science and medicine).

Although it is clear that what is usually called "deviant drinking" fits Zola's description, I am here concerned with only a small segment of the medical model of alcohol: I focus on the idea that a particular pattern of repetitive, usually heavy, and always consequential drinking behavior should, of itself, be considered an instance of disease. A closely related yet distinct issue is the belief that some prior condition, usually identified as "pathological," causes the drinking which is seen as a "symptom" of this prior, and analytically distinct, pathology. Nor am I concerned with medicine's jurisdiction over the pharmacological, physiological, or psychological effects on the body, although this jurisdiction is, nonetheless, political.[2] I am concerned with the assertion that there is a disease called alcoholism that is identifiable independent of the specification of any conditions believed to be causes or effects of it.

• • •

The Post-Prohibition Rediscovery: The Yale Center, Alcoholics Anonymous, and the Jellinek Model

As Gusfield (1975) has suggested, there was virtually no organized interest in the disease concept from the end of the nineteenth century until after prohibition. There was considerable interests, however, in science and the professionalization of scientific research in American universities (Ben-David, 1971: 139–168). As the moral crusade against alcohol waned, science and scientific work became established. This trend had a great impact on the solutions Americans would pose for a variety of problems. It was not likely that alcohol, popular and again legal after 1933, would be seen as the source of deviant drinking. Intoxication and drunkenness, when requiring control, were problems assigned to civil authorities or the state. But with the rise and achievements of science, the apparent irrationality of chronic drunkenness became a more intriguing and less tolerable mystery.

In this context even more than during Rush's time, science and medicine seemed to hold promise. Three developments, all beginning within a decade after repeal, provided the foundation on which a "new" conceptualization of chronic deviant drinking was to rise in the twentieth century: The Yale research center; the self-help group, Alcoholics Anonymous; and a more careful, largely non-psychiatric, specification of the claim "alcoholism is a disease," referred to here as the Jellinek model. These developments provided the moral and political foundation for the subsequent rise of the more than two hundred million dollar federal bureaucracy, the National Institute on Alcohol Abuse and Alcoholism (NIAAA), and an "alcoholism industry" (Trice and Roman, 1972: 11–12) of professional and other workers devoted to treating this disease.

The Yale Research Center

The major body coordinating support for scientific work in the mid-1930s was the Research Council on Problems of Alcohol, organized shortly after repeal (Keller, 1976). This council was composed disproportionately of physicians and natural scientists interested in finding the causes of alcoholism. One member of the committee was Howard Haggard, the physician-director of the Laboratory of Applied Physiology at Yale University. Although the Council was unsuccessful in raising substantial monies for alcohol research, the prominence of its members gave the work scientific respectability. One grant, however, was consequential. It was for a review of the literature on the biological effects of alcohol on humans. The Council called on E. M. Jellinek, who had been doing research on neuroendocrine schizophrenia, to administer the project.

Haggard and his colleagues at the Yale Laboratory were involved in alcohol metabolism and nutritional research, a study which was gaining attention through the journal he founded in 1940, *The Quarterly Journal of Studies on Alcohol.*[3] As this work became more interdisciplinary within the natural sciences, Haggard came to believe that adequate study required an even more comprehensive approach. He invited E. M. Jellinek to Yale where he became the director of a truly multidisciplinary Yale Center for Alcohol Studies. The Center, the Laboratory, and the *Journal* became the core of American research on alcohol.[4] One of the Center's most significant contributions to the idea that alcoholism is a disease was its Summer School program, begun in 1943. These annual sessions were educational programs for concerned citizens from around the country who were involved in policy formation in their local communities. A common concern was what to do about alcoholism and alcohol-related problems. Straus (1976) and Chafetz and Demone (1962) suggest that the slogan "alcoholism is a disease" was introduced intentionally by Center staff in an attempt to reorient local and state policy and thinking about "alcoholics." These summer sessions were a good opportunity to disseminate the idea and point out its moral and political implications for treatment and cure. Although only a small segment of the summer program was devoted to the disease question, it soon became a topic of interest among the lay audience. Critics of this idea (Seeley, 1962; Pattison, 1969; Room, 1972; Robinson, 1976) suggest that its appeal must be seen in historical perspective and should be understood in terms of its practical, humanitarian, and administrative consequences rather than on the basis of scientific merit.[5]

These sessions also provided an established organizational foundation for the rise of the National Council on Alcoholism, the leading voluntary association in the United States devoted to public education about the disease (Chafetz and Demone, 1962; Paredes, 1976). The National Council known initially as the National Committee for Education on Alcoholism, was established in 1944 by three women: a former alcoholic, a journalist, and a psychiatrist. Mrs. Marty Mann, a one-time member of Alcoholics Anonymous, saw the National Committee as supplementing the work of A. A. for public education against ignorance about alcoholism's disease status. In the spring of 1944, these women met with Jellinek and determined that the National Committee "plan" be introduced in the Yale Summer School program. At the time of the original incorporation of the National Committee, its close connection with the Yale Center is evidenced by the Committee's officers: Howard Haggard was named President; E. M. Jellinek was Chairman of the Board; Professor Seldon Bacon of Yale was secretary, and Professor Edward Baird, also of Yale, was the Committee's legal counsel (Chafetz and Demone, 1962:141). Although the National Council become organizationally independent of the Yale Center in 1950, the association was propitious for the disease concept, as suggested by Chaftez and Demone (1962:142):

> NCA then began to search for a formula, something which would translate the basic facts of alcoholism into easily understood and remembered phrases. This resulted in the well known concepts or credo: Alcoholism is a disease and the alcoholic a sick person. The alcoholic can be helped and is worth helping. This is a public health problem and therefore a public responsibility.

Alcoholics Anonymous

In 1935 Alcoholics Anonymous was founded by two men, one of whom was a physician. Another physician, Dr. W. D. Silkworth, suggested to these founders the idea that alcoholism is an allergy of the body, the result of a physiological reaction to alcohol (Jellinek, 1960:160). Although medical opinion was generally skeptical of this questionable formulation (Jellinek, 1960:86–88), the concept of alcoholism as a mark of physiological sensitivity rather than moral decay was appealing and the allergy concept came to occupy a central although implicit place in A. A. ideology.

This theory had an additional advantage over other versions of the disease concept common during the early decades of the century that suggested alcoholism was a mental illness, a notion opposed strongly by A. A. (Trice and Roman, 1970). The appeal of allergy rests precisely in its identity as a bona fide medical or "disease" condition; people with allergies are victimized by, not responsible for, their condition. Trice and Roman (1970) suggest that much of the apparent success of A. A. involves the process of removing a stigmatized label and replacing it with a socially acceptable identity, such as "sick," "repentant," "recovered," or "controlled."

Two themes relevant to A. A.'s implicit disease concept are found in the first and third of the famous "Twelve Steps" to recovery, printed originally in *Alcoholics Anonymous* (1939). The first and most important step is, "We admitted we were powerless over alcohol—that our lives had become unmanageable." This is precisely the concept of "loss of control," a key idea in the early writing on alcoholism as a disease. Step three is "(We) have made a decision to turn our will and our lives over to the care of God as we understood him." Representatives of A. A. are quick to note that although this language sounds traditionally religious, such terms are to be interpreted broadly and on the basis of the individual's own biography. In discussing the interpretation of step three, Norris (1976) says:

> This turning over of self direction is akin perhaps to the acceptance of a regimen prescribed by a physician for a disease. The decision is made to accept reality, to stop trying to run things, and to let the "Power greater than ourselves" take over.

This partial description of the role of A. A. recalls Parsons's (1951) discussion of the sick role. Norris's suggestion that "God" might be interpreted to be a physician is perhaps not an extreme exaggeration given a doctor's control over the legitimacy of sickness and disease designations and admission to treatment.

The success attributed to the A. A. program in helping drinkers "recover" from alcoholism has become part of popular wisdom and is largely unchallenged, despite the lack of systematic empirical evidence. The effect of A.A. programs and ideology on thinking about alcoholism has been humanitarian and educational. The generally high regard for the program throughout the country serves to reinforce the disease concept implied in its approach. This pattern of regard is evidenced by recent research showing that a majority of physicians who agreed that alcoholism is a disease felt that referring such cases to A. A. was the best professional strategy (Jones and Helrich, 1972).

The Jellinek Model

The Yale Center and Alcoholics Anonymous provided important structural vehicles for the spread and popularization of the disease definition. Without the research and writing of Jellinek, and later Mark Keller (neither of whom, incidently, are physicians), this idea would probably have remained largely undeveloped. By comparison with previous efforts, Jellinek's work on the disease concept was brilliant and stimulated further research and writing. His reputation as a medical researcher, coupled with his being the director of the Yale Center, established his work as worthy of serious consideration. Excluding Howard Haggard, no one of Jellinek's stature since Rush had chosen to address the question at length.

In a series of articles beginning shortly after his arrival in New Haven and subsequently in a comprehensive manuscript, *The Disease Concept of Alcoholism* (1960), Jellinek (1941, 1946, 1952) set out his understanding of what it meant to call alcoholism a disease. In the early paper with psychiatrist Bowman (1941) as first author, Jellinek raised the question of alcoholism as an addiction. Using data obtained from a questionnaire in an issue of the A. A. *Grapevine*,[6] he constructed his well-known phase progression of the disease (Jellinek, 1946). A revision and extension was published in 1952 titled "The Phases of Alcohol Addiction," which appeared initially under the auspices of the Alcoholism Subcommittee of the World Health Organization, of which Jellinek was a member. Five phases of the progressive disease of alcohol addiction[7] were presented in terms of characteristic drinking and drinking-related behaviors. A major purpose of this paper, beyond presenting the phase progression, was to resurrect and clarify a distinction central to the disease concept. Drinking behavior that results in problems of living, or problem drinking, while important in its own right, was to be kept quite distinct from drinking behavior indicative of disease.[8] Such a distinction is important for the viability of the disease view: first because it serves to define the boundaries within which medicine could (and should, according to Jellinek) operate; second, because it suggests that forms of deviant drinking not properly called disease should be "managed only on the level of applied sociology, including law enforcement" (Jellinek, 1952). Non-disease forms of drinking behavior are here defined as moral problems to be met on moral terms; disease forms are, by contrast, medical problems and deserve the attention and treatment of the medical profession. Without defining alcoholism,[9] Jellinek proposes two subcategories of this larger entity: "alcohol addicts" and "habitual symptomatic excessive drinkers." Although both types have "underlying psychological or social pathology" that leads to drinking, only the former, after a number of years, develops a "loss of control", becomes addicted to alcohol, and is therefore diseased.

"Loss of control" as the distinction between the disease and non-disease types of alcoholism is elaborated in Jellinek's major work, *The Disease Concept of Alcoholism* (1960), which provides an exhaustive review of relevant research and a clearer description of the kinds of behaviors typically called "alcoholism." Using Greek letters to designate distinct types, Jellinek describes four major categories: Alpha, Beta, Gamma, and Delta (1960:36–39). The first two, Alpha and Beta, are not distinct disease entities: Alpha is the symptomatic drinking discussed in the 1952 essay; Beta refers specifically to all physical disease conditions resulting from prolonged substantial drinking, for example, polyneuropathy, gastritis, and cirrhosis of the liver. Only the Gamma and Delta types qualify as disease entities and are defined by four key elements, three of which are unambiguously physiological and common to both: 1) acquired increased tissue tolerance to alcohol, 2) adaptive cell metabolism, and 3) withdrawal symptoms. These three conditions lead to "craving" or physical dependence on alcohol. In addition, Gamma alcoholics lose control over how much they drink, which involves a progression from psychological to physiological dependence. Jellinek identified this type as most typical of the United States; as causing the greatest personal and social damage; and as the type of alcoholism recognized by Alcoholics Anonymous. The Delta alcoholic differs from Gamma in losing control not over quantity of intake, but rather over the ability to abstain for a significant period. As a result, this type of alcoholic, while suffering from the disease of alcoholism, rarely experiences the devastating consequences of the Gamma type. Jellinek suggests that the Delta drinking pattern is characteristic in certain European countries, particularly France. Although the disease is seen as a product of drinking, in neither case are the initial causes important in identifying the disease itself.

Jellinek's explicit development of addiction as the defining quality of the disease was a necessary condition for the contemporary medicalization of deviant drinking. Although addiction is itself not a particularly precise concept (See Coleman (1976) and Grinspoon and Bakalar (1976:177–178) for recent critiques), its contemporary association with narcotics and their physiological effects renders it a medicalized condition. Use of the term serves to locate the above forms of alcoholism in the body,[10] thus identifying them as legitimate problems for medical attention and intervention. Medicine reluctantly assumed responsibility. In 1956, The American Medical Association's Committee on Alcoholism (A. M. A., 1956) issued its well known statement encouraging medical personnel and institutions to accept persons presenting the syndrome of alcoholism defined by excessive drinking and "certain signs and symptoms of behavioral, personality, and physical disorder." A key sentence in the statement asserts:

> The Council on Mental Health, its Committee on Alcoholism, and the profession in general recognizes this syndrome of alcoholism as illness which justifiably should have the attention of physicians (A. M. A., 1956:750).

State and local medical societies soon created their own committees on alcoholism based on this reaffirmation of an idea that had already achieved a certain degree of official recognition. Keller (1976a) notes that "Alcohol Addiction" and "Alcoholism" were included in the first volume of the Standard Classified Nomenclature of Disease issued by the National Conference on Nomenclature of Disease in 1933 and approved by the American Medical Association. The significance of the 1956 statement was to reiterate this and other previous definitions. Regardless of how many American physicians agreed with the A.M.A. statement, the formal re-endorsement of the idea that alcoholics fall properly within medical jurisdiction became compelling "evidence" in support of the disease concept.[11] In this context, Jellinek's (1960:12) comments on whether his Gamma and Delta types are "really" diseases are instructive:

> Physicians know what belongs in their realm.
> . . . a disease is what the medical profession recognizes as such.
> . . . the medical profession has officially accepted alcoholism as an illness, whether a part of the public likes it or not, and even if a minority of the medical profession is disinclined to accept the idea.

Almost impatiently, the concept's leading proponent argues that diseases are what physicians say they are and since physicians, as represented by their major professional organization, have said so, alcoholism is a disease and that should settle the matter!

Since Jellinek's death in 1963, the leading spokesman for the disease concept has been Mark Keller, long time colleague of Jellinek at the Yale Center and editor of the *Journal of Studies on Alcohol,* a position he has held since its inception in 1940.[12] In two early essays, Keller (1958, 1962) attempted to develop a definition of alcoholism consistent with the disease view but useful also in epidemiological and survey research. In the first essay, he defines alcoholism as a "chronic behavioral disorder" in which repeated drinking exceeds "dietary and social uses of the community" and causes harm to the drinker's health and social and economic functioning. The two key and familiar elements are that the drinking is deviant and causes harm. Although ambiguous on the question of disease, Keller agrees with Jellinek's position that persons apparently addicted to alcohol suffer from the disease of alcoholism. In a subsequent essay, Keller (1962) provides a "medical definition" of alcoholism as a "psychogenic dependence on or a physiological addiction to" alcohol, the defining characteristic of which is "loss of control." He translates the latter idea in behavioral terms: "Whenever an alcoholic starts to drink it is not certain that he will be able to stop at will." In an attempt to show the links between harm due to drinking, loss of control, and the existence of disease, Keller gives revealing insight into the intellectual core of the idea that chronic drunkenness is a disease:

The key criterion, for all ill effects, is this: Would the individual be expected to reduce his drinking (or give it up) in order to avoid the injury or its continuance? If the answer is yes and he does not do so, it is assumed—admitting it is only an assumption—that he cannot, hence that he has "lost control over drinking," that he is addicted to or dependent on alcohol. This inference is the heart of the matter. Without evident or at least reasonably inferred loss of control, there is no foundation for the claim that "alcoholism is a disease," except in the medical dictionary sense of diseases . . . caused by alcohol poisoning . . . (Keller, 1962).

In order to extend the research use of the disease concept, Keller applies canons of reason and medicine to the behavioral puzzle of repeated, highly consequential drinking: (1) If one drinks in an excessive, deviant manner, (2) so as to bring deprivation and harm to self and others (3) while remaining impervious to pleas and admonitions based on this "obvious" connection, (4) the person is assumed not to be in control of his or her will (regardless of desire); (5) such lack of control is then "explained" by the medical concept disease and the medicalized concept addiction, inherent in which is the presumption of limited or diminished responsibility. Resting on the inference of loss of control in a cultural system in which values of rationality, personal control, science, and medicine are given prominence, the assertion that alcoholism is a disease becomes an affirmation of dominant cultural and institutional values on which empirical data are never brought to bear. Indeed, it is precisely this quality of the question that holds the key to its viability as well as its controversy: it is a statement not for scientific scrutiny but for political debate.

Keller's (1976a) most recent defense of the idea supports this contention. In a style at once more polemical and less cautious that that of his mentor Jellinek, Keller reiterates that alcoholism is a "dysbehaviorism" typified by deviant drinking that causes harm; that "It is the same as alcohol addiction and classified as a chronic disease of uncertain etiology and undetermined site." Wishing to base his argument on logic, Keller defines disease to mean the same as "disablement" of physical or mental functioning, in effect saying that alcoholism is a behavior disorder that impairs typical functioning and is therefore a disease because disease is a disablement. Using this circular and inclusive argument Keller proceeds to defend the disease concept against all detractors, both real and imagined, taking liberty with the critical arguments he chooses to cite.[13] Keller's defense has a particularly *ad hominem* quality illustrated by the following remarks concerning skeptic's motives (1976a):

It is possible that some people look with envy—unconscious, of course—at those fellows who are having an uproariously good time at everybody else's expense, getting irresponsibly drunk and then demanding to be cared for and coddled—at public cost yet.

Another motive is apparent in those who, not being M.D.'s, think they know better than doctors how to treat alcoholism. . . . It is understandable that some people would feel uncomfortable—they might even perceive it to be illegal—to be treating a disease without a license to practice medicine. But if only it is not a disease—why, then they are in business![14]

Not only are the critics' characters under attack, but, as Keller's discussion makes clear, they also run the risk of definition as anti-medical, unhumanitarian and, perhaps worst, modern day moral crusaders. His attempts at "logic" notwithstanding, Keller is primary a disciple arguing that the disease formulation is revealed truth, and that skeptics and detractors, whether physicians or social scientists, are heretics. Such, of course, is the quality of ideological debate.

Conclusions

The purpose of this paper has been to develop a social historical overview of the major structural and cultural supports of the idea that certain forms of deviant drinking behavior should be considered as instances of disease. I have not attempted to defend the empirical validity of this idea. Indeed, such an attempt would produce a tautological discussion. The question of whether or not a given condition constitutes a disease involves issues of politics and ideology—questions of definition, not fact. The disease concept of alcoholism has a long history in America and has been supported both by medical and non-medical people and organizations for a wide variety of reasons. That certain forms of deviant drinking are now or have been for more than one hundred and fifty years medicalized is not due to a medical "hegemony," but reflects the interests of several groups and organizations assuming, or being given, responsibility for behaviors associated with chronic drunkenness in the United States. The disease concept owes its life to these variously interested parties, rather than to substantive scientific findings. As such, the disease concept of alcoholism is primarily a social rather than a scientific or medical accomplishment.

Notes

1. The medicalization of a variety of forms of deviance and social control is discussed in Conrad and Schneider (Forthcoming), which contains a considerably expanded version of this paper.
2. Seldon Bacon has pointed out to me that the recent controversy over alcohol use among pregnant women attests to the political nature of even these "obvious" medical questions.
3. This journal, which in 1975 became *The Journal of Studies on Alcohol* is issued monthly, is perhaps the key international publication on alcohol research, its tenure of continuous publication being second only to the *British Journal of Addiction*, which began in 1892 as *The British Journal of Inebriety*.
4. In 1962 the Yale Center was moved to Rutgers—the State University, where it remains one of the most prestigious of the few such centers in the world. Straus (1976) provides some insight into the social and political history leading to this move. He suggests that the wide publicity the Yale Center received was an embarrassment to the University because of the substance of the Center's work, and that its interdisciplinary quality was perceived as inappropriate in the context of the traditional departmental structure of the University.
5. Trice and Roman (1968) suggest some unintended consequences of adopting the sick role that may serve to perpetuate and perhaps reinforce the individual's self-definition as one who cannot control his or her drinking.
6. The A. A. *Grapevine* began publication in 1944 and continues as a monthly magazine comprised of items written mainly, although not exclusively, by alcoholics themselves about A. A. and alcoholism (Norris, 1976).
7. Jellinek called these phases the prealcoholic symptomatic phase, the prodromal phase, the crucial phase (wherein loss of control develops), and the chronic phase. The retrospective "discovery" of these phases is not unlike similar discovery processes discussed recently for hyperactivity (Conrad, 1976) and child abuse (Pfohl, 1977). Analysis of such diagnostic categories from a sociology of knowledge perspective suggests that they represent a particular organization of information that serves or reinforces values, assumptions, or beliefs held by the discoverers. Using disease as his guiding assumption, Jellinek decidedly increased the probability of "discovering" phase movement and progression given the processural, temporal imagery that this concept conveys (Fabrega, 1972; Room, 1974).
8. Recent research by Cahalan and Room (1974) on problem drinking among American men suggests the importance of distinctions between "problem drinkers" and "alcoholics" to be less than once thought and perhaps misleading in terms of the typical history of drinking problems. This and previous research (Trice and Wahl, 1958) also questions the popular notice of the inevitable progression of alcoholism. For a thorough, critical review of these and other disease propositions, see Pattison, et al. (1977).
9. In avoiding a conceptual definition of alcoholism, Jellinek is not unlike many if not most students of the problem (see Bacon, 1976, for a complete and critical discussion of the definitional chaos in this field of study).

10. The medicalization of deviance does not depend solely on the presence of physiological dimensions. Other conditions, such as the availability of relevant and efficacious technology, moral and ethical considerations, and a supportive political context, must be considered (see Conrad, 1976: 92–100, for a preliminary discussion).
11. Keller's (1967a) faith in the disease status of alcoholism and physician's abilities to diagnose it is steadfast: ". . . I have never met a physician who could not diagnose alcoholism if he was willing."
12. Keller has recently assumed the position of editor emeritus for the *Journal*.
13. For example:

    Sociologists, no less humane [than social workers], object to classifying alcoholism as a disease because that involves labeling people. This concern is especially touching in the case of alcoholism and alcoholics, labels that tend to stigmatize (Keller, 1976a).

    Keller gives no citation to support this allegation and although frequent reference is made to "social scientist" critics, work cited in this regard appears to be by psychiatrists and other physicians, e.g. Thomas Szasz.
14. Fingarette (1970) discusses the impact of the disease concept of alcoholism in the law and in key United States Supreme Court rulings based thereon.

References

Alcoholics Anonymous, Alcoholics Anonymous. New York: A. A. World Services, 1939.

The American Medical Association, "Report of the board of trustees: Hospitalization of patients with alcoholism." Journal of The American Medical Association 162 (October 20):750, 1956.

Bacon, Selden D., "Concepts." Pp. 57–134 in W. Filstead, J. Rossi, M. Keller (eds), Alcohol and Alcohol Problems, Cambridge, Massachusetts: Ballinger, 1976.

Ben-David, Joseph, The Scientist's Role in Society. Englewood Cliffs, N.J.: Prentice-Hall, 1971.

Berger, Peter L., and Thomas Luckmann, The Social Construction of Reality. Garden City, N.Y.: Anchor, 1966.

Bowman, K. M., and E. M. Jellinek, "Alcohol addiction and chronic alcoholism." Quarterly Journal of Studies on Alcohol 2:98–176, 1941.

Cahalan, Don, and Robin Room, Problem Drinking Among American Men: A Mongraph. New Brunswick, N.J.: Rutgers Center for Alcohol Studies, 1974.

Chafetz, Morris E., and Harold W. Demone, Jr., Alcoholism and Society. New York: Oxford University Press, 1962.

Coleman, James W., "The myth of addiction." Journal of Drug Issues 6(Spring):135–141, 1976.

Conrad, Peter, Identifying Hyperactive Children: The Medicalization of Deviant Behavior. Lexington, Massachusetts: D. C. Heath, 1976.

Conrad, Peter and Joseph W. Schneider, From Badness to Sickness: A Sociology of Deviance and Social Control. St. Louis; Mosby, Forthcoming.

Fabrega, Horacio Jr., "Concepts of disease: Logical features and social implications." Perspectives in Biology and Medicine 15(Summer):583–616, 1972.

Fingarette, Herbert, "The perils of Powell: In search of a factual foundation for the 'disease concept of alcoholism.' " Harvard Law Review 83:793–812, 1970.

Freidson, Eliot, The Profession of Medicine. New York: Dodd, Mead, 1970.

Grinspoon, Lester, and James B. Bakalar, Cocaine. New York: Basic Books, 1976.

Gusfield, Joseph, "Categories of ownership and responsibility in social issues: alcohol use and automobile use" Journal of Drug Issues 5(Fall):285–303, 1975.

Holzner, Burkart, Reality Construction in Society. Revised Edition. Cambridge, Mass.: Schenkman, 1972.

Jellinek, E. M., "Phases in the drinking history of alcoholics." Quarterly Journal of Studies on Alcohol 7:1–88, 1946.

———. "Phases of alcohol addiction." Quarterly Journal of Studies on Alcohol 13:673–684, 1952.

———. The Disease Concept of Alcoholism. Highland Park, N.J.: Hillhouse, 1960.

Jones, R. W., and A. R. Helrich, "Treatment of alcoholism by physicians in private practice: a national survey." Quarterly Journal of Studies on Alcohol 33:117–131, 1972.

Keller, Mark, "Alcoholism: nature and extent of the problem." The Annals of the American Academy of Politcal and Social Science 315:1–11, 1958.

————. "The definition of alcoholism and the estimation of its prevalence." Pp. 310–329 in D. J. Pittman and C. R. Snyder (eds), Society, Culture and Drinking Patterns, New York: Wiley, 1962.

————. "Problems with alcohol: An historical perspective." Pp. 5–28 in W. Filstead, J. Rossi, M. Keller (eds.), Alcohol and Alcohol Problems, Cambridge, Massachusetts: Ballinger, 1976.

————. "The disease concept of alcoholism revisited." Journal of Studies on Alcohol 37(September). 1694–1717, 1976a.

Kittrie, Nicholas, The Right to be Different. Baltimore: Johns Hopkins Press, 1971.

Lender, Mark, "Drunkenness as an offense in early New England: A Study of Puritan attitudes." Quarterly Journal of Studies on Alcohol 34:353–366, 1973.

Levine, Harry Gene, "The discovery of addiction: Changing conceptions of habitual drunkenness in America". Journal of Studies on Alcohol 39 (January): 143–174, 1978.

MacAndrew, Craig, "On the notion that certain persons who are given to frequent drunkenness suffer from a disease called alcoholism." Pp. 483–501 in S. C. Plog and R. B. Edgerton (eds.), Changing Perspectives in Mental Illness, New York: Holt, Rinehart, and Winston, 1969.

Mulford, Harold, "Alcoholics," "Alcoholism" and "Problem Drinkers": Social Objects in the Making. Washington, D.C.: National Center for Health Statistics, Department of Health, Education and Welfare, 1969.

National Conference on Nomenclature of Disease, A Standard Classified Nomenclature of Disease of Disease. H. B. Logie (ed.) New York: Commonwealth Fund, 1933.

Norris, John L., "Alcoholics anonymous and other self-help groups." Pp. 735–776 in R. Tarter and A. Sugerman (eds.), Alcoholism. Reading, Massachusetts: Addison-Wesley, 1976.

Paredes, Alfonso, "The history of the concept of alcoholism." Pp. 9–52 in R. Tarter and A. Sugerman (eds.), Alcoholism. Reading, Massachusetts: Addison-Wesley, 1976.

Parsons, Talcott, The Social System. New York: The Free Press, 1951.

Pattison, E. M., "Comment on the alcoholic game." Quarterly Journal of Studies on Alcohol 30:953, 1969.

Pattison, E. M., Mark Sobell, and Linda Sobell, Emerging Concepts of Alcohol Dependence. New York: Springer, 1977.

Pfohl, Stephen J., "The 'discovery' of child abuse." Social Problems 24(February):310–323, 1977.

Pitts, Jesse, "Social control: the concept." International Encyclopedia of the Social Sciences. no. 14 New York: Macmillan, 1968.

Robinson, David, From Drinking to Alcoholism: A Sociological Commentary. New York: Wiley, 1976.

Roman, Paul M., and H. M. Trice, "The sick role, labelling theory, and the deviant drinker." International Journal of Social Psychiatry 14: 245–251, 1968.

Room, Robin, "Drinking and disease: Comment on 'the alcohologist's addiction'." Quarterly Journal of Studies on Alcohol 33(December):1049–1059, 1972.

————. "Governing images and the prevention of alcohol problems." Preventive Medicine 3:11–23, 1974.

Seeley, John R., "Alcoholism is a disease: implications for social policy." Pp. 586–593 in D. J. Pittman and C. R. Snyder (eds.), Society, Culture and Drinking Patterns. New York: Wiley, 1962.

Spector, Malcolm, and John I. Kitsuse, Constructing Social Problems. Menlo Park, California: Cummings, 1977.

Straus, Robert, "Problem drinking in the perspective of social change 1940–1973." Pp. 29–56 in W. Filstead, J. Rossi, M. Keller (eds.), Alcohol and Alcohol Problems. Cambridge, Massachusetts: Ballinger, 1976.

Szasz, Thomas, The Manufacture of Madness. New York: Dell, 1970.

Trice, H. M., and Paul Roman, Spirits and Demons at Work: Alcohol and Other Drugs on the Job. Ithaca, New York: New York State School of Industrial and Labor Relations, Cornell University, 1972.

————. "Delabeling, relabeling, and alcoholics anonymous." Social Problems 17:538–546, 1970.

Trice, H. M., and Richard, J. Wahl, "A rank order analysis of the symptoms of alcohlism," 1958.

Wilkerson, A. E., A History of the Concept of Alcoholism as a Disease. Unpublished doctoral dissertation, University of Pennsylvania, 1966.

Zola, Irving K., "Medicine as an institution of social control." Sociological Review 20:487–504, 1972.

17. Alcohol and Health

U.S. Department of Health and Human Services

Women

Because of the low rates of heavy drinking among women compared with the rates among men, most surveys of drinking patterns and problems have included relatively little information on women who have high consumption levels and high levels of alcohol-related problems. A national survey was conducted in 1981 to overcome these limitations by oversampling women who drank moderately to heavily or who had histories of drinking-related problems. Results of this survey provide a more accurate and detailed picture of women's drinking patterns and problems (Wilsnack et al. 1984a, b, 1985).

A comparison of results from this survey with the results of eight surveys conducted in the 1970s revealed no evidence of a major increase in alcohol consumption by women over the 10-year period. Women remained predominantly abstainers (39 percent) or light drinkers (38 percent), with increasing abstinence after the age of 50. One change from patterns of the 1970s was an apparent increase in alcohol consumption among middle-aged women (ages 35 to 64), with more drinkers and more heavier drinkers in this age group than were found in the earlier surveys. Contrary to expectations, there was no increase in drinking or in heavier drinking in the youngest age group (ages 21 to 34). A pattern of increased heavy drinking in the middle years (ages 35 to 64) was also found by Fillmore (1985) in a cross-sectional study of drinking patterns among 10-year birth cohorts.

Wilsnack's 1981 survey found that women of lower educational or economic status were more likely to be abstainers. Half the women with household incomes under $10,000 were abstainers, as were 68 percent of women with no more than an eighth-grade education, compared with 39 percent for all women surveyed. However, low-income women who did drink were more likely to drink heavily or to drink to intoxication.

Comparisons of women's drinking levels by marital status indicated that women who were divorced or separated or who had never married were relatively unlikely to be abstainers and were relatively likely to be heavier drinkers, whereas most widows were abstainers and very few were heavier drinkers. However, these patterns can largely be accounted for by age differences.

Married women with paid employment outside the home were found to be somewhat less likely than full-time homemakers to be heavier drinkers. However, moderate drinking was more common among married women who worked, particularly among those with part-time jobs. Among women with full-time employment who had never married, 49 percent were moderate or heavier drinkers, significantly more than any of the women in the married categories. Similarly, 41 percent of the women who were divorced or separated and were employed full time were moderate or heavier drinkers.

Women's drinking patterns and consequences were strongly associated with the drinking behavior of significant others. There was a close relationship between women's drinking behavior and the number of significant others such as husbands, siblings, and close friends whom they perceived as frequent drinkers. Women with husbands or partners whom they described as frequent

From U.S. Department of Health and Human Services, ALCOHOL AND HEALTH from the *Sixth Special Report to the U.S. Congress on Alcohol and Health from the Secretary of Health and Human Services.* January 1987.

drinkers were more likely to report heavier drinking, drinking-related problems, or symptoms of alcohol dependence. However, the women who described their husbands or partners as problem drinkers rather than frequent drinkers were actually less likely to report problems or dependence symptoms of their own.

Although researchers have acknowledged a strong association between domestic violence and high levels of alcohol consumption, the nature of the relationship is not clear. One reason is that battered women, although they make frequent use of emergency room services, are often not identified as battered. In a study by Russell (1982), there was a high rate of problem drinking among battering husbands, especially among those married to women who specifically identified themselves as battered. In 63 percent of these cases, the women reported that their husbands were sometimes, usually, or always drinking when they were violent.

A study of wife rape found that in 20 to 25 percent of cases the husband was drinking at the time of the rape (Russell 1982). However, these respondents were not asked specifically about alcohol involvement, and it was thought that alcohol consumption in these cases was thus greatly underestimated.

A survey of 1,000 battered wives found that those who used the police as a source of help were more likely than the other battered women to report that their husbands always or usually had been drinking at the time of the battering (Bowker 1984). They further reported that drinking was always or usually the major reason for the violent behavior.

The 1981 survey was the first study to obtain detailed data on drinking and reproductive dysfunction from a representative national sample of women (Wilsnack et al. 1984a). Dysmenorrhea, heavy menstrual flow, and premenstrual discomfort were found to increase with drinking level. There was a particularly strong association of such disorders with at least one 3-ounce (six-drink) drinking episode per week. Women who averaged 1.5 ounces or more of ethanol per day, or who experienced at least five 3-ounce drinking episodes per week, had higher rates of most types of gynecologic surgery. A history of miscarriage or stillbirth, premature birth, birth defects, and infertility was found to be associated with the highest levels of alcohol consumption.

Other studies that controlled for potentially confounding variables, including smoking, confirmed a strong association between fetal mortality and drinking during pregnancy (Harlap and Shiono 1980; Kline et al. 1980; Prager et al. 1984). Harlap and Shiono (1980) also determined that drinking and smoking were independent risk factors for spontaneous abortion, with the effect of drinking greater than that of smoking. Prager et al. (1984) further showed that smoking and drinking were independently and additively associated with low birth weight.

• • •

ˆdolescents

Since 1975, the National Institute on Drug Abuse (NIDA) has conducted an annual nationwide survey of about 17,000 high school seniors on the use of drugs, tobacco, and alcohol. The 1984 survey found that reported use of alcohol, as well as of nearly all illicit drugs (particularly marijuana), had declined since 1980 (Johnston et al. 1985). However, the 1985 survey (Johnston et al. 1986) revealed that this declining trend had leveled off for most drugs and that use of cocaine had in fact increased. Despite this halt in the decline of drug use, alcohol consumption continued a steady, though gradual, decline.

In 1985, nearly 5 percent of high school seniors drank every day, fewer than the 1979 high of 7 percent but still representing daily alcohol use by 1 in 20 students. Episodes of heavy drinking (five or more drinks at a time) during the preceding 2 weeks were reported by 37 percent of the seniors, a significant drop from the 1983 level of 41 percent and the lowest level since 1975.

Despite the decline in alcohol use between 1980 and 1985, the proportion of users remained high. Most high school seniors in 1985 (92 percent) reported having used alcohol at least once. More than half of the seniors (56 percent) reported that their first use of alcohol occurred before the 10th grade, nearly 10 percent of them as early as the 6th grade. During the year preceding the 1985 survey, only 14 percent did not use any alcohol. Two-thirds of the seniors had used alcohol during the preceding month, and 20 percent reported drinking during the preceding year but not during the preceding month. Nearly one-third of the seniors (30 percent) said that most or all of their friends got drunk at least once a week; only 18 percent stated that none of their friends got drunk at least once a week.

Frequent and heavy drinking were more prevalent among male students, with more than twice as many males as females drinking daily and nearly half the male students (45 percent) reporting heavy drinking in the preceding 2 weeks compared with 28 percent of the female students. Both percentages represent decreases from the respective 1984 levels of 48 and 30 percent.

A national poll by the Gallup Organization found that, in 1984, 59 percent of adolescents 13 to 18 years old were at least occasional consumers of alcohol and an additional 17 percent had tried alcohol at least once (Gallup 1984b). Two-thirds of those polled had used alcohol before their 16th birthdays. A large majority (83 percent) had friends who were regular users of alcohol (Gallup 1984a). One-third of all those interviewed and more than half of those over age 16 said that all or most of their friends were regular drinkers.

Followup surveys of students 1, 2, and 3 years after graduation from high school examined the interrelated effects of education, occupation, and living arrangements on drug and alcohol use (Johnston et al. 1985). Education and occupation per se had little impact, but clear trends were associated with living arrangements. Alcohol use decreased among those who were married and living with a spouse, remained relatively unchanged among those living with parents, and increased among those living alone or with others in apartments, dormitories, or military quarters.

The 1985 survey included followup studies of graduates who were 1 to 4 years past high school, with a specific focus on college students (Johnston et al. 1986). Patterns of alcohol use among the college students did not vary substantially from use among nonstudents in that age group except for the frequency of occasional heavy drinking (five or more drinks at a time during the preceding 2 weeks). Among the college students, 45 percent drank at this level, compared with 41 percent for the group as a whole and 37 percent for high school seniors. However, the college students reported slightly lower rates of daily drinking (5 percent) than was true for their age group as a whole (6 percent).

When seniors in the 1985 survey were questioned about their perceptions of the degree of risk associated with various levels of alcohol use, 24 percent reported that they perceived a great risk in consumption of one or two drinks nearly every day; 43 percent believed that there was a great risk in occasional heavy drinking (five or more drinks at a time once or twice each weekend); and 70 percent perceived a great risk in consumption of four or five drinks nearly every day (Johnston et al. 1986). However, 10 years earlier, these figures were, respectively, 22, 38, and 64 percent. Thus, although the data suggest a liberal attitude toward the use of alcohol, they also appear to reflect an increasing awareness of the risks of heavy alcohol consumption.

The Elderly

According to the U.S. Bureau of the Census, in 1983 there were nearly 26 million persons in the United States age 65 years or older, more than 11 percent of the population. It is estimated that, by the year 2000, 12.2 percent of the population will be 65 years old or older, and by the year 2025 that figure will rise to 17.2 percent (Williams 1984).

Alcohol abuse is less prevalent among the elderly than among younger age groups. However, estimates of the prevalence of alcohol-related problems in the older age groups vary considerably. Holzer et al. (1984) found that rates of alcohol abuse exceeded 10 percent among men under age 40, but were less than 5 percent among men over age 60 and less than 1 percent in older women. Preliminary data from an epidemiologic study of mental disorders by NIMH indicate that, although alcohol abuse and dependence constitute the most common psychiatric disorder for men and the fifth most common disorder for women, people over the age of 65 have the lowest rates of abuse for both sexes (Robins 1984).

The reasons for the lower prevalence of alcohol abuse in the elderly are not clear. The statistics could reflect actual drops in individual consumption, underreporting of consumption, early death from problems caused by heavy alcohol use, or a combination of these factors. A recent study that followed a population of more than 1,500 men 28 to 84 years old for a 9-year period showed no drop in individual consumption with increasing age (Glynn et al. 1984).

The relatively low prevalence of alcohol abuse among older persons may be due to the reduced tolerance to alcohol that is associated with aging. The biological aging process includes many changes that can influence the body's responses to alcohol (Straus 1984). The proportion of body fat increases, while the volume of body water decreases. Because alcohol is distributed in body water, a given amount of alcohol per unit of body weight will produce a higher blood alcohol concentration in an older person. Changes in hormone levels; in rates of absorption, metabolism, and elimination; and in tissue sensitivity also act to decrease the quantity of alcohol that an older person can consume without adverse effects.

Decreases in individual consumption may also be related to an increase in adverse health effects. About one-fourth of the people in this country over age 65 take prescribed medications (Williams 1984), and the interactions of these drugs with alcohol may pose particularly significant health risks.

There are two significantly different types of elderly problem drinkers: those who begin to abuse alcohol earlier in life and continue into old age and those who do not develop alcohol-related problems until their later years (Holzer et al. 1984; Williams 1984). The early-onset drinkers account for about two-thirds of the elderly problem-drinking population. Their long-term alcohol abuse often results in severe medical problems, particularly degenerative diseases of the liver, brain, heart, intestinal tract, and pancreas. Fewer than one-third of elderly problem drinkers are late-onset drinkers who usually begin problem drinking in response to such major late-life stresses as the death of a spouse or other person close to them, retirement, reduced income, poor health, or geographic relocation.

A possible third group of elderly alcoholics has recently been suggested, consisting of people with a history of light or moderate drinking interspersed with occasional binge episodes (Williams 1984). These so-called intermittent drinkers may respond to late-life depression, loneliness, and anxiety with frequent periods of heavy drinking.

The Homeless

It is not possible to determine accurately the size of the homeless population, but according to esimates by the U.S. Department of Housing and Urban Development, there are roughly 250,000 to 350,000 homeless persons in the United States and their numbers are increasing (USGAO 1985). Although the homeless traditionally have been viewed as mostly alcoholics, drug addicts, and transients, this subpopulation now includes increasing proportions of the elderly, women, children, minorities, the unemployed, displaced families, and the mentally ill. Many interrelated factors contribute to the increasing numbers of homeless persons, but alcohol abuse remains among the most important (USGAO 1985).

Recent surveys in eight U.S. cities found estimates of alcohol abuse among the homeless ranging from less than 20 percent to 45 percent (Mulkern and Spence 1984). These studies focused mainly on shelter users and on men, although the two studies that did include significant numbers of women found overall problem drinking rates of 25 percent and 32 percent. Although interpretation of these investigations was hampered by inadequate sampling and by the lack of uniform methodology, it is clear that a significant proportion of the homeless are alcohol abusers.

A comparison of homeless alcoholic women at a New York City shelter with alcoholic women interviewed at treatment agencies found that the homeless women were heavier drinkers, were somewhat older (average age 46 years versus 41 years for agency-treated women), and were less likely to be married (Corrigan and Anderson 1984). A higher proportion of the homeless women were black (39 percent, compared with 21 percent of the agency-treated women).

A demographic study of 1,000 homeless persons in Ohio found that 21 percent were self-reported alcohol abusers (Roth and Bean 1985). Those with alcohol problems were more likely than the total sample to be men (94 percent versus 78 percent), were older (median age 41 years versus 33 years), were more likely to be divorced (45 percent versus 20 percent), were less likely to be currently married (3 percent versus 11 percent), and were more likely to have been in jail (87 percent versus 51 percent). The group with alcohol problems had been homeless twice as long; 24 percent of the alcohol abusers had been homeless for 2 years or more, compared with 13 percent of the others in the study.

Homeless persons who drink heavily are especially susceptible to certain health problems (Wright 1985). Trauma is much more prevalent among drinkers than among nondrinkers in the homeless population; a New York study indicated that 42 percent of drinkers showed evidence of trauma, compared with 18 percent of nondrinkers. Homeless problem drinkers run higher risks of thermoregulatory disorders, the most serious of which is frostbite that may lead to gangrenous infection. Peripheral vascular disorders, such as edema and cellulitis, are common. Physical debilitation and poor personal hygiene can lead to ulcers, septicemia, and gangrene. Homeless drinkers are considered to be more susceptible to infestations of scabies and lice. One commonly used treatment for such infestations has bee.. associated with neurological side effects and may be contraindicated for alcohol users. Homeless persons generally exhibit active tuberculosis rates 100 to 200 times the rate observed for the general population. Heavy drinkers are considered to be at greater risk for tuberculosis because of their generally more debilitated condition, and sharing of bottles is a possible source of tuberculosis infection.

Minority Groups

Blacks

Blacks are the largest ethnic minority in the United States, numbering more than 27 million in 1983—about 12 percent of the total population and 92 percent of the nonwhite population. Thus, when research studies designate racial groups only as white or nonwhite, data on nonwhites can be considered as reasonably representative of blacks. Despite the large size of the black population and the high rate of alcohol-related problems within this population, relatively little alcohol-related research has focused specifically on blacks (Lex 1985; Herd in press).

Results of national surveys in 1979 and 1983 indicated that blacks of both sexes had higher rates of abstention than whites (Clark and Midanik 1982; Malin et al. 1986). Among drinkers, white men were more likely to be heavy drinkers than black men. The reverse was true for female drinkers, with black women more likely to drink heavily than white women. A large-scale survey in California confirmed these patterns and found significant age-group differences between black and white men (Caetano 1984). Consumption among white men was high among 18- to 29-year-olds but declined after age 30, whereas consumption among blacks was relatively low between the ages of 18 and 29 but rose sharply among those in their 30s.

A national survey in 1984 further confirmed these age-group patterns among black and white men (Herd in press). Among women, the 1984 survey found similar racial differences in the age distribution of drinking patterns. This survey also confirmed higher rates of abstention among blacks for men (29 percent versus 23 percent for whites) and women (46 percent versus 34 percent). However, contrary to earlier findings, white women in the two heaviest drinking categories (those who drink at least once a week and, at least sometimes, consume five drinks at a time) proportionately outnumbered black women, with 13 percent heavy drinkers versus 8 percent for black women (Herd in press).

Among white men, increasing income levels were found to be associated with increases in heavy drinking, but among black men, rates of heavy drinking fell with increasing income. For both black and white women, increasing income was associated with increases in frequent, as opposed to heavy, drinking.

A nationwide survey of 5,000 high school students in the 10th through 12th grades revealed that there were twice as many abstainers reported among black students as among white students (Lowman et al. 1983). Among black students, 41 percent of females and 34 percent of males reported that they abstained, whereas only 18 percent of white females and 20 percent of white males were self-reported abstainers. Black students who did drink consumed less alcohol and drank less frequently than white students. There were four times as many heavier drinkers among white students, with 16 percent drinking at least once a week and consuming at least five drinks on each occasion. Only 4 percent of blacks drank at that level. Demographic differences did not adequately explain the large differences in alcohol use, but many of the black abstainers reported that they used marijuana. Although similar levels of marijuana use were reported by both black and white students, 24 percent of black marijuana users were self-reported alcohol abstainers, compared with only 4 percent of white marijuana users.

Blacks, especially black men, are at high risk for certain alcohol-related causes of mortality and morbidity, particularly liver cirrhosis and such associated disorders as fatty liver and hepatitis. Blacks have an extremely high incidence of cancer of the esophagus, with incidence rates several times higher than those for whites (Herd in press). Alcohol is considered to be a major causal factor in the development of this type of cancer (Page and Asire 1985; Cann 1986; Lieber et al. 1986).

186

The cirrhosis mortality rate was higher for whites than for nonwhites from the mid-1930s until the mid-1950s, when cirrhosis mortality in nonwhites began a steep rise. The nonwhite cirrhosis mortality rate doubled in the 1960s and, between 1950 and 1972, it increased 242 percent, from 7.4 to 25.3 deaths per 100,000 population (NIAAA 1985b). Cirrhosis death rates for whites rose only 58 percent during the same period. Despite a downward trend after 1972, the cirrhosis death rate for nonwhites has continued to far exceed the rate for whites.

Cirrhosis death rates for both white and nonwhite men have been consistently higher than those for women, often more than double the female rate. In 1972, the cirrhosis death rate for nonwhite men was nearly twice the rate for white men, twice the rate for nonwhite women, and more than four times the rate for white women. The rate for nonwhite women increased 203 percent from 1950 to a peak in 1973, compared with an increase of 50 percent for white women over the same period. After 1973, there was a steady decline in cirrhosis death rates for all race and sex groups, but the white-nonwhite mortality ratios were unchanged in 1980; nonwhite mortality rates remained nearly twice the white rates (20.0 and 11.1 deaths per 100,000, respectively). The elevated nonwhite mortality rates may reflect the different age patterns of heavy drinking in the black and white populations.

Herd (1985) noted an association between cirrhosis mortality and major demographic shifts in the black population, whereby regional trends in mortality appeared to reflect blacks' migration and urbanization. In major areas of black migration influx, such as the urban North and the coastal South, cirrhosis death rates for nonwhites rose steeply between 1949 and 1970, but rates remained low in the Deep South where there is a large and relatively stable rural black population. In contrast, cirrhosis mortality rates for whites rose more in the Deep South than they did in the urban North during the same period.

A similar geographic pattern emerged in national surveys of clients in alcohol treatment programs. In the urban northeastern States, the proportions of blacks in treatment in 1980 and 1982 were two to three times higher than their proportions in the States' populations. However, in the interior South, the number of blacks in treatment was generally proportional to their representation in the population (Herd 1985).

Despite late onset of heavy drinking, blacks were shown to enter treatment at younger ages than whites. Blacks between the ages of 35 and 44 had the highest rates of admission to treatment programs, whereas the peak ages for whites entering treatment were between 45 and 54 (Herd 1985).

Hispanics

In 1980 there were nearly 15 million Hispanics in the United States, more than 6 percent of the total population (U.S. Bureau of the Census 1980). Hispanics are a heterogeneous group with diverse cultural, national, and racial backgrounds. Hispanic men have relatively high rates of alcohol use and abuse, while Hispanic women have high rates of abstention.

Alcocer (1982) reviewed the relatively few existing studies of alcohol use by Hispanics in this country. However, these studies did not provide a full epidemiologic picture of alcohol use and abuse by Hispanics because they focused mainly on relatively small and homogeneous populations.

The first large-scale nationwide survey of drinking patterns and alcohol problems in a truly representative sample of Hispanics was conducted by Caetano (in press). The survey found that, among Hispanic women, nearly half (47 percent) abstained and an additional 24 percent drank less than once a month. In contrast, only 22 percent of the men were abstainers, and 36 percent drank heavily or moderately heavily, that is, drank at least once a week and at least sometimes consumed five or more drinks at a sitting. This study also revealed that Hispanic men drink more heavily in their 30s than in their 20s, with consumption declining only after age 40.

In Hispanics of both sexes, after age 60 there was a significant increase in the number of abstainers as well as a decrease in the number of heavy drinkers. Among women, consumption increased markedly in middle age, with a considerable rise in consumption by women in their 40s and 50s. However, after the age of 60, 88 percent of women abstained or drank less than once a month, and none drank heavily. In both sexes, drinking levels increased with increasing education and income level, a finding that confirmed earlier studies. Persons in the higher income brackets and with higher educational attainment had lower rates of abstention and higher rates of heavy drinking.

Analysis of survey data by national origin showed that Mexican American men had both the highest rate of abstention and the highest rate of heavy drinking when compared with Hispanics of Cuban, Puerto Rican, or other Latin American origin. Mexican American women drank more heavily than women in the other groups but also had a high rate of abstention. Puerto Rican women were predominantly moderate drinkers; they had the lowest rate of abstention and included very few heavy drinkers.

A survey of Mexican Americans in five western States (Christian et al. 1985) also found a relatively high rate of abstention, particularly among women, with 64 percent of women and 25 percent of men abstaining. This study of Mexican Americans also confirmed Caetano's (1984) findings of increased abstention rates in middle age, particularly after the age of 55, and of decreased abstention with increasing levels of education and income.

Comparison with drinking levels by birthplace revealed that first-generation Hispanic men, those born in the United States to foreign-born parents, had decreased levels of abstention and increased levels of heavy drinking, compared with foreign-born Hispanic men (Caetano in press). More than half (54 percent) of first-generation Hispanic men drank heavily or moderately heavily, compared with 38 percent of foreign-born Hispanic men. First-generation Hispanic women had lower rates of abstention but higher rates of infrequent light drinking than women born abroad. Among Hispanic men born abroad, Mexicans had a rate of heavy drinking six times higher than that of any other national group, together with a low rate of abstention. In contrast, foreign-born Mexican American women had a high rate of abstention and almost no heavy drinking.

Self-reported prevalence of drinking-related problems (symptoms of dependence, social problems, health problems, and accidents) was very high among foreign-born Mexican American men. Only 75 percent of foreign-born Mexican American men reported no alcohol problems, compared with 95 percent of foreign-born Puerto Ricans, 98 percent of Cubans, and 81 percent of other Latin American men (Caetano in press).

In contrast to problem rates for white men in the same sample and for men in the general population, the rate of alcohol problems among Hispanic American men did not drop between their 20s and their 30s but remained high until their 40s. Problem rates among women in their 20s were high. These women reported rates for some problems (salience of drinking behavior, impaired control over alcohol consumption, belligerence, and health problems) not substantially below those of men in the same age group, even though the rate of heavy drinking among the men was eight times higher (Caetano 1984).

American Indians and Alaskan Natives

There are about 1.5 million American Indians and Alaskan Natives in the United States, less than 1 percent of the total population (U.S. Bureau of the Census 1980). American Indians have rates of alcohol abuse and alcoholism several times higher than rates in the general population. However, as pointed out in comprehensive reviews of recent research (Lex 1985; Heath in press), drinking practices and consequent problem levels vary widely across tribal groups. Of more than 280 diverse American Indian populations, some are characterized by binge drinking followed by periods of sobriety, while other groups remain almost totally abstinent. In still other populations, moderate drinking is the norm. Alcohol problems among American Indians appear to have a strong correlation with economic factors such as unemployment and low income levels and with marital and family instability.

American Indian men between the ages of 25 and 44 have the highest rates of alcohol consumption; both total consumption and numbers of drinkers decline after age 40 (Lex 1985). Long-term heavy drinkers over age 40 make up a relatively small proportion of the American Indian population. American Indian adolescents have high rates of consumption, with 42 percent of male drinkers and 31 percent of female drinkers reporting alcohol problems, compared with 34 percent of white male and 25 percent of white female adolescent drinkers (Lex 1985).

The rate of American Indian hospital discharges involving alcohol-related illnesses or injuries in 1979 was more than three times the rate for the general population (Lex 1985). Accidents, liver cirrhosis, alcoholism, homicide, and suicide are among the 10 leading causes of death among American Indians, and all of these are, or may be, alcohol related. Accidents, homicide, and suicide occur most frequently among people in the younger age groups.

Accidents, the second most frequent cause of death among American Indians after heart disease, account for about 20 percent of deaths, and an estimated 75 percent of those accidents are alcohol related (Lex 1985). Accidents account for nearly one-fourth of the deaths among American Indian men and are particularly prevalent among Alaskan Natives. Accidents are consistently the leading cause of death in Alaska, accounting for 23 percent of all deaths in 1983, compared with 4.5 percent for the United States as a whole. The 1983 death rate for accidents was 146 per 100,000 among Alaskan Natives, compared with 82 per 100,000 for all Alaskans and 39 per 100,000 for the general U.S. population (Kelso and DuBay in press).

For the 3-year period from 1977 to 1979, the age-adjusted American Indian and Alaskan Native combined mortality rate for alcohol psychosis, alcoholism, and alcoholic cirrhosis of the liver was 57.3 per 100,000 population, compared with a rate of 7.4 per 100,000 for the overall population of the United States (Lex 1985). From 1978 to 1983, the alcoholism death rate for Alaskan Natives remained fairly constant at 30 to 36 per 100,000 compared with 7 to 8 per 100,000 for white Alaskans (Kelso and DuBay in press). From 1974 to 1983, Alaskan Natives accounted for more than half of the deaths from alcoholism in Alaska, although they constituted only about 15 percent of the population of the State.

Liver cirrhosis is the fourth-ranked cause of death among American Indians, causing 6 percent of all deaths, compared with 1.4 percent of deaths in the total U.S. population. Using 1980 national mortality statistics, Bertolucci et al. (1985b) estimated that, in 1980, American Indian men lost an estimated 527 years of potential life per 100,000 population due to alcoholic cirrhosis. In comparison, black men lost an estimated 253 years of potential life per 100,000 population, and white men 99 years. The comparable rates for women were 349 years for American Indians, 121 years for blacks, and 40 years for whites.

Homicide is the cause of 3.3 percent of deaths among American Indians, more than double the rate for the U.S. population as a whole. An estimated 90 percent of Indian homicide deaths are alcohol related (Lex 1985).

The rate of suicide among American Indians, about 22 per 100,000 population, is almost double the rate for the overall population (Heath in press). However, among tribes, rates vary from 8 to 120 per 100,000 population. Suicide rates are particularly high among Alaskan Natives, with a high in 1973 of 518 suicide attempts per 100,000 population (Kelso and DuBay in press). Between 1975 and 1981, the suicide rate among Alaskan Natives declined, dropping from 43 percent to 18 percent of all Alaskan suicides. An estimated 80 percent of all American Indian suicide deaths are alcohol related (Lex 1985).

American Indian women appear to be particularly susceptible to alcohol-related problems. Although they drink less than men, they account for nearly half of all American Indian cirrhosis deaths. Also, American Indians appear to be at particular risk for FAS.

Asian Americans and Native Hawaiians

Asian Americans, who make up less than 2 percent of the population of the United States, have very low levels of alcohol use and abuse. A comparison of racial patterns of alcohol consumption among whites, blacks, Hispanics, and Asians in Oakland, Calif., found that Asian Americans of both sexes drank significantly less than whites, blacks, or Hispanics (Klatsky et al. 1983).

It is often assumed that all Asian Americans have similar drinking practices and similar problem levels regardless of national origin. However, Asian Americans have a great diversity of cultural backgrounds, with origins in China, Japan, the Philippines, Korea, India, Vietnam, and other Asian countries, and recent studies have shown that there are significant differences in consumption patterns among Asian Americans of different origins (Klatsky et al. 1983; Kitano et al. 1985; Sue et al. 1985; Ahern in press, Murakami in press).

A survey comparing the drinking patterns of Chinese, Japanese, and Koreans in Los Angeles with those of other Californians showed very high levels of abstention, with 67 percent of Koreans, 55 percent of Chinese, and 47 percent of Japanese abstaining, compared with 13 percent of the general population of California (Kitano et al. 1985; Sue et al. 1985). Abstention rates were significantly higher for Asian females than for males, with 81 versus 56 percent for Koreans, 74 versus 48 percent for Chinese, and 63 versus 36 percent for Japanese.

The Chinese in this study had significantly lower rates of heavier drinking (defined as four or more drinks per day) than the other groups, with only 8 percent drinking at this level, compared with 21 percent of Japanese, 14 percent of Koreans, and 17 percent of other Californians. Among males, the Japanese and Koreans had the highest proportion of heavy drinkers (26 and 24 percent, respectively), while 12 percent of Chinese and 16 percent of other California men were heavier drinkers. Among females, there were no Chinese in the heavier-drinker category and only 0.8 percent of Koreans, compared with 12 percent of Japanese and 18 percent of other California women.

Murakami (in press), in a recent survey of alcohol consumption by the four major ethnic groups in Hawaii, found that Native Hawaiians consumed somewhat less alcohol than Caucasians but significantly more than Japanese or Filipinos. In all groups, men drank more than women. The proportion of heavier drinkers, defined as those who consumed 1 or more ounces of ethanol (two or more drinks) per day, among Native Hawaiians was 11 percent, compared with 14 percent for Caucasians, 7 percent for Filipinos, and 5 percent for Japanese. More than half the Japanese and Filipinos were abstainers, compared with 41 percent of Native Hawaiians and 31 percent of Caucasians.

Ahern (in press), in a review of earlier studies, presented data suggesting that Native Hawaiians, as well as other non-Caucasian ethnic groups, are underrepresented in treatment facilities in proportion to their estimated numbers of heavier drinkers, defined as those who consumed 2 or more ounces of pure alcohol (four or more drinks) per day during the month preceding the survey. In 1979, 41 percent of all such heavy drinkers in Hawaii were Caucasian, but they represented 71 percent of treatment admissions. Native Hawaiians accounted for 19 percent of the State's alcohol abusers in 1979 but only 10 percent of admissions. Japanese, Filipinos, and Chinese had lower proportions of alcohol abusers (11, 9, and 2 percent, respectively), and these groups accounted for even lower percentages of treatment admissions (4, 2, and 0.2 percent, respectively).

Between 1975 and 1980, Native Hawaiians were at less risk than Caucasians for liver cirrhosis, with an estimated 6.8 deaths per 100,000 population versus 12.1 per 100,000 for Caucasians. However, alcoholic Caucasians had significantly lower death rates from liver cirrhosis than Japanese, Chinese, and Filipinos, and Caucasian male alcoholics had significantly fewer cases of organic brain syndrome. During this period, Native Hawaiians were at greater risk than the general State population for only three of eight alcohol-related causes of death: homicide, motor vehicle accidents, and suicide (Ahern in press).

Costs of Alcohol Abuse

In 1980, alcohol abuse in the United States was estimated to cost $89.5 billion. Lost employment and reduced productivity ($54.7 billion) accounted for more than half this amount. Health care for accidents and illnesses related to alcohol abuse, including alcoholism, liver cirrhosis, cancer, and diseases of the pancreas, was estimated to cost $10.5 billion. (These estimates are not comparable to an earlier assessment of costs based on 1977 data because of differences in methodology, among other factors.)

Projections of the 1980 estimate to future years, adjusting only for inflation and population changes, indicate that, in 1983, alcohol abuse cost the United States almost $117 billion. Of this amount, nearly $71 billion is attributed to lost employment and reduced productivity and $15 billion to health care costs.

Summary

In 1984, the estimated per capita consumption of alcohol in the United States was the equivalent of 2.65 gallons of pure alcohol. This is the amount of alcohol one would obtain from approximately 50 gallons of beer, or 20 gallons of wine, or more than 4 gallons of distilled spirits. This was the lowest level of consumption since 1977. After reaching a peak in 1980 and 1981, apparent consumption began a gradual decline. In the single year from 1983 to 1984, apparent per capita consumption decreased or remained unchanged in 43 States and the District of Columbia; only 7 States showed an increase.

Half the alcohol consumed in the United States is accounted for by the 10 percent of the drinking population who drink the most heavily. About one-third of the U.S. population are light drinkers, one-third are moderate-to-heavy drinkers, and one-third are abstainers. There are more abstainers among women than among men, and among older people of both sexes than among younger adults.

Alcohol is associated with a wide variety of diseases and disorders. The greatest chronic health hazard of alcohol is liver disease. In 1983, cirrhosis of the liver caused 28,000 deaths and was the ninth leading cause of death at all ages in the United States. Cirrhosis death rates are higher for men than for women and higher for nonwhites than for whites. Cirrhosis mortality has been declining, and the mortality rate for 1983 was the lowest recorded since 1959.

Accidental death, suicide, and homicide are significant causes of death, particularly for young men under age 34. Nearly half of these violent deaths are alcohol related, and victims are intoxicated in about one-third of drownings, homicides, boating deaths, and aviation deaths, and in about one-fourth of suicides.

There was a significant decrease in the number of alcohol-related traffic fatalities from 1980 to 1984. The proportion of fatally injured drivers who were legally intoxicated (in most States, having a blood alcohol concentration of 0.10 percent or more) dropped from 50 percent in 1980 to 43 percent in 1984.

An estimated 18 million persons 18 years old and older experience problems as a result of alcohol use. These may be dependence symptoms, such as binge drinking or loss of control over drinking behavior, or negative personal consequences, such as problems with health, work, or personal relationships. Patterns in problem prevalence tend to parallel patterns of heavy drinking with regard to sex, age, and ethnic background.

Nearly half of convicted jail inmates were among the influence of alcohol at the time of comitting the criminal offense, and more than half of those who had been drinking were drunk at the time. More than half of the persons convicted of violent crimes had been drinking at the time of the offense.

Women drink significantly less heavily than men and have fewer drinking-related problems, but the level of drinking for women in their middle years (ages 35 to 64) has increased. Higher rates of gynecologic and obstetric problems, including stillbirth and birth defects, are associated with higher drinking levels.

Drug use (especially marijuana use) among high school seniors declined from 1980 to 1984 and leveled off in 1985, except for cocaine use, which increased. However, alcohol use continued a steady decline from 1980 to 1985. In 1985, 1 out of 20 high school seniors drank every day, 92 percent had used alcohol at least once, and 30 percent reported that most or all of their friends got drunk at least once a week. One-third of adolescents aged 16 to 18 reported that most or all of their friends drank regularly.

People over the age of 65 consume less alcohol than younger adults, and they have a lower prevalence of alcohol abuse. Decreases in individual consumption may be due to the lowered tolerance for alcohol that is associated with aging. Elderly long-term alcohol abusers are at high risk for adverse health effects. Major late-life stresses may affect levels of alcohol abuse in the elderly.

There are an estimated 250,000 to 350,000 homeless persons in the United States, including growing numbers of women, children, the elderly, the unemployed, minorities, and the mentally ill. The homeless have a high rate of alcohol-related problems and are particularly susceptible to many health problems.

Blacks have higher rates of abstention than whites. Among drinkers, black men are less likely to drink heavily than white men, but the reverse is true for women. The incidence of alcohol-related medical problems, particularly liver cirrhosis and cancer of the esophagus, is very high among blacks. Cirrhosis mortality rates for blacks are twice as high as the rates for whites.

Hispanic men in this country have a high rate of alcohol use and abuse and a high rate of cirrhosis mortality. Nearly half of the Hispanic women are abstainers, and another fourth drink less than once a month, while less than one-fourth of the men abstain. First-generation American-born Hispanic men drink more heavily than foreign-born Hispanics.

American Indians and Alaskan Natives appear to have very high rates of alcohol abuse and alcoholism, although there is great variation among tribal groups. Even though many tribes remain almost totally abstinent, the rate of alcohol-related illness and injury among American Indians is three times the rate for the general population. Accidents, most of them alcohol related, are the second most common cause of death and account for nearly one-fourth of deaths among American Indian men. Homicide and suicide rates are double the rates for the general population. Liver cirrhosis is the fourth-ranked cause of death among American Indians.

Asian Americans, regardless of national origin, have very low levels of alcohol use and abuse. The percentage of abstainers is very high in all Asian American groups, particularly among women, with the highest abstention rates among Koreans and Chinese. Chinese of both sexes and Korean women have the lowest levels of heavier drinking, and those with the highest levels among males are Japanese and Koreans. In Hawaii, Native Hawaiians have higher rates of consumption than Japanese, Filipinos, or Caucasians.

Complex interactions of demographic, social, economic, and biological factors determine whether a person drinks, how much and how often that person drinks, and what the individual response will be to alcohol. Age, sex, and ethnic background are particularly significant determinants of a person's drinking patterns and susceptibility to drinking problems. Successful prevention and treatment of alcohol abuse and alcoholism must be based on a knowledge and understanding of these factors.

18. New Careers for Moral Entrepreneurs: Teenage Drinking

Robert L. Chauncey *

The NIAAA and Teenage Drinking

The National Institute on Alcohol Abuse and Alcoholism (NIAAA) began operating on May 6, 1971. Some nine months later, it received its first citations in *Reader's Guide to Periodical Literature,* for brief articles in *Time* (1972) and *Newsweek* (1972) which claimed the preeminence of alcohol among abused drugs. The following year, NIAAA commissioned a survey on teenage alcohol abuse, whose findings were reported in 1974 with great effect. A *Time* cover story (1974) quoted Morris Chafetz, then Director of NIAAA: "The switch is on. . . . Youths are moving from a wide range of other drugs to the most devastating drug—the one most widely misused of all—alcohol." Similar stories appeared in all major news magazines, many newspapers, and a variety of other periodicals. The following year, NBC broadcast a two hour television special entitled "Sarah T.: Portrait of a teenage alcoholic." NIAAA was of course trumpeting this message in its own publications, and in dealings with Congress and the White House.

> Across the nation, more teenagers—and even preteenagers—are drinking than ever before. (NIAAA, 1975: 2)
>
> The Committee notes with chagrin that the problem of teenage alcoholism continues to rise. . . . With this in mind, the Committee directs the NIAAA to develop a comprehensive public education and information dissemination program dealing specifically with teenage alcoholism programs. (U.S. Senate Committee on Appropriations, 1976: 72)
>
> Adequate consideration (should) be given to the needs of special population groups that are at high risk for developing alcohol problems or (are) inadequately served. Among such groups are women, youth, the disabled, (etc.) (recommendation of the President's Commission on Mental Health, reported in NIAAA, 1978).

As a result of this interest, the NIAAA announced the development of a five-year, 83 million dollar "National Teenage Alcohol Education Program" (*The Alcoholism Report,* January 14, 1977: 6–7).

This publicity has not been lost on academics and practitioners, as Blane and Hewitt's (1977) survey revealed approximately 475 books, monographs, dissertations, pamphlets and journal articles dealing with teenage drinking published between 1960 and 1971, but listed some 675 citations from 1972 to 1975. The general public was similarly influenced as a 1975 Gallup poll showed that, for the first time, more than half of the respondents considered alcohol to be a serious local youth problem (NIAAA, 1976).

These trends were mirrored in a flurry of programmatic activities. In San Diego, for example, at least three outpatient and one inpatient programs for youthful problem drinkers have been started since 1977. The county Department of Substance Abuse, in their "alcoholism plan" for

*The work for this paper was supported by an NIAAA training grant award.

1977–78, perceived an increase in youthful drinking and assigned youth action teams to each of their newly created neighborhood recovery centers. A youth and alcohol task force was organized in the summer of 1977 by a confederation of community agencies. At their organizing meeting, over fifty agencies were represented. The Drug and Narcotic Education program (DANE) of the San Diego city school district was recently modified to include counseling for alcohol abuse. Various private agencies began education and prevention programs in the schools. Young Alcoholics Anonymous members established several "young people's" A. A. meetings throughout the county. Local radio and television news departments offered "analyses" of the problem. Simultaneously, a statewide "Youth and Alcohol Day" was sponsored by the State Office of Alcoholism. A "State-wide Youth Advisory Board on Alcohol" was initiated as a result of this "Day."

Interestingly, this wave of alarm over youthful alcohol abuse has no precedent in U.S. history (Smart, 1976: 2, 15–16).[1] During the long contests over the sale and use of alcoholic beverages, scarcely a mention was made of youthful drinking (Pittman, 1877; Dorchester, 1884; Fehlandt, 1904; Peabody, 1905). Youths were considered primarily in reference to "schoolhouse laws" which prohibited the sale of liquor within a specified distance from a school, and as the victims of their parents' alcohol abuse (Clubb, 1856: 72, 89; Wines and Koren, 1897: 193). In this century, the *Readers' Guide to Periodical Literature* reveals but a scattered few articles on youth and alcohol through the 1960's.[2] The themes of these articles include personal accounts (*Ladies Home Journal,* 1914), psychologically weak children who drink heavily (*Time,* 1943), foreign children who are encouraged to drink heavily by their parents (*Time,* 1954), and the ever-present danger of alcohol abuse *one day becoming* a problem among our youth (Breg, 1937; Hein, 1962). In 1951, *Newsweek* somewhat whimsically reported the results of a survey of Harvard undergraduates by a Harvard student which found widespread periodic drunkenness among the student body. The article concluded that a Harvard dean was "extremely skeptical" of these conclusions (see also Straus and Bacon, 1953: 38–43).

This absence of general concern over teenage drinking had coexisted, from at least the late nineteenth century, with a societal perception of occasional heavy drinking as a characteristic of college life (e.g. *Ladies Home Journal,* 1914: 6, Warner, 1970: 46–50), including periodic disclosures of deaths from excessive alcohol ingestion as a part of some initiation ritual (e.g. Straus and Bacon, 1953: 38). Yet why did this awareness and periodic outrage fail to produce a general sense of alarm comparable to the reaction of the mid-1970's?

Two possibilities emerge. Either the extent of the problems associated with teenage drinking have grown dramatically in recent years and the diligence of the newly created NIAAA served to publicize this burgeoning problem heretofore clouded by misinformation and blithe ignorance; or the NIAAA, in an effort to sustain itself, has seized on an emotionally charged topic certain to generate demands for a variety of educational and treatment programs.

Teenage Drinking and Problem Drinking

An exhaustive survey of the teenage drinking literature was recently completed by Blane and Hewitt (1977) at the behest of the NIAAA. After reviewing some 1100 documents, their conclusions were singularly critical of the view that teenage drinking has grown rapidly over the past few years, and that problem drinking among this population has reached epidemic proportions. Let me outline their findings.

1. The prevalence of use among teenagers remained stable during the 1966–75 period (II-14).

2. There was no demonstrable shift upward or downward in prevalence of use for girls during this 10 year period (II-16).
3. The mean age of first drink had not changed significantly from the 1951–65 period to the 1966–75 period (II-17-18).
4. There appears to be no upward shift in frequency of use from 1966 to 1975 (II-19).
5. Lifetime prevalence of intoxication among teenagers remained the same during this period (II-21).
6. "Limited evidence suggests that collegians today drink more often and become intoxicated more often than collegians of twenty-five years ago; the data, however, are sparse and open to varying interpretations (IV-22)."
7. Alcoholism, as medically defined, is a rarity among children, adolescents, and young adults (VI-16-17).
8. Despite widespread belief, data on the drinking habits of children of alcoholics "are extremely limited" (VIII-1).

While Blane and Hewitt (1977) are careful to add that many teenagers do drink to excess, and many of these suffer adverse consequences, there are no clear indications of a *growing* problem involving adolescents and alcohol (see also Blane and Chafetz, 1978). Selden Bacon (1977: 214) has offered perhaps the most succinct summary of this literature.[3]

> It is incorrect to say there were *no* measurements of youthful drinking after 1950. But they were certainly (a) few, (b) rather unrepresentative, (c) crude, and (d) whether by intention of surveyors or not, utilized to excite interest in the pathologic. Perhaps indirect evidences, together with assumptions that they "must" signal increased drinking, were more important bases for this widely spread assertion.

Notwithstanding these criticisms, a steady stream of messages emerging from NIAAA have voiced alarm over the growing problem of teenage drinking.[4] For example, Morris Chafetz, as Director of NIAAA, announced at the widely covered 1974 news conference:

> All of the signs and statistics over the past couple of years have pointed to the fact that the switch is on among young people—from a wide range of other drugs to alcohol (Chafetz, 1974:1)

Yet he failed to mention one carefully done investigation which suggested this shift. Instead, he argued:

> For example, we have been finding that arrests of young people for public drunkenness are occurring in larger numbers and at earlier ages. Alcoholics Anonymous groups for alcoholic teenagers are springing up around the country, where there were none before 1970. Even among pre-teens—children between 9 and 12 years old—alcoholism is becoming more and more common. (Chafetz, 1974:1)

Unfortunately, all of these perceptions are easily disputed. The F.B.I.'s *Uniform Crime Reports* of 1975 (p. 185) shows a *decrease* in arrests for drunkenness between 1970 and 1975 among male and female juveniles. An A. A. membership survey found "no discernible trend regarding either young or older members" (*The Alcoholism Report,* Dec. 27, 1975: 6), as young people's A. A. groups have proven to be short lived or populated by those best described as young at heart. Finally, the difficulties in defining "alcoholism" remain numerous and the number of children suffering physiological addiction to the drug remain miniscule (Blane and Hewitt, 1977: VI-16-17; Smart, 1977: 223).

Later in the news conference, Chafetz cited figures from the recently released *Second Special Report to the U.S. Congress on Alcohol and Health* which suggested that the number of juvenile drinkers and the frequency of juvenile drinking was increasing. (That these findings have been subsequently criticized by a variety of investigators need not indicate any impropriety in their initial and unqualified acceptance by the NIAAA.) Yet after this statement, Chafetz added:

> In placing the Report figures in perspective, the *near-universal* use of alcohol within the teenage population is not nearly as troubling as the fact that it has been accompanied by a high rate of alcohol misuse and abuse. . . . (I)f we adopt a problem-drinking criterion (for teenagers) of getting "high" or "tight" at least once a week, preliminary estimates . . . indicate that approximately five percent of the students are problem drinkers. Among male high school seniors, nearly one out of seven reports getting drunk at least once a week—that's 52 times a year. Twenty-three percent of all students, including 36 percent of male high school seniors, report getting drunk at least four times a year—a frequency that some experts, including myself, believe is indicative of a developing alcoholism problem. (Chafetz, 1974: 2; emphasis added)

The Alcoholism Report (July 26, 1974: 2) quoted Chafetz's initial reaction to these findings on "problem drinking" teenagers: "That just blows my mind. I think that is phenomenal."

Less than a year later, in his waning days as Director, Chafetz reversed his field by attempting to defuse the issue and seeking to blame the media for the uproar over teenage drinking. He was strangely silent concerning his own media presentation.

> The NIAAA Director (Chafetz) said it was "unfortunate" that the news media have "gone the usual route" on teenage drinking and "blown it out of proportion." "What they're going to do," he said, "is intensify the problem." . . . "I think there are reasonable ways to approach the situation without terrifying everyone," he said. (*The Alcoholism Report*, May 9, 1975: 5–6)

While one can only speculate on the causes of Chafetz's reversal, it clearly did not influence his successor, Ernest Noble.

> "(W)hile great strikes have been made in the field of alcoholism, I feel that the tide has by no means been arrested." "In fact," he said, "in some areas, the problems of alcoholism have become worse in this country." . . . (Noble) cited the problem of teenage drinking as one of the worsening areas. (*The Alcoholism Report*, Nov. 28, 1975:2)
>
> I would like to indicate that we have a devastating problem with alcohol amongst youth in our country at this time. We feel that the problem at this state is of epidemic proportion. (Testimony before the U.S. Senate Alcohol and Drug Abuse Subcommittee, March 24–25, 1977:5)

It is interesting to note how Noble reacted to Blane and Hewitt's review. In testifying before the Senate Alcohol and Drug Abuse Subcommittee, Noble failed to mention the reported stable rate of drinking and problem drinking among teenagers during the previous ten years, implying the persistence of increases which characterized the fifties and early sixties.

> Noble recited findings from a comprehensive review, by Howard Blane and Linda Hewitt, who analyzed some 120 surveys of junior and senior high school drinking practices between 1941 and 1975. He said the percentage of young people getting drunk has more than doubled from 1965 to 1974. . . . (*The Alcoholism Report*, April 8, 1977: 9)

The following year, before the Senate Labor and H.E.W. Appropriations Subcommittee, Noble completely ignored Blane and Hewitt in stating:

> Every indication points to the conclusion that the teenagers in our country are not only drinking more, but that they are drinking earlier and experiencing more problems with alcohol. . . . (*The Alcoholism Report*, March 10, 1978:6)

This manipulation of teenage drinking as a public and political issue by the NIAAA offers self-preservation as a dominant motive behind the campaign. This is not to demean the agency or its employees, but merely to emphasize the entrepreneurial aspect of welfare organizations, especially ones as highly bureaucratized as the NIAAA. Trice and Roman (1972: 44) have offered similar comments.

> While recognizing the dedication and humanitarianism of the professionals and nonprofessionals in these agencies, we must also recognize that their work is embedded in organizational structures and superstructures strikingly similar to the organization of business and industry in terms of the significance of the competition. Simply, the aim of various problem industries is the accumulation of new programs, jobs and resources, which in turn may yield greater social prestige and power. Thus, we warn against ready acceptance of definitions of the scope of problems from those whose future authority and power hinge heavily on public acceptance of these definitions.

Adopting the view of NIAAA as a large business will aid in explaining the need to create social issues from behaviors like teenage drinking. More particularly, the position of the NIAAA relative to its competition (other H.E.W. agencies) and certain key aspects of its product (alcohol problems) will be explored.

The NIAAA, as a young bureaucracy, faces stiff competition for funds from older, better established, and more insulated bureaucracies. Additionally, the particular behavior which NIAAA regulates poses difficulties of a magnitude not shared by other agencies.

Discussing the first of these issues, the position of the NIAAA with respect to its competition, can be illustrated by examining federal budget figures. The proximal agencies in the federal bureaucracy to NIAAA are the National Institute on Drug Abuse (NIDA) and the National Institute on Mental Health (NIMH). NIDA and NIAAA were created out of NIMH, and the three agencies were lodged in 1974 under the umbrella of the new Alcohol, Drug Abuse and Mental Health Agency (ADAMHA). Throughout the period 1968–1977, federal expenditures for alcohol problems were much lower than the expenditures for drug abuse or for mental health. In 1977 NIAAA's budget was a little over one-third of the NIMH budget and one-half of the NIDA budget.

While the reasons for this fiscal inequality likely stem from the longer history of the NIMH and the impetus initially provided to it by President Kennedy, and the drug scare of the late 1960's and early 1970's which frightened society into handsomely funding NIDA, the result clearly suggests the need of the NIAAA to escalate its promotional efforts and thereby improve its position among the competition.[5] This necessity has been underscored by recent attempts to subsume alcohol programs into "substance abuse" or "chemical dependency" programs. Trice and Roman (1972: 12) report:

> The alcoholism industry has occasionally captured the limelight with its own brand of militancy and fervor. These efforts, however, are presently overshadowed by the demons associated with other drugs. Without a doubt there are dissimilarities between the impacts of alcohol and other drugs . . . but it is intriguing and almost humorous to observe the resistances created by the suggestion that alcohol and drug-problem agencies join forces in their activities (usually on the basis of the

contention that alcohol *is* a form of drug). Such suggestions sometimes create frantic responses such as intense arguments that alcohol problems are completely unique and that "everyone will lose" if the two sets of efforts are put together. These resistances clearly reflect the vested interests which might be lost through a merger, as well as the greater stigmatization associated with illegal drug abuse: problem drinkers and their caretakers might have their reputations damaged by becoming associated with "drug fiends."[6]

The cultural conflict surrounding alcohol use has also made the growth of NIAAA more difficult. Most adults value the occasional use of alcohol, in moderate amounts within socially acceptable circumstances. Accordingly, messages focussing on the dangers of drinking and efforts to limit its supply through prohibition, taxation or dilution are not met with enthusiasm. The insistence of alcohol workers on counseling abstinence rather than "responsible drinking" further isolates these programs from public support.[7]

Finally, the insistence of the alcoholism movement on separating themselves from other forms of drug abuse has left them with an artificially narrow area of responsibility. By comparison, NIDA can explore the abuse of a wide assortment of illegal drugs, prescription drugs, patent medicines, and chemicals found in commonly consumed foods. NIMH, in turn, can concern itself with a variety of ever changing labels for behaviors subsumed under the psychoses, neuroses, character disorders, and organic disorders, and measure the efficacy of a spiraling number of therapies. NIAAA, on the other hand, has defined itself into a corner. Only the ingestion of alcohol in liquid form is of concern. Although therapies abound, the basis of most long-term efforts still centers on Alcoholics Anonymous. So rather than publicize the rise of new problems or the efficacy of new treatments, NIAAA has attempted to develop itself through publicizing the variety of people who are risking the onset of alcoholism by the heavy drinking which characterizes certain segments of the population. Among the groups cited for special attention include youth and the elderly, workers and the handicapped, women and homosexuals, blacks and migrant workers, native Americans, Spanish-speaking Americans, Asian Americans, rural Americans, and the children of alcoholics from any category whether or not mentioned above. These overlapping groups are not actually perceived by NIAAA as suffering from the same ailment, but are viewed as reacting to unique social situations in ways which necessitate unique education/prevention efforts and unique treatments for those who succumb to the disease.

The Legitimation of a Social Problem

By viewing the NIAAA as an agency faced with significant competition for federal dollars and widespread public apathy which often borders on opposition, its attempts to create new social problems and expand the controversy surrounding pre-existing ones are not surprising. What is surprising is the perceptionist view of social problems as being created solely by victims and sympathizers who then force a reaction from the autonomous, monolithic bureaucracy which feeds on misery while doing as little as possible to ameliorate it. While the federal bureaucracy in total may operate by its own logic and on its own power, various elements of it are continually being re-organized, re-classified, expanded and reduced. The edifice persists, but its various inhabitants (interests and constituencies) prosper and perish. The precarious existence of the dwellers should not be confused with the permanence of the structure.

Assuming that public controversy over a behavior or situation can be created by a government agency and thereby meet the perceptionist criterion for the creation of a social problem, the issue of *legitimizing* this problem becomes important. The perceptionists have argued that problems created by protesters become legitimized by government recognition. Does it follow that government initiated problems become legitimized by public recognition?

Blumer's (1971: 303) use of the term "social endorsement" clearly describes the concept of legitimacy which remains vague in Spector and Kitsuse's work (1973: 147; 1977: 142).

> Yet after gaining initial recognition, a social problem must acquire social endorsement if it is to be taken seriously and move along in its career. It must acquire a necessary degree of respectability which entitles it to consideration in the recognized arenas of public discussion. . . . (Without this endorsement) the asserted problem may be regarded as insignificant, as not worthy of consideration, as in the accepted order of things and thus not to be tampered with, as distasteful to codes of propriety, or as merely the shouting of questionable or subversive elements in a society. (Blumer, 1971: 303)

Hence, a problem created by a government agency does not become legitimate by its birthright, but must be accepted as a topic worthy of debate by some elements of the population. Yet Blumer (1971: 301) and Spector and Kitsuse (1973: 147; 1977: 142) add that a social problem is not fully established until *action* is undertaken in its behalf. In a problem emerging from protesters, action is defined as the implementation of an official program (Blumer) or as the rejection of official meliboratives and the substitution of alternative efforts (Spector and Kitsuse). It seems to follow, then, that action on an officially created problem implies some public participation in an officially sanctioned program (agreeing to wage and price restraints, driving more economical cars, submitting to free innoculation programs, providing clients for community mental health centers, etc.) or in some alternative. In this sense, the *legitimacy* of an officially created social problem, as defined here, is established by the arousal of public controversy or discussion *coupled with* the popular participation in some ameliorative program. How legitimate, then, is the problem of teenage drinking?

Public Reaction to Teenage Drinking

As mentioned above, the NIAAA-sponsored 1974 national survey on teenage drinking received wide media coverage and was followed by a growing public concern about teenage drinking (as measured in a 1975 Gallup poll) and the initiation of a variety of educational and treatment programs. While a degree of public concern and debate persists,[8] the amount of current program activity appears minimal. In San Diego, none of the three outpatient programs for teenage problem drinkers initiated since 1977 was able to generate a sufficient number of referrals to survive. The youth action teams assigned to the county's eight neighborhood recovery centers have not materialized. The youth and alcohol task force to be composed of representatives from a number of community agencies moribund. The DANE program of the city schools has never been able to gain the trust of heavy users, according to its former director, and has recently been diluted by other counseling functions. The surviving young people's A. A. meetings are rarely attended by teenagers. Although it is premature to evaluate the efforts of the state youth advisory board, its president recently stated that educational prevention services are more important than outpatient or residential services because so few teenagers are actually addicted to alcohol. The single surviving inpatient facility has been reclassified as a substance abuse program. It presently houses five adolescents.

San Diego is not unique in its failure to generate alcohol abuse programs. From the summer of 1977 to the summer of 1978, the *NIAAA Information and Feature Service* cited the existence of four treatment programs throughout the nation. A 1977 NIAAA pamphlet, entitled *Guide to Alcohol Programs for Youth* describes nine exemplary programs, but openly states:

> Unfortunately, a common deficiency in these programs is the lack of good evaluative research and longitudinal followup of program participants. All of the programs described here have been operating 2 years or less and their newness alone makes it difficult to judge their success.

There appear to be two reasons for this typical difficulty in producing community action. Heading the list must be the confusion surrounding the offensive behavior itself. The variety and inadequacy of definitions of alcoholism are well known (i.e. Siegler and Osmond, 1974; Clark, 1975; Ries, 1977), and exacerbated when preceded by the term "adolescent." Bacon (1976: 1015), for one, questions equating the drinking behavior of a thirteen-year-old and a seventeen-year-old, and of artificially excluding ten to twelve-year-olds and eighteen-year-olds. More significantly, Blane and Hewitt (1977: VI-7-8) report that the failure to distinguish acute from chronic effects of alcohol may lead to erroneous diagnoses of alcoholism among drinking youth.

> Young people drink infrequently relative to adults, but when they do drink, they are more apt to drink in large amounts. They are therefore a group at risk for suffering acute effects of alcohol (intoxication, blackouts, gastric distress, "hangover"), behavioral concomitants of intoxication (uncoordination and disinhibition, including belligerence, crying, "silliness," raucousness, impulsive behavior, poor judgment), and negative social and impersonal consequences (fights, impaired driving, fractured relations with friends and relatives, destruction of property, job difficulties, arrests or other involvement with police). Some of the behaviors enumerated are identical to behaviors which contribute to a diagnosis of alcoholism. . . . Given this partial coincidence of acute and chronic behavioral signs, it is only too easy to confound them in attempting to arrive at a definition of alcoholism appropriate to young people. . . . A positive diagnosis of alcoholism can be made only in the presence of substantial chronic effects; acute effects in the absence of chronic effects do not warrant a diagnosis of alcoholism.

The term "problem drinking" is similarly made more problematic when used to describe adolescents. While Cahalan and Room's (1974: 240–42) index of problem drinking may be appropriate to adult males, it seems inadequate for teenagers.[9] Moreover, the essential nature of indices like this one—defining problem drinking as a break from routine, expected behaviors caused or sustained by the ingestion of alcohol—is inapplicable to teenagers who have yet to achieve a stable mode of functioning, whose struggles toward maturity are in fact *characterized by* instability. In addition, many of the "problems" of teenage problem drinking stem from the legal status of underage use, making it difficult to distinguish between teenagers whose excessive drinking has led to personal problems and teenagers whose problems stem not from alcohol but from the illegality of drinking it.

The concept of alcohol abuse is more difficult to deal with than alcoholism or problem drinking. Although not rigorously defined by the NIAAA, the dictionary definition of abuse and the assumption that alcohol abuse is not synonymous with alcoholism or problem drinking implies a pattern of drinking which might be viewed as excessive or inappropriate, but not addictive, leading to consequences which are negative but not (as yet) "problematic." The arbitrary nature of criteria for "excessive" drinking is clear. Subjective evaluations of "impropriety" depend, of course, as much on the audience as the behavior. Since the drinking habits of teenagers seem to be highly correlated with those of their parents (e.g. Barnes, 1977) and peer group (e.g. Bacon and Jones, 1968: 51), it appears unlikely that teenagers who consume a higher than average amount of alcohol (or consume it more regularly or frequently) will receive much of a reaction from unofficial others. Reactions of official others are generally termed "problematic" and suffer from the vagaries discussed above.

For some, the sheer use of alcohol by adolescents is the social problem that demands attention. Our society habitually places higher standards of conduct on adolescents, prohibiting the young from drinking alcohol, engaging in sex, seeing "excessively" violent or "pornographic" movies, fighting wars, driving cars, and involving themselves in other Mephistophelian delights which are somehow made less dangerous and/or sinful by the experience of adulthood. The young are to be taught gradually about these forbidden fruits, yet premature partaking is prohibited. The single exception to this dogma is alcohol, where teenagers and occasionally preteenagers may be allowed to imbibe limited quantities under adult supervision. With the widespread use of alcohol among adults and the acceptance of supervised, circumscribed adolescent use, the doctrinaire appeal against teenage drinking has not gained many adherents.

The result of these definitional ambiguities is an inability to clearly distinguish those teenagers who have an alcohol problem from those who do not. If teenage alcohol addiction cannot be clearly differentiated from non-addiction, if problems due to drinking cannot be clearly differentiated from problems due to other causes, if abuse cannot be clearly differentiated from normal use, and if legal proscriptions against teenage use are openly flaunted by most parents, then alcoholism workers will undoubtedly suffer difficulties in trying to rally public support for the proposed adolescent alcohol programs necessary to legitimize and maintain teenage drinking as a social problem.[10]

The second general problem inhibiting the production of community action against teenage drinking is the socially constructed discrimination between *alcohol* abuse and *drug* abuse, as mentioned above. Despite a media campaign aimed toward the public recognition of alcohol as a drug, the NIAAA refuses to become aligned with drug treatment agencies. This position is reinforced by the legal distinction between alcohol and other recreational drugs. Teenagers, of course, are not oblivious to these creations. Although drug using adolescents generally use alcohol as well (e.g. Blane and Hewitt, 1977: VI-17, 19; Wechsler and Thum, 1973: 1223), they tend to identify themselves as drug users, "loadees" or "stoners" rather than drinkers. For example:

You know, you take some joints and some pills and you feel nice, man. You're not out there endangering other people's lives—driving recklessly, stumbling all over. It's just not as messy. You don't look as messy. For a long time, drugs—I guess with the psychedelics too—there was just something more spiritual about them, or something. Alcohol was just like low grade or something.

R1: It was more cool around people to get high and stuff, you know, big thing. Beer was, you know, just a normal thing. Drugs was to be cool.

R2: Like if you were on acid, or you'd be drinking beer and then you'd take acid, that was something else, you know? You'd just keep on drinking. Same with like PCP—angel dust—if you were on that you just kept on drinking beer. You didn't keep on doing angel dust or you didn't keep on taking LSD, you just kept on drinking beer.

R1: You could talk around other people, say "I really got fucked up on some acid last night." And beer, it's just getting drunk. You don't flip out or nothing. Like acid, you can tell somebody your trip, that you really had a good one, stuff like that. That's cool. All the stoners, they like, there ain't much to talk about drinking. But when you get into drugs, it's more interesting— about getting busted and dealing and ripping people off.

Noting these attitudes of the NIAAA and teenage drinkers, it is not surprising to find polydrug abusing teenagers typically coming or getting sent to drug abuse agencies, while alcohol abuse facilities generally screen out these teenagers who primarily abuse drugs other than alcohol. As a result, drug agencies remain active while teenage alcohol programs wither or fail to germinate.

These two broad conceptual problems which hinder effective public reaction to the claims made by NIAAA provide a background for the more specific conditions and behaviors serving to obfuscate teenage alcohol abuse from those individuals socially mandated to care for these adolescents—parents, physicians, counselors, school personnel, and police officers.

The following observations are based on field work in the San Diego area. Approximately fifty interviews were conducted with professionals from a variety of state, county and private agencies, schools, psychiatric hospitals, criminal justice personnel, and a number of private physicians. An additional fifteen interviews were conducted with alcohol and drug abusing adolescents. Another fifteen student "peer counselors", each with a "caseload" of about a dozen students, were also contacted.

Parents and Teenage Drinking

The act of teenage drinking, though generally illegal, is not problematic to a great many parents. For example, Blane and Hewitt (1977: III-77) report that parents were found to be the most common source of alcohol for teenagers in several surveys, while many children have their first drink at home with their parents (1977: V-13-14). Among the teenagers interviewed for this study, all (save one) reported their parents knew of their drinking and were not initially alarmed by it. This benign neglect was justified in two ways. First, several parents thought their children were merely trying to mimic the adults.

> She (my mother) thought it was cute—such a little kid drinking.
> The first couple of times (my parents caught me drinking) they just thought it was funny and, oh well, she'll get sick and never do it again.

Other parents felt that drinking was not problematic so long as their children stayed out of trouble.

> I was told earlier that I could drink, smoke marijuana or take pills as long as I kept it okay, as long as I did nothing strange or out of the ordinary. As long as I kept up the responsibilities I had.

> I: You said your mom was pretty cool at first about drinking and taking drugs.
> R: Well, she didn't like it, but as long as you're not making an ass of yourself and you're not getting into trouble, and you're doing it close to home. Well, she'd rather that I did it at home. I liked that at first, everybody came over to my house, . . . it's cool.

Two studies of the family reactions to adult drinkers provide some clues to explain the perception of a transformation from benign neglect to an attempt at corrective action. Jackson (1954) speaks of wives becoming concerned about their husbands' "socially inappropriate drinking", generally referring to drinking that was clearly excessive for the occasion. This pattern occurred with two of my informants.

> Well, I don't think they realized before when they found me drunk. I don't think they realized how much I was drinking. But they did catch me this other time, though, when they did think it was serious. . . . They caught me with a whole quart, smoking cigarettes. That was the only thing different. They realized how much I had been drinking. I guess it upset them, and that I was smoking too.

I: Did your parents know you were drinking?

R: Yeh, they knew. But I wasn't drinking that much at that time. So it really didn't bother them. And I got away with it most of the time. They confronted me and hasseled me about it when they found out.

I: When they found out you were drinking?

R: Yes. Like I'd come home from a friend's house and they'd smell it on me. Then they'd rap with me. You know, sit down and rap with me for two hours.

Yet the concept of social inappropriateness demands an evaluation of the audience as well as the one accused of acting inappropriately. It can be suggested that one explanation for the often cited relationship between the drinking habits of parents and their children is the tendency of heavy drinking parents to constrict the category of socially inappropriate drinking far more than do parents who drink moderately. Simply put, heavy drinking parents "produce" heavy drinking children in part by defining their (the teenagers') heavy drinking as appropriate. This contention can be supported by comparing the parental use of other drugs with their tolerance of this behavior. For example, the parents who regularly use drugs were rather blasé about the drug use of their children.

She (mother) knew that I was smoking pot and drinking. But she didn't have any idea of on what scale. And so (we'd tell her) once in a while we'd smoke a joint and everyday we could get high. And that's what she thought because she believed me. (Later) We got into conversations about getting high and so forth, we said acid, and she's telling me the only acid you ever get is cut with aspirin and speed. Kids these days don't get no acid. She didn't believe me.

I: Did you (and your mother) ever smoke dope together?

R: Yes, a couple of times. But that was after I was living with my dad.

I: Were you doing anything else when you were still living with your mom?

R: Yes, the valiums. She said she'd rather have me smoking pot than doing drugs like that.

Contrast this reaction to the more dramatic one characteristic of the parents who do not use drugs.

I: Did he (guardian) know you were smoking dope?

R: A friend of mine gave me two pipes that had never been used. I put them in my pocket, thinking he wouldn't search me there, but I came home one day and those pipes were just sitting on the table. He beat the shit out of me.

I: Did your parents know you were using?

R: O yeh, they busted me. It must have been the first time I had any marijuana around the house. I hid it in this box and I stashed the box away somewhere and they found the box and opened it up and found the pot. They knew about it. And I got busted. . . .

To further complicate matters, drinking can hardly be considered socially inappropriate to family members who are not aware of it. The ability of teenagers to hide their drinking from their parents is another significant limiting factor on the family's ability to construct a response.

I: Where would you drink?

R: At the house because my mom and dad always worked. We would drink there while they were at work.

I: Did your parents know you were drinking?

R: No.

I: How come?

R: I didn't want them to find out, so they didn't.

I: Who would you drink with?

R: Buddies.

I: At home at all?
R: Never at home.
I: Where would you generally drink?
R: At home.
I: With your parents?
R: No. They didn't allow it. But I would just sneak it.

Wiseman (in preparation) suggests that while alcoholic husbands also attempt to hide their drinking, these efforts become undermined by certain forms of "evidence"—the husband's inability to fulfill his familial responsibilities (chief among these is balancing the family budget) and the appearance of radical personality changes (leading to an occurrence of bad scenes and violence). But what family responsibilities do adolescents have? None in my sample had part time jobs (when they lived at home) or contributed to the family budget in any way. None did very well in school, but only after expulsion did parents respond. One boy adequately summarized his responsibilities and those of his peers.

I: What do you mean by responsibilities?
R: School, household chores, being home when I was supposed to, not trying to kill my little sister, and just being a kid—a little thirteen-year-old kid.

Similarly, adolescence is a time for personality changes and increased conflict with parents. When these changes and conflicts become viewed as excessive, parents and teenagers ignore the possible role of drug and/or alcohol abuse and presume that the teenager is troublesome because he/she is undergoing a troublesome stage on the path to maturity.

I was kind of, you might say, uncontrollable. It's been said about a lot of kids. Well, I was one of them.
    I started getting high, getting drunk. I don't know, just having the screwed attitude—where it don't matter. I'm going to be cool with my friends and get high.
I: Did you ever think you were an alcoholic?
R: No, not really. I just got busted a lot for it.
I: Why not?
R: Just for going out and having a good time? Just going out and getting drunk? I wouldn't bother anybody but they'd bother me. . . . Except sometimes I just drink a little too much and I get blanked out, and start fighting. . . . That's what its like when you're young. Everybody I know when they're young will drink until they're gone.

The work of Sampson, Messinger and Towne (1962), Freeman and Simmons (1963) as well as Jackson and Wiseman, suggests that many husbands and wives will eventually define their spouses' behavior as problematic and needing treatment through an exhaustion of their tolerance (or efforts to normalize) rather than as a result of increasingly deviant behavior. This decision is postponed in accordance with the ability of the problematic spouse to negotiate with the non-alcoholic spouse through promises to repent and eliminate the offending behavior, attempts to blame the non-alcoholic spouse for the offending behavior, efforts to reminisce about better times, and so on. Teenagers are also quite adept at these negotiations.

My mom tried to take me down to this counseling place, family counseling, to see what was wrong with me. I went there with her once. I thought she was going to commit me into the place. I just started to cry to get her so I could go back home. I conned her into it and she let me come back home.

205

I used the whole guilt trip on them and everything. . . . I manipulated them into thinking pretty much what I wanted them to think.

My old man would get violent every once in a while. But it was no really big deal. I would just kind of shine him on.

I don't know why I lasted there (home) so long and why they just didn't kick me out. They had people telling them (to do this) but they just loved me so much they just kept holding on until they got into a program called Alanon and started finding out. . . .

The general acceptance of teenager drinking, the subjective nature of socially inappropriate drinking, the tendency of teenagers to drink furtively, the general expectation of problematic behavior during adolescence, and the ability of teenagers to negotiate with parents implies a parental inability or reluctance to seek help for their heavy drinking teenagers. Accordingly, although all the teenagers interviewed were eventually assigned to a treatment facility, none of them were placed there by their parents as a direct result of drinking or drug abuse. On two occasions, the police were called by parents who felt threatened by their teenagers.

In a third family, the parents, frightened by withdrawal symptoms, called a doctor in preparation for an admission to a mental hospital.

In the other cases, the family played little or no role in the eventual assignment of the teenager to a treatment facility.[11] This assignment was generally made by a judge or probation officer after the teenager had been arrested for a rather serious offense—not officially associated with alcohol or drug abuse.

Since action taken to legitimate teenager drinking as a social problem is unlikely to originate from parents,[12] the aid of other agents must be solicited.

The Medical Profession and Teenage Drinking

Physicians generally maintain themselves through a voluntary rather than conscripted patient population. Accordingly, they are not likely to see large numbers of heavy drinking teenagers. In addition, physicians are generally reluctant to consider alcoholism as a true disease[13] and are hesitant to treat it themselves (e.g. Marden, 1977: 349; Cook, 1976: 1898–99; Hare and Wilkins, 1976). Regarding teenage drinkers, Mandell and Ginsburg (1976: 189–91) report that few physicians routinely take data from adolescent patients about their use of alcohol, offering alcohol abusers a good chance of escaping detection.

The segregation of hospitalized adolescents furthers the disinclination to diagnose and treat instances of teenager alcohol abuse. Most hospitals have an adolescent or children's ward distinct from the rest of the hospital. In another wing resides the alcoholism or detox unit. A common complaint among alcoholism workers in this unit is the lack of communication between themselves and the adolescent unit. They argue that youthful drinkers are treated for physical discomforts or classified as adolescent adjustment reactions (in psychiatric facilities), while the primary problem of alcohol abuse (in the eyes of the alcoholism workers) remains undisclosed.

Psychiatrists face an interesting situation in attempting to treat teenage drinkers. The psychiatric classification system (DSM II) includes only one category applicable to adolescents, entitled "Behavior Disorders of Childhood and Adolescence". Under this category are the following diagnoses: hyperkinetic reaction, withdrawing reaction, overanxious reaction, runaway reaction, unsocialized aggressive reaction, group delinquent reaction, other reaction (Kaplan, 1972; 75–76). Nowhere in the description of these reactions is the use of drugs or alcohol implicated. It seems likely, then, that most adolescent psychiatric patients, at least initially, are not labeled as alcoholics or alcohol abusers. However, DSM II does state that for adolescent disorders which are "more stable, internalized, and resistant to treatment", the therapist should consider diagnoses submerged under the psychoses, neuroses, and personality disorders (Kaplan, 1972: 75–76). Thus, after some exposure to an adolescent alcohol abuser, the psychiatrist is officially permitted to opt for a diagnosis of alcoholism, a label clearly defined as a personality disorder. Yet DSM II provides a caveat: "If the alcoholism is due to another mental disorder, both diagnoses should be made (Kaplan, 1972: 71)." So, for an adolescent to be *treated as an alcoholic* by a psychiatrist following DSM II, he/she must first be moved beyond the adolescent adjustment labels and then be cleared of any underlying mental deficiency which creates the drinking behavior. While many, perhaps most psychiatrists consult DSM II only for insurance or other official matters, the psychiatric ambiguity surrounding the teenage drinker is nicely summarized within its obtuse directives.

A common refrain among alcoholism workers called on the medical profession to better "educate" itself and its future members about the disease nature of alcoholism. This enhanced education, if realized, would more firmly place alcoholism beneath the legitimating umbrella of medical science and thereby provide better treatment for the increased number of alcoholics encouraged to step forward and receive it. Although this scenario is consistent with the growing trend to medicalize deviance under the rubric of mental health enhancement, it omits at least two imposing problems not found in present patient categories. First, while Freud could suggest properties of certain disorders not considered within then-standard medical conceptions, and thereby spawn the development of a new medical discipline, the ambiguities surrounding alcoholism do not portend a similar development. Without a segment of the medical profession especially organized to ameliorate alcoholism, the alcoholism industry cannot hope to match the growth of the mental health enterprise. Perhaps the best chance for the medical acceptance of alcoholism lies with developing physiological and psychological conceptions of *addiction,* allowing specialists in this more legitimated area to treat the causes and consequences of the interaction between the drug and the individual (e.g. Knott, 1973: 266). This prospect, however, would remove the term "alcoholism" from the general lexicon (making it as superfluous as "heroinism" or "marijuana-ism") and be severely opposed by the alcoholism workers fervently united in the concept of their unique malady.

Second, medical concepts of deviance attempt to remove responsibility for the distressing behavior from the actor and place it on involuntary mechanisms. Although patients are implicitly held responsible for certain physical conditions—such as venereal disease (Becker, et al., 1961: 323–24; Roth, 1972: 844) and injuries suffered as a result of brawls, suicide attempts and the like (Glaser and Strauss, 1965: 83)—the medical profession and the public at large do not generally blame patients for their illnesses (Parsons, 1951: 440; Siegler and Osmond, 1974: 17). Although some evidence indicates that psychiatrists may expect their patients to take a larger part in effecting their improvement than physicians expect of their patients (i.e. Sobel and Ingalls, 1968; Viscott, 1972: 41), this prodding is a far cry from the dominant perspective of alcoholism which holds the alcoholic *primarily responsible* for his/her recovery. The A. A. literature, for example, repeatedly stresses the overriding importance of self-help in this enterprise. The following comments, taken from pamphlets distributed by alcoholism agencies in San Diego, underscore the prominence of this theme.

> This is a specialized treatment program designed to help teenagers free themselves from dependence on drugs and alcohol.
> Responsibility starts with the willingness to acknowledge that you are cause in the matter.
> Emphasis on self-help, peer relationships and caring is the philosophy of—.

This experience . . . is designed to provide the participant with meaningful tools to effectively deal with problems associated with alcohol use.

Individuals admitted to the short term residential program and sober and desiring assistance with their acknowledged problem of alcoholism.

'The most challenging problem we face in the field of alcoholism is to bring about the bankruptcy of the alibi structure in the drinker long before it would occur in the ordinary course of events.' (pamphlet quoting E. M. Jellinek)

With this emphasis on self-help alcoholism workers have effectively undercut one of the chief advantages of the sick role for the alcoholic and undermined the scope of the physician's role as architect of recovery. Without some modifications in the disease concept of alcoholism which would increase the rewards for potential doctors and patients, it is difficult to imagine much improvement in the willingness of doctors to treat alcoholics and the desire of alcoholics to be treated by physicians.

Social Agencies and Teenage Drinking

As mentioned above, the distinctions created between alcohol abuse and the abuse of other drugs, coupled with the large number of teenage polydrug users (including alcohol) has produced a wealth of drug programs for juveniles but a dearth of alcohol programs. However, there are several family counseling centers and a number of *adult* alcohol facilities which do occasionally see teenage drinkers.

The effectiveness of family counseling centers is unfortunately limited primarily because (to use the parlance of social workers) alcohol abuse is generally not the "presenting factor" of adolescent clients. The adolescent has been brought to the counselor for any one of a variety of reasons (centering around behavior which causes "trouble"), with alcohol abuse becoming significant only after the counselor has explored the case in some detail. If alcohol abuse is suspected (very often it is not because these counselors, perhaps legitimately, focus on locating problems within familial interaction patterns rather than on substance abuse per se), it becomes a delicate process for the counselor to raise this suggestion to parents and teenagers (who have come voluntarily) bent on denying the possibility. Accordingly, few alcohol abusing teenagers are isolated and treated in these agencies.

Teenagers report feeling uncomfortable in adult alcohol programs. While part of the discomfort is simply due to age differences, the tendency of some long term members to discount the possibility of alcoholism among the young is also responsible. Moreover, the competition for status through the glorification of past drinking experiences, a popular pastime among A. A. members, generally finds the teenager short of episodes and consumptive capabilities. The differences between the purported histories of the adult members and the teenage initiates also reinforces the common teenage attempts at denial. The teenager can justifiably assert the significant differences between his/her drinking and that of the self-proclaimed adult alcoholics.

These drawbacks of family counseling centers and adult alcoholism programs are certainly not irremediable, but, as with the situation surrounding physicians and psychiatrists, they do not portend the stimulation of much interest in teenage drinking as a social problem.

Schools and Teenage Drinking

San Diego county schools typically suspend students who are either caught drinking or using drugs while at school or who are obviously suffering from the consequences of such use. Any staff member who witnesses these behaviors is to contact the school disciplinarian and, if necessary, the school nurse. Following the suspension, the school disciplinarian may schedule conferences with parents, send the child for outside counseling (if the school district has a contract with a local agency), fill up the child's free periods with classes or duties, etc. The San Diego city schools operate in a similar fashion, with the addition of their "social concerns" counselors who rotate among a number of schools offering information and advice about a variety of maturational problems—drug and alcohol use among them.

Although county and city school districts do not compile the total number of suspensions by cause, it appears that few students are suspended for using or abusing alcohol. For example, one principal of a high school with 2,000 students reported five suspensions for this offense in the 1977–78 school year. Another principal remarked that he had known only one alcoholic student in his ten year tenure. Similarly, a school counselor recalled seeing about ten students in four years for drug or alcohol problems, while another was able to refer but two students to a drug counseling program in the last year and a half.

The paucity of suspensions for alcohol abuse is primarily the result of a paucity of students using alcohol at school or coming to school after drinking. As one principal noted:

> Alcohol is probably the most dangerous drug, but the problem is not terribly noticeable in school. It is outside of school—evenings, weekends—but schools can do little about this.

It appears that the heavy drinking and drug abusing students are less likely to be regular school attenders (Kandel, 1975; Marden and Kolodner, n.d.: 29–30; Blane and Hewitt, 1977: VI-17), and that students showing the effects of alcohol or drugs in school are often shielded by their friends. The following comment is not atypical.

> I got to school and said I can't go to school. I'm really wasted. I could hardly walk. As soon as I got to school it really hit me. So I was sitting in the smoking area on first break and all I can remember is telling my buddy to get me out of here, I've got to get out of here. I was laying on the ground. All the counselors were looking at me. My buddy grabs me and lays me on the football field because I live a little ways from there. And he just left me.

Not surprisingly, a self-fulfilling prophecy also works to limit the number of suspensions.

> Once kids have a reputation as troublemakers, many teachers discourage them from returning to class. 'Come to class if you're going to work.' These kids take up much time (the teachers must help the student catch up with his/her work), are disciplinary problems, and the teachers feel they are poor risks for the future. (school counselor)

Of those students who do use drugs while at school or who come to school after using drugs, many escape punishment as a result of staff members' ignorance, unease, or paternalism.

> I: Did anybody at school know you were drinking?
> R: No, not really. I was going to a Catholic school. They're a bunch of good people there and they didn't know—ignorant.

Some teachers will refer (drug abusing students) to counselors, some try to deal with the problem themselves, and many do nothing because they don't know what to do. They feel uncomfortable in the situation. (school counselor)

I felt uncomfortable dealing with drinking and drugs because I didn't know the symptoms or what to do—how to help. I felt the same way about gay students. I couldn't bring myself to deal with this until this year. (school counselor)

One counselor and one teacher (on two different occasions) wanted to talk to me about it (drinking and using drugs), off the record. But I never did.

Other staff members reflect on more systemic obstacles to the isolation and treatment of alcohol abusing students.

The counselor's major function is getting the kids through the system. This takes a lot of work. Drug counseling must be viewed as secondary. (school counselor)

Almost all parent contacts with counselors revolve around grades or chances for college. No one asks about the child's happiness, communication problems, and so on. Administrators reflect this view. Their primary concern is with academics. 'Let's not get too idealistic.' (school counselor)

Most teachers will ignore the problem. They're getting paid to teach, not to do counseling or police work. They come in to teach, eat their lunch in their office areas, and leave as soon as possible. They're not around for any potential crisis situations—monitoring dances or taking tickets at ball games. (school disciplinarian)

While some may differ with this disciplinarian's assessment of the dedication and commitment of teachers, few will argue against the necessary focussing of school activities on the basic education function. Within the boundaries of parental authority and pecuniary frugality, public schools can do little more than isolate a few miscreants and recommend help for recidivists. If enhanced drug education programs for current and future teachers might increase the number of abusing students brought to official attention, it will not alter the basic good sense of most heavy drug and alcohol abusing students to stay away from school when partaking.

Police and Teenage Drinking

According to Reiss (1971) and others, most police work stems from citizen complaints rather than direct police observation. Since teenage drinking is generally a furtive activity which rarely involves a potential outsider-complainant, police are not likely to become aware of a signifcant percentage of youthful liquor law violators. Even when violations do become known, police in San Diego generally avoid filing juvenile contact reports (the juvenile equivalent of an arrest). A sampling of field observations supports this contention.

Kids show no fear of drinking in public—on the beach or on the strand.
Many bikes have receptacles to hold beer cans.

There goes one kid on a skateboard with a half-gallon of vodka.

The police van just cruised slowly down the strand. They said nothing to kids on bikes drinking beer.

When reports are filed, juvenile diversion programs attempt to separate most alcohol offenders from more serious offenders and repeaters. Those in the first category are released to their parents while the latter are punished for the crimes committed subsequent to or coincidental with the alcohol use rather than offered treatment for an alcohol problem.

Diversion programs thrive because of the obvious advantages inherent in limiting the number of cases processed through the criminal justice system. The absence of readily available treatment alternatives for juvenile drinkers coupled with the move to decriminalize alcohol abuse has also contributed to this strategy. Clearly, if alcoholism workers continue to press for a disease concept of alcoholism, they cannot expect the criminal justice system to supply their facilities with clients.

Conclusion

The perceptionist view of social problems, as most clearly elucidated by Spector and Kitsuse, has been shown to portray a distorted and oversimplified image of the creation of these phenomena. First, this perspective seriously understates the historical variety of cross cutting values and interest groups responsible for shaping contemporary public policy. Second, the perceptionist view of officialdom fails to fully consider the conflicts between segments of the government for financial power and visibility which provide the chief motivation for the attempted creation of social problems. Third, by portraying the bureaucracy as self-serving and obstructivistic, this view fails to recognize that all organizations are basically self-serving but that agency competition often forces officials to create issues which might otherwise not be raised (or might not have received as much public notice). Perhaps more importantly, the perceptionist position was shown to omit the possibility of social problems being *legitimated* as well as *created* by *public attitudes and public action.*

With regard to teenage drinking in particular, the legitimation efforts of alcoholism workers have been hindered by the ambiguity of the problematic behavior, the cultural cross currents surrounding the use of alcohol, the portrayal of alcohol addiction as a disease, the discrimination between the abuse of alcohol and the abuse of other drugs, and several resultant tendencies and situations which hamper the production of social action against this behavior.

It would, of course, be highly reasonable to recommend the end of efforts to create a social problem for teenage drinking. The opposing argument, which suggests the need to exaggerate claims and expand problem areas to generate sufficient income for the beneficial work being done now by NIAAA and the need for additional programs in the future, is easily countered. First, the ceaseless creation of social problems dilutes federal resources by transferring them from problems already defined, resulting in less than adequate treatment of old and new alike. Second, as Fry (1977) and Cloward and Piven (1974) have shown, many social programs tend to benefit not the target population but the various professional classes employed to aid them. Third, Trice and Roman (1972: ix) suggest the existence of programs which "are far more disruptive and costly than the actual deviant patterns themselves." Finally, the regular production of unanticipated and purportedly devastating problems tends to produce (if it has not already produced) a lack of public confidence in all social programs.

Unfortunately, a cessation of bureaucratic sensationalism over teenage drinking will not help those adolescents who suffer a variety of adverse consequences from the ingestion of alcohol. Instead, there is some evidence to suggest (e.g., Institute of Medicine, 1978) that bureaucratic claims about problematic teenagers in general, rather than alcohol abusers in particular, would more closely approximate the behavior of teenagers and more likely lead to community-sponsored ameliorative action. Of course, this more generally defined problem would not help the NIAAA gain fiscal equality with NIMH and NIDA.

The role of social science ends with suggestions of social policy. Yet in this era of fiscal conservatism and antipathy toward large social programs, sociologists can serve their scientific and political goals by wedding social problems theory with studies of government activity. Undoubtedly, the offspring will be beneficial to both professional understanding and practical assessments of individual agency efforts. In my own view, careful analyses of government programs may help save the most worthy from the growing horde of indiscriminate budget cutters by attempting to separate political strategies from behavioral consequences.

Notes

1. Although Straus (1977: 242) and Bacon (1977: 104) claim a long history of concern with teenage drinking in this country, they reported earlier on the generally lighthearted and satiric responses to their college drinking study (Straus and Bacon, 1953: 39–43), which suggest something less than widespread alarm over this issue.
2. A review of the *New York Times* indices for this century yields an identical conclusion.
3. For a variety of criticisms of the data on teenage drinking, see O'Gorman, et al., 1977.
4. Perusing issues of the *NIAAA Information and Feature Service* over the last five years will provide the reader with ample support for this statement.
5. According to Morris Chafetz (in a taped interview with Joseph Gusfield), President Nixon opposed the creation of NIAAA, signing the bill only at the behest of a wealthy contributor. In any event, Nixon certainly failed to provide the kind of open support for alcohol programs that President Kennedy provided for mental health initiatives.
6. Even a hint of a merger raises the alarm among alcoholism workers. For example:
   A proposal by Administrator Gerald L. Klerman to centralize initial review of all discretionary grants and research contracts at the Alcohol, Drug Abuse and Mental Health Administration (ADAMHA) generated a solid wall of opposition in the alcoholism field with battle lines extending to Capitol Hill. The proposal—already approved by HEW Secretary Joseph A. Califano, Jr.—escalated rapidly into an overriding policy issue seen by alcoholism interests as freighted with crucial implications for the programmatic integrity of NIAAA. (*The Alcoholism Report*, March 24, 1978: 1)
7. The August 25, 1978 issue of *The Alcoholism Report* (p. 6) quoted acting Director Loran Archer on this issue.
   At the same time, Archer spoke out strongly for abstinence as a treatment goal. He said the notion puzzled him that somehow abstinence could be 'harmful'. He said: 'I've never known anyone who has been harmed by abstinence from alcohol, or abstinence from smoking. What I am concerned about is the fact that people can be at risk when you set other goals.' Archer said that although not everyone will achieve complete, life-time abstinence, 'it's still a very appropriate goal.'
8. In the first six months of 1978, the *New York Times Index* included three references to drinking among teenagers and college students. The March, 1977 to February, 1978 volume of the *Readers Guide to Periodical Literature* listed five articles under "Alcohol and Youth".
9. Among the scales comprising the drinking problems score, the "problem with wife", "job problems", and "financial problems" scales are clearly inapplicable to most teenagers. Since drinking under the age of eighteen is illegal in all states, the "police problems" scale is inappropriate. As the impact of alcohol on health is rarely evident for many years, the "health and injury problems" scale also seems inapplicable for teenage drinkers. A general difference in the tolerance levels of adult and adolescents would dictate a change in the "heavy drinking" scale, while the tendency of teens to drink furtively, infrequently and in large quantities (primarily due to the illegality of the behavior) would obviate the "binge drinking" scale.
10. There are, of course, programs focussing on the treatment of alcohol abusing adolescents. Yet comparing this number with the plethora of adult alcohol programs, drug abuse programs and mental health clinics suggests the extent of community response to each of these.
11. The single exception to this statement involves a mother who knew of an alcohol treatment facility as a result of her membership in A. A. She suggested her son might be more happy there than at home.

12. Cook (1976: 1899), Jackson (1954) and Wiseman (in preparation) suggest that adult alcoholics and their families also rarely seek professional help. The paucity of articles indexed in the *Journal of Studies on Alcohol* under the topic "self-referral/alcoholism treatment" also supports this conclusion. Between 1974 and August, 1978, only two such articles were listed.
13. Out of six medical dictionaries consulted, only one used the term "disease" to describe alcoholism.

References

Bacon, Margaret and Mary Brush Jones, *Teenage Drinking.* New York: Crowell, 1968.

Bacon, Selden D., "Defining adolescent alcohol use: Implications for a definition of adolescent alcoholism" *Journal of Studies on Alcohol.* 37(7): 1014–19, 1976.

———. "Words about alcohol: Their meaning in study, public relations, and policy-making" in Patricia O'Gorman, Sharon Stringfield and Iris Smith (eds.) Defining Adolescent Alcohol Use: Implications Toward a Definition of Adolescent Alcoholism. Proceedings of the 1976 conference of the National Council on Alcoholism, Washington, D.C., 1977.

Barnes, Grace M., "The development of adolescent drinking behavior: An evaluative review of the impact of the socialization process within the family." *Adolescence.* 12 (Winter): 571–91, 1977.

Becker, Howard S., Blanche Geer, Everett C. Hughes and Anselm L. Strauss *Boys in White: Student Culture in Medical School.* Chicago: University of Chicago Press, 1961.

Berger, Bennett M., "Comments on Mel Kohn's paper." *Social Problems* 24(1): 115–20, 1976.

Blane, Howard T. and Morris E. Chafetz, " 'Must guard against overreaction' " *Focus on Alcohol and Drug Issues* 1(3, May–June): 5–6, 1978.

Blane, Howard T. and Linda Hewitt, Alcohol and Youth—An Analysis of the Literature, 1960–1975. Prepared for the NIAAA, 1977. (NTIS#PB-268-698)

Blumer, Herbert, "Social problems as collective behavior." *Social Problems* 18 (Winter): 298–306, 1971.

Breg, W. Roy, "Alcohol in youth's world." *Journal of the National Educational Association,* 26 (7):237, 1937.

Cahalan, Don and Robin Room, *Problem Drinking Among American Men.* New Brunswick, New Jersey: Rutgers Center of Alcohol Studies, 1974.

Chafetz, Morris E., Statement by Morris E. Chafetz, M.D., Director, National Institute on Alcohol Abuse and Alcoholism, News Conference on Youth and Alcohol, New York, New York, October 1, 1974.

———. A transcribed interview, conducted by Joseph R. Gusfield on November 16, 1977.

Clark, Walter B., "Conceptions of alcoholism: Consequences for research." *Addictive Diseases.* 1(4): 395–430, 1975.

Cloward, Richard and Francis Fox Piven, "The professional bureaucracies: Benefit systems as influence systems." Pp. 7–27 in R. Cloward and F. F. Piven (eds.) *The Politics of Turmoil.* New York: Pantheon, 1974.

Clubb, Henry Stephen, *The Maine Liquor Law: Its Origin, History, and Results, including a Life of Hon. Neal Dow.* New York: Fowler and Wells, 1856.

Cook, Gloria, Review of A. K. J. Cartwright, S. J. Shaw and T. A. Spratley's Designing a Comprehensive Community Response to Problems of Alcohol Abuse. London: Maudsley Alcohol Pilot Project. In *Journal of Studies on Alcohol.* 37(12): 1897–99, 1976.

Dorchester, Daniel, *The Liquor Problem in All Ages.* New York: Phillips and Hunt, 1884.

Douglas, Jack D., *Defining America's Social Problems.* Englewood, New Jersey: Prentice-Hall, 1974.

Fehlandt, August F., *A Century of Drink Reform in the United States.* Cincinnati: Jennings and Graham, 1904.

Ferrari, Art, "Social problems, collective behavior and social policy: Propositions from the war on poverty." *Sociology and Social Research.* 59(January): 150–62, 1975.

Freeman, Howard E. and Ozzie Simmons, *The Mental Patient Comes Home.* New York: John Wiley and Sons, 1963.

Fry, Lincoln J., "Research grants and drug self-help programs: What price knowledge?" *Journal of Health and Social Behavior.* 18 (December):405–17, 1977.

Fuller, Richard C. and Richard Myers, "The natural history of a social problem." *American Sociological Review.* 6(June): 320–28, 1941.

Glaser, Barney G. and Anselm L. Strauss, *Awareness of Dying.* Chicago: Aldine, 1965.

Gusfield, Joseph R., *Symbolic Crusade: Status Politics and the American Temperance Movement*. Urbana: University of Illinois Press, 1963.

Hare, B. D. and R. H. Wilkins, "A general-practice study of the commonest presenting symptoms of alcoholism." *Journal of the Royal College of General Practitioners*. 26: 140–42, 1976.

Hein, Fred V., "How teens set the stage for alcoholism." *Today's Health*. 40(June): 36–7+, 1962.

Institute of Medicine, Adolescent Behavior and Health: A Conference Summary. Sponsored by the National Institute of Drug Abuse, June 26, 27, 1978.

Jackson, Joan K., "The adjustment of the family to the crisis of alcoholism." *Quarterly Journal of Studies on Alcohol*. 15:562–86, 1954.

Kaplan, Howard I., "Classification of child psychiatric disorders." Pp. 45–94 in Alfred M. Freedman and Howard I. Kaplan (eds.) *The Child: His Psychological and Cultural Development II, 1972*.

Kitsuse, John I. and Malcolm Spector, "Toward a sociology of social problems: Social conditions, value-judgements, and social problems." *Social Problems* 20(4):407–19, 1973.

Knott, David H., James D. Beard and A. Alan Fischer, "Alcoholism—The physician's role in diagnosis and treatment." Pp. 265–75 in Howard F. Conn, Robert E. Rakel and Thomas W. Johnson (eds.) *Family Practice*. Philadelphia: W. B. Saunders, 1973.

Kunitz, Stephen J., "Some notes on physiologic conditions as social problems." *Social Science and Medicine*. 8(April): 207–11, 1974.

Ladies Home Journal, "Young man who quit." Volume 31: 6, 1914.

Lauer, Robert H., "Defining social problems: Public and professional perspectives." *Social Problems*. 24 (1): 122–30, 1976.

Mandell, Wallace and Harold M. Ginzburg, "Youthful alcohol use, abuse and alcoholism." Pp. 167–204 in Benjamin Kissin and Henri Begleiter (eds.) *The Biology of Alcoholism IV: Social Aspects of Alcoholism*. New York: Plenum, 1976.

Marden, Parker G. and Kenneth Kolodner, "Alcohol use and abuse among adolescents." Unpublished report distributed by NCAI (#026533).

Marden, Philip, Review of D. Robinson's From Drinking to Alcoholism: A Sociological Commentary. New York: Wiley, 1976, in *Journal of Studies on Alcohol*. 38 (2):348–52, 1977.

Merton, Robert K., "Social problems and sociological theory." Pp. 793–845 in Robert K. Merton and Robert Nisbet (eds.) *Contemporary Social Problems* (3rd edition). New York: Harcourt-Brace-Jovanovich, 1971.

———. "The sociology of social problems." Pp. 3–43 in Robert K. Merton and Robert Nisbet (eds.) *Contemporary Social Problems* (4th edition). New York: Harcourt-Brace-Jovanovich, 1976.

Moynihan, Daniel Patrick, "The professionalization of reform." Pp. 245–58 in Joseph R. Gusfield (ed.) *Protest, Reform, and Revolt: A Reader in Social Movements*. New York: John Wiley and Sons, 1970.

Newsweek, "The no. 1 drug problem" February 28: 54, 1972.

NIAAA, "Young people and alcohol" *Alcohol Health and Research World*. Summer, pamphlet, 1975.

———. "Gallup poll indicates most citizens view youth drinking as serious problem" NIAAA Information and Feature Service, May 25, 1976.

———. "U.S. commission to study alcohol problems urged" NIAAA Information and Feature Service, August 11, 1978.

Nisbet, Robert, "The study of social problems" Pp. 1–25 in Robert K. Merton and Robert Nisbet (eds.) *Contemporary Social Problems* (3rd. edition). New York: Harcourt-Brace-Jovanovich, 1971.

———. *Sociology as an Art Form*. London: Oxford University Press, 1976.

O'Gorman, Patricia, Sharon Stringfield and Iris Smith, eds. Defining Adolescent Alcohol Use: Implications Toward a Definition of Adolescent Alcoholism. Proceedings of the 1976 conference of the National Council on Alcoholism, Washington, D.C., 1977.

Peabody, Francis Greenwood, *The Liquor Problem: A Summary of Investigations Conducted by the Committee of Fifty, 1893–1903*. Boston: Houghton, Mifflin and Company, 1905.

Pittman, Robert C., *Alcohol and the State: A Discussion of the Problem of Law as Applied to the Liquor Traffic*. New York: National Temperance Society, 1877.

Reiss, Albert J., Jr., "Putting sociology into policy" *Social Problems* 17 (Winter): 289–94, 1970.

———. The Police and the Public. New Haven: Yale University Press, 1971.

Ries, Janet K., "Public acceptance of the disease concept of alcoholism." *Journal of Health and Social Behavior*. 18(September): 338–44, 1977.

Ross, Robert and Graham L. Staines, "The politics of analyzing social problems." *Social Problems* 20 (Summer): 18–40, 1972.

Roth, Julius A., "Some contingencies of the moral evaluation and control of clientele: The case of the hospital emergency system." *American Journal of Sociology* 77(5): 839–56, 1972.

Sampson, Harold, Sheldon L. Messinger and Robert D. Towne, "Family processes and becoming a mental patient." *American Journal of Sociology.* 68: 88–96, 1962.

Schneider, Joseph W., "Deviant drinking as disease: Alcoholism as a social accomplishment." *Social Problems.* 25(4): 361–72, 1978.

Sidey, Hugh, "The presidency: 531,600 tons of dollars" *Time* 113 (6-Feb. 5): 17, 1979.

Siegler, Miriam and Humphry Osmond, *Models of Madness, Models of Medicine.* New York: Macmillan, 1974.

Smart, Reginald G., *The New Drinkers: Teenage Use and Abuse of Alcohol.* Toronto: Addiction Research Foundation of Ontario, 1976.

————. "Alcohol misuse and alcoholism among young people" Pp. 221–32 in O'Gorman, et al., 1977.

Sobel, Raymond and Ardis Ingalls, "Resistance to treatment: Explorations in the patient's sick role." Pp. 324–34 in Stephan Spitzer and Norman Denzin (eds.) *The Mental Patient: Studies in Sociology of Deviance.* New York: McGraw-Hill, 1968.

Spector, Malcolm and John I. Kitsuse, "Social problems: A reformulation." *Social Problems* 21(2): 145–58, 1973.

————. Constructing Social Problems. Menlo Park, California: Cummings, 1977.

Straus, Robert, "Conceptualizing alcoholism and problem drinking" Pp. 242–48 in O'Gorman, et al., 1977.

Straus, Robert and Selden Bacon, *Drinking in College.* New Haven: Yale University Press, 1953.

Time, "Child dipsomaniacs" June 14: 48, 1943.

————. "The wine drinkers" July 12: 45, 1954.

————. "Pot and alcohol: Some new views" February 28: 51, 1972.

————. "Alcoholism: New victims, new treatments" April 22: 75–81, 1974.

Trice, Harrison M. and Paul M. Roman, *Spirits and Demons at Work: Alcohol and Other Drugs on the Job,* Ithaca: New York State School of Industrial and Labor Relations, Cornell University, 1972.

U.S. Senate Committee on Appropriations, Departments of Labor and Health, Education, and Welfare and Related Agencies Appropriation Bill, 1977. Calendar #942, report #94-997, June 26, 1976.

Viscott, David S., *The Making of a Psychiatrist.* New York: Arbor House, 1972.

Warner, Harry S., "Alcohol trends in college life: Historical Perspectives." Pp. 45–80 in George L. Maddox (ed.) *The Domesticated Drug.* New Haven: College and University Press, 1970.

Weber, Max, *The Methodology of the Social Sciences.* Translated and edited by Edward A. Shils and Henry A. Finch. New York: Free Press of Glencoe, 1949.

Wechsler, Henry and Denise Thum, "Teenage drinking, drug use, and social correlates." *Quarterly Journal of Studies on Alcohol.* 34(4-A): 1220–27, 1973.

Wines, Frederick H. and John Koren, *The Liquor Problem in its Legislative Aspects.* Boston: Houghton, Mifflin and Company, 1897.

Wiseman, Jacqueline P., *The Other Half: Wives of Alcoholics.* In preparation.

19. Sociological Perspectives on Drunk Driving

Ellen Ziskind Berg

The social problem of drunk driving is produced by our lifestyle: it is "the predictable result of how alcohol and cars fit into the daily lives of Americans" (Ross 1985). Increasingly in the public eye, drunk driving and responses to it are of concern to sociologists interested in criminology, public policy, and social movements. This article will briefly profile work being done in each of these areas.

Criminology

Drunk driving is a criminal offense, punishable by law. The question of whether legal interventions effectively deter drunk driving has been examined by H. Laurence Ross and Gary D. LaFree of the University of New Mexico (1983). An important legal intervention which they evaluate is the introduction of "Scandinavian-type . . . laws which define the offense in terms of blood-alcohol concentrations, measurable by instruments" (Ross and LaFree 1983: 18). Their survey of the responses to these laws in a number of countries shows an initial decline in drunk driving which, however, is not sustained. When punishment is not certain or not severe, the deterrence effect of these interventions is short-lived. Ross and LaFree write: "Deterrent effects have been found in virtually all well-designed studies of significant interventions, in many countries throughout the world. However, these effects universally disappear over time. . . . One possible explanation for this is the fact that the very low levels of actual likelihood of punishment are insufficient to continue an initial impression of reasonable certainty of punishment for the law violator" (1983: 25).

This suggests that certain, swift, and severe penalties might act as an effective deterrent. Laws providing for this would have appeal, Ross and LaFree argue, because they are aimed at the deviants rather than at social customs or institutions, because they satisfy a psychological need for retribution, and because there is widespread belief at an intuitive level that punishments do deter illicit behavior. Ultimately, however, Ross and LaFree think the enactment of such laws is unlikely because of the fiscal costs and the level of police intrusiveness into daily life they would require. Concluding that legal interventions which aim at deterrence are politically impractical, the authors suggest that other policy alternatives which make drinking less appealing or crashes less catastrophic are more promising solutions to the problem of drunk driving. They write: ". . . It strikes us as more rational policy to expermient along these lines in the hopes of finding economically sound mitigants than to follow the chimera of deterrance-based solutions that experience repeatedly shows to be inadequate in the context for which they are proposed" (1983: 33).

Public Policy

Dean Gerstein of the National Research Council (the research arm of the National Academy of Sciences) directed a study, by an interdisciplinary panel, of "alternative policies affecting the prevention of alcohol abuse and alcoholism" (1985: v). The panel issued its report in 1981 and in 1985 Gerstein, in collaboration with Steve Olson, published *Alcohol in America: Taking Action to Prevent Abuse.*

Gerstein and Olson note that only half of alcohol-related problems are caused by confirmed alcoholics, while half are caused by moderate drinkers—on occasions when they are immoderate. They are concerned in their book with articulating policies that target this second group. Thus they present preventive measures which are "nonpersonalized approaches that act throughout the drinking population. . . . (These measures) seek to change the incentives, opportunities, risks, and expectations that surround drinkers in society" (1985: 24–25). The measures they suggest fall into three broad categories: (1) those which "affect the price and availability of alcohol;" (2) those which "seek to alter drinking practices more directly through various forms of education and persuasion," and (3) measures which "make the world a safer place in which to drink" (1985: 25–26).

Honing in on the problem of drunk driving, Gerstein and Olson insist that no single measure can solve the problem, but that a multidimensional package of preventive measures can make a significant difference. They propose both deterrence-oriented measures aimed at specific offenders and institutional changes aimed at all drinkers. They write: "Beefed-up surveillance and tougher penalties for drunk drivers are two approaches that must be part of the solution. . . . At the same time, there are many other preventive options that should not be overlooked. . . . Higher taxes on alcohol, changes in the drinking age, responsible oversight by servers, educational campaigns, safer cars and highways, and steps to deal with repeat offenders all have at least a theoretical capability to reduce drunk driving" (1985: 43–44).

Measures aimed at changing the social context so that drunk driving is less likely very often meet institutional resistance—from the liquor industry, restauranteurs and bartenders, and the auto industry. Counterbalancing this resistance is a growing tide of citizen support for at least some changes.

One of the preventive measures proposed by Gerstein and Olson is raising the drinking age. Publically popular, this measure has been studied by Alexander C. Wagenaar (1983).

In a brief history of the ups and downs of the drinking age Wagenaar says that after prohibition it was generally established at twenty-one, to remain there until 1970–75 when, following the change in voting age, many states lowered it. By 1975 there was clear evidence that a lower drinking age meant more traffic fatalities among young people, and the age-lowering trend was reversed. Sixteen states increased their drinking age between 1976 and 1983. The issue now is whether further increases are warranted, and what the optimal age should be.

Wagenaar's research shows that "approximately 20 percent of all alcohol-related crashes involving young drivers can be prevented by removing legal access to alcoholic beverages" (1983: 101). Thus, he concludes, it is warranted on public health grounds to raise the drinking age to twenty-one. As further justification for this position Wagenaar presents evidence that the restriction of this privilege is constitutional and that it has popular support.

But, Wagenaar continues, there are some counter arguments to consider. Alcohol is an important part of adult life, for which adolescents must be prepared. It can be argued that phasing in the privilege of drinking may better prepare the young person to handle liquor well. There is no move toward prohibition at this time—indeed the positive value of alcohol in lubricating social situations and relieving the tensions of contemporary life is generally recognized. Therefore, a policy to strive for is one which prepares young people for an adulthood of responsible drinking.

The decisions about policy rest, of course, with the public and their representatives. Increasingly the public has become aware of, concerned about, and organized around the issue of drunk driving.

Social Movement

The attention of sociologists interested in the dynamics of social movements has been caught by the proliferation of citizen groups around the issue of drunk driving. Three which began in response to specific tragedies but which have grown beyond their original locales are Remove Intoxicated Drivers (RID), Mothers Against Drunk Driving (MADD), and Students Against Drunk Driving (SADD).

MADD, the most viable of these groups, has been the focus of several research projects. Frank Weed of the University of Texas–Arlington, reported on his research on MADD chapter leadership and programs at the ASA Meetings in 1985. Weed did telephone interviews with three officers in each of 112 randomly selected chapters (at the time MADD had 320 chapters).

He found that "the typical local chapter officer is female, age 42, has attended college, and is involved in several community organizations" (1985: 9). Additionally, they or members of their families have quite often been victims of drunk driving accidents. Forty-six percent of the chapter presidents had lost a member of her family in an accident.

Asking about their program, Weed found a consensus that MADD is concerned first and foremost with developing public awareness and education, then with court monitoring and promoting new law, and finally with victim assistance. As might be expected of an organization which has spawned so many chapters since its founding in 1980, MADD officers generally feel they enjoy strong community support. The resistance they do report comes, Weed notes, from groups which fall into two categories: purveyors and servers of liquor and members of the legal establishment who must take the brunt of MADD's criticism of the legal process.

Craig Reinarman, Northeastern University, also reported on his MADD research at the 1985 SSSP Meetings. He offers an extended and probing account of MADD's history, in which he chronicles not only its impressive growth and accomplishments but also its "growing pains."

MADD was begun in 1980 by Candy Lightner, following the death of her daughter Cari, and Lightner's consequent initiation into the criminal justice system. Her grief was joined by anger when she learned that the man who killed Cari was "both on probation for previous DUI (Drinking Under the Influence) convictions and out on bail for another hit-and-run DUI offence a few days before" (1985: 4). In sum, Reinarman says, "Her passion, commitment, and status as an aggrieved mother gave her substantial charismatic credibility and moral legitimacy and she quickly attracted adherents" (1985: 5).

By way of accomplishments, Reinarman notes MADD's success in focusing media attention on itself and on the drunk-driving issue: ". . . MADD has affected what Foucault calls a 'shift of gaze' with regard to drinking-driving in the U.S." (1985: 7). He notes the considerable success MADD has enjoyed in generating legislation which reflects its "victims' rights focus" (1985: 5). The centerpiece of this accomplishment is the 1984 federal law which will cut federal highway funds to states which do not raise the drinking age to twenty-one.

On the other hand, Reinarman cites a number of "growing pains" which MADD has suffered. These include tensions between MADD's board and Mrs. Lightner over the division of organizational responsibilities, an unauthorized loan to her of $8,200, a high salary for Mrs. Lightner, and high administrative and fundraising costs which led ultimately to the refusal of the Council of Better Business Bureaus' "Philanthropic Advisor Service" (1984) and the National Charities Information Bureau to recommend MADD as a charity (1985).

Reinarman's larger concern is with MADD's exclusive focus on drunk drivers and its refusal to endorse preventive policies which take aim at the liquor industry. (MADD does not support increased taxes on alcohol or the regulation of advertising, for instance.) He writes: "Like the National Rifle Association and other anti-gun control advocates who have long held that 'guns don't kill people, people kill people,' MADD's strategy from the start has been to argue that alcohol is not the problem, drunk drivers are" (1985: 18). This limited focus has produced financial support from the liquor industry, which naturally prefers a delimited focus.

Two contextual factors seem to Reinarman to give support to the MADD position. The first is a shift in thinking about alcohol-related problems. By MADD's inception in 1980 the disease paradigm, which defined recent thought about alcoholism, was losing its hegemony and a more pluralistic, "disaggregative approach to alcohol problems" was taking hold (1985: 22). This "scientific and public policy ferment in the alcohol arena seems," Reinarman writes, "to have given intellectual elbow room to those calling attention to alcohol-related problems like drinking-driving" (1985: 23).

The second factor he notes is political; namely, "the intersection of the politics of MADD and the political culture of Reagan and the New Right" (1985: 23). MADD's individualist focus, its concern with retribution, and its willingness to condone public intervention in areas of private mortality all, Reinarman says, are compatible with conservatism as it has developed from the "Law and Order" campaigns of the Nixon years to the present. "MADD's discourse seems very much in sync with the now-dominant mode of discourse eminating from the Administration," Reinarman claims (1985: 25). The legislative program of MADD, with its emphases on finding and punishing alcohol abusers, seems to Reinarman to introduce legal intervention into areas of behavior previously immune, and thus to "at least raise questions about, if not a momentum toward, the further constriction of civil liberties" (1985: 31). The discourse MADD has introduced and defined is, he believes, "born of and suited to an age in which the powers that be are intent upon shifting the agenda away from social welfare toward social control" (1985: 33).

MADD continues to be a hot research topic. For instance, John McCarthy of Catholic University is currently collecting data for a study which will use MADD chapters in various areas to assess "the importance of four factors which social movement theory says are important to the growth of citizen action: widespread common understandings of the problems and its solution, the increased capacity to mobilize which has flowed from expanded political opportunity, the flow of state resources to local areas designed to encourage citizen action, and the existence of local structures of relationships of individuals who can be expected to be interested in organizing around the issue" (1984: 8). Results of this analysis are still forthcoming.

Sociologists are contributing to scholarly and public understanding of the drunk-driving issue by analyzing it through criminology, public policy, and social movements. The work cited is characteristic, though not exhaustive of the contributions being made from these perspectives.

References

McCarthy, John D. 1984. "The Causes and Consequences of the Citizens' Movement Against Drunk Driving." Proposal to the National Science Foundation.

Olson, Steve and Dean R. Gerstein. 1985. *Alcohol in America: Taking Action to Prevent Abuse.* Washington, DC: National Academy Press.

Reinarman, Craig. 1985. "Social Movements and Social Problems: 'Mothers Against Drunk Drivers,' Restrictive Alcohol Laws and Social Control in the 1980s." Paper presented at the Society for the Study of Social Problems Annual Meeting, Washington, DC, August 23–26.

Ross, H. Laurence. 1985. "Can We Make the Problem Go Away?" *The New Mexican,* December 22.

Ross, H. Laurence and Gary D. LaFree. 1983. "Deterrence in Criminology and Social Policy." Paper presented to the National Academy of Sciences Symposium on "Knowledge in Social and Behavioral Science: Discoveries and Trends Over Fifty Years." Washington, DC.

Wagenaar, Alexander C. 1983. *Alcohol, Young Drivers, and Traffic Accidents.* Lexington, MA: Lexington Books/D. C. Heath and Co.

Weed, Frank J. 1985. "Grass-roots Activism and the Drunk Driving Issue: A Survey of MADD Chapters." Paper presented at the 80th Annual Meeting of the American Sociological Association, Washington, DC, August 26–30.

Chapter V
Tobacco

We are in the midst of an intense controversy over how cigarette smoking will be defined in the United States. At stake is whether tobacco is seen as a harmful drug or a benign habit and the symbolic definition of smoking as socially approved or illegitimate. The tobacco industry denies that smoking "causes" health problems; some U.S. governmental agencies encourage tobacco farming and exports; local, state and Federal governments collect billions of dollars in tobacco taxes; and smokers claim constitutional rights. Other agencies of the U.S. government, health and antismoking advocates are attempting to place restrictions on cigarette smoking, to define its use as dangerous, smokers as deviant and, some would say, to denigrate smokers.

The scientific evidence regarding the health effects of smoking cigarettes is overwhelming and persuasive. Cigarette smoking is addicting; nicotine produces a physical dependence. This addiction is probably why so many smokers continue to smoke and why it is so hard to quit. About 2.5 million deaths a year worldwide are associated with cigarette consumption. The harmful smoke from cigarettes is the prime risk factor in lung cancer where death rates are related to the average number of cigarettes smoked daily. Risks of dying from cancer of the larynx are 6-10 times higher for cigarette smokers; risks of dying from cancer of the esophagus are 2-6 times higher. Other kinds of cancers are also increased by cigarette smoking. The risk of premature coronary disease is increased 2-3 times for smokers. Risks of respiratory diseases, such as chronic bronchitis and death from emphysema, also rise dramatically with cigarette smoking. These risks and others are dose-related, and we must be careful to speak in terms of "probability" because smoking does not inevitably affect everyone who smokes.

If the use of cigarettes was newly discovered, if there were no vested interests at play and given what we know about tobacco's harmful effects, it is extremely unlikely that the Food and Drug Administration would ever allow cigarettes on the market. Yet reality intrudes, in this case the political power of the tobacco industry. The tobacco industry vigorously denies that smoking causes health problems. It is an industry with over 55 million regular customers in the United States with annual sales over $20 billion. The industry has quite a public relations and legal task: it must entice new customers (smoking is increasing among women and teenagers) to replace those who quit or die; it must keep cigarettes on the market with as few restrictions as possible; it must fend off lawsuits; and, above all else, it must protect the legitimacy of its product in the eyes of the public. In sum, it has quite an advertising job. Many would argue it has succeeded all too well—so well in fact that we do not normally think of tobacco as a "drug," much less a drug whose dangers are well-known, very costly to society, and clearly documented.

The articles in this chapter help to explore the battle over the social definition of tobacco. The first article by Blair looks at why this harmful drug is legal and socially acceptable in America today, that is, the successful selling job done by the tobacco industry. The second article by Daynard explores the strategy of making tobacco companies liable for the damage and death caused by their product. He depicts the battle between the tobacco industry and antismoking advocates. The last piece by Chandler estimates the costs of tobacco smoking to society and reviews the effects of cigarette smoke on nonsmokers. Chandler explores antismoking efforts and advocates a change in social policy.

20. Why Dick Can't Stop Smoking
The Politics Behind our National Addiction

Gwenda Blair

Every morning my husband coughs and gags for about ten minutes. Some days he wakes up choking. On others he is fine until he stands up, then doubles over retching. After 15 or 20 minutes, he can finish a sentence without gasping, walk across the room without bending over in pain, even pick up our two-year-old son without dropping him. Then he gets dressed, has a cup of coffee and lights his first cigarette of the day.

During the next 16 or so hours that he is awake, he will smoke two packs of cigarettes. He will enjoy only a few puffs, and he will give up smoking at least 40 times. Sometimes he gives it up more than once during the course of a single cigarette. During the 16 years—half his life—that he has smoked, he has stopped occasionally for a few weeks or even months. In such periods, he is able to do little else but search for an occasion—sad, happy or insignificant, any one will do—to justify having a cigarette.

To dismiss this as one man's neurosis would be a mistake. Dick is only one of a number of people I know whose lives ultimately revolve not around jobs, friends, families, lovers or politics, but around their seemingly incurable attachment to smoking. Probably only eating, sleeping, working or watching television involves more Americans more continuously than does smoking. According to Department of Health, Education, and Welfare figures, about a quarter of the country's population smokes, and one-sixth, or 37 million people, will die prematurely from it. On a day-to-day basis, that means that, every two minutes, possibly five teenagers will begin smoking—shortening their lives by an average of 5 ½ minutes with every cigarette—and one of them will die prematurely because of it. As much as we need to know why Johnny can't read or what makes Sammy run, an even more pressing question is, why can't Dick stop smoking?

Dick's biggest problem is that nicotine—one of the most rapid and fatal of poisons, also used commercially as an insecticide—is physically addictive. It is the soma, not the psyche, that shrieks loudest when smokers try to stop. Recently, Columbia University psychologist Stanley Schachter found that when smokers try to give up the weed, withdrawal from nicotine creates anxiety, which in turn results in acidic urine. This flushes nicotine faster than usual and thus triggers the physical need to light up another cigarette so as to bring the amount of nicotine in the body back up to the usual level of addiction.

More specifically, according to Dr. Hamilton Russell of the Institute of Psychiatry, London, it is the level of nicotine in the brain that is crucial to the highly dependent smoker. Nicotine reaches the brain within a few moments after the first drag, but within 20 to 30 minutes—precisely the time lag between cigarettes for most heavy smokers—the nicotine has dissipated to other organs, and another fix is needed to counter the change in brain wave activity, as registered in an EEG taken at that time.

Our ample supplies of tobacco and social tolerance of both smoking and withdrawal symptoms ("I need a cigarette") make its addictive property nearly invisible. Nevertheless, this is precisely why tobacco is one of the country's most profitable and, in turn, most politically powerful industries.

Tobacco's promoters never stop working. Their activities range from contributions to political campaigns (including the full-time energies of a Philip Morris executive as the only big-business representative on Jimmy Carter's 1976 campaign staff) and support for well-placed members of Congress to the advertisements that make most of the nation's press afraid to print stories like this.

The tobacco industry has also been astoundingly successful. Few Americans remain ignorant for long, for example, of any new cigarette brand that is introduced, yet how many know that:

- According to a 1967 British government survey of teenagers who smoked more than one cigarette, 85 percent become regular users.
- Former drug addicts and alcoholics who have been surveyed consider it's harder to give up tobacco than heroin or booze.
- The former director of HEW's National Institute on Drug Abuse, Dr. Robert Dupont, estimates that only 10 to 15 percent of the people alive today who ever used heroin are still addicted, whereas more than 66 percent of those still living who ever smoked cigarettes are current daily smokers.
- Chemically and pharmacologically, nicotine is related to such central nervous system stimulants as methylphenidate and the amphetamines, which are even more addictive than heroin and other opiates.
- Both drug and alcohol addicts can tolerate drug-free periods, whereas only 2 percent of all cigarette users are intermittent smokers.

Yet despite these classic symptoms of addiction, tobacco is categorized as neither drug nor food (although U.S. taxpayers paid $29.4 million in 1975 to include it in the U.S. Food for Peace export program). The legally required warning label on cigarette packs implies that some sort of inspection has occurred, but tobacco is ignored by the Food and Drug Administration. It is also specifically exempt from regulation by the Consumer Product Safety Commission or the Environmental Protection Agency. And the more than 300 possible cigarette additives, including oxidizers to make them burn better (cigarettes are the leading cause of fatal home fires), preservatives and enhancers designed to compensate for reduced taste in newer low-tar brands, need not even be disclosed, much less examined for carcinogenic or other effects.

What's more, it is understandably difficult for Dick and this country's other 53 million smokers to accept that going through the physical and psychological trauma of getting the cigarette monkey off their backs is really worth it, since they'll still be exposed to countless other pollutants in America's on-going game of cancer roulette. Smokers can get almost as much relief without even quitting by just switching to one of the low-tar brands that now account for a quarter of the market and half the advertising dollars. Not only do low-tars let smokers satisfy and exhibit concern for their own health (and that of those around them, who will now be exposed to fewer milligrams of tar every time a cigarette is lit), but these brands also let new smokers become addicted more smoothly, without that initial revulsion that used to turn off at least some potential smokers.

The federal government has followed the same line of thought. Until last year, HEW's preventive efforts against smoking had been budgeted at under $1 million a year, whereas more than $40 million had been spent over the last decade in attempts to develop a "safe" cigarette—the only case in which the government itself had financed a major effort to develop a less harmful consumer product. Indeed, the chimera of a safe smoke is so powerful that, when the National Cancer Institute released a study last August showing that low-tars are "less hazardous," the media and the tobacco industry ignored the chief researcher's careful insistence that there is no safe level of smoking, and they virtually heralded low-tars as a solution. Relieved consumers, in turn, pushed up sales of Carlton cigarettes, deemed least hazardous, by 124 percent.

Smokes and Popes

The other major reason that Dick continues to smoke is simply that cigarettes represent not only the good life, but the American way of life. To begin with, every year the United States consumes more cigarettes (4,064 per year for every American) than does any other country in the world. This is only fitting since cigarettes have played a significant—if little appreciated—role in making the United States one of the world's most heavily industrialized nations.

One of the major problems among workers in the Industrial Age, particularly those in routine lower-level jobs, is tedium. Cigarettes provide the ideal solution: at about ten minutes apiece (plus occasional coffee breaks to give the day a few high points), smokes not only help pace out a day—on the production line, in the typing pool, behind a lunch counter or waiting on a welfare line—but they give you a steady flow of small rewards to keep on trucking. No wonder, according to the U.S. Department of Agriculture, cigarettes are the first luxury item poor people buy.

Data from Germany after World War II indicates that even under conditions of extreme deprivation, and in situations where food rations were under 1,000 calories a day, smokers still bartered eats for smokes. (Soviet concentration-camp memoirs indicate the same pattern.) Smokers' need for nicotine was so overwhelming that some also picked up butts off the street, begged tobacco, prostituted themselves or stole other goods that could be traded for cigarettes. In fact, nicotine addiction is so powerful that Consumers Union researchers have speculated that it may have contributed to the conversion by early North American Indian tribes from hunting and fishing to settled agriculture in order to have a guaranteed supply of tobacco.

Unlike smallpox and venereal disease, smoking was already here when Columbus arrived. A clay pipe found in California has been carbon-dated to 7000 B.C. and the specific use of tobacco goes back at least to 4th-century Mayan priests in Mexico. As the postmark used by the Tobacco Institute, the major tobacco lobby, proudly proclaims, tobacco was "America's First Industry." And it soon became the equivalent to small change at home as well as the major commodity in trade with Europe.

Opposition to tobacco's use began early, too. At the beginning of the 17th century, King James I of England named tobacco and papism as evils against which he vowed to do life-long battle. Pope Innocent X agreed with half of King James' list of evils and excommunicated smokers. Other early tobacco adversaries were Ottoman Emperor Amurat IV who condemned smokers to death, one Czar who resorted to nose-slitting, and the Shah Sifi who had smokers impaled. Most recently, U.S. Secretary of Health, Education, and Welfare Joseph Califano, Jr., has labeled smoking to be "slow-motion suicide." And it has all been to such little avail that tobacco is now grown and smoked worldwide, from Russia to New Zealand, although American tobacco is still considered among the finest.

Cigarettes proved a handy taboo in many ways. With only the defiant flick of a match, anyone, from soldiers on the front to women struggling to liberate themselves from traditional roles, could signal a bold stance to the world. In this century, improvements in tobacco cultivation and processing that made cigarettes easier to inhale, plus public acceptance of women smoking, have caused such an increase in the number of smokers that eyebrows do not even go up when a gentleman offers a lady a Tiparillo. Yet, for many, cigarettes still remain a basic symbol of mystery, daring and sexuality. Cigarettes appeal so strongly to a gut anti-authoritarian instinct that they continue to be smoked in spite of—or, in some cases, because of—steadily mounting evidence of danger.

Beauty Pageants in Niger

For a while, all this seemed to be coming to an end. During the 1960s, as the civil rights movement, the Vietnam War and the women's movement were changing the course of history, Americans were also cutting down on smoking after a 1964 Surgeon General's report linked smoking to disease and death.

Today, there are fewer smokers than in 1964 (except among teenage girls, whose usage of cigarettes has quintupled in that period, possibly because of cigarette ads' exploitation of women's liberation), but today's smokers are smoking more. Simple population growth will increase the number of smokers to 60.2 million by 1980—not a bad record given that a 1975 U.S. Public Health Service poll found that 84 percent of all adult Americans consider cigarette smoking "enough of a health hazard for something to be done about it," and 82 percent believe it frequently causes disease and death.

Even the cigarette companies are not relying on cigarette sales to stay up forever. Now that 33 states and many more cities and counties have restricted smoking in certain public areas, the industry is busily diversifying into other products, from dog food to beer, as a hedge against the future. Less well-publicized in this country, the cigarette industry is also following what might be called "the infant-formula model"—shifting their sights from the developed world, where consumption may level off, to a vast Third World market eager for symbols of Western affluence and still unencumbered by health and advertising regulations. According to Worldwatch Institute, typical promotional efforts include the Gitane beauty pageant in Niger and Gauloise ads in Africa that stress that cigarette as a mark of high status and virility. Such aggressive marketing is also evident in giant multinationals, like Philip Morris International, whose Marlboro man now sponsors tennis matches and bridge tournaments for the booming Egyptian market. Since 1965, PMI has increased the number of its Asian, African and Latin American affiliates and licensing arrangements from 2 to 13 and from 2 to 9, respectively. As a result, sales of more than 160 brands PMI markets internationally in 170 countries have increased a healthy 18 percent annually over the last decade.

With a 1977 U.S. cigarette advertising outlay of $422 million, or about $2 for every American, what is truly amazing is that only about 25 percent of the population smokes. Of course you don't win a ball game or a war by just sitting on your butt, so the cigarette companies are continually exploring other promotional ideas. Brown & Williamson, for example, is paying each of 1,500 Volkswagen owners $20 a month to paint their cars "Kool" green with a big "9" (to represent that cigarette's tar content); they've also started four other Volkswagen campaigns to promote their low-tar brands. Wary of proposals to the government asking it to prohibit the use of human models in cigarette ads, in 1977 B&W also launched a series of 20 scenic color ads that showed no people, but suggested "a human presence" by including homes in the background.

Other companies have sponsored tennis tournaments (Decade, Virginia Slims), special show-ings of movie classics (Benson & Hedges), jazz and country-music festivals (Kool), ethnic festivals (R. J. Reynolds), gold championships (Kent, Carlton, Doral), and sweepstakes with prizes of mink coats (Max) and a farm in Vermont (Kool). The introduction of commercials into movie theaters also offers new promotion posibilities, which include recycling old television cigarette ads (already done in overseas movie houses).

"Screw the Proletariat"

This display of Madison Avenue ingenuity helps keep tobacco the nation's fifth-largest cash crop. Last year's retail sales of tobacco products totaled $17 billion—equal to the entire gross national product of Greece. It's enough to support 600,000 tobacco farm families and 76,000 workers in the cigarette manufacturing industry, as well as providing revenue to cigarette vendors and government agencies on all levels.

This money also buys a lot of protection. The most obvious is the cigarette lobby in Wash-ington, described by Senator Edward Kennedy as "probably the most effective lobby on Capitol Hill." At the Tobacco Institute, the industry's chief lobby, the promotion of tobacco begins as soon as you enter the waiting room, which is dominated by a large wall-sized display case containing row on row of cigarette packs (presumably all 168 brands now on the market) mounted on black velvet. In the inner offices used by the Institute's staff of 56, bumperstickers and posters on the wall range from "Enjoy Smoking" and "Califano is Dangerous to My Health" to "Screw the Proletariat." But the Institute's official strategy depends not so much on smart-ass slogans as it does on a combination of never surrendering the offensive and stonewalling to the death.

Inspired perhaps by the four-volume set of Nixon's memoirs on his bookshelf, the Institute's vice president, Bill Dwyer, painted a picture of the tobacco industry as a pitiful helpless giant. "We're trying to re-establish a controversy in this country," he told me as he chain-smoked Benson & Hedges. "Most people believe beyond the shadow of a doubt that smoking is dangerous. We're going *against* popular prejudices, and that's *very* difficult."

Dwyer calls tobacco "one of life's natural pleasures," which, like all other basic pleasures, is subject to continual attack from busybodies and do-gooders. The message he and the people from the Institute deliver to hundreds of civic organizations, schools and local media each year is that there has been no "conclusive" cause and effect established between smoking and health but "merely inferences from statistics," and that people should listen to both sides and then decide for them-selves.

Dwyer does not have a logical argument in favor of tobacco as much as he has a stray col-lection of quips and quotes. When you question him about statistical links between cigarettes and lung cancer, for example, he immediately becomes a walking compendium of other peoples' say-ings: "Cancer is a biological, not a statistical, problem." "Smoking is one of the leading causes of statistics." "Statistics are like a bikini bathing suit: what they reveal is interesting; what they conceal is vital."

Repeatedly, Dwyer used his audience (me) as the example to back up his point: "If you can decide not to smoke on your own, why not let others do the same?" When asked how independent a decision about smoking could be, given its addictive properties and the industry's massive ad-vertising budget, he replied that there is no addictive effect, and that ads influence only the brand choice of those who already smoke, "just as soap ads only talk to consumers about buying Tide instead of Fab, not about whether to wash."

This skilled persuasion on the public-relations level is backed up by widespread campaign contributions to Congressional candidates. By the end of September of 1978, the Institute's political-action committee, the Tobacco People's Public Affairs Committee (TPPAC), had already given money to 157 members of the House (more than one-third of its members) and 15 senators—a gift list that included a number of committees with jurisdiction over smoking programs. By the time of the November 1978 elections, the TPPAC gave away about $61,000 to its friends running for office. Many of the same candidates received support from other tobacco public affairs committees, such as the newly formed Farmers and Friends PAC of Raleigh, North Carolina. Organized by tobacco growers, this group wants to arrange a voluntary check-off system for the country's one-half million tobacco farmers, and estimates of its potential receipts range from $200,000 to $3 million.

The lobbyists' results are impressive. On Capitol Hill, it has meant not only that initiatives such as removing tobacco from the Food for Peace export program have been defeated, but that many issues concerning smoking are raised only minimally if at all. A typical example is an early September hearing held by the House Subcommittee on Tobacco. Subcommittee chairman Representative Walter Jones (D-N.C.) called eight medical and other experts who testified that cigarette smoke is not a health hazard. Nine other members of Congress, all from tobacco states and an unusually high number for a hearing, were on hand, but there was no report of probing questions. Anti-smoking groups had not been informed of the hearing ahead of time. By the hearing's close, the Tobacco Institute was ready with a three-page press release.

The executive branch has also done its part to counter anti-smoking developments with neutralizing and, occasionally, openly pro-smoking gestures. On the same day that the American Medical Association issued a 14-year study, financed by the nation's largest tobacco companies, linking cigarette smoking to maladies from indigestion and the common cold to cancer, President Carter made a well-publicized visit to tobacco country in North Carolina. After a few jibes at Califano, Carter said that he saw "no incompatibility" with annual price-support for tobacco farmers and pursuit of a "good health program." Subsidies to the tobacco industry totaled $35 million in 1977, in additiion to a little-known $123 million in federally guaranteed loans to foreign countries for purchases of American tobacco.

Smoking Under Attack

The tobacco institute's most active opposition, the "ruthless" anti-smoking forces of which Bill Dwyer complained, have their headquarters about a mile away from the Institute's plush digs. Action on Smoking and Health operates from two, cramped, third-floor walk-up rooms on the edge of the George Washington University campus. "Sue the Bastards" says the poster next to the desk of ASH's founder John Banzhaf. Over a decade ago, Banzhaf forced radio and television stations to provide free time for anti-smoking messages; today, ASH is doing just that. The first organization to file suit to force airlines to provide separate no-smoking sections, and, along with others, has also sued for smoke-free workplaces and public space, ASH is now after the FDA to reclassify nicotine as a drug. (If, by the way, you want to get involved in anti-smoking efforts, ASH is your best bet. It can put you in touch with groups in your community. Contact ASH at 2000 H Street NW, Washington, D.C. 20006;(202)659–4310.)

One of the major problems with the anti-smoking movement, according to Banzhaf, is that although there are more than 1,000 small, local anti-smoking groups, there is no strong, well-financed national nonsmokers' rights group. The three major organizations that are in a position

228

to exercise leadership, the American Cancer Society, the American Heart Association and the American Lung Association, are "worse than useless," he charges. "They only use a tiny percentage of the millions they take in for anti-smoking activities, but people think giving them money is the way to fight cigarettes. The result is like having Phyllis Schlafly head of NOW."

Nevertheless, nonsmokers have been alarmed and moved to action by findings that it is dangerous to be around cigarettes whether you are actually smoking or not. Tearing eyes, painful coughs and estimates that a nonsmoker inhales the equivalent of up to six cigarettes merely by being in the same room with smokers have gradually roused a growing number of nonsmokers to declare that smoking is one American way of death they refuse to accept. Recent research has also found that the annual cost of cigarette-related illnesses may be as high as $18 billion, more than seven times the tax revenues that have so far rationalized smoking for some government purse watchers, and a further burden that nonsmokers are increasingly unwilling to assume. As a result, anti-smoking incidents are mounting continually: from the Washington, D.C., woman who poured water over the cigar of a recalcitrant smoker in a restaurant to the New Jersey telephone company worker who successfully sued for a smoke-free workplace.

Over 500 anti-smoking ordinances were introduced around the country in 1976, and there have been no retreats yet in those areas where the restrictions passed. This momentum could grind to a halt, however, after the defeat last November of California's Proposition 5. This statewide anti-smoking measure was successfully opposed by some $5 million spent to defeat it, financed mainly by five major cigarette companies and consisting largely of skillful television and radio spots linking the attack on smoking to Big Government.

On the national level, HEW Secretary Califano's anti-smoking offensive, announced last January, includes a proposed ban on cigarette smoking in commercial airplanes, a study on whether to raise cigarette taxes (8¢ a pack since 1951) to discourage consumption and a stepped-up program of anti-smoking education. A few weeks later, a widely publicized study issued by the National Commission on Smoking and Public Policy, a group sponsored by the American Cancer Society, criticized the ACS for inaction on smoking and called for stronger measures. The Civil Aeronautics Board followed suit with a decision to ban smoking of cigars and pipes on airplanes.

What is needed now is massive, continual support for smokers who want to stop and encouragement for others not to start. Above all, this means public acknowledgement of the seriousness of cigarette addiction. One of lobbyist Bill Dwyer's favorite arguments is that "more people are familiar with the official cigarette warning label than they are with the First Amendment," and therefore smokers are simply exercising their right of choice. But when researchers find that nine out of ten smokers wish to stop, that six out of ten have tried and failed, and that present smoke-cessation techniques, most of which rely on will power or aversion techniques, have a failure rate of more than 75 percent, smoking looks far less like free will than enslavement.

To ban cigarettes outright would doubtless be as futile as Prohibition, but there is much that could be done. Probably the single most important anti-smoking measure would be to drastically restrict cigarette advertising—either completely or to restrict it to straightforward information like that in financial "tombstone" ads. A total ban on advertising is scarcely a novel idea, for it has already been adopted in Italy, Iceland, Finland, Sweden and Norway.

The evidence that such a ban would lead to an immediate drop in consumption is not yet clear, but one thing it surely would lead to is far more vigorous coverage of smoking's dangers by newspapers and magazines—which have reaped about $800 million growth of tobacco advertising in the eight years since cigarettes left the airwaves. (In an average year, for instance, *TV Guide* carries $20 million worth of cigarette advertising; *Time,* $15 million; and *Playboy,* $12 million.

Parade magazine, the Sunday newspaper supplement, gets a whopping 80 percent of its ad revenue from tobacco.) Without this financial tie, major magazines other than *Reader's Digest,* the *New Yorker, The Washington Monthly* and *Good Housekeeping* (the only four that do not accept cigarette ads) might open their pages to the in-depth coverage of cigarette hazards they have thus far avoided. A survey a year ago by the *Columbia Journalism Review* failed to find a *single* comprehensive article about the dangers of smoking in the previous seven years in any major national magazine accepting cigarette advertising. [*Editor's Note:* The *Columbia Journalism Review* evidently omitted the then relatively new *Mother Jones* from its survey. But the magazine's experience in regard to cigarette advertising has been instructive. Hugh Drummond, M.D., *MJ*'s medical columnist in 1977 and early 1978, repeatedly attacked cigarettes in his articles. One column, in December 1977, linked cigarettes with cancer of the lungs, throat, mouth, esophagus, pancreas and bladder, as well as with emphysema and heart disease. Drummond ended his article by noting the irony with "one company—Philip Morris—manufactures both cigarettes and hospital equipment." Several months later, despite *MJ*'s rapidly rising circulation, R. J. Reynolds abruptly cancelled $18,000 worth of cigarette advertising scheduled to run in the magazine. No explanation was given.]

Other critical measures that should be taken include:

- Officially labeling cigarettes "addictive" rather than simply "habit forming." This would at least channel anti-smoking attention and funds toward relevant projects such as addiction studies and massive preventative campaigns to discourage nonsmokers from taking even a puff under the illusion that they "can always stop when they want to."
- Anti-smoking ads.
- Strict enforcement of existing laws against the sale of cigarettes to minors.
- Research into why some people don't smoke.
- More smoke-cessation counseling and clinics with Medicaid and Blue Cross reimbursement, which will also furnish follow-up studies, so that we can begin to learn what, if anything, will work.
- Making cigarette companies legally liable for the effect of their products, a tactic now being tested by Melvin Belli in a suit he has filed on behalf of the children of a woman who died of lung cancer.
- Development of alternative uses for tobacco. One of the most promising is extraction of fraction-1, a protein that contains more nutritional value than standard animal protein and that could develop into one of the world's primary nutrition sources.

Such measures would mean increasing the federal anti-smoking budget many times over the $30 million Secretary Califano has requested, but it would be well worth it considering the 322,000 lives lost each year to cigarette-related diseases. And it would certainly be cheaper than the heavy price we all pay by allowing our society to be so shaped by a practice we already know to be deadly to body and spirit alike.

21. Tobacco Liability Litigation as a Cancer Control Strategy

Richard A. Daynard

Since the 1930s there has been a steadily rising trend in cigarette-induced cancer deaths in the United States, reaching about 120,000 such deaths in 1984 (*1*). This trend reflects a similar trend in cigarette consumption that began about 20 years earlier. While total U.S. cigarette consumption has been falling 1%–2% annually since 1982, even at that rate of decline several million more Americans will die from cigarette-induced cancers before the epidemic concludes. Obviously, any viable strategy for further reducing cigarette consumption deserves high priority among cancer control strategies.

Reasons for Viewing Tobacco Liability Litigation as a Cancer Control Strategy

Successful products liability suits against cigarette manufacturers on behalf of diseased smokers and their families would be likely to reduce future cigarette consumption dramatically. Briefly stated, they could shift billions of dollars of health and productivity costs from families and third-party payers to cigarette companies, forcing increases in cigarette prices and consequent large drops in consumption, especially among children and teenagers. They may drive home the point about the dangers of smoking, while forcing the industry to stop its deceptive advertising, promotion, and public relations. Finally, materials documenting the industry's disinformation campaign, discovered by plaintiffs' attorneys in the litigation process, may hinder industry lobbying efforts against other anti-smoking strategies.

Products liability suits have achieved similar effects with respect to asbestos and other dangerous products.

Economic Effects.

Products liability suits transfer costs, albeit inefficiently, from injured parties to the manufacturers of defective or unreasonably dangerous products. Plaintiffs include the injured person, his immediate family, and—by "subrogation"—whoever has paid his medical bills. Plaintiffs' attorneys bear the cost of pressing the suits and, where successful, share in the judgment or settlement. It is, however, the defendants' costs that are most relevant from a public health standpoint.

Defendants pay their own attorneys' fees, plus whatever judgments or settlements are reached. Attorneys' fees and other costs in successfully defending a single smokeless tobacco products liability case in 1986 were estimated at $15 million (*2*). This may have contributed to a consequent price increase and sharp decline in smokeless tobacco use. Cigarette manufacturers obviously spend much more to defend the 120+ cases currently pending against them. However, since sales and profits from cigarettes are many times those from smokeless tobacco, the recent cigarette price increases may not have been motivated by a need to pass along defense costs.

From Richard A. Daynard, TOBACCO LIABILITY LITIGATION AS A CANCER CONTROL STRATEGY, which originally appeared in *Journal of the National Cancer Institute*, Vol. 80, NO. 1, March 2, 1988, pp. 9–13.

But five or ten successful tobacco liability suits should impact quickly and heavily. Thousands of suits, distributed widely throughout the United States, can be expected. The six major cigarette companies will have to retain counsel in every large city. Fresh liability insurance will cease to be available, while the manufacturers' financial statements will have to reflect enormous contingent liabilities. Industry executives and directors will have to decide whether to try to absorb current liability costs, to raise prices to cover them, or to raise prices even further to cover the average additional liability exposure incurred with each additional pack sold.

The amount of exposure is very substantial. The annual cigarette-caused medical costs and productivity losses, divided by annual cigarette sales, have been conservatively estimated at $2.17/pack (3). Of course, every affected smoker will not sue, and every meritorious suit will not succeed. On the other hand, the manufacturers have to cover their defense costs as well, and punitive damages may raise some judgments well above the amounts needed for compensation.

Furthermore, even a relatively small price increase—such as $.25/pack—will have very significant consumption effects. Price increases of 10% have been shown to produce overall consumption decreases of 4%, with 14% decreases among males 12–17 years old (4). Since 50% of smokers begin by age 14 (5) and the great majority by age 18, the reductions in smoking by children and teenagers may be the most relevant for cancer control purposes. In any event, the hypothesized $.25/pack, 20%, price increase would produce long-term reductions of at least 10,000 cigarette-caused cancer deaths annually, and possibly much more.

Information/Disinformation.

Public education against smoking faces the problems of abstractness and diminishing marginal effectiveness. In an age of "celebrities," neither statistics nor even anonymous diseased lungs make the point that "real" people actually suffer and die from cigarette-induced diseases. Furthermore, new reports of the adverse health effects of cigarettes make little impression on people who already know at some level that cigarettes are dangerous. But the first few nationally publicized cases of particular individuals suing cigarette companies for their disease—and the first few such cases in each local media market—will focus media and public attention on the plaintiffs' cigarette-induced suffering, as well as exciting widespread discussion and debate on the larger issues of personal and corporate responsibility.

This debate has already produced a salutary shift in the industry's public relations. Public statements by industry representatives portray smokers who would sue cigarette companies for their lung cancer, emphysema, or peripheral vascular disease as people who knowingly and voluntarily accepted these risks. Since the industry *still* denies the reality of these and other health risks, their new position is essentially that "anyone foolish enough to believe us deserves the disease he gets." This is surely not the most effective posture for selling cigarettes: It is at least possible that some portion of the dramatic drop in smoking incidence reported between 1985 and 1986 was attributable to this public relations shift.

Successful cases are likely to produce even more dramatic changes in the industry's communicative behavior. Continuing deceptions, ranging from not admitting that smoking causes a range of diseases to actively misrepresenting the state of scientific knowledge (6), are likely to outrage jurors and judges, making substantial punitive damage awards more likely. Industry lawyers are likely to advise their clients and their clients' public relations and lobbying representatives to stop the active denials and perhaps actually to admit the dangers. Advertising campaigns using juvenile culture heros, young models, people engaged in active sports, and so forth may have to be curtailed for similar reasons.

Success of Tobacco Industry Lobbying.

A wide variety of anti-smoking efforts fail as a result of the tobacco industry's lobbying power. Recent efforts to regulate cigarette design and advertising have been completely thwarted, and efforts to regulate cigarette use in public places have met only partial success.

Information obtained by plaintiffs' attorneys through the "discovery" process in tobacco products liability cases will document industry "stonewalling" and disinformation campaigns, as well as publicize the actual ingredients of commercially available cigarettes. The resulting public embarrassment to the industry will likely make future lobbying efforts significantly more difficult.

Relevant Legal Doctrines

A successful lawsuit requires a viable legal theory. The common law of most states offers products liability attorneys a variety of possible theories, any or all of which may be available in tobacco cases.

The "failure-to-warn" theory has gotten the most attention, though it may be the hardest to prove in the cigarette context. While any significant differential between the manufacturers' and the ordinary customers' knowledge of the dangers of smoking should be sufficient to invoke this theory, the public seems wedded to the absurd notion that there has been no such differential at least since warnings started appearing on cigarette packs in 1966. In any event, three U.S. Circuit Courts of Appeals have decided, perhaps erroneously, that Congress intended to "preempt" failure-to-warn claims once the warning started appearing (7–9). Inadequacy of pre-1966 warnings can still be proved and may even be more relevant since the warnings received or not received before addictions set in may be the ones that really matter.

A related theory is "overpromotion," that a manufacturer may not deliberately subvert the consumers' understanding of the warnings which it is legally required to display. Thus the manufacturer of chloromycetin was held liable for suggesting to doctors that the required warnings of aplastic anemia were overstated (10). Of course, cigarette manufacturers and their public relations representatives continue to urge, contrary to the mandated warnings, that smoking has not been proved to cause any disease. The major problem with this theory is that the three Circuit Court preemption decision used language broad enough to preclude claims based on post-1966 overpromotion: Whether they really intended this indefensible result will be tested in future litigation.

Even if the cigarette manufacturers did not "know" that their products were lethal, they certainly had enough information no later than 1950 (11,12) to be under a moral and legal obligation to test whether their products were toxic. If they performed the relevant tests, they would have found their cigarettes toxic; since they have continued publicly to deny the dangers, they would be guilty of actionable misrepresentation. If, on the other hand, they failed to test, they are guilty of negligence, since the relevant tests, properly conducted, would have demonstrated toxicity.

If cigarettes have been improperly designed or manufactured, in that a feasible alternative design, or simply more careful manufacturing techniques, would have avoided some of their dangers, then their manufacturers are liable to any one injured as a result of these unnecessary dangers.

Evidence recently discovered by plaintiffs' attorneys and anti-smoking activists strongly suggests that the industry has known for many years how to make cigarettes that are less likely to cause cancer. For example, the Liggett & Myers Tobacco Co. obtained a patent in 1977 for tobacco mixed with palladium and magnesium nitrate hexahydrate: The patent claimed that while tar from ordinary cigarettes produced 38 tumors after 79 weeks when applied to the skin of 50 mice, tar from the treated cigarettes produced only one tumor in a similar test (13).

Similarly, the R. J. Reynolds Tobacco Co. recently announced a new "smokeless" cigarette and publicly claimed: "Since the tobacco does not burn, a majority of the compounds produced by burning tobacco are eliminated or greatly reduced, including most compounds that are often associated with the smoking and health controversy" (14). Private representations on the same subject made the same day to federal health officials were allegedly even more explicit (15). The new device, which is described in a patent as producing "wet total particulate matter having no mutagenic activity, as measured by the Ames test" (16), appears to be quite similar to the device described in a 1966 patent (17).

Evidence is beginning to appear suggesting that at least some brands of cigarettes may contain non-tobacco carcinogenic substances. Thus a former maintenance employee at a cigarette plant submitted an affidavit in a pending case that chemicals that came in barrels "marked with skull and crossbones" were sprayed on all tobacco and were not washed off: The chemical was later identified as dimethyl 2,2-dichlorovinyl phosphate (18). Furthermore, a materials analyst retained by the plaintiff's attorneys in the same case discoverd 35 inorganic fibers (man-made or asbestos-like) in a sample of cigarette ash under a transmission electron microscope: The equivalent number for an entire cigarette would be 46 million (19). Similarly, both hydrazine residues and polonium-210 have been found in cigarettes. None of these are naturally contained in tobacco: If their presence and carcinogenicity are proved, the cigarettes that contain them could easily be found defective.

Finally, it may be possible to win a case on the basis of the inherent dangers of tobacco. Most states permit juries to find liability if a product is more dangerous than an ordinary consumer would expect, or if its risks exceed its benefits, or even if it is simply unreasonably dangerous. While many courts may be reluctant on their own authority to find wanting a generic product like tobacco, at least one court (in Louisiana) has taken that step with respect to asbestos, and others may follow. It is clear that any of these tests, fairly applied, would make tobacco product manufacturers strictly liable for the deaths and diseases that their products cause.

There are also legal theories under which the industry as a whole, including the Tobacco Institute (its lobbying and public relations arm) and the Council for Tobacco Research, could be held liable. One is "civil conspiracy," based on evidence that the manufacturers may have gotten together beginning in the 1950s to plan and implement a strategy for marketing cigarettes in the face of the developing scientific evidence of their dangers. Another is a "Good Samaritan" theory: that the companies, having publicly pledged in 1954 to investigate the possible dangers of smoking, were obliged to carry out their promise and take reasonable action based on what they found.

Required Inputs

To succeed in its purpose of reducing cigarette consumption, the tobacco products liability strategy requires the cooperation of a) doctors willing to testify, b) attorneys willing to invest, c) organization(s) willing to perform clearinghouse functions, d) judges willing to apply settled legal doctrine, e) juries willing to relax the impulse to blame smoker victims, and f) legislatures and law-making coalitions willing not to interfere.

Doctors

Medical testimony is, of course, needed both from the treating physicians and from experts in relevant fields. While any physician should be competent to testify to the causal link between smoking and lung cancer, cigarette manufacturers still deny this link in their pleadings and find some scientists willing to testify against it in court. The causation defense is more powerful where science is less certain: thus, on the relationship between moist snuff use and tongue cancer, a snuff manufacturer was able to persuade a jury that no causal link exists (20).

Testimony is needed not only from oncologists but also from epidemiologists (on the methodology of causal attribution), from historians of medicine (on the state of medical knowledge when the plaintiff began smoking), from toxicologists (on the proved effects of cigarette smoke and its components), from pathologists (on both the diagnosis and diagnostic methodology), from psychiatrists (on nicotine dependence), and perhaps from other medical specialists. Nonmedical experts are also needed on such issues as the purpose and effect of cigarette advertising, the chemical composition of cigarettes and cigarette smoke, nature of addiction, and methods of comparing the risks and "benefits" of smoking.

Medical experts have been very forthcoming, often waiving their fees. Doctors have, however, been more reluctant to take other supportive steps, with only a few publicly supporting the strategy or referring cases to attorneys or to the Tobacco Products Liability Project.

Attorneys

The prosecution of products liability cases is financed by plaintiffs' attorneys, who look to contingent fees obtained in successful cases to finance their enterprise. The financial attractiveness of any given case depends on the likely cost of bringing it to completion, the likelihood of success, and the damages likely to be awarded or obtained in settlement.

Tobacco products liability cases are at present extremely expensive to bring, since the cigarette companies defend them with unprecedented ferocity and the plaintiffs' attorneys have no succesful models to emulate, no "cookbooks" to follow. Trials are delayed by complicated pretrial skirmishing, and the paucity of relevant experience, combined with the strength and complexity of public feelings on the issue, makes it impossible to estimate the prospects for eventual success in any given case. While the majority of products liability cases are settled before trial, the cigarette manufacturers have refused to settle any cases against them, thereby maximizing the costs to attorneys contemplating such cases. It is unlikely that attorneys will be able to recoup their costs in litigating their first tobacco case through fees earned in that case.

Attorneys are sometimes attracted to new fields in the hope of obtaining recognition and additional cases, recouping their initial investment further down the line. Attorneys are also sometimes motivated by a desire to prove that they can succeed where others have failed, and even sometimes by a desire to do justice. Some combination of these three factors has motivated a small number of highly competent attorneys to press forward with tobacco products liability cases.

Organization(s)

The costs of bringing tobacco products liability cases have been reduced, and their prospects for success brightened, by the Tobacco Products Liability Project. The purpose of the Project is to help lawyers avoid some mistakes made in the first wave of tobacco liability cases in the 1960s by sharing information with each other and with medical authorities, as well as generally to explain and promote the strategy.

The Project, located in Boston, MA, at Northeastern University School of Law, holds annual meetings of physicians, attorneys, and others who support this strategy; convenes plaintiffs' lawyers to discuss tactics on a more frequent basis; submits *amicus curiae* briefs in important cases; does legal and other backup research; and explains and advocates the strategy to a variety of audiences. It created and works closely with a reference service for lawyers—the *Tobacco Products Litigation Reporter*—and publishes its own newsletter for nonlawyers—*Tobacco on Trial*.

The defendants, however, are even better organized. The six cigarette manufacturers have mounted a "joint defense." They work out a common strategy for defending each case and exercise tight central control over local counsel, thereby ensuring that, for example, an attorney representing one of them in Montana does not repeat the recent faux pas of one of their attorneys in admitting that smoking causes lung cancer and other diseaes (15).

Furthermore, the industry in its defense vastly outspends the plaintiffs' attorneys and the Project. It is, therefore, well positioned to take advantage of any inadequacies in preparation and coordination among plaintiffs' attorneys. As a practical matter, for the strategy to succeed, the Project may need additional financial support, and plaintiffs and their attorneys may need some measure of sympathetic understanding from judges and juries.

Judges

The strategy requires judges to apply in an even-handed manner legal principles developed with respect to products less lethal than cigarettes. Many of the principles supporting tobacco products liability cases—such as that toxic as well as traumatic injuries are compensable and that some awareness of the danger by plaintiffs does not bar recovery where the manufacturer had more precise information—were established by 1973 in the asbestos cases (21). Other legal doctrines—such as that compliance with regulatory standards does not prevent a jury from determining that a reasonable manufacturer would have done more—were settled even earlier (22). Since judges generally have life tenure, they should not be as susceptible as legislators to tobacco industry pressure to bend principle for the industry's benefit.

Surprisingly, three appellate courts have ignored settled interpretative principles in deciding that the Federal Cigarette Labeling and Advertising Act preempts failure-to-warn claims in cigarette products liability suits (7–9). Their decisions have made these cases more difficult—but by no means impossible—to bring.

Many judges, however, have applied existing principles to tobacco cases, developing especially useful precedents with respect to the scope of discovery of tobacco industry documents and the ability of plaintiffs' attorneys to share the results.

Juries

Jurors need to be convinced to relax their impulse to blame the victims of tobacco-induced disease. A dominant notion, even among smokers, is that "anyone stupid enough to smoke deserves what he gets." Ignored, in this reasoning is that most smokers became addicted as teenagers (5), that most have tried unsuccessfully to quit, and that few have had an accurate notion of the range and magnitude of the dangers presented by smoking (23). Also ignored is the role played by the tobacco industry in encouraging the addiction and in publicly denying the dangers that, in the litigation context they insist lay plaintiffs should have been fully aware of.

Increasing public awareness of the addictiveness of tobacco use can be expected to reduce the prejudice against smokers. Nor will smokers be thought to have knowingly accepted the additional risks posed by carcinogenic contaminants. Furthermore, detailed evidence of unsavory tobacco industry behavior may redirect some public animosity toward the industry.

In the first cigarette case to go to a jury this decade, *Galbraith* v. *R. J. Reynolds Tobacco Co.*, the jury found for the defendant on a 9–3 vote (*24*). The three holdouts would have voted for the plaintiff despite a paucity of evidence that he had died of a tobacco-related disease. The impulse to hold the tobacco industry accountable for the damage that it causes is potentially as strong as the impulse to blame the victim.

Legislatures

The tobacco industry thus far has been able to defeat most proposed anti-smoking measures both in Congress and the state legislatures. Thus it is a strength of the tobacco products liability strategy that it does not require affirmative legislative support. It can, however, be defeated by hostile legislation.

The tobacco industry by itself is not strong enough to obtain legislation protecting itself from products liability suits. The limited protection that it has received from the recent judicial interpretation of the Federal Cigarette Labeling and Advertising Act is not supported by the legislative history of that Act. But, ever resourceful, it combined in 1987 with pharmaceutical manufacturers and other groups—in one state including plaintiffs' malpractice attorneys!—to obtain products liability "reforms" designed to protect their special interests. Thus while earlier such reforms impacted evenly on various industries, three states adopted statutes in 1987 that either explicitly (California) or indirectly (New Jersey and Ohio) made bringing tobacco products liability suits especially difficult.

Prospects

As of the end of 1987 there were about 125 cases against the tobacco industry pending in 17 states. Two—*Horton* v. *American Tobacco Co.*, pending in the Mississippi state court (*25*), and *Cipollone* v. *Liggett Group, Inc.*, pending in the New Jersey federal court (*26*)—were scheduled for trial in January 1988.

Perhaps the greatest difficulty confronting the tobacco products liability strategy is the inference that, since no case has yet been won, the cases must simply not be winnable. This is buttressed by the tobacco industry's extraordinary record of emerging unscathed from over three decades of convincing evidence of the lethal consequences of smoking. This difficulty will not go away until a case is won.

Until a case is won, most lawyers, public health advocates, and journalists will likely stay on the sidelines. The typical citizen will probably continue to think that someone who "chose" to smoke should not be permitted to sue a tobacco company. The tobacco companies will probably be able to continue to make legislative deals, even with doctors and lawyers who do not think they are giving up anything of substance by agreeing to ban tobacco products liability suits.

Once a case is won, the general perception of the value of the strategy should change rapidly. The useful economic, educational, and political effects described at the beginning of this commentary would follow.

References

1. Office on Smoking and Health. Smoking-attributable mortality and years of potential life lost—United States, 1984. MMWR 1978;36:694.
2. Wall Street Journal, June 23, 1986:2.
3. Office of Technology Assessment. Smoking-related deaths and financial costs. Washington, DC: US Congress, Sept. 1985.
4. WARNER KE. Smoking and health implications of a change in the federal cigarette excise tax. JAMA 1986;255:1028–1032.
5. JOHNSTON LD, O'MALLEY PM, BACHMAN JG. Use of licit and illicit drugs by America's high school students 1975–1984. Bethesda, MD: National Institute on Drug Abuse, 1985.
6. Federal Trade Commission. In the matter of R. J. Reynolds Tobacco Co., Inc., Dkt No. 9206. Tobacco Products Litigation Rptr 1986;1.7:8.3–8.6.
7. *Cipollone v. Liggett Group, Inc.,* 789 F.2d 181, 1.5 TPLR 2.129 (3rd Cir. 1986), cert. denied (1987).
8. *Stephen v. American Brands,* 825 F.2d 312, 2.8 TPLR 2.157 (11th Cir. 1987).
9. *Palmer v. Liggett Group, Inc.,* 825 F.2d 620, 2.8 TPLR 2.149 (1st Cir. 1987).
10. *Stevens v. Parke Davis & Co.,* 107 Cal. Rptr 45, 507 P.2d 653 (1973).
11. DOLL R, HILL AB. Smoking and carcinoma of the lung. Br Med J 1950;2:739–748.
12. WYNDER EL, GRAHAM EA. Tobacco smoking as a possible etiologic factor in bronchogenic cancer. JAMA 1950;143:329–336.
13. US Patent No. 4,055,191. Tobacco Products Litigation Rptr 1987; 3.1:8.1–8.13.
14. R. J. Reynolds Tobacco Co. Press release of Sept. 14, 1987. Tobacco Products Litigation Rptr 1987; 2.10:5.123–5.125.
15. DAVIS RM. Memorandum of Sept. 22, 1987, to D. Tolsma. Tobacco Products Litigation Rptr 1987;3.1:8.14–8.15.
16. European Patent Application No. 85111467.8 (R. J. Reynolds' 1985 patent). Partially reprinted in Tobacco Products Litigation Rptr 1987;2.10:8.66–8.69.
17. US Patent No. 3,258,015 (1966). Partially reprinted in Tobacco Products Litigation Rptr 1987;2.10:8.70–8.71.
18. DICKERSON WW. Affidavit in *Horton v. American Tobacco Co.,* Sept. 8, 1987. Tobacco Products Litigation Rptr 1987;2.9:3.583–3.584.
19. LONGO WE. Affidavit in *Horton v. American Tobacco Co.* Tobacco Products Litigation Rptr 2.9:3.585–3.586.
20. *Marsee v. US Tobacco Co.,* Dkt No. 84–2777, US District Court, W. D., Oklahoma, 1984.
21. *Borel v. Fibreboard Paper Products Corp.,* 493 F.2d 1076 (5th Cir. 1973), cert. denied, 419 US 869 (1974).
22. American Law Institute. Restatement 2nd Torts sec. 288C(1965).
23. Federal Trade Commission. Staff report of the cigarette advertising investigation, chap 3. Washington, DC: FTC, 1981.
24. *Galbraith v. R. J. Reynolds Tobacco Co.,* Dkt No. 144417, Santa Barbara Superior Court, Dec 23, 1985.
25. *Horton v. American Tobacco Co.,* Dkt No. 9050, Circuit Court of Holmes County, MS.
26. *Cipollone v. Liggett Group, Inc.,* Dkt No. 83-2864SA, US District Court, New Jersey.

22. Banishing Tobacco
Nonsmokers Demand Clean Air

William U. Chandler

Tobacco causes more death and suffering among adults than any other toxic material in the environment. Increasingly, evidence shows that nonsmokers as well as smokers are at risk. It is now feared that *involuntary* exposure to cigarette smoke causes more cancer deaths than any other pollutant. Protecting nonsmokers from cigarette smoke will require a marked change in society's treatment of tobacco, one that could also help eliminate its direct threat to users themselves.

No country takes action against tobacco commensurate with the cost it imposes. The global use of tobacco has grown nearly 75% over the past two decades. The direct health costs, the health risks to passive smokers, and the economic costs have grown proportionally.

The worldwide cost in lives now approaches 2.5 million per year, almost 5% of all deaths. Tobacco kills 13 times as many Americans as hard drugs and eight times as many as automobile accidents. Passive smokers (those who must inhale the smoke of others' cigarettes) are perhaps three times likelier to die of lung cancer than they would be otherwise. Smoking by mothers diminishes the physical and mental capabilities of their children, and in many countries more than one-fifth of children are exposed to smoke in this way. These statistics add up to a cost that is increasingly viewed not only as unnecessary but as intolerable.

Most efforts to control tobacco are merely attempts to control or color information about the product. No national tobacco control effort has been launched with the vigor of campaigns against drugs or toxic chemicals, though hard drugs and chemicals claim far fewer victims than tobacco.

Health leaders in government, international organizations, and public-interest groups have also failed in this fight, as high levels of tobacco use continue in industrial countries and explosive growth of cigarette smoking occurs in Eastern bloc countries and China.

The Epidemic Spreads

Smoking is increasing at 2.1% per year, faster than world population. Over a billion people now smoke, consuming almost 5 trillion cigarettes per year, an average of more than half a pack a day.

Smoking rates remain high around the world, especially among men. In Bangladesh, two-thirds of men smoke, spending on average 5% of their household income on tobacco. In Czechoslovakia, 57% smoke; in south-central European Russia, two-thirds of adult males smoke. And while smoking among women remains very low in many countries, teenage girls in the United States now smoke more than boys do.

One ironic result of campaigns to reduce smoking in the absence of a more general effort to control tobacco has been the marked increase in the use of "smokeless" tobacco. The use of "chew" or "snuff" in the United States has increased by over 40% in the last two decades. Surveys in some

Adapted from William U. Chandler, *State of the World 1986.* Copyright © 1986 by Worldwatch Institute. Reprinted with permission.

localities show that 20–40% of high-school boys chew tobacco or use snuff. Unfortunately, these forms of tobacco are strongly linked to oral cancer, an effect seen in India, where chewing— and oral cancer—is common.

Smoking prevalence among young people is changing, sometimes for the better, other times not. Although American, British, Norwegian, and Swedish children appear to be starting this habit later in life and are less likely to smoke, this is not the case elsewhere. More young people than adults smoke in Eastern bloc countries, Canada, and Egypt. In some schools surveyed in Santiago, Chile, two-thirds of the students smoked. Even in developing societies—among Polynesians, for example—smoking rates reach levels exceeding 50% in children.

Measuring smoking by educational level also reveals significant trends. There is an inverse relationship between educational level and smoking in the United States, the Soviet Union, and elsewhere. Over 60% of U.S. adult males with only a primary education smoke, while less than 20% of men with an advanced degree are smokers. This relationship appears to hold in most of Western and Eastern Europe. It is true for women as well, at least in the United States, with the exception that women who have only a grade-school education seldom smoke. In these countries, at least, smoking thus no longer symbolizes fashion, status, and upward mobility, but the opposite.

The Direct Cost of Addiction

No avoidable condition claims more adult lives than tobacco addiction. Over 2 million smokers die worldwide each year from heart disease, lung cancer, and emphysema—smoker's disease, as it is called—caused by their addiction. Additional thousands die as a result of fires caused by cigarettes and from cancers caused by tobacco consumed as snuff or chew. Almost one-fifth of all U.S. deaths can be traced to the use of tobacco.

From 15 to 30% of all heart attacks in the United States and perhaps a third in the United Kingdom are caused by smoking. Smoking is also the leading cause of death from cardiovascular disease for those middle-aged or younger in West Germany, Scandinavian countries, and Australia.

Smoking carries special risks for young women. One study of women under age 50 found the risk of heart attack to be 10 times greater in women who smoked two packs per day. The authors attributed two-thirds of the heart attacks in the group to smoking.

A Canadian study found that females who smoked heavily were 7 to 34 times more likely to have a heart attack. Significantly, it also found that women who both smoked heavily and took birth-control pills were 8 to 39 times more likely than nonsmokers to have heart attacks. The authors concluded that women under 35 could safely take the pill without additional risk of heart attack, but only if they did not smoke.

A review of the epidemiology of heart attacks in women found that female heart-attack victims die on average 19 years earlier than other women. Unfortunately, young women are the group in industrial nations whose rate of smoking is increasing fastest.

Active smoking accounts for an estimated 85% of lung cancer. International comparisons of lung-cancer rates and earlier smoking habits show a strong correlation. Nonindustrial societies with high smoking rates have high lung-cancer rates; Polynesians and New Zealanders have little industry, smoke heavily, and have high rates of lung cancer. These trends implicate smoking over industrial air pollutants as the cause of cancer.

Cancer of the bladder, pancreas, lip, mouth, esophagus, and pharynx can also be traced to the use of tobacco, though alcohol plays a strong role in the last two types. The use of tobacco may also be linked with cervical cancer and stomach cancer, although these connections are less clear.

Smoking kills 52,000 Americans each year through bronchitis and emphysema. Fires caused by cigarettes kill between 2,000 and 4,000 Americans each year. And passive smoking may cause 5,000 lung-cancer deaths each year in the United States alone. Altogether, smoking causes 10–25% of deaths in Europe and the United States.

Economic Costs

Several nations have attempted to estimate the direct economic cost of smoking. In the United States, smoking's toll amounts to $12–35 billion per year—3–9% of all healthcare costs. Smoking claims a similar proportion of the total health-care expenditures in Australia, Canada, Switzerland, and the United Kingdom.

Lost income and work due to death and illness caused by smoking cost the United States $27–61 billion a year. Thus, health expenditures plus economic losses in that country range from $38–95 billion, or $1.27–3.17 per pack. These totals do not include the cost of tobacco itself—about $30 billion per year. Nor do they include the suffering borne by victims and their families.

These costs do not include the environmental and agricultural costs of tobacco production. Tobacco curing consumes 1–2% of all wood burned each year in Kenya and Tanzania and one-third of all wood harvested in Malawi, where harvesting far exceeds sustainable yields. Many agricultural countries, including Brazil, China, India, Pakistan, and Zimbabwe, dedicate between 0.5 and 7% of cropland to tobacco, with the United States and China using slightly less than 1% in this way. If planted in grain, this land would be sufficient to feed 10–20 million people.

Some economists argue that the jobs and incomes created by the tobacco business must be counted as benefits. Even if other uses of land were not available, tobacco's economic costs alone would exceed its "benefits" by more than two to one.

Tragically, the cost in lives and money can only be expected to grow. Seventy-three percent more tobacco is consumed now than 20 years ago, so without a sudden drop in smoking, lung-cancer deaths, for example, will almost certainly increase by 50% by the turn of the century. At the current rates, the next 20 years would also witness a 50% increase in bronchitis and emphysema.

Ironically, it may take the growing realization of this habit's high costs for passive smokers to actually bring about effective action. For no matter how convincing the direct costs may be to rational thinkers, smokers—being addicted—may not be able to act rationally to solve the problem.

Victims of Others' Smoke

Sidestream smoke—which wafts from a smoker's cigarette to an involuntary smoker—puts into the surrounding air 50 times the amount of carcinogens inhaled by the user and has been linked to lung cancer and respiratory disease. The scale of these effects has only recently attracted attention, and much more work is urgently needed to define their total impact.

Passive smoking has been correlated with lung cancer in more than 10 studies. One study in Japan found that wives who did not smoke but who lived with heavy smokers were twice as likely to die of lung cancer as wives of men who did not smoke. Studies in Greece, West Germany, and the United States have yielded similar results.

One recent effort to quantify the risk of ambient tobacco smoke to nonsmokers estimated that passive smoking in the United States causes more cancer deaths than all regulated industrial air pollutants combined. The cost in lives may be as high as 5,000 nonsmokers per year, or one-third the cases of lung cancer not directly attributable to smoking.

Nonsmokers are quite likely to have no choice about breathing tobacco smoke. In the United States, people typically spend 90% of their time indoors. Some 63% of U.S. workers are exposed to tobacco smoke, and over 60% of all households have at least one smoker. Altogether, only 14% of Americans escape being exposed to tobacco smoke in the home or at the workplace.

Effects on Children

Passive smoking places unborn children at serious risk. Nicotine, numerous toxic chemicals, and radioactive polonium may all interfere with fetal development, whether the mother smokes or chews tobacco. Furthermore, studies in both industrial and developing countries show that smoking by pregnant women reduces infants' weight at birth by roughly one-tenth. Because birthweight is a key factor in infant mortality, tobacco use seriously endangers infants' lives.

Smoking can also cause premature delivery and spontaneous abortions. Epidemiologist R. T. Ravenholt estimates that smoking causes 50,000 miscarriages in the United States each year. Nineteen percent of the firstborn infants of Italian women who smoke were premature, twice the rate for nonsmokers.

Unfortunately, women in many countries are smoking in record numbers, even while pregnant. Each year, at least 3 million newborns—the estimated number of live births to women who smoke—are potentially handicapped by their mothers.

Children with parents who smoke experience much higher rates of respiratory illness, including colds, influenza, bronchitis, asthma, and pneumonia. One British study published almost 10 years ago showed that children under age 1 whose mothers smoke more than one pack a day are twice as likely to get bronchitis and pneumonia. This finding has been repeatedly corroborated.

In addition, the evidence indicates that parental smoking retards child development. One study found that lung capacity in boys was reduced 7% by their mothers' smoking. If the teenage boys also smoked, their lung capacity was reduced by 25%. The effect of passive smoking in children can last a lifetime because it delays physical and intellectual development and because the longer people are exposed to carcinogens, the more likely they are to develop lung cancer.

Parents who smoke may also reduce the intellectual development of their children. One study in Italy found that children whose mothers smoked learned to read more slowly than those of nonsmokers. In the United States, the learning ability of 11-year-olds whose mothers smoke has been shown to lag by six months.

Antismoking Efforts to Date

When a recent medical journal editorial writer rhetorically asked "What if smoking killed baby seals?" he was making the point that environmental and health activists do not give tobacco the priority it deserves.

Nor have governments assumed their traditional role in protecting public health by acting decisively to reduce tobacco's threat. They move swiftly to remove from the market unsafe medicines. They conduct paramilitary operations to destroy fields of marijuana or opium but not tobacco, a far deadlier crop. They pay for expensive cleanup operations to remove toxic chemicals from the human environment. But not only do they fail to take these actions for tobacco, which is often more deadly to both users and innocent—or passive—victims, they even support efforts to stabilize the tobacco industry.

Equating smokers with baby seals—as victims rather than willing participants—helps clarify some confusion that contributes to inactions on tobacco. Many people assume it is enough to warn tobacco users, through the media and with labels on tobacco products, of the risks they take and then leave to them the responsibility for their own health. But the independence and voluntary nature of this choice is questionable on three counts.

First, tobacco is strongly addictive. Studies have shown that only 15–30% of children who try more than one cigarette ever succeed in quitting. Pharmacologically, tobacco acts like heroin in hooking its victims.

Second, smoke harms more than just the smoker, through the effects of sidestream smoke.

Third, when governments act inconsistently in their management of tobacco with respect to other dangerous products that they ban, they confuse tobacco users. Asbestos, heroin, and DDT are banned to protect public health; tobacco is not. This implicitly signals that those responsible for health consider tobacco to be different and normal to use.

Forbidding the sale of tobacco would be consistent with the prohibition of the sale of addictive drugs that harm the user and others. Banning tobacco would also be consistent with the control of strong carcinogens.

Some people argue that individuals should be able to do whatever they want in the privacy of their own homes. This is an acceptable, even admirable attitude favoring civil liberties. But the limit to one's pursuit of happiness begins at the point where it clearly harms others. If smokers are to be permitted to harm themselves but forbidden to harm their children, spouses, or co-workers, they will have to smoke in their backyards. Because control of tobacco use in private homes is both politically and practically unacceptable, the only realistic way to protect children—if parents fail to do so—is to control the product itself.

Societies urgently need to examine how to better control tobacco use, for the current strategy of informational campaigns is not working well.

Absolute cigarette consumption has fallen over the last 10 years in only a dozen countries. Of these, only four had moderate to strong antismoking policies, while eight had weak ones. Reduction in countries with weak policies can be attributed to economic decline, specifically to higher costs of imported cigarettes and reduced per capita income. Overall, income and cigarette price seem to have much more influence on consumption than the current generation of antismoking policies.

A dozen countries have had strong antismoking measures—by today's standards—but have experienced strong growth in tobacco. Tobacco advertising is prohibited in Poland and restrictions are placed on smoking in public, yet that nation ranks among the highest in per capita cigarette consumption in the world. Advertising bans and other antismoking policies exist in China, East Germany, and the Soviet Union, but smoking nevertheless continues at very high levels, at least among men.

Finland, Norway, and Sweden, in contrast, have imposed advertising bans and required strong warnings on tobacco labels, and they have experienced better results. Norway's antismoking policy is exceeded in strength by only four other countries, and tobacco consumption has declined by almost 15% since the imposition of that policy. Sweden's policy has been somewhat weaker than those of other Scandinavian countries, but consumption is down about 3% since 1974, about the time its policy was initiated.

Bulgaria, Hungary, and the Soviet Union have the strongest policies in the world. Bulgarians now smoke 2% fewer cigarettes than 10 years ago, while the Soviets and the Hungarians use 8% and 4% more, respectively.

Countries with weaker policies but better results include Belgium, the Netherlands, and the United Kingdom. These governments permit advertising in print but forbid it on electronic media. They have negotiated voluntary warnings on tobacco products with the tobacco industry. Perhaps most importantly, they have conducted vigorous antismoking educational campaigns. Cigarette consumption has declined 20% or more over the last 10 years in these nations. The per capita consumption level in each is below the average for industrial countries, though well above the mean for the world. Only in the United Kingdom, however, is consumption lower than 20 years ago.

Some countries have had dramatic declines in cigarette consumption without even trying. Drops in consumption of 7–32% in Bolivia, Chile, and Zaire can be attributed to their economic difficulties: Their antismoking policies are among the weakest in the world.

Changes in income affect tobacco consumption, though the strength of the income effect depends on a country's stage of development. A statistical analysis of 29 industrial and developing countries suggested that, overall, cigarette consumption increases about 3% for every 10% rise in income. This relation apparently does not hold for industrial countries. Consumption seems more related to price and social attractiveness in countries such as the United States, where price increases of 10% appear to reduce consumption by 3–4%. The largest decline ever in U.S. cigarette use occurred, in fact, in 1983, when the government imposed a tax of about 8% of the retail price.

Stronger Medicine

Health advocates have generally dismissed stronger medicine for dealing with smoking and tobacco. The U.K. Royal College of Physicians, for example, the first governmental body in the world to launch a campaign to save the health of smokers, has conceded that banning tobacco is impractical. The physicians compared such a move to prohibition, fearing that it would be unenforceable and would lead to criminality.

An alternative approach is inherent in a new movement to protect passive smokers: banishing tobacco. This campaign includes either the prohibition of smoking in the workplace and in public buildings or the strict limitation of smoking to specified areas. Its leaders insist that despite the continued sale, advertising, and use of tobacco, nonsmokers—the majority in most societies—have every right not to be exposed to the carcinogens, carbon monoxide, and irritants in tobacco smoke. Such a campaign can make three important contributions.

First, by banishing tobacco use from places where innocent people are exposed, thousands of lives may be saved. Second, forcing smokers to give up their habit while in the presence of nonsmokers will provide them with an added impetus to quit. And third, by stigmatizing tobacco use as dangerous and antisocial, the passive smokers' rights movement can make smoking socially unattractive. This should reduce the attraction of smoking for children.

Nonsmokers have an important ally in the workplace: employers. Companies, at least in the United States, are rapidly realizing two things. First, most of their employees do not smoke and do not like to breathe the smoke of others. Second, smokers cost employers money. Surveys indicate that the combination of inefficiency and ill health as a result of smoking wastes about 7% of a smoker's working time. They also suggest that smokers cost employers at least $650 each per year. Smokers add to insurance and cleaning costs, and they reduce nonsmoker employee morale.

American industry is responding rapidly to the nonsmoker movement. A number of well-known industries have prohibited smoking on the job for most employees. A few refuse to hire smokers. In 1984, one-tenth to one-fourth of the top 1,000 businesses in publishing, insurance, finance, pharmaceuticals, and scientific equipment industries in the United States implemented new policies to banish smoking.

Schizophrenic Policies

A particular difficulty in banishing tobacco is the role of government in promoting tobacco use. This schizophrenic state of affairs persists not just in the market-oriented west, but also in centralized economies. China, the Soviet Union, and India, for example, grow their own tobacco. The state-owned tobacco industry in China is being carefully nurtured and expanded rapidly even as another part of the government is telling the Chinese that smoking is bad for them.

In the United States, the U.S. Department of Agriculture administers a price-support system to protect tobacco producers. Western European nations subsidize tobacco farmers with about $660 million in price supports each year. Ironically, the systems protect small, inefficient farmers who earn higher prices than they would without the subsidy. As tobacco use varies negatively in response to price, smoking is being directly reduced by price supports.

There is a more subtle effect, however. The tobacco industry gains the powerful political support of the small farmer. The added political clout helps counter antismoking forces. Moreover, it retains the appealing appearance of official tolerance and even endorsement of the use of tobacco. Any child about to start smoking could be inclined to think that the U.S. government sees tobacco use as desirable.

The overall situation of antismoking efforts, then, is at best a standoff in industrial countries and a rout in developing ones. At the current rate, Western countries will not see a major improvement in the health effects of smoking for many decades, but Eastern and developing countries will see a rapid worsening. It falls to world health leaders to bolster their antismoking efforts. Unfortunately, one lead agency, the World Health Organization, allots less than 1% of its budget to this problem, though it calls smoking "the most important preventable health problem in the world." Its current budget for the mid-1980s has no funds for actively reducing tobacco's toll.

Recommended Policies

Effective policies fall into four categories. The first, continuation of the informational campaign, is worthwhile as a foundation for the others.

The second step is for those countries that have low smoking rates and no tobacco industry to ban smoking altogether. This will eliminate the epidemic's threat to them and reduce foreign exchange losses for a nonproductive product.

The third approach is for those nations that must be politically pragmatic to at least protect the health of the innocent. Banishing tobacco from public buildings, the workplace, restaurants, and public meeting places should be considered a minimum level of protection.

United Nations organizations could do well to establish no-smoking policies for their employees, especially those who work with children and the poor, for they are unavoidably going to be viewed as symbols of modernity and success.

The fourth level involves the power of economic tools to eliminate smoking. A tax of $1.25 to $3.15 per pack—the estimated cost of smoking—would reduce smoking in Western nations by as much as 40% over time. Any tax increase, even of 5–10¢ per pack, would rapidly encourage light smokers to quit and, more importantly, would discourage the young and poor from starting. Additionally, tobacco-support systems can be dismantled in order to signal that governments now wish to discourage the use of tobacco. This move would be productive even where such a step would lower the price of cigarettes.

These measures will not be easy, nor will they solve the tobacco problem. They will not, for example, assure that children will be protected in the home against the smoke of their parents. They will not protect the newborn from their mothers' smoking.

New measures will not assure that smokers will quit or that innocent young people will not become addicted before realizing that their new habit kills one out of four users. But without more responsible efforts on the part of the health professions and public-interest organizations, even these efforts will be held in abeyance.

Chapter VI
Marijuana and the Psychedelics

Among the drugs considered in this volume, marijuana and the psychedelics are probably those most closely associated with the hippie movement and the youth counterculture of the 1960's. However, marijuana has enjoyed a long, if somewhat circuitous history in American society. During the colonial era, for example, marijuana served as a legal cash crop, providing the raw material for cloth, rope, varnish, lamp oil, and even bird seed. By the early 1900's, in a manner similar to the opiates, alcohol and cocaine before it, marijuana had become a popular medical aid for a number of minor physical maladies. Beginning early in the present century and returning in the 1960's and 1970's, marijuana gained widespread use and a folklore reputation as a recreational intoxicant. Most recently, marijuana has received some attention in medical circles for its potential in treating glaucoma, asthma, certain nervous system disorders and cancer patients undergoing chemotherapy. Despite these potential medical uses, however, marijuana's major notoriety in America today, stems from its status as a major illegal cash crop and the high potency, domestic hybrid, sinsemilla.

Presently, as throughout its history in this country, marijuana as a recreational drug is commonly ingested via smoking. The most recent medical evidence, however, suggests that this smoking of marijuana may be more hazardous than tobacco smoking in the long run, given the level of toxic substances released in the smoke and the fact that the marijuana user typically holds the smoke in his/her lungs longer that a cigarette smoker.

Psychedelics, such as LSD, mescaline and psilocybin, have effects which are primarily psychological in nature. These effects include sensory distortion, synesthesia or the perceived overlapping of the senses, and a heightened sense of awareness and self-consciousness. The psychedelics are also characterized by very potent effects from relatively small doses, rapid tolerance, and infrequent dependence.

Despite some similarities to the effects of marijuana, psychedelics have enjoyed a much shorter and less varied history in this country. With the exception of the use of peyote as a part of religious rituals by the Native American church, the psychedelics are probably most well known in conjunction with Timothy Leary's famous dictum "tune in, turn on, drop out" and the youth culture's use of LSD. Prior to this time period and the creation of laws against the use of LSD and other psychedelics, however, such drugs were utilized for such varied purposes as U.S. Army experimentation in search of psychological "nerve gases" and the treatment of psychiatric illnesses and terminally ill cancer patients.

This chapter begins with the article by Rubin and Comitas on ganja in Jamaica. As this reading indicates, the differential effects and uses that marijuana has among the working class of Jamaica in comparison to the youth of America are closely related to the distinct cultural conditions, ways of life, and social definitions and expectations for this drug in these two societies. The second article by Bonnie and Whitebread analyzes the early folklore and mythology about marijuana at the beginning of the 20th century based upon the introduction of this drug from Mexico and the Carribean. Again providing a focus upon social context, Bonnie and Whitebread document how the spread of this mythology about the effects and impacts of marijuana produced dramatic consequences for the formulation of public attitudes and related social policy legislation in the early 1900's.

Given the particular importance of set and setting for marijuana and the psychedelics, laws and social attitudes may be expected to significantly affect the effects of these drugs. Following this logic, the concluding article by Howard Becker argues that such expectations can serve as an importance source of informal social control and subcultural therapy in preventing negative drug experiences associated with the psychedelics through supportive peer group definitions, beliefs, and related practices.

23. Cannabis, Society and Culture

Vera Rubin and Lambros Comitas

• • •

Recent research points to the development of two major cultural complexes related to the use of cannabis: the "*ganja* complex" and a sociocultural configuration that may be termed the "marihuana complex" stemming from the psychedelic context of cannabis use in the United States and its diffusion to Western-oriented youth in other societies (Rubin 1974). The traditional "set and setting" of the Jamaican *ganja* user differs significantly from that of the marihuana user. The contrasts between the Western and traditional modes of use are germane to an understanding of man's relationship to cannabis and cultural factors that influence reactions to cannabis.

The comparatively late spread of marihuana smoking to middle-class youth in the United States has been attributed to the "electronic origins" of the cultural revolution of the 1960s. Following McLuhan's theory of the "message" of the media, it is postulated that "psychedelic fallout, in the form of music, light-shows, new cinematic techniques . . . inundated" the United States "with the mystique of the electrochemical turn on" (Zinberg and Robertson 1972:67). Even the phrases "tune-in," "turn-on" and "turn-off" are derived from television. For the television generation, it may be said that "electronics preceded chemistry" as a technique for "alteration of consciousness" (Geller and Boas 1969).

In the United States, however, reactions to marihuana have differed dramatically during various periods. Marihuana as a mood-altering substance was generally unknown when it was first introduced in the United States from Mexico after World War I (Weil 1972). Panic reactions were common during the early period of its use, but such reactions became increasingly rare after the mid-1930s. As marihuana use spread, less anxiety was attached to it. Any drug can trigger a state of extreme anxiety, as has frequently been observed, whether or not the panic reaction has a pharmacological basis. Nevertheless, allegations about the physical, social and moral "dangers" of marihuana re-emerge in cyclical waves that may reflect the Zeitgeist more than the pharmacological properties of the plant. As McGlothlin (1974) indicates: "The data clearly show that the amount of THC taken by the typical U.S. marijuana user is quite small in comparison to that consumed in cultures where cannabis has been used for many years. Certainly, the estimated 5 mg of THC per occasion for casual users is almost trivial. This supports the argument that factors other than the pharmacological effects have played an important role in the recent adoption of marijuana use by large numbers of middle-class youth."

Recognition that the pharmacological action of a drug is mediated by "set and setting" is on the increase. "It is quite possible for the combined effects of set [individual expectation] and setting [total physical and social environment] to completely overshadow the pharmacological action of a drug. . . . The more the drug can be considered psychoactive (in that a principal reason for ingesting the substance is related to desired changes in mood, emotion, perceptions), the more set and setting are crucial" (Zinberg and Robertson 1972:95; see also Becker 1963; and Weil 1972).

The "set" of the individual is culturally conditioned and the "social environment" modifies the cannabis-man relationship. If the "electrochemical turn-on" was the background for marihuana use in the United States, in Jamaica, the traditional folk pharmacopoeia serves as the background for the use of *ganja*. Furthermore, an established body of folklore about *ganja* use conditions the psychocultural expectations and reactions of both smokers and nonsmokers. The nature of reactions to the first experience, whether positive or adverse (similar to "novice anxiety reactions"), generally determines whether the initiate becomes a regular smoker. Idiosyncratic differences in initial reactions are recognized and respected in the *ganja* subculture and help to support the neophyte in becoming—or not becoming—a smoker.

For example, the 29 smokers of the project sample who reported a positive first experience recalled feelings of sociability and "merriment," that is, making jokes in Jamaican idiom. None had recollections of uncontrolled laughter as is occasionally reported in the United States or the "merry mania" described by the Indian Hemp Drugs Commission (Great Britain 1969). Frequently recalled reactions to the first experience by the Jamaican smokers were "meditation," "concentration," "relaxation" and "visions."

Hallucinations

Cultural variables undoubtedly condition hallucinogenic reactions to cannabis. The vivid accounts of reactions to hashish smoking by Baudelaire, Gautier and their contemporaries, provided the backdrop for Western cultural expectations and social concerns. Gautier's fantastic description of his reactions to "the greenish paste" focused on the bizarre: "Hallucination, that strange guest had set up his dwelling place in me" (Solomon 1966: 168). Even in less baroque Western literature, cannabis has been classified as a hallucinogen, along with lysergic acid diethylamid (LSD), mescaline and psilocybin.

The Jamaican data make it clear that "hallucinations are not an invariable consequence of marijuana use" (Fort 1970–71: 519). In the Jamaican working-class setting, hallucinogenic reactions are apparently neither regularly sought nor generally experienced. The one exception to this, reported by subjects from a rural area generally in relation to their initial smoking experience, is the vision of a "little lady" who dances and beckons the smoker, usually in a congenial manner. The initial vision was never repeated. Probing produced a few reports about occasional, non-specific hallucinations, said to have been experienced by others and always attributed by the narrator to excessive use or use of *ganja* with alcohol.

A significant psychological difference distinguishes hallucinations from visions; hallucinations are usually idiosyncratic phenomena which may be triggered by personality and/or pharmacological factors; visions are culturally patterned experiences, related to "set and setting," usually in the context of a *rite de passage*. The quantity and potency of the initial "smoke" by the Jamaican subjects would not warrant a pharmacological explanation of the phenomenon and certainly not of the patterned cultural content of the vision.

Similar folk uses and reactions to other plants, not generally considered hallucinogens, have been reported. Tobacco *(Nicotiana spp.),* for example, which has been used in folk medicine and magic by American Indians is also "a vehicle for ecstacy." Wilbert reports that among the Warao Indians of Venezuela the role of tobacco as a vehicle of the vision quest is "obviously [a] cultural conditioning toward specific ecstatic experiences that have nothing to do with the chemical action of the tobacco plant itself" (1972:80).

Some observers, apparently baffled by the diversity of reactions attributed to cannabis, ascribe these phenomena to an innate, if unknown, characteristic of the plant. Thus, psychopharmacological studies have given rise to the suggestion that "the same drug can cause opposite changes in behavior" (Wolstenholme and Knight 1965: 52). These studies have not made clear, however, whether such apparently contradictory reactions might be related to differences in dosage, frequency, THC content or psychological "set and setting." Some researchers have concluded that titration, or control of the dosage, explains differences in reactions (Grinspoon 1970–71), but others hold the view that "the psychological effects of marijuana are as varied as the range of human personality and as complex as the multiple factors which influence the user each time he smokes" (Bloomquist 1967). A recent pharmacological report, e.g., presents the "lassitude/violence" dichotomy: "At a behavioural level, the subject may experience lassitude to the point of sedation or hyperactivity, hypersensitivity to stimuli and irritability to the point of violence." The authors note, however, "These widely differing observations may at least in part be explained in terms of differences in the composition of the Cannabis sativa, differences in concentration of active principles and individual variations in respose to Cannabis" (Davis and Persaud 1970: 107).

A survey of the literature, "The Cannabis Habit," by Murphy concluded: "It seems probable that cannabis has a highly complex influence, dependent on personality and culture as well as the drug itself" (1963:21). In a similar vein, Jones has pointed out that "the effects of psychoactive drugs on behavior and experience are often independent of the drug's pharmacologic effect" (1971:164).[1] Research findings of the present study bolster the opinion that reactions to cannabis use depend more on the individual's personality, beliefs and expectations than on the pharmacology of the plant itself.

Both as stimulant and sedative, for sacred or secular use, *ganja* fits into working-class life styles in Jamaica and the regular user's reactions to *ganja* stem from this sociocultural framework. Chronic *ganja* smokers do not report "vivid ideas crowding the brain," or tendencies to violence or to debauchery[2] and wild sex orgies. Such reactions would violate working-class mores. Individual psychosomatic reactions generally reinforce situational sociocultural expectations—endurance, energy, problem solving, alleviation of hunger or invigoration of appetite, enhancement of memory or relaxation—as the situation requires.

Ganja and Society

At this point, some questions might be raised about possible consequences to the greater society in terms of socioeconomic development. In Jamaica, *ganja* use is integrally linked to all aspects of working-class social structure; cultivation, cash crops, marketing, economics; consumer-cultivator-dealer networks; intraclass relationships and processes of avoidance or cooperation; parent-child, peer and mate relationships; folk medicine; folk religious doctrines; *obeah* and gossip sanctions; personality and culture; interclass stereotypes; legal and church sanctions; perceived requisites of behavioral changes for social mobility; and adaptive strategies. Although the structural linkages to society as a whole were not part of the research project and are difficult to investigate, the working-class *ganja* culture obviously cannot be disassociated from the overall social structure.

There is little if anything to indicate that extensive use of *ganja* is causally related to poverty in Jamaica. High rates of unemployment and even higher rates of underemployment, debilitating health factors such as malnutrition, yaws and intestinal parasites, restrictions on emigration, lack of capital for small-scale investment are all chronic conditions antedating the widespread use of *ganja* in Jamaica. "Failure lies everywhere," one subject remarks, "when the crop is scanty, work is scanty." Under the circumstances, even though they are small-scale operations, cultivation of *ganja* as a cash crop and the distribution of *ganja* provide welcome, if illegal and arduous, sources of income: "The only way you can get a penny to send the children to school."

> Herbs selling is a small man's speculation—[the money] even though small usually come in the time of need. So is not people love to deal with ganja so much why the average people that deal with it deal with it. But is a necessity. The necessity is a bigger achievement. [Even if] the fee is small, it can still boil a pot of porridge for five hungry children.

In fact, economic reasons are frequently given to support the continued use of *ganja*. Anti-*ganja* legislation is sometimes seen in terms of economic advantage: *ganja* is "good if sell and mek yu get a good piece of money." For some individuals, the cultivation of *ganja* may even provide enough cash for investment in small legitimate enterprises that could not otherwise be funded.

Ganja use in many ways is central to the life style of active participants in the *ganja* subculture. Acquiring and affording *ganja*, anticipated beneficial effects, fear of detection and the sense of community in sharing in an illicit activity all contribute to the importance of *ganja* to the individual. Nevertheless, there are structural restraints on compulsive use. Seasonal variations, availability of cash for purchase, on-the-job restrictions against smoking, and intensity of police surveillance, fear of *obeah* and "science" and awareness of local informers inhibit excessive use and constrain smoking in public. In this regard, the regular *ganja* smoker is unlike the alcoholic or compulsive gambler, both in terms of felt needs and of a compulsion to invest in a "habit" regardless of consequences. Although rum is a common working-class drink, smokers of *ganja* say that they "rather it to rum" and cite therapeutic, behavioral and work benefits as reasons for their choice. As contrasted with the many positive benefits of *ganja*, alcohol is considered harmful not only to the individual drinker but to his interpersonal relations.[3] Given recent scientific findings on the deleterious personal and social effects of alcohol, *ganja* may well be "a benevolent alternative." Certainly there appears to be considerably less risk to the society of work loss from *ganja* than from alcohol.

Ganja smokers dispute alleged links of *ganja* to crime, violence and insanity, attributing antisocial behavior to underlying personality and predisposition rather than to the plant. These observations are supported by the Indian Hemp Drugs Commission Report of 1894 which noted that the effect of *ganja* is to bring into play the "natural disposition of the user" (Great Britain 1969:264); more than half a century later, various researchers independently have been rediscovering some of the findings of the Commission. For example, "The underlying personality is the determining factor in criminal behavior" (Charen and Perelman 1946:676–677); and the general observation has been made by Nowlis that no "drugs, per se, produce addiction, criminal behavior, sexual excess . . ." (1970–71:532).

Contrasts in reaction to cannabis are becoming apparent within Jamaica itself, as a sociocultural phenomenon. Position in the social system is undoubtedly the single most significant variable in conditioning attitudes to *ganja* smoking. While members of the upper levels of the working class, particularly devout church members, share the middle-class view that *ganja* smoking is psychologically and physically damaging, a precipitant of violent, anti-social and "revolutionary" acts, smokers apparently agree with Brotman and Suffet that "it is not necessary to explain drug use by invoking some version of social pathology" (1971:242).

252

Cannabis use recently has spread to some segments of the middle class, although it is not as pervasive and it carries a different set of psychocultural expectations, such as concepts of enhancement of creativity, pleasure in listening to music, escape from boredom, return to a "childlike" state of absorption in details and search for the "ultimate experience" in sex. Smoking or ingesting small amounts of *ganja* is reported to induce voracious hunger and to act as an instant aphrodisiac.[4]

Sociocultural and individual variations in usage and reactions must be analyzed in relation to the chemical content of the cannabis and quantity consumed.[5] Working-class users regularly consume far more *ganja,* in all forms, for much longer periods, than middle-class users. They are also more familiar with the plant and its products in terms of quality and use the most potent grades available seasonally.

Cannabis and Other Drugs

Concern in the United States about allegations that there is "no doubt that marijuana has long been important in the rites of initiation to heroin use—and for a medley of other drugs"[6] do not apply to Jamaica. After a century of use of cannabis for medicinal and psychoactive purposes, Jamaican working-class users do not experiment with other drugs. Heroin and "hard" drugs, generally, are unknown in Jamaica. Amphetamines and barbiturates are rarely, if at all, used in the working class, which relies by tradition on folk medicines and has limited access to costly prescriptions or patent medicines. The few cases of heroin toxicity that had come to the attention of physicians all involved tourists. The concern that cannabis is "the half-way house to heroin" is simply not borne out by the Jamaican data.

Implications for the Future

Data from the research project suggests that Jamaicans are starting to smoke *ganja* regularly at younger ages than in the past. Taking this trend into account, along with the increase in life expectancy over the past few decades, an increase in the average number of years of regular use can be expected in the future. Despite the array of formal and informal sanctions against *ganja,* its use has been increasing in the working classes and is spreading to other sections of the population. There appears to be every likelihood that this diffusion will continue. In due course, *ganja* may have as widespread a distribution as tobacco and alcohol.

Summary

Judging from the clinical data, the physical risk to the individual appears to relate primarily to *smoking per se,* given long-term chronic smoking of *ganja* mixed with regular tobacco, in spliffs and chillum pipes, in addition to heavy consumption of regular tobacco cigarettes. The only significant medical differences between smokers and non-smokers were differences in statistical trends in lung function and hematology. Kalant and Kalant (1968) point out that respiratory consequences correlated with chronic cannabis smoking may be due to smoke components unrelated to the psychoactive properties. While more clinical research is required to follow up these leads and, if possible, to isolate the effects of tobacco smoking from the effects of cannabis-tobacco smoking, at present it appears that the risk of chronic cannabis smoking may parallel the risks of chronic tobacco smoking.

The psychiatric findings do not bear out any of the extreme allegations about the deleterious effects of chronic use of cannabis on sanity, cerebral atrophy, brain damage or personality deterioration. There is no evidence of withdrawal symptoms or reports of severe overdose reactions or of physical dependency.[7] The psychological findings show no significant differences between long-term smokers and non-smokers.

Over the past one hundred years, the *ganja* complex has developed and proliferated in Jamaican society and is extraordinarily well integrated into working-class life styles. *Ganja* serves multiple purposes that are essentially pragmatic, rather than psychedelic: working-class users smoke *ganja* to support rational task-oriented behavior, to keep "conscious," fortify health, maintain peer group relations and enhance religious and philosophical contemplation. They express social rather than hedonistic motivations for smoking.[8]

Ganja as an energizer is the primary motivation given for continued use. The concern of many in the United States that marihuana creates an "amotivational syndrome" and a "reduction of the work drive" is not borne out by the life histories of Jamaican working-class subjects or by objective measurements, which indicate that acute effects may alter the rate and organization of movement and the expenditure of energy during work, but that heavy use of *ganja* does not diminish work drive or the work ethic.

There is no evidence of any causal relationship between cannabis use and mental deterioration, insanity, violence or poverty; or that widespread cannabis use in Jamaica produces an apathetic, indolent class of people. In fact, the *ganja* complex provides an adaptive mechanism by which many Jamaicans cope with limited life chances in a harsh environment. Legislative repeal of the mandatory sentence for possession, following the presentation of the *ganja* report to the Jamaican Government, was a major step in the decriminalization of a traditional cultural practice that goes back to remote horizons.

The failure of policy makers to realize the importance of informal social controls in preventing drug abuse is beginning to be recognized. Michael Sonnenreich, Vice-President of the National Coordinating Council on Drug Education in the United States, observed that drug-taking is socially controlled "when it is routinized, ritualized and structured so as to reduce to a minimum any drug-taking behavior which the surrounding culture considers inadvisable. From this analysis there should follow a new approach" (*ICAA News* 1974:5). The multidisciplinary findings reported in this volume highlight the underlying role of culture in regulating the use of *ganja* and conditioning reactions to it—within a structured system of social controls.

Notes

1. New light may come from current research on operant conditioning for conscious control of bodily functioning, being undertaken at the Langley Porter Neuropsychiatric Institute and other research centers in the United States. Mechoulam's research on metabolites may also throw light on adverse psychosomatic reactions reported (see Mechoulam 1970 and Mechoulam *et al.* 1970).
2. The Hemp Drugs Commission found no tendency to "debauch" with *ganja,* as occurred with alcohol (Great Britain 1969:186). Grinspoon discusses at length Baudelaire's extensive use of opium and alcohol and limited experience with hashish and suggests that "most of the effects he attributed to hashish were in fact produced by opium" (1971:80).
3. Beaubrun (1974) cites a high correlation between extroversion and heavy drinking; with a preponderance of cyclothymic personalities who are successful in Western cultures, alcohol becomes the "establishment" choice while personality attributes in the "culture of poverty" may lead to cannabis preference.
4. Laboratory analysis of samples submitted to the Jamaica Project by several middle-class users reveal only "traces" of THC, supporting the thesis that psychocultural expectations condition individual reactions to cannabis.

5. Reports on the potency of plant samples submitted by the subjects, assayed in NIMH laboratories in the United States, and project data on quantity and frequency of use are included in Appendices III and IV in original source.

6. See discussion by Brill in symposium on "Drug Abuse: Legal and Ethical Implications of the Non-Medicinal Use of Hallucinogenic and Narcotic Drugs" (1968:80–81). See also Nahas (1973:285) on cannabis and multiple-drug use: "All available evidence indicates that regular *Cannabis* consumption conditions the user psychologically as well as pharmacologically to the use of other mind-altering drugs."

7. The U.S. DHEW report notes that "Death from an overdose of cannabis is apparently extremely rare and difficult to confirm" (1972:13). The matter of "lethal overdosage" of marihuana is undoubtedly extremely rare; as Weil observes: "On the basis of experiments in cats, one can estimate (roughly) that a possible lethal dose of marijuana for a person of average weight would be a pound and a half taken as a single oral dose." No such heroic dosages have been reported in *ganja* folklore. Cases of acute collapse have been reported in the literature following intravenous use of cannabis, but "acute toxic physical reactions to marijuana are relatively rare." According to Weil, "marijuana [is] among the least toxic drugs known to modern medicine" (Weil 1972:48).

8. The Canadian Commission, for example, reports that: "the simple pleasure of the experience" appears to be a major factor in cannabis use among students and adults as "part of a largely hedonistic life style in which happiness and pleasure are taken as self-evidently valid goals of human life." The Report notes that this is not a trivial motivation; "it is an old and universal theme of human history. Man has always sought gratifications of the kind afforded by the psychotropic drugs" (Canada 1970:160, 155–56).

24. The Alien Weed

Richard J. Bonnie and Charles H. Whitebread, II

The practices of smoking marihuana and of growing it for that purpose filtered into the United States from the south in the early years of the twentieth century. Transported by Mexicans and West Indians, the plant and its intoxicant use encountered a hostile political and social climate. Gradually during the ensuring quarter-century, criminal prohibitions appeared on the statute books of nearly every state where the drug was used. Well into the 1930s, however, marihuana-smoking attracted little concerted attention from the national policy and opinion apparatus, which was deeply engaged in drug matters of much wider social impact than the limited, regional use of this new drug. Thus, the story of marihuana policy in the United States begins as a series of distinctly local tales.

Beginning around 1900 in the towns along the Mexican border and a decade later on the Gulf coast; the practice of marihuana-smoking entered the United States at two independent points. The users in the two areas differed, as did the degree of public awareness of the phenomenon and nature of the public perception. During the twenties the use of the drug spread from these points of entry in two directions, and with two distinct identities: it traveled north and west from the border, taking along an ethnic identity, and north and east from New Orleans, with its identity as a fungible narcotic and enslaver of youth.

Marihuana Crosses the Rio Grande

Political chaos at home and economic opportunity in the United States significantly augmented the migration of Mexicans to Texas and New Mexico at the turn of the century.[1] In Mexican districts of the border towns and in major cities these immigrants continued to smoke and grow marihuana as they had done at home. Cultivation of the plant was a major industry in the vicinity of Mexico City, the mountains of Thalpam, and in surrounding Mexican provinces, and a steady supply of marihuana easily crossed the border into Laredo, El Paso, San Antonio, Nogales, and other border towns and major cities. Laredo was of major importance because it was linked directly to the Mexico City area by the Mexican National Railroad. The demand for the plant was significant enough that in 1917 a United States government investigator reported that several importing firms commercially distributed marihuana to other points in the region, particularly to San Antonio. One company, in business only three months, had five hundred pounds of marihuana in stock at the time of the investigation. Retailers, mostly local grocers, openly advertised.[2]

The demand for "Rosa Maria" was satisfied not only by garden plants and bulk Mexican imports but also by one-ounce packages sold over the counter in drug stores. Since no prescription was required for its purchase, the corner druggist was a useful source of the weed. In fact, a mail-order business grew up; one druggist in Floresville, Texas, sent marihuana by mail to twenty customers in Texas, Arizona, New Mexico, Kansas, and Colorado. Although medical application of

From Richard J. Bonnie and Charles Whitebread, II, THE ALIEN WEED from *The Marihuana Conviction: A History of Prohibition of Marihuana in the United States* (Charlottesville, Va.: University Press of Virginia, 1974), pages 32–52 as abridged. Reprinted with permission.

the drug was apparently limited by this time, major pharmaceutical houses still manufactured it in "herb" package as well as in tincture and extract form.[3]

Marihuana-smoking was probably a casual adjunct to life in the Mexican community—a relaxant, a folk remedy for headaches, a mild euphoriant cheaply obtained for two cigarettes for a dollar. But within the Mexican community, marihuana had also achieved a potent folklore status which spread to the Americans more quickly than did the drug.

According to contemporary reports, a common Mexican saying "Esta ya ledio las tres" ("you take it three times") referred to the exhilarating effects of three inhalations of marihuana. The first puff was said to induce a feeling of well-being; the second allegedly provoked extreme elation coupled with activity; and the third was reputed to make the smoker oblivious to danger, quarrelsome, delirious, destructive, and conscious of superhuman strength.[4]

A drug with such obnoxious properties soon attracted the attention of the law enforcement officials of El Paso, characterized as a "hot bed of marihuana fiends"[5] where use of the drug was reportedly common not only among Mexicans but among "Negroes, prostitutes, pimps and a criminal class of whites."[6] In response, El Paso passed an ordinance banning sale and possession of the drug in 1914.[7] According to one interested physician who traveled along the border towns around 1920, passage of this ordinance was precipitated by a major fight allegedly involving a marihuana user.[8]

Similar anecdotes were common. One police captain reported three years later:

> I have had almost daily experiance [sic] with the users of [marihuana] for the reason that when they are addicted to the use they become very violent, especially when they become angry and will attack an officer even if a gun is drawn on him, they seem to have no fear. I have also noted that when under the influence of this weed they have abnormal strength and that it will take several men to handle one man where under ordinary circumstances one man could handle him with ease.[9]

The captain of detectives concluded that marihuana produced "a lust for blood," rendering the user "insensible to pain" and capable of "superhuman strength when detained or hindered from doing whatever [he is] attempting to do."[10] The chief of police wondered why the Mexican government did not feed the "marihuana dope" to its armies to get the civil war over with because the soldiers would then fight instead of looting and hunting as they were prone to do.[11]

Actually, marihuana was in common use in Mexican army. A U.S. Customs officer who served at the international bridge at El Paso and was a self-declared authority on "marihuana fiends" did not think the drug helped the Mexican army much. In his view, marihuana users became irresponsible and strayed aimlessly about. . . .

American authorities were particularly concerned that the troops stationed along the border under General Pershing in 1916 might become infected with the marihuana vice. When a federal investigator learned from an El Paso druggist that numerous American soldiers had sought cannabis packages upon their return from expeditions across the border, he interviewed almost every military official along the border. All of them denied any knowledge of the practice.[12]

However, an army physician stationed in Texas at this time recalled nine years later: "Mexican Laborers were about the only ones I knew of to use it in the United States. They use it, get "hopped up," are picked up by the police who send them [to the hospital] for treatment. We would keep them five or six weeks and send them back. After the guard went down to Mexico and came back, I saw the first white people who smoked the plant. Soldiers who had been on the border smoked cigarettes of marihuana either straight or mixed with tobacco."[13] This hypothesis is farther supported by the fact that use of marihuana was prohibited at Fort Sam Houston by order of the commanding general in July 1921.[14]

Apart from its possible infusion into the American military, marihuana-smoking in Texas appears to have been confined primarily to lower class Mexicans. Marihuana use was a lower class phenomenon in Mexico as well; it is therefore of particular interest that several states of the Mexican Republic adopted a restrictive public policy at about the same time marihuana appeared in the southwestern United States. Mexican authorities, even more class-conscious than their American counterparts, were particularly apprehensive about its use in the army, fearing it might contaminate the upper classes. The Mexican aristocracy's position is clearly reflected in a 1917 editorial, translated from a Spanish-language San Antonio newspaper:

> [The hemp] plant is terribly noxious when used as a narcotic, from which a dangerous vice is acquired by those who make a bad use of it, as happens among the lower classes in Mexico. . . .
> The men who smoke this herb become excited to such an extent that they go through periods of near frenzy, and worse, it is always aggressive as the crimes which have been committed in garrisons, armories, barracks, and the humble suburbs of Mexico [attest].
> In the South of the United States, this menacing evil has begun to appear, especially in the army and among the Negroes. . . .
> [T]he authorities . . . [must] uproot this malicious vice in its incipiency as it is growing even in the army among members of distinguished families and also as it is happening in Mexico among young men of good society; this, of course, is doubly lamentable.[15]

On 15 March 1920 the Department of Public Health of the Federal Government of Mexico published a "regulation concerning commerce in products that may be utilized to encourage vices degenerating the race and concerning the cultivation of plants that may be employed for such purpose," wherein the "cultivation and commerce of marihuana" was strictly prohibited.[16]

Class consciousness was a recurrent element in marihuana prohibition even in its infancy. Mexican-American patricians appealed to sentiments of Negro inferiority, and European-American officials appealed to sentiments of Mexican inferiority. Most interesting is the fact that Mexican-American physicians painted a more fantastic account of the drug's effects than did the El Paso police. Dr. Lopez, a member of the Association of Military Surgeons of the United States and former director of the General Hospital in Mexico City, alleged that smoking marihuana "causes hallucinations of both eye and ear," rendering the person under its influence "actually crazy and irresponsible for the time being." "Continued use of the drug," he observed, "causes the body to wear away as is the case with other drug fiends."[17] Dr. Francisco de Ganseca, a graduate of the National School of Medicine in Mexico City, contended that "madness is the final result," the drug being "worse than opium as it not only destroys the life of the person who smokes it, but causes him to take the lives of others."[18] Another Mexican-American doctor contended that a person "under [marihuana's] influence may see a friend and imagine that he is an enemy and kill him."[19]

From all accounts, marihuana use and tales of its destructive effects were prevalent in the border towns of Texas and New Mexico after 1910. One botanist from the U.S. Department of Agriculture noted in 1925 that "the plant . . . is used a great deal . . . in Texas, Arizona and New Mexico, especially by the Mexicans. I have been told that a few years ago two guards in the penitentiary at Tucson, Arizona, were killed by a Mexican, while under the influence of the drug."[20] An army botanist observed that the drug was used by Mexican railroad laborers and by inmates of the prison at Yuma, Arizona, and that a former superintendent of this prison had declared that "under its baneful influence reckless men become bloodthirsty, trebly daring and dangerous to an uncontrollable degree." This same observer quoted an American consul from Nogales who noted in 1911 that use of the drug "causes the smoker to become exceedingly pugnacious and to run amuck without discrimination."[21]

The Mexican marihuana folklore apparently make a deep impression on any American who came in contact with the drug or its alien users. Having no reason to suspect the veracity of such tales, law enforcement officials and local representatives of the Customs and Agriculture departments of the federal government agitated for state and federal legislation to combat the "killer weed." The deputy sheriff of El Paso persuaded a local Food and Drug inspector to bring the matter to the attention of the chief of the Bureau of Chemistry in the federal Agriculture Department, the man with primary enforcement responsibility under the Food and Drug Act. Without any further investigation, the bureaucracy responded with the necessary administrative action: in 1915, after an official request by the secretary of agriculture, the secretary of the treasury issued a decision under the Food and Drug Act prohibiting importation of cannabis for other medical purposes.[22] (The Act itself required only that any quantity of cannabis contained in a retail produce by explicitly designated on the label.)

• • •

Mexican immigration during the first third of the twentieth century increased enormously; the Bureau of Immigration records the entry of 590,765 Mexicans from 1915 to 1930. Two-thirds of these people remained in Texas. The others settled in states in the Rocky Mountain area, most of them as farm laborers.[23] During this period practically every state west of the Mississippi River passed antimarihuana legislation: California and Utah in 1915; Colorado in 1917; Texas in 1919; Iowa in 1921; New Mexico, Arkansas, Nevada, Oregon, and Washington in 1923; Idaho, Kansas, Montana, and Nebraska in 1927; Wyoming in 1929; South Dakota in 1931; and North Dakota and Oklahoma in 1933.[24] Whether motivated by outright ethnic prejudice or by simple discriminatory lack of interest, the proceedings before each legislature resembled those in Texas and New Mexico in 1923. There was little if any public attention and no debate. Pointed references were made to the drug's Mexican origins, and sometimes to the criminal conduct which inevitably followed when Mexicans used the "killer weed."

In 1931 the Texas legislature finally prohibited possession of marihuana. By now alcohol prohibition had withdrawn any philosophical barrier to making possession illegal. The *San Antonio Light* reported that: "At last the state legislature had taken a definite step toward suppression of traffic in a dangerous and insanity-producing narcotic easily compounded of a weed (marihuana) indigenous to this section. . . . This newspaper has urged the passage of prohibitory legislation and is gratified that the solons at Austin have acted, even if tardily, in the suppression of traffic in a drug which makes the addict frequently a dangerous or homicidal maniac."[25]

Setting out to enforce the new law by destroying patches of the weed, a local agent emphasized the difficulty of his task. There were a lot of patches to destroy because "consumption of this 'tobacco' has been very heavy among Mexicans and Negroes."[26]

The earliest marihuana prohibitions in the West were adopted by California and Utah in 1915.[27] Satisfactory explanations for these incipient legislative responses remain elusive. On the one hand, it is clear that these prohibitions were directed at a drug with which someone was familiar. In California the drug was specifically added to a preexisting comprehensive antinarcotics package. And the Utah prohibition even extended to possession of pipes for smoking the drug. On the other hand, it does not appear likely that sufficient numbers of immigrants would have arrived in either state by this early date to arouse interest in them and their unusual habits. (There is much evidence of a sizable Mexican colony in Los Angeles fifteen years later.)[28] We can only speculate.

In California it is possible that (Asian) Indian cannabis use inspired the same collision of curiosity and fear which had been aroused by Chinese opium prohibitions a generation earlier. In connection with preparation for the first House Conference in 1912, one of the U.S. delegates joined Dr. Wright of the State Department in requesting the inclusion of cannabis in the international accords. Henry J. Finger of the California Board of Pharmacy reported the concern of Californians, particularly in San Francisco, over a "large influx of Hindoos . . . demanding cannabis indica" and their claim that they would attract "the whites into their habit."[29]

• • •

The Battle of New Orleans

While Mexican immigrants were introducing marihuana to the border states and the Southwest, Caribbean sailors and West Indian immigrants were introducing the habit to ports along the Gulf of Mexico. Although use in the border states remained essentially an alien phenomenon, contemporary accounts suggest that marihuana-smoking became well established among certain segments of the native population in Houston, Galveston, and particularly in New Orleans.

Although there is evidence that some marihuana came to these areas from Mexico by way of Tampico and El Paso, most of it was smuggled in by enterprising sailors from Cuba and other points in the Indies. Around 1925 Dr. Frank Gomila, commissioner of Public Safety of New Orleans, began his campaign for federal legislation to supplement the Treasury Department's ineffectual 1915 ban on importation for nonmedical purposes. He observed that the traffic was quite organized, amounting to thousands of kilograms a year: "The custom was to keep [marihuana] in warehouses or storerooms for further distribution. It was sold by the wholesaler to the retailer who in turn put the 'weed' through a process known as 'sweating.' The dried leaves and stems were soaked in sugar water and dried on butcher's brown papers."[30]

If Gomila and the newspapers can be believed, the demand in New Orleans in the mid-twenties was so great that the "peddlers" were able to become exceptionally prosperous by dividing the market. One had exclusive jurisdiction over the blacks unloading the fruit boats, another over the lobby in a certain hotel, and so on. Marihuana was, of course, also available at local pharmacies without a prescription before 1919 in Texas and before 1924 in Louisiana. After that, marihuana had to be bought on the street unless the user could obtain or forge a prescription.

Druggists in Houston reported in 1917 that their marihuana purchasers were no longer predominantly Mexican, but increasingly white—"sporting" women (prostitutes), gamblers, pimps, and "hop heads," some of whom were allegedly "having difficulty in obtaining their usual supply of dope."[31] In Galveston the story was much the same. One druggist characterized his marihuana clientele as "Mexicans, a low class of whites, and East Indians coming off the boats." Another referred to "Mexicans, Negroes, and chauffeurs, and a low class of whites such as those addicted to the use of habit-forming drugs, and hangers-on of the underworld."[32] Gomila suggests that in New Orleans about the same time, the previously unknown practice rapidly became "more and more of common knowledge among the vicious characters of the city."[33]

Different pictures emerge of the marihuana user in El Paso and San Antonio on the one hand and New Orleans and Galveston on the other. In the border towns he was a Mexican laborer, indolent to some, volatile to others. Local authorities were, by and large, unable to generate any significant public or political interest, although there were no political objections to making the Mexican weed illegal.

In the port cities, however, the marihuana user was a "dope fiend," the basest element of American society. He was a narcotics addict, a pimp, or a gambler; she was a prostitute. Marihuana was simply "another narcotic" in a city with a major "narcotic problem." The issue was always open to sensationalism. Even before public attention was excited, however, the prevalence of marihuana use came to the attention of the president of the Louisiana State Board of Health, Dr. Oscar Dowling. On 21 August 1920 he advised the governor of the increasing availability of marihuana, a "powerful narcotic, causing exhiliration, intoxication, delirious hallucinations, and its subsequent action, drowsiness and stupor. . . ." Apparently the drug had come to his attention through the arrest, conviction, and incarceration of a twenty-one-year-old musician convicted of forging a doctor's name to a prescription.[34]

At the same time, Dr. Dowling wrote to the surgeon general of the United States, Dr. Hugh Cummings, to advise him of the increasing traffic in morphine, opium, and marihuana, and to seek federal cooperation. It is interesting that Dr. Dowling was simultaneously involved with federal officials in the effort to close the New Orleans morphine clinics;[35] within a few years, none of the morphine clinics were open, and a maintenance approach to narcotics addiction was to be foreclosed for a half-century.[36]

Very little, however, was done about the marihuana issued until the press seized upon it. In the fall of 1926 the *New Orleans Item* dispatched an army of reporters among the smoking and selling population. A series of articles published by the more widely circulated *Morning Tribune* (both papers were owned by the same publishing company) exposed the immense profits being made peddling "muggles" or "moota" and commented upon the volatile effects of the drug upon its "addicts." It was reported that marihuana "numbs the sense, creates wild fancies and has a hypnotic effect upon the user, making his will easily subordinated to that of others."

What emerged from these articles, however, was not a vision of addicts on the streets and pushers on the docks. Rather, the public was encouraged to believe that the peddlers were men who lurked on playgrounds seeking to entrap young minds. "Over two hundred children under fourteen are believed to be addicted to the marihuana habit," the paper reported, and at least forty-four schools were infected.[37]

Although it was quite clear that the "addicted" children were street-wise youths drawn from the same socioeconomic classes as the adult users, the impact was no less pointed. In those innocent early days of the juvenile court movement, harassed social workers, pastors, teachers, and club women tended to attribute delinquent behavior to any identifiable defect in the physical and social environment—in this case the marihuana menace.

Local policy makers wasted no time. The New Orleans Police Department immediately launched a roundup. They arrested more than 150 persons for violation of a law which had lain dormant for two years.[38] Dr. Dowling reportedly soon circulated "a warning to parents, guardians and teachers of children against this menace."[39] The Women's Christian Temperance Union jumped on the bandwagon, focusing their attacks on the "soft drink" bars which had sprung up all over New Orleans during prohibition: "The soft drink stand and the corner drug store have taken the place of the saloon as a social meeting place. Here is where marihuana and liquors can sometimes be bought."[40]

Beyond these immediate effects, a more substantial result of the local policy reaction in New Orleans was the formation of a tightly knit coterie of New Orleans law enforcement, public health, and social welfare officials, who would carry their antimarihuana campaign to Washington, with ultimate success.

Marihuana Comes to the Big Cities

The West Indies was one source for the marihuana that arrived in the port cities of America. Not long after the practice became established in the Gulf area, it seems to have appeared on a much smaller scale in New York City. During the twenties the commercial traffic which steamed up the Mississippi from New Orleans and Texas also spread Mexicans and marihuana to Chicago, Kansas City, Cleveland, Detroit, St. Louis, and other major commercial centers.

Large communities of Mexican laborers penetrated the industrial region on the southern shore of Lake Michigan during the 1920s. By 1930 the Mexican population in Chicago alone had reached approximately 30,000. Judging from all contemporary accounts, the "white" population, which included many second generation immigrants, exhibited considerable distaste for the new immigrants and their different habits of life. The Mexican customs and police prejudice were a highly cumbustible mixture, apparently resulting both in a disproportionately large number of Mexicans being arrested and in a belief among the "whites" that Mexicans were inherently lawless.[41]

• • •

It is in this context that we must view the Mexican laborers' use of marihuana or "muggles" which apparently took local officials by surprise in 1927. One law enforcement official reported: "There are about 7,000 Mexicans in Gary, 10,000 in Indiana Harbor and 8,000 in South Chicago. . . . The Mexicans depend on the steel mills, railroads, and construction gangs for employment. Many are drifters when slack labor conditions prevail. . . . [T]wenty-five percent of these Mexicans smoke marijuana. In fact, many of them make their living by raising and peddling the drug."[42]

Such a situation seemed likely to infect the rest of the community. As in New Orleans, reports started to appear that high school students were smoking the weed.[43] Then the dam broke. Since neither state nor federal legislation prohibited sale of marihuana, the local United States attorney declared war, armed with an internal revenue statute prohibiting production and transfer of "a cigarette substitute" on which tax had not been paid. In June 1929 he raided wholesale houses' "believed to have disposed of large quantities of marihuana cigarettes, sold to school pupils and other youthful thrill-seekers," and arrested nine men, "most of them Mexicans."[44] At the same time, local officials began to use a statute which prohibited transfer of "any cigarette containing any substance deleterious to health."[45]

The *Chicago Tribune,* lobbying heavily for antimarihuana legislation then pending before the Illinois legislature, breathlessly reported the day-to-day progress of the enforcement activity.[46] Every stall in the legislature earned a banner headline.

BAN ON HASHISH
BLOCKED DESPITE
RAVAGES OF DRUG

In an article appearing in June 1929 the paper noted: "The number of addicts is growing alarmingly according to authorities, because of the ease with which [marihuana] can be obtained. The habit was introduced a dozen years ago or so by Mexican laborers . . . but it has become widespread among American youths . . . even among school children." The specter of substitution was also rasied: "There being no legal ban such as makes other drugs scarce, 'loco weed' is cheap. The rush of its popularity in Chicago and all over the country since the oncoming of Prohibition is partly explained by the price of cigarettes, 3 for 50 cents or at most 30 cents apiece." Apparently the bill had been waylaid in a Senate committee by one senator, a druggist from Chicago, who "declared that the seed of the plant is used as birdseed." The *Tribune* was not convinced. They contacted a birdseed seller who disputed the senator's contention, but whatever the senator's reason, he successfully killed the bill.[47]

To place the Tribune's epidemic description in perspective, it should be noted that representatives of the major local pressure groups (the WCTU, the Immigrant's Protective League, and the National Federation of Women Clubs) who became heavily involved in the marihuana issue several years later were essentially unfamiliar with marihuana even after the *Tribune* campaign. Cannabis was produced and dispensed in the United States for medical use throughout the period of the first antinarcotics legislation. The drug was mentioned in the poison laws of nine states,[48] and in the course of bringing the pharmaceutical manufacturers, pharmacies, and physicians under regulatory control, a handful of states had enacted tighter restrictions on cannabis. In 1911 Louisiana prohibited refills of prescriptions containing cannabis or opiates, cocaine, chloroform, or hyoscyamics.[49] Maine (1913), Massachusetts (1914), Vermont (1915), and Rhode Island (1918) all barred the sale of cannabis without a prescription as part of comprehensive regulatory laws.[50]

These early cannabis laws in the East were passed not in response to street use, since the intoxicant use of marihuana had not yet appeared in the Northeast, but rather in anticipation of future problems. The medical establishment in the Northeast was already familiar with the psychoactive properties of cannabis and with literary descriptions of the virtues of hashish. For example, Victor Robinson reported in 1912 on the nature of acute intoxication on the basis of self-administration and observation of ingestion by friends. His report was widely circulated.[51] Among the most moralistic of the antinarcotics reformers there was little doubt that effective elimination of the curse of the "drug habit evil" demanded strict control over any and all potentially intoxicating substances to which addicts might resort once the opiates and cocaine became more difficult to obtain. Several authorities who spearheaded the development of the Harrison Act had even urged the inclusion of cannabis in that act despite the fact that the drug had not yet attracted any habitual users. The State Department's Dr. Hamilton Wright, who coordinated domestic and international aspects of the mushrooming antinarcotic movement, Cornell University's Dr. Alexander Lambert, who later became president of the AMA, and the Agriculture Department's Dr. Harvey Wiley, who had shepherded the Pure Food and Drug Act through Congress, all testified in favor of covering cannabis by federal law.[52]

In response to these reform sentiments, the drug industry vehemently protested, contending that cannabis was an insignificant medicine which had no place in antinarcotics legislation. . . . Charles West, chairman of the NWDA's (National Wholesale Druggists Association) legislative committee, argued in 1910 that "cannabis is not what may be called a 'habit-forming drug.'"[53]

The industry successfully resisted the inclusion of cannabis in federal legislation. But the reformers' purification sentiment easily accounts for the drug's inclusion in the initial Eastern prohibitions, especially after 1914 when the states were pressed to implement the national policies declared in the Harrison Act. This hypothesis is supported by the New York experience.

• • •

As late as 1918 a state legislative committee which had exhaustively investigated the narcotics problem in New York did not mention marihuana.[54] Nevertheless, by 1921 at least one writer noted an increase in marihuana use. He sounded the alarm in the title to his work—*From Opium to Hashish*—and raised new fears. Marihuana could be used as a substitute not only for opium

263

and morphine but also for alcohol, which had recently been suppressed by the Volstead Act.[55] Marihuana was not the only focus of the substitution argument, as one commentator had warned in 1919: "Cocaine in particular is in great demand. When prohibition is in force, persons, especially drinkers from compulsion of habit who have been robbed of the daily drink, will naturally resort to cocaine."[56]

By 1923 the *New York Times* referred to marihuana as the city's "latest habit-forming drug" when reporting its exhibition at a women's club meeting.[57] In 1927 the legislature included marihuana in its list of "habit-forming drugs" in a comprehensive narcotics bill.[58] . . . The 1927 New York law was drafted by an AMA committee; we suspect, therefore, that the inclusion of cannabis was not attributable to any significant increase in use in the city. If marihuana use was increasing, however, it was not attracting attention. During the period from 1914 to 1927 the New York newspapers were replete with articles dealing with narcotic addiction; yet only four brief references were made to marihuana in the *New York Times*.[59] Public concern was focused on drug problems at the time of the 1927 act; yet none of the postenactment comments on the act referred to marihuana.[60]

Probably the best description of the nature of marihuana use in New York about this time appears in a 1930 report by a federal agent on the basis of an undercover survey. He portrayed a smalltime, unorganized traffic with a limited ethnic clientele. One user said she "got her supply . . . from Spaniards and East Indians working as members of the crew on boats belonging to the United Fruit Lines and other boat lines touching South American, Mexican and Cuban ports. . . ." Another woman revealed that

> her husband was a steward on the Bull Line Ships running between Cuba, Mexico and South American countries; that the marihuana was purchased by her husband in Cuba and he brought it into the United States in 10 and 15-pound lots, and he could bring in a larger quantity on order . . . (and) that she made up the packages of marihuana for sale to the trade, which consisted mostly of Spaniards, East Indians, Filipinos, and a few Americans, both white and colored.[61]

In New York during the first quarter of the twentieth century, a reforming zeal impelled an attack on the narcotics menace, particularly after prohibition. Every intoxicant posed a threat, whether or not its use was common. Judging from contemporary accounts, marihuana use was rare outside areas of ethnic concentration. Thus, the enactment of statutory proscriptions in 1927 was axiomatic and did not constitute a matter of public concern, even within the medical and law enforcement communities.

Local Prohibition: A Legend Disputed

It has become fashionable in recent years to attribute the illegal status of marihuana to the Federal Bureau of Narcotics and its long-time head, Harry J. Anslinger. Such a theory has been particularly popular among those seeking to alter the existing public policy since it implies that what was done by one man is not entitled to the deference which a more broadly based policy would enjoy.

However, the recent public policy emerged in a more subtle, less controversial fashion. Although the federal narcotics bureaucracy, with Commissioner Anslinger at the helm, was to become marihuana's leading antagonist in the mid-thirties, a restrictive public policy toward the drug was well rooted locally before that time. During the "local" phase of marihuana prohibition, lasting roughly from 1914 to 1931, twenty-nine states, including seventeen west of the Mississippi, prohibited use of the drug for nonmedical purposes. (Four more states did so in 1933.)

The most important feature of this initial prohibitory phase is that marihuana was inevitably viewed as a "narcotic" drug, thereby invoking the broad consensus underlying the nation's recently enunciated antinarcotics policy. This classification emerged primarily from the drug's alien character. Although use of some drugs—alcohol and tobacco—was indigenous to American life, the use of "narcotics" for pleasure was not. Evidently, drugs associated with ethnic minorities and with otherwise "immoral" populations were automatically viewed as "narcotics." The scientific community shared this social bias and therefore had little interest in scientific accuracy.

From this instinctive classification of marihuana with opium, morphine, heroin, and cocaine flowed the entire set of factual supports on which narcotics prohibition rested. Marihuana was presumed to be addictive, its use inevitably tending to excess. Since its users—Mexicans, West Indians, blacks, and underworld whites—were associated in the public mind with crime, particularly of a violent nature, the association applied also to marihuana, which had a similar reputation in Mexican folklore. Since the nation was preoccupied during the twenties with lawlessness, especially among the foreign born, this association was a strong one.

To the idea of an alien cancer in the social organism was added the inevitable fear that it would spread. In New Orleans, Denver, and Chicago the specter of a doped school population was the cornerstone of the prohibitory effort. And during alcohol prohibition, paralleled by the local phase of marihuana prohibition, it was naturally imperative to suppress a drug which frustrated alcohol users might substitute for their customary intoxicant.

In short, marihuana prohibition was a predictable phenomenon. In states where either Mexicans or the weed had appeared, suppressing its use required no public clamor or citizens' movement; soon after being apprised of its presence, local lawmakers invoked the criminal law, and some also turned to Washington for assistance.

NOTES

1. The Bureau of Immigration recorded the entry of 590,765 Mexicans into the United States between 1915 and 1930. Of these, upwards of 90 percent in each year were to be resident in the twenty-two states west of the Mississippi, and more than two-thirds were to reside in Texas alone. Information compiled from Tables, Immigrant Aliens, by States of Intended Future Residence and Race on Peoples, published annually from each fiscal year from 1915 to 1930 in *Commissioner General of Immigration Annual Report*.

2. "Report of Investigation in the State of Texas, Particularly along the Mexican Border, of the Traffic in, and Consumption of the Drug Generally known as 'Indian Hemp' or *Cannabis Indica,* known in Mexico and States Bordering on the Rio Grande as 'Marihuana'; Sometimes also referred to as 'Rosa Maria,' or 'Juanita,' " filed by R. F. Smith to Dr. Alsberg, chief of the Bureau of Chemistry, United States Department of Agriculture, 13 Apr. 1917, pp. 10–12, in Federal Bureau of Narcotics files (hereafter cited as "1917 Investigation").

3. Ibid., pp. 13–15.

4. M. V. Ball, "Marihuana: Mexican Name for Cannabis, Also Called Loco Weed in Certain Parts of Texas," May 1922, in the "Report of Committee Appointed by the Governor of the Canal Zone, April 1, 1925, for the Purpose of Investigating the Use of Marihuana and Making Recommendations Regarding Same and Related Papers" (Balboa Heights, Canal Zone), pp. 55–60. (The Canal Zone Report is an unpublished document hereafter cited as "Canal Zone Report," 18 Dec. 1925. The related Papers are a group of heretofore unpublished documents, hereafter cited as "Canal Zone Papers," which may be found in

the National Archives. A copy of these materials is on deposit with the University of Virginia Law Library in Charlottesville, Va. Page references are to the latter copy, which has been ordered chronologically and paginated by the authors.)

5. "1917 Investigations," p. 9.
6. Ibid., p. 13.
7. Ibid., p. 9.
8. Ball, "Marihuana: Mexican Name for Cannabis."
9. "1917 Investigation," p. 36.
10. Ibid., p. 37.
11. Ibid., p. 35.
12. Ibid., p. 9.
13. Testimony of Dr. Hesner before Committee on Use of Marihuana, 5 Dec. 1925, "Canal Zone Papers," p. 31.
14. W. E. Safford, economic botanist, to Dr. E. R. Hodge, chemist, Medical Department, U.S. Army, "Canal Zone Papers," pp. 106–7.
15. "1917 Investigation," pp. 17(d)–17(e).
16. Mexico Department of Public Health," Regulations Concerning Commerce in Products That May Be Utilized to Encourage Vices Degenerating the Race, and Concerning the Cultivation of Plants That May Be Employed for Such Purpose," 15 Mar. 1920, "Canal Zone Papers," pp. 130–32.
17. "1917 Investigation," p. 176.
18. Ibid., p. 29.
19. Ibid., p. 30.
20. Paul C. Standley, associate curator, Division of Plants, Smithsonian Institution, to Mr. Holger Johansen, 18 June 1925, "Canal Zone Papers," pp. 15–16.
21. Safford to Hodge.
22. Treasury Decision 35719, 25 Sept. 1915.
23. See p. 1, supra.
24. *State Laws* (1931), pp. 44, 48, 112, 194, 200, 306. See citations to map.
25. *San Antonio Light,* 4 May 1931 (editorial).
26. Agent-in-charge to commissioner, 26 Aug. 1931 and 9 Sept. 1931.
27. *State Laws* (1931), p. 289.
28. P. S. Taylor, "Crime and the Foreign Born: The Problem of the Mexican," National Commission on Law Observance and Enforcement (Wickersham Commission), *Report on Crime and the Foreign Born,* report no. 10 (Washington, D.C.: GPO, 1931), pp. 201–15 (hereafter cited as Taylor, "Crime and the Foreign Born," *Wickersham Report,* no. 10).
29. H. J. Finger to Dr. Hamilton Wright, 2 July 1911, in *Preliminary Inventories,* no. 76, Records of United States Participation in International Conferences, Commissions and Expositions, no. 39, "Correspondence of Wright with Delegate Henry J. Finger, 1911" (Washington, D.C.: National Archives, 1955), quoted in Musto, "The Marihuana Tax Act of 1937," *Archives of General Psychiatry,* 26 (1972), 101–8.
30. F. R. Gomila and M. C. Gomila Lambow, "Present Status of the Marihuana Vice in the United States," in *Marihuana: America's New Drug Problem,* ed. R. Walton (Philadelphia: Lippincott, 1938), p. 29.
31. "1917 Investigation," pp. 72–79.
32. Ibid., pp. 80–84.
33. Gomila and Lambow, p. 29.
34. Dowling to governor of Louisiana, 21 Aug. 1920, United States surgeon general's files.
35. Dowling to Acting Surgeon General Periz, 3 Dec. 1920; Treasury Department Report on Investigation of Narcotics Dispensory Programs, 25 Mar. 1921. (In the files of the surgeon general for the period 1921–23.)
36. See generally A. Lindesmith, *The Addict and the Law* (Bloomington: Indiana Univ. Press, 1965), pp. 135–61; King, "Narcotic Drug Laws and Enforcement Policies," *Law and Contemporary Problems,* 22 (1957), 124–26. For a savage contemporary attack on the clinic system by a well-known supporter of the law enforcement strategy, see Stanley, "Narcotic Drugs and Crime," *Journal of Criminal Law and Criminology,* 12 (1921), 110.
37. Gomila and Lambow, pp. 29–31; WCTU, *Marihuana* (1928).

38. WCTU, *Marihuana* (1928).
39. Ibid., p. 1.
40. Ibid., p. 3.
41. Taylor, "Crime and the Foreign Born," *Wickersham Report,* no. 10, pp. 220–35.
42. Memorandum from Arthur F. Paul, chief, Chicago Station Food, Drug, and Insecticide Administration, U.S. Department of Agriculture, to chief, Central District, 27 June 1929, p. 4.
43. Ibid., p. 1; *Chicago Tribune,* 3 June 1929.
44. *Chicago Examiner,* 22 June 1929.
45. *Chicago Examiner,* 19 June 1929.
46. *Chicago Tribune,* 17 Oct. 1929; see also *Chicago Tribune,* 1 July 1928, where an article entitled "New Giggle Drug Puts Discord in City Orchestras" reported that marihuana addiction was common among local musicians. The paper noted that marihuana "is an old drug but was generally introduced into the country only a few years ago by the Mexicans. It is like cocaine. In the long run, it bends and cripples its victims. A sort of creeping paralysis results from long use."
47. *Chicago Tribune,* 3 June 1929.
48. *State Laws* (1912), pp. 18–19.
49. Ibid., p. 124.
50. Ibid., pp. 34–41.
51. V. Robinson, "An Essay on Hasheesh: Historical and Experimental," *Medical Review of Reviews,* 18 (1912), 159–60, 300–312. Dr. Robinson's essay was reprinted in book form by E. H. Ringer of New York in 1912 and appeared in a second edition in 1925.
52. U.S., Congress, House, Committee on Ways and Means, *Hearings on Importation and Use of Opium,* 61st Cong., 3d sess., 14 Dec. 1910 and 11 Jan. 1911.
53. Ibid., 11 Jan. 1911.
54. New York, Senate, Joint Legislative Committee to Investigate the Laws in Relation to the Distribution and Sale of Narcotic Drugs, *Final Report* (Albany, 1918), Doc. no. 35.
55. Simon, "From Opium to Hash Eesh," *Scientific American,* Nov. 1921, pp. 14–15.
56. Weber, "Drugs and Crime," *Journal of Crime and Criminology,* 10 (1919), 370.
57. *New York Times,* 11 Jan. 1923, p. 24, col. 1.
58. New York, *New York Laws* (1927), ch. 672, p. 1695.
59. In addition to the Women's Club demonstration noted at n. 59, supra, the *New York Times* (29 Dec. 1925, p. 10, col. 7) reported that the drug had been banned in Mexico. One year later, the paper reported the results of the Panama Canal Zone study on the effects of marihuana, noting the investigator's conclusion that no legislation was necessary to prevent sale or use of the drug (21 Nov. 1926, sec. 2, p. 3, col. 1). The *Times* later reported that a Mexican family was said to have gone insane from eating marihuana (6 July 1927, p. 10, col. 6).
60. See *New York Times,* 25 Mar. 1927, p. 4, col. 6; 6 Apr. 1927, p. 13, col. 2.
61. Memorandum from Ralph H. Oyler, FBN agent-in-charge, New York, to Acting Commission Anslinger, 6 June 1930.

25. Social Bases of Drug-Induced Experiences

Howard S. Becker

In 1938, Albert Hoffman discovered the peculiar effects of lysergic acid dieythlamide (LSD-25) on the mind. He synthesized the drug in 1943 and, following the end of World War II, it came into use in psychiatry, both as a method of simulating psychosis for clinical study and as a means of therapy.[1] In the early 1960's, Timothy Leary, Richard Alpert and others began using it with normal subjects as a means of "consciousness expansion." Their work received a great deal of publicity, particularly after a dispute with Harvard authorities over its potential danger. Simultaneously, LSD-25 became available on the underground market and, although no one has accurate figures, the number of people who have used or continue to use it is clearly very large.

The publicity continues and a great controversy now surrounds LSD use. At one extreme, Leary considers its use so beneficial that he founded a new religion in which it is the major sacrament. At the other extreme, psychiatrists, police and journalists allege that LSD is extremely dangerous, that it produces psychosis, and that persons under its influence are likely to commit actions dangerous to themselves and others that they would not otherwise have committed. Opponents of the drug have persuaded the Congress and some state legislatures to classify it as a narcotic or dangerous drug and to attach penal sanctions to its sale, possession, or use.

In spite of the great interest in the drug, I think it is fair to say that the evidence of its danger is by no means decisive.[2] If the drug does prove to be the cause of a bona fide psychosis, it will be the only case in which anyone can state with authority that they have found *the* unique cause of any such phenomenon; a similar statement applies to causes of crime and suicide. Whatever the ultimate findings of pharmacologists and others now studying the drug, sociologists are unlikely to accept such an asocial and unicausal explanation of any form of complex social behavior. But if we refuse to accept the explanations of others we are obligated to provide one of our own. In what follows, I consider the reports of LSD-induced psychoses and try to relate them to what is known of the social psychology and sociology of drug use. By this means I hope to add both to our understanding of the current controversy over LSD and to our general knowledge of the social character of drug use.

In particular, I will make use of a comparison between LSD use and marijuana use, suggested by the early history of marihuana in this country. That history contains the same reports of "psychotic episodes" now current with respect to LSD. But reports of such episodes disappeared at the same time as the number of marihuana users increased greatly. This suggests the utility of considering the historical dimension of drug use.

I must add a cautionary disclaimer. I have not examined thoroughly the literature on LSD, which increases at an alarming rate.[3] What I have to say about it is necessarily speculative with respect to its effects; what I have to say about the conditions under which it is used is also speculative; but is based in part on interviews with a few users. I present no documented conclusions, but do hope that the perspective outlined may help orient research toward generalizations that will fit into the corpus of sociological and social psychological theory on related matters.

The Subjective Effects of Drugs

The physiological effects of drugs can be ascertained by standard techniques of physiological and pharmacological research. Scientists measure and have explanations for the actions of many drugs on such observable indices as the heart and respiratory rates, the level of various chemicals in the blood, and the secretion of enzymes and hormones. In contrast, the subjective changes produced by a drug can be ascertained only by asking the subject, in one way or another, how he feels. (To be sure, one can measure the drug's effect on certain measures of psychological functioning—the ability to perform some standardized task, such as placing pegs in a board or remembering nonsense syllables—but this does not tell us what the drug experience is like.)[4]

We take medically prescribed drugs because we believe they will cure or control a disease from which we are suffering; the subjective effects they produce are either ignored or defined as noxious side effects. But some people take some drugs precisely because they want to experience these subjective effects; they take them, to put it colloquially, because they want to get "high." These recreationally used drugs have become the focus of sociological research because the goal of an artificially induced change in consciousness seems to many immoral, and those who so believe have been able to transform their belief into law. Drug users thus come to sociological attention as lawbreakers, and the problems typically investigated have to do with explaining their lawbreaking.

Nevertheless, some sociologists, anthropologists and social psychologists have investigated the problem of drug-induced subjective experience in its own right. Taking their findings together, the following conclusions seem justified.[5] First, many drugs, including those used to produce changes in subjective experience, have a great variety of effects and the user may single out many of them, one of them, or none of them as definite experiences he is undergoing. He may be totally unaware of some of the drug's effects, even when they are physiologically gross, although in general the grosser the effects the harder they are to ignore. When he does perceive the effects, he may not attribute them to drug use but dismiss them as due to some other cause, such as fatigue or a cold. Marihuana users, for example, may not even be aware of the drug's effects when they first use it, even though it is obvious to others that they are experiencing them.[6]

Second, and in consequence, the effects of the same drug may be experienced quite differently by different people or by the same people at different times. Even if physiologically observable effects are substantially the same in all members of the species, individuals can vary widely in those to which they choose to pay attention. Thus, Aberle remarks on the quite different experiences Indians and experimental subjects have with peyote[7] and Blum reports a wide variety of experiences with LSD, depending on the circumstances under which it was taken.[8]

Third, since recreational users take drugs in order to achieve some subjective state not ordinarily available to them, it follows that they will expect and be most likely to experience those effects which produce a deviation from conventional perceptions and interpretations of internal and external experience. Thus, distortions in perception of time and space and shifts in judgments of the importance and meaning of ordinary events constitute the most common reported effects.

Fourth, any of a great variety of effects may be singled out by the user as desirable or pleasurable, as the effects for which he has taken the drug. Even effects which seem to the uninitiated to be uncomfortable, unpleasant or frightening—perceptual distortions or visual and auditory hallucinations—can be defined by users as a goal to be sought.[9]

Fifth, how a person experiences the effects of a drug depends greatly on the way others define those effects for him.[10] The total effect of a drug is likely to be a melange of differing physical and psychological sensations. If others whom the user believes to be knowledgeable single out certain effects as characteristic and dismiss others, he is likely to notice those they single out as characteristic of his own experience. If they define certain effects as transitory, he is likely to believe that those effects will go away. All this supposes, of course, that the definition offered the user can be validated in his own experience, that something contained in the drug-induced melange of sensations corresponds to it.

Such a conception of the character of the drug experience has its roots, obviously, in Mead's theory of the self and the relation of objects to the self.[11] In that theory, objects (including the self) have meaning for the person only as he imputes that meaning to them in the course of his interaction with them. The meaning is not given in the object, but is lodged there as the person acquires a conception of the kind of action that can be taken with, toward, by and for it. Meanings arise in the course of social interaction, deriving their character from the consensus participants develop about the object in question. The findings of such research on the character of drug-induced experience are therefore predictable from Mead's theory.

Drug Psychoses

The scientific literature and, even more, the popular press frequently state that recreational drug use produces a psychosis. The nature of "psychosis" is seldom defined, as though it were intuitively clear. Writers usually seem to mean a mental disturbance of some unspecified kind, involving auditory and visual hallucinations, an inability to control one's stream of thought, and a tendency to engage in socially inappropriate behavior, either because one has lost the sense that it is inappropriate or because one cannot stop oneself. In addition, and perhaps most important, psychosis is thought to be a state that will last long beyond the specific event that provoked it. However it occurred, it is thought to mark a more-or-less permanent change in the psyche and this, after all, is why we usually think of it as such a bad thing. Over-indulgence in alcohol produces many of the symptoms cited but this frightens no one because we understand that they will soon go away.

Verified reports of drug-induced psychoses are scarcer than one might think.[12] Nevertheless, let us assume that these reports have not been fabricated, but represent an interpretation by the reporter of something that really happened. In the light of the findings just cited, what kind of event can we imagine to have occurred that might have been interpreted as a "psychotic episode?" (I use the word "imagine" advisedly, for the available case reports usually do not furnish sufficient material to allow us to do more than imagine what might have happened.)

The most likely sequence of events is this. The inexperienced user has certain unusual subjective experiences, which he may or may not attribute to having taken the drug. He may find his perception of space distorted, so that he has difficulty climbing a flight of stairs. He may find his train of thought so confused that he is unable to carry on a normal conversation and hears himself making totally inappropriate remarks. He may see or hear things in a way that he suspects is quite different from the way others see and hear them.

Whether or not he attributes what is happening to the drug, the experiences are likely to be upsetting. One of the ways we know that we are normal human beings is that our perceptual world, on the evidence available to us, seems to be pretty much the same as other people's. We see and hear the same things, make the same kind of sense out of them and, where perceptions differ, can explain the difference by a difference in situation or perspective.[13] We may take for granted that the inexperienced drug user, though he wanted to get "high," did not expect an experience so radical as to call into question that common sense set of assumptions.

In any society whose culture contains notions of sanity and insanity, the person who finds his subjective state altered in the way described may think he has become insane. We learn at a young age that a person who "acts funny," "sees things," "hears things," or has other bizarre and unusual experiences may have become "crazy," "nuts," "loony" or a host of other synonyms.[14] When a drug user identifies some of these untoward events occurring in his own experience, he may decide that he merits one of those titles—that he has lost his grip on reality, his control of himself, and has in fact "gone crazy." The interpretation implies the corollary that the change is irreversible or, at least, that things are not going to be changed back very easily. The drug experience, perhaps originally intended as a momentary entertainment, now looms as a momentous event which will disrupt one's life, possibly permanently. Faced with this conclusion, the person develops a full-blown anxiety attack, but it is an anxiety caused by his reaction to the drug experience rather than a direct consequence of the drug use itself. (In this connection, it is interesting that, in the published reports of LSD psychoses, acute anxiety attacks appear as the largest category of untoward reactions.)[15]

It is perhaps easier to grasp what this must feel like if we imagine that, having taken several social drinks at a party, we were suddenly to see varicolored snakes peering out at us from behind the furniture. We would instantly recognize this as a sign of delirium tremens, and would no doubt become severely anxious at the prospect of having developed such a serious mental illness. Some such panic is likely to grip the recreational user of drugs who interprets his experience as a sign of insanity.

Though I have put the argument with respect to the inexperienced user, long-time users of recreational drugs sometimes have similar experiences. They may experiment with a higher dosage than they are used to and experience effects unlike anything they have known before. This can easily occur when using drugs purchased in the illicit market, where quality may vary greatly, so that the user inadvertently gets more than he can handle.

The scientific literature does not report any verified cases of people acting on their distorted perceptions so as to harm themselves and others, but such cases have been reported in the press. Press reports of drug-related events are very unreliable, but it may be that users have, for instance, stepped out of a second story window, deluded by the drug into thinking it only a few feet to the ground.[16] If such cases have occurred, they too may be interpreted as examples of psychosis, but a different mechanism than the one just discussed would be involved. The person, presumably, would have failed to make the necessary correction for the drug-induced distortion, a correction, however, that experienced users assert can be made. Thus, a novice marihuana user will find it difficult to drive while "high," but experienced users can control their thinking and actions so as to behave appropriately.[17] Although it is commonly assumed that a person under the influence of LSD must avoid ordinary social situations for 12 or more hours, I have been told[18] of at least one user who takes the drug and then goes to work; she explained that once you learn "how to handle it" (i.e., make the necessary corrections for distortions caused by the drug) there is no problem.

In short, the most likely interpretation we can make of the drug-induced psychoses reported is that they are either severe anxiety reactions to an event interpreted and experienced as insanity, or failures by the user to correct, in carrying out some ordinary action, for the perceptual distortions caused by the drug. If the interpretation is correct, then untoward mental effects produced by drugs depend in some part on its physiological action, but to a much larger degree find their origin in the definitions and conceptions the user applies to that action. These can vary with the individual's personal makeup, a possibility psychiatrists are most alive to, or with the groups he participates in, the trail I shall pursue here.

271

The Influence of Drug-Using Cultures

While there are no reliable figures, it is obvious that a very large number of people use recreational drugs, primarily marihuana and LSD. From the previous analysis one might suppose that, therefore, a great many people would have disquieting symptoms and, given the ubiquity in our society of the concept of insanity, that many would decide they had gone crazy and thus have a drug-induced anxiety attack. But very few such reactions occur. Although there must be more than are reported in the professional literature, it is unlikely that drugs have this effect in any large number of cases. If they did there would necessarily be many more verified accounts than are presently available. Since the psychotic reaction stems from a definition of the drug-induced experience, the explanation of this paradox must lie in the availability of competing definitions of the subjective states produced by drugs.

Competing definitions come to the user from other users who, to his knowledge, have had sufficient experience with the drug to speak with authority. He knows that the drug does not produce permanent disabling damage in all cases, for he can see that these other users do not suffer from it. The question, of course, remains whether it may not produce damage in some cases and whether his is one of them, no matter how rare.

When someone experiences disturbing effects, other users typically assure him that the change in his subjective experience is neither rare nor dangerous. They have seen similar reactions before, and may even have experienced them themselves with no lasting harm. In any event, they have some folk knowledge about how to handle the problem.

They may, for instance, know of an antidote for the frightening effects; thus, marihuana users, confronted with someone who had gotten "too high," encourage him to eat, an apparently effective countermeasure.[19] They talk reassuringly about their own experiences, "normalizing" the frightening symptom by treating it, matter-of-factly, as temporary. They maintain surveillance over the affected person, preventing any physically or socially dangerous activity. They may, for instance, keep him from driving or from making a public display that will bring him to the attention of the police or others who would disapprove of his drug use. They show him how to allow for the perceptual distortion the drug causes and teach him how to manage interaction with non-users.

They redefine the experience he is having as desirable rather than frightening, as the end for which the drug is taken.[20] What they tell him carries conviction, because he can see that it is not some idiosyncratic belief but is instead culturally shared. It is what "everyone" who uses the drug knows. In all these ways, experienced users prevent the episode from having lasting effects and reassure the novice that whatever he feels will come to a timely and harmless end.

The anxious novice thus has an alternative to defining his experience as "going crazy." He may redefine the event immediately or, having been watched over by others throughout the anxiety attack, decide that it was not so bad after all and not fear its reoccurrence. He "learns" that his original definition was "incorrect" and that the alternative offered by other users more nearly describes what he has experienced.

Available knowledge does not tell us how often this mechanism comes into play or how effective it is in preventing untoward psychological reactions; no research has been addressed to this point. In the case of marihuana, at least, the paucity of reported cases of permanent damage coupled with the undoubted increase in use suggests that it may be an effective mechanism.

For such a mechanism to operate, a number of conditions must be met. First, the drug must not produce, quite apart from the user's interpretations, permanent damage to the mind. No amount of social redefinition can undo the damage done by toxic alcohols, or the effects of a lethal dose of an opiate or barbituate. This analysis, therefore, does not apply to drugs known to have such effects.

272

Second, users of the drug must share a set of understandings—a culture—which includes, in addition to material on how to obtain and ingest the drug, definitions of the typical effects, the typical course of the experience, the permanence of the effects, and a description of methods for dealing with someone who suffers an anxiety attack because of drug use or attempts to act on the basis of distorted perceptions. Users should have available to them, largely through face-to-face participation with other users but possibly in such other ways as reading as well, the definitions contained in that culture, which they can apply in place of the common-sense definitions available to the inexperienced man in the street.

Third, the drug should ordinarily be used in group settings, where other users can present the definitions of the drug-using culture to the person whose inner experience is so unusual as to provoke use of the common-sense category of insanity. Drugs for which technology and custom promote group use should produce a lower incidence of "psychotic episodes."

The last two conditions suggest, as is the case, that marihuana, surrounded by an elaborate culture and ordinarily used in group settings, should produce few "psychotic" episodes.[21] At the same time, they suggest the prediction that drugs which have not spawned a culture and are ordinarily used in private, such as barbiturates, will produce more such episodes. I suggest possible research along these lines below.

Non-User Interpretations

A user suffering from drug-induced anxiety may also come into contact with non-users who will offer him definitions, depending on their own perspectives and experiences, that may validate the diagnosis of "going crazy" and thus prolong the episode, possibly producing relatively permanent disability. These non-users include family members and police, but most important among them are psychiatrists and psychiatrically oriented physicians. (Remember that when we speak of reported cases of psychosis, the report is ordinarily made by a physician, though police may also use the term in reporting a case of the press.)

Medical knowledge about the recreational use of drugs is spotty. Little research has been done, and its results are not at the fingertips of physicians who do not specialize in the area. (In the case of LSD, of course, there has been a good deal of research, but its conclusions are not clear and, in any case, have not yet been spread throughout the profession.) Psychiatrists are not anxious to treat drug users, so few of them have accumulated any clinical experience with the phenomenon. Nevertheless, a user who develops severe and uncontrollable anxiety will probably be brought, if he is brought anywhere, to a physician for treatment. Most probably, he will be brought to a psychiatric hospital, if one is available; if not, to a hospital emergency room, where a psychiatric resident will be called once the connection with drugs is established, or to a private psychiatrist.[22]

Physicians, confronted with a case of drug-induced anxiety and lacking specific knowledge of its character or proper treatment, rely on a kind of generalized diagnosis. They reason that people probably do not use drugs unless they are suffering from a severe underlying personality disturbance; that use of the drug may allow repressed conflicts to come into the open where they will prove unmanageable; that the drug in this way provokes a true psychosis; and, therefore, that the patient confronting them is psychotic. Furthermore, even though the effects of the drug wear off, the psychosis may not, for the repressed psychological problems it has brought to the surface may not recede as it is metabolized and excreted from the body.

Given such a diagnosis, the physician knows what to do. He hospitalizes the patient for observation and prepares, where possible, for long-term therapy designed to repair the damage done to the psychic defenses or to deal with the conflict unmasked by the drug. Both hospitalization and therapy are likely to reinforce the definition of the drug experience as insanity, for in both the patient will be required to "understand" that he is mentally ill as a precondition for return to the world.[23]

The physician then, does *not* treat the anxiety attack as a localized phenomenon, to be treated in a symptomatic way, but as an outbreak of a serious disease heretofore hidden. He may thus prolong the serious effects beyond the time they might have lasted had the user instead come into contact with other users. This analysis, of course, is frankly speculative; what is required is study of the way physicians treat cases of the kind described and, especially, comparative study of the effects of treatment of drug-induced anxiety attacks by physicians and by drug users.

Another category of non-users deserves mention. Literary men and journalists publicize definitions of drug experiences, either of their own invention or those borrowed from users, psychiatrists or police. (Some members of this category use drugs themselves, so it may be a little confusing to classify them as non-users; in any case, the definitions are provided outside the ordinary channels of communication in the drug-using world.) The definitions of literary men—novelists, essayists and poets—grow out of a long professional tradition, beginning with De Quincey's *Confessions,* and are likely to be colored by that tradition. Literary descriptions dwell on the fantasy component of the experience, on its cosmic and ineffable character, and on the threat of madness.[24] Such widely available definitions furnish some of the substance out of which a user may develop his own definition, in the absence of definitions from the drug-using culture.

Journalists use any of a number of approaches conventional in their craft; what they write is greatly influenced by their own professional needs. They must write about "news," about events which have occurred recently and require reporting and interpretation. Furthermore, they need "sources," persons to whom authoritative statements can be attributed. Both needs dispose them to reproduce the line taken by law enforcement officials and physicians, for news is often made by the passage of a law or by a public statement in the wake of an alarming event, such as a bizarre murder or suicide. So journalistic reports frequently dwell on the theme of madness or suicide, a tendency intensified by the newsman's desire to tell a dramatic story.[25] Some journalists, of course, will take the other side in the argument, but even then, because they argue against the theme of madness, the emphasis on that theme is maintained. Public discussion of drug use tends to strengthen those stereotypes that would lead users who suffer disturbing effects to interpret their experience as "going crazy."

An Historical Dimension

A number of variables, then, affect the character of drug-induced experiences. It remains to show that the experiences themselves are likely to vary according to when they occur in the history of use of a given drug in a society. In particular, it seems likely that the experience of acute anxiety caused by drug use will so vary.

Consider the following sequence of possible events, which may be regarded as a natural history of the assimilation of an intoxicating drug by a society. Someone in the society discovers, rediscovers or invents a drug which has the properties described earlier. The ability of the drug to alter subjective experience in desirable ways becomes known to increasing numbers of people, and the drug itself simultaneously becomes available, along with the information needed to make its use effective. Use increases, but users do not have a sufficient amount of experience with the drug to form a stable conception of it as an object. They do not know what it can do to the mind, have no firm idea of the variety of effects it can produce, and are not sure how permanent or dangerous the effects are. They do not know if the effects can be controlled or how. No drug-using culture exists, and there is thus no authoritative alternative with which to counter the possible definition, when and if it comes to mind, of the drug experience as madness. "Psychotic episodes" occur frequently.

But individuals accumulate experience with the drug and communicate their experiences to one another. Consensus develops about the drug's subjective effects, their duration, proper dosages, predictable dangers and how they may be avoided; all these points become matters of common knowledge, validated by their acceptance in a world of users. A culture exists. When a user experiences bewildering or frightening effects, he has available to him an authoritative alternative to the lay notion that he has gone mad. Every time he uses cultural conceptions to interpret drug experiences and control his response to them, he strengthens his belief that the culture is indeed a reliable source of knowledge. "Psychotic episodes" occur less frequently in proportion to the growth of the culture to cover the range of possible effects and its spread to a greater proportion of users. Novice users, to whom the effects are most unfamiliar and who therefore might be expected to suffer most from drug-induced anxiety, learn the culture from older users in casual conversation and in more serious teaching sessions and are thus protected from the dangers of "panicking" or "flipping out."

The incidence of "psychoses," then, is a function of the stage of development of a drug-using culture. Individual experience varies with historical stages and the kinds of cultural and social organization associated with them.

Is this model a useful guide to reality? The only drug for which there is sufficient evidence to attempt an evaluation is marihuana; even there the evidence is equivocal, but it is consistent with the model. On this interpretation, the early history of marihuana use in the United States should be marked by reports of marihuana-induced psychoses. In the absence of a fully formed drug-using culture, some users would experience disquieting symptoms and have no alternative to the idea that they were losing their minds. They would turn up at psychiatric facilities in acute states of anxiety and doctors, eliciting a history of marihuana use, would interpret the episode as a psychotic breakdown. When, however, the culture reached full flower and spread throughout the user population, the number of psychoses should have dropped even though (as a variety of evidence suggests) the number of users increased greatly. Using the definitions made available by the culture, users who had unexpectedly severe symptoms could interpret them in such a way as to reduce or control anxiety and would thus no longer come to the attention of those likely to report them as cases of psychosis.

Marihuana first came into use in the United States in the 1920's and early '30's, and all reports of psychosis associated with its use date from approximately that period.[26] A search of both *Psychological Abstracts* and the *Cumulative Index Medicus* (and its predecessors, the *Current List of Medical Literature* and the *Quarterly Index Medicus*) revealed no cases after 1940. The disappearance of reports of psychosis thus fits the model. It is, of course, a shaky index, for it depends as much on the reporting habits of physicians as on the true incidence of cases, but it is the only thing available.

The psychoses described also fit the model, insofar as there is any clear indication of a drug-induced effect. (The murder, suicide and death in an automobile accident reported by Curtis, for instance, are equivocal in this respect; in no case is any connection with marihuana use demonstrated other than that the people involved used it.)[27] The best evidence comes from the 31 cases reported by Bromberg. Where the detail given allows judgment, it appears that all but one stemmed from the person's inability to deal with either the perceptual distortion caused by the drug or with the panic at the thought of losing one's mind it created.[28] Bromberg's own interpretation supports this:

> In occasional instances, and these are the cases which are apt to come to medical attention, the anxiety with regard to death, insanity, bodily deformity and bodily dissolution is startling. The patient is tense, nervous, frightened; a state of panic may develop. Often suicide or assaultive acts are the result [of the panic]. The anxiety state is so common . . . that it can be considered a part of the intoxication syndrome.[29]
>
> The inner relationship between cannabis [marihuana] and the onset of a functional psychotic state is not always clear. The inner reaction to somatic sensation seems vital. Such reactions consisted of panic states which disappeared as soon as the stimulus (effects of the drug) faded.[30]

Even though Bromberg distinguishes between pure panic reactions and those in which some underlying mental disturbance was present (the "functional psychotic state" he refers to), he finds, as our model leads us to expect, that the episode is provoked by the user's interpretation of the drug effects in terms other than those contained in the drug-using culture.

The evidence cited is extremely scanty. We do not know the role of elements of the drug-using culture in any of these cases or whether the decrease in incidence is a true one. But we are not likely to do any better and, in the absence of conflicting evidence, it seems justified to take the model as an accurate representation of the history of marihuana use in the United States.

The final question, then, is whether the model can be used to interpret current reports of LSD-induced psychosis. Are these episodes the consequence of an early stage in the development of an LSD-using culture? Will the number of episodes decrease while the number of users rises, as the model leads us to predict?

LSD

We cannot predict the history of LSD by direct analogy to the history of marihuana, for a number of important conditions may vary. We must first ask whether the drug has, apart from the definitions users impose on their experience, any demonstrated causal relation to psychosis. There is a great deal of controversy on this point, and any reading of the evidence must be tentative. My own opinion is that LSD has essentially the same characteristics as those described in the first part of this paper; its effects may be more powerful than those of other drugs that have been studied, but they too are subject to differing interpretations by users,[31] so that the mechanisms I have described can come into play.

The cases reported in the literature are, like those reported for marihuana, mostly panic reactions to the drug experience, occasioned by the user's interpretation that he has lost his mind, or further disturbance among people already quite disturbed.[32] There are no cases of permanent derangement directly traceable to the drug, with one puzzling exception (puzzling to those who report it as well as to me). In a few cases the visual and auditory distortions produced by the drug reoccur weeks or months after it was last ingested; this sometimes produces severe upset among those who experience it. Observers are at a loss to explain the phenomenon, except for Rosenthal, who proposes that the drug may have a specific effect on the nerve pathways involved in vision; but this theory, should it prove correct, is a long way from dealing with questions of possible psychosis.[33]

The whole question is confused by the extraordinary assertions about the effects of LSD made by both proponents and opponents of its use. Both sides agree that it has a very strong effect on the mind, disagreeing only as to whether this powerful effect is benign or malignant. Leary, for example, argues that we must "go out of our minds to use our heads,"[34] and that this can be accomplished by using LSD. Opponents[35] agree that it can drive you out of your mind, but do not share Leary's view that this is a desirable goal. In any case, we need not accept the premise simply because both parties to the controversy do.

Let us assume then, in the absence of more definitive evidence, that the drug does not in itself produce lasting derangement, that such psychotic episodes as are now reported are largely a result of panic at the possible meaning of the experience, that users who "freak out" do so because they fear they have permanently damaged their minds. Is there an LSD-using culture? In what stage of development is it? Are the reported episodes of psychosis congruent with what our model would predict, given that stage of development?

Here again my discussion must be speculative, for no serious study of this culture is yet available.[36] It appears likely, however, that such a culture is in an early stage of development. Several conceptions of the drug and its possible effects exists, but no stable consensus has arisen. Radio, television and the popular press present a variety of interpretations, many of them contradictory. There is widespread disagreement, even among users, about possible dangers. Some certainly believe that use (or injudicious use) can lead to severe mental difficulty.

At the same time, my preliminary inquiries and observations hinted at the development (or at least the beginnings) of a culture similar to that surrounding marihuana use. Users with some experience discuss their symptoms and translate from one idiosyncratic description into another, developing a common conception of effects as they talk. The notion that a "bad trip" can be brought to a speedy conclusion by taking thorazine by mouth (or, when immediate action is required, intravenously) has spread. Users are also beginning to develop a set of safeguards against committing irrational acts while under the drug's influence. Many feel, for instance, that one should take one's "trip" in the company of experienced users who are not under the drug's influence at the time; they will be able to see you through bad times and restrain you when necessary. A conception of the appropriate dose is rapidly becoming common knowledge. Users understand that they may have to "sit up with" people who have panicked as a result of the drug's effects, and they talk of techniques that have proved useful in this enterprise.[37] All this suggests that a common conception of the drug is developing which will eventually see it defined as pleasurable and desirable, with possible untoward effects that can however be controlled.

Insofar as this emergent culture spreads so that most or all users share the belief that LSD does not cause insanity, and the other understandings just listed, the incidence of "psychoses" should drop markedly or disappear. Just as with marihuana, the interpretation of the experience as one likely to produce madness will disappear and, having other definitions available to use in coping with the experience, users will treat the experience as self-limiting and not as a cause for panic.

The technology of LSD use, however, has features which will work in the opposite direction. In the first place, it is very easily taken; one need learn no special technique (as one must with marihuana) to produce the characteristic effects, for a sugar cube can be swallowed without instruction. This means that anyone who gets hold of the drug can take it in a setting where there are no experienced users around to redefine frightening effects and "normalize" them. He may also have acquired the drug without acquiring any of the presently developing cultural under-standings so that, when frightening effects occur, he is left with nothing but current lay conceptions as plausible definitions. In this connection, it is important that a large amount of the published material by journalists and literary men places heavy emphasis on the dangers of psychosis.[38] It is also important that various medical facilities have become alerted to the possibility of patients (particularly college students and teenagers) coming in with LSD-induced psychoses. All these factors will tend to increase the incidence of "psychotic episodes," perhaps sufficiently to offset the dampening effect of the developing culture.

A second feature of LSD which works in the opposite direction is that it can be administered to someone without his knowledge, since it is colorless, tasteless and odorless. (This possibility is recognized in recent state legislation which specifies *knowing* use as a crime; no such distinction has been found necessary in laws about marihuana, heroin, peyote or similar drugs.) It is reported, for instance, that LSD has been put in a party punchbowl, so that large numbers of people have suffered substantial changes in their subjective experience without even knowing they had been given a drug that might account for the change. Under such circumstances, the tendency to in-terpret the experience as a sudden attack of insanity might be very strong.[39] If LSD continues to be available on the underground market without much difficulty, such events are likely to continue to occur. (A few apocalyptic types speak of introducing LSD into a city water supply—not at all impossible, since a small amount will affect enormous quantities of water—and thus "turning a whole city on." This might provoke a vast number of "psychoses," should it ever happen.)

In addition to these technological features, many of the new users of LSD, unlike the users of most illicit recreational drugs, will be people who, in addition to never having used any drug to alter their subjective experience before, will have had little or nothing to do with others who have used drugs in that way. LSD, after all, was introduced into the United States under very reputable auspices and has had testimonials from many reputable and conventional persons. In addition, there has been a great deal of favorable publicity to accompany the less favorable—the possibility that the drug can do good as well as harm has been spread in a fashion that never occurred with marihuana. Finally, LSD has appeared at a time when the mores governing illicit drug use among young people seem to be changing radically, so that youth no longer reject drugs out of hand. Those who try LSD may thus not even have had the preliminary instruction in being "high" that most novice marihuana users have before first using it. They will, consequently, be less prepared for the experience they have. (This suggests the prediction that marihuana users who experiment with LSD will show fewer untoward reactions than those who have had no such experience.)[40]

These features of the drug make it difficult to predict the number of mental upsets likely to be "caused" by LSD. If use grows, the number of people exposed to the possibility will grow. As an LSD-using culture develops, the proportion of those exposed who interpret their experience as one of insanity will decrease. But people may use the drug without being indoctrinated with the new cultural definitions, either because of the ease with which the drug can be taken or because it has been given to them without their knowledge, in which case the number of episodes will rise. The actual figure will be a vector made up of these several components.

A Note on the Opiates

The opiate drugs present an interesting paradox. In the drugs we have been considering, the development of a drug-using culture causes a decrease in rates of morbidity associated with drug use, for greater knowledge of the true character of the drug's effects lessens the likelihood that users will respond to those effects with uncontrolled anxiety. In the case of opiates, however, the greater one's knowledge of the drug's effects, the more likely it is that one will suffer its worst effect, addiction. As Lindesmith has shown,[41] one can only be addicted when he experiences physiological withdrawal symptoms, recognizes them as due to a need for drugs, and relieves them by taking another dose. The crucial step of recognition is most likely to occur when the user participates in a culture in which the signs of withdrawal are interpreted for what they are. When a person is ignorant of the nature of withdrawal sickness, and has some other cause to which he can attribute his discomfort (such as a medical problem), he may misinterpret the symptoms and thus escape addiction, as some of Lindesmith's cases demonstrate.[42]

This example makes clear how important the actual physiology of the drug response is in the model I have developed. The culture contains interpretations of the drug experience, but these must be congruent with the drug's actual effects. Where the effects are varied and ambiguous, as with marihuana and LSD, a great variety of interpretations is possible. Where the effects are clear and unmistakable, as with opiates, the culture is limited in the possible interpretations it can provide. Where the cultural interpretation is so constrained, and the effect to be interpreted leads, in its most likely interpretation, to morbidity, the spread of a drug-using culture will increase morbidity rates.

Conclusion

The preceding analysis, to repeat, is supported at only a few points by available research; most of what has been said is speculative. The theory, however, gains credibility in several ways. Many of its features follow directly from a Meadian social psychology and the general plausibility of that scheme lends it weight. Furthermore, it is consistent with much of what social scientists have discovered about the nature of drug-induced experiences. In addition, the theory makes sense of some commonly reported and otherwise inexplicable phenomena, such as variations in the number of "psychotic" episodes attributable to recreational drug use. Finally, and much the least important, it is in accord with my haphazard and informal observations of LSD use.

The theory also has the virtue of suggesting a number of specific lines of research. With respect to the emerging "social problem" of LSD use, it marks out the following areas for investigation: the relation between social settings of use, the definitions of the drug's effects available to the user, and the subjective experiences produced by the drug; the mechanisms by which an LSD-using culture arises and spreads; the difference in experiences of participants and non-participants in that culture; the influence of each of the several factors described on the number of harmful effects attributable to the drug; and the typical response of physicians to LSD-induced anxiety states and the effect of that response as compared to the response made by experienced drug culture participants.

The theory indicates useful lines of research with respect to other common drugs as well. Large numbers of people take tranquilizers, barbiturates and amphetamines. Some frankly take them for "kicks" and are participants in drug-using cultures built around those drugs, while others are respectable middleclass citizens who probably do not participate in any "hip" user culture. Do these "square" users have some shared cultural understandings of their own with respect to use of these drugs? What are the differential effects of the drugs—both on subjective experience and on rates of morbidity associated with drug use—among the two classes of users? How do physicians handle the pathological effects of these drugs, with which they are relatively familiar, as compared to their handling of drugs which are only available illicitly?

The theory may have implications for the study of drugs not ordinarily used recreationally as well. Some drugs used in ordinary medical practice (such as the adrenocortical steroids) are said to carry a risk of provoking psychosis. It may be that this danger arises when the drug produces changes in subjective experience which the user does not anticipate, does not connect with the drug, and thus interprets as signs of insanity. Should the physician confirm this by diagnosing a "drug psychosis," a vicious circle of increasing validation of the diagnosis may ensue. The theory suggests that the physician using such drugs might do well to inquire carefully into the feelings that produce such anxiety reactions, interpret them to the patient as common, transient and essentially harmless side effects, and see whether such action would not control the phenomenon. Drugs that have been incriminated in this fashion would make good subjects for research designed to explore some of the premises of the argument made here.

The sociologist may find most interesting the postulated connection between historical stages in the development of a culture and the nature of individual subjective experience. Similar linkages might be discovered in the study of political and religious movements. For example, at what stages in the development of such movements are individuals likely to experience euphoric and ecstatic feelings? How are these related to shifts in the culture and organization of social relations within the movement? The three-way link between history, culture and social organization, and the person's subjective state may point the way to a better understanding than we now have of the social bases of individual experience.

Notes

1. See "D-lysergic Acid Diethylamide—LSD," *Sandoz Excerpta,* 1 (1955), pp. 1–2, quoted in Sanford M. Unger, "Mescaline, LSD, Psilocybin and Personality Change," in David Solomon, editor, *LSD: The Consciousness-Expanding Drug,* New York: Berkley Publishing Corp., 1966, p. 206.
2. On this point, to which I return later, the major references are Sydney Cohen, "Lysergic Acid Diethylamide: Side Effects and Complications," *Journal of Nervous and Mental Diseases,* 130 (January, 1960), pp. 30–40; Sydney Cohen and Keith S. Ditman, "Prolonged Adverse Reactions to Lysergic Acid Diethylamide," *Archives of General Psychiatry,* 8 (1963), pp. 475–480; Sydney Cohen and Keith S. Ditman, "Complications Associated with Lysergic Acid Diethylamide (LSD-25)," *Journal of the American Medical Association,* 181 (July 14, 1962), pp. 161–162; William A. Frosch, Edwin S. Robbins and Marvin Stern, "Untoward Reactions to Lysergic Acid Diethylamide (LSD) Resulting in Hospitalization," *New England Journal of Medicine,* 273 (December 2, 1965), pp. 1235–1239; A. Hoffer, "D-Lysergic Acid Diethylamide (LSD): A Review of its Present Status," *Clinical Pharmacology and Therapeutics,* 6 (March, 1965), pp. 183–255; S. H. Rosenthal, "Persistent Hallucinosis Following Repeated Administration of Hallucinogenic Drugs," *American Journal of Psychiatry,* 121 (1964), pp. 238–244; and J. Thomas Ungerleider, Duke D. Fisher and Marielle Fuller, "The Dangers of LSD: Analysis of Seven Months' Experience in a University Hospital's Psychiatric Service," *Journal of the American Medical Association,* 197 (August 8, 1966), pp. 389–392.
3. Hoffer's recent review of this literature, for which he disclaims completeness, cites 411 references (Hoffer, *op. cit.*)
4. See, for instance: New York City Mayor's Committee on Marihuana, *The Marihuana Problem in the City of New York,* Lancaster: Jacques Cattell Press, 1944, pp. 69–77; and C. Knight Aldrich, "The Effect of a Synthetic Marihuana-Like Compound on Musical Talent as Measured by the Seashore Test," *Public Health Reports,* 59 (1944), pp. 431–433.
5. I rely largely on the following reports: Howard S. Becker, *Outsiders,* New York: The Free Press, 1963, pp. 41–58 (marihuana); Alfred R. Lindesmith, *Opiate Addiction,* Bloomington: Principia Press, 1947 (opiates); Richard Blum and associates, *Utopiates,* New York: Atherton Press, 1964 (LSD); Ralph Metzner, George Litwin and Gunther M. Weil, "The Relation of Expectation and Mood to Psilocybin Reactions: A Questionnaire Study," *Psychedelic Review,* No. 5, 1965, pp. 3–39 (psilocybin); David F. Aberle, *The Peyote Religion Among the Navaho,* Chicago: Aldine Publishing Co., 1966, pp. 5–11 (peyote);

Stanley Schacter and Jerome E. Singer, "Cognitive, Social and Physiological Determinants of Emotional State," *Psychological Review,* 69 (September, 1962), pp. 379–399 (adrenalin); and Vincent Newlis and Helen H. Newlis, "The Description and Analysis of Mood," *Annals of the New York Academy of Science,* 65 (1956), pp. 345–355 (benzedrine, seconal and dramamine).

Schacter and Singer propose a similar approach to mine to the study of drug experiences, stressing the importance of the label the person attaches to the experience he is having.

6. Becker, *op. cit.*
7. Aberle, *op cit.*, and Anthony F. C. Wallace, "Cultural Determinants of Response to Hallucinatory Experience," *Archives of General Psychiatry,* (July, 1959), pp. 58–69 (especially Table 2 on p. 62). Wallace argues that ". . . both the subjective feeling tone and the specific content of the hallucination are heavily influenced by . . . the cultural milieu in which the hallucination, and particularly the voluntary hallucination, takes place." (p. 62).
8. Blum, *et al., op. cit.*, p. 42.
9. See the case cited in Becker, *op. cit.*, pp. 55–56.
10. The studies cited in footnote 5, *supra,* generally make this point.
11. See George Herbert Mead, *Mind, Self and Society,* Chicago: University of Chicago Press, 1934, and Herbert Blumer, "Sociological Implications of the Thought of George Herbert Mead," *American Journal of Sociology,* 71 (March 1966), pp. 535–544.
12. See the studies cited in footnote 2, *supra,* and the following reports of marihuana psychoses: Walter Bromberg, "Marihuana: A Psychiatric Study," *Journal of the American Medical Association,* 113 (July 1, 1939), pp. 4–12; Howard C. Curtis, "Psychosis Following the Use of Marihuana with Report of Cases," *Journal of the Kansas Medical Society,* 40 (1939), pp. 515–517; and Marjorie Nesbit, "Psychosis Due to Exogenous Poisons," *Illinois Medical Journal,* 77 (1940), 278–281.
13. See Alfred Schutz, *Collected Papers,* vols I and II, The Hague: Martinus Nijhoof, 1962 and 1964, and Harold Garfinkel, "A Conception of and Experiments with 'Trust' as a Condition of Stable Concerted Actions," in O. J. Harvey, editor, *Motivation and Social Interaction,* New York: Ronald Press Co., 1963, pp. 187–238.
14. See Thomas J. Scheff, *Being Mentally Ill: A Sociological Theory,* Chicago: Aldine Publishing Co., 1966.
15. See Frosch, *et al., op. cit.,* Cohen and Ditman, "Prolonged Adverse Reactions . . . ," *op. cit.,* and Ungerleider, *et al., op. cit.* It is not always easy to make a judgment, due to the scanty presentation of the material, and some of the reactions I count as anxiety are placed in these sources under different headings. Bromberg, *op. cit.,* makes a good case that practically all adverse reactions to marihuana can be traced to this kind of anxiety, and I think it likely that the same reasoning could be applied to the LSD reports, so that such reactions as "hallucination," "depression" and confused (to use Ungerleider's categories) are probably reactions to anxiety.
16. Although LSD is often said to provoke suicide, there is very little evidence of this. Cohen, *op. cit.,* after surveying 44 investigators who had used LSD with over 5,000 patients, says that the few cases reported all occurred among extremely disturbed patients who might have done it anyway; Hoffer, *op. cit.,* remarks that the number is so low that it might be argued that LSD actually lowers the rate among mental patients. Ungerleider reports that 10 of 70 cases were suicidal or suicide attempts, but gives no further data.
17. See Becker, *op. cit.,* pp. 66–72.
18. By David Oppenheim.
19. Cf. the New York City Mayor's Committee on Marihuana, *op. cit.,* p. 13. "The smoker determines for himself the point of being 'high,' and is over-conscious of preventing himself from becoming "too high." This fear of being 'too high' must be associated with some form of anxiety which causes the smoker, should he accidentally reach that point, immediately to institute measures so that he can 'come down.' It has been found that the use of beverages such as beer, or a sweet soda pop, is an effective measure. A cold shower will also have the effect of bringing the person 'down.' "
20. *Ibid.,* and Becker, *op. cit.*
21. I discuss the evidence on this point below.
22. It may be that a disproportionate number of cases will be brought to certain facilities. Ungerleider, *et al., op. cit.,* say (p. 392): "A larger number of admissions, both relative and real, than in other facilities in the Los Angeles area suggests the prevalence of a rumor that 'UCLA takes care of acid heads,' as several of our patients have told us."

23. See Thomas Szasz, *The Myth of Mental Illness,* New York: Paul B. Hoeber, Inc., 1961.
24. For a classic in the genre, see Fitzhugh Ludlow, *The Hasheesh Eater,* New York: Harper and Brothers, 1857. A more modern example is Alan Harrington, "A Visit to Inner Space," in Solomon, *op. cit.,* pp. 72–102.
25. Examples are J. Kobler, "Don't Fool Around with LSD," *Saturday Evening Post,* 236 (November 2, 1963), pp. 30–32, and Noah Gordon, "The Hallucinogenic Drug Cult," *The Reporter,* 29 (August 15, 1963), pp. 35–43.
26. Bromberg, *op. cit.,* Curtis, *op. cit.,* and Nesbit, *op. cit.*
27. Curtis, *op. cit.*
28. See Table 1 in Bromberg, *op. cit.,* pp. 6–7.
29. *Ibid.,* p. 5.
30. *Ibid.,* pp. 7–8.
31. Blum, *et al., op. cit.,* p. 42.
32. See footnote 2, *supra.*
33. Rosenthal, *op. cit.*
34. Timothy Leary, "Introduction" to Solomon, *op. cit.,* p. 13.
35. Frosch, *et al., op. cit.* and Ungerleider, *et al., op. cit.*
36. The book by Blum, *et al., op. cit.,* attempts this, but leaves many important questions untouched.
37. Ungerleider, *et al.,* deny the efficacy of these techniques (pp. 391–392): "How do we know that persons taking LSD in a relaxed friendly environment with an experienced guide or 'sitter' will have serious side effects? We have no statistical data to answer this, but our impression (from our weekly group sessions) is that bad experiences were common with or without sitters and with or without 'the right environment.' This does not minimize the importance of suggestion in the LSD experience."
38. For journalistic accounts, see Kobler, *op. cit.;* Gordon, *op. cit.;* R. Coughlan, "Chemical Mind-Changers," *Life,* 54 (March 15, 1963); and H. Asher, "They Split My Personality," *Saturday Review,* 46 (June 1, 1963), pp. 39–43. See also two recent novels in which LSD plays a major role: B. H. Friedman, *Yarborough,* New York: Knopf, 1964; and Alan Harrington, *The Secret Swinger,* New York: World Publishing Co., 1966.
39. Cf. Cohen and Ditman, "Complications. . . . ," *op. cit.,* p. 161: "Accidental ingestion of the drug by individuals who are unaware of its nature has already occurred. This represents a maximally stressful event because the perceptual and ideational distortions then occur without the saving knowledge that they were drug induced and temporary."
40. Negative evidence is found in Ungerleider, *et al., op. cit.* Twenty-five of their 70 cases had previously used marihuana.
41. Lindesmith, *op. cit.*
42. *Ibid.,* cases 3, 5 and 6 (pp. 68–69, 71, 72).

Chapter VII
Heroin

Heroin was first produced in 1898. It was named for its "heroic" powers to cure morphine addiction, which was widespread in America because of its medical use during the Civil War. Heroin is chemically derived from morphine and then smuggled into the United States from Southeast Asia, Mexico, the Far East, the Middle East, and Europe. Like other opiate-derivatives (morphine, codeine, laudanum, etc.), heroin is a potent painkiller which reduces sensory perception and depresses bodily functions. It is also highly addicting, however, in its pure form it is relatively nontoxic—unlike alcohol and tobacco. Heroin has a fairly narrow safety zone between an effective and life-threatening dose, thus "overdoses" are a real medical concern.

Typically, heroin addicts inject heroin that is only about 5 percent pure. The imminent medical dangers of heroin, including overdoses, result not from the drug itself but from the way in which addicts use the drug and the way they live their lives. Common addict medical problems like tetanus, hepatitis, pneumonia, gangrene and even many of the "overdoses" are generally related to the social circumstances of the addicts' world and, more specifically, the way they inject drugs with needles that are usually unsterile and often shared. The most life threatening problem addicts face today—high risk for contracting AIDS—also results from their use of shared needles and their lifestyle.

The selections in this chapter focus on the world of the addicts and their impact on the larger community. None of the serious social problems discussed in these readings—crime, unsuccessful treatment programs, an ineffectual criminal justice system, and AIDS—need to be the serious problems that they are. Rather, these problems largely exist as a consequence of the black market for heroin and the way addicts use the drug. This black market, in turn, thrives because heroin is totally prohibited; the high cost of heroin, its low purity, and the addict subculture are all a result of heroin's legal status and ineffective treatment programs.

The first article by Faupel and Klockars examines the complicated drug-crime connection by addressing the classic policy debate regarding the heroin addict's extensive criminal activity; does addiction promote criminal activity because of the heavy financial burden placed on the addict which cannot be met through normal jobs or is it prior involvement in a criminal subculture that promotes criminal solutions to financing drug habits? The authors' findings have serious implications for treatment and enforcement alternatives. The selection by Johnson and colleagues pursues the themes of treatment and law enforcement. They show that the two major avenues of social control for addicts, methadone maintenance treatment programs and the criminal justice system, are successfully "avoided" by addicts.

The third article by Des Jarlais and Friedman is a very sobering and important contribution to understanding why intravenous drug users are a major risk group for AIDS in the United States. About one-quarter of the adult cases of AIDS in the United States occur among intravenous drug users. While these figures are alarming, Des Jarlais and Friedman point to strategies of AIDS risk reduction which clearly follow from a sociological understanding of the behavioral factors they cite.

26. Drugs-Crime Connections: Elaborations from the Life Histories of Hard-Core Heroin Addicts*

Charles E. Faupel
Carl B. Klockars

The debate over the nature and extent of the relationship between heroin use and criminal activity is a long-standing one which has generated a voluminous literature. A 1980 survey (Gandossey et al., 1980) lists over 450 citations to books, articles, and research reports which directly or indirectly bear upon the heroin-crime relationship. Since 1980 the study of this relationship has continued, and several large-scale quantitative studies (Anglin and Speckart, 1984; Ball et al., 1981, 1983; Collins et al., 1984, 1985; Johnson et al., 1985) generally support the thesis that an increase in criminality commonly occurs in conjunction with increased heroin use in the United States. These studies, together with a host of others preceding them (e.g., Ball and Snarr, 1969; Chein et al., 1964; Inciardi, 1979; McGlothlin et al., 1978; Nash, 1973; Weissman et al., 1974) have moved the focus of the debate from the empirical question of whether or not there is a heroin-crime connection to empirical and theoretical questions about the dynamics of that connection.

In particular, two hypotheses, neither of which is new, currently occupy center stage in the drugs-crime controversy. The first, stated by Tappan a quarter of a century ago, maintains that the "addict of lower socio-economic class is a criminal primarily because illicit narcotics are costly and because he can secure his daily requirements only by committing crimes that will pay for them" (1960:65–66). This hypothesis maintains that heroin addict criminality is a consequence of addiction, albeit an indirect one. As physical dependence upon and tolerance for heroin increase, and the cost of progressively larger dosages of heroin increase proportionally, the addict is driven to criminal means to satisfy his or her habit. Empirically, this hypothesis predicts a linear increase in heroin consumption and a corresponding increase in criminal activity necessary to support it. In contrast, a second hypothesis maintains that the "principal explanation for the association between drug abuse and crime . . . is likely to be found in the subcultural attachment" (Goldman, 1981:162) comprised of the criminal associations, identifications, and activities of those persons who eventually become addicted. The basis for this hypothesis can only be understood in the context of the contemporary socio-legal milieu in which narcotics use takes place. Since the criminalization of heroin in 1914, the social world of narcotics has become increasingly intertwined with the broader criminal subculture (Musto, 1973). Consequently, would-be narcotics users inevitably associate with other criminals in the highly criminal copping areas of inner cities, and, indeed, are often recruited from delinquent and criminal networks. Through these criminal associations, therefore, the individual is introduced to heroin, and both crime and heroin use are facilitated and maintained. Empirically, this second hypothesis predicts increases in heroin use following or coinciding with periods of criminal association and activity.

From Charles E. Faupel and Carl B. Klockars, DRUGS-CRIME CONNECTIONS: ELABORATIONS FROM THE LIFE-HISTORIES OF HARD-CORE HEROIN ADDICTS. Copyright © 1987 by the Society for the Study of Social Problems. Reprinted from *Social Problems*, Vol. 34, No. 1, February, 1987, pp. 54–68, by permission.

A shorthand title for the first hypothesis is "Drugs cause crimes"; for the second "Crimes cause drugs." Each, as we shall see below, is subject to a number of qualifications and reservations; but each, as we shall also see below, continues to mark a rather different approach to understanding the drugs-crime connection. Furthermore, each hypothesis has quite different policy implications associated with it.

Methodology

Our contribution to understanding the dynamics of the drugs-crime connection is based upon life-history interviews with 32 hard core heroin addicts in the Wilmington, Delaware area. We purposely selected the respondents on the basis of their extensive involvement in the heroin subculture. All of the respondents had extensive contact with the criminal justice system. At the time of interview, 24 of the 32 respondents were incarcerated or under some form of correctional authority supervision (e.g., supervised custody, work release, parole, or probation). While this places certain limits on the generalizations that can be made from these data, the focus of this study is the dynamics of addiction among heavily-involved street addicts. For example, controlled users or "chippers" will not have experienced many of the dynamics reported here. Similarly, physicians, nurses, and middle class "prescription abusers" are not typically subject to many of the constraints experienced by lower-class street users. Hence, it is important to emphasize that the findings we report here are intended to describe "hard core" urban heroin addicts.

Women are slightly overrepresented, constituting 14 of the 32 respondents. Ethnically, the sample consists of 23 blacks and nine whites; Hispanics are not represented because there is not a sizable Hispanic drug-using population in the Wilmington area.

Respondents were paid five dollars per hour for their interview time, which undoubtedly contributed to the 100 percent response rate. The interviews ranged from 10 to 25 hours in length, with each interview session averaging between three and four hours. With a single exception, all of the interviews were tape recorded and transcribed. Respondents were promised confidentiality and, without exception, they spoke openly of their drug, crime, and life-history experience.

The incarcerated respondents and most of the street respondents were selected with the aid of treatment personnel who were carefully instructed regarding the goals of the research and selection criteria. This strategy proved invaluable for two reasons. First, by utilizing treatment personnel in the screening process, we were able to avoid the time-consuming task of establishing the "appropriateness" of respondents for the purposes of this research; the treatment personnel were already intimately familiar with the drug-using and criminal histories of the respondents. Second, the treatment personnel had an unusually positive relationship with Wilmington-area drug users. The treatment counselor in the prison system was regarded as an ally in the quest for better living conditions, appeals for early release, etc., and was regarded as highly trustworthy in the prison subculture. His frequent confrontations with prison authorities over prisoner rights and privileges enhanced his reputation among the inmates. Similarly, the treatment counselor who aided in the selection of street respondents was carefully selected on the basis of his positive involvement with street addicts. His relationship with area addicts is a long-standing and multifaceted one. His reputation among street addicts was firmly established when he successfully negotiated much needed reforms in one of the local treatment agencies. Because of the long-standing positive relationship they had with area addicts, this initial contact by treatment personnel greatly facilitated our establishing necessary rapport.

After a few initial interviews were completed, several broad focal areas emerged which formed the basis for future questioning. Respondents were interviewed regarding: (1) childhood and early adolescent experiences which may have served as *predisposing factors* for eventual drugs/criminal involvement; (2) *initial encounters* with various types of drugs and criminality; (3) the *evolution* of their drug and criminal careers; (4) their patterns of activity during *peak periods* of drug use and criminality, including descriptions of *typical days* during these periods; (5) their *preferences* for types of crimes and drugs; (6) the *structure of understanding* guiding drug use and criminal activity; and (7) their perceptions of the nature and effectiveness of *drug treatment*. Structuring the life-history interviews in this way insured that most relevant career phases were covered while at the same time it permitted the respondents a great deal of flexibility in interpreting their experiences.

Drugs Cause Crimes Versus Crimes Cause Drugs

One of the earliest strategies for testing the Drugs-cause-crimes versus Crimes-cause-drugs hypotheses involved trying to establish a temporal sequence to drug use and criminal behavior. If it can be established that a pattern of regular or extensive criminal behavior typically precedes heroin addiction, that finding would tend to support the Crimes-cause-drugs hypothesis. Conversely, if a pattern of regular or extensive criminality tends to develop after the onset of heroin addiction, that finding would tend to support the Drugs-cause-crimes hypothesis. Previous research on this question is mixed, but mixed in a systematic way. Most of the early studies found little criminality before the onset of opiate addiction (Pescor, 1943; Terry and Pellens, 1928). Later studies, by contrast, have shown a high probability of criminality preceding heroin addiction (Ball and Chambers, 1970; Chambers, 1974; Jacoby et al., 1973; Inciardi, 1979; O'Donnell, 1966; Robins and Murphy 1967).

Our life-history interviews are consistent with the findings of the recent studies. All of our respondents reported some criminal activity prior to their first use of heroin. However, for nearly all of our respondents, both their criminal careers and their heroin-using careers began slowly. For the respondents in our study, a median of 3.5 years elapsed between their first serious criminal offense and subsequent involvement in criminal activity on a regular basis. Likewise, all of our respondents reported at least occasional use of other illicit drugs prior to their first experience with heroin. Moreover, many of our respondents indicated that they spent substantial periods of time— months and even years—using heroin on an occasional basis ("chipping" or "chippying"), either inhaling the powder ("sniffing" or "snorting"), injecting the prepared ("cooked") mixture subcutaneously ("skinpopping"), or receiving occasional intravenous injections from other users before becoming regular users themselves. Perhaps most importantly, virtually all of our respondents reported that they believed that their criminal and drug careers began independently of one another, although both careers became intimately interconnected as each evolved. In the earliest phases of their drug and crime careers, the decision to commit crimes and the decision to use drugs were choices which our respondents believe they freely chose to make and which they believe they could have discontinued before either choice became a way of life (also see Fields and Walters, 1985; Morris, 1985).

Drug and Crime Career Patterns

From our interviews it appears that two very general factors shape and influence the drug and crime careers of our respondents, not only during the early stages of each career but as each career evolves through different stages. The first of these factors is the *availability* of heroin rather than the level of physical tolerance the user has developed. "The more you had the more you did," explains "Mona" a thirty-year-old female. "And if all you had was $10 than that's all you did. . . . But if you had $200 then you did that much." Addicts are able to adjust to periods of sharply decreased availability (e.g., "panic" periods when supplies of street heroin disappear) by reducing consumption or by using alternative drugs (e.g., methadone). They are also able to manipulate availability, increasing or decreasing it in ways and for reasons we discuss below.

As we use the term, availability also means something more than access to sellers of heroin who have quantities of the drug to sell. By availability we also mean the resources and opportunities to buy heroin or obtain it in other ways as well as the skills necessary to use it. In short, availability is understood to include considerations of all of those opportunities and obstacles which may influence a heroin user's success in introducing a quantity of the drug into his or her bloodstream.

The second general factor shaping the drugs and crime careers of our life-history interviewees is *life structure*. By "life structure" we mean regularly occurring patterns of daily domestic, occupational, recreational, or criminal activity. Recent ethnographic accounts of heroin-using careers in several major cities reveal that, like their "straight" counterparts, most addicts maintain reasonably predictable daily routines. (Beschner and Brower, 1985; Walters, 1985). Throughout their lives our respondents fulfilled, to one degree or another, conventional as well as criminal and other subcultural roles. In fact, during most periods of their crime and drug careers, our interviewees spent far more time engaged in conventional role activities than in criminal or deviant ones. Many worked conventional jobs. Women with children performed routine housekeeping and child-rearing duties. Many leisure-time activities did not differ from those of non-addicts. These hard core addicts spent time grocery shopping, tinkering with cars, visiting relatives, talking with friends, listening to records, and watching television in totally unremarkable fashion.

Life structure in the hard core criminal addict's life can be also provided by some rather stable forms of criminal activity. Burglars spend time staking out business establishments. Shoplifters typically establish "runs," more or less stable sequences of targeted stores from which to "boost" during late morning, noon, and early afternoon hours, saving the later afternoon for fencing what they have stolen. Prostitutes typically keep a regular evening and night-time schedule, which runs from 7 P.M. to 3 A.M. Mornings are usually spent sleeping and afternoons are usually occupied with conventional duties.

It is within this structure of conventional and criminal roles that buying ("copping"), selling ("dealing"), and using ("shooting") heroin takes place. For example, shoplifters typically structure their runs to allow times and places for all three activities. Likewise, prostitutes seek to manage their drug use so that neither withdrawal symptoms ("joneses") nor periods of heroin-induced drowsiness will interfere with their work. In order to meet the demands of criminal or conventional roles, addicts in our sample often used other drugs (e.g., marijuana, barbiturates, alcohol, amphetamines, methadone) to alter their moods and motivations, saving heroin as a reward for successfully completing a job or meeting other obligations.

Figure 1 • A Typology of Heroin Use Career Phases

Availability	Life Structure	
	High	*Low*
High	The Stabilized Junkie	The Free-Wheeling Junkie
Low	The Occasional User	The Street Junkie

A Typology of Career Patterns

These two dimensions—*availability* and *life structure*—are critical to understanding the dynamics of addict careers. According to our respondents, differences in the ways addicts manage these functions and variations in these two dimensions that are beyond the control of addicts combine to produce fairly distinct patterns, periods, or stages in their careers. The interaction of availability and life structure may be understood to describe addict career phases that are familiar to participants or observers of the heroin scene.

In Figure 1, we identify four such familiar career phases, each of which is marked by a different interaction of heroin availability and life structure. It is important to note that while each denotes an addict type, none of the "types" imply a single career pattern. That is, throughout their drug-crime careers, addicts typically move through periods in which they may at one time be described as one type and later as another. In our discussion of each type, we describe some of the ways in which transitions seem to occur.

The Occasional User—Low Availability/High Life Structure.

Initiates into the heroin-using subculture typically begin as occasional users. For the beginning heroin user, a variety of factors typically serve to limit the availability of heroin. The initiate has usually not spent enough time in the heroin subculture to develop extensive drug connections. In addition, the beginner must be taught how and where to buy heroin, and also must learn how to use it. Moreover, the typical beginning heroin user is unlikely to have sufficient income to maintain any substantial level of heroin consumption, and is most unlikely to have either the connections or the knowledge necessary to increase availability through low-level dealing or through shrewd buying and reselling as experienced addicts sometimes do.

In addition to these factors which tend to limit the availability of heroin to the beginning user and hold him or her to an occasional user role, a variety of factors related to life structure also tend to oblige the beginning heroin user to play an occasional user role, or at least to do so until that life structure can be modified to accommodate a higher level of heroin use. In many cases beginning heroin users are young, dependent, involved in school, and bear family roles and obligations which are not easily changed. Likewise, adult role obligations, such as full-time employment, housekeeping, and child rearing, can be altered so as to be compatible with occasional patterns of heroin use, but not without considerable difficulty if those patterns include high or even moderately high levels of addiction.

One of our respondents, "Belle," explained how she and her husband, "Taps" maintained a very long period of occasional use, due largely to Taps' determination to keep his full-time job:

> I know of people that does half a bag generally. Do you understand what I'm saying? That they automatically live off of half a bag and got a jones. Like I said, Taps worked—and he would shoot no more than half a bag of dope at any time he took off and wouldn't do no wrong. He would not do no wrong. He worked each and every day. And this is what I told you before—I said I don't know how he had a jones and worked, but he worked every day.

Moreover, Belle went on to explain that when the life structure Taps provided for her lapsed—and availability increased—she did not remain an occasional user:

> Taps had me limited a long, long time. I mean a long time limited to nothing but a half a bag of drugs, until he completely stopped hisself. Then when he stopped, I went "Phwee!"—because I didn't have anybody to guide me. I didn't have to take half a bag and divide it in half for him. And I went from one bag to more.

"Ron," another addict in our sample, played the role of "occasional user" without interruption for nearly eight years. During this period he consumed an average of $10–15 in street heroin per day, while holding down a full-time job and living with his mother, who refused to allow him to use drugs in her home. Toward the end of the eight-year period he became a "tester" for a local drug dealer, a role which increased the availability of heroin. At about the same time, he also lost his job, and moved out of his mother's home. Having lost the support of the stable routine imposed by his job and living arrangements at the same time heroin became more readily available to him in his role of "tester," his drug use escalated dramatically within a very short time.

Interestingly, the low availability/high life structure pattern of occasional use, which typically marks the beginning addict's entrance into the drug-using world, is characteristic of many addicts' attempts to leave it. Many formal drug rehabilitation programs impose conditions of low (or no) heroin availability combined with high life structure upon addicts enrolled in their programs (Faupel, 1985). Likewise, as Biernacki (1986) and Waldorf (1983) have extensively demonstrated addicts who attempt to quit on their own often seek to do so by limiting or eliminating altogether their contacts with addict friends, self-medicating with "street" methodone, and devoting themselves intensively to some highly demanding routine activity such as a full-time job or caring for young children.

The Stabilized Junkie—High Availability/High Life Structure.

For the occasional user to become a stabilized junkie, heroin must become increasingly available in large and regular quantities, and his or her daily structure must be modified to accommodate regular heroin use. Making heroin regularly available in sufficiently large quantities is not only a matter of gaining access to reliable sources of supply of the drug; it also involves learning new and more sophisticated techniques for using and obtaining it as well as getting enough money to be able to buy it regularly.

During the time beginning addicts play occasional user roles, they typically learn the fundamentals of copping, cooking, cutting, and spiking. These are all drug-using skills that take time to learn. It was not uncommon for the addicts in our sample to report that a sharp increase in their level of heroin use followed their learning to shoot themselves. When an occasional user learns to self-inject and no longer requires the more knowledgeable drug-using friends to "get off," this new level of skill and independence, in effect, increases the availability of heroin.

Likewise, copping skills and contacts which might have been sufficient to support occasional use require upgrading to support the needs of the stabilized junkie. The would-be stabilized junkie who must rely solely on low-quality, "street" heroin, who gets "ripped" by paying high prices for "bad dope," or who is totally dependent on what quality or quantity of heroin a single supplier happens to have available must seek to stabilize both the quantity and quality of regularly available heroin. Doing so seems to require extending and developing contacts in the drug subculture. In the words of one of our respondents:

> . . . you got to start associating with different people. You got to be in touch with different people for the simple reason that not just one person has it all the time. You got to go from one person to the other, find out who's got the best bag and who hasn't. . . . You want to go where the best bag is for your money, and especially for the money *you're* spending. You got to mingle with so many different people.

Making, developing, and maintaining the contacts that are helpful if not absolutely necessary to stable heroin use seem to invite natural opportunities for the most common modification in the stabilized junkie's life structure: dealing. From the point of view of the would-be stabilized junkie, dealing has two major advantages over most other forms of routine daily activity. First, it can be carried on in the course of the stabilized junkie's search for his or her own supply of drugs and, second, it can be a source of money for the purchase of drugs or a source of drugs itself. Dealing can be rather easily accommodated to the needs of both availability and life structure.

All of our respondents reported that at some time in their drug-using careers they had played the role of dealer, if only occasionally. Becoming an occasional dealer is almost an inevitable consequence of becoming a competent, regular user. A stabilized junkie will not only be approached to "cop" for occasional users and addicts whose suppliers are temporarily out of stock, but the stabilized junkie will come to recognize occasions on which especially "good dope" can be purchased and resold at a profit to drug-using friends.

Because the work of dealing drugs on a small scale does not require much more time or effort than that which goes into buying drugs regularly for one's own use, dealing also has another advantage which makes it an attractive activity for the stabilized junkie. Namely, it can be carried on as a source of drugs or income without undue interference with whatever other "hustle," if any, constitutes the stabilized junkie's additional source of support. This is particularly true if, in the course of carrying on the hustle—be it theft, shoplifting, pimping, prostitution, bookmaking, or dealing in stolen property—the stabilized addict is likely to come into contact with other drug users.

The extent to which dealing can be carried on along with other hustles depends, of course, both on the nature of that hustle and on the extent of the dealing. The stabilized junkie will tend to divide his or her hustling efforts between dealing and other hustles with an eye toward which one delivers the highest profit. However, dividing those efforts will also involve other considerations such as the stabilized junkie's personal preference for one type of work, life style and community reputation considerations, opportunities to practice one type of hustle or another, and the physical demands each type of hustle tends to require. Among female heroin users, a rather common accommodation to the profits and opportunities of dealing and those of other hustles is a live-together arrangement with a male user. In this division of labor each tries to conduct their outside hustle during hours when the other can be at home to handle dealing transactions. An important feature of this arrangement is that, if necessary, it can be structured so as to permit the stabilized female junkie to be at home for housekeeping and child-rearing as well as dealing.

The Free-Wheeling Junkie—High Availability/Low Life Structure.

Although most heroin users spend some portion of their drug-using careers as stabilized junkies and many manage to live for years with high heroin availability and highly-structured daily routines, at least two properties of the stabilized junkie's situation tend to work against the maintenance of stability. One is the pharmacological property of heroin. It is a drug to which users tend to develop a tolerance rather rapidly, although as Zinberg (1984) has demonstrated, such tolerance is neither necessary nor universal. Moreover, as we have pointed out earlier, numerous factors in the social setting of heroin use mitigate the destabilizing effect of the drug. Work routines, household duties, and even subcultural roles all serve to structure drug consumption. However, in the absence of external structures of constraint, or when such routines are temporarily disrupted, the pharmacological properties of heroin tend to destabilize the lifestyle of the addict further. In sum, contrary to popular belief, heroin use does not inevitably lead to a deterioration of lifestyle. Rather, the physiological dynamics of narcotics use tend to be most destabilizing under conditions where life structure is already weak and incapable of accommodating the physiological demands imposed by increased tolerance.

The other property of the stabilized junkie's life which tends to undermine stability is the hustle the junkie uses to finance his or her habit. According to our respondents, it is not hard times or difficulties in raising money through hustles which tend to destabilize the stabilized junkie's life. "You can adjust yourself to a certain amount of drugs a day," explained Belle, "that you don't have to have but just that much." In addition to reducing their drug consumption, stabilized junkies accommodate themselves to such lean periods by substituting other drugs for heroin, working longer and harder at their hustling, or changing the type of hustle they work.

On the contrary, it is the unusual success, the "big sting" or "big hit," that tends to destabilize the stabilized junkie's high degree of life structure. The "big sting" or "big hit" can come in many forms. One of our respondents—an armed robber who usually limited his robbing to street mugging, gas stations, and convenience stores—"hit" a bank, which to our respondent's surprise, produced a "take" of over $60,000. He increased his heroin consumption dramatically and, while doing so, abandoned virtually all the stabilizing routines which marked his life prior to his windfall take. In another instance, a relatively stable junkie dealer was "fronted" several thousand dollars of heroin on consignment. Instead of selling it as he had agreed to do, he absconded with it to another state, shot up most of it himself, and gave the rest away. In still another case, a relatively low-level burglar/thief came across $10,000 in cash in the course of one of his burglaries. He took the money to New York where he intended to cop a "big piece" that he could bring back to the city in which he lived and sell for a nice profit. However, instead of selling it, he kept it for his own use and his habit rapidly increased from a stable three bags per day to nearly a "bundle"— 25 bags per day.

Although the "big hit" or "big sting" appears to be the most common precipitator of the transition from the status of stabilized or occasional heroin user to the status of free-wheeling junkie, many other variants of similar destabilizing patterns are common. The stabilized junkie may not be the one who makes the big sting. It may be his or her spouse, roommate, paramour, addict friend, or regular trick who receives a windfall of drugs or money and invites the stabilized junkie to share in the benefits of good fortune. "Goody," a part-time street prostitute, moved in with a big-time drug dealer who provided her with all the heroin she wanted in exchange for domestic services, sexual favors, and some modest help in cutting and packaging drugs. Although her supply of drugs was virtually limitless, she took her childraising obligations and responsibilities very seriously and they kept her to a modest level of use. However, after a year of domestic living she began to miss the "street" life and the friends she had there and to resent her total ("bag bitch") dependence on her dealer boyfriend. She returned to the street and used the money she earned from " 'hoing," and "ripping" her tricks to purchase drugs in addition to what she got at home for free. This behavior not only destabilized her drug use, but it also disrupted her home life to such an extent that she parted with her dealer and returned to the street full-time. Interestingly, this return to prostitution, theft, and robbery as her sole means of support forced her to develop a new life structure and abandon the free-wheeling pattern into which she had drifted when she had a dual source of supply.

Unless heroin addicts are disciplined by a life structure to which they are so committed and obligated that it effectively prevents them from doing so, they will expand their consumption of heroin to whatever level of use the availability of drugs or funds to buy them makes possible. What marks the career stage of the free-wheeling junkie is the almost total absence of structures of restraint. In the words of "Little Italy," who described a "free-wheeling" stage of his addict career:

> I can remember, I wouldn't be sick, I wouldn't need a shot. . . . And some of the guys might come around and get a few bags [and say] "Hey man, like I don't have enough money. Why don't you come down with me?" . . . I'm saying [to myself], "Oh-oh, here I go!" and I would shoot drugs I didn't even need to shoot. So I let it get out of control.

The problem for the free-wheeling junkie is that the binge cannot last forever and is typically fairly short-lived. After a month or two of free-wheeling heroin use—during which time the free-wheeling junkie may have no idea of how much heroin he or she is consuming daily—not only is a modest usage level unsatisfying but the life structure within which he or she might support it is likely to have been completely abandoned or at least be in severe disrepair.

The Street Junkie—Low Availability/Low Life Structure.

At the point in a free-wheeling junkie's career when heroin availability drops precipitously and life structure does not provide the support necessary to stabilize heroin use, the free-wheeling junkie may manage to rebuild that life structure and accommodate to a new and lower level of availability. To the extent that this rebuilding and accommodation can be managed, the free-wheeling junkie may be able to return to the life of a stabilized junkie. However, if the rebuilding of life structure cannot be managed, the free-wheeling junkie may become a street junkie.

Street junkies most closely approximate the public stereotype of heroin addicts, if only because their way of life—both where and how they live—make them the most visible variety of heroin addict. Cut off from a stable source of quality heroin, not knowing from where his or her next "fix" or the money to pay for it will come, looking for any opportunity to make a buck, getting "sick" or "jonesing," being pathetically unkempt and unable to maintain even the most primitive routines of health or hygiene, the street junkie lives a very difficult, hand-to-mouth existence.

In terms of our typology, the street junkie's life may be understood as a continuous but typically unsuccessful effort to stabilize life structure and increase heroin availability. The two problems are intimately related in such a way that, unless the street junkie can solve both problems at once, neither problem will be solved at all. That is, unless the street junkie can establish a stable life structure, he or she will be unlikely to increase the availability of heroin. Likewise, unless the street junkie is able to increase the availability of heroin, he or she will be unlikely to establish a stable life structure.

To illustrate how this relationship works in less abstract terms, it is helpful to begin with a description of what low life structure means in the life of the street. Goldstein (1981:69) captures the tenor of the street junkie's situation nicely when he observes that

[if] any single word can describe the essence of how street opiate users "get over," that word is *opportunism*. Subjects were always alert to the smallest opportunity to earn a few dollars. The notion of opportunism is equally relevant to predatory criminality, nonpredatory criminality, employment, and miscellaneous hustling activities.

The cause of the street junkie's opportunism is his or her failure to establish a stable life structure which regularly produces enough income to support an addiction. Consequently, the street junkie's life is a series of short-term crimes, jobs, and hustles. Street junkies steal or rob when opportunities arise to do so. For a price or in exchange for heroin, they will "cop" for an out-of-towner, "taste" for a dealer, "tip" for a burglar, rent their "works" to another junkie, sell their "clinic meth" and food stamps, or share their "crib" (accommodations) with a junkie who needs a place to "get off" or a "hoe" who needs a room to take her "tricks." They will do odd jobs, wash cars, paint apartments, deliver circulars, move furniture, carry baggage, or snitch to the police. The problem is not only that this opportunistic crime, hustling, or legitimate work pays very little, but that none of it is stable. While one or more of these activities may produce enough income today, none of them may be counted on to do so tomorrow. Moreover, because typical street addict crimes pay so little, because such crimes must be repeated frequently to produce any sizable income, and because they are so unpredictably opportunistic, the chance that the street addict will be arrested sooner or later is very, very high. This was the unfortunate experience of Little Italy who, after falling out with his supplier, was forced to discontinue drug sales as a major means of income and turned to armed robbery to support his use.

I know today, I can say that if you don't have a plan you're gonna fuck up man. . . . Now those robberies weren't no plan. They didn't fit nowhere . . . just by the spur of the moment, you know what I mean? I had to find something to take that place so that income would stand off properly, 'cause I didn't have a plan or didn't know anything about robbery . . .

As Little Italy's experience demonstrates, street junkies lives are further complicated by the fact that "big dealers"—vendors of quantities of good quality heroin—often refuse to sell to them. The reasons they refuse are directly related to the instability of street junkies' lives. Because street junkies can never be certain when and for how much they will "get over," they are frequently unable to afford to buy enough drugs to satisfy their "jones." In the face of such a shortage they will commonly beg drugs from anyone they know who might have them or have access to them, try to "cop short" (buy at less than the going rate), attempt to strike a deal to get drugs loaned or "fronted" (given on consignment) to them on a short-term basis, or, if necessary, engage in opportunistic hustling. Also, because street junkies are the type of addict most vulnerable to arrest they are also the most likely category of addict to be "flipped" by police into the role of an informant. Usually street junkies will be promised immunity from prosecution on the charge for which they were arrested if they "give up" somebody "big." Given the frequency with which street addicts "come up short," the relatively small amount of profit to be made in each individual transaction with them, and the higher than normal risk of police involvement, few "big dealers" are willing to put up with all of the attendant hassles and hustles that dealing with street junkies typically involves.

While there are exceptions—the most common being big dealers who are relatives of street junkies or their friends of long standing—street addicts are mainly limited to "street dope," heroin that has been repeatedly "stepped on" (diluted) as it is passed from the highest level of dealer to the lowest. In fact, some studies (Leveson and Weiss, 1976:119) have shown that as much as 7 percent of street dope may have no heroin in it at all, while other studies (Smith, 1973) show a heroin concentration of from 3 to 10 percent in street dope as compared with an average concentration of nearly 30 percent in bags seized from "big dealers." The irony in this situation is that, as a consumer of "street dope," the street addict pays a higher per/unit price for heroin than any other person in the distribution chain. Furthermore, this very low and often unpredictable quality of heroin available to the street junkie serves to destabilize his or her life structure further.

Research and Policy Implications

The life-history data presented here have some important research and policy implications which merit brief consideration. Particularly relevant are the implications for: (1) the nature of the drugs-crime connection itself; (2) drug law enforcement and (3) treatment policy.

The Drugs-Crime Connection

As we have pointed out above, early studies examining the relationship between drug use and crime have utilized the strategy of establishing the temporal priority of the onset of drug use versus criminality. While the earliest of these studies tended to find that drug use preceded the onset of criminal behavior, virtually all of the studies conducted since 1950 have found a reverse pattern, thus posing once again the perplexing question of the theoretical nature of the relationship between drug use and criminal behavior. Because the methodologies employed in these "sequence" studies are incapable of examining the dynamic nature of this relationship over time, they have succeeded in raising theoretical questions which continue to beg for explanation. More recent studies—particularly those of Ball et al. (1981, 1983) and Johnson et al. (1985)—have moved beyond the sequence issued by examining drug-using and criminal behavior on a daily or weekly basis over a period of time. These longitudinal methodologies represent a major breakthrough toward establishing the dynamic nature of the drugs-crime relationship.

This study further contributes to the emerging "post-sequence" literature by examining the drugs-crime nexus in the broader context of addict careers. Perhaps the most significant finding to emerge from our data is that the relationship between heroin use and crime is not necessarily consistent throughout the career of the addict. During the "occasional user" phase, for example, the issue is a moot one for many addicts; their limited level of drug use is quite affordable with a legitimate income, and any criminal activity that does take place is often quite spurious to drug use. During the "stabilized junkie" and "free-wheeling junkie" periods, the level of drug use seems to be largely a function of availability, typically enhanced through criminal income. Rather than *drug use causing crime,* however, it seems more accurate to suggest that *crime facilitates drug use* during these periods. Quite the reverse is the case during the "street junkie" phase, where availability through normal channels is lacking but the addict lacks the necessary structure to regulate his or her drug needs. Under these conditions the drug habit does indeed appear to "cause" crime in the manner commonly depicted.

Moreover, the life history data reveal that the relationship between drugs and crime is more dynamic than phrasing the issue in terms of "cause" typically suggests. In addition to providing necessary income for the purchase of heroin, criminal activity also serves to *structure* the drug using behavior of the addict. Crime thus provides the addict with a daily routine which for many addicts actually serves to limit or at least regulate their drug use.

In short, the respondents in this study have revealed that the relationship between drug use and criminal behavior is far more complex and dynamic than previous research has suggested. While in any given instance, it may be possible to specify a causal sequence, our data suggest that any generalizations suggesting a simple cause-effect scheme fail to capture the complexity of the drugs-crime connection throughout an addict's career.

Drug Law Enforcement

Since the passage of the Harrison Act in 1914, drug law enforcement in the United States has been dominated by the "criminal model" of drug use (Inciardi, 1974). While variously articulated, this model understands drug use as primarily a *criminal* issue which should be addressed by imposing criminal sanctions on both users and dealers, and by taking steps to prevent the import and distribution of heroin. Insofar as there is a relationship between drug use and other criminal behavior, the narcotics user is understood to be a criminal, first and foremost, whose drug using behavior is an important and contributing component in an extensive pattern of related criminal behavior.

Not surprisingly, the criminalization of heroin has profoundly affected the dynamics of the drugs-crime nexus. Virtually all of the post-1950 studies have found that criminal histories preceded expensive drug-using histories of the respondents in their samples as suggested by the subculturally based "Crimes cause drugs" model. Our life-history data support and qualify the implications for the criminal model suggested by these studies. While our respondents do report criminal involvement prior to their first exposure to heroin, the drug-using histories began quite independently of their criminal involvement. Throughout their early "occasional use" phase, most of these individuals were supporting their drug use without relying on a stable income from systematic criminal activity. As their careers progressed, however, they cultivated criminal skills and associations which played an important role in facilitating a greatly expanded level of heroin use.

However, our research suggests that even if such enforcement efforts rightly characterize the drugs-crime connection, enforcement approaches may not have their intended effects of controlling or suppressing drug use or the crimes related to it. We find no reason to conclude that enforcement efforts may have an effect on very early periods in addict careers. During the period of occasional use, addicts can easily adjust to dramatic variations in the level of supply of heroin and our respondents report little need to support such occasional use through systematic criminal activity. Even in those periods of the hard-core addict's life history which we have described as characterized by a "stabilized junkie" model, our respondents report being able to adjust to periods in which heroin supplies are sharply reduced, only to return to previous levels of use when their channels of supply are restored. Moreover, our respondents report that during stabilized junkie periods in their life histories they cultivated a variety of sources of supply. Given this variety, not only could they choose vendors who appeared to offer the best quality product, but they could adjust relatively easily to the temporary or permanent loss of a supplier. Unless enforcement efforts managed a simultaneous elimination of virtually all of these sources of supply, we would not anticipate that they would have much effect on the stabilized junkie's pattern of stable use, nor on the criminal activity which the stabilized junkie typically pursues to support it. Likewise, enforcement efforts may not be expected to have much impact on hard-core addicts during "free-wheeling" phases in their life histories. Particularly insofar as these periods are precipitated by "big scores" or "big hits" and marked by short-term, unlimited availability of drugs or the money to purchase them, enforcement is already too late.

The street junkie, by contrast, faced with the lack of ready availability of adequate supplies of heroin and without the necessary life structure to constrain his or her felt need for drugs, is most vulnerable to law enforcement activity. Indeed, our data would suggest that the effectiveness of current law enforcement efforts is largely limited to this career phase. The addict in this situation is often confronted with the alternative of arrest or informing on other addicts. Either alternative almost inevitably imposes a criminal transition in the career of the addict. Arrest typically culminates either in treatment or incarceration, both which impose a disengagement from street routine. Even if the addict subsequently returns to the street, the conditions of availability and life structure will be profoundly altered. While informing on other addicts may buy more time on the street, this alternative will only further alienate the street junkie from the subculture. While such a strategy of "flipping" informants may be helpful in locating "big dealers," its overall impact in limiting the availability of drugs to nonstreet junkies appears negligible unless, as we have suggested, all major dealers are "hit" simultaneously. Unless our drug policies give balanced weight to educational and treatment efforts, law enforcement effectiveness appears relegated to the already vulnerable "street junkie."

Treatment Policy

Narcotics treatment in the United States has also been characterized by an overriding concern with the anti-social behavior associated with heroin use. Methadone maintenance is currently the dominant model of treatment, and has generated a voluminous literature addressing its effectiveness as a deterrent to crime (see, for example, Dole et al., 1968, 1969; Gearing, 1974; Judson et al., 1980; Lukoff and Quatrone, 1973; Nash, 1973; Newman and Gates, 1973). These and other studies have reported widely varying effects of methadone treatment upon criminality ranging from a 99.9 percent reduction (Gearing, 1974) to an actual *increase* in crime following admission to treatment (Lukoff and Quatrone, 1973). Unfortunately, our understanding of the effect of methadone maintenance on criminality is severely limited because of the many methodological difficulties associated with these studies (Faupel, 1981).

However, our data suggest that to the extent that a long-term reduction in criminality is a central goal of drug treatment, treatment policy must attend to more than simply the physiological demand for heroin. Drug-free residential programs, in particular, attempt to reduce availability by imposing abstinence for a substantial period of time. Beyond simply curtailing access to heroin, however, successful treatment will require provision for an alternative life structure which facilitates and rewards conventional behavior, thus reducing demand as well. We would argue that such an agenda not only requires renunciation of past routines but also the facilitation of long-term alternative behavior patterns through a concerted effort at community reintegration (see Dembo et al., 1982; Faupel, 1985; Goldbart, 1982; Hawkins, 1979). Involvement in conventional employment, voluntary associations, and even organized leisure-time activities should tightly structure the addicts' daily routine. Just as importantly, since access to drugs is largely a function of social networks, renunciation of "street" relationships and subsequent integration into supportive conventional social networks should serve to reduce availability and demand simultaneously.

References

Anglin, M. Douglas and George Speckart. 1984 Narcotics Use and Crime: A Confirmatory Analysis. Unpublished Report, University of California Los Angeles.

Ball, John C. and Carl D. Chambers. 1970 The Epidemiology of Heroin Use in the United States. Springfield, IL: Charles C. Thomas.

Ball, John C., Lawrence Rosen, John A. Flueck and David Nurco. 1981 "The criminality of heroin addicts when addicted and when off opiates." Pp. 39–65 in James A. Inciardi (ed.), The Drugs-Crime Connection. Beverly Hills, CA: Sage Publications.

Ball, John C., John W. Shaffer and David Nurco. 1983 "The day to day criminality of heroin addicts in Baltimore: a study of the continuity of offense rates." Drug and Alcohol Dependence 12:119–42.

Ball, John C. and Richard W. Snarr. 1969 "A test of the maturation hypothesis with respect to opiate addiction." Bulletin of Narcotics 21:9–13.

Beschner, George M. and William Brower. 1985 "The scene." Pp. 19–29 in Bill Hanson, George Beschner, James M. Walters and Elliot Bovelle (eds.), Life with Heroin: Voices from the Inner City. Lexington, MA: Lexington Books.

Biernacki, Patrick. 1986 Pathways from Heroin Addiction: Recovery without Treatment. Philadelphia: Temple University Press.

Chambers, Carl D. 1974 "Narcotic addiction and crime: an empirical overview." Pp. 125–42 in James A. Inciardi and Carl D. Chambers (eds.), Drugs and the Criminal Justice System. Beverly Hills, CA: Sage Publications.

Chein, Isidor, Donald L. Gerard, Robert S. Lee and Eva Rosenfeld. 1964 The Road to H: Narcotics, Juvenile Delinquency, and Social Policy. New York: Basic Books.

Collins, James J., Robert L. Hubbard and J. Valley Rachal. 1984 Heroin and Cocaine Use and Illegal Income. Center for Social Research and Policy Analysis. Research Triangle Park, NC: Research Triangle Institute.

———. 1985 "Expensive drug use and illegal income: a test of explanatory hypotheses." Criminology 23:743–64.

Dembo, Richard, James A. Ciarlo and Robert W. Taylor. 1983 "A model for assessing and improving drug abuse treatment resource use in inner city areas." The International Journal of Addictions 18:921–36.

Dole, Vincent P., Marie E. Nyswander and Alan Warner. 1968 "Successful treatment of 750 criminal addicts." Journal of the American Medical Association 206:2708–11.

Dole, Vincent P., J. Waymond Robinson, John Orraca, Edward Towns, Paul Searcy and Eric Caine. 1969 "Methadone treatment of randomly selected criminal addicts." New England Journal of Medicine 280:1372–75.

Faupel, Charles E. 1981 "Drug treatment and criminality: methodological and theoretical considerations." Pp. 183–206 in James A. Inciardi (ed.), The Drugs-Crime Connection. Beverly Hills, CA: Sage Publications.

———. 1985 "A theoretical model for a socially oriented drug treatment policy." Journal of Drug Education 15:189–203.

Fields, Allen and James M. Walters. 1985 "Hustling: supporting a heroin habit." Pp. 49–73 in Bill Hanson, George Beschner, James M. Walters and Elliot Bovelle (eds), Life with Heroin: Voices from the Inner City. Lexington, MA: Lexington Books.

Gandossy, Robert P., Jay R. Williams, Jo Cohen and Hendrick J. Harwood. 1980 Drugs and Crime: A Survey and Analysis of the Literature. National Institute of Justice. Washington, DC: U.S. Government Printing Office.

Gearing, Frances R. 1974 "Methadone maintenance treatment five years later—where are they now?" American Journal of Public Health 64:44–50.

Goldbart, Stephen. 1982 "Systematic barriers to addict aftercare program implementation." Journal of Drug Issues 12:415–30.

Goldman, Fred. 1976 "Drug markets and addict consumption behavior." Pp. 273–96 in Drug Use and Crime: Report of the Panel on Drug Use and Criminal Behavior. National Technical Information Service publication number PB–259 167. Springfield, VA: U.S. Dept. of Commerce.

———. 1981 "Drug abuse, crime and economics: the dismal limits of social choice." Pp. 155–81 in James A. Inciardi (ed.), The Drugs-Crime Connection. Beverly Hills, CA: Sage Publications.

Goldstein, Paul. 1981 "Getting over: economic alternatives to predatory crime among street drug users." Pp. 67–84 in James A. Inciardi (ed.), The Drugs-Crime Connection. Beverly Hills, CA: Sage Publications.

Hanson, Bill, George Beschner, James M. Walters and Elliot Bovelle. 1985 Life with Heroin: Voices from the Inner City. Lexington, MA: Lexington Books.

Hawkins, J. David. 1979 "Reintegrating street drug abusers: community roles in continuing care." Pp. 25–79 in Barry S. Brown (ed.), Addicts and Aftercare. Beverly Hills, CA: Sage Publications.

Inciardi, James A. 1974 "The villification of euphoria: some perspectives on an elusive issue." Addictive Diseases 1:241–67.

———. 1979 "Heroin use and street crime." Crime and Delinquency 25:335–46.

Jacoby, Joseph E., Neil A. Weiner, Terence P. Thornberry, and Marvin E. Wolfgang. 1973 "Drug use in a birth cohort." Pp. 300–43 in National Commission on Marijuana and Drug Abuse, Drug Use in America: Problem in Perspective, Appendix I. Washington, DC: U.S. Government Printing Office.

Johnson, Bruce D., Paul J. Goldstein, Edward Preble, James Schmeidler, Douglas S. Lipton, Barry Spunt and Thomas Miller. 1985 Taking Care of Business: The Economics of Crime by Heroin Abusers. Lexington, MA: Lexington Books.

Judson, Barbara, Serapio Ortiz, Linda Crouse, Thomas Carney and Avram Goldstein. 1980 "A follow-up study of heroin addicts five years after admission to a methadone treatment program." Drug and Alcohol Dependence 6:295–313.

Leveson, Irving and Jeffrey H. Weiss. 1976 Analysis of Urban Health Problems. New York: Spectrum.

Lukoff, Irving and Debra Quatrone. 1973 "Heroin use and crime in a methadone maintenance program: a two year follow-up of the Addiction and Research Corporation Program: a preliminary report." Pp. 63–112 in Gil J. Hayim, Irving Lukoff and Debra Quatrone (eds.), Heroin Use in a Methadone Maintenance Program. Washington, DC: U.S. Department of Justice, National Institute of Law Enforcement and Criminal Justice.

McGlothlin, William H., M. Douglas Anglin and Bruce D. Wilson. 1978 "Narcotic addiction and crime." Criminology 16:293–315.

Morris, Richard W. 1985 "Not the cause, nor the cure: self-image and control among inner city black male heroin users." Pp. 135–53 in Bill Hanson, George Beschner, James M. Walters and Elliot Bovelle (eds.), Life with Heroin: Voices from the Inner City. Lexington, MA: Lexington Books.

Musto, David. 1973 The American Disease: Origins of Narcotic Control. New Haven, CT: Yale University Press.

Nash, George. 1973 "The impact of drug abuse treatment upon criminality: a look at 19 programs." Upper Montclair, NJ: Montclair State College.

Newman, Robert G., Sylvia Bashkow and Margot Gates. 1973 "Arrest histories before and after admission to a methadone maintenance treatment program." Contemporary Drug Problems 2:417–24.

O'Donnell, John A. 1966 "Narcotic addiction and crime." Social Problems 13:374–85.

Pescor, Michael J. 1943 "A statistical analysis of the clinical records of hospitalized drug addicts." Public Health Reports Supplement, 143.

Robins, Lee N. and George E. Murphy. 1967 "Drug use in a normal population of young Negro men." American Journal of Public Health 570:1580–96.

Smith, Jean Paul. 1973 "Substances in illicit drugs." Pp. 13–30 in Richard H. Blum and Associates (eds.), Drug Dealers—Taking Action. San Francisco: Jossey Bass.

Tappan, Paul. 1960 Crime, Justice and Correction. New York: McGraw-Hill.

Terry, Charles E. and Mildred Pellens. 1928 The Opium Problem. New York: The Haddon Craftsman.

Waldorf, Dan. 1983 "Natural recovery from opiate addiction: some social-psychological processes of untreated recovery." Journal of Drug Issues 13:237–80.

Walters, James M. 1985 " 'Taking care of business' updated: a fresh look at the daily routine of the heroin user." Pp. 31–48 in Bill Hanson, George Beschner, James M. Walters and Elliot Bovelle (eds.), Life with Heroin: Voices from the Inner City. Lexington, MA: Lexington Books.

Weissman, James C., Paul L. Katsampes and Thomas A. Giacienti. 1974 "Opiate use and criminality among a jail population." Addictive Diseases 1:269–81.

Zinberg, Norman E. 1984 Drug Set and Setting: The Basis for Controlled Intoxicant Use. New Haven, CT: Yale University Press.

27. Avoidance of Methadone Treatment and the Criminal Justice System

Bruce D. Johnson, Paul J. Goldstein, Edward Preble, James Schmeidler, Douglas S. Lipton, Barry Spunt, and Thomas Miller

> I have to pay a $200 fine. . . . I think they want me off the street. I have to get on a program. . . . Forget it. I'd rather be in jail.
>
> Kit G.

Despite their high crime rates, criminal incomes, and economic consequences, many heroin abusers are quite successful at avoiding or limiting their contacts with the two major institutions of social control that address their behavior: methadone treatment programs and the criminal justice system. Our analysis suggests that subjects who are the most criminal and the heaviest heroin users are the least likely to be in treatment. Similarly, they had relatively few arrests and typically were unlikely to receive severe punishment by the criminal justice system.

Methadone Treatment

This section compares criminal offender types and heroin users in terms of whether they were in a methadone treatment program at any time during their reporting period. The absence of such treatment has important implications for drug-treatment and criminal justice policy makers.

A cautionary note is in order here. The data presented in this section do not provide a basis for evaluating the success of methadone maintenance programs. Our recruitment patterns, in fact, had the effect of selecting respondents for whom methadone treatment was likely to have a marginal impact. Specifically, we were unlikely to recruit many types of methadone clients, such as those who held full-time jobs, who spent most of their time with family, or who otherwise avoided the street scene. Moreover, our recruitment methods resulted in over-selection of methadone clients who were continual abusers of drugs and alcohol and the most troublesome for clinics to manage. Thus, when we did recruit heroin abusers who were enrolled in methadone programs, such subjects would be among the least successful in the program and the most criminally active.

Background Characteristics

Respondents were classified as having some methadone treatment if they reported using legal methadone on 2 percent or more days during their reporting period. Among our 201 subjects, 26 percent (N = 52) had some methadone treatment, and 74 percent were not in methadone treatment during their reporting period.

Table 1 shows few differences in the characteristics of these two groups of subjects. Subjects with and without some methadone treatment did not differ by sex, ethnicity, age, neighborhood of residence (East or Central Harlem), marital status, education, type of work, nor the use during the prior year of illicit methadone, cocaine, or other drugs.

Reprinted by permission of the publisher, from *TAKING CARE OF BUSINESS: The Economics of Crime by Heroin Abusers* by Bruce D. Johnson, Paul J. Goldstein, Edward Preble, James Schmeidler, Douglas S. Lipton, Barry Spunt, and Thomas Miller (Lexington, Mass.: Lexington Books, D.C. Heath and Company, Copyright 1985, D.C. Heath and Company).

Table 1. Characteristics of Subjects without and with Some Methadone Treatment

Characteristic	Any Methadone Treatment in Reporting Period? (percentage)		
	None (N = 149)	Some (N = 52)	Significance of Chi Square
Sex			
Male	77%	71%	ns
Female	23	29	
Age			
Under 26	17	4	
26–30	27	29	
31–35	22	29	ns
36–40	14	21	
41 and older	20	17	
Ethnicity			
Black	56	52	
Hispanic	44	48	ns
Other			
Number of arrests			
None	19	9	
1–5	38	45	ns
6 or more	43	45	
Number years incarcerated			
None	42	25	
1–4	37	52	ns
5 or more	21	23	
Number years heroin use			
5 and under	27	20	
6–10	26	34	
11–15	25	23	ns
16 and over	22	23	
Frequency of heroin use in year prior to interview			
Daily	66	53	
Weekly	27	28	.07
Monthly	7	19	
Average daily amount heroin used/day in year prior to interview			
$20 and under	37	56	
$21–$50	38	20	.05
Over $50	25	24	

Characteristic	Any Methadone Treatment in Reporting Period? (percentage)		
	None (N = 149)	Some (N = 52)	Significance of Chi Square
During year prior to interview:			
Percentage addicted to			
No drugs	5%	8%	ns
Heroin	75	75	ns
Illegal methadone	3	8	ns
Cocaine	9	10	ns
Alcohol	20	14	ns
During year prior to interview			
Major means of support			
Theft	50	28	
Drug business	17	37	.03
Working	16	14	
Other	16	21	
Criminal income			
$1,000 and under	44	41	
$1,001–$5,000	25	23	ns
$5,001–$10,000	18	18	
Over $10,000	14	18	
Drug expenditures			
$1,000 and under	17	33	
$1,001–$5,000	41	38	
$5,001–$10,000	20	14	ns
Over $10,000	22	14	
Shoplifting frequency			
Daily	11	5	
Weekly	22	36	
Monthly	21	17	ns
None	46	43	
Burglary frequency			
Weekly or daily	14	2	
Monthly	19	13	.06
None	67	85	
Robbery frequency			
Weekly or daily	7	8	
Monthly	16	20	ns
None	77	72	
Drug business frequency			
Daily	20	24	
Weekly	15	27	ns
Monthly	13	12	
None	53	38	

ns Not significant.

Although it might be anticipated that those without methadone treatment might be more criminally active than subjects with such treatments, both groups reported a similar number of prior arrests, years of incarceration, and years of heroin use. Both groups reported about the same frequency of heroin use and daily amounts of heroin used per day in the year prior to interview. Both groups had similar percentages addicted to heroin, alcohol, and cocaine. Finally, both groups engaged in shoplifting, burglary, robbery, and drug-business activities with the same frequency in the year prior to their interviews.

One difference between the two groups was in their major means of support. Those without methadone treatment were more likely to report theft as their major means of support, and those with some methadone treatment reported more involvement in the drug business in the year prior to interview.

Given that subjects reporting some methadone treatment had similar backgrounds, self-reported drug abuse, and criminal histories as those not receiving such treatment, what then differentiates the two groups? The next section looks at the types of criminals and heroin abusers who were not receiving methadone treatment.

Criminality, Heroin Abuse, and Methadone

Table 2 identifies the types of criminal offenders and heroin users who had no methadone treatment during their reporting period. For this table, the criminal offender typology has been collapsed to eliminate the dealer–nondealer distinction. Respondents were classified in a hierarchical order of *robbers, burglars, thieves,* and *none of these* (drug dealers, low-level distributors, and prostitutes). Among daily heroin users, 92 percent or more of the robbers, burglars, and thieves had no methadone treatment during their reporting periods. Among irregular heroin users, about three-fifths had no methadone treatment. Among the sixteen robbers and burglars who were irregular heroin users, about 44 percent had no methadone treatment.

Methadone treatment is more likely to affect clients if they take their medication daily, as directed. Less than half of any group of subjects with some methadone treatment, however, used methadone on a substantial proportion (66 percent or more) of their reporting days.

Table 2 shows that among daily heroin users most (98 percent) avoided methadone treatment for a substantial proportion of their reporting days. Among regular heroin users, the findings are similar, with the exception that 74 percent avoided methadone completely and 91 percent avoided using methadone on a substantial proportion of days; these figures include both those with no and with some treatment.

Among the irregular heroin users, over half of the sixteen robbers and burglars had some methadone treatment, but about only a third of these took methadone on two-thirds of their days. Thus, only among irregular heroin users were high proportions in methadone treatment and likely to be taking their methadone as expected.

Were Those without Methadone Treatment Avoiding It?

Although we did not ask detailed questions about why respondents were not in methadone treatment, considerable ethnographic evidence suggests that many persons avoided entry into methadone treatment or denied their need for it. A parallel research project, the Tristate Ethnographic Project (Hunt, Lipton, and Spunt 1983; Hunt et al. 1982, 1984; Goldsmith et al. 1984) found that street heroin abusers not in methadone programs held a variety of folk beliefs about methadone and gave other reasons why they would not enter programs (although many had been enrolled previously). Our field experience also indicated an avoidance of methadone and other treatment programs.

Table 2. Percentage of Criminal Offenders and Heroin Users Avoiding, or with No Routine, Methadone Treatment during Their Reporting Period *(percentage)*

Nondrug Criminal Offender Group	Heroin User Group			
	Irregular	Regular	Daily	Average All R's
Percentage in cell (offender/drug user group) with no methadone treatment				
None of these	65%	93%	50%	75%
Thief	61	64	95	71
Burglar	44	65	92	68
Robber	43	87	92	83
Total	57	74	90	74
Percentage of group not using methadone on 66 percent or more of reporting days[a]				
None of these	82	100	75	89
Thief	79	89	100	88
Burglar	56	80	100	80
Robber	71	100	100	96
Total	75	91	98	89
Number of cases on which above percentages are based				
None of these	17	15	4	36
Thief	28	28	20	76
Burglar	9	20	12	41
Robber	7	15	26	48
Total	61	78	62	201

[a]Denominator includes both those with no and with some methadone treatment.

Three-quarters of our subjects were not in methadone treatment during the interview period. On several occasions, such subjects would comment that they wanted to get off drugs or alcohol and needed help. "Maybe" they would go into treatment. One or two even planned to go into treatment. But at the next interview, they would invariably have done nothing about it: Something else came up, they forgot about it, they were still thinking about it, or they had some other similar excuse.

Although the clear purpose of this study was to investigate the actual economic and criminal behavior of these subjects without making moral judgments or trying to rehabilitate them, the staff, in consultation with the Institutional Review Board, had agreed to aid subjects in securing treatment admission. That is, if a subject was ready to go into treatment, a staff member would refer him to the program of his choice and help him gain admission. With one exception (see below), expression of interest by noninvolved subjects in treatment was not followed by a decision to seek admission.

The one exception occurred in 1979 when a twenty-six-year-old subject who had been a severe alcoholic for many years, passed out in the storefront from intoxication. He was taken to a nearby detoxification center, where he spent eight days *drying out;* he resumed his drinking shortly after.

A more typical respondent was twenty-six-year-old Kit G. (see vignette 29), who indicated that he had never entered a treatment program. During his interviews, Kit expressed strong opinions about methadone: "I don't like methadone. It's worse than heroin. You should know that." (4/3/80) "I hate meth. It's death." (4/28/80) Toward the end of his reporting cycle, he *kicked the habit* and abstained for 13 days. After completing his reporting cycle, Kit visited the storefront on 5/6/80, during which the following dialogue occurred:

Kit: I started shooting up again. I don't know why. My friend had some money and he treated me to about $50 to $60 a day of heroin. I have to get on a program.
Q: But you don't like methadone.
Kit: I think it's shit. I mean a drug-free program.
Q: You mean like Project Return.
Kit: Yeah, How long do I have to stay there?
Q: About eighteen months.
Kit: Forget it. I'd rather be in jail.

Kit would appear to speak for many subjects in preferring jail to either a methadone or drug-free treatment program that requires a long-term commitment (also see Hanson et al. 1985; Goldsmith, et al. 1984; Hunt, Lipton, and Spunt 1983). Clearly, however, more information about these respondents is needed to disentangle complex patterns of avoidance, admission, use, and termination of methadone treatment.

Vignette 29
Kit G.: The Nonimpact of a Burglary Arrest on a Robber–Dealer — Compulsive Heroin Use, Serious Criminality, Voluntary Abstinence, and Treatment Avoidance

---

Kit G. (Hispanic male, age 26) was a robber–dealer and regular heroin user. He would have been a daily user, but he had an arrest and a thirteen-day period of self-imposed abstinence.

Kit G. came to the United States from Puerto Rico in 1975, was married, had one child, and lived with his family. He attempted to conceal his addiction from his wife. He had been mainlining heroin for five years at the time of his recruitment and supported his habit (which was close to $150 daily) through a variety of crimes, including drug dealing, burglary, and robbery.

Kit had five arrests in Puerto Rico and three in New York. His first arrest was in 1969, in Puerto Rico, at age 15, for attempted murder. "This guy hit my little brother and sent him to the hospital, so I went back and I got a gun from my friend and when I found him I shot him." Kit was convicted and spent two years in jail and three years on probation in Puerto Rico. Kit also spoke of committing robberies, mostly as a strong-arm man, while in Puerto Rico. Two of Kit's arrests in New York were for possession of marijuana, but he was released both times.

On 4/3/80, Kit reported a robbery. "I took a watch and wallet from a guy on the street, told him to keep walking without looking back. He had $150 cash. Sold the watch for $85." He used $160 of heroin. "I gave about $10 worth of heroin to a friend; he was sick." He also shoplifted three mangoes, three oranges, and some rice, beans, and milk. Gave his wife $60.

On 4/4/80, Kit sold about $1,000 worth of heroin during twenty transactions for which he earned $175 in cash and $50 worth of heroin. He purchased $150 of heroin but used

$100. "I gave two quarters to friends." He reported, "I don't usually like to deal, but I'm sick, I need money." He sold for a dealer whose regular dealer was arrested. Gave his wife $30.

On 4/5/80, Kit sold $1,200 of heroin and $700 of cocaine during 22 transactions; earned $100 worth of heroin. "Same dealer as yesterday. I woke up late. I could've dealt more." He also assaulted a young man and received the downpayment for beating up a man. "I had to pay $75 to hospital for son; he had a fever; Ok now, home."

On 4/6/80, Kit reported no dealing. "They turned me loose. They heard I was shooting a lot of heroin. I never beat them but they probably think I will." He received the final payments for beating up the young man. He used $100 of heroin, $10 of cocaine. "I had three quarts of beer; I drank fast, so my wife will think I'm drunk. But I was high." He also received $1,000 from a former drug-dealer associate:

> A few years ago in P.R., we took off a numbers man (three of us). I got caught by the police, sentenced to three to five years; did two in jail and three in the street. He still owes me $3,000 from then. This guy is now a dealer and has a few people working for him. If he don't pay me my money, I'm going to have to kill him. I think he knows that so he'll pay. I hope he knows it. I ran into him last week by mistake. He didn't want to see me.

On 4/7/80, Kit committed the burglary reported in vignette 9. He bought $200 of heroin, used $150, and saved $50 for the next day. "Hit the vein wrong. Arm was swollen and hurts." He asked the interviewer, "I've got four guns home. Do you want to buy one?" Interviewer: "No. What kind of guns do you have?" "I have a .38, a .25, a .22, and a shotgun."

On 4/8/80, Kit mugged a guy for $120 and used $125 of heroin.

On 4/9/80, Kit and partner burglarized an apartment. Got $500 cash, which they split. Kit used $150 of heroin; gave $40 to his wife.

On 4/10/80, Kit dealt $3,000 worth of heroin in fifty transactions, earning $115 cash and $150 of heroin.

On 4/11/80, Kit dealt $600 of heroin in about twelve transactions and earned $50. He used $75 worth of heroin before committing a burglary, which led to his third arrest in New York.

Kit and a partner were caught leaving a building with $200 in cash, a box of jewelry, and a color television:

> I told him [partner], "Let's take the money and jewelry," but he wanted the TV; that's why we got caught. Monday night, Tuesday, and Wednesday were the worst days I ever spent in my life [in jail, with no drugs]. They didn't give me anything; I almost kicked the habit.

Kit pled guilty. He showed the interviewer his court papers on 4/15/80:

> I have to pay a $200 fine. If I don't pay I'll go to jail. I have $163 on me. I need $40 more for the fine. The D.A. won't give me no time to pay. I think they want me off the street.

After his release from jail, Kit got $250 in heroin, rebagged it, sold it for $550, and used the profit to help pay his fine.

In the following week, the dealer who owed him money (4/6/80), gave him $300 worth of heroin. He used $100 on each day, 4/15-17/80, and didn't commit any crimes on those days.

On 4/18/80, Kit and a partner burglarized a dealer's apartment. The partner got all the coke, and Kit got all the heroin (twelve-five half-quarters worth about $1,375), which he used at the rate of $300 a day from 4/18-21/80:

> I don't know how much coke, I think it was more than the heroin. Two days he shot it (cocaine) up. I left my gun in the apartment, .38 caliber. We also had a box of jewelry and five guns, but we left them when he came back and heard us in the apartment. He shot the lock off the door. We just made it out the windows (ground floor) and through the back yard.

In the following week, 4/22-28/80, Kit finished using $130 of heroin from the previous burglary. Then: "I kicked the habit with nothing. I'm getting tired of fooling around. All my money goes on drugs. I feel lousy, I feel sick."

He stayed around home most of the time. Except on 4/26/80: "I hit this guy in the street and knocked him out. I took $40 off him. I didn't want to do it. I robbed the guy because I needed the money for the rent. They're looking to kick me out. If I don't need money for drugs, it's always something else."

The following week, 4/29 to 5/5/80, for reasons we don't know, he avoided all drugs and didn't commit any crimes.

Criminal Justice System

A variety of recent studies of juveniles (Duford and Elliott 1982; Duford, Elliott, and Huizinga, 1983a, 1983b; Elliott and Huizinga, 1984; Elliott, Duford and Huizinga, 1983) and heroin users (Inciardi and Chambers 1972; Inciardi 1979, 1984; Ball 1982) have begun to document that the most serious offenders are more likely to have one or more arrests and incarcerations than less serious offenders. These studies also show that the higher the rates of criminal activity, the lower the rates of arrest per 100 self-reported crimes. For example, Inciardi (1979, 1984) reported that the arrest rate was under one per 100 robberies, burglaries, thefts, and other crimes among heroin-abusing males in Miami.

A major thread emerging from the research of Chaiken and Chaiken (1982a, 1982b) is that even among offenders arrested and offically processed, their official arrest and incarceration history is a poor predictor of their actual (self-reported) behavior and crime rate. For example, Chaiken and Chaiken found that among their inmate subjects, official records of arrests for robbery, assault, and drug sales would identify only about 10 percent of all self-reported violent predators (who did those crimes).

Our recruitment and follow-up techniques were not designed to answer questions about how often high-rate offenders are arrested and incarcerated. We did not obtain official criminal justice histories, so we did not know how many of our subjects had been arrested or incarcerated. We had only self-reported arrest and incarceration information. That information was frequently sketchy about what happened at court. Moreover, subjects who were arrested and incarcerated for a long time during the study period would have been lost to contact without our knowing why.

On a few occasions, however, subjects were arrested during or between their reporting cycles. This generally meant they were in jail for a few days awaiting arraignment. Further hearings on the case would typically occur after the reporting cycle, so we did not learn the outcome of the case.

We did, however, ask our subjects whether they had ever been arrested or incarcerated. Eighty-four percent of the subjects reported an arrest, and the mean number of arrests was eight (see table 3). Moreover, 62 percent reported an incarceration, and they had served 2.7 years in jail or prison prior to our interviews. In short, most heroin abusers had not escaped apprehension and incarceration. Moreover, as table 3 shows, robber–dealers and daily heroin users had slightly more official contacts with the criminal justice system from less-serious active offenders, but the differences were seldom statistically significant.

Almost all (95 percent) robber–dealers had been arrested, and three-fifths reported six or more arrests; the average was twelve arrests. Low-level burglars had the same pattern of arrests. Low-level robbers and burglar–dealers had the same number of arrests as drug dealers and low-level distributors. Overall, the mean number of arrests did not differ significantly by criminal-offender type or heroin-user group. Examining the number of lifetime arrests, the chi square value was barely significant at the .05 level for the criminal-offender types, but it was significant for the heroin-user groups. That is, daily heroin users were more likely to have six or more arrests than regular and irregular heroin users.

Similarly, the average subject reported under three years of incarceration during ten or more years of heroin use and fifteen to twenty years since reaching age 16. The number of years of incarceration (jail plus prison) was not significantly associated with the criminal-offender typology. The mean number of years of incarceration was just (.05 level) associated with the heroin-user groups.

If criminal behavior in previous years of heroin abuse was similar to that reported during the interviews, our subjects had spent relatively little time during their criminal careers in jail or prison, although they had been arrested several times.

Despite their high crime rates and economic consequences, robber–dealers and other serious offender types were arrested irregularly and generally for low-seriousness crimes. For example, we showed that three of the ten most active robbers had been arrested, but not for robbery. Rather, they were arrested on a less serious charge. Subjects typically entered a plea and were sentenced to time served, a fine, probation, or a few months in jail. Upon release, they quickly returned to crime and drug use.

Vignette 29 outlines the thirty-three-day reporting cycle of Kit G. Kit's burglary arrest was a common one. He was out of jail shortly and raised the money for his fine by committing more crimes. Kit's arrest illustrates the problem described by Chaiken and Chaiken (1982b): identifying serious offenders who are arrested on relatively less serious charges. Kit's official New York criminal record probably (we do not know) included his two arrests for selling marijuana and the current burglary, not a long or serious record. It is unlikely that it included his prior juvenile imprisonment in Puerto Rico for assault. Thus, the district attorney likely assumed that Kit was a low-level offender arrested for his first household burglary. He was willing to accept a plea in exchange for a fine as a sentence.

Kit's criminal lifestyle, however, was extraordinarily diverse and serious. He was a violent predator (as defined by Chaiken and Chaiken). During a twenty-day period, Kit committed a contract assault and another assault during a robbery. He committed two burglaries of residences, one of a commercial establishment, and one of a drug dealer. He committed two thefts and sold thousands of dollars worth of heroin and cocaine. He also was well armed with guns and frightened even a former associate (now a drug dealer) who owed him money from his days in Puerto Rico.

Table 3. Prior Arrests and Incarcerations among Criminal Offenders and Heroin-User Groups

	Lifetime arrests[a]				Number of Years Incarcerated[b]			
	Mean Number	None (%)	1–5 (%)	6+ (%)	Mean Number	None (%)	1–5 (%)	6+ (%)
All subjects	8.2	16	40	44	2.7	38	44	18
Criminal offender types								
Robber–dealer	12.2	5	32	63	4.4	26	37	37
Low-level robber	5.5	14	46	41	2.2	36	55	9
Burglar–dealer	5.6	0	58	42	2.2	33	58	8
Low-level burglar	12.7	6	22	72	3.9	22	44	33
Thief–dealers	10.1	10	45	45	2.4	28	59	14
Low-level thieves	7.2	31	36	33	2.5	51	31	17
Drug dealers	5.2	20	60	20	1.2	40	50	10
Low-level distributors	5.7	27	33	40	2.5	53	27	20
None of above	2.4	40	60	0	1.0	60	40	0
Significance Level	.07		.04		ns		ns	
Heroin-user group								
Daily	9.8	16	29	56	5.6	30	43	27
Regular	8.1	22	32	46	2.9	39	48	14
Irregular	7.0	11	59	30	3.3	43	41	16
Significance Level	ns		.01		.04		ns	

[a]Percentages add to 100 for each row.
ns Not significant

During almost all of this heavily criminal period, he was using heroin daily and in large amounts ($100 a day or more). Despite his heavy consumption, he suddenly went cold turkey at home by himself and abstained from heroin for almost two weeks. During the thirteen days of heroin abstinence, Kit committed only one crime (an assaultive robbery) to obtain rent money. But then he relapsed into heroin abuse again and refused to consider treatment entry (see above).

In many respects, Kit's behavior represents almost all extremes of drug-related crime in New York City. He was extremely active in all forms of crime while using heroin daily, but quite inactive when abstinent. He had been active in serious crimes since his early childhood and served time as a juvenile in Puerto Rico. His arrest record was short and nonserious in New York City, but his actual behavior was very serious.

The implications are clear. The criminal justice system is unlikely to detect and severely punish serious offenders like Kit because the appropriate information is not available. The treatment system will also never see them because of their avoidance behavior.

References

Ball, John C. 1982. The hyper-criminal opiate addict. Paper prepared for the Interdisciplinary Research Center, New York.

Chaiken, Jan, and Marcia Chaiken, 1982a. *Varieties of criminal behavior.* Santa Monica, Calif.: Rand.

Chaiken, Jan, and Marcia R. Chaiken with Joyce E. Peterson. 1982b. *Varieties of criminal behavior: Summary and policy implications.* Santa Monica, Calif.: Rand.

Duford, Franklyn W., and Delbert Elliott. 1982. *Identifying the career offender: Assessing the deterrent effect of arrests on criminal behavior and career patterns.* Boulder, Colo.: Behavioral Research Institute.

Duford, Franklyn W., Delbert Elliott, and David Huizinga. 1983a. *Assessing the seriousness hypothesis with self-reported data: A study of chronic offenders.* Boulder, Colo.: Behavioral Research Institute.

———. 1983b. *Characteristics of career offending: Testing four hypotheses.* Boulder, Colo.: Behavioral Research Institute.

Elliott, Delbert S., Franklyn W. Duford, and David Huizinga. 1983. The identification and prediction of career offenders utilizing self-reported and official data. Boulder, Colo.: Behavioral Research Institute.

Elliott, Delbert S., and David Huizinga. 1984. *The relationship between delinquent behavior and ADM problems.* Boulder, Colo.: Behavioral Research Institute.

Goldsmith, Douglas S., Dana E. Hunt, Douglas S. Lipton, and David Strug. 1984. Methadone folklore: Beliefs about side effects and their impact on treatment. *Human Organization* 43(4):330–340.

Hanson, Bill, George Beschner, James Walters, and Elliott Bovelle, eds. 1985. *Life with heroin: Voices from the inner city.* Lexington, Mass.: Lexington Books.

Hunt, Dana E., Douglas S. Lipton, Douglas Goldsmith, and David Strug. 1982. *Problems in methadone treatment: The influence of reference groups.* New York: Division of Substance Abuse Services. Also in *Behavioral Intervention Techniques in Drug Abuse Treatment,* edited by J. Grabowski, M. Stitzer, and J. Henningfield, 8–22, Monograph Series 46, Rockville, Md.: National Institute on Drug Abuse. 1984.

———. 1984. Street pharmacology: Uses of cocaine and heroin in the treatment of addiction. *Drug and Alcohol Dependence* 13:375–87.

Hunt, Dana E., Douglas S. Lipton, and Barry Spunt. 1983. Patterns of criminality among methadone clients and current narcotics users not in treatment. Paper presented at the American Society of Criminology, Toronto, Canada, November.

Inciardi, James A. 1979. Heroin use and street crime. *Crime and Delinquency* 25(July):335–346.

———. 1984. *Criminal justice.* Orlando, Fla.: Academic Press.

Inciardi, James A., and Carl D. Chambers. 1972. Unreported criminal involvement of narcotic addicts. *Journal of Drug Issues* 2:57–64.

28. HIV Infection Among Intravenous Drug Users: Epidemology and Risk Reduction

Don C. Des Jarlais and Samuel R. Friedman

Introduction . . .

In this paper, we will review current research on AIDS and HIV seroprevalence among IV drug users in the United States and Europe, on behaviors associated with HIV exposure among IV drug users, and on current and potential risk reduction among IV drug users. Research on AIDS among IV drug users is still at a relatively early stage. Many of the studies reviewed here have been presented at scientific conferences but have not yet been published in final form. Nevertheless, areas of consistency are emerging across studies that can serve to guide future research. Given the urgency of the need to prevent additional HIV infection, they will also have to guide public health policy decisions.

Epidemiology of AIDS and HIV infection among IV Drug Users

Probably the best single piece of information for predicting whether an individual IV drug user is likely to have been exposed to HIV is geographic location. Tables 1 and 2 show seroprevalence rates among IV drug users studied in different parts of the United States and Western Europe. While differences in recruitment of the samples undoubtedly account for some of the differences in seroprevalence rates, there is still very great geographic variation, from 2% in New Orleans (Ginzburg, personal communication, 1986) to approximately 70% in Milan [2].

In the United States, the New York City area clearly has the highest seroprevalence rate. This area also has had the greatest number of cases of AIDS among IV drug users—throughout the epidemic over 75% of the IV drug use AIDS cases in the USA have been from the states of New York and New Jersey (CDC AIDS Surveillance, personal communication: drug users with male homosexuality as a risk factor not included).

Studies of HIV seroprevalence among IV drug users in Europe also show a wide range. There is a general north-south difference, with higher rates among IV drug users in southern Europe. This gradient also applies within some countries, e.g. France (Brunet, personal communication, 1986) although not in the United Kingdom where Edinburgh has the highest seroprevalence rates.

In Europe, Italy and Spain have high seroprevalence rates and the greatest numbers of AIDS cases among IV drug users, 187 cases and 93 cases, respectively. Over 50% of the AIDS cases in each of these two countries have been among IV drug users. France with 58 and the Federal

From Don C. Des Jarlais and Samuel R. Friedman, HIV INFECTIONS AMONG IV DRUG USERS. Reprinted with permission from *AIDS*, Vol. 1, No. 2 (1987). Copyright © 1987 by Gower Academic Journals.

From the New York State Division of Substance Abuse Services, 55 W 125 Street, New York, NY 10027 and the *Narcotic and Drug Research, Inc. 55 W 125 Street, New York, NY 10027, USA.

Sponsorship: This research was supported by grant R01 DA 03574 from the National Institute on Drug Abuse. The views expressed in the article do not necessarily reflect the opinions of the New York State Division of Substance Abuse Services, Narcotic and Drug Research, Inc. or the National Institute on Drug Abuse.

Table 1. HIV seroprevalence among intravenous drug users in the United States.

Location	Date of sera collection	Reference
High seroprevalence 50% or higher		
Manhatten, NYC	1984	[7]
Northern New Jersey	1984	[8]
Moderate seroprevalence: 20-49%		
Bronx, New York	1985	[11]
Boston	1985	(Hutchinson, Craven, personal communication, 1987)
Low seroprevalence: 5-19%		
Chicago	1984	[21]
San Francisco	1984	[21]
	1985	[9]
Washington, DC	1985	(Ginzburg, personal communication, 1986)
Very low seroprevalence: less than 5%, but greater than 0%		
New Orleans	1985	(Ginzburg, personal communication, 1986)
Southern New Jersey	1984	[8]

Table 2. HIV seroprevalence among intravenous drug users in Western Europe.

Location	Date of sera collection	Reference
High seroprevalence: 50% or greater		
Southern Italy	1985	[41]
	1985	[2]
Spain	1985	[42]
	1985	[43]
Edinburgh, Scotland	1985	[6]
Moderate seroprevalence: 20-49%		
Berlin, FDR	1985	[44]
	1985	[2]
Zurich, Switzerland	1985	[45]
Amsterdam, Holland	1985	[10]
Dublin, Ireland	1985	[46]
Low seroprevalence: 5-19%		
Copenhagen, Denmark	1985	[5]
Stockholm, Sweden	1985	(Helgessen, personal communication, 1986)
Very low seroprevalence: less than 5%, but greater than 0%		
Yugoslavia	1985	(Data from Yugoslavia, Department of health)
Glasgow, Scotland	1985	[47]

Republic of Germany with 41 are the other two European countries with high numbers of IV drug user AIDS cases, and Switzerland, with 18, must be considered to have a high number relative to its population (Brunet, personal communication: IV drug users with male homosexual risk behavior not included).

The explanation for the great differences in HIV seroprevalence rates within the USA and Europe is a major problem in the epidemiology of HIV among IV drug users. Part of the explanation clearly is the date of first introduction of the virus into the local group of IV drug users. Historically collected sera from IV drug users show the first seropositive sample from New York City was collected in 1978 [3], from northern Italy in 1979 [2], from the Federal Republic of Germany in 1982 [4], and from Denmark in 1984 [5].

The studes of historically collected sera also show that, once the virus has been introduced into a local community of IV drug users, very rapid spread is possible. In southern Manhattan, seroprevalence rose to over 40% by 2 years after the first seropositive sample [3]. In Edinburgh, seroprevalence rose to approximately 50% within 2 years of the first seropositive sample [6], and in Milan to approximately 50% within 4 years after the first seropositive sample [2].

Behavioral Factors Associated with Seropositivity

There have been only a limited number of studies that examine different behavioral factors associated with sharing of injection equipment and HIV seropositivity [7–11]. Despite the limited number of studies, the findings permit some conclusions about behavioral factors associated with sharing equipment and HIV seropositivity.

The frequency of drug injection was associated with seropositivity in the studies from New York area [7,8,11]. This finding is consistent with the pre-AIDS observations that sharing drug injection equipment was normal behavior among IV drug users. The more one injected, the more frequently one would use equipment that another person had already used, and the more likely one was to become infected with HIV.

The second behavioral factor that has been associated with HIV exposure in different studies has been the use of 'shooting galleries' as a place to inject drug [7,8] (Chaisson, personal communication). Shooting galleries are places where IV drug users can rent injection equipment, which is returned to the owner and then rented to the next customer. They provide for sharing drug injection equipment with large numbers of other drug users. Use of shooting galleries may be considered the functional equivalent of having large numbers of homosexual partners in the early stages of the AIDS epidemic among gay men.

In addition to frequency of injection and the use of shooting galleries as factors associated with HIV exposure among IV drug users, there are two demographic variables that should be mentioned. These variables are not consistently associated with HIV exposure across studies, but have sufficiently important policy implications that they deserve to be mentioned. Females have had higher rates of HIV exposure in studies conducted in Manhattan [7] and West Berlin [4]. In addition, prostitutes were found to have higher seroprevalence rates in Manhattan [12] and the Bronx [11]. HIV exposure among prostitutes does not appear to be the result of transmission from customers. In a national study of HIV exposure among prostitutes, Darrow and colleagues found that the use of shooting galleries and unprotected sexual intercourse with IV drug using boyfriends was associated with HIV exposure, but not the total number of sexual contacts [13]. When multivariate analyses were done in these studies, male–female differences and differences between IV drug using female prostitutes and IV drug using females who did not report prostitution generally lost statistical significance. Nevertheless, it is clear that IV drug using women, almost all of whom are of childbearing age, will present a growing problem for *in utero* transmission. To the extent that female-to-male transmission does occur in North America and Western Europe (the efficiency of this transmission is currently a subject of intense debate) IV drug using prostitutes are an important potential source of heterosexual transmission.

Studies of ethnic differences in HIV exposure among IV drug users have found that minority group members have higher rates than whites in Manhattan [7], the Bronx [11], and San Francisco [9]. Multivariate analyses (controlling on drug injection frequency and use of shooting galleries) usually caused these differences to lose statistical significance, but it is clear that in the USA, HIV has spread more extensively among non-white IV drug users. This will present complicated public health problems to limit further spread among minority IV drug users and the associated heterosexual and *in utero* transmission.

In Europe, there are not yet sufficient data to address the question of seroprevalence among ethnic groups. Potentially higher rates of IV drug use within immigrant communities and the ease with which IV drug users can cross national boundaries, however, indicate potential difficulties in conducting AIDS prevention efforts for IV drug users.

There is currently very little evidence for a simple relationship between HIV seroprevalence among IV drug users and the legal restrictions on the sale of sterile needles and syringes. The most convincing evidence comes from Edinburgh, where the legal supply of sterile equipment was restricted (through police persuading pharmacists not to sell needles and syringes to drug users) at about the time that HIV was introduced into the community. This was followed by very rapid spread of the virus among IV drug users, reaching approximately 50% within 2 years after the virus was introduced into the area[6].

Italy provides the strongest counterexample. Sterile needles and syringes are legally available without prescription; indeed they are often sold in supermarkets. This legal availability has not prevented the rapid spread of HIV among IV drug users in the northern part of the country.

In the United States, prescriptions are required for the sale of needles and syringes in only 12 states [14]. Most of the states with high concentrations of IV drug users do require prescriptions, e.g. New York, New Jersey, California and Illinois, but not all do, e.g. Missouri and Louisiana. New Jersey has areas of both high and very low seroprevalence.

In Europe, only Sweden currently requires prescriptions. France and Switzerland only recently removed prescription requirements as AIDS prevention measures. Again there is no simple relationship to AIDS among IV drug users, as Switzerland is considered to have a relatively 'high' rate of HIV infection among IV drug users, France an 'average rate' and Sweden a 'low' rate [15].

Needle exchange programs, in which IV drug users may return used needles and syringes in exchange for sterile ones, have been in operation in Holland for several years and have recently been established in the United Kingdom, and at the time of writing were being considered in France and New York. There are, however, no data yet indicating that these programs have been successful in reducing the spread of HIV.

This current lack of a simple relationship between the legal restrictions on the purchase and possession of needles and syringes should not be considered surprising. The data in Tables 1 and 2 largely represent spread of HIV before any awareness among IV drug users of the dangers of AIDS. As noted above, the sharing of drug injection equipment was a normal part of the IV drug use subculture before any awareness of AIDS. Thus, the extent to which an increased availability of sterile equipment when coupled with an awareness of AIDS will reduce HIV infection among IV drug users must be considered an open question at this point.

Despite the wide variation in seroprevalence rates in the USA and Western Europe, the risk factor studies conducted to date show a limited number of behavioral factors that are typically associated with HIV exposure. Frequency of drug injection and use of shooting galleries (sharing equipment with large numbers of other IV drug users) appear to be frequently associated with HIV exposure, suggesting that effective prevention programs need to focus on reducing these two factors. Belonging to an ethnic minority group and engaging in prostitution may be additional risk factors, indicating the need for prevention programs that include special components for prostitutes and incorporate ethnic differences. Before considering prevention strategies, however, it is necessary to consider the question of whether IV drug users are capable of changing AIDS related risk behavior.

Current AIDS Risk Reduction Efforts Among IV Drug Users

The impression that drug users are 'self-destructive' has led many public officials to conclude that IV drug users will not change their behavior to avoid AIDS. (In addition to this belief, there are real social organizational and physiological impediments to AIDS risk reduction among IV drug users [1,16].) While there have been only a limited number of studies of behavior change among IV drug users in response to the threat of AIDS, all of them have shown substantial numbers of IV drug users adopting some form of AIDS risk reduction.

In 1984, all of a sample of 59 methadone maintenance patients whom we interviewed had heard of AIDS; 55 (93%) of them knew that IV drug use is a mode of transmission of the disease. The majority (61%) of these subjects also were able to name at least one AIDS symptom correctly, with the most frequently named symptoms being weight loss (36%) and fatigue (31%). Fifty-nine per cent of the subjects reported some form of risk reduction to avoid AIDS; 54% reported changes in injection-related behavior. The most common changes were increased use of clean needles and/ or the cleaning of needles, reported by 31%, and reducing needle sharing, reported by 29%. Fourteen per cent reported reducing their level of IV drug injection. (These subjects were primarily injecting cocaine, for which methadone has no chemotherapeutic effect.) Fifty-one per cent of the group also reported that friends had changed their behaviors to avoid AIDS [16].

In the summer of 1985, Selwyn et al. [17] studied IV drug users in jail (n = 115) and methadone maintenance clients (n = 146) with findings remarkably similar to those from our methadone maintenance subjects. Ninety-seven per cent of the two Selwyn samples knew that sharing needles could transmit AIDS. Over 60% of these subjects reported risk reduction. Reducing (or eliminating) needle sharing was the most common form of risk reduction in both samples.

Support for the validity of these reports from individual IV drug users can be seen in studies of the marketing of illicit needles and syringes in New York City. These studies show evidence of a large-scale change in the demand for sterile needles and syringes for injecting drugs. In the spring of 1985, we conducted interviews with people selling needles and syringes in the drug dealing areas of New York City [18]. Eighteen out of 22 needle sellers reported that sales had increased over the previous year, four specifically mentioned AIDS as the reason for the increased demand.

The increased demand for sterile needles and syringes is sufficiently strong to support a market in 'counterfeit' sterile needles. The people selling needles and syringes were also asked if they had ever sold used needles as new; 10 out of 21 (48%) reported that they occasionally repackaged used equipment and then sold it as new. This 'counterfeit' sterile needle phenomenon had not been observed in the city before awareness of AIDS, and indicates both the strength of the increased demand for sterile equipment and the hazards of relying upon an illicit market for sterile drug injection equipment.

315

In the fall of 1985, we observed additional AIDS related changes in the marketing of needles and syringes for illicit drug injection. Some needle sellers were including an extra needle with the sale of a 'set' of a needle and syringe. If the first needle gets clogged, it can immediately be replaced with the extra needle. This reduces the chances that a clogged needle would lead an IV drug user to rent or borrow a used needle. Finally, drug dealers have been including a new set of works as a marketing device with $25 and $50 bags of heroin [19].

These studies of changes in the marketing of illicit sterile needles in New York not only suggest that the self-reported changes in needle use by drug users are valid; they also suggest that AIDS risk reduction is occurring among IV drug users who are not in treatment. (The great majority of IV drug users are not in treatment at any point in time, and IV drug users in treatment inject drugs at levels greatly reduced from those out of treatment. The changes in the marketing of illicit needles and syringes should therefore be seen as primarily resulting from an increased demand for sterile equipment from IV drug users not in treatment.)

Both concern about AIDS and risk reduction to avoid exposure to the virus have developed among IV drug users in the New York metropolitan area, where HIV seroprevalence is approximately 50%, and where there are almost 3000 IV drug users who have already developed CDC (Centers for Disease Control) surveillance definition AIDS. An important question for control of the epidemic among IV drug users in other areas is whether risk reduction will occur before extensive spread of the virus and/or development of large numbers of cases of AIDS among IV drug users. Preliminary data from Amsterdam and San Francisco are encouraging on this point.

In Amsterdam, the HIV seroprevalence rate among IV drug users is estimated to be between 25% and 35%, and, to date, there have been only a few cases among IV drug users. Preliminary studies nevertheless indicate that significant risk reduction is occurring. In a retrospective study of self-reported behavior change over a 6-month period among 164 IV drug users, Coutinho and his colleagues found both a decline in the percentage who inject more than once per day, and an increase in the percentage using the 'needle exchange' to obtain sterile needles and syringes [20].

HIV seroprevalence among IV drug users in San Francisco is estimated to be between approximately 10 and 20% [9,16]. Biernacki and Feldman [22] have been conducting ethnographic research on IV drug users not in treatment in that city. They report that AIDS is already a topic of 'grave concern' among IV drug users there, and that the drug users want to learn how to protect themselves against exposure, including how to sterilize needles and syringes. Before any widespread prevention campaigns aimed at IV drug users, a 'substantial minority' had already reduced the numbers of people with whom they would share drug injection equipment.

Prevention Strategies

The AIDS risk reduction discussed above has primarily been the result of information carried by the mass media and by the oral communication networks within the IV drug use subculture, rather than the result of any public prevention efforts. Specifically targeted prevention efforts should be able to produce greater levels of AIDS risk reduction among IV drug users than have been observed to date.

In discussing AIDS prevention among IV drug users, it is important to avoid stereotyping all IV drug users as the same. There are important differences among current and potential IV drug users that will require different strategies for successful AIDS prevention. The epidemiological studies suggesting that ethnic minorities and prostitutes may have higher HIV seroprevalence rates indicate a need for prevention programs that consider the special circumstances of these groups.

In addition to these considerations, specific prevention programs should include the likelihood of future IV drug use as a major consideration. Conceptualizing prevention programs in terms of the likelihood of future IV drug use provides three target groups for AIDS/HIV prevention:

(1) those who have not begun IV drug use;
(2) those who are willing to enter treatment to eliminate IV drug use, and
(3) those who are unwilling to enter treatment and/or those for whom present forms of treatment are unlikely to be successful.

People Who Have Not Begun IV Drug Use

The ideal point for prevention of AIDS among IV drug users would be to prevent initiation into IV drug use. This would not only prevent needle sharing transmission of HIV; it would also prevent the many other health and social problems associated with IV drug use.

Educational programs about the dangers of AIDS and IV drug use are already being developed for use in secondary schools. While such programs certainly should be supported, there are likely to be limits on their effectiveness. First, drug prevention programs based on fear arousal have not been very successful in the past [23], particularly if the fear is associated with a low probability event or there is a long time period between the 'risky' drug use and the adverse consequences. Second, many people who eventually become IV drug users drop out of school well before they make decisions about injecting drugs.

Prevention programs targeted at reducing initiation into IV drug use may have to operate outside school settings. Rather than merely disseminating information about the dangers of AIDS, they may also have to focus on teaching skills needed to resist social pressures to begin injecting drugs (similar to cigarette smoking prevention programs that focus on teaching skills to resist initiation into cigarette smoking). Such programs undoubtedly are more difficult to operate than the in-school programs, but they will be necessary to reach those at highest risk for beginning drug injection. Programs working with people at high risk of beginning injecting also pose some difficult policy/strategic questions such as: should they focus only on preventing drug injection (the AIDS danger), or should they be broader and focus on any use of such drugs as cocaine and heroin, or broader still and try to focus on any illicit drug use? Preventing non-injected drug abuse is a valid public health goal in itself, but may dilute efforts to reduce the AIDS-specific problem of initiation into drug injection.

Reducing initiation into IV drug use may be the most effective long-term strategy for reducing the spread of HIV through sharing drug injection equipment. Given the likelihood that IV drug users will be active heterosexuals and have children, it may also be a necessary strategy for reducing heterosexual and *in utero* transmission. Yet we know very little about how AIDS has (or has not) affected initiation into IV drug use. This is clearly a critical area for research on long-term prevention.

Preventing AIDS through reducing initiation into IV drug use certainly will be required as part of a long-term effort to control AIDS. The number of current IV drug users at risk for HIV infection, however, is sufficiently large to require extensive prevention programs.

Current IV Drug Users Who Would Enter Treatment

Entering treatment has been associated with large reductions in the rate of IV drug use, particularly for heroin injection [24]. Fear of AIDS, among other reasons, will undoubtedly lead significant numbers of IV drug users to seek treatment for their drug use. Current data from New

Jersey, where people entering treatment are specifically asked their reasons for entering, show that approximately half of the IV drug users now entering give fear of AIDS as one of their reasons for entering treatment [25].

For the USA as a whole and in some parts of Europe, however, the availability of treatment was significantly less than the demand even before the AIDS epidemic. Expanding the treatment system could significantly reduce IV drug injection and transmission of HIV among IV drug users. Users who had not been exposed would greatly reduce their chances of being exposed, and users who had already been exposed would greatly reduce their chances of exposing others. The economics of treating AIDS (approximately $100 000–150 000 per case in New York) versus providing drug abuse treatment (approximately $3000 per patient year) also argue for expansion of the treatment network.

Unfortunately, there are real factors other than finances that currently limit the availability of drug abuse treatment. Drug abuse treatment has general approval within Western society, but is particularly subject to local neighbourhood opposition. In addition, methadone maintenance treatment, which tends to be the most acceptable treatment modality to large numbers of IV drug users, also tends to have the least degree of acceptance among the general public and by the criminal justice system.

Finally, if there is to be significant reduction of HIV transmission through increased treatment, the program expansion will have to be on a large scale. Based on our New York experience, we would estimate that there are approximately six IV drug users not in treatment for every one currently in treatment. Thus, to control HIV transmission among IV drug users through additional treatment would require a massive expansion of the treatment system, not just an incremental expansion.

IV Drug Users Who Do Not Wish to Enter Treatment

There are many current IV drug users who wish to reduce their chances of exposure to HIV but do not wish to enter treatment. In addition, treatment is not likely to be immediately successful in eliminating IV drug use for many who do enter. The studies in New York and elsewhere indicate that these IV drug users who are very likely to continue injecting drugs will try to modify their needle use behavior to avoid AIDS.

One strategy for reducing the spread of HIV among people who are likely to continue injecting drugs is to increase the legal availability of sterile needles and syringes. This has been the subject of much public discussion in New York, New Jersey and California, though none of these states has adopted any program to provide sterile drug injection equipment to IV drug users. Concern about AIDS among IV drug users has also led to public discussion of increasing legal availability of sterile injection equipment in France and Sweden, and to removal of prescription requirements in Switzerland, and establishment of needle exchanges in the United Kingdom. Increasing the legal availability of hypodermic needles has received support among public health officials. It has generally been opposed by law enforcement officials, who predict that it either would not be effective because IV drug users would not change their behavior, or that it would be 'too' effective and increase the number of IV drug users by removing the threat of AIDS.

The actual effects of increasing the legal availability of sterile needles and syringes are unknown. Almost no data have been systematically collected about the relationships between the legal availability of sterile equipment and levels of IV drug use prior to the AIDS epidemic. Even if such prior information were available, it is questionable whether it could be generalized to the AIDS situation, since the threat of AIDS may be radically changing many aspects of IV drug use.

The preliminary findings from Amsterdam indicate that IV drug users will return equipment (so that disposal of the used equipment is not a major problem), that there has been no decrease in demand for either methadone or drug-free treatment, and that there has been no increase in IV drug use [26]. There is as yet no evidence that the needle exchange program has reduced spread of HIV, but such effectiveness may depend upon the increasing concern about AIDS and use of the needle exchange noted above [20].

In light of the current lack of information regarding the legal distribution of sterile equipment to IV drug users as a method of preventing AIDS, the National Academy of Sciences–Institute of Medicine has specifically called for research in the United States on this topic [27].

A related method of attempting to reduce HIV transmission among IV drug users who are very likely to continue injecting illicit drugs is education about not sharing needles and on how to 'clean' needles properly in order to kill HIV. The United States Public Health Service has called for research on increasing the use of sterile equipment by IV drug users not in treatment [28]. Printed information is being distributed in several parts of the USA, sometimes supplemented with face-to-face instruction on how to sterilize needles. (The messages emphasize that stopping drug injection is the only certain method for avoiding HIV infection from contaminated works.) Such programs are currently operational in New York City, New Jersey, San Francisco, Baltimore, Chicago and Washington, DC.

Interactions Among Prevention Strategies

It is possible to see 'inconsistencies' among these strategies for preventing AIDS among groups that differ according to the likelihood of future IV drug injection. Providing for any form of 'safer injection' may be viewed as encouraging non-injectors to start injecting drugs, and as discouraging current IV drug users from entering treatment and stopping IV drug use. Because these perceived inconsistencies may lead to failure to develop any AIDS prevention programs among IV drug users, several brief comments are appropriate.

First, the abuse of psychoactive substances is associated with a variety of complex social and health problems. A mixture of educational, therapeutic and law enforcement methods is utilized to try to minimize these problems. This mixture of strategies has been adopted because no single approach has been effective by itself. Because a mixture of strategies is used, it is relatively easy to find numerous 'logical inconsistencies' between the different methods. Conflict between therapeutic and law enforcement approaches to reducing addiction certainly has existed throughout the history of drug abuse in the United States [29–31]. Adaptation to this conflict has usually been through the use of separate agencies with separate missions and the setting of priorities when working with individuals, with a current consensus that neither approach is likely to be sufficiently effective by itself. AIDS is a new and potentially catastrophic problem associated with drug abuse. Use of a single strategy to try controlling AIDS among IV drug users is no more likely to be successful than use of a single strategy is in controlling the overall problem of drug abuse in society.

The second comment concerns our very limited ability to predict just what does 'encourage drug abuse' and what does prevent HIV infection among IV drug users. The mass media coverage of AIDs among IV drug users in New York City appears to have led to both an increase in the use of sterile equipment and, to a smaller extent, a decrease in the frequency of injection. Data from Amsterdam indicate that the needle exchange program has not led to any increase in drug injection nor to a reduction in the demand for either methadone or drug-free treatment [26], but has not yet led to an observable reduction in the spread of HIV [10].

Preliminary data from New York (Kleinman, personal communication, 1986), New Jersey [25] and San Francisco (Newmeyer, personal communication, 1986) indicate that educating IV drug users in how to sterilize illicit drug injection equipment leads many of them to want to enter treatment for their drug abuse. Consistency on the need to prevent HIV infection appears to be overriding any potential inconsistency between sterilizing needles versus entering treatment to stop IV drug use. Efforts to prevent AIDS through increasing the use of sterile equipment and through providing drug abuse treatment to stop IV drug use may be mutually reinforcing strategies rather than contradictory ones.

Given the heterogeneity among current (and potential) IV drug users, it is highly unlikely that any single approach to the prevention of HIV infection will be sufficient for all IV drug users. Determining the optimal mixture of strategies will require careful evaluation of different prevention programs integrated with monitoring of the spread of the virus. The mixture of strategies to maximize the prevention of AIDS can be expected to vary in different communities and across time in a single community.

HIV Antibody Testing and AIDS Prevention

HIV antibody testing has been advocated as a potentially powerful technique for reducing the transmission of HIV [28]. There are only limited data on the effects of HIV testing on AIDS-related behavior in IV drug users. Two papers were presented at the Paris conference showing dramatic short-term reductions in needle use transmission behavior following feedback of test results [32,33]. Both of these studies were conducted within treatment settings, the decision to provide counseling was supported by the treatment staff, there was extensive pre-test counselling, the testing was totally voluntary, and extensive precautions were taken to assure confidentiality of the test results. When HIV antibody testing is done without these extensive supports, there appears to be no net positive effect on AIDS risk behavior, and a potential for harm to the individuals participating [25]. Even with the intensive supports, antibody test feedback is likely to produce increases in anxiety and depression [32]. In terms of reducing AIDS risk behavior, it is probably a mistake to think of 'antibody testing' as a prevention technique. Instead, one should think of intensive counselling with testing as an adjunct to the counselling.

Self-Organization and AIDS Prevention

Although there are no data on the competitive efficacy of the 'causes' of AIDS risk reduction among gay men, organizations of gay men have been very active in promoting risk reduction. Despite the inherent difficulties in creating formal organizations of IV drug users, there is the potential that self-help organizations of current and/or former IV drug users might be able to create new social norms that would discourage the sharing of drug injection equipment.

The most developed form of drug user formal organization is undoubtedly the Dutch 'junkiebonden' (drug users' unions, or JBs). The JBs formed in the early 1980s as an attempt by drug users to influence government drug laws and the way in which Dutch drug treatment programs were run. They initiated a needle exchange program in response to the danger of hepatitis. More recently, they have been an essential vehicle for distributing syringes and needles as part of the official Dutch anti-AIDS needle exchange programs, and they have written their own pamphlets and conducted other educational efforts. They have not yet been able to plan and implement a broad plan for subcultural change to reduce HIV transmission, but they have established a degree of self-awareness and identity among Dutch IV drug users that will be a valuable resource for collective efforts at mutual protection (for more detail about the JBs, including analyses of their strengths and weaknesses, see [34,35]).

In New York, former IV drug users, methadone patients, health professionals, and current drug users have set up an explicitly AIDS-oriented organization to educate IV drug users about AIDS, give support to the sick, give drug users a voice in AIDS policy, and do whatever they can to reduce HIV transmission to and by IV drug users. Their activities have included going into drug selling areas to teach users about AIDS; visiting shooting galleries and negotiated with their owners to have sterile works on hand as well as bleach, clean cotton, clean plastic cups, garbage bags, and other equipment; and conducting training sessions for drug program staff and clients.

Another, more limited, form of drug user organization has taken place in some drug treatment program. Here, staff members have initiated discussion groups to work through what the existence of HIV means for the lives of participants and to help individuals figure out how to cope with their changed environment. In some cases, the drug users in these groups have become interested in spreading the facts about AIDS, and their ideas about how drug users can protect themselves, to other program clients and to drug users on the streets. These self-help groups seem to offer an opportunity both for effective outreach and also for the development of support among their active participants for self-protective behavior [36].

Heterosexual and *In Utero* Transmission of HIV

While this paper is restricted to reviewing current data on the sharing of drug injection equipment and the transmission of HIV, a brief discussion of heterosexual and *in utero* transmission is also needed. As noted in the introduction, once HIV becomes established within a local group of IV drug users, they can become the predominant source for both heterosexual and *in utero* transmission in the area.

Both our 1984 data on risk reduction among methadone patients [16] and the Selwyn *et al.'s* 1985 data on methadone patients and IV drug users in prison [17] showed risk reduction for heterosexual transmission, although this was reported by smaller percentages than were reporting IV drug use risk reduction. The number of public health messages for heterosexuals to use condoms has been increasing rapidly in both the United States and Europe, and there are some drug abuse treatment programs in the USA and Europe that are now distributing condoms as a regular activity. Voluntary antibody testing may be particularly helpful in reducing heterosexual and *in utero* transmission from IV drug users as it would at least identify seronegatives who would have little worry of transmitting the virus. The situation is quite difficult for seropositive IV drug users. The danger of heterosexual transmission may lead sexual partners to break off relationships at a time when the newly informed seropositive needs psychological and social support [32]. To decide permanently against having children would have great psychological cost for many IV drug users.

Consideration of the difficulties in preventing heterosexual and *in utero* transmission reinforces the need to prevent HIV transmission through sharing of drug injection equipment.

Natural History of HIV Infection in IV Drug Users

There has been very little study of the outcomes of HIV infection in IV drug users. One study found that two out of eight seropositive IV drug users developed AIDS within 3 years [37], and we found an annual incidence of 4% for development of AIDS in a 9-month follow-up [38]. These rates are similar to the rates for the development of AIDS among seropositive gay men in New York City. There are, however, two aspects of the natural history of HIV infection that could increase motivation for behavior change/risk reduction among IV drug users.

First, in our cohort study, high levels of continued drug injection were associated with increased rates of HIV-related immunosuppression (T4 cell loss) in seropositive IV drug users. If AIDS prevention efforts include a warning that continued injection may increase immunosuppression, this may lead seropositive IV drug users to reduce their levels of drug injection and therefore the likelihood that they would transmit HIV to others. (Provision of drug abuse treatment for seropositives may be needed for this to have an effect on a public health scale level.)

The second aspect of the natural history of HIV infection among IV drug users is the possibility that AIDS deaths greatly underestimate the number of fatal outcomes of HIV infection in the group. Since HIV was first introduced into the IV drug use group in New York City, there has been a dramatic increase in the annual numbers of recorded deaths among IV drug users from approximately 250 in 1978, to approximately 2000 in 1986 [13,33]. Deaths from AIDS account for only half of this increase, with non-pneumocystis pneumonia and endocarditis being among the rapidly growing other causes of death among IV drug users in New York City. There has also been an epidemic increase in tuberculosis among IV drug users over the same time period [40]. Research on possible relationships of HIV infection to the 'non-AIDS' excess deaths and to the increase in tuberculosis is currently being conducted. If IV drug users perceive HIV infection as likely to lead to a variety of serious health problems in addition to the possibility of developing AIDS, their motivation to reduce AIDS risk behavior could be strengthened.

Summary

Research on the epidemiology of HIV infection among IV drug users is still at a relatively early stage. Multi-location studies that would permit better geographic comparisons are greatly needed. Multi-method studies within single geographic areas are also needed to assess possible biases with respect to sample recruitment and data collection procedures. The continuation of the epidemic provides a changing historical context that complicates any comparisons. Despite these problems, there are some consistencies that can be seen across studies.

Studies of HIV seroprevalence among IV drug users show wide variation among cities in the United States and Europe. The time that the virus was introduced into the IV drug using group within the city is one factor in explaining these differences; other cross-city factors have yet to be identified. Once HIV has been introduced into the IV drug use group within a particular geographic area, there is the possibility of rapid spread up to seroprevalence levels of 50% or greater. Thus, a currently low seroprevalence rate should not be seen as a stable situation.

Frequency of injection and sharing of equipment with multiple other drug users (particularly at shooting galleries) have been frequently associated with HIV exposure. Being female, ethnicity (in the USA) and engaging in prostitution also may be associated with increased risk for HIV exposure, suggesting that prevention programs should include special consideration of sex and ethnic differences.

Studies of AIDS risk reduction show that substantial proportions of IV drug users are changing their behavior to avoid exposure to HIV. This risk reduction is probably more advanced in New York, with its high seroprevalence and incidence of cases, but is also occurring in cities with lower seroprevalence and limited numbers of cases. The primary forms of risk reduction are increasing the use of sterile equipment, reducing the number of needle sharing partners, and reducing the

322

frequency of injection. These behavior changes are very similar to the frequently identified behavioral risk factors associated with HIV exposure, suggesting that they should be effective in at least slowing the spread of HIV among IV drug users. No linkage of risk reduction to decreases in sero-conversion has yet been shown, however, and greater risk reduction is clearly required.

A variety of prevention strategies will probably be needed to reduce the spread of HIV among IV drug users. Prevention of initiation into drug injection is an undeniable long-term goal for the control of HIV infection, but there is very little research being conducted in this area. Increasing the availability of drug abuse treatment and increasing the use of sterile equipment among people who continue to inject have been two commonly suggested means for reducing the spread of the virus among current IV drug users. While it is possible to see contradiction between these two strategies, the very limited available data from places where both have been put into effect indicate that the two strategies probably reinforce each other rather than detract from each other. While there is considerable evidence that AIDS prevention is quite feasible among IV drug users, the present state of knowledge on how best to achieve this is limited. Much more research and demonstration activity is needed.

References

1. Des Jarlais D C., Friedman S R, Strug D: AIDS among intravenous drug users; a sociocultural perspective. *In* The Social Dimensions of AIDS: Methods and Theory edited by Feldman D, Johnson T. New York: Praeger, 1986, pp. 11–126.
2. Verani P: Seroprevalence among intravenous drug abusers in Italy. Presented at Workshop on Epidemiological Surveys on AIDS: Epidemiology of HIV Infections in Europe Spread among Intravenous Drug Users and the Heterosexual Population. Berlin, November 12–14, 1986.
3. Novick D M, Kreek M J, Des Jarlais D C, Spira T J, Khuri E T, Ragunath J, Kalyanaraman V S, Gelb A M, Miescher A: Abstract of clinical research findings: therapeutic and historical aspects. *In* Problems of Drug Dependence 1985: Proceedings of the 47th Annual Scientific Meeting, The Committee on Problems of Drug Dependence, Inc. NIDA Research Monograph 67, edited by Harris L J. Washington, DC: USGPO, 1985, pp. 318–320.
4. Rex W: Increase of HIV Seroprevalence among IVDA in West Berlin prisons since 1982. Presented at Workshop on Epidemiological Surveys on AIDS: Epidemiology of HIV Infections in Europe Spread among Intravenous Drug Users and the Heterosexual Population. Berlin, November 12–14, 1986.
5. Worm A M: Incidence of HIV antibodies in IV drug abusers and prostitutes in Copenhagen. Presented at Workship on Epidemiological Surveys on AIDS: Epidemiology of HIV Infections in Europe Spread among Intravenous Drug Users and the Heterosexual Population. Berlin, November 12–14, 1986.
6. Robertson J R, Bucknall A B V, Welsby P D, Roberts J J K, Inglis J M, Peutherer J F, Brettle R P: Epidemic of AIDS related virus (HTLV-III/LAV) infection among intravenous drug users. Br Med J 1986, **292**:527–529.
7. Cohen H, Marmor M, Des Jarlais D C, Spira T, Friedmans S R, Yancovitz S: Risk factors for HTLV-III/LAV seropositivity among intravenous drug users. Presented at the International Conference on the Acquired Immune Deficiency Syndrome (AIDS). Atlanta, April 14–17, 1985.
8. Weiss S H, Ginzburg H M, Goedert J J, Biggar R J, Mohica B A, Blattner W A: Risk for HTLV-III exposure and AIDS among parenteral drug abusers in New Jersey. Presented at the International Conference on the Acquired Immunodeficiency Syndrome (AIDS). Atlanta, April 14–17, 1985.
9. Chaisson R E, Moss A R, Onishi R, Osmond D, Carlson J R: Human immunodeficiency virus infection in heterosexual intravenous drug users in San Francisco, AM J Public Health 1987, **77**:169–172.
10. Van den Hoek J A, Van Zadelhof A W, Goudsmit J, Coutinho R A: Risk factors for LAV/HTLV-III infection among drug users in Amsterdam. Presented at the International Conference on AIDS. Paris, June 23–25, 1986.
11. Schoenbaum E E, Selwyn P A, Klein R S, Rogers M F, Freeman K, Friedland G H: Prevalence of and risk factors associated with HTLV-III/LAV antibodies among intravenous drug abusers in methadone programs in New York City. Presented at the International Conference on AIDS. Paris, June 23–25, 1986.

12. Des Jarlais D C, Wish E, Friedman S R, Stoneburner R, Yancovitz S, Mildvan D, El-Sadr W, Brady E, Cuadrado M: Intravenous drug use and heterosexual transmission of human immunodeficiency virus: current trends in New York City. New York State J Med 1987, **87**:283–285.
13. Darrow M: Risk Factors among prostitutes. Presented at Workshop on Epidemiological Surveys on AIDS: Epidemiology of HIV Infections in Europe Spread among Intravenous Drug users and the Heterosexual Population. Berlin, November 12–14, 1986.
14. National Association of State Boards of Pharmacy. Survey of Pharmacy Law, 1983–1984. Chicago, 1983.
15. Ancelle R. Buning E: Incidence and problems of AIDS and HIV infections in European Community countries. Presented at Workshop on Epidemiological Surveys on AIDS: Epidemiology of HIV Infections in Europe Spread among Intravenous Drug Users and the Heterosexual Population. Berlin, November 12–14, 1986.
16. Friedman S R, Des Jarlais D C, Sotheran J L, Garber J, Cohen H, Smith D: AIDS and self-organization among intravenous drug users. Int J Addict 1987, **22**:201–220.
17. Selwyn P A, Cox C P, Feiner C, Lipschutz C, Cohen R: Knowledge about AIDS and high-risk behavior among intravenous drug abusers in New York City. Presented at Annual Meeting of the American Public Health Association. Washington, DC, September 1985.
18. Des Jarlais D C, Friedman S R, Hopkins W: Risk reduction for the acquired immunodeficiency syndrome among intravenous drug users. Ann Intern Med 1985, **103**:755–759.
19. Des Jarlais D C, Hopkins W: Free needles for intravenous drug users at risk for AIDS: current developments in New York City. N Engl J Med 1985, **313**:23.
20. Coutinho R A: Preliminary results of AIDS studies among IVDA in Amsterdam. Presented at Workshop on Epidemiological Surveys on AIDS: Epidemiology of HIV Infections in Europe Spread among Intravenous Drug Users and the Heterosexual Population. Berlin, November 12–14, 1986.
21. Spira T J, Des Jarlais D C, Bokos D, Onichi R, Kiprov R, Kalyanaraman V S: HTLV-III/LAV antibodies in intravenous drug users—comparisons of high and low risk areas for AIDS. Presented at the International Conference on the Acquired Immune Deficiency Syndrome (AIDS). Atlanta, April 14–17, 1985.
22. Biemacki P, Feldman H: Ethnographic observations of IV drug use practices that put users at risk for AIDS. Presented at the XV International Institute on the Prevention and Treatment of Drug Dependence. Amsterdam/Noordwijkerhout, the Netherlands, April 6–11, 1986.
23. Schaps E. DiBartolo R, Churgin S: Primary Prevention Research: A Review of 127 Program Evaluations. Walnut Creek, California: Pyramid Project, Pacific Institute for Research and Evaluation, 1978.
24. Simpson D D, Savage J L, Sells S B: Data Book on Drug Treatment Outcomes: Followup Study of 1969–1972 Admissions to the Drug Abuse Reporting Program (DARP). Institute of Behavioral Research Report 78–10. Fort Worth: Texas Christian University, 1978.
25. Jackson J: Developing a community approach. Presented at AIDS in the Drug Abuse Community and Heterosexual Transmission. Newark, March 31–April 1, 1986.
26. Buning E: Amsterdam's drug policy and the prevention of AIDS. Presented at the Conference on AIDS in the Drug Abuse Community and Heterosexual Transmission. Newark, March 31–April 1, 1986.
27. National Academy of Sciences. Institute of Medicine Confronting AIDS: Directions for Public Health, Health Care, and Research. Washington, DC: National Academy Press, 1986.
28. U.S. Public Health Service. Public Health Service Plan for the Prevention and Control of AID and the AIDS Virus: Report of the Coolfont Planning Conference. June 4–6, 1986.
29. Musto D F: The American Disease: Origins of Narcotic Control. New Haven: Yale University, 1973.
30. Courtwright D T: Dark Paradise: Opiate Addiction in America before 1940. Cambridge: Harvard University Press, 1982.
31. Inciardi J: The War on Drugs: Heroin, Cocaine, Crime and Public Policy. Palo Alto: Mayfield, 1986.
32. Casadonte P, Des Jarlais D C, Smith T, Novatt A, Hemdal P: Psychological and Behavioral Impact of Learning HTLV-III/LAV Antibody Test Results. Presented at the International Conference on Acquired Immunodeficiency Syndrome (AIDS). Paris, June 23–25, 1986.
33. Cox C P, Selwyn P A, Schoenbaum E E, O'Dowd M A, Drucker E: Psychological and behavioral consequences of HTLV-III/LAV antibody testing and notification among intravenous drug abusers in a methadone programs in New York City. Presented at the International Conference on Acquired Immunodeficiency Syndrome (AIDS). Paris, June 1–5, 1986.

34. Des Jarlais D C, Friedman S R: An overview of AIDS among intravenous drug users; epidemiology, natural history and prevention. Proceedings of ICAA Drug Institute (in press). Amsterdam: Nordwykerhoud.

35. Friedman S R, Des Jarlais D C, Sotheran J L, Garber J, Cohen H, Smith D: AIDS and self-organization among intravenous drug users. Int J Addict 1987, 22:201–220.

36. Friedman S R, Des Jarlais D C, Goldsmith D S: An overview of current AIDS prevention efforts aimed at intravenous drug users. J Drug Issues (in press).

37. Goedert J J, Biggar R, Weiss S, Eyster M, Melbey M, Wilson S, Ginzburg H, Grossman R, DiGioia H, Sanchez W, Giron J, Ebbessen P, Gallo R, Blattner W: Three year incidence of AIDS among HTLV-III-infected risk group members: a comparison of five cohorts. Science 1986, 231:992–995.

38. Des Jarlais D C, Friedman S R, Marmor M, Cohen H, Mildvan D, Yancovitz S, Mathur U, El-Sadr W, Spira T J, Garber J, Beatrice S T, Abdul-Quader A S, Sotheran J L: Development of AIDS, HIV seroconversion, and co-factors for T4 cell loss in a cohort of intravenous drug users. AIDS, 1987, 1:105–111.

39. Stonebuner R L, Guigli P, Kristal A: Increasing mortality in intravenous narcotic users in New York City and its relationship to the AIDS epidemic: is there an unrecognized spectrum of HTLV-III/LAV-related disease? Presented at the International Conference on AIDS. Paris, June 23–25, 1986.

40. Stoneburner R L, Kristal A: Increasing tuberculosis incidence and its relationship to acquired immunodeficiency syndrome in New York City. Presented at the International Conference on Acquired Immunodeficiency Syndrome (AIDS). Atlanta, April 14–17, 1985.

41. Angarano G. Pastore G, Monno L, Santantonio F, Luchera N, Schiraldi O: Rapid spread of HTLV-III infection among drug addicts in Italy. Lancet 1985, II:1302.

42. Camprubi J: SIDA: Prevalencia de la infeccion por VIH en los ADVP. Situacion actual y posibilidades de actuacion. Comunidad y Drogas 2:9–22.

43. Rodrigo J M, Serra M A, Aguilar E, Del Olmo J A, Jimeno V, Aparisi L: HTLV antibodies in drug addicts in Spain. Lancet 1985, II:156–157.

44. Hunsmann G, Schneider J, Bayer H: Seroepidemiology of HTLV-III/LAV in the Federal Republic of Germany. Klin Wochenschr 1985, 63:233–235.

45. Schupbach J. Haller O, Vogt M, Luthy R, Joller H, Oelz O, Popovic M, Sarngadharan M G, Gallo R C: Antibodies to HTLV-III in Swiss patients with AIDS and pre-AIDS and in groups at risk for AIDS. N Engl J Med 1985, 312:265–270.

46. Shattock A G, Kaminski G Z, Hillary I B: HTLV-III serology, AIDS and ARC cases in Ireland. Presented at the International Conference on AIDS. Paris, June 23–25, 1986.

47. Follett E A C, McIntyre A, O'Donnell B: HTLV-III antibody in drug abusers in the West of Scotland: the Edinburgh connection. Lancet 1986, I:446–447.

Chapter VIII
Cocaine and the Amphetamines

This chapter deals with the drug category of the major stimulants, cocaine and the amphetamines. Throughout the past century in American history, both of these drugs have enjoyed a somewhat mixed reputation. Most recently, the illegal international trade in cocaine has become tied to foreign policy issues and related questions about tacit U.S. approval of, and even possible CIA participation in, drug trafficking operations involving several Central American countries. Prior to the turn of the 20th century, however, cocaine was hailed as a medicine with important curative properties for those suffering from depression, overfatigue and related psychological and physical ailments. As medical practice began to establish the risks of overstimulation, psychological dependence and cocaine psychosis in the late 1800's and early 1900's, the use of cocaine as a medical drug began to decline while its use as a recreational drug increased.

At the same time that this change was taking place, the development of cheaper and longer lasting synthetic amphetamine stimulants arose to take the pharmaceutical place of cocaine. Indeed, from the early part of this century up until the 1960's, the amphetamines have often been utilized not only for depression and related ailments, but also for weight loss, to boost the performance of athletes, to keep truck drivers awake during long hauls without sleep and even for aiding college students preparing for exams. During the 1960's, the so-called "speedfreak" came on the drug scene increasingly moving the amphetamines from legal, medicinal to illegal, recreational uses. Following crackdowns on the illegal production, distribution and use of amphetamines, the 1970's and 1980's have seen the re-emergence of cocaine as a drug of choice, first as the high class, expensive drug of the successful professional set, and more recently in the form of "crack" as a popular intoxicant among young people.

This chapter's first article by Cooter takes on the question of whether or not the use of stimulants (in this case, amphetamines) does in fact improve athletic performance. Given the numerous rumors and related allegations in recent years about the use of amphetamines and cocaine by professional and amateur athletes, Cooter presents important and timely information on this issue.

The Grinspoon and Bakalar article provides recent information regarding the effects, usage patterns and risks that exist for cocaine. Focusing in particular on the increasing use of cocaine by young adults as well as the recognition that there are substantial numbers of psychologically dependent individuals who use cocaine frequently and in large quantities, this article notes the related health risks and consequences. Grinspoon and Bakalar also note the increased risks that occur with intravenous ingestion and the use of freebase cocaine or "crack."

The final selection by Adler draws upon her undercover participant observation research to describe the fast-paced and extravagant lifestyle of those who heavily use and illegally traffic in cocaine. Adler also details the particular ways in which the attitudes of these dealers impact their relationships with the women and children in their lives. Although Adler's article does not specifically touch upon the recent foreign policy issues for cocaine, clearly the amounts of money involved in the black market for this drug serve as a seductive lure to individuals with various financial and political motivations.

29. Amphetamine Use: Physical Activity and Sport

G. Rankin Cooter

• • •

The Problem

It is speculated that a large number of athletes at many levels of skill and ability have at one time or another resorted to drug use in an attempt to improve performance in sport competition. In the last decade the use of drugs by athletes has increased at an alarming rate. Of particular importance is a classification of drugs known as amphetamines (more commonly denoted as "pep pills," "greenies," "uppers," and various other names). The use and abuse of the amphetamines for the purpose of performance enhancement is well documented in the literature. Peak documentation appeared in 1969, with the articles by Gilbert in *Sports Illustrated* (1969a, 1969b, 1969c) and in the early 1970's in Dave Meggyesy's (1970) article and Jim Bouton's (1970) book which describe amphetamine use by professional football and baseball players respectively. Many articles have also implied wide-spread use of amphetamines by collegiate and to a lesser extent by junior and senior high school athletes (Furlong, 1971).

Primary abuse appears to be in professional sports. However, the banning of ergogenic drugs from the 1968 Olympic Games; Bowie Kuhn's 1971 ruling prohibiting baseball players' use of drugs; the banning of drug use by NFL professional football players; and recent FDA and AMA regulations, have apparently resulted in a somewhat reduced "up-front" utilization of amphetamines by athletes. But amphetamine availability to the athletes certainly continues, as evidenced by the recent *Playboy* interview of Pete rose (*Playboy,* 1979) and articles in *Sports Illustrated—* "Speed Is All The Rage" (Underwood, 1978), *Reader's Digest—* "Drugs and the Athlete: A Growing Threat" (Amdur, 1978) and in *Science—* "Drugging of Football Players Curbed by Central Monitoring Plan, NFL Claims." (Marshall, 1979). In fact, California psychiatrist Arnold Mandell reports that of 87 professional football players surveyed, 75 had used amphetamines with doses ranging from 5 mg to a dangerously high 150 mg per Sunday (Mandell, 1978). In an exclusive *Playboy* interview the renowned professional baseball player Pete Rose stated: "Well, a lot of guys might think there are certain days you might need a greenie, an upper." When *Playboy* asked Rose if he would take a greenie, he replied that he might take one and that there might be someday when he played a doubleheader that he mentally needed a lift. He added, "A doctor isn't going to write a prescription that is going to be harmful to my body." (*Playboy,* 1979.) These statements seem to indicate, as Mandell feared, that amphetamine abuse remains rampant and that professional players' (who set examples for youngsters) attitudes have not changed in spite of Kuhn's rulings on drug prescriptions. The documented accounts in these articles clearly suggest continued use of amphetamines by professional athletes, yet professional sport leagues contend that abuse is not severe enough to warrant tests prior to competition which would detect amphetamine presence. Even urine analysis attempts at recent Olympic Games have been undermined by the failure of several Eastern athletes to report for such tests. (Amdur, 1979; Marshall, 1979).

Amphetamines: What Are They?

The amphetamines are central nervous system and cardiovascular stimulants and are classified as pressor or sympathomimetic amines. They are chemically and pharmacologically related to epinephrine or ephedrine but are greater nervous system stimulants. Amphetamines stimulate activity of the post-ganglionic sympathetic nerves, and possibly facilitate synaptic transmission in the spinal cord (Kalant, 1958; Thompson & Schuster, 1968). They also may increase attention transmission and alertness due to the promotion of norepinephrine (or other catecholamine) release or accumulation in the brain (Goth, 1974). The increased feeling of alertness often masks fatigue and produces a false sense of well-being.

The knowledge that soldiers in the German army were using amphetamines to prolong their muscular endurance and attention span during World War II, prompted a series of field studies into the ergogenic effects of amphetamines by American researchers. Findings from these studies confirmed that amphetamine increases attention and cerebral activity; increases blood pressure (Beyer, 1939); enhances neural transmission, causes vasoconstriction in the splanchnic area; increases blood sugar (due to increased glycogenolysis or glycogen to glucose conversion); increases metabolism and oxygen uptake; and causes pupil dilation (Hahn, 1960; Leake, 1958; Thompson & Schuster, 1968). Due to increased muscular tension and cardiovascular activity, there is increased proprioceptive bombardment of sensory nerve impulses, especially from bones and joints to the brain stem (Leake, 1958). This results in a feeling of alertness and awareness, which has been demonstrated both behaviorally and electroencephalographically; and the increased awareness is accompanied by an increase in psychic and motor activity (Thompson & Schuster, 1968). But amphetamine abuse may produce extreme psychological dependence, severe general fatigue (over a period of time), mental depression, insomnia, irritability, headaches, constipation or other metabolic disturbances, and personality change. (Kalent, 1958; Kastrup and Boyd, 1975; and Leake, 1958).

According to the American Medical Association's Council on Scientific Affairs report, amphetamines were the country's tenth most abused drug in 1974–1975. (Council, 1978.) Thus, it is apparent that amphetamine abuse does not occur only in the athletic domain. The Fourth Report by the Select Committee on Crime in 1971 revealed that the U.S. Army consumed more amphetamines than the entire British or American Armed Forces during World War II. The total official issue between 1966–69 was 225 million standard dose tablets. Several studies indicate amphetamines are abused by students of high school and college age and drug use varied from 11 to 81% of the students (primarily 20–30%) surveyed. (Grinspoon and Hedblom, 1975.)

Amphetamine and Performance in Sport

The literature reveals conflicting reports regarding the effects of amphetamines on various sport and/or psychomotor skills. This may be due to serious methodological problems characterizing many of the reported studies. In numerous instances sufficient controls or precision, which drug research demands, are conspicuously absent. Often the results are confounded. Therefore, the reader is obliged to apply certain considerations when critically reviewing the research literature regarding amphetamine and sport performance.

The first consideration is the type of amphetamine used and its general purpose in the research. There are three major amphetamine compounds reported in the literature: amphetamine sulfate (benzedrine), d-amphetamine (dextro), and meth-amphetamine. Amphetamine sulfate has one-half the central nervous system stimulation effect but more cardiovascular effect than does d-amphetamine. Meth-amphetamine is a potent central nervous system stimulant, has a considerable pressor effect on blood vessels, and is used for the same purpose as amphetamine sulfate, except it is more powerful. Therefore, when evaluating the effect of amphetamine on muscular strength, reaction time, or sport skill performance, it is crucial to consider the type of amphetamine administered, since each produces different psychological effects.

A second consideration is absorption time and metabolism prior to the drug's application in the experimental protocol. Research indicates that 48 hours is necessary for complete metabolism of most drugs (Thompson & Schuster, 1968). Much reported research in the literature suffers from failure to account for optimal absorption time. The third consideration relates to physical and emotional environmental factors (i.e., temperature, humidity, and emotional state of the subject), which are the most commonly ignored variables in drug research. These factors may affect circulation, absorption rate, and metabolic rate (Thompson & Schuster, 1968). Additional considerations which tend to confound findings in the literature are the presence of other drugs in the test organism, failure to control for age, weight, sex, physical condition, and body composition of subjects—all of which may alter the effect of the drug. Other methodological shortcomings in reported amphetamine research include generalizing results obtained from animal studies to humans; lack of double-blind designs with human subjects; dosage differences (some based on kg of body weight and others with no weight consideration); task variability (aerobic contrasted to anaerobic); lack of a control group; small group size; lack of randomization of order of treatments; lack of control on confounding psychological effects; and individual variation in response to drugs (i.e., tolerance). The literature in drug research must be reviewed carefully, and internal as well as external validity requirements must be met. Stringent controls are necessary for meaningful statistical research and conclusions. The purpose of this paper, therefore, will be to present selected research literature within three areas: (a) amphetamine and reaction time, (b) amphetamine and muscular strength, and (c) amphetamine and cardiorespiratory endurance.

Amphetamine and Reaction Time

Very little properly controlled research has been conducted on the effects of amphetamine on reaction time or movement time, even though these are probably the two most important psychomotor reactions in athletic performance. Several studies have indicated no improvement (Blyth, Allen & Lovingood, 1960; Cuthbertson & Knox, 1947; Kornetzky, 1958; Rasch, Pierson & Burbaker, 1960). However, since many of the subjects in these studies were fatigued because data were collected in field settings, methodological controls were not as stringent as they probably would have been in a laboratory environment. Therefore, findings in these studies should be reviewed cautiously. In contrast, Smith and Beecher (1959) reported that amphetamine caused improvements in fatigued or bored subjects on simple tasks and had decreasing impact upon tasks with increasing complexity. In a later study using doses of 15 mg, Lovingood, Blythe, Peacock, and Lindsay, (1967) found significantly faster reaction times as a result of amphetamine administration as did Ivy (1971) who utilized doses of 4, 8 and 12 mg per 70 kg of body weight. Results, therefore, appear to be contradictory and this is likely due to methodologically weak research designs. Additional research is certainly needed in order to determine if reaction or movement time is enhanced by the administration of the amphetamines.

Amphetamine and Strength

The effects of amphetamine on muscular strength have also been somewhat controversial. Motivation for maximal performance in tests of strength is difficult to regulate and assess in infrahuman as well as human subjects. In addition, construction of valid test instruments for use with animals is problematical and maximal effort is difficult to obtain in animals. Blyth, et al. (1960) administered 5 mg d-amphetamine and a placebo before measuring hand grip and dynamometric back, and leg strength (isometric) in human subjects. No significant strengths gains were observed. Ivy (1971) also reported no greater strength gains in a group receiving 4, 8 and 12 mg of d-amphetamine per 70 kg of body weight in comparison to performance by a placebo group. Many other studies report findings which are in conflict with results in both the Blyth, et al. and Ivy studies. Lovingood, et al., in their 1967 study, utilized a larger dosage (15 mg of d-amphetamine) and found a significant increase in grip strength. Ikai and Steinhaus (1961) utilized 30 mg of amphetamine and also found statistically significant strength gains. Adamson and Finley (1965), Danysz, Smietans, and Panck (1967), and Graham and Bos (Note 1) all found significant isometric strength gains when 10 to 15 mg of amphetamines were administered. The evidence is overwhelming that 15 mg of amphetamine or d-amphetamine will increase strength, with only Ivy's study reporting to the contrary. Ivy's study, however, was apparently well controlled and dosages were adjusted according to body weight. Dosages seem to be of critical importance in such studies as so the variables of body size and weight. Also, isotonic muscular strength as opposed to isometric (contraction against resistance which is practically unyielding) should be employed as a dependent variable in such research designs.

Amphetamine and Endurance

Early studies in the area of cardiorespiratory endurance were field studies geared primarily toward the delay of fatigue and boredom and the improvement of alertness. Most of these investigations, many of which were conducted under auspices of the military, were poorly controlled and lacked appropriate statistical procedures necessary to the derivation of valid conclusions.

Several early studies (Knoefel, 1943; Cuthbertson & Knox, 1947; and Lehmann, Straub and Szakall, 1939) have attempted to investigate the effects of amphetamine on cardiorespiratory endurance, but serious weaknesses in design and analysis of data as well as procedures for collecting data have rendered their findings practically useless.

In 1959 Smith and Beecher attempted a series of six experiments on almost 800 performances of swimmers, weight throwers, and runners. A double-blind study was utilized to determine the effects of amphetamine and secobarbital (to mask subjective effects of the amphetamines) on cardiorespiratory performance. Experiment 4, in which nine subjects ran 4.5 to 12.7 miles, was the cardiorespiratory phase of the study. Dosages of 7, 14, or 21 mg of amphetamine per 70 kg of body weight and 50 mg of secobarbital per 70 kg were administered to all subjects. Smith and Beecher concluded that in the majority of the cases (about 75%) the performances were improved. Superficially, this study seems to be the most valid and best controlled of all of the studies thus far. However, Pierson (1961) has indicated that data collection (i.e., self timing of performances), statistical techniques, and interpretation of results are questionable. Some of the methodological problems inherent in the Smith & Beecher study were a lack of consistent temperature control (25–69% F), varied wind velocity 8–23 miles per hour (in fact, some data were discarded due to strong winds), the utilization of motivational devices (confounding), self-timing, and the use of unconventional statistics (William, 1974). Once again, the consumer of scientific reports which focus upon cardiorespiratory endurance and amphetamine use is handicapped in his quest for definite conclusions about this relationship. So much of the available findings derive from spurious sources that the impact of amphetamine upon endurance remains unclarified.

However, two recent laboratory studies were apparently procedurely sound and their conclusions deserve to be integrated within the acceptable scientific body of literature. Williams and Thompson (1973), using subjects with a mean age of 24, administered a placebo—5, 20, or 15 mg of d-amphetamine per 70 kg of body weight—and a repeated measures design (dosages and bouts 3 days apart to allow for complete drug metabolism). All subjects pedalled to exhaustion on a bicycle ergometer. No improvement in endurance due to any of the three treatment dosages was observed. A study by Cooter and Stull (1974) was conducted on 23 male Wistar rats. Dosages of 4, 8, 12 and 16 mg of amphetamine sulfate per kg of body weight and a placebo were administered 30, 60, 90, or 120 minutes prior to testing. Each animal swam all 17 conditions (randomly assigned) to the apparent stages of drowning. None of the 16 experimental conditions produced significant improvements in maximally timed swimming performance nor was improvement noted in subjects in the control condition. The study was conducted under stringent environmental conditions (i.e., 34°C water, controlled lighting, handling, etc.).

Practical Implications

Those who administer, teach or perform in competitive sport programs should recognize a three-fold responsibility concerning the use of the amphetamines: (1) They should be able to recognize symptoms of amphetamine abuse, (2) they should be willing to provide education to athletes relative to misconceptions about improved performance due to amphetamine use and (3) coaches and trainers should avoid use of amphetamines in their own teaching and performance frameworks. The abuse may very well be to no avail in any case as the *literature does not provide acceptable evidence of sport skill performance enhancement due to amphetamine use.* At best, amphetamines may produce small gains in reaction time but there certainly is no conclusive evidence that amphetamine enhances either strength, power, endurance, or sport performance. Again, it must be noted that very little methodologically sound laboratory research has been conducted on any of these variables using human subjects.

Of additional importance in this area are the legal ramifications for coaches who permit students or athletes to participate in sport activities while under drug influence. Coaches and teams may be held liable in courts of law for their sanction of drug use among athletes. In fact, several National Football League players have recently won large settlements from their teams for drug-related injuries (Marshall, 1979). Also, physical activity under conditions of extreme heat and humidity (over 80°F and 70% relative humidity) may cause death in drug abusing sport participants, probably due to hyperadrenergic effects which may precipitate cardiac arrest (Council on Scientific Affairs, 1978). Drug interaction with medication or other pharmacologic agents may also produce dangerous cardiac or central nervous system reactions in athletes as well. Physical educators, athletes and coaches are obliged to be aware of these potential problems.

Within the typically administered dosage range (5–15 mg) most persons report enhanced alertness and less awareness of fatigue due to amphetamine. Therefore, many athletes, undoubtedly, use amphetamines in an effort to facilitate competitive performance. However, stimulants are not a magical source of energy (mental or physical) but push the user to a greater expenditure of his own energy resources to a hazardous (or masked) level of fatigue. One of the greatest hazards facing the athlete may be his or her incapability to accurately evaluate physical condition (fatigue), or mood. Jim Bouton (1970) and Dave Meggyesy (1970), both former professional athletes, have elaborated upon those dangers.

Finally, amphetamine use may produce a negative cumulative or total effect upon athletic skill performance since small performance gains (if existent) may be offset by a loss of homeostasis (physiologic balance) particularly with regard to central nervous system circulatory function. (4)

Summary and Conclusions

(1) Amphetamine has been extensively abused by the general population as well as by sport participants.
(2) Strength, endurance and power are probably not significantly enhanced by the amphetamines, however the literature is not conclusive especially in the strength area.
(3) Small reaction time gains may be obtained by administration of amphetamine.
(4) The legal ramifications are such that coaches who condone or permit amphetamine usage may be legally liable in a court of law (as has been the case in professional sports).
(5) Other drug or medication interaction with amphetamine may present CNS or cardiovascular dangers (i.e., stroke, heart attack, hypertension).
(6) Amphetamine in large doses tends to cause extreme aggressiveness as has been demonstrated in professional football linemen's overaggressiveness, leading to injury of other players. (Underwood, 1978)
(7) Personality changes, insomnia, irritability, headaches, and psychological dependence may occur with continual amphetamine abuse.
(8) One of the most serious aspects of amphetamine abuse is the masking of fatigue and poor performance due to a stimulation of the CNS and a loss of the biological feedback mechanisms.
(9) A urinalysis check prior to performance in professional sport is the simplest method to curb amphetamine abuse.
(10) "In schools where academic or intellectual excellence and personal freedom are stressed, drugs are used more frequently than in schools where social activities and sports absorb most of the student energies." (Grinspoon and Hedblom, 1975)

Notes

Graham, G., and Bos, R. *The effect of dextro-amphetamine sulfate on integrated action potentials and local muscular fatigue.* Paper presented at the American Association for Health, Physical Education and Recreation National Convention, Houston, 1972.

References

Beyer, K. H. Benzedrine sulfate and metabolism. *Journal of Pharmacology and Experimental Therapeutics,* 66:323–324, 1939.

Blyth, C. S., Allen, E. M. and Lovingood, B. W., Effects of amphetamine (dexedrine) and caffeine on subjects exposed to heat and exercise stress. *Research Quarterly,* 31:553–559, 1960.

Bouton, J., *Ball four.* Cleveland: World, 1970.

Cooter, G. R. and Stull, G. A., The effect of amphetamine on endurance in rats. *Journal of Sports Medicine and Physical Fitness,* 14:120–126, 1974.

Council on Scientific Affairs, Clinical Aspects of Amphetamine Abuse, *Journal of American Medical Association,* 240 (21):2317–2319, 1978.

Cuthbertson, D. P. and Knox, J. A. C., The effects of analeptics on the fatigued subject. *Journal of Physiology,* 106:42–58, 1947.

Danysz, A., Smietans, J. and Panek, W., The influence of 2-dimethylaminethanol (DMAE) on the mental and physical efficiency in man. *Activitas Nervosa Superior,* 9:417, 1967.

Furlong, W. B., How "speed" kills athletic careers. *Today's Health,* February, pp. 30–33; 62–66, 1971.

Gilbert, B., Drugs in sport: Problems in a turned on world. *Sports Illustrated,* June 23, pp. 64–72. (a), 1969.

Gilbert, B., Drugs in sport: Something extra on the ball. *Sports Illustrated,* June 30,pp. 30–43. (b), 1969.

Gilbert, B., Drugs in sport: High time to make some rules. *Sports Illustrated.* July 7, pp. 30–35. (c), 1969.

Goth, A., *Medical Pharmacology* (7th ed.). St. Louis: Mosby, 1974.

Grinspoon, L. and Hedblom, P., *The Speed Culture.* Cambridge, MA: Harvard University Press, 1975.

Hahn, F., Analeptics. Pharmacological Reviews, 12:447–530, 1960.

Ikai, M. and Steinhaus, A. H., Some factors modifying the expression of human strength. *Journal of Applied Physiology,* 16:157–163, 1961.

Ivy, J., *The effect of amphetamine on reaction, movement and completion time in relation to time intervals and dosage levels.* Unpublished master's thesis, University of Maryland, 1971.

Kalant,O. J., *The amphetamines: Toxicity and addiction.* Springfield, Ill.: Thomas, 1958.

Karpovich, P. V., Effect of amphetamine sulfate on athletic performance. *Journal of American Medical Association,* 170:558–561, 1959.

Kastrup, E. K. and Boyd, J. R. (Eds.), *Facts and Comparisons.* St. Louis, MO: Facts and Comparisons, Inc., 1975.

Knoepfel, P. K., The influence of phenisoprophy amine and phenisopropyl methylamine on work output. *Federation Proceedings,* 2:83, 1943.

Kornetzky, C., Effects of meprobamate, phenobarbital and detroamphetamine on reaction time and learning in man. *Journal of Pharmacology and Experimental Therapeutics,* 123:216–219, 1958.

Leake, C. D., *The amphetamines.* Springfield, Ill.: Thomas, 1958.

Lehman, G., Straug, H. and Szakall, A., Pervitin als leistungssteigerndes Mittel. *Arbeitsphysiologie,* 10:680–691, 1939.

Lovingood, B. W., Blyth, C. S., Peacock, W. H. and Lindsay, R. B., Effects of d-amphetamine sulfate, caffeine and high temperature on human performance. *Research Quarterly,* 38:64–71, 1967.

Mandell, A., "The Sunday Syndrome" *Proceedings, National Amphetamine Conference,* (San Francisco, CA), September, 1978.

Marshall, E., "Drugging of football players curbed by central monitoring plan, NFL claims." *Science,* February 16, pp. 626–628, 1979.

Meggyesy, D., The football racket. *Look,* November 17, pp. 66–77, 1970.

Pierson, W., Amphetamine sulfate and performance: A critique. *Journal of American Medical Association,* 177:345–347, 1961.

Playboy Interview: Pete Rose, *Playboy,* September, pp. 77–108, 1979.

Rasch, P., Pierson,W. R. and Brubaker, M. L., The effect of amphetamine sulfate and meprobamate on reaction time and movement time. *International Angew Physiology,* 18:280–284, 1960.

Shepard, R., *Alive man: The physiology of physical activity.* Springfield, Ill.: Thomas, 1972.

Smith, G. and Beecher, H., Amphetamine sulfate and athletic performance. *Journal of American Medical Association,* 170:542–557, 1959.

Thompson, T. and Schuster, C. R., *Behavioral pharmacology.* Englewood Cliffs, N.J.: Prentice-Hall, 1968.

Underwood, J., "Speed is all the rage." *Sports Illustrated,* August 28, pp. 30–36, 1978.

Williams, M. H., *Drugs and athletic performance.* Springfield, Ill.: Thomas, 1974.

Williams, M. H. and Thompson, J., Effect of variant dosages of amphetamine upon endurance. *Research Quarterly,* 44:417–422, 1973.

30. The Further Social Evolution of Cocaine

Lester Grinspoon and James B. Bakalar

· · ·

Cocaine in the Americas Today

Although cocaine use has increased greatly since the early 1970s, it is not clear whether it is still on the rise. Part of this increase is due to economic and political conditions in Bolivia and Peru, where coca is grown, and in Colombia, where it is processed into cocaine. The economy of Bolivia has become dependent on cocaine, and everyone from poor peasants to rich traffickers profits from it. Cocaine accounts for half of Bolivia's foreign exchange, and peasants can earn many times more from growing coca than from any other crop. After a recent revolution established a democratic government, the army was paid by the United States to occupy a region where much coca is grown for illicit cocaine production. As a result, the value of Bolivian currency went down 30 percent in one day. The heat of the peasant union has rejected a United States government proposal to provide money to substitute other crops for coca.[1] United States congressmen continually talk of cutting off military and economic aid as a punishment, but the money involved is insignificant in comparison to the fruits of the coca traffic. Eradication programs financed by the United States have not yet been successful, because coca will grow almost anywhere in the country, and spraying alone will not kill the plant unless it is first cut down to the stump. Large areas of the country are controlled by cocaine traffickers. In Peru, new coca cultivation was outlawed by the government as early as 1964. Nevertheless, the acreage devoted to coca has since increased 600 percent. According to the U.S. State Department, coca production in Bolivia and Peru rose 40 percent from 1980 to 1984.[2]

Until recently the biggest cocaine traffickers have been Colombians. They financed plantations, processed coca paste into cocaine, and arranged to smuggle the cocaine into the United States and distribute it. They became rich and highly visible, investing in legitimate businesses, starting their own newspapers and political parties, and promoting philanthropies. Colombians responded with nationalistic pride to U.S. government demands for an extradition treaty that would allow these drug dealers to be tried in the United States. Colombia was earning more foreign exchange dollars from cocaine than from coffee. But a problem of coca paste smoking among urban youth and the murder of a minister of justice finally caused the Colombian government to take action, and many of the big traffickers have now fled the country. There is some evidence that their operations are being relocated in Panama, Miami, and Brazil.[3]

Given the expansion of the cocaine industry, it would seem that cocaine use in the United States must be steadily increasing, but the figures are somewhat ambiguous. The National Household Survey found that, in 1974, 5.4 million people had tried cocaine. By 1982, this figure had risen to 21.6 million. The number of current users (those who had used cocaine in the last month) rose from 1.6 million in 1977 to 4.2 million in 1982.[4] In 1976, according to one survey, 6 percent of high school seniors had tried cocaine; in 1982 it was 20 percent.[5] About twenty million people

From *COCAINE: A DRUG AND ITS SOCIAL EVOLUTION,* Revised Edition, by Lester Grinspoon and James B. Bakalar. Revised edition copyright © 1985 by Lester Grinspoon and James Bakalar. Copyright © 1976 by Lester Grinspoon and James Bakalar. Reprinted by permission of Basic Books, Inc., Publishers.

in the United States have used cocaine at least once and four million use it at least once a month. The National Institute on Drug Abuse reported in its 1982 annual survey that among young adults (aged 18 to 25) the proportion who had ever used cocaine rose from 9.1 percent in 1972 to 27.5 percent in 1979, and then leveled off at 28.3 percent in 1982. Twenty-nine percent of high school dropouts and 34 percent of college graduates have tried cocaine. In 1982 only 12 percent had used the drug more than ten times, and only 7 percent had used it in the previous week—a smaller percentage than in 1979—and most had used it on only one or two days. Only 1.3 percent of young adults had used cocaine as often as five days in the previous month. Of those older than twenty-five, 6.4 percent had ever used cocaine, and .5 percent had used it in the previous month. Among youths under 18, 5.2 percent had used cocaine, compared to 4.8 percent in 1972, and only 1.4 percent had used it in the previous month (the same percentage as in 1972 and less than in 1979).[6]

The President's advisor on drug abuse policy and the head of the National Institute on Drug Abuse have both said that cocaine abuse may be in decline. Yet the National Narcotics Intelligence Estimate concluded that 70 percent more cocaine entered the United States in 1983 than in 1981.[7] Cocaine, now a 30-billion-dollar-a-year business, is the most popular recreational drug in the United States after alcohol and marihuana, and, as we will see, problems created by cocaine abuse are increasing. The most plausile explanation is that the same number of people (or fewer people) are using *more* cocaine now, either because compulsive use is increasing or, more likely, because the average dose of street cocaine has become less diluted with sugars and other adulterants. In fact, the average purity of street cocaine is reported to have risen from 28 percent in 1982 to 40 percent in 1983.[8]

Acute Effects of Cocaine

Until recently scientific knowledge about cocaine use and abuse was very limited, and most of it was based on studies more than fifty years old. There were no controlled experiments on human beings, and the clinical literature was sparse, affected by the limitations of an earlier era. Partly because cocaine has gained so much popularity on the street, scientific understanding of its effects has advanced considerably in the last ten years. Although there have been no surprising discoveries, we have filled some gaps and put our knowledge on a sounder basis.

In a 1976 controlled, double-blind experiment, cocaine, dextroamphetamine, and a placebo were administered intravenously to nine experienced cocaine users.[9] Heart rate, blood pressure, respiratory rate, and mood all increased as the cocaine dose was raised from 4 to 32 mg. Major effects were experienced only at doses of 16 mg and above; subjects rated doses of 24 and 32 mg as among the highest they had ever taken. A 10 mg dose of dextroamphetamine produced effects equivalent to 8 to 16 mg of cocaine, and subjects usually had trouble distinguishing between the two drugs, although the effects of dextroamphetamine were sometimes perceived as lasting longer. The authors of this study concluded that the stimulant action of cocaine resembles that of amphetamine.

In another controlled study intranasal (snorting) and intravenous routes were compared. Nineteen experienced cocaine users took doses of 10 mg and 25 mg both intranasally and intravenously, and 100 mg intranasally only. The 10 mg intranasal dose had no subjective or observable physiological effects. With 25 mg there was a rise in systolic blood pressure (but no other physiological effects) and some euphoria (the most commonly reported feeling was relaxation). One hundred mg affected mood strongly; it also raised heart rate and diastolic blood pressure, but not respiratory rate or body temperature. Intravenously taken cocaine had strong physiological and mood effects even at the 10 mg dose. At 25 mg, the effect on blood pressure, was equivalent to 20 mg of oral dextroamphetamine. Twenty to thirty minutes after the 25 mg intravenous dose, and forty-five to sixty minutes after the 100 mg intranasal dose, a few subjects suffered mild lethargy, irritability and a desire for more cocaine.[10] It is worth noting again that the average street dose of cocaine is about 20 to 50 mg when taken intranasally. Changes in behavior are more clearly correlated with dose than are physiological changes, and they occur at much lower doses. For example, monkeys press levers for a dose as low as .05 mg per kg (the equivalent of 3.5 mg in a 70 kg man).[11]

Cocaine reaches a peak concentration in the blood fifteen to sixty minutes after it is snorted and declines gradually over a period of three to five hours. The peak of the subjective intoxication comes at three to five minutes, possibly because the blood concentration is increasing faster or because more cocaine is reaching the brain. Eating cocaine produces just as high a concentration in the blood as snorting, but it takes longer, appearing in the blood after thirty minutes and peaking after fifty to ninety minutes. The subjective feeling of intoxication is also just as great, although it is delayed proportionately.[12]

The cardiovascular effect of cocaine subsides long before it starts to leave the blood. When it is snorted, levels of cocaine in the blood reach a peak in 60 minutes. By that time, the heart rate is almost back to normal. Tolerance to both subjective and cardiovascular effects increases rapidly with repeated use over a short time. In one experiment, volunteers were given 96 mg of cocaine intranasally, followed by 32 mg intravenously an hour later. The intravenous injection caused almost no increase in subjective effect and only a small increase in heart rate, even though it greatly raised blood levels of the drug. When six 32 mg intravenous injections were given in an hour, only the first had a significant effect on heart rate and subjective intoxication, despite continuously rising blood levels.[13]

• • •

Acute Emergencies

Until the late 1970s, studies of recreational users suggested that undesirable effects were not common.[14] However, some authorities familiar with the street scene insisted even then that both laboratory experiments and surveys tended to underestimate the number and severity of problems.[15] Physicians at rock mucis concerts, for example, reported cocaine-induced acute anxiety reactions with symptoms including high blood pressure, racing heart, anxiety, and paranoia.[16] Tactile and other hallucinations and delusions were occasionally noticed, as well as instances of cocaine psychosis in habitual cocaine abusers.[17]

Severe physical poisoning and death from the toxic effects were once rare. A 1974 paper recorded only six cases of death from cocaine poisoning between 1970 and 1973, and in every case the cocaine was apparently either injected intravenously or eaten in large quantities.[18] Another study found five documented cases of cocaine-related death and contributed nine more, three of which involved cocaine alone, always taken intravenously (the other cases also involved alcohol, morphine, or other drugs). In a three-year survey of Dallas County, Texas, researchers found 2 deaths in which cocaine was present among 228 deaths caused by drugs.[19] From May 1975 to April 1976, medical examiners reported 57 cocaine-related deaths to the federal Drug Abuse Warning Network (DAWN), including 6 (out of 4,668 drug-related deaths) that involved cocaine alone.[20]

Another study used data from coroners and medical examiners' offices over an area with a population of 63 million. In the period from 1971 to 1976, 111 fatalities were found in which cocaine was somehow involved. Twenty-five of these cases were not toxic overdoses, but deaths by murder, suicide, or accident related to drug use. There was an increase from two deaths associated with cocaine in 1971 to twenty-nine in the first six months of 1976. Of the twenty-six deaths associated with cocaine alone, four (15.4 percent) were from oral cocaine, either suicides or smuggling incidents; two (7.7 percent) were from intranasal use; the rest resulted from intravenous injection or unknown methods of administration. Six of the twenty-six were suicides. Deaths from a combination of opiates and cocaine were more common than deaths from cocaine alone.[21]

The increase from two deaths to twenty-nine between 1971 and 1976 indicates both an increase in cocaine use and a greater awareness of cocaine in the medical and legal systems. Evidence of serious acute reactions to cocaine continues to emerge, although the precise numbers are not clear. It has been noted that angina and myocardial infarction can be produced by cocaine's constriction of blood vessels and speeding up of the heart rate. Intravenous injection can paralyze the respiratory centers of the brain and produce cardiac arrest. Other dangers include abnormally high body temperatures, heart arrhythmias, and stroke. After a cocaine crash, suffocation may occur in sleep by choking on mucus due to an obstructed airway.[22] Cocaine and alcohol are a particularly dangerous combination for drivers: the alertness induced by cocaine may falsely convince the driver that he is not drunk, and the effect of the cocaine then wears off sooner than the effect of the alcohol. Death from snorting cocaine, although rare, is being reported more often.[23]

A New York metropolitan area survey conducted in 1981 found cocaine-related emergency room admissions up 121 percent from 1979 to 1980, up 17 percent from 1980 to 1981, and up 47 percent from 1981 to 1982. Medical emergencies recorded by the DAWN network rose from 0.7 to 2.3 per 10,000 emergency cases between 1976 and 1981.[24] Between 1977 and 1980 DAWN reported an increase of cocaine-related deaths; from zero to fifty-six in Miami, and from thirteen to seventy-nine in New York City. Emergency room entries in the first quarter of 1984 were equal to the number for all of 1978; nearly half of these patients were over thirty years old, compared with 21 percent in 1978.[25] It is even possible that deaths from cocaine, once undercounted, are now overcounted, because when cocaine is used in combination with sedatives or depressants it is often hard to tell which drug has caused the death.

Cocaine Dependence

The rise in emergency room visits and deaths from acute intoxication is real and regrettable. More significant, however, from a social standpoint are the spreading consequences of chronic cocaine abuse. . . . The most disturbing thing we encountered in our research and interviews was the difficulty some people had in leaving cocaine alone. It has become apparent that cocaine dependence can create serious health and social problems for a substantial minority of users—estimates range from 5 percent to 30 percent. An unknown proportion are finding it necessary to seek professional help to rid themselves of the cocaine habit.

When access is limited, laboratory animals can take cocaine daily for years with no apparent ill effects.[26] But when unlimited access to intravenous cocaine is provided, caged animals will kill themselves with it. In one recent experiment, for example, intravenous cocaine was made available twenty-three hours a day (at a rate 0.2 mg per kg of body weight per injection) to monkeys. They developed hyperactivity, tactile hallucinations, severe weight loss, tremors, and convulsions. All died within five days. Methamphetamine and dextroamphetamine had similar effects.[27]

Dependence potential varies with the route of administration. For example, animal experiments continue to show that intravenous cocaine is possibly the most powerful of drug reinforcers.[28] Monkeys will also smoke a cocaine cigarette and chew cocaine-based gum; in fact, they prefer a cocaine cigarette to a lettuce cigarette. However, they do not chose cocaine gum over ordinary sugar gum.[29]

Obviously cocaine craving can become a serious problem, particularly for those who have constant access to the drug. The progress in human beings is insidious. One takes a second snort to counteract a mild letdown feeling, and then a third, a fourth, and so on. Cocaine is taken for energy in the afternoon at work or to wake up early in the morning. Users steal to get money for cocaine; freebase smoking and intravenous injection often lead to a preoccupation with cocaine to the exclusion of everything else. Clearly, this dependence has much in common with other addictive behavior, especially amphetamine dependence and alcoholism. Symptoms include: needing cocaine to work, using it when alone, bingeing, inability to turn it down, thinking about it constantly, dreaming about it, inability to stop using it for any length of time, problems at work and at home, spending all one's savings on it or borrowing, stealing, and dealing to pay for it, and needing alcohol or sedatives to sleep. Even people who are using cocaine no more than a few times a week may be in some difficulty.

Contrary to what we and most other researchers once believed, it has now become clear that tolerance to cocaine can arise— not only during a single session of drug use, but also over a period of time. Animals in experiments have shown a tolerance to the cardiac and respiratory stimulant effects.[30] Cross-tolerance to amphetamine and amphetamine congeners has also been reported experimentally;[31] and tolerance to cocaine disappears faster than tolerance to amphetamines when the drug is discontinued. Cocaine snorters report a 50 percent decrease in sensitivity to the drug after several years of use.[32] Freebasers almost always find themelves increasing the dose without any greater effect. One theory that accounts for this increased tolerance is that by blocking the reuptake of dopamine and norepinephrine in the brain's mood-regulating centers, cocaine at first heightens the effect of these neurotransmitters but then depletes them, so that more of the drug is required for the same effect.

The controversy about reverse tolerance or sensitization to some of cocaine's effects continues. There are reports of both tolerance and sensitization.[33] Clinically, seizures are being reported with increasing frequency in chronic cocaine users, although these are self-reports and may be unreliable. In some studies, animals show increasing hyperactivity and stereotyped movements from an hour or two after each of a series of daily injections of the same large dose.[34] This increased sensitivity may endure for up to seven weeks after the drug is discontinued.[35] There is still no agreement about the reasons for the sensitization effect. Sensitization may partly explain why stimulant-induced psychoses occur mainly in chronic abusers who take a higher dose than usual for a short time.

Adverse Effects of Chronic Use

We are now in a position to know more about the kinds of problems that cocaine abusers develop. Any kind of chronic cocaine use can produce exaggerated sensitivity to light, sound, smell, and touch sensations, which may result in pseudohallucinations. For example, "snow lights" (flashes in the peripheral visual field) may be followed by halos around light sources, moving geometric patterns, vibrating walls, and animated shadows. Ringing in the ears may develop into imaginary voices.[36] Cocaine psychosis is also being reported more frequently.[37] Recently reported effects of intravenous injection include skin infections, tetanus, polyarteritis nodosa (inflamed and broken arteries), internal fungus infections, and acquired immune deficiency syndrome.[38]

In one study, five hundred callers to a cocaine information hotline were interviewed. They admitted using cocaine to attain euphoria and energy, and sometimes for sexual purposes (21 percent). Fewer than half were using cocaine every day, but 80 percent said they had a letdown or crash when they stopped, and 70 percent used alcohol or narcotics to calm down. The main undesirable physical effects, reported by more than half of the callers, were fatigue, sinus headaches, nasal problems (runny noses and cracked, bleeding, or ulcerated nasal membranes), and sexual problems. Twenty-six percent said they had had seizures or loss of consciousness at least once. Insomnia, loss of interest and ability to concentrate, anxiety, depression, and irritability were reported by more than 65 percent. Fifty-four percent usually used cocaine when alone, 61 percent believed they were addicted, and 73 percent said they had lost control. Nine percent had made a suicide attempt, 45 percent had stolen money, and 38 percent had trafficked in cocaine. Twenty-six percent had been divorced or lost a lover because of it, 17 percent had lost a job, and 12 percent had been in traffic accidents related to cocaine.[39]

Having observed closely some people before and during heavy involvement with cocaine—people for whom cocaine is not merely an occasional and casual experience but an omnipresent desire—we believe that there may appear to be subtle changes in their personalities during the period of heavy abuse. They appear to have become more irritable and less patient. Their relationships with people close to them seem less warm, and they put more distance between themselves and the people who play an important part in their lives. Put differently, they apparently become more narcissistic, placing themselves even more emphatically than before at the center of their universe. As a result, they have lost some of their capacity for empathy; for example, although they may understand intellectually the hardship that their involvement with cocaine imposes on others, they seem less able to feel this concern, to acknowledge it emotionally. It is as though cocaine has become so important to them that part of the ego is no longer able to respond emotionally to people and concerns once highly valued.

Freebasing

• • •

Free base cocaine was introduced into the United States in the early 1970s. At that time a few users began to sprinkle cocaine hydrochloride on tobacco or marihuana and smoke it in a cigarette or pipe, but this did not produce an effect distinctly different from snorting. Soon it was discovered that free base cocaine is much more convenient for smoking than cocaine HCL or even the cocaine sulfate found in South American *base,* because it is more volatile and decomposes less on heating. Free base is purer and more concentrated than coca paste. It is precipitated from a water solution of cocaine hydrochloride by the addition of an alkaline substance such as baking sode or ammonium hydroxide, and then either filtered out or dissolved in ether, which is removed by evaporation. Extraction kits are sold by drug paraphernalia shops, but actually very little equipment is needed except baking soda, water, glassware, and a heat source. Base is smoked in a glass water pipe equipped with fine-mesh steel screens designed to trap the drug as it melts. More than a million people have experimented with this practice, called basing or freebasing. According to some reports, 10 percent of cocaine users now freebase exclusively.[40]

The effects and dangers of smoking either coca paste or free base resemble those of intravenous cocaine injection. The blood concentration rises just as fast, and the intoxication is similar—a rush of pleasure lasting a few minutes, followed by an afterglow.[41] In an experimental study, 50 mg of cocaine base placed in a pipe (of which only 36 mg was actually inhaled) produced a slightly more intense intoxication and a slightly stronger craving than 20 mg of cocaine hydrochloride injected intravenously.[42] The average amount placed in a pipe bowl for smoking seems to be about 80 mg; how much of this is actually inhaled depends on the smoking technique used. After tolerance develops, the dose may be increased to as high as 250 mg.[43]

Freebasers or coca paste smokers generally use more cocaine than those who take it through the nose. With freebasing, intense euphoria subsides into irritable craving after a few minutes, and many smokers do not stop until either they, or their drug supplies, are exhausted. Users have been known to smoke continuously for three or four days without sleep, using up to 150 grams of cocaine in seventy-two hours.[44] Habitual cocaine smokers suffer from a full range of ill effects, including exhaustion, insomnia, weight loss, headaches, tremors, sore throat and mouth, swollen tongue, blurred vision, lost sex drive, and seizures. They become jittery, depressed, unable to concentrate, and may develop hallucinations and paranoid delusions. They dream about cocaine, lose control over violent impulses, and develop work, marital, and money problems. The alcohol or sedatives used to counteract the jitteriness and paranoia or to induce sleep may create a dual dependency. And the craving and withdrawal depression make it hard to give it up.[45] The cost can run to hundreds, even thousands of dollars a week, and many freebasers must traffic in cocaine to pay for their habit. Among cocaine abusers forced to seek treatment at hospitals, clinics, and crisis centers, a disproportionately high number are freebasers.

One special danger of cocaine smoking is the proximity of highly flammable ether (or rum when it is used instead of water as a coolant in the pipe) to an open flame. The danger is enhanced because the user is suffering from loss of coordination produced by cocaine or a combination of cocaine and alcohol. Another danger is lung damage that reduces the capacity to exchange gases. Presumably the vasoconstrictor action of cocaine eventually irritates blood vessels in the lung, just as it irritates blood vessels in the nose. Deficiencies in lung function are indicated by tests after only a few months of smoking.[46] The measured deficiencies have not yet been correlated with respiratory symptoms, but death from pulmonary edema (fluid collection in the lungs) has been reported.[47]

Cocaine Abusers

Who are the chronic cocaine abusers and how many are there? Evidence is fragmentary, but the problem is substantial and probably still growing. According to the records of the Drug Abuse Warning Network (DAWN), from May 1975 to April 1976, cocaine, either alone or in combination with other drugs, was involved in only 3.6 percent of cases at drug crisis intervention centers and in less than 1 percent of drug cases in hospital emergency rooms.[48] The Client-Oriented Data Acquisition Process (CODAP) reported that 1.2 percent of clients appearing at federally funded drug treatment facilities from 1975 to 1976 (about 650 clients in all) said cocaine was their primary drug of abuse. Another 4 percent reported cocaine as a secondary drug problem.[49] From 1976 to 1980 the number of people seeking treatment for cocaine related problems in publicly funded programs rose 500 percent.[50] Drug treatment program admissions reported to the National

Institute of Drug Abuse that involved cocaine primarily rose from 1.2 percent to 5.8 percent between 1976 and 1981 and to 9 percent by 1983. If intravenous use of heroin and cocaine in combination (speedballing) is included, the total is 17 percent. These estimates do not include private drug treatment programs.[51]

Several studies give a clearer idea of the current situation among those seeking treatment for cocaine abuse. An information hotline established in May 1983 received 350,000 calls in the first year—nearly 1,000 calls a day. In a random sample of 500 of these callers, the average age was thirty. Two thirds were men, and 88 percent were white. Three hundred six were snorting cocaine, 103 were freebasing, and 91 were injecting it intravenously. Half were using cocaine daily. The average amount spent on cocaine in the previous week was $637. More than half said they would use more if the price went down. In another hotline survey, 78 percent of the callers were male and 50 percent earned more than $25,000 a year, (the mean family income in the United States).[52] This suggests that cocaine abuse is not a habit confined to the rich.

Among inpatients at a drug dependence clinic in a Chicago hospital, the number being treated for cocaine dependence rose from one out of 125 in 1979 to 89 out of 125 in 1983. At that time their mean age was thirty; 69 percent were men, 61 percent had some college education, and 4 percent had doctoral level degrees. Fifty percent were employed at the time of admission. Seventy-five percent were freebasers and 56 percent used cocaine daily. Eighty-seven percent had been using cocaine less than four years, and 37 percent had been using it less than six months. Almost all used alcohol with cocaine, and 26 percent used heroin. Forty-three percent smoked marihuana daily. Seventy-five percent had had no previous treatment for drug dependence. The authors of the study identified three groups of cocaine abusers in the clinic: (1) persons who had abused numerous drugs but had no previous treatment; (2) persons who had previously been treated for drug dependence; and (3) somewhat older patients who had little previous drug experience and had been using cocaine for only a few months.[53]

Among 136 patients who sought treatment for cocaine abuse at clinics in Denver and Aspen, Colorado, the mean number of years of education was fourteen; 57 percent snorted cocaine, 33 percent injected it intravenously, and 10 percent were freebasers. Twenty-seven percent used cocaine more than three times a day, 15 percent two to three times a day, and 30 percent once a day to twice a week. Thirty-four percent also abused alcohol.[54] At the detoxification unit of the Haight-Ashbury Free Clinic in San Francisco, the proportion of patients seen for cocaine problems rose from 1 percent in 1970 to 3.5 percent in early 1980 and 6 percent in the first half of 1981—six people a day.[55]

Ronald Siegel was able to follow fifty cocaine users (out of a group of ninety-nine) from 1975 to 1983. They were given questionnaires and personality tests and were interviewed at eighteen-month intervals. All fifty started as intranasal users, but by 1978, 10 percent were mainly freebasers. This percentage did not increase in the last five years of the study. Only a few had experimented with intravenous use by 1983. The amount of cocaine use tended to rise, but only a minority had lost control. In 1975 the average amount taken by intranasal users was 1 to 4 grams a month. From 1978 to 1983, it rose to 1 to 3 grams a week. Freebasers used an average of 1 gram a day from 1975 to 1978. From 1978 to 1983 they used 1.5 grams a day. Through the period 1975 to 1978, 75 percent remained social or recreational users. From 1978 to 1983, 50 percent remained social or recreational users, and 32 percent became situational users who took cocaine to perform specific work tasks or relieve boredom up to four to five times a week. By this time there were also eight intensive and five compulsive users, all of whom were freebasers. So four fifths of the cocaine users who were followed up for nine years remained either social-recreational users or situational users. Almost all the cocaine users, including intensive and compulsive users, had periods of abstinence for up to a few months.

None of the social users (but 18 percent of the situational users) reported some toxic psychological and physical crises. All of the intensive and compulsive users reported acute crises, with compulsive users experiencing them very often. On psychological tests these compulsive users showed increased egocentricity, body concerns, and disturbed social adjustment. Intensive and compulsive users had high levels of paranoia, depression, sleep disturbances, poor impulse regulation, and other problems. Other drugs used by the group during the last six years of the study were alcohol (70 percent); methaqualone (30 percent); marihuana (24 percent); hallucinogens (18 percent); and Valium (13 percent).

Siegel concludes that many social users do not develop serious problems even when their incomes increase and they are able to buy more of the drug (most of these subjects had started as students). But he also notes that the average dose of the social, recreational, and situational users did increase, as did negative effects. He makes no comment on the forty-nine users who dropped out of the study except to note that eight of them, refusing further interviews, said they had stopped using cocaine entirely.[56]

Cocaine has always been popular among opiate addicts. It is now also a growing problem among methadone maintenance clients. In a 1982 study of 348 clients, 36 percent had used cocaine at least once in the week before the interview; 28 percent used it one to six times a week, and 7 percent even more often. Most preferred intravenous injection. Clients who had recently started treatment were no more likely to use cocaine than those who had been taking methadone for years. The most frequent users of cocaine used heroin at the same time (speedballing). The clients who took the treatment most seriously and complied best with the regulations were less likely to be involved with cocaine, but even among them, 20 percent used it occasionally. Many clients regarded cocaine as safer (less physically addicting) than narcotics, sedatives, or tranquilizers. They were also influenced by its high social status in the non-addict world. But cocaine was risky for these clients. Unlike heroin, cocaine can be injected repeatedly every few minutes; so the potential cost is almost unlimited. The need to pay for it and the way of life associated with it forced the clients in the program into hustling and drug dealing. They bought cocaine in the same places where heroin was sold, and heavy cocaine use was often a road back to the life of a street addict.[57]

What kinds of people become cocaine abusers? Studies indicate that many hospitalized abusers suffer from depressive disorders of varying severity: bipolar (manic-depressive) disorder or cyclothymia (a mild form of bipolar disorder). A smaller group may have the adult version of the syndrome known in children as hyperactivity or attention deficit disorder; its symptoms are physical restlessness, impulsiveness, and unstable feelings.[58] But as in many cases of drug abuse, it is often hard to distinguish preexisting problems from the effects of the drug itself.

Beyond this, the development of cocaine abuse seems to depend on access, accident, life stresses, and cultural influences. Like amphetamines, cocaine provides a feeling of energy, control, and confidence. It counters depression and loneliness, bolsters shaky self-esteem, and helps users keep up with the pace of modern life and cope with a world in constant change. Not only the bored rich but also salesmen, entertainers, and others who need to be constantly "on" may be attracted to cocaine. Many people in our society have an exaggerated need for self-sufficiency and are driven toward an unrealistic ideal of achievement. The use of stimulants continues to fit the Western cultural emphasis on activity, efficiency, speed, and aggressiveness. Cocaine has also become identified with wealth, sexuality, and social status, and cocaine abusers, like amphetamine abusers, are sometimes caricatures of the pathological features of the society in which they live.

• • •

Notes

1. Brinkley, "Bolivia in Turmoil."
2. Ibid.
3. Alan Riding. "Shaken Colombia Acts at Last on Drug," *New York Times,* September 11, 1984, p. 1.
4. Edgar H. Adams and Jack Durell, "Cocaine: A Growing Public Health Problem," in *Cocaine: Pharmacology, Effects, and Treatment of Abuse,* edited by John Grabowski. National Institute on Drug Abuse Research Monograph 50. (Rockville, Md.: National Institute on Drug Abuse, 1984).
5. P. M. O'Malley, J. G. Bachman, and L. D. Johnston, "Period, Age, and Cohort Effects on Substance Abuse Among American Youth, 1976–1982," *American Journal of Public Health* 74 (1984): 682–688.
6. Judith D. Miller, ed., *National Survey on Drug Abuse: Main Findings 1982* (Washington, D.C.: U.S. Government Printing Office, 1983).
7. Joel Brinkley, "Rampant Drug Abuse Brings Call for Move Against Source Nations," *New York Times,* September 9, 1984, p. 1.
8. Arnold M. Washton et al., "Adolescent Cocaine Abusers," *The Lancet,* 2, no. 8405 (1984): 746.
9. Marian W. Fischman et al., "Cardiovascular and Subjective Effects of Intravenous Cocaine in Rats," *Archives of General Psychiatry* 33 (1976): 983–989.
10. R. B. Resnick, R. S. Kestenbaum, and L. K. Schwartz, "Acute Systemic Effects of Cocaine in Man: A Controlled Study by Intranasal and Intravenous Routes of Administration," in *Cocaine and Other Stimulants,* edited by E. H. Ellinwood, Jr. and M. M. Kilbey (New York: Plenum Press, 1977).
11. Marvin C. Wilson et al., "Acute Pharmacological Activity of Intravenous Cocaine in the Rhesus Monkey," *Psychopharmacology Communications* 2 (1976): 251–261.
12. C. Van Dyke et al., "Cocaine: Plasma Concentrations After Intranasal Applications in Man," *Science* 191 (1976): 859–861; C. Van Dyke et al., "Oral Cocaine: Plasma Concentrations and Central Effects," *Science* 200 (1978): 211–213.
13. Marian W. Fischman and Charles R. Schuster, "Experimental Investigations of the Actions of Cocaine in Humans," in *Cocaine 1980,* edited by F. R. Jerí (Lima, Peru: Pacific Press, 1980).
14. Ronald K. Siegel, "Cocaine: Recreational Use and Intoxication," in *Cocaine: 1977,* edited by R. C. Petersen and R. C. Stillman. National Institute on Drug Abuse Research Monograph 13 (Washington, D.C.: U.S. Government Printing Office, 1977); D. Waldorf et al., *Doing Coke: An Ethnography of Cocaine Users and Sellers* (Washington, D.C.: Drug Abuse Council, 1977).
15. D. R. Wesson and D. E. Smith, "Cocaine: Its Use for Central Nervous System Stimulation Including Recreational and Medical Uses," in *Cocaine: 1977,* edited by R. C. Petersen and R. C. Stillman. National Institute on Drug Abuse Research Monograph 13 (Washington, D.C.: U.S. Government Printing Office, 1977).
16. R. T. Rappolt, G. R. Gay, and D. S. Inaba, "Propranolol in the Treatment of Cardiopressor Effects of Cocaine," *New England Journal of Medicine* 295 (1976): 448.
17. Wesson and Smith, "Cocaine."
18. K. R. Price, "Fatal Cocaine Poisoning," *Journal of the Forensic Science Society* 14 (1974): 329–333.
19. G. D. Lundberg et al., "Cocaine-related Death," *Journal of the Forensic Sciences* 22 (1977): 402–408.
20. R. C. Petersen, "Cocaine: An Overview," in *Cocaine: 1977,* edited by R. C. Petersen and R. C. Stillman. National Institute on Drug Abuse Research Monograph 13 (Washington, D.C.: U.S. Government Printing Office, 1977).
21. B. S. Finkle and K. L. McCloskey, "The Forensic Toxicology of Cocaine (1971–1976), *Journal of the Forensic Sciences* 23 (1978): 173–189.

22. Vincent J. M. DiMaio and James C. Garriott, "Four Deaths Due to Intravenous Injection of Cocaine," *Forensic Sciences International* 12 (1978): 119–125; George R. Gay, "Clinical Management of Acute and Chronic Cocaine Poisoning," *Annals of Emergency Medicine* 11 (1982): 562–572.

23. G. D. Lundberg et al., "Cocaine-related Death"; Charles V. Wetli and Ronald K. Wright, "Death Caused by Recreational Cocaine Use," *Journal of the Americn Medical Association* 241 (1979): 2519–2522.

24. N. J. Kozel, R. A. Crider, and E. H. Adams, "National Surveillance of Cocaine Use and Related Health Consequences," Center for Disease Control, *Morbidity and Mortality Weekly Report* 31 (20) (1982): 265–73.

25. Gay, "Clinical Management of Acute and Chronic Cocaine Poisoning."

26. C. E. Johanson, "Assessment of the Dependence Potential of Cocaine in Animals," in *Cocaine: Pharmacology, Effects, and Treatment of Abuse,* edited by John Grabowski. National Institute on Drug Abuse Research Monograph 50 (Rockville, Md.: National Institute on Drug Abuse, 1984).

27. C. E. Johanson, R. L. Balister, and K. Bonese, "Self-administration of Psychoactive Drugs: The Effects of Unlimited Access," *Pharmacology, Biochemistry, and Behavior* 4 (1976): 45–51.

28. C. E. Johanson and C. R. Schuster, "A Choice Procedure for Drug Reinforcers: Cocaine and Methylphenidate in the Rhesus Monkey," *Journal of Pharmacology and Experimental Therapeutics* 193 (1975): 676–688; James Woods, "Behavioral Effects of Cocaine in Animals," in *Cocaine: 1977,* edited by R. C. Petersen and R. C. Stillman. National Institute on Drug Abuse Research Monograph 13. (Washington, D.C.: U.S. Government Printing Office, 1977); S. R. Goldberg and R. T. Kelleher, "Reinforcement of Behavior by Cocaine Injections," in *Cocaine and Other Stimulants,* edited by E. H. Ellinwood, Jr. and M. M. Kilbey (New York: Plenum Press, 1977); Johanson, "Assessment of the Dependence Potential of Cocaine in Animals."

29. R. K. Siegel et al., "Cocaine Self-administration in Monkeys by Chewing and Smoking," *Pharmacology, Biochemistry, and Behavior* 4 (1976): 461–467.

30. Masaji Matsuzaki et al., "Cocaine: Tolerance to Its Convulsant and Cardiorespiratory Stimulating Effects in Monkeys," *Life Sciences* 19 (1976): 193–204.

31. William V. Woolverton, David Kandel, and Charles R. Schuster, "Tolerance and Cross-tolerance to Cocaine and d-Amphetamine," *Journal of Pharmacology and Experimental Therapeutics* 205 (1987): 525–535; N. J. Leith and R. J. Barrett, "Self-stimulation and Amphetamine: Tolerance to d and l Isomers and Cross-tolerance to Cocaine and Methylphenidate," *Psychopharmacology* 74 (1981): 23–28, 47. Ronald K. Siegel, "Cocaine Smoking." *Journal of Psychoactive Drugs* 14 (1982): 271–359.

32. Ronald K. Siegel, "Long-term Effects of Recreational Cocaine Use: A Four-Year Study," in *Cocaine 1980,* edited by F. R. Jerí. (Lima, Peru: Pacific Press, 1980).

33. Matsuzaki et al., "Cocaine: Tolerance of Its Convulsant and Cardiorespiratory Stimulating Effects in Monkeys"; Marvin C. Wilson and John M. Holbrook, "Intravenous Cocaine Lethality in the Rat," *Pharmacological Research Communications* 10 (1978): 243–256.

34. R. M. Post and H. Rose, "Increasing Effects of Repetitive Cocaine Administration in the Rat," *Nature* 260 (1976): 731–732; Sam Castellani, Everett H. Ellinwood, and M. Marlyne Kilbey, "Behavioral Analysis of Chronic Cocaine Intoxication in the Cat," *Biological Psychiatry* 13 (1978): 203–215.

35. M. M. Kilbey and E. H. Ellinwood, Jr., "Reverse Tolerance to Stimulant-Induced Abnormal Behavior," *Life Sciences* 20 (1977): 1063–1076.

36. Ronald K. Siegel, "Cocaine Hallucinations," *American Journal of Psychiatry* 135 (1978): 309–314.

37. Carlos Carbajal, "Psychosis Produced by Nasal Aspiration of Cocaine Hydrochloride," in *Cocaine 1980,* edited by F. R. Jerí (Lima, Peru: Pacific Press, 1980).

38. Joseph B. Michelson, Stanley D. Freedman, and Douglas G. Boyden, "Aspergillus Endopthalmitis in a Drug Abuser," *Annals of Ophthalmology* 14 (1982): 1051–1054; Harold M. Ginzburg, "Intravenous Drug Users and the Acquired Immune Deficiency Syndrome," *Public Health Reports* 99 (1984): 206–212.

39. Arnold M. Washton, Mark S. Gold, and A. C. Pottash, "Cocaine Hotline: Survey of 500 Callers," *Psychosomatics* 25 (1984): 771–778.

40. For a thorough review of cocaine smoking, see Ronald K. Siegel, "Cocaine Smoking," *Journal of Psychoactive Drugs* 14 (1982): 271–359.

41. D. Paly et al., "Cocaine Plasma Levels After Cocaine Paste Smoking," in *Cocaine 1980,* edited by F. R. Jerí (Lima, Peru: Pacific Press, 1980).

42. M. Pérez-Reyes et al., "Free-base Cocaine Smoking," *Clinical Pharmacology and Therapeutics* 32 (1982): 459–465.
43. Siegel, "Cocaine Smoking," p. 315.
44. Siegel, "Cocaine Smoking Disorders: Diagnosis and Treatment," *Psychiatric Annals* 14 (1984): 728–732.
45. F. R. Jerí et al., "The Syndrome of Coca Paste," *Journal of Psychedelic Drugs* 10, no. 4 (1978): 361–370; F. R. Jerí et al., "Further Experience with the Syndromes Produced by Coca Paste Smoking," *Bulletin on Narcotics* 30, no. 3 (1978): 1–12.
46. Roger D. Weiss et al., "Pulmonary Dysfunction in Cocaine Smokers," *American Journal of Psychiatry* 138 (1981): 1110–1112.
47. R. James Allred and Steven Ewer, "Fatal Pulmonary Edema Following 'Freebase' Cocaine Abuse," *Annals of Emergency Medicine* 10 (1981): 441–442.
48. R. C. Petersen, "Cocaine: An Overview," in *Cocaine: 1977,* edited by R. C. Petersen and R. C. Stillman. National Institute on Drug Abuse Research Monograph 13 (Washington, D.C.: U.S. Government Printing Office, 1977).
49. Siegel, "Cocaine: Recreational Use and Intoxication."
50. Antoinette A. Helfrich et al., "A Clinical Profile of One Hundred Thirty-Six Cocaine Abusers," in *Problems of Drug Dependence,* edited by Louis S. Harris. National Institute of Drug Abuse Research Monograph 43 (Washington, D.C.: U.S. Government Printing Office, 1983).
51. Adams and Durell, "Cocaine: A Growing Public Health Problem."
52. Washton, "Cocaine Hotline: Survey of 500 Callers."
53. Sidney H. Schnoll et al., "Characteristics of Cocaine Abusers Presenting for Treatment." Personal communication, 1984.
54. Helfrich et al., "A Clinical Profile of One Hundred Thirty-Six Cocaine Abusers."
55. Gay, "Clinical Management of Acute and Chronic Cocaine Poisoning."
56. Ronald K. Siegel, "Changing Patterns of Cocaine Use: Longitudinal Observations, Consequences, and Treatment," in *Cocaine: Pharmacology, Effects, and Treatment of Abuse,* edited by John Grabowski. National Institute on Drug Abuse Research Monograph 50 (Rockville, Md.: National Institute on Drug Abuse, 1984).
57. Dana E. Hunt et al., "An Instant Shot of 'Ahh': Cocaine Use Among Methadone Clients," *Journal of Psychoactive Drugs* 16 (1984): 217–227.
58. H. D. Kleber and F. Gawin, "Cocaine Abuse: A Review of Current and Experimental Treatments," in *Cocaine: Pharmacology, Effects, and Treatment of Abuse.* National Institute on Drug Abuse Research Monograph 50 (Rockville, Md.: National Institute on Drug Abuse, 1984).

31. The Dealing Lifestyle

Patricia A. Adler

I have just described how the networks of social relationships which surrounded Southwest County dealers and smugglers provided an element of community and stability in their lives. Juxtaposed against this dimension of rational organization, drug traffickers' lifestyle of hedonism represented the irrational, compelling force.

Southwest County dealers and smugglers led lives that were seldom dull. Abandoning the dictates of propriety and the workaday world, they lived spontaneously and intensely. Drug traffickers rejected society's normative constraints which mandated a lifestyle of deferred gratification, careful planning, and sensible spending. Instead, they embraced the pursuit of self-indulgence. Whether it was the unlimited availability of their favorite drugs, the illusion of the seemingly bottomless supply of money, the sense of power and the freedom they attained, their easy access to sexual satisfaction, or merely the excitement associated with the continual dangers they faced, the dealing crowd was strongly driven by the pleasures they derived from their way of life. This lifestyle was one of the strongest forces that attracted and held people to the drug trafficking business. It was therefore largely responsible for the set of traits which comprised the dealers' personality; only those people who found the reward system enticing enough to merit assuming the risks were persuaded to strive for greater involvement in this world.

In this chapter I examine salient characteristics of the dealers' and smugglers' lifestyle and sketch a rough portrait of their common social psychological traits, in order to better understand the dual motivations of hedonism and materialism in the drug world's upper echelons.

The Fast Life

The lifestyle associated with big-time dealers and smugglers was intemperate and uninhibited. Dubbed the fast life,[1] or "flash," it was characterized by a feeling of euphoria. So pleasurable was life that nobody worried about paying the bills, running out of drugs, or planning for the future. Dealers and smugglers plunged themselves fully into satisfying their immediate desires, whether these involved consuming lavish, expensive dinners, drugging themselves to saturation, traveling hundreds of miles to buy a particular item that caught their eye, or "crashing" (sleeping) for 15–20 hours at a time to make up for nights spent in unending drug use. Those who lived in the fast land sought an intensity that disdained the boredom of security and the peace of calm quietude. They were always on the run, rushing back and forth between partying and doing business, often intermingling the two. Schedules and commitments were hard to maintain, since people were apt to pursue the unexpected at any time or get caught in a run of drug consumption that could last for hours or even days. One coke dealer commented on the frequency of his partying:

> When we're sitting around the house with friends that are into dealing it always turns into a party. We do a lot of drugs, drink a lot, and just speed rap all night. . . . It's a full time thing; we're basically decadent 24 hours a day.

Those who lived the fast life were the *beautiful people,* bedecked with expensive adornments such as flashy clothes, jewelry, and sports cars. When they entered a restaurant or bar they ordered extravagantly and tipped lavishly. They grew up to reattain a childlike innocence by escaping the unpleasant responsibilities of adult life, while seizing the opportunity to surround themselves with anything money could buy. In their own eyes, they were the ultimate "in crowd."

The dealers' and smugglers' fast life emulated the jet set with all of its travel, spending, and heavy partying.[2] Private planes were diverted to carry a smuggler's entourage off for a week in Las Vegas where they all drank, gambled, and saw the shows. At other times it was off to the Pacific Islands for sunbathing and tropical drinks, to the mountains for skiing, or to famous spas, where they luxuriously exercised and rejuvenated themselves. In contrast to those children of inherited wealth, though, dealers and smugglers had to work for their money. Their lifestyle was characterized by a mixture of work and play, as they combined concentrated wheeling and dealing with unadulterated partying. Yet, like jet-setters, they ultimately became bored and sought ever-greater excitement, usually turning to drugs for their most intense highs.

Members of the "glitter crowd" were known for their *irresponsibility* and *daring,* their desire to live recklessly and wildly. They despised the conservatism of the straight world as lowly and mundane. For them, the excitement of life came from a series of challenges where they pitted themselves against the forces that stood in their way. Although they did not create arbitrary risks, dealers and smugglers were gamblers who enjoyed the element of risk in their work, being intoxicated with living on the edge of danger. They relished more than just the money; they reveled in the thrill-seeking associated with their close scrapes, their ever-present danger, and their drug-induced highs. Gone was the quiet, steady home life of soberly raising children and accumulating savings, as they set themselves on a continuous search for new highs. They exalted freedom, the ability to pick up and "blow" without having to answer to anybody. One dope chick who had spent the past several years moving from relationship to relationship with various big dealers discussed her sense of freedom:

Now I can do anything I want and not have to worry about someone telling me not to do it. One day I just woke up and said to my little girl, "Honey, pack your clothes. We're going to Hawaii."

Drug dealers lived for the present, surrounding themselves with the maximum pleasures they could grab. They did not, as the middle class ethos suggested, live in reduced comfort so that they could enjoy the fruits of their labor at a later date. In fact, the reverse was true. The beautiful people seized their happiness now and deferred their hardships for the future; they lived for the moment and let tomorrow worry about paying the tab. One dealer's old lady elaborated on this *mañana* effect:

It was always like, tomorrow, tomorrow. You write a check, you think you'll cover it tomorrow. It was like that. We went through a lot of stuff like that.

Money lay at the base of their exhilarating madness, more money than most could ever have imagined. The gigantic profits that could be accumulated after even a short period of smuggling or heavy dealing could run into hundreds of thousands of dollars a year,[3] which seemed like an endless supply to most participants. Sometimes they became so overcome by their material wealth that they just gloried in it. One novice dealer exclaimed:

We were like little children in a big fancy palace playhouse. We'd dump all our money on the living room floor and we'd roll in it.

349

Most initiates could not imagine how to spend this much at first, but they soon learned. After even a short period they found themselves laughing when hundred dollar bills came out of laundered shirt pockets, crumpled and torn from the wash. By then money had become something to be spent without care on the fulfillment of any whim. One member of a smuggler's crew recalled:

> Money meant nothing to me. Like, if some guy gave me a $100 bill I'd go out and burn it or cut it in half for all I cared.

This overabundance drove them to generate new needs, to search out new avenues of spending. As one dealer illustrated:

> At the height of my dealing I was making at least 10 grand a month profit, even after all my partying. When you have too much money you always have to look for something to spend it on. I used to run into the stores every day to find $50, $60 shirts to buy because I didn't know what else to do with the money, there was so much.

Drugs were also a big part of the fast life. Smugglers and dealers took personal consumption for themselves and their entourage as a basic cost of doing business, to be siphoned out before profits could accumulate, so drugs flowed freely, without care for expense. High-potency marijuana and hashish were smoked in moderation by many, most noticeably among the marijuana traffickers. Alcohol, particularly wine and champagne, was consumed regularly, often along with other drugs. Cocaine, however, was used heavily, its presence pervading the entire dealing community. They typically "coked" themselves to saturation, and it was not uncommon for a dealer to snort more than an ounce a week (market value: $2,000–$2,200) during periods of heavy partying. One cocaine dealer estimated how much he and his old lady took out for their "own heads":

> As much as we wanted, which was a lot. We used a couple of grams a day at least, that was nothing. We could go through a quarter [of an ounce], you wouldn't believe it. We used big ziplocs, the large size, for our personal stash. We'd stick a big spoon in it and just dump it out on the mirror. One time I dropped an ounce down the front of my shirt when I went to take a toot [snort] and the bag ripped. I just brushed it off, it was nothing.

One of the reasons dealers and smugglers went through large quantities of cocaine so quickly was that they built up a short-term tolerance to its effects. Early phases of contact with the drug usually brought on a subtle rush of warmth, and feelings of affection for surrounding people.[4] This might be accompanied by a brief seizure of diarrhea, a loss of appetite, and a feeling of acceleration. After a half hour or so the warmth faded and the speed effect intensified. The usual reaction was either to moderate this overintensity with alcohol or marijuana or to pass around another series of "lines" and snort some more. This pattern could continue for hours or days until the participants became so "wired" (tense) that they found themselves gritting their teeth and passing up further offers. Sleep usually came only with great difficulty, and then often did not last long, as individuals awakened, often exhausted, with a slightly bitter drip down the backs of their throats.

After people had been exposed to heavy cocaine use for a period of weeks, they usually noticed a slight change in its effects. They required larger quantities to generate and sustain that buzzing feeling of warmth ("the rush"). Their loss of appetite and sleeplessness diminished, so that people who used it to lose weight soon noticed a reduction in its effectiveness. These changes, although indicative of a shift in individuals' patterns and quantity of usage, were not associated with any physical withdrawal symptoms when the drug was unavailable, such as heroin and barbiturate users experience (Grinspoon and Bakalar 1976).

The great appeal of cocaine snorting rested on two main characteristics of its effects: internal and interpersonal. Psychologically, individuals achieved a sense of happiness and well-being. They felt as if their problems were temporarily solved and that everything was wonderful, that they could do no wrong. This was associated with great sensations of safety and power. However, coke was even more strongly a social drug, helping to facilitate intimate lines of communication between people. One pilot voiced a commonly held opinion concerning cocaine's aphrodisiac effects:

Coke and chicks! Yeah, man, whenever I have some I make sure all the ladies know, cause it really turns them on, they really dig it.

Beyond these casual relationships, serious coke users used the drug to enhance interaction with others. One ounce dealer described the effect it had within his group of friends:

Coke helps you get past the stupid front games. Our little sessions at night with coke show the closeness that comes from the coke raps. You have such tight friends in such a short amount of time—it's all right there.

Another dealer discussed how cocaine affected his relationship with his wife:

She and I have such a severe communication gap that it's probably 50 percent of the reason cocaine persists the way it does. When we get together in the evenings it smooths the way for us to relate, for us to have our special time together as lovers. We probably couldn't go on together for long without it.

Dealers and smugglers began consuming cocaine in even larger quantities in the late 1970s when "freebasing" became a popular fad. This involved altering the refined drug's condition into a smokable state. Chemical kits which contained the solvent that transformed coke into base became widely available in headshops. Jean described her fascination with this drug experience:

You start by mixing the coke with the solvent. You pour it out with an eyedropper onto the dish and it fluffs up like little white trees—like snow, it's pretty. Half of the Jones [the high] is watching that stuff form, scraping it up, putting it into the waterbase pipe—you have to use a torch to keep the heat on it all the time—it forms oils and resins. And as it drops down through the pipe it starts to swirl—half the Jones is in that whole process of smoking it. The other half is in the product. It's like you got hit by a train, it hits you so heavy, but then it goes away so fast that you use so much.

Yet along with the intense highs came some equally intense lows. An experienced freebaser recalled some of his more unpleasant episodes:

Lows? It's like when you can't get up to go to the bathroom and your mind goes by itself. When you're up pacing the floor—your mind, but your body's not. When you're so wired and exhausted and you just want to sleep but you can't. You lie there staring at the ceiling for about 24 hours straight. You're so fucked up you're embarrassed to go out of the house. Falling asleep in public bars. I've been so fucked up I couldn't go in to work and my six-year-old kid had to call in sick for me.

Getting into the habit of consistently freebasing (called "being addicted" by some) broke several dealers and smugglers in Southwest County. Many individuals, once introduced to freebasing, found it increasingly difficult to moderate their drug use. It was an allure that compelled continuing use more than any other drug popular with this subculture. Because larger and more frequent doses of cocaine were used when smoking base, two people could easily consume a quarter to a half ounce of cocaine during a single night's "run" (sitting of continuous usage). Some heavy users freebased for as long as seven or eight days straight without sleep. One person I knew went through $20,000 worth of cocaine in a week this way, while another used $60,000 worth in a month. Only the richest and most successful dealers and smugglers could afford to sustain such an expensive drug diet. Freebasing, however, could become all-consuming, leaving little time for the business of earning money. Thus some people committed themselves to sanatoriums for rehabilitation when they realized that they had reached this level of involvement. Still others quit the business altogether (some with the help of Narcotics Anonymous), as one former pound dealer explained:

> Once I got into base I realized I could never deal again, because you can't have the product or you might get into doing it again.

Another component of life for Southwest County's beautiful people was the *casual sex scene.* Although many members of the community were married and had children, they openly broke the bonds of marital fidelity to explore their sexual urges. Casual attractions, although not the only mode of sexual fulfillment, were a commonly accepted part of life. This open sexual promiscuity was legitimated by the predominance of the hedonistic ethos which infused the dealing and smuggling community. The ease with which they engaged in casual sexual relations indicated their openness toward sexual self-indulgence as a subculturally accepted norm, overriding the contrary sexual mores of the greater society.

Many male dealers and smugglers went out with their male friends to pick-up bars, looking for one-night stands. Some kept old ladies on the side and set them up in apartments. They also played musical old ladies, shifting from one to another as they got tired of each one. Extramarital flings were not limited to the men, though, as married women frequently went out for a night with the "girls" and did not come home until sunrise. Marital relationships often became taken for granted in the light of this emphasis on immediate attractions, and divorce was common.

Dealers' old ladies formed an interesting part of the drug scene, because although their role was occasionally active, it was more often passive. Some women ran their own drug businesses. Of these, most entered dealing through the connections they made while living with a male dealer. Typically, after a breakup, these women needed money and realized that they had the knowledge to attempt doing business on their own. Not all women who tried to establish themselves as drug traffickers were successful, however. This lack of success rested, in part, on certain qualities essential to the profession and in part on the reactions men had to working with them. Blum et al. (1972:47) offered a discussion of why there were fewer women dealers in their sample which is relevant to my sample as well:

> Dealers suggest first that women do not always have the personality for it, that they are too paranoid. They also say that women are victims of the double standard; their being in the dealing business is generally disapproved. Some observed that women are less business-oriented in general and so are less likely to be entrepreneurs in peddling drugs. Some contend that women are in general less competent; others hold that women, as the girl friends or sexual partners of dealers and users, can get their drugs free and need not worry about drugs or money. Finally, some of our dealers point out that women cannot do as well in dealing because men, who comprise the majority of the business network, are not comfortable dealing with them or do not trust them.

Some Southwest County dealers echoed these sentiments, as one marijuana trafficker complained:

Among the guys I know, a lot of them are reluctant to deal with girls. Girls don't seem to bend as well as guys do. Like girls seem to be a lot more highstrung, or they get more emotional if something doesn't go down right. Like guys seem to have more patience involved in it. . . . And girls are a lot more greedier than guys, they want a bigger cut normally for some strange reason.

This was not a universal complaint. Others found nothing wrong with working with women and did not reject them as associates. One cocaine dealer gave his view on women dealers:

Out here there's lots of them, as equal with guys. The first person who gave me my first front was a lady and I'm still good friends with her. I really have no preference for dealing with either sex.

Most people agreed, though, that men chauvinistically bent the rules for the "ladies." For instance, women were given more time to pay back money they owed, and were less likely to have to adhere to standard operating procedures for dealing, such as weighing or performing tests for quality on drugs that they sold. This chauvinism could be favorably manipulated, as one female dealer admitted:

Chicks have a great advantage, especially when you use it in an unfair way, which you can when you're a chick.

Women, as I have discussed, were also used by male dealers and smugglers as employees. Smugglers felt that women were less vulnerable to the suspicions of police or border agents. Positions in which women were often employed included transporting money or drugs, locally, around the country, or across international lines, and operating stash houses.

The majority of women in Southwest County's drug world took a more passive role, however. A crowd of dope chicks formed part of the entourage which surrounded big dealers and smugglers. Universally beautiful and sexily clad, they served as prestigious escorts, so that dealers could show them off to other members of the community. The motivation for these women was to share in the fast life's drugs, money, glamor, and excitement, as one dealer's wife explained:

Some chicks use their looks as a way of getting a man or some coke or their money or whatever. Those girls are like prostitutes—they put themselves where they know they can accomplish what they're really looking for.

In return, they were expected not to intrude on any of their companions' social or business relations. One dope chick offered this explanation of the reciprocal relationship:

I guess he just wanted someone to look pretty and drive his Pantera, so that people would say, hey so-and-so's got a real foxy-looking chick.

Beyond appearance, dealers looked on these women as sex objects. A married smuggler explained the rules of the game:

Sex is important in that they can make love to that lady because they're stimulated by her. They're gonna live with her and ball her, but yet they can make love to another lady too.

When it came to personality, however, less dynamic stimulus was required. A major coke dealer was frank about his colleagues' attitudes on this point:

> The guys want a chick who will hang on their arm and go places with them and they don't really have to relate to her, because they would actually prefer if the chick was dumb enough to where they could leave her with a couple of bottles of wine and say I'm going out to do some business, I'll see you in the morning. They want a chick who will accept where she's at and have enough brains to know when to shut up.

Children of the drug world experience an upbringing that was very different from children of the larger culture. When their parents went out to a party they were often left home alone. Some were enrolled in boarding schools to offer their parents greater freedom. In divorced households they were often bounced back and forth from one parent to the other as the adults fluctuated in their financial and household stability. When parents dealt or partied in the home, only slight efforts were made to hide their actions from the children. However, as the party progressed or the children aged and became more aware, it was increasingly impossible to diguise what was happening. Other parents made no attempt to camouflage their promiscuous or drug-related activities. They took their children with them when they slept around or partied, allowing them to view what went on without censorship.

The result of this treatment was generally a premature precocity and independence on the children's part. Given the responsibility for viewing, understanding, and accepting this adult behavior, children adapted rapidly. They learned about the nature of drugs: what they were worth and what effects they generated. They also learned to amuse and take care of themselves in the absence of parental protectiveness.

In some cases, their experience with drugs came firsthand. From earliest infancy these children were "tinydopers" (see Adler and Adler 1978), becoming passively intoxicated through the inhalation of smoke in the air. As they got older, however, they were permitted to take an occasional toke on the communal marijuana cigarette. Parents varied in how regularly they gave their children drugs. Some made marijuana available to children whenever it was requested, either bringing them into the smoking circle or rolling "pinners" (tiny, thin joints) for the youngsters to smoke on their own. One dealer, when queried about the possible dangers of offering drugs to young children, replied:

> What the hell! It grows in the ground, it's a weed. I can't see anything wrong with doing anything, inducing any part of it into your body any way that you possibly could eat it, smoke it, intraveneously, or whatever, that it would ever harm you because it grows in the ground. It's one of God's treats.

Other parents offered marijuana to their children only occasionally. These parents made the decision to let their children have access to marijuana for one of the following special reasons: (1) as a reward for a child's good behavior in the past, present, or anticipated future; (2) out of guilt, to compensate children for neglecting them in other ways; (3) as a source of adult entertainment, because children behave amusingly when under the influence; or (4) as a medicinal aid, to help children fall asleep or to alleviate their cranky moods.

Children of the dealing crowd eventually outgrew their cuteness as tinydopers, however, and some graduated to become "tinydealers." Moving into junior high and high school, 13- and 14-year-old dealers were capable of making large sums of money by selling ounces of marijuana and grams or half-grams of cocaine to their peers. One smuggler commented on this second generation of dealers:

> These are kids who've been raised with this lifestyle, easy money, drugs around all the time—their parents are still heavy dealers now. All these kids and all their friends have access to the drug and they're ripping off their parents. Or else they're dealing on their own through their parents' connections or through their parents' friends' kids. . . . What the hell are the parents going to do? They're not setting the example themselves so what can they do? They have no relating to the kids anyway.

Thus these children grew up in their parents' image. It is not unusual to see a community transmit its norms, values, and occupational preferences from one generation to the next. In fact, this commonly occurs with some regularity, even when that community constitutes a subculture that stands off from the norms of the greater culture. The unusual thing here was the fact that drug use and drug trafficking, acts which are usually reserved for more mature members of a community, were allowed for children, a sacred group in most societies. This violation of a cross-cultural taboo further stigmatized the drug dealing subculture as highly deviant.

The Dealing Personality

Drug dealers and smugglers entered the business from many walks of life. However diverse their origins, though, they were all attracted to certain joys and pressures inherent in the dealing life. As a self-selecting group, they held key common traits which I have compiled into a portrait of their collective social psyche.

The most noticeable and significant characteristic was the *dealer's ego*. Dealers and smugglers had a highly elevated sense of self-esteem. This was, in part, based on their degree of success in completing challenging business transactions, where they had to constantly maneuver to overcome such obstacles as the law, untrustworthy dealers, human error, mechanical failure, climatic disaster, and a host of other unforseeable difficulties. Money also served to inflate their egos, not only because of the amounts they could earn but because of the consumable items on which they were forced to spend it (for security reasons). Another feature contributing to the dealers' egos was the *power* of their position. They controlled the flow of drugs to lower-level dealers, which affected others' ability to do business, to earn money, and to obtain a personal supply of drugs. They could thus make or break their associates through the extension or withholding of their favors.

Dealers and smugglers also derived ego-gratification from their social status in the community. Although many differences exist between the drug dealing culture and lower-class culture, Miller's (1958) discussion of the importance of "rep" among juvenile street gangs highlights the infamy dealers earned from their personal exploits: recognition among peers became an end in itself. They greatly enjoyed the *prestige* of others' knowledge about the deviant nature of their occupation, the volume they were capable of handling, and the amount of money they made. Many dealers thus relished the spread of their reputations, dangerous though this was, because it fed back to their egos and made them feel important.

Closely interwoven with power and prestige was the attribute of being *sexy*. It was part of a dealer's macho image of himself and others to be sexually attractive to women. One tactic they used to seduce women was to impress them with their status as dealers. Many females found this a "turn on" because of the glamor, money, thrills, and risk associated with evading the law and handling forbidden substances. Dealers were also known to have a ready supply of cocaine, which was perceived as an enticement and enhancement to sexual activity. During sexual hunting, then, a dealer might breach his safety precautions and reveal his identity and activities to an available woman.[5]

Interestingly, the dealer's ego stands in contrast to another egotistical personality syndrome: the "little man" complex. While the latter refers to a condescending attitude arising out of an inferior physical stature, dealers and smugglers as a group were overwhelmingly large in size. Before meeting a new drug trafficker I could expect that, at minimum, he would be six foot two and weigh 180 pounds. The reasons for this also lay in self-selection, for although violence was rare in Southwest County, it was fairly common in the drug world more generally. Regardless of whether an individual ever had to resort to violence it lay behind all business relationships as a lurking threat. As Moore (1977:43) has noted, "muscle" in the drug world refers to one's perceived capacity for violence more than its continued demonstration. Thus people who felt unsure of their ability to be aggressive or to physically defend themselves were less likely to venture into drug trafficking. This was also part of the reason why the dealing and smuggling ranks were more heavily populated by men than by women. The dealer's ego was the "big man's" ego.

Another characteristic of dealers and smugglers was the high level of *tension* which pervaded their existence. Inherent in their occupation were certain pressures of time, money, and the law, which made them highly vulnerable to emotional stress. Dave spoke about his underlying worries:

> I realize I might lose everything again completely. I may get busted and go away for quite awhile. I guess I have a gambling sickness, like I'm gambling on my life. It's crazy. I try and push the worry about getting busted out of my mind but I think about it quite a bit. It's a heavy toll.

Tension also built up from the intensity of their lifestyle, as they both worked and partied to extreme degrees. Here, as the pressure to seek thrills mounted, dealers became more frazzled. This was exacerbated by their extended periods of heavy cocaine use which left them jittery, on edge, and prone to quick flare-ups of anger.

Set against this enduring mood of tension were more intense and short-lived spells of "paranoia."[6] All dealers and smugglers knew the feeling of paranoia. Although they generally rode the crest of enthusiasm and confidence, their constant flirtation with great risk caused them to occasionally experience flashes of vulnerability. These came when they claimed their drug-laden suitcases at airports, passed through metal detectors, crossed international borders while carrying drugs, or most often, as one smuggler described, for seemingly little reason:

> You can be up for hours totally high on a utopia type of thing, but if things start going slow, like if a deal's going down and it seems to be taking too long, paranoia totally sets in, unbelievably sets in, like one minute after the load's supposed to arrive.

In order to deter such attacks of paranoia, dealers and smugglers developed a series of *rationalizations* which were multifunctional. One set functioned as "accounts" (Scott and Lyman

1968), helping drug traffickers to convince themselves that their activities were "cool," that for some reason they were safe from the law. One cut-ounce cocaine dealer attributed this to his "karma":

> I really believe it's karma—cause and effect. What you're putting out gets back. The types of deals and business that I'm doing are so minor and nonoffensive that I don't think they want me.

Others based their sense of safety on their degree of caution, criticizing colleagues for their shady associates or loose behavior, while being blind to these very elements in their own mode of operating. These delusions were all part of their internal cover-up.

Dealers' and smugglers' rationalization extended beyond their self-deceptions to their use of techniques of legitimation and neutralization (see Sykes and Matza 1957), designed to help them deal with society's reactions to their being deviant. They knew that they were breaking the law, but they saw nothing morally wrong with their activities. Providing a commodity that people eagerly bought did not give them criminal self-conceptions. One smuggler offered an analogy that combined both the "denial of injury" and "rejecting the rejector" neutralizing themes:

> Even the straight people who've made a lot of money have done it illegally one way or another to get up there. Even look at the Kennedys—Kennedy was a bootlegger. I look at running grass and selling grass right now, is the same thing as the bootleggers did in the 1920s with booze. And nobody looks down on them. Like I don't feel like I'm pushing anything which is hurting anybody.

A final personality characteristic shared by dealers and smugglers was a sense of *invulnerability,* a feeling that they were surrounded by a protective shell so that nothing bad could happen to them. Despite the dangers and tensions with which they lived, drug traffickers did not always brood on disaster; in fact, they generally ignored that possibility. When not stricken by pangs of paranoia, they commonly felt inordinately safe, flaunting their illegal activities and gains within the group. Their moods thus vacillated erratically, seesawing up and down from one extreme to the other.

The trait was partly tied to their heavy drug use, as their extended cocaine consumption generated an aura of "magical omnipotence," a bubble which was artificially inflated only to be continually punctured and reinflated. Using cocaine also created a subtle detachment from reality so that they tended to forget about their ever-present danger. But dealers' and smugglers' feelings of invulnerability also indicated that they had developed a subconscious coping strategy where they removed constant worries about their personal safety from their immediate zones of relevance in order to normalize their occupation and lifestyle.

Motivations for Dealing

Two dominant motivations fueled the drive to traffic in drugs: *hedonism* and *materialism.*[7] The latter was the more readily apparent of the two, and has been cited by most sociological accounts of other illegal occupations as the primary enticement (see Cameron 1964; Ianni 1972; Langer 1977; Letkemann 1973; Plate 1975; Sutherland 1937). Certainly, none of the dealers or smugglers I observed could have earned as much money in as short a time by legitimate means. Their drug profits enabled them to surround themselves with the kind of material possessions they coveted: fine food, clothes, cars, electronic equipment, and, above all, money itself, as a symbol of success and power. The lure of extravagant wealth thus served to both recruit and hold people to this enterprise.

A second source of motivation, more compelling than the first, however, was the hedonism inherent in the lifestyle. Southwest County drug traffickers pursued a style of life filled with the pleasures of unlimited drugs, sexual promiscuity, personal power, high status, freedom, risk, and excitement. Yet the acceptance of hedonism as a forceful motivation underlying criminal behavior remains controversial in the literature. Some studies, particularly those focusing on materialism, have decried this as a secondary, irrelevant, or nonexistent dimension of deviant occupations, considering illegal work as mundane as its legal counterpart (Inciardi 1975; Letkemann 1973; Sutherland 1937). Others, however, have pointed to the thrills, sexual opportunities, and deviant lifestyle as equal in their attraction and reward to materialistic compensations (see Jackson 1972; Maurer 1974; Roebuck and Frese 1976; Miller 1978). For Southwest County dealers and smugglers, the fast life became the central part of their existence. While they might have been initially drawn to trafficking out of materialism, they soon became addicted to it out of hedonism. Once people had become sufficiently exposed to the enchantment of the fast life, enamored with their feelings of importance, and used to wantonly consuming money and drugs, they were willing to continue drug trafficking to support themselves in this style. The myriad pleasures reinforced one another, overwhelming even the once soberly directed individuals. Thus, the dealing lifestyle, through its unmitigated hedonism, both attracted pleasure-seeking individuals into the drug business and transformed others, through its concentrated decadence, into pleasure seekers, combining its thrust with materialism in ensuring their continuance in this line of work.

Notes

1. This fast life resembled, although it did not exactly correspond to, Rosenbaum's (1981:23) depiction of the ghetto heroin user's lifestyle.
2. Ironically, it seemed that in the 1980s the jet set began to emulate the dealing crowd. In an article entitled, "Drugs and the High Life," *Newsweek* (1983) discussed the cases of over a dozen "trend-setting jet-setters" who were arrested for allegedly smuggling large quantities of cocaine.
3. I sat down once with a commercial marijuana smuggler and we figured out that if he did one run per week (which was his average frequency) during the prime season of October to April and incurred no unexpected losses due to arrest, theft, or accidental mishap, he could clear a profit of $800,000 per year. This figure did not include a deduction for the expense of his personal drug consumption (and that of his crew or entourage), because most dealers and smugglers considered this a perquisite of the business rather than part of their net profit. This salary represented the upper end of the profit scale, since commercial marijuana smuggling was the most lucrative type of operation I witnessed. There was a vast difference between how much dealers and smugglers earned. When compared to legitimate work, dealers' profits were quite high, but the big money was always in smuggling.
4. Waldorf et al. (1977:32) referred to the feelings of affection people experienced that faded after the drug effect wore off as "cocaine friendships."
5. Elsewhere (Adler and Adler 1980), I have referred to this breaching of safety precautions to impress others, especially women, as "the irony of secrecy in the drug world."
6. In the dealer's vernacular, this term was not used in the clinical sense of an individual psychopathology rooted in early childhood traumas. Instead, it resembled Lemert's (1962) more sociological definition which focused on such behavioral dynamics as suspicion, hostility, aggressiveness, and even delusion. Not only Lemert, but also Waldorf et al. (1977) and Wedow (1979) have asserted that dealers' feelings of paranoia could have a sound basis in reality, and were therefore readily comprehended and even empathized with by others.
7. See Miller 1978:232 for another discussion of the role of hedonism and materialism in motivating deviant work.

Chapter IX
Treatment and Policy

Chapter 9 focuses on treatment and policy responses to drug use. These two issues illustrate some of the options pursued in dealing with America's drug problems.

For example, all of us are familiar with Alcoholics Anonymous, the most widely used and visible drug program in the world. AA is a non-profit, loosely structured organization that serves men, women and children from all racial and class backgrounds. This service is provided free of charge, although limited donations are accepted. But what about the alcoholic who needs to be hospitalized and has no insurance; or the heroin addict who needs to ride the subway for an hour to reach a methadone clinic; or the multi-addicted person serving time in the local jail? Can treatment options expand to reach such a disparate group?

A variety of policy options have been pursued in the search for an answer to America's drug problems. The legal drinking age has been lowered and raised as if there is some optimal time period when all individuals become more responsible drinkers. Taxes on cigarettes rise steadily but only children under a certain age are banned from purchasing them. The criminal justice system seems forever engaged in attempting to stem the tide of any number of drugs that manage to creep inexorably over the U.S. border. And some local school boards are resorting to urine analysis to deal with in-school drug problems.

Weisner and Room start this chapter off by discussing data on the relationship between ideology, money and drug treatment. They discuss recent California legislation that has had a dramatic impact on how alcoholics are treated in the state's health care system. Kleinman, Lukoff and Kail follow up with an inside view of the limitations of methadone as a treatment panacea for heroin addicts.

The Public Citizen Health Research Group argues effectively for the limited use of tranquilizers as a treatment option, but only in conjunction with counseling between a doctor and patient. Basing their arguments on emergency room data, this research group also states that tranquilizer use is the number one drug abuse problem in the U.S.

Gronfein traces the introduction of psycho-tropic drugs for patient care in his discussion of deinstitutionalization. He argues that such drugs only served to facilitate a policy response to care that had emerged out of a concern with institutional overcrowding rather than the therapeutic needs of patients.

Finally, in the last selection, we argue that America's response to drug abuse tends to overlook the relationship between social, legal and medical components. Instead, drug policies tend to be single-minded in their focus on control. As a result it is not surprising that we never get beyond a criminal justice response to our more serious drug problems.

This chapter presents a rather gloomy outlook for the immediate resolution of a range of serious drug related concerns. A more comprehensive and holistic approach to drug use and abuse is the beginning stage of this resolution.

32. Financing and Ideology in Alcohol Treatment

Constance Weisner
Robin Room

• • •

The way U.S. society has handled its alcohol and mental health problems has changed radically since the 1950s. Sociologists have characterized these changes as "the medicalization of deviance" or "the rise of the welfare state." In fact, the changes have been so complex that they defy such simple characterization. Some believe that the power of the medical profession over alcohol and mental health problems has declined (Bunce *et al.,* 1981:159). On the other hand, while there were certainly shifts in professional ideology and changes in bellwether treatment institutions in the late 1940s and 1950s, mental health services did not change drastically until the late 1960s and early 1970s, and alcohol services until after 1970. The expansion of both services coincided with the beginning of a period of conservative politics and fiscal crisis. As a result the federal government tried to pass the cost of these changes on to the state governments. While these changes increased the availability and responsiveness of services, they also included a strong element of social control (Morgan, 1981b:243).

The timing of the changes also affected the way the new services were financed, and their relation to the bureaucratic organization of government and to their clients. Where these services were traditionally provided by civil servants, most of the new services were provided by non-government agencies operating on contract. There are two main forms of such contractual financing of services. First, services can be provided on behalf of, and paid for by, the government under a master contract for a specific period of time. These are called "contract agencies." Second, services can be provided and paid for on a case-by-base basis under an insurance or other third-party coverage stimulated by, or subsidized by, the government. These are called "private treatment agencies."

The shifts in the scope, structure, and financing of alcohol services emerged in response to changes both in the specific field of alcohol treatment and in the larger society. For example, the rise of contractual relations in human services reflects a variety of motivations, including moves by government to cut costs, the rise of an ideology of accountability in the provision of professional services, the emergence of alternative services, and the movement of entrepreneurial and investment groups into the human services "industries." But the shifts in scope, structure, and financing have in turn deeply affected the ideology and functioning of the services.

This paper is a case study of changes in alcohol services in California since 1970. First, we review the history of the modern alcohol treatment system. Second, we discuss the nature of, and reasons for, the major changes in the scope, funding, and delivery of alcohol services which have taken place in the public sector since 1970. Third, we describe how private treatment agencies have rapidly developed as third-party payments have grown. Fourth, we analyze how these changes have transformed the social ecology and functions of the alcohol treatment system. Finally, we discuss the implications of the changes for treatment ideology and practice and for the characteristics of the client population.

We collected the data for this paper from 1979 to 1984. We analyzed Weisner's (1981) study of workers in 65 different human service agencies in one northern California county. Weisner's fieldwork for this paper included attendance at: more than 200 meetings of agency administrators in three Northern California counties; meetings of regional health planning task forces; meetings of the county alcohol program administrators of nine Northern California counties; state treatment conferences; and state legislative hearings and task forces. Secondary data sources included state and county plans and policy statements, and a variety of documents describing and analyzing relevant legislation, and lobbying and marketing by the treatment and insurance industries. Surprisingly, we found remarkably little documentation of the changes under study. Extensive inquiries have failed to reveal statistical or fiscal data for California on the shift from government-run services to contracting agencies. In the absence of such data, we based our conclusions on our fieldwork and discussions with county alcohol administrators and many individual agency directors.

Development of the Modern Alcohol Treatment System

After the Second World War, state governments shouldered most of the responsibility for providing treatment for mental health and alcohol problems in the United States. These services were concentrated in large public mental hospitals. Beginning in the 1950s, in California as well as in other states, a variety of smaller, community-based therapeutic institutions slowly grew up alongside the traditional state system. These included halfway houses and community outpatient clinics. While many of these institutions were originally supported by charities or churches, a few were funded by state or local governments. Right from the start, the community-based programs differentiated between alcohol problems and mental health problems, and established separate institutions for both. Even the literature on halfway houses in the mental health field (Rausch with Rausch, 1968) and in the alcohol field (Cahn, 1970; Martinson, 1964) remained quite separate. The separation reflected the influence of the nascent alcoholism movement, with its view of alcohol problems as a disease and its perception that alcoholics were not well served in mental health institutions (Roizen and Weisner, 1979:77; Wiener, 1981).

In 1954, somewhat later than in many other U.S. states, California established a state commission to deal with alcoholism. In 1957, these alcohol functions were transferred to California's Department of Public Health (Reynolds, 1973:76). Thereafter, responsibility for alcoholism remained separate from California's Department of Mental Hygiene. By the early 1960s the state was supporting a few pilot alcoholism clinics in communities (Morgan, 1980:131), including a few halfway houses (Martinson, 1964:432). By the mid-1960s, the federal government had committed itself to a policy of encouraging the treatment of alcohol and mental problems at the community level. It began providing what was originally seen as "start-up" money for community mental health centers, with alcoholism treatment as an optional service. In 1967, federal legislation setting up the Social and Rehabilitation Services agency offered an opportunity—quickly seized by California—for states to secure federal funds which would match state funds on a percentage basis for the rehabilitation of alcoholics (Reynolds, 1973:101). In the early 1970s, with the separation of the National Institute on Alcohol Abuse and Alcoholism (NIAAA) from the National Institute of Mental Health, substantial federal funds became available to community alcoholism programs from mental health treatment—a policy already established in California.

In the meantime, in the early 1970s California stopped treating alcoholics in state psychiatric hospitals. Between 1950 and 1972, alcoholic first admissions to these hospitals dropped from 34.9 to 13.9 per 100,000 persons aged 20 and older. During the same period, alcoholic involuntary commitments dropped from 37.3 to 0.4. Alcoholic admissions disappeared entirely in the following years (Cameron, 1982:132). This change was part of a general trend at both the national and state levels in the late 1960s and 1970s to use community-based agencies rather than large state hospitals for dealing with mental health problems (Lerman, 1981:77). By 1975, the number of residents in state mental hospitals was one-third of what it had been in 1955 (President's Commission on Mental Health, 1978:9). But whereas in the United States as a whole alcoholic admissions to mental health hospitals fell less than other admissions, in California the change was much more sharply focused on alcoholic admissions. By the early 1970s, the phasing out of alcohol treatment services in California public psychiatric hospitals was so complete that information on them was no longer collected and published (Cameron, 1982:132).

At all levels of government—federal, state, and local—the largest growth in government support specifically for alcoholism treatment came during the 1970s. Yet many of the parameters for that expansion were set in the previous decades. In 1957, California passed legislation establishing programs to treat alcoholism not through a state-operated civil service agency, but rather through "contract and cooperat(ion) with local governmental agencies and voluntary nonprofit organizations" (quoted in Reynolds, 1973:76). The advent of federal project grants for alcoholism treatment reinforced this move to establish services in both local government and nonprofit organizations.

Meanwhile, federal health and social programs began providing subventions to individuals thereby supporting and transforming local treatment agencies. Federal social security and disability insurance payments had originally not been available to institutionalized individuals. But in the 1960s, these restrictions were relaxed (Lerman, 1981:77). At the same time, the federal government established new health and social programs such as Medicare, Medicaid, and food stamps. These indirect subventions were available whether treatment was offered by local government, by a nonprofit agency, or by a for-profit firm. However, it was not unitl the federal government encouraged the extension of health insurance to cover alcoholism treatment in the late 1970s that private, for-profit agencies penetrated the alcohol service industry.

California ceded control of alcoholism treatment programs to the counties in the 1970s. State plans became essentially compilations of county plans. Judging by the difficulty that federal surveys have had in assembling complete data on the use of alcohol services in California, the devolution of authority from state to county was greater than in other states.

Although the federal money for mental health and alcohol services was originally sent directly to local agencies, state governments—and in California also the county governments—fought sustained and increasingly successful campaigns through the 1970s to interpose their control. The various resulting programs of "revenue sharing" and "block grants" that, in terms of federal-state relations, went under the rubrics of "decentralization" and "new federalism," were seen by local agencies as a centralization of powers in the state or county governments.

The Public Alcohol Treatment System Since 1980

There were a wide range of public treatment programs available in most counties in California in the first half of the 1980s. In most metropolitan communities, publicly-funded services consisted of social model (non-medical) detoxification units with medical back-up, halfway houses, information and referral services, drop-in centers, outpatient counseling services, occupational program consultants, prevention/education services, and drunk driving programs. There were as many as 25 different agencies providing these services in counties with populations ranging from 500,000 to one million. Most of these services were also available in rural counties, though some were combined in a much smaller number of agencies, or shared between counties. Room (1980) suggests that the U.S. population in treatment for alcoholism increased at least 20-fold between 1942 and 1976. Attempts to document changes in the number of individuals treated for alcohol problems in California since 1950 have proved difficult, due to changes in institutional responsibility and changing definitions of alcoholism, as well as poor and unsystematic record-keeping within and across agencies.

Funding for the public alcohol treatment system increased rapidly over a relatively short time span. In California in 1980, the total state-administered budget for alcohol programs was over $70 million; of this total, $6 million was from federal subventions, $8 million from county funds, $37 million from state funds, and $19 million from client fees and insurance reimbursements (California, Department of Alcohol and Drug Programs, 1980:43). Direct federal grants (outside the state budget) added about another $10 million. This represents a substantial growth from the total 1972–73 budget of slightly over $26 million (California, Human Relations Agency 1972:37).

When money for alcohol treatment in California first became available in the 1960s, most of the services were initially provided through the counties by civil service agencies, often county hospitals. With the sudden injection of funding from NIAAA and the state in the early 1970s, many California counties began to contract out many of their services rather than to include them under their civil service systems.

This phenomenon was not unique to the alcohol field. Terrell and Kramer (1982:1), in their study of contracting for human services in nine northern California counties, note that "indeed, while governmental responsibilities for ensuring public welfare have enlarged tremendously in the years since 1965, the scale of public provision has been increasingly checked by the development of new instruments like vouchers, tax incentives, and contracting." All of the counties studies were contracting out for mental health services. Terrell and Kramer found "in three agency areas (aging, community action, mental health) over 70 percent of all expenditures are made via nonprofit social agencies. In two other areas (social services, general revenue sharing), over one-fifth and one-third of the funds, respectively, are contracted out" (1982:20). They describe the origins of contracting:

> Contracting for social welfare first became a major option for service delivery in the 1960s within a context of rapidly expanding federal spending and the inability of many public agencies to handle increased responsibilities. Major changes in the political culture of the 1970s contributed to the expanded use of nonprofit organizations as the disenchantment with bureaucracies and the backlash against taxes and spending made nongovernmental arrangements appealing. In addition, the emergence of public policy themes such as decentralization, deinstitutionalization, privatization, and 'social targeting' all gave further impetus to voluntary community-based services (1982:2).

Terrell and Kramer were unable to document the shift from county-run to contracted programs.[1] Our attempts to document this change across California were likewise unsuccessful.[2] This is partly due to the many changes in jurisdiction in the state government. During the 1960s, the responsibility for alcohol services shifted between three different departments. Even after 1970, when state and federal legislation called for a single state agency, there were changes in the way the agency related to the state departments of mental health, drug abuse, and public health in 1973, 1974, 1976, and 1978. These institutional changes were reflected at the county level as well, with the result that records of funding arrangements are scattered through different departments

TABLE 1. *Funds Allocated to County-Operated Programs and to Programs Run by Private Contractors*[1]

County	Mid 1970s[2]		1982–83	
	Percent County-run programs	Percent Contracted programs	Percent County-run programs	Percent Contracted programs
Alameda	87[3]	13	16[3]	84
Contra Costa	92	8	20	80
Los Angeles	34	66	19	81
Orange	62[4]	38	37[4]	63
Santa Clara	63	37	26	74
San Diego	38	62	0	100
San Francisco	39	61	26	74

Notes:
1. These amounts represent the counties' total alcohol funds from federal, state, and local sources. Percentages are rounded off.
2. Because of jurisdictional changes in location of alcohol programming and inconsistent availability of alcohol-specific budget figures for the 1970s from county to county, the same baseline years are not presented: Orange was 1975-76; Alameda 1976-77; Santa Clara, San Diego and San Francisco 1977-78; and Los Angeles 1978-79.
3. Includes funds spent for central program administration.
4. Includes some client fees.

and do not always specifically mention alcohol services. This same situation has made it difficult to document other areas of the history of alcohol services financing as well, such as the amounts of money spent by third party payments for alcoholism treatment.

Since statistics were not available for California as a whole, we collected information from the County Alcohol Program Administrations of the seven counties which receive the bulk of federal and state funds (90 percent of the residential services budget, 65 percent of the detox budget, and 60 percent of the halfway house budget) (California, Department of Alcohol and Drug Programs, 1983). Table 1 shows the shift from county to contract programs from the middle 1970s to 1982–83. The data do not reflect the full extent of the shift, as most counties did not have specific statistics for their alcohol programs until the years indicated in the table. One county, Contra Costa, reported that in 1974–75 it spent 100 percent of its funds on county-operated programs. Staff from other counties said that county-operated programs received higher percentages prior to the years for which they had records.

The counties decided to contract out alcohol services for a number of reasons, including the sudden arrival of money and the immediate need to provide services; a more responsive labor force; the lower cost of providing services outside of local government; and the freedom to hire employees outside the civil service system. The shift can also be seen as an extension of how funds were being channeled from one level of government to another. Each level of govenment appeared to be contracting with the one below it. In addition, with a mandate to construct a comprehensive system, local alcohol treatment administrators first disbursed money to existing programs, many of them in the private or voluntary sectors; in some cases they funded the entire program, and in other cases only certain service components. A limited number of new programs were then started to fill some of the remaining gaps. Many alcohol treatment administrators said they felt it made sense to give the new treatment funds to organizations that had a proven record. Moreover, by at least partially funding a wide variety of alcohol treatment institutions, the administrators were able to maintain control over—and claim credit for—many more programs.

As Salamon and Abramson (1982:37) note, the tradition of government "partnership" with non-profit entities such as the alcohol treatment contract agencies actually has deep roots in U.S. history. But the 1960s and early 1970s saw an increase in the federal government's use of contract relationships for social and health services. In some cases, such as the neighborhood health centers legislation and the Amended Food Stamp Act of 1977, the federal government actually forced nonprofit rather than local government governance by disqualifying programs run by local government from participation (National Association of State Alcohol and Drug Abuse Directors, 1984; Sardell, 1983:488). Federal subventions, both contractual funding and subventions through individual entitlements, have indeed transformed the financial base of the nonprofit sector. Salamon and Abramson (1982:44) estimate that in 1980, for the United States as a whole, 58 percent of the revenues of social service agencies and 36 percent of the revenues of health care agencies came from federal programs. They also estimate that 20 percent of federal funding for nonprofit agencies came in direct contracts, 27 percent through state or local governments, and 53 percent through individual-level subventions (1982:45).

California's state alcohol problems agency, the Department of Alcohol and Drug Programs, was authorized from its inception to contract either with local governments or with nonprofit agencies. Since the early 1970s, the state has contracted exclusively with the counties. But California set a precedent for contracting with nonprofit agencies by providing subventions to some halfway houses in 1961; by the Late 1960s this practice was widely imitated in other states. Cahn (1970:150) refers to "quasi-public halfway houses":

> These are organized under voluntary auspices but with public funds, most often provided by the state alcoholism authority for meeting deficits. . . . In some states the state alcoholism authority also helps finance the original capital investments. . . . Several quasi-public institutions are in states whose mental hospitals do not accept alcoholics for treatment; they offer some of the programs normally available in the specialized wards of state mental institutions.

This suggests that in the late 1960s subventions for halfway houses were a special case; the primary state relationship for other treatment agencies was with local governments. In contrast, Aiken and Williams' (1982) review of "state and local programs on alcoholism" gives prominent billing to "private non-profit providers" for all kinds of services, in discussing intergovernment relations as well as relationships between government and the private sector (1982:338).

Government subvention of nonprofit halfway houses carried over to the county level in California, but has progressively expanded to include most other treatment modalities and agencies. This enthusiasm for contracting with private agencies was even extended in the 1970s to contracts with for-profit firms to manage the county general hospital (Shonick and Roemer, 1982:188).

The Growth of Private For-Profit Agencies

The use of private hospitals and sanitaria for the treatment of alcohol problems in the United States extends back to the "inebriate asylums" of the late 19th-century (Corwin and Cunningham, 1944:9). Through the 1920s and 1930s such hospitals were the only institutions available for treating alcoholism. The lack of other treatment alternatives played an important role in the birth of Alcoholics Anonymous (AA) (Blumberg, 1977).[3] Until the 1980s, however, there were relatively few private hospitals, and they served primarily an affluent clientele.

Since the mid 1970s, state and federal government action transformed the arena of private, for-profit treatment facilities for alcohol problems. Quite early in its existence, NIAAA decided that health insurance for alcoholism was the best way to assure a stable funding base for alcoholism treatment. Rodwin (1982) has detailed the steps NIAAA took to bring this about. State alcoholism agencies joined this effort; by September 1981, 33 of 50 states had passed legislation requiring group health insurance providers to offer optional coverage for alcohol treatment. Rodwin points out a number of factors responsible for the increase in health insurance for alcohol treatment services, including an environment of concern about alcoholism (partly due to NIAAA's campaign and pressure by the alcoholism movement); the federal Health Maintenance Organization Act of 1973, which required all Health Maintenance Organizations to provide alcoholism services in order to qualify for federal subsidies; and the growth of employee-assistance programs in industry, which made management interested in health insurance for such services. The growth of hospital-based facilities was also encouraged by the existence of substantial excess capacity in many hospitals, after a period of federally-financed overbuilding.

> In 1979, the National Drug and Alcoholism Treatment Utilization Survey indicated that 32 percent of all funding for alcohol treatment centers came from third party health insurance- both public and private. Private health insurance alone contributed 18 percent of all funding. Although this is still significantly lower than the share of private health insurance for other medical services (almost 30 percent) . . . it would seem reasonable to pronounce NIAAA's campaign to promote health insurance an "admirable success" in reaching its goals (Rodwin, 1982:17).

These government initiatives resulted in a phenomenal growth of private, hospital-based alcoholism programs. These programs were most often for inpatients and lasted about four weeks. They emphasized therapy based on the disease concept, education about the medical effects of alcoholism, and attendance at AA meetings. Documentation of this growth is incomplete because no agency has consistently kept records.[4] Moreover, the classification of alcoholism treatment and beds was not consistent within or between hospitals, and was often recorded under various labels in order to obtain health insurance reimbursement.

Attempts to document the growth in private programs in California through state and county records were frustrating, since hospital beds for alcoholism treatment were listed under categories such as medical surgery, acute psychiatry and, most recently, chemical dependency. Another reason the growth has not been charted is that it has been difficult for researchers to gain access to information from these facilities (Rodwin, 1982). In 1983 there were at least 96 private residential alcohol programs in California (*Alcoholism: The National Magazine,* 1983; Moore, 1981). The California State Health Planning Department has had such a large number of requests for licenses for chemical dependency rehabilitation hospitals since that classification was legislated by the state in 1983 that they have asked the regional Health Service Administration offices to do assessments of need. On the national level, a 1982 survey by the National Institute on Alcohol Abuse and Alcoholism found that most alcoholism treatment units in the United States were privately owned, that third party payment dollars had increased since 1979, and "that much of the overall increase in the private sector was accounted for by a steady growth in the number of units owned by profit-making organizations." Private sector treatment was found to have increased 48.2 percent between 1979 and 1982 (U.S. National Institute on Alcohol Abuse and Alcoholism, 1984:46).[5]

This growth brought problems in its wake. The excess capacity in general hospitals and the preference of health insurance carriers for hospital-based programs meant that the treatment offered by these programs was often very expensive. Profitable corporations emerged which leased empty wards of hospitals and installed chains of alcohol treatment centers. For example, in 1982 American Medical International, a corporation owning a large number of health facilities and listed on the New York and London stock exchanges, purchased 24 Raleigh Hills alcoholism treatment facilities (U.S. Journal of Drug and Alcohol Dependence, 1982). In 1983, Comprehensive Care Corporation (Comp Care), one of the major California private groups, began reorganizing due to "rapid growth into more than a $400 million company. The company has posted record earnings each year since its formation in 1972, earning $10.8 million on revenues of $89.4 million in the fiscal year ending last May 31, and $3.3 million on revenues of $25.8 million for the first quarter of this fiscal year" (Lewis, 1983:7). In 1982, the National Council on Alcoholism (NCA), the leading voluntary organization in the field, set up a group to examine "treatment financing issues," noting that "the proprietary treatment sector which flourished in the past several years is coming under increased scrutiny by the media, public and private insurors, and by public officials at both the state and national levels, in a manner which is not unlike that for the nursing home industry several years ago" (National Council on Alcoholism, 1982:1). The NCA chairman's letter which announced the study listed several reasons for conducting it, including:

1. The explosive growth of hospital-based alcoholism treatment programs in response to the liberalization of insurance coverage, and under-utilization of acute care hospital beds.
2. Growing disillusionment among insurors with the high cost of hospital-based rehabilitation programs, where it is not unusual for treatment to cost between $6,000 and $10,000.
3. Adverse publicity for one of the largest proprietary treatment chains, Raleigh Hills hospitals, which has focused on allegations of profiteering under Medicare, deficient patient care, misleading advertisements, and a controversial form of treatment.
4. Lack of agreement among professionals in the field as to what is the most effective treatment for alcoholism (National Council on Alcoholism, 1982:1).

The growing alcohol treatment industry has formed its own organization to protect its interests and has hired many veterans of the alcoholism movement to project a favorable image. Industry representatives reacted strongly to questioning by the administration of the Alcohol, Drug and Mental Health Administration about the high cost of alcoholism treatment by stressing that treatment must be hospital-based to be reimbursable (Lewis, 1982:5).

Changing Functions and Characteristics of Alcohol Treatment

By 1974, Harold Hughes, the sponsor of the Comprehensive Act of 1970, was becoming distressed at the rapid growth in the size and power of the public and private establishment for the treatment of alcoholism. He described it as "a new civilian army that has now become institutionalized. The alcohol and drug industrial complex is not as powerful as its military-industrial counterparts, but nevertheless there are some striking similarities" (Hughes quoted in Wiener, 1981:3). In retrospect, however, we can see that the system has grown and changed even more radically since Hughes spoke; yet there has been little explicit discussion of these changes and of their relationship to the ideology of the treatment enterprise itself.

The combined effect of the growth of the contract agency system and of the private hospital-based treatment chains and services has been an enormous growth in treatment capacity for alcoholism. In the course of this growth, requests for a demonstration of need for services have been readily met by recourse to the concept of the hidden alcoholic and to surveys which suggest that the number of alcoholics in the population is 10 times the number in treatment. The problems involved in using survey data to estimate need have been discussed by alcohol researchers (Cahalan, 1976; Room, 1980). Most of those identified in surveys as having alcohol-related problems are not inclined to volunteer for treatment.

Yet the beds and treatment slots must be filled. The old state mental hospital system, with its civil-servants and continuing budget, could take years to respond to changes in the patient load. But public, contract-based services and private programs must respond to such changes in days. The private hospital-based treatment services are reimbursed under health insurance contracts for each service performed for each client, and a lack of clients immediately makes revenues fall. The contract agencies must account to the county or other government funding agencies for the services they provide. As government fiscal crises tighten budgets, the contract agencies are also under pressure to make up shortfalls by taking on clients who can pay for treatment.[6]

Although in theory the public and private programs do not compete for the same clients, in practice this does happen. At meetings between agencies—for example, county level Alcohol Advisory Board meetings and regional Health Service Administration planning meetings—private hospitals appeal to public programs to refer clients who can afford to pay, since public programs are intended for those who are unable to pay. Public programs respond that they also need paying clients.

Thus, treatment agencies must show considerable entrepreneurship in dealing with agencies, institutions treating other social and health problems, and potential individual clients. The administrators of public contract agencies have become adept at recognizing and profiting from new opportunities. In the counties we studied, when Boards of Supervisors were pushed to provide generalized services for disfranchised groups, such as ethnic groups or women, they often called on contract agencies in the alcohol treatment system, even though the request for help had not specifically mentioned alcohol (Roizen and Weisner, 1979; Weisner, 1981). If the political process demanded special services for a new special population—ethnic minorities, women, gays, the disabled—an alcohol counselor from that population was found and a new service added to the county's list of alcohol services. If stiffened drunk driving laws funneled a new stream of clients into treatment, agencies responded almost overnight by changing their functions. At the level of the individual case, staff learned strategies in intervention and confrontation to widen the agency's outreach.

The public alcohol treatment system is affected by many of the same needs and resources, conflicts and contradictions, and historical, political, and economic pulls as other institutions within the larger welfare system. But it has some characteristics which make it particularly flexible in meeting broader social and political needs. First, the tremendous growth of the treatment system has created an unusual need for a sufficiently large clientele to warrant continued and even increased funding (Room, 1980). Second, the drive for a legitimate place within the social service bureaucracy has fostered a desire for an articulate, non-marginal clientele, in contrast to the more disreputable public drunk (Kurtz and Regier, 1975). Third, the potential to draw funds from a variety of sources has often rested on an ability to expand the types of problems defined as alcohol-related, and thus within the treatment system (Roizen and Weisner, 1979:82; Wiener, 1981:157). Fourth, as the treatment system has expanded, it has continued to strive for respectability, often by cementing relations with other institutions (Weisner, 1981:127).

The history of both the public and private alcohol treatment systems has made them vulnerable to pressures to redefine service populations and functions, and, in general, to accommodate other institutions. Expanding definitions of domestic violence has been just one example of these pressures: strategies for handling domestic violence have emerged which emphasize alcohol problems, though the research literature is skeptical of a causal link (Morgan, 1981a). But the program administrators knew that funds were more likely to be available for alcohol treatment than for family counseling (Weisner, 1981). The impact of extending alcohol funding to other problem areas has been twofold: it has assisted individual agencies in coping with fiscal problems, and it has propagated a broader definition of alcohol-related problems (Morgan, 1981a).

Providing services on a contractual basis has facilitated such rapid shifts in the public system. The funding of such agencies is not as secure; they must reapply annually. Their employees do not have the security of employment that civil service employees have. They are the ones most likely to be asked to make changes when a new service is needed, since the county run programs are more entrenched and difficult to change. Alcohol treatment agencies have had to be increasingly competitive and have had to redefine their functions and services in accordance with politically determined priorities. For instance, one county we studied had a contract program to provide information and referral and short-term counseling for alcoholism in 1982. The following year its program shifted to coordinating drunk driving referrals between the courts and other treatment agencies, and developing a prevention program using volunteers.

Contract services which have survived in an environment of competition for resources have developed local political connections as a self-protective device; but they remain exposed to political shifts at several levels of government. At the very least, they are obligated to stay on good terms with the county, rather than with their own boards of directors. As a result, they often face intractable dilemmas. While they must respond to their boards, they are frequently issued contradictory directives. In one county, many agencies responded by trying to secure their funding sources, often at the expense of their community constituencies and even their boards of directors. The boards in some cases ceased functioning, or existed in name only (Roizen and Weisner, 1979).

Shifts in Alcoholism Treatment

The changes we have described in both public and private agencies have transformed the way alcoholism is combined with other problems in the counties we have studied. In an unstable environment, there is a premium on arranging a stable supply of clients. It is a major coup for a halfway house to sign a contract to provide services for a labor union. Personnel departments of large corporations are besieged by offers to contract for employee assistance programs. Public service advertising by hospital-based alcoholism treatment units, aimed more at the family than at the individual alcoholic, are now a regular part of television in California.

In the public system, the search for new and more stable sources of clients has led to the courts. An increasing number of clients in alcohol treatment come from the criminal justice system; in some cases the courts are the main souce (Boscarino, 1980:403; Clarke, 1975:220; Dunham and Mauss, 1982:7; Morrissey, 1981; Speiglman and Weisner, 1982:10; U.S. National Institute on Alcohol Abuse and Alcoholism 1982:3; Weisner, 1981, 1983). Perhaps no other social agency is as well situated to provide a steady flow of clients as the criminal courts. The coercion of the courts ensures that the referred case arrives, and often can be used to induce the client to pay for treatment. We found that by 1981 the trickle of cases from the courts to alcoholism treatment in California had increased to a flood. Clients were referred not only for public drunkenness and drunk driving, but also for wife battery, child abuse, robbery, forgery, and assault. Nevertheless, by the middle of 1982, because of tough, new drunk driving laws, drunk drivers began to be one of the dominant treatment groups throughout California. There are many mechanisms of referral, from formal diversion procedures to conditions of probation, sentencing, and parole. Defense attorneys often advise their clients to volunteer for treatment in the hope of a shorter sentence (Speiglman and Weisner, 1982:5). While social action groups such as Mothers Against Drunk Driving have been influential on tougher legislation regarding drunk driving, the public alcohol treatment system has lobbied for penalties including treatment as well as traditional sanctions.

The private alcohol treatment system has grown more in response to the need to fill hospital beds rather than to a line of people waiting to be treated. Here too, coercion—albeit sometimes more subtle than in the public system—has become a prominent marketing strategy. One coercive strategy focuses on the family of persons with alcohol problems. The family is helped to confront the alcoholic with the seriousness of the problem and persuade him or her to seek treatment (Melody, 1980). The rationale for this strategy is that, when faced with evidence and an ultimatum from the family, the individual will stop denying the problem and agree to seek treatment. Often the individual's employer is involved. The rapid spread of employee assistance programs with their strategy of constructive confrontation has coincided with the growth of private programs and increased health insurance coverage. Private programs have documented the cost of alcoholism to industry and actively market their programs there. While it seems illogical to the outsider that persons who remain sufficiently stable to have retained their jobs should be in hospitals rather than outpatient programs, many industries and unions contract exclusively with hospital programs.

As we have seen, both public and private treatment systems are under pressure to find clients who can pay fees. As a result, coercion is increasingly intrinsic to the client-gathering process. These changes have brought striking shifts in treatment.

Changes in the Process and Ideology of Treatment

The flood of clients referred from the courts has been accompanied by changes in treatment philosophy. The original ideology of Alcoholics Anonymous (AA) and the alcoholism movement was highly oriented toward the client's motivation and voluntary treatment. AA waited for people to come in the door. Being properly motivated and receptive to the recovery process was considered crucial to recovery. Within the space of a few years, however, the barrier between voluntary and involuntary clients dissolved. The movement's rhetoric shifted to accommodate the realities of gathering clients. Programs became expert in "breaking through denial"; indeed, the whole rhetoric of intervention revolves around the concept of denial. Public programs use the threat of jail as a therapeutic tool (Weisner, 1981:51). The same change in attitude is found in private programs, which intervene to precipitate a crisis: the alcoholic thus hits bottom sooner, breaks through denial more easily, and becomes more receptive to treatment (Roman and Trice, 1967).

The people who provide treatment do not appear to have stopped to consider the implications of the new rhetoric—though some of the originators of the ideas have (Roman, 1980). There is certainly little self-consciousness about it. The 1982 annual California Alcohol Conference, sponsored by statewide treatment organizations, had as its theme "Breaking Down Barriers" with an emphasis on "networking and developing productive coalitions among alcohol programs and allied human service and law enforcement agencies for greater impact on individual and community denial" (California State Alcohol Treatment Conference, 1982:1). Workshops in intervention are some of the most popular and available training courses for those working in alcohol treatment (Faulkner Training Institute, 1983; Johnson Institute Seminars, 1983; Scripps Memorial Hospital, 1984).

Treatment goals have also changed. In one county, agencies under contract with the county alcohol administration stated in their contracts with the county that they would attempt to keep two-thirds of their clients out of the criminal justice system for at least six months (Speiglman and Weisner, 1982:23). The mixture of coerced and voluntary clients also has affected the treatment atmosphere. When some members of a therapy group bring attendance cards to be signed for their probation officers or employers, it changes the atmosphere of the group as a whole.

Currently in California counties, alcohol treatment providers do not have the prerogative of screening out drunk driver clients entering court-mandated programs. However, where the provider does have the power to screen cases, as with other coerced clients seeking treatment to avoid jail, there are ethical dilemmas. The agencies have no control over the context in which treatment is presented to the clients, nor over what other alternatives are offered. This may greatly influence how clients present themselves and what attitude they take to therapy. Traditionally, providers have not hesitated to terminate their relationship with clients who were not successfully participating in treatment. However, with the need to keep the new treatment slots filled, programs often feel pressured to retain clients who are not appropriate or who are not committed. Providers must also consider that clients may lose their jobs or go to jail if treatment is terminated. Even discharging clients for reasons which are based solely on medical or clinical grounds can have potentially dire consequences.

However, with other clients, a reverse problem exists. In some programs, such as drunk driving, where the treatment system is taking over a whole category of clients with which the court has long been frustrated, judges really do not want individuals returned to them unless they fail drastically. The courts thus make it very difficult for agencies to get rid of these clients.

Role Conflicts for Therapists

In both the public and private programs, in the counties we have studied, the changing environment of treatment has created ambiguities about responsibility. Who is the provider responsible to—the alcoholic, the family, the employer, the judge or the probation officer? In the pubic sector, at treatment conferences and meetings of administrators, agency directors consistently mention the reality of the pressure to be responsible to the criminal justice system or to groups which are powerful in deciding where the handling of clients such as drunk drivers should take place (California Senate Committee on Health and Welfare, 1981; California State Alcohol Treatment Conference, 1981; Northern California Conference on Drunk Driving, 1982). Agency officials speak without apparent defensiveness of the need to convince judges and Mothers Against Drunk Driving that they are punishing as well as treating criminal justice clients. Indeed, during interviews for a pilot study in one county most of these clients described their agency experience as "doing time." Counselors show little compunction in forcing clients to attend sessions and abstain from drinking by threatening to return them to the courts.

Our fieldwork has found that as public programs have become dependent on the criminal justice system for clients, they become threatened by potential policy changes—such as shortening the programs—which would change the existing arrangements. While counselors often play an empathic role during therapy, publicly they define their clients as dangerous and in need of longer-term programs. Agency staff are thus caught in a dual role: they must gain their clients' confidence while also presenting an unsympathetic view of clients to demonstrate the seriousness of the problem. In response to a recent court ruling (*People v. Municipal Court,* 1983) that treatment could not be a substitute for jail, treatment providers stressed how tightly structured their programs were and suggested that the judge increase the length of stay in the program to make it as long or longer than a jail sentence.

371

The situation within private agencies is not much different. As long as agencies have to market their programs and compete in courting referrals from employee assistance programs, their main alliances will be with the employers and unions rather than with individual clients. In both private and public agencies, the staff are caught in the uneasy compromise between a therapeutic model and model of social control and punishment which Christie (1965) described almost twenty years ago.

Compromises of Confidentiality

Alcoholism treatment has traditionally placed great emphasis on confidentiality and anonymity. The very name of Alcoholics Anonymous reflects a concern, and indeed an imperative, to maintain confidentiality (Beauchamp, 1980:50). Yet the new environment of treatment agencies compromises client confidentiality in the counties we have studied. In public programs, some counselors regularly discuss clients with probation officers. Others give only minimal information through written reports (Speiglman and Weisner, 1982). In private programs and in those public programs with contracts with employers, information on clients who have been referred by employers must be given. Similarly, counselors must report to the courts on the client's compliance or progress. In such cases, treatment is no longer a private matter between therapist and client. In both public and private programs, court-referred clients must sign release-of-information consent forms. Aiken and Weiner (1974) suggest that such clients may actually have less legal protection than they would in a conventional criminal justice setting.

Shift in Clientele

The new entrepreneurial environment has brought changes in economic and class characteristics of clients in the counties we have studied. Medicaid, which formerly supported some hospital-based care for very low income individuals, no longer covers costs, and clients having only Medicaid are therefore not accepted in private programs. These programs are populated by individuals who have private health insurance, whose employer will pay for their treatment, or whose family is sufficiently affluent to pay for the treatment. There have also been changes in the class composition of the clientele within public agencies. The public drunk, for whom the alcohol treatment system was first created (Kurtz and Regier, 1975), has been gradually pushed out the door. While the public alcohol treatment system in some counties is required by law, to make services available to indigents, just how seriously this charge must be taken has never been clarified. At the same time, agencies are under pressure from county administrations to collect fees. Examination of state management information statistics has shown that indigent claims are found in agencies which emphasize custody rather than treatment or cure and offer only short term services (Speiglman and Weisner, 1982:33; Weisner, 1983). The most common treatment locations for indigents are drop-in centers and social model detoxification units, which are in effect one-to-three day, non-medical drying-out stations.

An obvious way in which referrals from criminal justice have resulted in class bias is that treatment programs often only accept clients who can pay. If defendants cannot pay, their attorneys are less likely to request treatment and judges are more hesitant to refer (Speiglman and Weisner, 1982; Weisner, 1981). In the counties we have studied, drunk driving programs are often structured in such a way that only those who can pay are referred to them, while other offenders receive jail sentences or have their driver's licenses suspended. Many of the clients referred by the courts and employee programs are thus closer to the profile of problem drinkers in the general population than to the traditional alcoholic (Room, 1977:81). While historically the treatment field has only concerned itself with alcoholism, its ideology has always allowed for a definition of those with alcohol problems as early-stage alcoholics. But, increasingly, the field is extending its jurisdiction beyond alcoholism to include also alcohol problems. In the public system, agencies have quite explicitly enlarged the scope of their responsibility to alcoholism *and* alcohol problems.

Both public and private programs have incorporated into their conceptual understanding of alcoholism, and into their treatment population, the idea of co-alcoholism. The co-alcoholic is anyone who is affected by someone else's alcoholism. It originally referred to family members.[7] However, it is now frequently heard in reference to friends, employers, and even the community. While mental health and alcohol therapists have long advocated family participation in treatment, only alcohol treatment has carried the concept to the point of giving it a name and labeling it as a disease—we do not hear of co-schizophrenics or co-drug addicts. In an environment of flexible adaptation to changing definitions of problems—and thus to new populations—it has not been difficult to make a case for the need to treat this population. Agencies are interested in this group because they are attractive clients compared with the chronic alcoholic (Weisner, 1981:23). More importantly, co-alcoholics represent a whole new group for treatment—one that may be as large as the alcoholic population itself.

Conclusion

Those who treat alcohol problems fall into two very different groups. One group talks of "recovering alcoholics" and espouse the Alcoholics Anonymous philosophy, related self-help strategies, and nonprofessionalized treatment agencies. A second group, made up of medical and psychiatric personnel in hospital and clinical settings, has a more traditional psychotherapeutic approach. Despite their differences, these groups have traditionally agreed that it is futile to help people who do not voluntarily seek help and acknowledge their alcoholism. Thus, in the past, clients were not accepted for treatment unless they admitted they were alcoholics (Roizen and Weisner, 1979; Sterne and Pittman, 1965). Itinerant alcoholics knew they had to make this admission if they wished to receive services—even if only food and lodging—from alcohol-oriented agencies (Bibby and Mauss, 1974; Wiseman, 1970:239).

This ideology and rhetoric have undergone dramatic change. Treatment providers now emphasize aggressive outreach and intervention; they talk of confrontation and constructive coercion as tools of a tough love which will overcome denial. The providers themselves have not changed, only the rhetoric. Some would suggest that this shift is related to a drift toward a more punitive approach to alcohol problems in U.S. society (Mäkelä et al., 1981:107, 111). However, as our research indicates, the shift reflects radical changes in the size, structure, and financing of the alcohol treatment system itself.

Notes

1. Paul Terrell, February 6, 1984: personal communication.
2. At numerous times in the past we have attempted to find these statistics from various departments in the state and local governments, including the California State Department of Health Services, the California Department of Alcohol and Drug Programs, and the Contra Costa-Alameda County Health Services Administration. We have also had personal communication with the directors and some staff members of the alcohol administrations of the seven counties receiving approximately 75 percent of the state administered budget.

3. Alcoholics Anonymous was founded by Bill W. in 1935. (Consistent with principles of anonymity in the organization, the literature does not use his last name). One of the strains which influenced the formation of AA was dissatisfaction with mental hospital treatment for alcoholism.

4. Data on the number of private hospitals with alcoholism programs in the middle 1970s and on the amount of third party payment expenditure from then on were not available from either state or local governments.

5. The survey also found that while alcohol treatment in outpatient services decreased (community health centers by 8 percent and free-standing outpatient centers by 17.7 percent) since 1979, there was an increase in hospital-based alcoholism treatment units reporting. "Units in mental and psychiatric hospitals increased by 13 percent, and units in other specialized hospitals as well as general hospitals (including Veterans Administration hospitals) increased by 10 percent;" (U.S. National Institute of Alcoholism and Alcohol Abuse, 1984:45). This is a reflection of the increase of third party payment fees for hospital-based care.

6. The county-run and county-contracted programs charge fees on a sliding scale from being free to $16.00 per hour for outpatient services. Some of them charge no fees or accept General Assistance payments for residential services; the most expensive programs charge $750 per month.

7. The term "co-alcoholic" appears to have emerged in the early 1970s in the therapeutic self-help literature directed at relatives—particularly wives—of alcoholics. The term does not appear in the 1982 edition of the *Dictionary of Words About Alcohol* (Keller *et al.,* 1982) and is apparently not used in the literatures of Al Anon, family therapy, and transactional analysis. While some early usages in the self-help literature avoid imputing responsibility to the "co-alcoholic" for the "alcoholic's" behavior, or regarding "co-alcoholism" as a disease (Coudert, 1972:173), the term has increasingly taken on these attributes. "There are literally millions of wives today who are afraid to act lest their alcoholic mates increase their drinking, leave them, or refuse to support them. . . . I call them co-alcoholics, for a person who shares the attitudinal problems of an alcoholic is the closest thing to being an addict. . . . The problem is that wives of alcoholics contract the twin malady of co-alcoholism. . . . It has become incurable co-alcoholism if the co-alcoholic cannot endure sharing the alcoholic's pain and its ramifications while he is abstaining. It is the most tragic kind of chronic co-alcoholism when the co-alcoholic cannot endure to have the alcoholic sober!" (Fajardo, 1976:6,67).

References

Aiken, Carl and Diane Tabler Williams. 1982 "State and local programs on alcoholism." Pp. 325–355 in National Institute of Alcohol Abuse and Alcoholism, Alcohol and Health Monograph 3: Prevention, Intervention and Treatment: Concerns and Models, Rockville, MD: U.S. Department of Health and Human Services.

Aiken, Robert and Sheldon Weiner. 1974 "The interface of mental health and judicial systems: Early impressions of an ASAP-related treatment effort." Pp. 292–301 in Morris Chafetz (ed.), Proceedings of the Third Annual Alcoholism Conference of the National Institute on Alcohol Abuse and Alcoholism. Washington, DC: Department of Health, Education and Welfare.

Alcoholism: The National Magazine. 1983 "National Alcoholism Treatment Center Directory, 1983–1984," 3 (March/April):1–38.

Anonymous. 1939 Alcoholics Anonymous: The Story of How Many Thousands of Men and Women Have Recovered from Alcoholism. New York: Works Publishing.

Benton, Bill. 1978 Social Services: Federal Legislation vs. State Implementation. Washington, DC: The Urban Institute.

Beauchamp, Dan. 1980 Beyond Alcoholism. Philadelphia, PA: Temple University Press.

Bibby, Reginald and Armand Mauss. 1974 "Skidders and their servants: Variable goals and functions of the skid row rescue mission." Journal for the Scientific Study of Religion 13(4):421–436.

Birch and Davis Associates, Inc. 1981 Increasing Revenue from the Private Sector. Report to the California Department of Alcohol and Drug Problems. Rockville, MD: National Institute on Drug Abuse.

Blumberg, Leonard. 1977 "The ideology of a therapeutic social movement: Alcoholics Anonymous." Journal of Studies on Alcohol 38(11):2122–2143.

Boscarino, Joseph. 1980 "A national survey of alcoholism treatment centers in the United States: A preliminary report." American Journal of Drug and Alcohol Abuse 7(3,4):403–413.

Boyle, Mimi. 1979 "Contracting for human services: A preliminary working paper on public-private relations." Unpublished paper. San Francisco: United Way of California (November).

Bunce, Richard, Tracy Cameron, Patricia Morgan, James Mosher, and Robin Room. 1981 "California's alcohol experience: Stable patterns and shifting responses." Pp. 159–199 in Eric Single, Patricia Morgan, and Jan de Lint (eds.), Alcohol, Society and the State: 2. The Social History of Control Policies in Seven Countries. Toronto: Addiction Research Foundation.

Cahalan, Don. 1976 "Some background considerations in estimating needs for states' services dealing with alcohol-related problems." Unpublished paper for National Center for Health Statistics. Rockville, MD: National Institute on Alcohol Abuse and Alcoholism (July 27).

Cahn, Sidney. 1970 The Treatment of Alcoholics: An Evaluative Study: New York: Oxford University Press.

California, Department of Alcohol and Drug Programs. 1980 California Alcohol Program: Plan FY 1980–1981. Sacramento Department of Alcohol and Drug Programs.

———. 1982 Task Force Report: AB 541 First Offender Program. Report to the Legislature, State of California. Sacramento: Department of Alcohol and Drug Programs.

———. 1983 California Alcohol Program: Plan FY 1983–1984. Sacramento: Department of Alcohol and Drug Programs.

California, Human Relations Agency. 1972 California State Plan for Comprehensive Alcohol Abuse and Alcoholism Prevention, Treatment and Rehabilitation. Sacramento: Department of Alcohol and Drug Programs.

California, Senate Committee on Health and Welfare. 1981 Mental Health, Drugs, Alcohol and the Criminal Justice System: The Revolving Door. Sacramento, December 14.

California, State Alcohol Treatment Conference. 1982 Program Statement of the Seventh Annual Alcohol Conference, Asilomar, September 20–24.

Cameron, Tracy. 1982 "Trends in alcohol problems in California, 1950–1979." Pp. 125–141 in Norman Giesbrecht, Monique Cahannes, Jacek Moskalewicz, Esa Osterberg, and Robin Room (eds.), Consequences of Drinking. Toronto: Addiction Research Foundation.

Christie, Nils. 1965 "Temperance boards and interinstitutional dilemmas: A case study of a welfare law." Social Problems 1(14):415–428.

Clarke, S. George. 1975 "Public intoxication and criminal justice." Journal of Drug Issues 5(3):220–233.

Corwin, E. H. L. and Elizabeth Cunningham. 1944 "Institutional facilities for the treatment of alcoholism." Quarterly Journal of Studies on Alcohol 5(1):9–85.

Coudert, Jo. 1972 The Alcoholic in Your Life. New York: Warner Paperback Library.

Dunham, Roger and Armand Mauss. 1982 "Reluctant referrals: The effectiveness of legal coercion in outpatient treatment for problem drinkers." Journal of Drug Issues 12(1):5–20.

Fagan, Ronald and Nancy Fagan. 1982 "The impact of legal coercion on the treatment of alcoholism." Journal of Drug Issues (12(1):103–114.

Fajardo, Rogue. 1976 Helping Your Alcoholic before He or She Hits Bottom: A Tested Technique for Leading Alcoholics into Treatment. New York: Crown.

Faulkner Training Institute. 1983 "Intervention workshop." Brochure for a training workshop for alcohol treatment professionals. Austin, TX: Faulkner Training Institute.

Giesbrecht, Norman, Monique Cahannes, Jacek Moskalewicz, Esa Osterberg and Robin Rooms (eds.). 1983 Consequences of Drinking: Trends in Alcohol Problem Statistics in Seven Countries. Toronto: Addiction Research Foundation.

Glasscote, Raymond, Thomas Plaut, Donald Hammersley, Francis O'Neil, Morris Chafetz, and Elaine Cumming. 1967 The Treatment of Alcoholism: A Study of Programs and Problems. Washington, DC: The Joint Information Service of the American Psychiatric Association and the National Association for Mental Health.

Gordon, James. 1978 Final Report to the President's Commission on Mental Health of the Special Study on Alternative Mental Health Services (PCMH/P-78/08). Pp. 376–410 in Task Panel Reports, Volume 2, Appendix. Washington, DC: U.S. Government Printing Office.

Jain, Sagar. 1981 "Role of state and local governments in relation to personal health services." American Journal of Public Health 71(1):5–8 Supplement.

Johnson Institute Seminars. 1983 "Intervention skill development seminar." Brochure for a training workshop for alcohol treatment professionals. Minneapolis, MN: Johnson Institute.

Keller, Mark, Mairi McCormick and Vera Efron. 1981 A Dictionary of Words about Alcohol. Second Edition. New Brunswick, NJ: Rutgers Center of Alcohol Studies.

Kurtz, Norman and Marilyn Regier. 1975 "The uniform alcoholism and intoxication treatment act." Journal of Studies on Alcohol 36(11):1421–1440.

Lerman, Paul. 1981 Deinstitutionalization: A Cross-Problem Analysis. Rockville, MD: National Institute on Alcohol Abuse and Alcoholism.

Lewis, Jay. 1982 Alcoholism Report 10 (June 30):1–6. Minneapolis, MN: Johnson Institute.

———. 1983 Alcoholism Report 12 (December 16):1–8. Minneapolis, MN: Johnson Institute.

Mäkelä, Klaus, Robin Room, Eric Single, Pekka Sulkunen and Brendan Walsh. 1981 Alcohol, Society and the State: Vol. 1. A Comparative Study of Alcohol Control. Toronto: Addiction Research Foundation.

Martinson, Robert. 1964 "The California Recovery House: A sanctuary for alcoholics." Mental Hygiene 48(3):432–438.

Melody, Moya. 1980 "Care Units: Making money from the disease concept of alcoholism." Unpublished Master's thesis, Department of Journalism, University of California, Berkeley.

Moore, Jean (ed.). 1981 Directory of alcoholism treatment centers. Western edition, plus supplement. Sharton, CT: ATD Publications.

Morgan, Patricia. 1980 "The state as mediator: Alcohol problem management in the post-war period." Contemporary Drug Problems 9(1):107–140.

———. 1981a "From battered wife to program client: The impact of the state in the shaping of a social problem." Kapitalistate Issue 9:1–16.

———. 1981b "Systems in crisis: Social welfare and the state's management of alcohol problems." Contemporary Drug Problems 10 (Summer):243–261.

Morris, Mark. 1980 "Final evaluation of the Bay Diversion Project's first year." Unpublished report. California Office of Criminal Justice Planning, Contract # A-4188.

Morrissey, Elizabeth. 1981 "The role of life changes in the development of alcohol-related problems." Seminar presented to the Social Research Group Seminar, Berkeley, California, January 13. (University of Washington, Seattle; Alcoholism and Drug Abuse Institute).

National Association of State Alcohol and Drug Abuse Directors. 1984 "1983 Year in Review." Alcohol and Drug Abuse Report, December 1983 and January 1984:1–36.

National Council on Alcoholism. 1982 Letter of appointment of an ad hoc working group on alcoholism treatment issues, May 7, New York: National Council on Alcoholism.

Northern California Conference on Drunk Driving. 1982 Program statement of the Northern California Conference on Drunk-Driving, sponsored by the Bay Area Coalition on Alcohol Problems, San Mateo, CA.

President's Commission on Mental Health. 1978 "Report of the task panel on the nature and scope of the problem." Pp. 1–138 in Task Panel Reports, Volume 2, Appendix. Washington, DC: U.S. Government Printing Office.

Raush, Harold with Charlotte Raush. 1968 The Halfway House Movement. New York: Appleton Century Crofts.

Reynolds, Lynn. 1973 "The California Office of Alcohol Program Management: A development in the formal control of a social problem." Unpublished Ph.D. dissertation, School of Public Health, University of California, Berkeley.

Rodwin, Victor. 1982 "Health insurance and alcohol treatment services: A strategy for change or a buttress for the status quo?" Working paper, Berkeley, CA: Alcohol Research Group.

Roizen, Ron and Constance Weisner. 1979 Fragmentation in Alcoholism Treatment Services: An Exploratory Analysis. Report C-24, Berkeley, CA: Social Research Group.

Roman, Paul. 1980 "Medicalization and social control in the workplace: Prospects for the 1980s." Journal of Applied Behavioral Science 16(3):407–422.

Roman, Paul and Harrison Trice. 1967 "Alcoholism and problem drinking as social roles: The effects of constructive coercion." Paper presented at the annual meetings of the Society for the Study of Social Problems, San Francisco, August 26.

Room, Robin. 1977 "Measurement and distribution of drinking patterns and problems in general populations." Pp. 61–87 in Griffith Edwards, Mark Keller, James Mosher and Robin Room (eds.), Alcohol-Related Disabilities. Offset Publication 32. Geneva: World Health Organization.

————. 1980 "Treatment-seeking populations and larger realities." Pp. 205–224 in Griffith Edwards and Marcus Grant (eds.), Alcoholism Treatment in Transition. London: Croom Helm.

————. 1983 "Sociological aspects of the disease concept of alcoholism." Pp. 47–91 in Reginald Smart, Fredrick Glaser, Yedy Israel, Harold Galant, Robert Popham, and Wolfgang Schmidt (eds.), Research Advances in Alcohol and Drug Problems, Volume 7. New York and London: Plenum Press.

Salamon, Lester. 1981 The Federal Government and the Nonprofit Sector: Implications of the Reagan Budget Proposals. Washington, DC: The Urban Institute.

————. 1983 Nonprofit Organizations and the Rise of Third-Party Government: The Scope, Character, and Consequences of Government Support of Nonprofit Organizations. Working paper, Washington, DC: The Urban Institute.

Salamon, Lester and Alan Abramson. 1982 The Federal Budget and the Nonprofit Sector. Washington, DC: The Urban Institute.

Sardell, Alice. 1983 "Neighborhood health centers and community-based care: Federal policy from 1965 to 1982." Journal of Public Health Policy 4 (4):484–504.

Scripps Memorial Hospital. 1984 "Intervention." Brochure for a training workshop for alcohol treatment professionals. La Jolla, CA: Scripps Memorial Hospital.

Shonick, William and Ruth Roemer. 1982 "Private management of public hospitals: The California experience." Journal of Public Health Policy 3 (2):182–205.

Speiglman, Richard. 1981 "Beyond 'Nothing Works': The politics and ideology of alcohol treatment in diversion." Paper presented at the annual meetings of the American Sociological Association, Toronto, August 24–28.

Speiglman, Richard and Constance Weisner. 1982 "Accommodation to coercion: Changes in alcoholism treatment paradigms." Paper presented at the annual meetings of the Society for the Study of Social Problems, San Francisco, September 3–6.

Sterne, Muriel and David Pittman. 1965 "The concept of motivation: A source of institutional and professional blockage in the treatment of alcoholics." Quarterly Journal of Studies on Alcohol 26 (1):41–57.

Terrell, Paul. 1979 "Private alternatives to public human services administration." Social Service Review 53 (1):56–74. 1982 "Financing social welfare services." Pp. 381–410 in Neil Gilbert and Harry Sprecht (eds.), Handbook of the Social Services. Englewood Cliffs, NJ: Prentice-Hall.

Terrell, Paul and Ralph Kramer. 1982 "Degovernmentalizing public services: The use of voluntary social agencies by local government." Paper presented at the Seminar on Local Government Organization and Economy, Sigtuna Sweden, May.

U.S. Department of Health and Human Services. 1982 Prevention, Intervention and Treatment: Concerns and Models. Alcohol and Health Monograph Number 3. Washington, DC: National Institute on Alcohol Abuse and Alcoholism.

U.S. Journal of Drug and Alcohol Dependence. 1982 "AMI purchases Raleigh Hills." U.S. Journal of Drug and Alcohol Dependence. 6 (12):1.

U.S. National Institute on Alcohol Abuse and Alcoholism. 1981 First Statistical Compendium on Alcohol and Health. Washington, DC: U.S. Government Printing Office.

————. 1982 Statistical Report: National Institute on Alcohol Abuse and Alcoholism Funded Treatment Programs, Calendar Year 1980, Volume 4, Rockville, MD: National Institute on Alcohol Abuse and Alcoholism.

————. 1983 Comprehensive Report, Data from the September 30, 1982 National Drug and Alcoholism Treatment Utilization Survey (NDATUS). Rockville, MD: National Institute on Alcohol Abuse and Alcoholism.

————. 1984. "Epidemiological Bulletin 2: Changes in Alcoholism Treatment Services, 1979–1982." Alcohol Health and Research World, Winter 1983/84 8(2):44–47.

U.S. National Institute on Drug Abuse. 1981 Standard Metropolitan Statistical Area Statistics, 1980. National Institute on Drug Abuse Statistical Series E, Number 23. Washington, DC: U.S. Government Printing Office.

United Way of California. 1981 Government Contracts with Voluntary Organization. San Francisco: United Way.

Van Dusen, Katherine. 1981 "Net widening and relabeling." American Behavioral Scientist 24 (6):801–811.

Weisner, Constance. 1981 Community Response to Alcohol-Related Problems: A Study of Treatment Providers' Perceptions. Report C30, Berkeley, CA: Social Research Group.

————. 1983 "The alcohol treatment system and social control: A study in institutional change." Journal of Drug Issues 13 (1):117–134.

Wiener, Carolyn. 1981 The Politics of Alcoholism: Building an Arena Around a Social Problem. New Brunswick, NJ: Transaction Books.

Wiseman, Jacqueline. 1970 Stations of the Lost: The Treatment of Skid Row Alcoholics. Englewood Cliffs, NJ: Prentice-Hall.

Cases cited. People v. Municipal Court (Hinton), Cal. App.3d, 1983.

---

33. The Magic Fix: A Critical Analysis of Methadone Maintenance Treatment*

Paula Holzman Kleinman, and Irving F. Lukoff with the assistance of Barbara Lynn Kail

• • •

The methadone maintenance approach to the treatment of heroin addiction was hailed at its inception, a little more than ten years ago, as virtually a miracle cure. The authors of this paper studied the Addiction Research and Treatment Corporation, a large not-for-profit methadone maintenance program in New York City, for five years, and found that for most patients it was minimally effective as an agent of change. We will first review some of our own findings, then analyze the more sanguine reports of other programs. We find that reanalysis of most methadone programs reveals them to be considerably less successful than initial reports had suggested.

Methadone is a synthetic material whose chemical structure closely resembles that of heroin. It can replace heroin in the sense that it satisfies the addict's physiological need and thus alleviates withdrawal symptoms. Its first, experimental use as a treatment for heroin addiction was initiated by Drs. Vincent Dole and Marie Nyswander in 1964. Behind this attempt to find a chemical solution to the heroin problem were the negative experiences of the traditional psychotherapy and therapeutic community modalities.

Dole and Nyswander took the extreme position that psychological causation is unimportant in understanding addiction, and maintained that chronic heroin use produces metabolic changes in the body of the addict. Methadone was to provide treatment for the metabolic deficiency. The analogy was often made to insulin treatment of diabetics. Like the diabetic, the methadone-maintained patient was expected to need lifetime treatment. Methadone was seen as good for the patient because dirty hypodermic needles and the threat of hepatitis would be eliminated, and good for society because low-cost methadone would obviate the addict's need to steal.

In recent years, students of methadone treatment have questioned the metabolic change theory and some programs have experimented with the detoxification of patients who have been maintained on methadone for long periods of time. However in most programs, regardless of their theoretical basis, the normal treatment continues to be that the patient maintained on methadone must continue in treatment for life.

*The research on which this paper is based was supported by grant Nos. NI-71-046-G, NI-72-008-G, 73-NI-99-002-G, and 74-NI-99-0041 from the United States Department of Justice, Law Enforcement Assistance Administration, to the Addiction Research and Treatment Corporation Evaluation Team through the Vera Institute of Justice. The fact that the National Institute of Law Enforcement and Criminal Justice furnished financial support to the activity described in this publication does not necessarily indicate the concurrence of the Institute in the statements or conclusions contained herein. The authors appreciate the cooperation of the New York City Police Department, without whose help we would not have had access to official police records.

The A. R. T. C. Program

Three commonly accepted goals for addiction treatment attempts are: cessation of heroin use: assumption of employment or other socially productive activities; and cessation of criminal activities. An additional criterion, retention in the program, is a prior condition which must be met before any of the other three can be achieved.

Retention

In the A. R. T. C. program, thirty-seven percent of the patients were terminated during their first year in treatment, and an additional twenty-four percent left during their second year. Thus, a total of sixty-one percent were terminated before the end of the second treatment year.

Heroin Use

Because of validity problems with the index of positive morphines, or "dirty urines," which are described in our detailed evaluation of the program (Kleinman and Lukoff, 1975), we use methadone absences, rather than the more conventional "morphine positives," as our indicator of heroin use. This is a meaningful measure because most addicts experience withdrawal pains twenty-four to thirty-six hours after the last administration of methadone. The pressure to use heroin under these circumstances is great, unless forestalled by the next methadone administration. Thus, in a methadone program, a patient who fails to pick up his/her medication is very likely to be using heroin instead, particularly if his/her methadone absences are frequent in a limited time period.

In light of these considerations, it is indicative of serious deficiencies in the treatment system to find that thirty-eight percent of all patients had methadone absences twenty-six percent of the time or more during the last quarter of their first year in treatment. Half (forty-nine percent) missed medication from one to twenty-five percent of the time, and only thirteen percent never missed medication in the last quarter of the first treatment year.

. . . Even though the initial rate of missed medications is unexpectedly high, there is an improvement in missed medication rate with each successive year of treatment. However, this curve is based on all patients who entered treatment during the study period. We suspected that missed medication performance might vary by length of retention in the program, so we proceeded to control for this variable. In the face of the impossibility of identifying a true control group for a treatment population, this is a type of pseudo-control that offers additional analytical leverage.

In striking contrast to the picture of declining methadone absences, there was actually an *increase* in proportion of patients who missed medication, by year in treatment, when those retained for more than three years only are considered. The appearance of improvement is the artifactual result of the year-by-year attrition of those patients who had the highest rates of methadone absences at the outset.

These data suggest either that the program does nothing, and that those who, at admission, were determined to change simply do so on their own; or that the program does have some impact, but only upon those who are initially motivated to change.

Employment

Among those who remained in the program for one to two years, there was only a slight increase, from sixteen percent to twenty-one percent, in proportion employed for more than six months. However, among those retained for twenty-five to thirty-six months, the proportion rose nineteen percentage points, from sixteen percent to thirty-five percent, and among those retained for three years or more, it rose twenty-four percentage points, from twenty-two percent to forty-six percent. Although these are, perhaps, the most encouraging facts about the program, a caveat must be entered: Only two-fifths of all patients who entered were retained for more than two years, so that for the majority who entered treatment, there was virtually no change in employment status.

Criminal Behavior

Our analysis of patients' criminal behavior, which is based on the official records of the New York City Police Department, yields results which indicate only very modest post-program behavioral changes. The three right-hand bars in the first section of Chart 1 show the overall charge rates[1] in the year before, and the first and second years after, entry into treatment, and indicate how the data could be made to show a promising trend of decreasing crime. This type of analysis is perhaps the most common in evaluations of heroin treatment programs. When we look at the bar at the extreme left, showing the charge rate for the entire onset-to-entry period, we see that the two-years-after rate of ninety-six is actually *higher* than the onset-to-entry rate of seventy-five.

The remaining sections of Chart 1 reveal a pattern which further casts doubt on the effectiveness of methadone as an agent for crime reduction. When the overall charge rate is broken down by type of charge, we find that the rate of assaultive charges is higher two years after entry into the program than it was even in the peak of crime one-year-before entry period, while the rate of charges for misdemeanors, larcenies and felonies was almost as high in the two-years-after period as it was in the year before entry. The only real decline is in the drug-related charges.

CHART 1

Mean Charge Rate by Type of Charge and Time Period for A.R.T.C. Patients in the First Cohort*

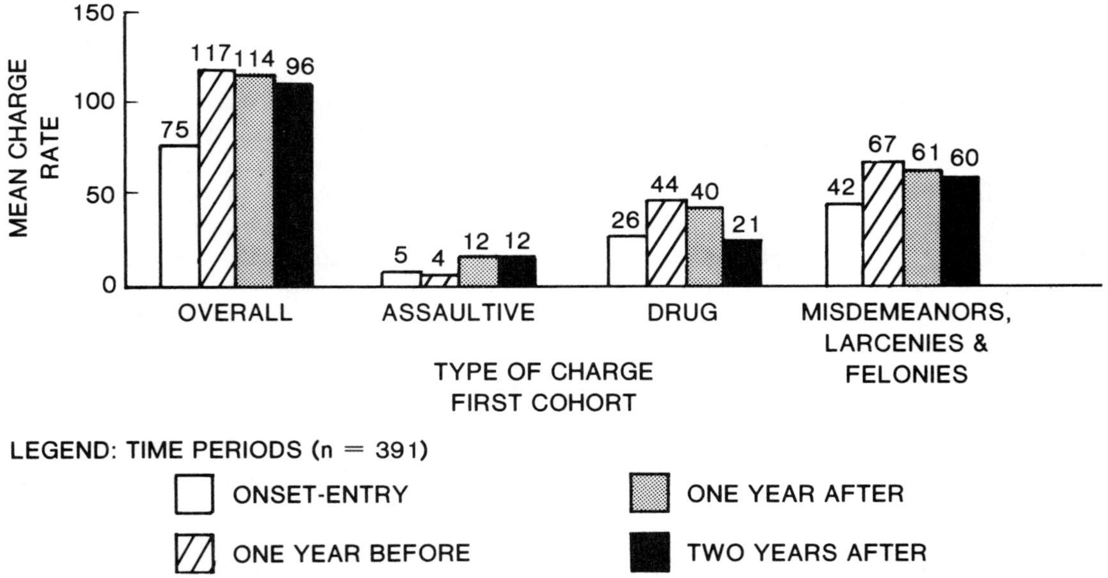

LEGEND: TIME PERIODS (n = 391)

☐ ONSET-ENTRY   ▨ ONE YEAR AFTER

▨ ONE YEAR BEFORE   ■ TWO YEARS AFTER

*This chart is limited to patients who entered treatment during the first year of the existence of the program. Nine percent of the patients in this cohort are missing information regarding criminal behavior.

When these patients are divided into length of retention categories, the above patterns are, in general, duplicated. The most prominent deviation is that among those retained for more than three years, the overall charge rate drops back to the level of the onset-to-entry period in the very first year after entry into treatment. But even in this group, the most dramatic decline occurs in the drug related, rather than in the more serious, charges (data not shown in tabular form).

In summary, we find that to the extent that pro-social changes occurred after entry into treatment, they were limited almost exclusively to that twenty-three percent of the patients who were retained in the program for more than three years. Moreover, these changes, in the areas of both heroin use and criminal behavior, occurred within the very first year after entry into treatment, and developed no further in succeeding years. Finally, even in this group productive changes were minimal: Fully twenty-five percent of the patients in this group had worked at no time during their more than three years of treatment; and while the level of crime dropped, it did not drop below the rate in the onset-to-entry period.

Other Methadone Maintenance Programs

Before one accepts the conclusion that the methadone maintenance approach is of limited value, one would want to know whether the A. R. T. C. program reviewed here is typical of other methadone programs or very much worse than average. We will grant, readily, that at first glance, data from other methadone programs appear to show much more favorable results. However, close scrutiny reveals that the bulk of these reports are based on analytic methods so weak that almost no conclusion can be drawn from them.

For example, consider the most simple datum, proportion retained in treatment. We find that most investigators report findings rendered meaningless by their failure to specify the time period under study. For example, an early report on the N. Y. C. Addiction Services Agency methadone program states, "The retention rate one year after admission for all patients . . . is seventy-six percent, and after two years sixty-five percent of all patients admitted remain in active treatment in the program" (Newman and Kagen, 1973: 797). This sounds like a commendably high retention rate, but the program opened in November 1970, and the report was delivered in March 1973. Only a very small proportion of the total could possibly, because of the reality of passing time, have been treated for two years. The sixty-five percent figure cited must refer to the proportion of all patients admitted who were still enrolled on the two-year anniversary of the program's existence. A large proportion of the total *might* have been admitted only one to three months before that anniversary. This example will have to stand for the numerous studies that commit the same or similar errors.

Only two studies, sound in this regard, were uncovered in a broad search. Maddux and McDonald (1973) measured retention by determining, individually for each of the first one hundred consecutively-admitted patients, whether he/she was in or out of the program on the one-year anniversary of his/her own admission date. They found that seventy-four percent had been retained for one year. Maddux and McDonald also show that while twenty-one percent of all patients had been employed at admission, sixty-five percent were employed one year after admission, an improvement considerably better than the A. R. T. C. rate.

However, the Maddux and McDonald figures are based on the first one hundred patients to enter into treatment in a small city. Results from *earliest* entries into almost any program have been found, by Wilmarth and Goldstein (1974), to be more positive than later results from the same program. Possible explanations of this effect are that the most highly motivated addicts are recruited earliest, and/or that staff morale and effort fade after a period of initial high enthusiasm. In any event, the Maddux and McDonald study is the only one we have found in which pre- and post-treatment employment figures can be reliably compared.

Gearing (1974), who has consistently found some of the most striking rates of success in the methadone literature, recently reported an increase in proportion employed in a more misleading way. A thirty-one percent increase in employment over a five year period is reported. Although the author asserts that the entire entry cohort was followed for the full five years, the table showing change in employment status claims to account for one hundred percent of the initial cohort, without use of categories for deceased, jailed, or lost contact. Because it is unbelievable that such categories would be unnecessary in following up a population of treatment drop-outs, the reader must infer that the five-year data are based on retainees only. Thus the reported increase in employment is greatly exaggerated.

Another general criticism that has been made of Gearing's work is that information comes almost exclusively from program records (Waldorf, 1973). A more reliable data source would be the patient him/herself, or, where possible, official records. Similar failure to show comparable pre- and post-treatment data plague all other employment analyses we have examined.

Many reports of the effects of treatment on criminal behavior are likewise flawed, because they fail to report post-program behavior of dropouts; are based on self reports rather than police records; or report results in terms of "man/months" in treatment, a procedure which misleadingly lumps individuals treated for one month with those treated for five years; or, most important, because they report on *all* arrests or all charges, and thus may simply be recording a temporary decline in drug charges, as shown in Chart 1.

In sum, although there is a vast literature evaluating methadone maintenance programs, only a small number reliably report positive findings. Our search of the literature, although necessarily not exhaustive, has been broad. In the absence of reliable positive findings, is there any sound basis for concluding that other programs are *not* successful? To some extent, the very absence of a firm body of positive findings supports such a conclusion. We do not suggest that all methodological lapses are motivated, but it is plausible to suggest that some are. In some cases; it is considerably more time-consuming and expensive to follow an air-tight procedure than a less rigorous one. For example, collection of data about type of crime requires lengthy and tedious coding of police records. On the other hand, the sorting of patients into separate categories of those who are retained and those who are terminated as of a given date is simple, and thus separate reportage of pre- and post-employment statistics could be accomplished easily.

Drs. Dole and Nyswander themselves now concede that, "the projections of ten years ago were overly optimistic. The great majority of heroin addicts in our cities remain on the streets. . . ." (Dole and Nyswander, 1976:2117). Dole and Nyswander attribute methadone's failures to an excessively restrictive set of federal rules and regulations; but whatever the cause, if even *they,* who have been among methadone's staunchest defenders for the last ten years, admit that the original projections were overly optimistic, then our negative assessment must be accepted as valid.

It is an ironic commentary on the history of methadone maintenance to note that before it was implemented on a large scale, a pilot program was inaugurated and evaluated. In other words, it appeared to follow the model often prescribed as essential to innovative social programs. Why, then, the sorry later developments which we have described? In part perhaps, the pilot program was over-rated because it restricted admissions only to selected and highly motivated patients; in part, the high involvement of the staff, including Drs. Dole and Nyswander, may have contributed to a "Hawthorne effect;" to some extent, too, the glowing initial evaluations may have been politically motivated.

Etzioni (1968) suggested that "short-cuts" to social change might prove more workable than large-scale, pervasive change attempts, and specifically identified methadone maintenance as an example of a promising short-cut. On the contrary, we propose that the attempted short-cut has proved to be a dead-end, one which has served to divert attention from efforts to develop effective strategies to bring about basic social change.

Note

1. The charge rate for each of the single-year time periods is computed by summing all criminal charges lodged against the individual in the time period in question, and multiplying by one hundred. Thus a person who had one charge in the year before entry into treatment would have a rate of 100 in that period. Rates for categories are formed by averaging the rates of all persons in that category.

    The formula for computing the charge rate in the entire period from onset of addiction to entry into treatment is:

$$\text{Charge Rate} = \frac{\text{Total number of charges in period}}{\text{Total number of months in period}} \times 100/.0833$$

    In this way, adjustment is made for the fact that the length of the onset-to-entry period varies by individual.

    The assaultive charge rate includes charges for assault, manslaughter, rape, homicide. Drug-related charges include criminal possession of dangerous drugs, criminally possessing a hypodermic needle. Misdeamenors, larcenies and felonies include burglary and forgery.

References

Dole, Vincent and Marie E. Nyswander, "Methadone maintenance treatment: A ten year perspective." Journal of the American Medical Association 235:2117–2119, 1976.

Etzioni, Amitai, "Shortcuts to social change." The Public Interest 12:40–51, 1968.

Gearing, Frances, "Methadone maintenance treatment five years later—where are they now?" American Journal of Public Health Supplement 64:44–49, 1974.

Kleinman, Paula H. and Irving F. Lukoff, Methadone Maintenance: Modest Help for a Few. Columbia University School of Social Work. Unpublished, 1975.

Maddux, James F. and Linda K. McDonald, "Status of 100 San Antonio addicts one year after admission to methadone maintenance." Drug Forum 2: 239–52, 1973.

Newman, Robert G. and James G. Kagan, "New York City Methadone Maintenance Treatment Program after two years—an overview." Proceedings Fifth National Conference on Methadone Treatment: 794–802, 1973.

Perkins, Marvin and Alex Richman, "Prevalence of participation in methadone programs" American Journal of Psychiatry 129: 447–50, 1972.

Waldorf, Dan, Careers in Dope, Englewood Cliffs: Prentice Hall, 1973.

Wilmarth, Steven and Avram Goldstein, Therapeutic Effectiveness of Methadone Maintenance Programs in the U.S.A. Geneva: World Health Organization, 1974.

34. Drug-Induced Tranquility

The Public Citizen Health Research Group

When former National Security Advisor Robert McFarlane recently had to go to the Bethesda Naval Hospital because of a drug abuse problem, it was not surprising that the drug involved was neither heroin nor morphine, nor was it cocaine or crack.

A federally funded program called the Drug Abuse Warning Network (DAWN) collects information from hospital emergency rooms and coroners' offices serving about one-third of the people in the country. During 1985, the latest year for which data are available, 13,501 people went to emergency rooms because of cocaine-related problems, 14,696 for morphine and heroin combined. But 18,492 people were treated for the number one drug abuse problem in the U.S.A., the family of tranquilizers and sleeping pills known as the benzodiazepines.

Although we are now spending hundreds of millions of dollars a year trying to solve the more traditional street-drug problems, the much-easier-to-get legitimate prescription drugs in the benzodiazepine family are taking their toll. The family of 11 drugs includes eight tranquilizers (VALIUM, XANAX, ATIVAN, TRANXENE, LIBRIUM, CENTRAX, SERAX, AND PAXIPAM) plus the three sleeping pills (DALMANE, RESTORIL, and HALCION).

The only significant differences between these 11 drugs is how they are pushed in the marketplace, as tranquilizers or sleeping pills, and the amount of time it takes to clear them from the body. As we will discuss later, they can all put someone to sleep, can induce tranquility, at least for a while, and they all share the adverse effects of addiction and other serious problems.

BENZODIAZEPINE PRESCRIPTIONS: 1985

Brand Name	(Generic Name)	Prescriptions Filled (Millions)
Tranqulizers		
Valium	(Diazepam)	23
Xanax	(Alprazolam)	11
Ativan	(Lorazepam)	10
Librium	(Chlordiazepoxide)	7
Tranxene	(Chlorazepate)	7
Centrax	(Prazepam)	2
Serax	(Oxazepam)	2
Paxipam	(Halazepam)	<1
Sleeping Pills		
Dalmane	(Flurazepam)	8
Halcion	(Triazolam)	7
Restoril	(Temazepam)	5

(Source: National Prescription Audit)

From The Public Citizen Research Group, DRUG-INDUCED TRANQUILITY, which originally appeared in *Health Letter*, Vol. 3, NO. 4 (April, 1987), pages 6–8. Copyright © 1987 by Health Letter, 2000 P St. NW, Rm 700, Washington, D.C. Reprinted by permission.

During 1985, Americans, persuaded by their doctors, filled 81 million prescriptions for these drugs, a total purchase of 3.7 billion pills. If every person in the country were a user, this would be equal to 15 pills per person per year. With the actual number of users being approximately 25 million, however, the average "sale" per person was 148 pills a year. As seen in the table below, there were 61 million prescriptions filled for the eight tranquilizers, 20 million for the three sleeping pills.

Sales of Valium have fallen from the record high of 61 million prescriptions in 1975 to 23 million in 1985 (only 38 percent of the earlier year). The other good news is that total benzodiazepine prescriptions—81 million in 1985—are not as high as the record for that total of 98 million, set in 1975 as well, but the family is making a comeback. As doctors and patients have learned about the dangers of Valium, the crafty drug-pushers have put 6 of the 11 benzodiazepines on the market since 1975, "positioning" them as not having the disadvantages, such as the "buzz," of Valium. Through an enormous amount of false and misleading advertising, the sales of the family, having fallen steadily from 1975 to 1981, have been on the rise since. For the tranquilizers, drugs like Xanax and Tranxene have replaced a good portion of lost Valium sales. As we have emphasized before, all of them have the same risks.

Are Benzodiazepines Killer Drugs?

Because he was, fortunately, too dumb to realize that the 20 or 25 Valium pills that he swallowed were not likely to kill him, Robert McFarlane is now alive. This low probability of death, even with massive doses, is common to all the benzodiazepines, just as it is for large doses of another well-known central nervous system depressant, alcohol. In all of these cases, the soporific properties of the drugs are likely to induce sleep before too much damage is done, at least in adults. But if Mr. McFarlane had downed a few drinks along with his Valium, (even if he had taken fewer pills) he might well be dead now. This was the fate of 492 benzodiazepine-using people in 1985 who wound up in the coroner's office, most commonly due to the combination of alcohol along with their favorite tranquilizer or sleeping pill. Although many of these unfortunate people were not attempting suicide, many did themselves in unintentionally, having underestimated the fatal properties of benzodiazepines in combination with drugs such as alcohol.

Are Benzodiazepines Addicting?

If you listen to the drug-makers, you might think that the only people who become addicted to benzodiazepines are those with a history of drug abuse or alcohol abuse. This is untrue, as several studies have shown that people without this kind of history often get addicted to members of the family. Another myth spread by the drug industry is that addiction only occurs if you use more than the recommended dose. Again, several studies have now shown that almost half of the people using the doctor-recommended dose of these drugs can become addicted, often after weeks or months of use. After such steady use, suddenly stopping the habit brings on withdrawal symptoms, within hours for the rapidly cleared drugs, in a day or two for the longer-lasting ones such as Valium. The easiest way to remedy the unpleasant nervousness, tremor, agitation, and other withdrawal symptoms is to go back to the drug, a behavior pattern which perpetuates the addictive state.

The benzodiazepines, considering their addictive properties and other dangers, are weakly regulated by the federal government, with five refills allowed with merely a phone call once the original prescription is filled. Added to this is the often poorly informed patient and doctor who, even after another office visit, may continue rewriting and rewriting prescriptions.

The result of the inadequate government regulation and inadequately informed doctors and patients is a massive amount of chronic, steady, long-term use of these drugs, even though there is no evidence they are effective for such periods of time.

A recent government study found that 2.9 million Americans were taking these drugs every day for at least four months and that 2.1 million of these people were daily users for a year or more. Many of these people are addicted to their benzodiazepines but this risk is not accompanied by any proven benefit.

Are Older People at Special Risk?

Addiction, death, confusion, memory loss, increased risk of an auto accident, poor coordination, impaired learning ability and slurred speech can happen to anyone of any age who uses these drugs. But older people are at special risk for several reasons.

As people age, there is a gradual impairment in many of the processes which get rid of drugs after they have been ingested or taken into the body by other routes of administration. As a result, higher levels of many of these drugs occur in older people than in their younger counterparts. Some researchers also think that, in addition, older people may be more sensitive to some of these drugs. Despite this evidence, doctors often give older people the same doses as younger people would get. Another problem resulting in a higher risk for older people who use benzodiazepines is the fact that older people are more likely to get a prescription for these drugs than younger people and, when they do, the prescription is much more likely to last for months, if not years.

Because of these factors, which place older people at greater risk from these drugs, the adverse effects mentioned above occur more commonly and are often more severe in older people. Further aggravating this situation is the fact that many of these "side effects" are easily attributed to growing old rather than being linked to the use of the tranquilizers or sleeping pills. The onset of memory loss, confusion, impaired coordination, or impaired learning in a younger person will more likely prompt an inquiry leading to the drug as culprit. But the same symptoms in an older person, especially if they develop more slowly, may well be attributed to "Well, he (or she) is just growing old, what do you expect?" This lack of suspicion allows the drug to keep doing the damage because the doctor keeps up the prescription.

In View of All of This, the Use of Benzodiazepines in Older People Is Not a Good Idea.

What Are the Alternatives to Using Benzodiazepines?

A recent well-controlled experiment suggests an important alternative to the use of benzodiazepines, not only in older people but for everyone. Ninety patients, mainly suffering from anxiety, were randomly divided into two groups when they went to see their family doctors. The first group was given the usual dose of one of the benzodiazepines. The people in the other group were given a small dose of a much safer treatment consisting solely of "listening, explanation, advice, and reassurance." The two treatments were equally effective in relieving the anxiety, but those getting the counselling were more satisfied with their treatment than were the others. Of interest was the fact that the doctors did not find that the several minutes they spent interfered with their work schedules.

Some patients with extreme anxiety do not immediately respond to brief counseling and there are some doctors, practicing good, careful medicine, who feel that a small fraction of anxious patients might benefit from a very brief course of treatment with a tranquilizer. But to protect both doctor and patient, the prescription should state "NO REFILL." The size of the prescription should also be limited to one week's treatment. By this time doctor and patient should have begun to understand the cause of the anxiety or sleeplessness, and further progress can occur without the use of more drugs. If the prescribing of these drugs was limited in these ways, the use of benzodiazepines would fall to less than one-tenth of the current levels as would the number of people addicted to, killed by, or otherwise damaged by these powerful drugs.

Helping to bring patients' anxiety down to tolerable levels through conversation is much safer and humane therapy than the current epidemic of 3.7 billion benzodiazepine pills bought each year. Even though they may earn a little less by spending a little more time talking with their patients, American doctors, who take in an average net income after expenses of $108,000 a year, will survive, and patients will be better off.

Making Important Decisions

We have all heard the phrase, "If you drink, don't drive." The idea is that if you are under the influence of alcohol, your coordination and your decision-making abilities are impaired. Similarly, those who engage in the two-(or one- or three-) martini lunch do not usually have the ability to make important decisions in the afternoon. The same kind of impairment occurs with the benzodiazepines. Part of the problem has to do with the proper weighing of opposing, often conflicting choices you have as you are deciding what to do. Clear thinking is just that, decision-making unencumbered by alcohol, hard drugs, or benzodiazepines. Whether the decisions have to do with yourself, your family, or your job, including important ones such as National Security Advisor, the outcome is more likely to make sense if the competing tensions are allowed to exist.

As Aldous Huxley said in *Brave New World Revisited,* written as the age of chemical tranquility was beginning,

"As things now stand, the tranquillizers may prevent some people from giving enough trouble, not only to their rulers, but even to themselves. Too much tension is a disease; but so is too little. There are certain occasions when we ought to be tense, when an excess of tranquillity (and especially of tranquillity imposed from the outside, by a chemical) is entirely inappropriate."

35. Psychotropic Drugs and the Origins of Deinstitutionalization*

William Gronfein

• • •

The treatment of the seriously mentally ill in the United States has undergone a series of radical transformations over the past 25 years. One of the principal changes was a marked reduction in the importance of state and county mental hospitals. In 1955 these institutions contained approximately 560,000 patients and accounted for almost half of all mental health patient care episodes; by 1977 they contained but 160,000 inmates and accounted for less than 10 percent of all mental health patient care episodes (Goldman et al., 1983; Kramer, 1977).

These sharp decreases in inpatient populations are one element in the complex of policies, philosophies, intentions, and facts which define the deinstitutionalization of the mentally ill. Deinstitutionalization has two goals. The first is the depopulation of state and county mental hospitals and other traditional institutions charged with the care of the mentally ill, and the second is the substitution of a network of community-based institutions to provide such care (Bachrach, 1978; General Accounting Office, 1977; Goldman et al., 1983). Deinstitutionalization has been sharply criticized for failing to implement its second goal, and much research has examined the problems created for patients, families, and communities (e.g., Arnhoff, 1975; Aviram and Segal, 1973; Aviram et al., 1976; Bachrach, 1976, 1978; Bassuk and Gerson, 1978; Becker and Schullberg, 1976; Braun et al., 1981; Freedman and Moran, 1983; Kirk and Therrien, 1975; Lerman, 1982; Morrissey, 1982; Rose, 1979; Segal and Aviram, 1978; Segal et al., 1974).

Deinstitutionalization is also grist for mills more explicitly analytic and sociological in character (e.g., Cohen, 1979; Estroff, 1981; Scull, 1977; Warren, 1981). The state hospital has been one of the densest symbols of disorder, estrangement, and exclusion to trouble the popular imagination, and has provided the central image for some of sociology's most influential treatments of social control. Goffman's (1961) delineation of total institutions, for instance, is based in part on his field work from 1955 to 1957 in St. Elizabeths, the public mental hospital serving the District of Columbia. Erikson's (1966) discussion of the persistence of exclusionary and segregative "deployment patterns" in the treatment accorded deviants in the United States likewise draws on the character of state hospitals prior to deinstitutionalization. The breakup of these models of social control is clearly a matter of both theoretical and practical importance.

Both the abrupt decline in state hospital populations which began in 1955, and the administrative, legislative, and judicial rulings at the state and federal levels which began in the late 1950s and early 1960s (Morrissey, 1982; Segal and Aviram, 1978) represented reversals of longstanding

*This research was supported in part by a grant from the Health Services Improvement Fund of Blue Cross/Blue Shield, and in part by NIMH grant MH16242. I would like to express my appreciation to Ron Angel, Yinon Cohen, Carol Selman, and three anonymous *Social Problems* reviewers for their helpful comments on earlier drafts. Any remaining errors of style or substance are, of course, my responsibility.

trends. Given the long domination of state and county mental hospitals over mental health services available to the seriously mentally ill (Pollack and Taube, 1975; Redick et al., 1973), a crucial question is why this institutional dominance ended when it did.

Since the turn of the century, state hospital populations had grown steadily, increasing four-fold from 1903 to 1955 (Council of State Governments, 1950; Kramer, 1977). During this period they were reviled as "bedlams," "snake pits," and "houses of horror" (American Psychiatric Association, 1949; Deutsch, 1948, Ward, 1946). The same critics who denounced these institutions urged that they be more generously funded, rather than depopulated (American Psychiatric Association, 1949, 1950, 1951, 1952, 1953, 1954; Beers, 1981; Deutsch, 1948). The Joint Commission on Mental Illness and Health (1961:190; emphasis in original) described publicly supported insane asylums with evident frustration as *"hospitals' that seem to have no defenders but endure despite all attacks."*

The timing of deinstitutionalization raises many questions regarding the relative roles played by such factors as intraprofessional rivalry (Morrissey, 1982), ideological change (Bachrach, 1976, 1978), the expansion of the welfare state (Lerman, 1982), and fiscal crisis (Rose, 1979; Scull, 1977). This paper examines the impact of psychotropic drugs on the decline of state and county mental hospital populations and on the evolution of a mental health policy which espouses as one of its principal aims the "eschewal, shunning, and avoidance" (Bachrach, 1978:573) of such institutions.

I examine the impact of the introduction of psychotropic drugs on state hospitals for several reasons. First, the move away from state and county hospitals is a crucial element in the deinstitutionalization of the mentally ill. While deinstitutionalization calls for the creation of community-based facilities to provide mental health care, a reduction in the importance of state and county hospitals is an essential prerequisite for this kind of substitution. Second, as noted above, state and county mental hospitals were institutional responses to deviance that had great practical and symbolic importance (Bucher and Schatzman, 1962; Council of State Governments, 1950; Deutsch, 1948; Dunham and Weinberg, 1960; Erikson, 1966; Goffman, 1961).

Third, the psychotropic drugs have been the subject of intense interest and controversy ever since their introduction in 1954 (Brill and Patton, 1957, 1959; Clark, 1956; Joint Commission on Mental Illness and Health, 1961; Kinross-Wright, 1955; Morrissey, 1982; Rose, 1979; Scull, 1977; Sedgwick, 1982). Two opposing positions have emerged with respect to their effects on state hospitals. The more orthodox view holds with Pollack and Taube (1975:49) that "there appears to be no question that the sudden decrease in the state mental hospital population in 1956 . . . was due to the widespread introduction of the psychoactive drugs into the mental hospitals" (see also Bachrach, 1976; General Accounting Office, 1977; Joint Commission on Mental Illness and Health, 1961; Pasamanick et al., 1967; Swazey, 1974). A number of "revisionist" authors (e.g., Aviram et al., 1976; Lerman, 1982; Rose, 1979; Scull, 1977; Segal and Aviram, 1978) downplay the importance of the drugs as a cause of deinstitutionalization and conclude with Sedgwick (1982:198) that this "straightforward 'pharmacological' explanation for the desegregation of patients . . . is . . . fatally flawed." These authors base their position on the methodological weaknesses of earlier studies that claimed to have demonstrated a drug effect on state hospital populations and on recent retrospective case studies showing that the expansion of federal health and welfare programs was more consequential in reducing state hospital populations than were the drugs (Aviram et al., 1976; Lerman, 1982; Scull, 1977; Segal and Aviram, 1978).

• • •

The Psychotropic Drugs and the Problem of Order

The Introduction of the Drugs

In 1953 Smith, Kline and French Labs began testing chlorpromazine, a new tranquilizing drug developed by the French firm of Rhone-Poulenc; in 1954 the American company received the approval of the Food and Drug Administration (FDA) to begin marketing the drug under the trade name Thorazine (Swazey, 1974). From the first, chlorpromazine was received with enthusiasm by the state hospitals. By 1956, two years after chlorpromazine had received the imprimatur of the FDA, at least 37 states were using chlorpromazine, reserpine—another psychoactive drug— or both (California State Senate Interim Committee on Treatment of Mental Illness, 1956), and 2000 articles had been written about the drugs (Kinross-Wright, 1956).

Such rapid diffusion was due in part to the efforts of the drug companies themselves. Smith, Kline and French Labs reorganized its entire sales force in order to market the drug, and lobbied state legislatures intensively in efforts to secure acceptance for Thorazine (Swazey, 1974). Both Smith, Kline and French and Ciba-Geigy (which marketed reserpine) underwrote conferences in 1955 to discuss the results of administering the drugs to state hospital inmates (Lhamonn, 1955; Smith, Kline and French, 1955).

These investments in public relations were profitable, particularly for Smith, Kline and French. In 1952 and 1953, the two years prior to the official introduction of Thorazine, Smith, Kline and French reported total earnings of $23,440,000 on $99,972,000 in sales. In the two years subsequent to the introduction of Thorazine, earnings totaled $75,560,000 on $196,280,000 in sales, an increase of over 300 percent (Smith, Kline and French, 1956).

Social Problems and the State Hospital

While entrepreneurial initiative may have aided the process of drug diffusion, the perceived properties of the drugs themselves were an important factor as well. As described in a number of clinical reports, the drugs appeared to offer a solution to one of the problems which perennially plagued the state hospitals: the maintenance of order. Publicly supported insane asylums in the 1950s were, and long had been, an uneasy marriage of hospital and prison (Fox, 1978; Rock et al., 1968; Rothman, 1971). These facilities had a clear carceral function which at times overrode any purely therapeutic mandate (Stanton and Schwartz, 1954). They were depositories as well as hospitals, receptacles into which the community could place those individuals whose presence in civil society had become intolerable (Fox, 1978; Grob, 1983; Rothman, 1971). The mechanism of involuntary commitment, which was by far the most common admissions procedure until the 1960s,[1] guaranteed that the community could maintain civil order by using legal procedures to compel patients to accept treatment, whatever wishes the patients may have had in this regard (Fox, 1978; Rock et al., 1968).

Involuntary commitment placed the state hospitals under compulsion as well as the patient. Hospitals were constrained to accept all those persons who had been committed for treatment, and thus lost the ability to regulate either the size or composition of its population (Greenley and Kirk, 1973; Rock et al., 1968). Just as the hospital's admissions decisions were shaped by community imperatives as well as by therapeutic desiderata, so too were its discharge decisions, since hospital administrators had to be sensitive to the anxieties of local communities.[2] (American Psychiatric Association, 1952; Stanton and Schwartz, 1954). While families and the police used the state hospital as a "last resort" for dealing with troubled individuals (Bittner, 1967; Sampson et al., 1962; Yarrow, et al., 1955), the hospital itself had no analogous option—the individuals who had been a problem of order for the outside community became a problem of order for the hospital's internal regime. Chronically short of resources and unable to regulate either inputs or outputs, the state hospitals accumulated large concentrations of very disturbed, psychotic, longstay patients[3] (Bucher and Schatzman, 1962; Council of State Governments, 1950; Deutsch, 1948; Kramer, 1957), who transformed these institutions into the "bedlams" described earlier.

Where Id Was, There Let Ego Be

State hospital physicians were genuinely impressed with what they saw when the drugs were introduced. As one review of drug-related research commented, "Reference to the psychiatric literature of the past year leaves one in no doubt that the chemotherapy of mental diseases has come of age . . ." (Kinross-Wright, 1956:187). The general level of enthusiasm was so high that one observer commented disapprovingly, "I have attended conferences on these drugs where the atmosphere approached that of a revivalist meeting" (Bowes, 1956:530).

Descriptions of the clinical trials of chlorpromazine, reserpine, and the other newly-synthesized psychotropics consistently emphasized their ability to control even the most disturbed and dangerous patients. For instance,

> Robert W. was admitted to the state hospital in a highly excited, homicidal state. His eyes were red and bulging, face suffused, restraint required. This patient was loud, screamed that he would kill someone, and communicated his sincerity in this purpose to attendants. . . . CPZ [chlorpromazine] administration was begun soon after admission. . . . In the course of two more weeks of hospitalization, this patient had quieted down, had lost his anxiety almost altogether, and was able to discuss his illness and his future plans in an objective and rational manner (Goldman, 1955a:73).

Within two months, Robert W. was discharged (Goldman, 1955b).

The drugs were particularly impressive in producing acceptable social behavior in chronic patients, some of whom had extensive experience with older somatic therapies.

> [A] 48 year old paranoid schizophrenic had spent most of the past two years in private and state mental institutions. She received electroshock, insulin treatment, and two prefrontal lobotomies without significant benefit. On admission, she was bellicose, sloppy in appearance, and actively hallucinating. . . . Improvement continued for three months on a maintenance dose of 75 mg. [of thorazine] daily. For the past four months, she has been symptom free, manages her home, goes to bridge parties, dresses well, and amazes her husband and friends with her affectionate friendliness (Kinross-Wright, 1955:56).

The new drugs were effective at the group level, too; entire wards were transformed. A study of the effects of reserpine on chronic, back ward patients in California's Modesto State Hospital commented that:

> Prior to this study, these wards presented the usual picture of wards of this type, namely 10 to 12 patients in seclusion, some also in camisoles or other types of restraints. . . . Owing to the raucous, hyperactive, combative, sarcastic, resistive, uncooperative patients, the ward was in a constant turmoil. . . . Patients have undergone a metamorphosis from raging, combative, unsociable persons to cooperative, cheerful, sociable, relatively quiet persons who are amenable to psychotherapy (California State Senate Interim Committee on Treatment of Mental Illness, 1956:31).

A report from the chronic disturbed ward of a large Canadian hospital details a similar transformation:

> Within two weeks of commencing treatment, a striking change had taken place. The patients on Frenqual had become more sociable, they were neater, cleaner, and tidier. . . . For the first time, the patients would read books and magazines instead of tearing them apart. Curtains could be left up instead of being pulled down. [The patients] appeared much more sociable. . . . Some who had previously banged their heads against the walls and covered their heads with their overcoats stopped responding to their hallucinations. It was most impressive (Bowes, 1956:532).

Modest gains were greeted with enthusiasm, since they were viewed against such dark and disturbing backdrops. Progress was measured by bridge parties and the ability to converse intelligently. As an official in the Maryland state hospital system remarked, "It is a distinct pleasure to think of these patients . . . going to the general dining room and eating with silverware" (California State Senate Interim Committee on Treatment of Mental Illness, 1956:134).

These startling improvements in the behavior of patients led to changes in the attitudes of staff. The possibility of instituting active therapy in place of a merely custodial regime led to the types of effects noted by Winfred Overholser (1958:214):

> A far greater interest [on the part of the staff] has been developed. The morale has been increased. A hopeful attitude has come about as patients who had been previously troublesome were noted to be cooperative and helpful, and to show other signs of improvement.

These salutary effects were thought to extend outside the hospital:

> Legislative bodies have shown a greater interest in the problems of mental illness now that a positive and easily administered therapy appears to be available. . . . Families have not only become more helpful but more demanding. . . . It seems not too much to say that the community is at last developing an attitude of far greater tolerance toward the discharged mental patient, a greater readiness to accept him back into the community . . . (Overholser, 1958:215).

Soon after they were introduced, the drugs began to appear indispensable in some quarters. In response to a California survey,[4] Missouri officials wrote, "Attendants here stated emphatically that if the institution discontinues the use of the drugs, they will refuse to work" (California State Senate Interim Committee on Treatment of Mental Illness, 1956:170).

The drugs had a marked impact on state hospital patients and on state hospital staffs. Previous therapies (electroconvulsive therapy, insulin shock, lobotomy) had produced more tractable patients, but these measures were sometimes dangerous and were difficult to use outside the hospital.[5] The drugs produced compliant patients and also had the advantage of being easily used in extramural settings.

The Effect of Psychotropic Drugs on Discharge Rates

The fact that psychoactive drugs could ameliorate disordered behavior at the individual level did not insure that they would produce significant changes in patterns of patient movement. Even though use of the drugs resulted in more manageable patients and prompted more favorable attitudes towards the release of patients among the general public, state hospital officials faced the problem of where to place patients newly ready for discharge. There were few facilities available for aftercare, and many of the patients had been hospitalized for so long that their families were reluctant to take them back (Brooks, 1958; Pennington, 1955).[6] The critical question of whether use of the drugs led to actual decreases in inpatient populations was addressed in a number of reports, although their results were sometimes contradictory (Boudwin and Kline, 1955; Brill and Patton, 1957; Epstein et al., 1962; Joint Commission on Mental Illness and Health, 1961). In the next section, I review historical evidence on aggregate changes in discharge rates before and after the drugs were introduced.

Historical Studies of Drug Effects

At the time of the drugs' introduction, opinions as to their effects on inpatient population movement patterns varied widely. Even collaborators disagreed about their impact. A paper jointly authored by James Boudwin and Nathan Kline (1955:77) stated that "Allowing for some relapse, it appears that a minimum of five percent of the chronic mental hospital population of the country could be discharged if adequately treated with chlorpromazine and/or reserpine," but Boudwin took the unusual step of explicitly disassociating himself from this estimate. Although the California State Senate survey (1956) did not inquire directly about the effects of the drugs on population size or discharge rates, 18 of the 37 states responding volunteered such information. The officials of ten states thought the drugs had increased discharge rates, decreased population size, or both, while the officials of the other eight states were of the opinion that the drugs had not had a noticeable effect.

A similar variability marks three major state-specific studies undertaken specifically to investigate the effects of the drugs on mental patients in the aggregate. They were done in New York (Brill and Patton, 1957, 1959), Michigan (Michigan Department of Mental Health, 1956), and California (Epstein et al., 1962). In New York, Brill and Patton (1959:495) concluded "that the abrupt population fall [from 1955 to 1956] was in material degree due to the introduction of the new drugs." However, their study was methodologically flawed—Brill and Patton appear to have inferred causation from correlation. That is, they assumed that because the drugs were introduced just prior to the population declines, the drugs must have been responsible for these unprecedented decreases. However, since they did not compare the release rates of treated and untreated patients, they could not determine whether it was the drugs or some other development which was linked to the population decreases.[7]

Studies conducted in Michigan and California which did compare the release or retention rates of treated and untreated patients found that the drugs did not exercise a significant effect on discharge rates. The Michigan report stated that the "data indicate that . . . the use of chlorpromazine and reserpine does *not* influence movement of patients out of the hospital" (Michigan Department of Mental Health, 1956:16, emphasis added), while the California study, which used data collected in 1956 and 1957 concluded that

> . . . where a difference is found between the retention rate of ataraxic drug treated patients and those not so treated, the untreated patients consistently show a somewhat *lower* retention rate (Epstein et al., 1962:44, emphasis in original).

More recent retrospective studies (Aviram et al., 1976; Lerman, 1982; Morrissey, 1982) have found that in states such as California the drugs were less important in generating decreases in inpatient populations than was the expansion of federal health and welfare programs in the 1960s.

International data also cast doubt on the strength of the relationship between the introduction of the psychotropic drugs and declines in hospital populations. In England, inpatient populations began to decline before the drugs were introduced (Brown et al., 1966; Mechanic, 1969; Scull, 1977) and, in France, inpatient populations increased for 20 years after the drugs were introduced (Sedgwick, 1982).

The evidence from the United States suggests that the impact of the introduction of the psychotropic medications on discharge rates across states was variable. The more careful studies done in California and Michigan indicate that the drug impact was minimal in these states. However, as we have seen, changes in inpatient populations from 1956 to 1965 were characterized by a high level of interstate variability. It is therefore possible that the studies done in Michigan and California, while well-executed, reflected conditions which were not representative of those occurring in other states.

Interstate Data on Discharge Rates

In order to investigate the impact of the drugs across a larger sample of states, I used data drawn from annual censuses conducted by the Public Health Service and the National Institutes of Mental Health, and include information on the 48 states of the continental United States and the District of Columbia. I compared the extent of operational deinstitutionalization—as indexed by discharge rates from state and county hospitals—before and after the drgus were introduced in 1954. Discharge rates were used as a proxy for operational deinstitutionalization for two reasons. First, if the drugs were to have an effect on any component of patient movement, it would most likely be through an increase in discharge rates, since they were employed mainly in hospital settings. Second, although the changes in inpatient population size are of primary interest, to use such changes as a measure of the drugs' effectiveness would be misleading. That is, if admissions also continued to increase, then increases in discharges might not be reflected in net population changes.

Discharge rates were computed using the method of Moon and Patton (1965). The number of live discharges from a state's hospitals in a given year was divided by the sum of the number of patients resident in those hospitals at the beginning of the year and the total number of admissions during the year. This quotient is multiplied by 100.

The state-level data I have assembled begin in 1946. Since the drugs were introduced in 1954, I have defined the period from 1946 to 1954 as the "predrug" preiod, and the period from 1955 to 1963 as the "postdrug" period. These periods are of equal length, and are long enough (nine years each) that the changes observed within them are not likely to be due to random fluctuations. The postdrug period ends in the year that John F. Kennedy declared his aim to reduce the inpatient loads of the nation's state and county mental hospitals by 50 percent (Foley and Sharfstein, 1983:160).

Two questions are of interest. First, were discharge rates subsequent to drug introduction higher than discharge rates prior to the introduction of the drugs? This question is crucial, since if there is no significant difference—or if "predrug" rates are actually higher than "postdrug" rates—then the drugs cannot be said to have exercised any significant influence on patient movement. Even if discharge rates in the 1955–1963 period were higher than those of the 1946–1954 period, it need not be the case that the drugs were responsible for the change. If discharge rates were already increasing prior to the introduction of the drugs, then any observed increase after

Table 1. Discharge Rates and Mean Yearly Percentage Change in Discharge Rates, 1946-1963

Mean Discharge Rate (S.D.)		Mean Yearly Percentage Change in Discharge Rates (S.D.)	
1946	4.8 (4.1)		
1947	5.9 (4.3)	1946-1947	22.6 (60.1)
1948	5.7 (4.0)	1947-1948	13.8 (55.0)
1949	6.1 (4.1)	1948-1949	13.9 (38.4)
1950	6.7 (4.3)	1949-1950	17.3 (47.6)
1951	7.3 (4.9)	1950-1951	12.0 (35.7)
1952	7.8 (5.3)	1951-1952	8.8 (29.7)
1953	8.6 (5.3)	1952-1953	16.4 (33.2)
1954	9.0 (5.7)	1953-1954	9.4 (26.7)
1955	9.8 (6.7)	1954-1955	9.9 (28.6)
1956	10.7 (6.3)	1955-1956	18.2 (36.1)
1957	11.5 (6.5)	1956-1957	9.1 (18.9)
1958	13.3 (6.8)	1957-1958	19.1 (23.3)
1959	14.1 (7.2)	1958-1959	7.4 (12.7)
1960	14.7 (7.5)	1959-1960	7.8 (18.1)
1961	16.9 (7.8)	1960-1961	22.4 (36.7)
1962	18.6 (8.2)	1961-1962	9.2 (13.6)
1963	20.4 (8.7)	1962-1963	13.0 (19.0)

1954 could simply be a continuation of an existing trend. Thus, the second question is, were rates of change in discharge rates higher in the postdrug period than in the predrug period? If so, we have some support for the argument that the drugs did contribute to operational deinstitutionalization. If not, the contribution of psychotropic drugs to higher postdrug rates becomes questionable.

Table 1 shows the mean discharge rate per state from 1946 to 1963, and the mean yearly percentage change in discharge rates over the same period. With a single exception (1948) the mean discharge rate in each year in the series was higher than in the previous year. Also, the standard deviation in each year was small relative to the mean, indicating that the distribution of individual discharge rates was not highly dispersed.

Mean yearly percentage *changes* in discharge rates behaved quite differently from the mean rates. There was little consistency in increases or decreases—the magnitude of the mean changed sharply at several points—and the large standard deviations relative to the mean indicate that individual states differed appreciably in their degree of yearly change. Thus, although states tended to have similar discharge rates in any given year, the degree to which these discharge rates changed from year to year was highly variable.

To compare discharge rates in the predrug and postdrug periods more exactly, I computed the mean discharge rate for each state for the total periods from 1946 to 1954 and from 1955 to 1963, and used these nine-year means to index each state's discharge rate within each period. The mean discharge rate within each period (over all states) is shown in Table 2, as is the mean percentage change within each period.

Table 2. Mean Discharge Rates and Mean Percentage Change in Discharge Rates, 1946-1954 and 1955-1963

	1946-1954	1955-1963
Mean Discharge Rate	6.84	14.44
(S.D.)	(3.93)	(6.14)
Mean Percentage Change		
in Discharge Rates	172.39	164.19
(S.D.)	(264.10)	(165.64)

The mean discharge rate per state was clearly higher from 1955 to 1963 (14.64) than it was from 1946 to 1954 (6.84). The difference between these two means (7.60) is statistically significant at the .001 level. Every state except the District of Columbia had a higher mean discharge rate from 1955 to 1963 than it did from 1946 to 1954.

Table 2 also presents a comparison of the percentage change in discharge rates between the predrug and the postdrug periods. This comparison shows that the overall percentage change in discharge rates was greater *before* the drugs were introduced than afterwards. From 1946 to 1954 the mean increase per state was 172.39 percent, while from 1955 to 1963 the mean increase was 164.19 percent. The mean difference per state between the percentage increase from 1955 to 1963 and the percentage increase from 1946 to 1954 was −8.20, indicating that on the average states showed a slightly greater relative increase in discharge rates *before* the drugs were introduced than they did afterwards. The difference between the two means was not statistically significant, however. Although the mean difference between the two periods was negative, 28 states showed a greater percentage increase in discharge rates from 1955 to 1963 than they did from 1946 to 1954, while the reverse was true for 17 states.[8]

Overall, these data do not provide strong support for the position that the introduction of the drugs in 1954 *produced* an increase in discharge rates. Table 1 shows quite clearly that discharge rates increased steadily from 1946 to 1954, a period in which the drugs had not yet been introduced. While it is true that discharge rates were higher after the drugs were introduced than they were before, the mean percentage increase in discharge rates from 1946 to 1954 was greater than the mean percentage increase from 1955 to 1963. Also, while a majority of the states did experience a greater increase in discharge rates after drug introduction than before, fully 40 percent of the states showed the reverse pattern.

Thus, increases in discharge rates which took place after the psychotropic drugs were introduced did not arise *de novo,* but represented an extension of a trend which had been in evidence for some time.[9] These results are consistent with earlier findings (Chittick et al., 1961; Kramer, 1959). A retrospective study done in Vermont's state hospital concluded that "no dramatic upswing in discharge rates is apparent with the advent of drug therapy in late 1954. Rather the picture for discharges in this period [1947 to 1958] is one of relatively smooth increases" (Chittick et al., 1961:20).

The fact that discharge rates were increasing *before* the advent of the drugs is itself an interesting finding. These early increases in discharge rates may have resulted from an acceleration of discharge rates for acute, short-stay patients, while chronic patients may have been affected more by the later increases. This possibility is suggested by the fact that one year release rates for first admissions in the predrug period were often quite high, while release rates for patients hospitalized for more than one year were quite low (Council of State Governments, 1950; Kramer, 1957; Pollack et al., 1959). Also, in Vermont chronic patients began to be discharged at an increasing rate only after the drugs were introduced, and the retention rate of schizophrenic first admissions (who were likely candidates for chronicity) was much lower after 1954 than it had been before (Chittick et al., 1961).

Drugs and Mental Health Policy

Reform and the State Hospital

From 1949 to 1954, the American Psychiatric Association (APA) sponsored a series of Mental Health Institutes. Attended largely by the superintendents of state and county hospitals, the proceedings of these Institutes provide a valuable picture of how the state hospitals were viewed by those who ran them.

Dr. Mesrop Tarumianz, superintendent of Delaware's single state hospital and a prominent member of the American Psychiatric Association, expressed the superintendents' general sentiments when he said, "I think that we should realize that conditions are abominable and obnoxious. There are no words in the dictionary that you can use to describe the conditions in mental hospitals" (American Psychiatric Association, 1949:12). Like other citizens concerned with the "abominable and obnoxious" conditions in the nation's mental hospitals, the superintendents' reform agenda gave demands for more money, more buildings, and more staff pride of place (American Psychiatric Association, 1952, 1953, 1954). A survey done at the 1949 meeting showed that 65 percent of the superintendents were engaged in construction projects (American Psychiatric Association, 1949:48). The 1951 Institute featured a session entitled "Appropriations: How Can Mental Hospitals Justify Requests for Increased Appropriations and Charges" (American Psychiatric Association, 1951), and every meeting from 1949 to 1954 featured seminars on how to convince state legislatures and budget officers to allocate more money.

Hospital growth seemed inevitable. Dr. Granville Jones, a Virginia superintendent, commented that "It is nice to plan rooms to meet the demand, but if you make the room too large, *sooner or later you are going to be overcrowded, and you are going to put two patients in a room designed for one*" (American Psychiatric Association, 1950:15, emphasis added). Confronted with an apparently inelastic demand for services, the superintendents felt that lobbying state legislatures for increased appropriations to expand the supply of hospital beds and personnel was eminently reasonable. Given the security burden which the hospital had to shoulder and the relatively ineffective means available for resocializing chronic psychotics prior to the introduction of the drugs, it is not surprising that most reform efforts turned to improvement rather than abolition.

The introduction of the drugs changed this situation markedly. They sparked intense clinical excitement and produced significant improvements in staff morale (Bowes, 1956; Ferguson, 1956; Overholser, 1958). The drugs also exerted a favorable effect (albeit indirectly) on outside audiences such as state legislatures, which became more interested in the problem of mental health care generally after psychoactive medications were introduced (Overholser, 1958).

The drugs were even given credit where credit was not their due, particularly in the matter of their effects on aggregate populations. The upward trend in discharge rates, for instance, had been in effect for a number of years, but was "noticed more frequently since the tranquilizing drugs came upon the scene" (Kramer, 1959:118). The Joint Commission on Mental Illness and Health (1961) credited psychotropics with reversing the "upward spiral" of state hospital populations. This assertion was based on the Brill and Patton studies (1957, 1959). Interestingly, the better designed Michigan study—which showed that the drugs did not increase discharge rates—was not mentioned by the Joint Commission even though it was available. Further, some observers in the middle 1950s (e.g., Clark, 1956) questioned the clinical results obtained with the drugs, since the clinical trials were seldom run under blinded conditions (cf. Scull, 1977).

Policy makers believed the psychotropic drugs could potentially launch a new era in the treatment of mental illness (Lyons, 1984). A recent report by the American Psychiatric Association on deinstitutionalization cited the psychotropic drugs as one of the four principal causes of the development of deinstitutionalization policy (Boffey, 1984). The Joint Commission on Mental Illness and Health, commissioned by the Congress to investigate mental health problems, wrote that "Drugs have revolutionized the management of psychotic patients in American mental hospitals, and probably deserve primary credit for the reversal of the upward trend of the upward spiral in the state hospital inpatient load" (Joint Commission on Mental Illness and Health, 1961:39). A National Institute of Mental Health (NIMH) sponsored investigation of the feasibility of treating schizophrenics in the community stated that "with tranquilizers, fewer patients need to be hospitalized . . . and patients [can be] more easily discharged. . . . [A]t all levels and in nearly all respects, tranquilizers have altered our hospitals and provided the impetus for community care" (Pasamanick et al., 1967:17).

A series of recent interviews with psychiatrists involved in the formulation of mental health policy in the 1950s and early 1960s shows a heavy reliance on the drugs, and former NIMH officials such as Robert Felix and Bertram Brown admit having "oversold" the drugs to the President and the Congress (Lyons, 1984). Most important, the drugs played a crucial role in President Kennedy's 1963 message to Congress. That speech is widely held to have ushered in the era of deinstitutionalization and community mental health (Bachrach, 1976; Bassuk and Gerson, 1978; General Accounting Office, 1977; Kramer, 1977). Kennedy gave the drugs credit for making his "bold new approach" possible:

> This approach rests primarily on the new knowledge and the new drugs acquired and developed in recent years which make it possible for most of the mentally ill to be successfully and quickly treated in their own communities and returned to a useful place in society (cited in Foley and Sharfstein, 1983:165).

It should be emphasized that the drugs were much more influential in the early period of deinstitutionalization than they were in the latter. As Morrissey (1982:148) has written, the drugs made the move away from the state hospital "plausible." While they did help "open the back door" of the state hospital, developments from 1965 onward—when deinstitutionalization accelerated markedly—were dependent on a number of other factors including: the emergence of a civil libertarian reform movement which transformed admission and discharge procedures (California Assembly Ways and Means Subcommittee on Mental Health Services, 1967; Morrissey, 1982); the expansion of federal health and welfare programs and the growth in nursing home capacity (Segal and Aviram, 1978; Shadish and Bootzin, 1981); and the development of fiscal crises in many states (Scull, 1977; Warren, 1981).

Conclusions

The effects of the psychotropic drugs on state and county hospitals and on deinstitutionalization lie somewhere between the "orthodox" and "revisionist" described earlier. The weight of the evidence presented here does not support the position that the introduction of the drugs was responsible for the increases in discharge rates that occurred after 1955. However, testimony from a number of sources does indicate that the advent of psychotropic medications was linked to the emergence of a new philosophy regarding what was possible and desirable in the provision of mental health care for the seriously mentally ill (Boffey, 1984; General Accounting Office, 1977; Joint Commission on Mental Illness and Health, 1961; Lyons, 1984).

The influences of the drugs on operational and policy deinstitutionalization were more a function of the environment into which they were introduced than a straightforward expression of their pharmacological properties. The reason discharge rates did not increase more sharply or inpatient censuses fall more dramatically after drug introduction in the United States may have had more to do with the short supply of alternative facilities in the community for state hospital inpatients than it had to do with any weakness in the drugs' capacities to influence behavior. By the same token, the contribution that the drugs made to the development of a policy of state and county hospital depopulation was not dictated by their pharmacology, since they could have been used as therapies which would promote inhospital adjustment as had electroconvulsive therapy, insulin shock, and lobotomy. To the extent that the drugs "led" to a policy of deinstitutionalization, they did so because they converged with the interests and needs of several different groups, including fiscal conservatives determined to save money and civil libertarian lawyers intent on attacking what they viewed as a repressive institution (Morrissey, 1982; Shadish and Bootzin, 1981).

The drugs, then, were an opportunity, not an imperative. That they stimulated deinstitutionalization does not mean that they had to do so. In an era in which institutional solutions to social problems were in favor, they might well have been used to buttress the internal order of the state hospital. Alone, psychotropic drugs could have had little impact on the actual size of patient populations, and the great acceleration in deinstitutionalization which occurred after 1965 owed much more to changes in the hospital's external environment than to the pacifying effects of these drugs on the internal environment of hospital wards.

Notes

1. In 1939, 90 percent of all admissions to state and county mental hospitals were involuntary (National Institute of Mental Health-Survey and Reports Section, 1974). A report prepared for the American Bar Foundation found that "In most states we studied the initial contact between the patient and the state hospital occurs when the patient arrives there under an order of commitment" (Rock et al., 1968:219).
2. Discussion among hospital psychiatrists at a 1952 meeting emphasized the importance of security considerations in the formulation of discharge decisions: "To the extent that the public considers our hospital as a place *where the mentally ill are not put away for the protection of the public and for no other purpose—to that extent will the public expect that the patient will not be discharged until there is no longer the slightest possibility of harm to himself or others"* (American Psychiatric Association, 1952:4, emphasis added).
3. Chronicity was very much the norm in state hospital inpatient populations, although a number of studies (e.g., Patton and Weinstein, 1960; Pollack et al., 1959; and Weinstein and Maiwald, 1974) found that cohorts of *admissions* often moved through the institutions with some celerity. In 1949, 63 percent of New Jersey state hospital patients had been in residence for five years or more, and 45 percent had been inpatients for more than ten years. In New York State during the same year, more than 60 percent of the inpatient population had been hospitalized for more than five years (Council of State Governments, 1950), and 49 percent of a sample of California state hospital patients discharged in 1956 had inpatient tenures of three years or longer (Miller, 1966). A form of treatment which was effective on this large core of long-stay patients—as the drugs appeared to be—was naturally of considerable interest.

4. In 1956 the California State Senate conducted a survey to determine how many states were using chlor-promazine, reserpine, or both, and to what effect. Thirty-seven states responded: in 13 cases, responses came from state hospital superintendents, and in 24 cases from the Commissioner of Mental Health or Public Welfare (or from the head of a similar state wide agency). In several cases, the response to the questionnaire was accompanied by a message from the state governor. The fact that the surveys were answered by highly placed civil servants indicates that they were taken seriously, and suggests that the data they provided were reliable.

5. Although electroconvulsive therapy (ECT) is now often used on an outpatient basis, ECT, insulin shock, and lobotomy in the early 1950s represented a more serious risk than is true at present. A 1955 review of extant treatment modalities for use in the care of the seriously mentally ill summarized the state of the art as follows: "Electroconvulsive therapy, although it is admittedly the most satisfactory available therapy for the affective disorders, is frightening to patients, traumatic to the osseous system, and some-times causes certain patients to become more disturbed and difficult to manage. Insulin coma therapy, although it did have certain definite advantages in the management and treatment of some cases of schizophrenia and chronic anxiety, is a potentially hazardous form of treatment, which requires addi-tional physical facilities, especially trained personnel, and constant and careful professional supervision" (Litteral and Wilkinson, 1955:63).

6. This report from a Mississippi state hospital illustrates the dependence of hospital discharge policy (and hence population size) on the extra-hospital environment: "In the six month period of this experiment, 42.8% of those taking reserpine were returned to their homes. *Many more were ready to return, but their relatives, especially husbands, would not come for them, so alienated had they become by long absence*" (Pennington, 1955: 107, emphasis added).

7. See Scull (1977:83–4) for a detailed critique of the Brill and Patton methodology.

8. Patients could be "on the books" of a hospital in one of two ways. They could be inpatients, in which case they were physically located within the hospital and were, of course, the hospital's responsibility. They could also be "in extramural care," which meant that although they were located physically outside the hospital, they remained the hospital's responsibility. Patients "in extramural care" could be read-mitted to the hospital without the necessity of a formal proceeding. Three states (Nevada, New Hamp-shire, and Pennsylvania) had discharge rates of zero in 1946, because all discharges in these states were made from extramural care. Therefore, the percentage change in discharge rates from 1946 to 1954 could not be computed for these states. Further, one state (Mississippi) showed a percentage increase of more than 13,000 percent from 1946 to 1954, owing to the fact that it discharged only 3 persons from the hospital in 1946; all other discharges were from extramural care. By 1954, however, most of its discharges came from the hospital, producing the huge percentage increase. Because Mississippi was in no way typical of the other states, I eliminated it from the computations involving percent change. Thus, the N for the comparison of percent change in the predrug and postdrug periods is 45, rather than 49, as it is for the comparison of mean discharge rates.

9. One problem with using the procedure just described is that it assumes that all the states began using the drugs at the same time (1954) and that they all used the drugs with the same degree of intensity. Data collected by the California State Senate survey (1956) show that of the 37 states responding, eight began using the drugs in 1953, 21 began using them in 1954, and eight began in 1955. When the amount of change in discharge rates in the five years before introduction was compared to the amount of change in discharge rates in the five years after the drugs were introduced for these 37 states, no statistically significant difference was found. Further, data on the amount of money spent on thorazine in the first six months of 1955 was reported for 12 states by the California survey. The amount spent did not show a statistically significant correlation with percentage changes in post introduction discharge rates; this remained true when the amount spent per patient was correlated with percentage changes in post drug discharge rates.

References

American Psychiatric Association. 1949 First Mental Hospital Institute-Better Care in Mental Hospitals. Washington, DC: American Psychiatric Association.

———. 1950 Second Mental Hospital Institute-Mental Hospitals. Washington, DC: American Psychiatric Association.

———. 1951 Third Mental Hospital Institute-Working Programs in Mental Hospitals. Washington, DC: American Psychiatric Association.

———. 1952 Fourth Mental Hospital Institute-Steps Forward. Washington, DC: American Psychiatric Association.

———. 1953 Fifth Mental Hospital Institute-Progress and Problems in Mental Hospitals. Washington, DC: American Psychiatric Association.

———. 1954 Sixth Mental Hospital Institute-The Psychiatric Hospital: A Community Resource. Washington, DC: American Psychiatric Association.

Arnhoff, Franklin W. 1975 "Social consequences of policy toward mental illness." Science 188:1277–84.

Aviram, Uri and Steven Segal. 1973 "Exclusion of the mentally ill." Archives of General Psychiatry 27:126–31.

Aviram, Uri, S. Leonard Syme and Judith B. Cohen. 1976 "The effects of policies and programs on reductions of mental hospitalization." Social Science and Medicine 10:571–78.

Bachrach, Leona. 1976 Deinstitutionalization: An Analytical Review and Sociological Perspective. DHEW Publication No. (ADM)76–351. Washington, DC: U.S. Government Printing Office.

———. 1978 "A conceptual approach to deinstitutionalization." Hospital and Community Psychiatry 29:573–78.

Bassuk, Ellen and Samuel Gerson. 1978 "Deinstitutionalization and mental health services." Scientific American 238:46–53.

Beers, Clifford Whittingham. 1981 A Mind That Found Itself. Pittsburgh: University of Pittsburgh Press.

Becker, Alvin and Herbert D. Schulberg. 1976 "Phasing out state hospitals: a psychiatric dilemma." New England Journal of Medicine 294:255–61.

Bittner, Egon. 1967 "Police discretion in emergency apprehension of mentally ill persons." Social Problems 14:278–92.

Boffey, Phillip K. 1984 "Community care for mentally ill termed a failure." New York Times Sept. 13: Al; B2.

Boudwin, James and Nathan Kline. 1955 "Use of reserpine in chronic non-disturbed psychotics." Pp. 71–78 in Jacques S. Gottlieb (ed.), An Evaluation of the Newer Psychopharmacologic Agents and their Role in Current Psychiatric Practice. Washington, DC: American Psychiatric Association.

Bowes, Angus H. 1956 "The ataractic drugs: the present position of chlorpromazine, frenqual, pacatal, and reserpine in the psychiatric hospital." American Journal of Psychiatry 113:530–39.

Braun, Peter, Gerald Kochansky, Robert Shapiro, Susan Greenberg, Jon Gudeman, Sylvia Johnson, and Miles F. Shore. 1981 "Overview: deinstitutionalization of psychiatric patients, a critical review of outcome studies." American Journal of Psychiatry 138:736–49.

Brill, Henry and Robert E. Patton. 1957 "Analysis of 1955–1956 population fall in New York state hospitals in first year of large scale use of tranquilizing drugs." American Journal of Psychiatry 114:509–17.

———. 1959 "Analysis of population reductions in New York state mental hospitals during the first four years of large scale use of tranquilizing drugs." American Journal of Psychiatry 116:495–508.

Brooks, George W. 1958 "Experience with the use of chlorpromazine and reserpine in psychiatry." Pp. 375–81 in Hirsch L. Gordon (ed.), The New Chemotherapy in Mental Illness. New York: Philosophical Library.

Brown, George W., Margaret Bone, Bridget Dalison, and John K. Wing. 1966 Schizophrenia and Social Care. London: Oxford University Press.

Bucher, Rue and Leonard Schatzman. 1962 "The logic of the state mental hospital." Social Problems 9:337–49.

California Assembly Ways and Means Subcommittee on Mental Health Services. 1967 The Dilemma of Mental Commitment in California: A Background Document. Sacramento, CA: California State Assembly.

California State Senate Interim Committee on Treatment of Mental Illness. 1956 First Partial Report. Sacramento, CA: California State Senate. Chittick, R. A., G. W. Brooks, F. S. Irons, and W. W. Deare.
———. 1961 The Vermont Story-Rehabilitation of Chronic Schizophrenic Patients. Burlington, VT: n.p.
Chu, Franklin and Sharland Trotter. 1974 The Madness Establishment. New York: Grossman.
Clark, Lincoln N. 1956 "Evaluation of the therapeutic effect of drugs on psychiatric patients." Diseases of the Nervous System 17:282–86.
Cohen, Stanley. 1979 "The punitive city: notes on the dispersal of social control." Contemporary Crises 3:339–67.
Council of State Governments. 1950 The Mental Health Programs of the Forty-Eight States. Chicago: Council of State Governments.
Deutsch, Albert. 1948 The Shame of the States. New York: Harcourt, Brace.
Dunham, H. Warren and S. Kirson Weinberg. 1960 The Culture of the State Mental Hospital. Detroit: Wayne State University Press.
Epstein, Leon J., Richard P. Morgan, and Lynn Reynolds. 1962 "An approach to the effect of ataraxic drugs on hospital release rates." American Journal of Psychiatry 119:36–47.
Erikson, Kai T. 1966 Wayward Puritans. New York: John Wiley.
Estroff, Sue E. 1981 Making It Crazy. Berkeley, CA: University of California Press.
Ferguson, John. 1956 "Improved behavior patterns in the hospitalized mentally ill with reserpine and methylphenidylacetate." Pp. 35–43 in Jacques S. Gottlieb (ed.), An Evaluation of the Newer Psychopharmacologic Agents and Their Role in Current Psychiatric Practice. Washington, DC: American Psychiatric Association.
Foley, Henry and Steven Sharfstein. 1983 Madness and Government. Washington, DC: American Psychiatric Association.
Fox, Richard W. 1978 So Far Disordered in Mind: Insanity in California, 1870–1930. Berkeley, CA: University of California Press.
Freedman, Ruth and Ann Moran. 1983 Wanderers in a Promised Land: The Chronically Mentally Ill and Deinstitutionalization. Unpublished report, Harvard Working Group on Mental Illness.
General Accounting Office. 1977 Returning the Mentally Disabled to the Community: Government Needs to Do More. Washington, DC: U.S. Government Printing Office.
Glasscote, Raymond, James W. Sussex, Elaine Cumming, and Lauren Smith. 1969 The Community Mental Health Center: An Interim Appraisal. Washington, DC: American Psychiatric Association.
Goffman, Erving. 1961 Asylums. Garden City, NY.: Doubleday.
Goldman, Douglas. 1955a. "The effect of chlorpromazine on severe mental and emotional disturbances." Pp. 19–40 in Chlorpromazine and Mental Health: Proceedings of a Symposium Held Under the Auspices of Smith, Kline and French, Philadelphia: Lea and Fabiger.
———. 1955b "The influence of chlorpromazine on psychotic thought content." Pp. 72–77 in William E. Lhamonn (ed.), Pharmacologic Products Recently Introduced in the Treatment of Psychiatric Disorders." Washington, DC: American Psychiatric Association.
Goldman, Howard H., Neal Adams, and Carl Taube. 1983 "Deinstitutionalization: the data demythologized." Hospital and Community Psychiatry 34:129–34.
Greenley, James and Stuart Kirk. 1973 "Organizational characteristics of agencies and the distribution of services to applicants." Journal of Health and Social Behavior 14:70–79.
Grob, Gerald. 1983 Mental Illness and American Society: 1875 to 1940. Princeton, NJ: Princeton University Press.
Gronfein, William. 1983 From Madhouse to Main Street: The Changing Place of Mental Illness in Post-World War II America. Unpublished Ph.D. dissertation, State University of New York at Stony Brook.
Joint Commission on Mental Illness and Health. 1961 Action for Mental Health. New York: Basic Books.
Kinross-Wright, Vernon. 1955 "The intensive chlorpromazine treatment of schizophrenia." Pp. 53–62 in William E. Lhamonn (ed.), Pharmacologic Products Recently Introduced in the Treatment of Psychiatric Disorders. Washington, DC: American Psychiatric Association.
———. 1956 "A review of the newer drug therapies in psychiatry." Diseases of the Nervous System 17:187–90.
Kirk, Stuart A. and Mark Therrien. 1975 "Community mental health myths and the fate of former hospitalized patients." Psychiatry 38:209–17.

Kramer, Morton. 1957 "Problems of research on the population dynamics and therapeutic effectiveness of mental hospitals." Pp. 145–72 in Milton Greenblatt, Daniel Levinson, and Richard H. Williams (eds.), The Patient and the Mental Hospital. Glencoe, IL: Free Press.

———. 1959 "Public health and social problems in the use of tranquilizing drugs." Pp. 108–43 in Jonathan O. Cole and Ralph W. Gerard (eds.), Psychopharmacology: Problems in Evaluation. Publication No. 583, National Academy of Sciences. Washington, DC: National Research Council.

———. 1977 Psychiatric Services and the Changing Institutional Scene: 1950–1985. DHEW Publication No. (ADM) 77–433. Washington, DC: U.S. Government Printing Office.

Lerman, Paul. 1982 Deinstitutionalization and the Welfare State. New Brunswick, NJ: Rutgers University Press.

Lhamonn, William E. (ed.). 1955 Pharmacologic Products Recently Introduced in the Treatment of Psychiatric Disorders. Washington, DC: American Psychiatric Association.

Litteral, Emmet B. and William E. Wilkinson. 1955 "The advantages, disadvantages, and limitations of the use of chlorpromazine as a substitute for certain somatic treatment methods in psychiatry." Pp. 63–72 in William E. Lhamonn (ed.), Pharmacologic Products Recently Introduced in the Treatment of Psychiatric Disorders. Washington, DC: American Psychiatric Association.

Lyons, Richard D. 1984 "How release of mental patients began." New York Times October 30:C1,C4.

Mechanic, David. 1969 Mental Health and Social Policy. Englewood Cliffs, NJ: Prentice-Hall.

Michigan Department of Mental Health. 1956 A Summary of Behavioral Changes in Patients and Changes in Hospital Ward Management Associated with the Use of Chlorpromazine and Reserpine Therapy in Michigan State Hospitals: Research Report 23. Lansing, MI: Michigan Department of Mental Health.

Miller, Dorothy. 1966 Worlds That Fail: Part II. Disbanded Worlds—A Study of Returns to the Mental Hospital. Sacramento, CA: California Department of Mental Hygiene.

Moon, Louis E. and Robert E. Patton. 1965 "First admissions and readmissions to New York State mental hospitals—a statistical evaluation." The Psychiatric Quarterly 39:476–86.

Morrissey, Joseph. 1982 "Deinstitutionalizing the mentally ill: processes, outcomes, and new directions. Pp. 147–76 in Walter Gove (ed.), Deviance and Mental Illness. Beverly Hills, CA: Sage Publications.

National Institute of Mental Health—Survey and Reports Section. 1974 Legal Status of Inpatient Admissions to State and County Mental Hospitals, 1972. Statistical Note No. 105. Washington, DC: U.S. Government Printing Office.

Overholser, Winfred. 1958 "Has chlorpromazine inaugurated a new era in mental hospitals?" Pp. 212–17 in Hirsch L. Gordon (ed.), The New Chemotherapy in Mental Illness. New York: Philosophical Library.

Pasamanick, Benjamin, Frank Scarpitti, and Simon Dinitz. 1967 Schizophrenics in the Community. New York: Appleton-Century Crofts.

Patton, Robert E. and Abbott S. Weinstein. 1960 "First admissions to New York civil state mental hospitals, 1911–1958." The Psychiatric Quarterly 34:245–74.

Pennington, Veronica M. 1955 "The use of reserpine (serpasil) in three hundred and fifty neuropsychiatric cases." Pp. 105–11 in William E. Lhamonn (ed.), Pharmacologic Products Recently Introduced in the Treatment of Psychiatric Disorders. Washington, DC: American Psychiatric Association.

Pollack, Earl, Philip H. Person, Morton B. Kramer, and Hyman Goldstein. 1959 Patterns of Retention, Release, and Death of First Admissions to State Mental Hospitals. DHEW Public Health Monograph No. 38. Washington, DC: U.S. Government Printing Office.

Pollack, Earl and Carl A. Taube. 1975 "Trends and projections in state hospital use." Pp. 31–55 in Jack Zusman and Elmer Bertsch (eds.), The Future Role of the State Hospital. Lexington, MA: D.C. Heath.

Redick, Richard V., Morton Kramer, and Carl A. Taube. 1973 "Epidemiology of mental illness and utilization of facilities among older persons." Pp. 199–232 in Ewald W. Busse and Eric Pfeiffer (eds.), Mental Illness in Later Life. Washington, DC: American Psychiatric Association.

Rock, Richard, Marcus A. Jacobson, and Richard M. Janopaul. 1968 Hospitalization and Discharge of the Mentally Ill. Chicago: University of Chicago Press.

Rose, Stephen. 1979 "Deciphering deinstitutionalization: complexities in policy and program analysis." Milbank Memorial Fund 57:429–60.

Rothman, David. 1971 The Discovery of the Asylum. Boston: Little, Brown.

Sampson, Harold, Sheldon Messinger and Robert A. Towne. 1962 "Family processes and becoming a mental patient." American Journal of Sociology 68:88–96.

Scull, Andrew. 1977 Decarceration: Community Treatment and the Deviant—A Radical View. Englewood Cliffs, NJ: Prentice-Hall.

Sedgwick, Peter. 1982 Psychopolitics. New York: Harper and Row.

Segal, Steven and Uri Aviram. 1978 The Mentally Ill in Community-Based Sheltered Care. New York: Wiley.

Segal, Steven, Jim Baumohl, and Elsie A. Johnson. 1974 "Falling through the cracks: mental disorder and social margin in a young vagrant population." Social Problems 24:387–400.

Shadish, William and Richard Bootzin. 1981 "Nursing homes and chronic mental patients." Schizophrenia Bulletin 7:488–98.

Smith, Kline and French. 1955 Chlorpromazine and Mental Health: Proceedings of a Symposium Held Under the Auspices of Smith, Kline and French. Philadelphia: Lea and Febiger.

———. 1956 Annual Report. Philadelphia: Smith, Kline and French.

Stanton, Alfred and Morris Schwartz. 1954 The Mental Hospital. New York: Basic.

Swazey, Judith. 1974 Chlorpromazine in Psychiatry. Cambridge, MA: MIT Press.

van der Vaart, H. Robert. 1978 "Variances, statistical study of." Pp. 1215–25 in William H. Kruskal and Judith M. Tanur (eds.), International Encyclopedia of Statistics. New York: Free Press.

Ward, Mary J. 1946 The Snake Pit. New York: H. Wolff.

Warren, Carol A. B. 1981 "New forms of social control: the myth of deinstitutionalization." American Behavioral Scientist 24:724–46.

Weinstein, Abbott and Albert Maiwald. 1974 "Trends in New York state mental hospital admissions and length of stay." Pp. 11–21 in The State Hospital-Past and Present. Hanover, NJ: Sandoz Pharmaceuticals.

Yarrow, Marion R., Charlotte G. Schwartz, Harriet J. Murphy, and Leila C. Deasy. 1955 "The psychological meaning of mental illness in the family." Journal of Social Issues 11:12–28.

36. Decriminalization: The Law, Society, and the User

Bruce K. Mac Murray, Thomas M. Shapiro, and Maureen E. Kelleher

Drug policy is one of those areas invested with enormous emotional ferment, but blessed with mixed logic and little social science insight. Present national policy focuses overwhelmingly on a law-enforcement approach aimed at punishing the drug user. Such efforts at legally controlling drug use have been marked by their failure, whether one looks at the dismal national experience involving the prohibition of alcohol (1919–1932) or at the ineffective seventy-year effort to eliminate heroin from the American drug scene.

Policy regarding drugs, whether legal or illegal, is a complex enterprise. Not only must pharmacological effects be addressed (such as increased probabilities of cancers, premature heart diseases, liver or brain damage), but so too should problems associated with the social conditions of use (for example, arrest or fear of arrest, stigmatization and deviance, and drug-related crime to secure illicit drug supplies) (Goode 1984). Particularly important in examining the social use of drugs is the recognition that many of associated problems are the direct or indirect result of drug enforcement policy. Thus, we believe it is time to start considering alternative policies aimed at reorienting national efforts away from criminalization and punishment and toward a concern with users, potential users, and related social problems.

Before changing any policy, however, it is prudent to examine the likely consequences such a change might entail, for drug policy touches on many wide-ranging issues. Among the more important to consider are the following: the legislation of morality and victimless crimes: the deterrence and social control of drug use; the legitimacy of the law and its impact by stigmatizing users; the organization of supplying and distributing legal and illegal drugs; the health of drug users; treatment options; and patterns of subsequent drug use. Discussions of these issues has been organized into three related and overlapping areas—the law, society, and the user.

In evaluating such policy options, we must be clear about our goals and biases. Placing the emphasis on the user and society, this paper suggests the following guidelines. First of all, it should be a fundamental aim of drug policy to minimize social disruption and harm to individuals. As such, policy should not pander to induced paranoia, victim-blaming, social stereotyping, or mere symbolic gestures. Furthermore, policy need not be, nor should it be, monolithic. Rather, it should be flexible and based on the specific drugs and related problems in question. Finally, in examining alternatives, we must remember that by maintaining present policy toward drugs we are also making a conscious choice, one to sustain the status quo.

This article will explore the implications of one alternative proposal—decriminalization. We choose decriminalization for a variety of reasons. First, decriminalization implies a reorientation of drug policy away from punitive law enforcement and toward education, rehabilitation, research, and treatment. Symbolic distinctions, commercial interest, and medical utility presently direct policy, producing a crazy patchwork of laws for different drugs (Kelleher, MacMurray, and Shapiro 1983). Second, decriminalization is worth exploring because it highlights the complexities and shortcomings of drug use and social control, which may have positive effects in sorting out drug policy.

Decriminalization typically involves the removal of a jail sentence for first-time possession of small amounts of a drug. The offense thus becomes a civil, rather than a criminal matter, and the offender pays a fine akin to that for a traffic violation. It should be noted that such a policy does not include a legal, regulated supply of drugs, but merely changes the penalty for personal possession and use.

The Law

This section discusses the relation of law and the criminal justice system to the use of illegal drugs. Of particular importance are the issues of: drug use as a victimless crime; the effect of deterrence through drug laws; and the implication of decriminalization policy on the criminal justice system.

Law and the Legislation of Morality

For a sociologist, law in general and criminal law more specifically is the attempt by society to formally lay out norms for the social control of acceptable and unacceptable conduct (Akers and Hawkins 1975). In most areas, there is relative consensus about these social rules for the protection of persons and their property (e.g., murder, assault, robbery and burglary). However, the content of some laws are more controversial. An example of one such area is for laws regarding what sociologists term, "victimless crimes."

Victimless crimes as defined by Schur (1965) involve ". . . the willing exchange, among adults, of strongly demanded but legally prescribed goods or services." Typically included in this category are such offenses as: prostitution, pornography, gambling, and illicit drug use. What distinguishes these crimes from others is that there is no victim harmed by their occurrence, or there is typically no complainant to report the crime and press charges. Following a civil libertarian perspective, some argue the law has no mandate to regulate such private consensual acts of individuals (Morris and Hawkins 1970; Szasz 1972). From this point of view, victimless crimes are prime candidates for potential decriminalization or legalization. Critics, however, maintain that no crimes are truly victimless as the offender and the broader society are both usually harmed by such behavior (Wilson 1975).

Law and Social Control

Laws serve to protect society from wrongdoing on the basis of two related processes: (1) instrumental control, and (2) symbolic features. As Gusfield notes (1963), law operates as an instrument by influencing behavior through enforcement and the arrest, conviction and punishment of law violators. However, just as importantly, the law also functions as a symbol designating and affirming the ideas of society. As such, the law provides a clear sense of what behavior is proper according to the moral norms; expresses the public value of a set of moral beliefs; and enhances the social status of one group, while stigmatizing as deviant those with differing views. In precisely this manner, criminal drug laws provide for both the official prosecution of law violators and also define such behaviors as immoral and antisocial.

The symbolic function of law is particularly important, because a society's criminal justice system, no matter how large in number or unlimited in resources, can never depend solely on enforcement to prevent or limit crime. Indeed, in the case of drugs (and other victimless crimes), one might expect particular reliance on the law's symbolic value and informal social control through the process of deterrence.

Deterrence and the Policy of Drug Criminalization

Deterrence is based on the assumption that people typically orient their behavior using rational decision making. For example, if the benefits from a particular drug are seen to outweigh the risks and costs associated with it, an individual should choose to use the drug. Deterrence of drug use, then, involves the process of raising the costs (and/or lowering the benefits) for drugs in order to make them seem less beneficial or desirable, and thus prevent their usage. Perhaps the most straightforward means to accomplish this goal is to pass laws against the use and possession of certain drugs, and vigorously enforce these laws to increase both the risk of apprehension and the punishment costs for such behavior.

Given the emphasis of current U.S. drug policy on deterrence and law enforcement, it seems appropriate to ask how effectively the criminalization of drugs works as a legal and social policy. More precisely, what are this policy's effects on drug use and related social behavior?

Brecher (1972) has noted several problems with the logic of deterrence as applied to drug behavior. First, much drug use is based on addiction. In such cases, usage is neither freely chosen nor based solely on rational criteria, making deterrence extremely difficult. Given this circumstance, laws penalizing addicts may be seen to "blame the victim" (Ryan 1971), rather than to provide treatment or rehabilitation to help ameliorate the problems of drug addiction.

Second, the illegality of drugs such as marijuana and LSD may lead to increased experimentation and recreational use, suggesting a "forbidden fruit" appeal for prospective users (Brecher 1972; Hellman 1975). Similarly, to the extent that criminalization is linked with claims about negative health, psychological, and behavioral effects that conflict with users' own drug experiences, the government, the law, and deterrence may all be seen to lose credibility (Hellman 1975).

Third, as criminalization attempts to deter, but does not and cannot entirely eliminate drug use, this policy leaves a tremendous consumer demand void. And as elementary economics tells us, if there is demand for a product or service, a supply will surely arise to meet it. If not by legitimate means, then through the establishment of a black market economy, as has clearly been the case with illegal drugs.

Drug criminalization also leads to additional problems, specifically in the area of enforcement. Because the use of illicit drugs is victimless, most sales transactions as well as private usage take place unbeknownst to the police. This situation forces law-enforcement agents to use techniques and procedures posing serious threats to the protection of constitutional civil liberties. These threats are particularly likely to occur with respect to surveillance, deception, unlawful or questionable searches and seizures, arrests without probable cause, selective enforcement, and harassment. Additionally, the heavy reliance on informers and undercover work places enforcement officers under extreme pressure and risk regarding perjury, corruption, and criminal involvement (Hellman 1975; Skolnick 1969).

In summary, while making certain drugs illegal serves to indicate society's social disapproval by punishing and stigmatizing users, such a policy does not remove the drugs from society and cannot guarantee the prevention of their use or abuse. Instead, this approach merely moves the drug from licit to illicit, and similarly from aboveground, legitimate use to underground, illegal behavior. And therein lies the problem. For much of what contemporary American society regards as most evil about drugs—drug-related crime, involvement with and financial support of organized crime, overdoses, and drug-poisoning, as well as the escapist "down and out" addict life-style—can all be seen as directly or indirectly linked with the criminalization of drugs.

Decriminalization as a Drug Policy

One proposed alternative to the present law-enforcement approach, though by no means universally endorsed, is decriminalization. This policy has recently been applied to the case of marijuana.

Among those proposing decriminalization for marijuana, probably one of the most influential sources was the National Commission on Marijuana and Drug Abuse. In 1972, this commission concluded that a policy of prohibition and the accompanying intrusion by the law into private behavior by citizens was inappropriate for offenses involving the personal possession of marijuana. In its place, the commission recommended a policy of discouragement based on decriminalization.

Following the release of this report, several states decided to implement a decriminalization policy. Beginning with Oregon in 1972 and ending most recently with Nebraska in 1979, decriminalization regarding possession and use of small quantities of marijuana is now the law (in one form or another) in eleven states.

With the passage of these laws, one can ask what effect decriminalization has had on the criminal justice system's handling of marijuana. Data available from states that have decriminalized suggest conclusions for two areas: law-enforcement costs and demands on criminal justice resources. Discussing the economic impact, Maloff (1981) reports that a California state evaluation found a substantial decrease in total arrests and citations for marijuana as well as little change in trafficking arrests. A significant increase occurred, however, in arrests regarding narcotics and other drug offenses. In Maloof's words, "Summing the total law-enforcement savings, California estimates that costs in the first half of 1976 were $12.6 million less than in a comparable period in 1975" (p. 317), not including increased fees from fines and bail forfeitures totaling $361,000 (a 79 percent increase).

A summary report on decriminalization for Maine noted a similar reduction in police costs, superior court trials, and imprisonment for marijuana possession along with an increase in guilty pleas and income from fines, thus turning a $332,600 government expense into a $16,900 profit for the state. Just as important, the report concludes that the change to decriminization, ". . . substantially improved the quality and uniformity of justice administered to marijuana possession defendants in Maine" (p. 318).

This section has sought to indicate how a criminalization approach to drug behavior is designed to operate utilizing law enforcement and deterrence. However, because of difficulties related to the victimless nature of illegal drug use, this prohibitionist approach has been a major failure in its mission. After examining some of the reasons for this result, the policy option of decriminalization is discussed as an alternative.

While such a policy seems quite appealing, however, there are problems and trade-offs with such a proposal. These issues will be discussed in the following sections focusing on decriminalization's likely impact on society and the drug user.

Society

The preceding section has shown how society can single out and define as illegal certain victimless crimes such as the use of illicit drugs. However, by choosing to legislate such moral norms (Duster 1970) and assign enforcement agents and the criminal justice system to act upon these laws, society almost inevitably creates a subgroup of deviants or criminals at the same time.

Focusing on the decriminalization of drugs and its potential impact on society, two primary themes need to be explored. First, one must examine the issue of deviance and whether decriminalization will alter the effect of this label for drug users. Will decriminalization affect the user subculture? Will the drug seem safer or more alluring? Second, one must address the issue involving the business of drugs, both legal and illegal. Does decriminalization affect the legal side of the drug industry in any meaningful way? Does it alleviate the fear of crime committed to support illegal drug habits?

Deviance and Decriminalization

Deviance is the classic sociological model for analyzing the use of drugs. Merton's (1968) retreatist mode of adaptation to disparity between goals and means provides one explanation for the drug user and his/her life-style. In his analysis, Merton argues that the drug user is a "double failure" who has given up the attempt to obtain a piece of the American dream by withdrawing from both legitimate and illegitimate occupational means, retreating instead to escape through drugs. More recently, Goode (1972; 1984) has challenged this position maintaining that the addict life-style is typically characterized by constant and demanding street hustling in order to financially support one's habit.

Labeling theorists, such as Lemert and Becker, have provided a slightly different perspective on deviance. Lemert's (1966) major contribution is his concept of secondary deviance, which involves dramatic changes in one's habits and life-styles in response to negative societal reactions such as arrest or incarceration. For example, Ray's (1961) research on heroin addiction and its related cycles of abstinence and relapse discusses the secondary status characteristics of the addict including the negative self-image as a bum, criminal, or someone who is mentally ill—all of which are highly stigmatizing. If heroin was decriminalized, perhaps the most adverse and damaging aspects of this labeling and resulting self-image could be contained or modified.

One example of recent stigma modification for drug users has occurred in terms of marijuana. In his research on the marijuana subculture of jazz musicians, Becker (1966) argues that the American values of the Protestant ethic and the emphasis on pragmatism and utilitarianism prevented acceptance of marijuana users during the 1950s and early 1960s. However, with the growing use of marijuana by middle-class college students in the 1960s and 1970s, society's view of marijuana has changed: possession penalties have been reduced nationwide; stigma has been tempered and usage more accepted; subcultural aspects have been modified away from a counterculture; and while still subject to arrest, users appear to be better integrated into mainstream society.

Trice and Roman (1970) suggest a different approach to reducing stigma through the process of delabeling. For example, by encouraging strict conformity to internal organization norms and creating a socially acceptable image of the reformed drinker, Alcoholics Anonymous has helped alleviate the stigmatizing negative stereotype of the alcoholic. NORML, an organization calling for the legalization of marijuana, uses another strategy emphasizing relabeling by organizing deviants (i.e., marijuana users) to work for the formal change of societal norms. A final approach involves the process whereby mandated professionals who initially take part in labeling behavior, process this deviance through treatment and create a highly visible delabeling ceremony pronouncing the user "cured" or rehabilitated.

Business and Drugs

The business of drugs, whether legal or illegal, is a profitable one. On the legal side, the pharmaceutical industry is one of the most profitable in the United States year in and year out (Silverman et al. 1981). However, critics point to problems with how this industry operates, including the amount of promotional money spent to persuade doctors to prescribe one company's drug over another's, or over the option of not prescribing any drugs at all. As a partial consequence of this promotion, Silverman and his coauthors argue, a large proportion of two classes of drugs are prescribed in this country: antibiotics and psychoactive drugs (such as stimulants, tranquilizers, and sedatives).

The overprescription of psychoactive drugs is a high profile controversy. Writers such as Chesler (1972) in her classic discussion of psychiatrists and more recently Hughes and Brewin (1979) both argue that American society in general, and women in particular, are being overly tranquilized through the prescribing practices of physicians. As a means to cope with stress, or simply to help one relax, tranquilizers such as Valium are prescribed to provide instant relief. However, because such legal drugs are habit-forming and physically addictive, overprescription also creates the possiblity for abuse and potential demand for illegally supplied psychoactive drugs. While the medical profession has begun to address some of these problems, users of psychoactive drugs remain the hidden addicts of America, in large part because the drugs involved are legal and because the users do not match the profile of the illegal street addict.

Graham's (1972) research on the scheduling of amphetamines in the federal Comprehensive Drug Abuse Prevention and Control Act of 1970 shows similar evidence that billions of amphetamines are overproduced in this country every year without medical justification. While these drugs are considered useful in treating narcolepsy and hyperkinesis, a more common use is for dietary purposes. Two results of this circumstance are overprescription and diversion of these drugs into illegal distribution channels. Graham notes that Senate and House debates on the 1970 bill focused primarily on the illegal street users or "speed freak" and virtually ignored other categories of abusers, such as housewives, students, businessmen, and truck drivers. Coupled with a wide-ranging examination of the entire American drug scene, decriminalization could contribute to a more well-rounded view of overall drug use and abuse in society, which in turn might lead to serious assessment of the impact of production, promotion, prescription, and overall profits of the legal drug business.

The illegal side of the drug business, of course, is also important to examine. As Salerno (1979) argues, the "American dichotomy" (p. 167) of guarding the separation of church and state while at the same time maintaining penal statutes for various victimless crimes (e.g., gambling, prostitution, and drug use) serves as a boon to organized crime. Tracing the history of illegal U.S. drugs from the Harrison Act in 1914 to the emergence of cocaine as a profitable drug in the 1970s, Salerno calls law-enforcement attempts a "convoluted miasma" (p. 182) involving organizational fragmentation, competition, and gerrymandering among a variety of enforcement agencies.

To improve this situation, Salerno suggests refocusing laws away from attempts to control and penalize the drug user. As a result, enforcement agencies could better target fewer, but more significant, cases against organized crime, and thus positively redirect resources. For users, a public health model similar to the British system might be instituted to maintain poor drug addicts' habits, while ignoring wealthy and other self-supporting users.

This type of public health policy when linked with decriminalization might also help reduce drug-related crime and its impact on society. While experts disagree on precise numbers, heroin addicts are seen as responsible for committing approximately 50 million crimes per year in this country (Ball et al. 1982), many of a serious nature. These crimes are often nonviolent in nature and are typically motivated by the need for income to support one's habit. Nevertheless, such crimes pose direct costs to the society by victimizing nonusers, and more indirectly through the public fear of crime.

This section has examined current drug policy and the alternative of decriminalization in terms of broad societal impacts. Of particular concern have been issues involving the stigmatization of users through criminal drug offenses, and the legal and illegal business of drugs. As has been suggested, present policy poses particular problems and imposes certain social costs which decriminalization might help relieve. In the next section, we turn to the effect of current policy and the option of decriminalization on the drug user.

The User

Previous sections have discussed the impact of decriminalization on law and the society. This final section examines how decriminalization might affect the user in the following areas: the general health and well-being of the user; the operation of available treatment facilities; and subsequent patterns of drug use.

Health and Well-Being for the User

One result which decriminalization alone would not produce is the regulation of quality for illicit drugs. For those drugs that become adulterated to increase black market profits, the user would be plagued by essentially the same health risks as under present criminalization policies. Thus, serious medical problems resulting from impurities and fillers in heroin, cocaine, marijuana, and other drugs would not be alleviated.

Decriminalization would also leave intact many societal causes of user health problems. For example, Goode (1972; 1984) points out that roughly one percent of all U.S. heroin addicts die every year as a result of the social conditions for heroin use. These deaths arise from the fact that heroin must be used illegally, not the pharmacological properties of the drug itself. What is typically sold on the streets as heroin can range from only 3–5 percent purity up to 15–20 percent, the bulk consisting of other, unknown substances. Deaths appearing to be from heroin overdose, then, may actually result from the enormous variability in the drug's potency or such impurities, a situation Brecher (1972) calls Syndrome X.

Other problems associated directly with illegality and commonly linked with heroin addicts in the United States include two diseases—hepatitis and tetanus—which are primarily the consequence of sharing unsterilized needles; as under conditions of drug purity and sanitary usage, heroin is relatively nontoxic (Goode 1972). Aside from physical dependence, which sets in motion all sorts of personal, financial and social problems, the use of heroin and other opiates does not cause permanent physiological damage.

One advantage which decriminalization offers for users is a change in psychological climate. For instance, the panic anxiety reaction characteristic of novice marijuana users is partly attributable to fear of being arrested and subsequent disclosure of such activity to parents, educators, other authorities, and peers (Becker 1967). In general, a drug user in a supportive and informed environment is likely to have a safer and more enjoyable experience than an uneasy novice in a hostile societal environment.

Evidence to support this claim can be found in several areas. For example, Becker (1967) describes the stages by which a drug like marijuana or LSD can become acculturated as individuals accumulate and share experience with new drugs. In this fashion a subcultural consensus develops about such matters as: the drug's subjective effects, the duration of these effects, appropriate dosages, predictable dangers and methods to cope with them, as well as when and where usage of the drug is appropriate.

Additionally, the social organization of drug use through subcultures and individuals' drug experiences can often produce a mode of stable usage. For instance, Jamaica provides stark contrast to the United States in terms of social attitudes toward marijuana use and, as a result, the subsequent experience of users is vastly different. Americans smoke marijuana for a variety of reasons: to relax, to enhance an experience, to alter subjective feelings, or simply to entertain themselves. In contrast, in the Jamaican countryside a very large amount of potent marijuana (ganja) is communally shared before engaging in strenuous physical labor. In these two contexts, the purpose, experience and meaning of marijuana are worlds apart (Rubin and Comitas 1976).

Decriminalization and User Patterns

Beyond the physiological and psychological health of drug users, another issue raised by decriminalization is what would happen to drug usage patterns. Decriminalization would lead some to expect a drastic increase in drug use in the absence of deterrence. However, there is evidence to contradict this popular notion.

Most significantly, research from Oregon, California, and Maine provide results on the effects of marijuana decriminalization efforts since the 1970s. Using crude impact measures, similar findings were reported in all three states; consumption patterns for marijuana appear to have changed little or not at all. Thus, although it is premature to reach conclusions about the long-range effects of decriminalization, this policy change has certainly not had alarming consequences in promoting marijuana use in the short run. In sum, removal of the legal deterrence for personal use has not opened the "flood gates" to massive abuse as critics had feared.

Conversely, the 1973 "get tough" drug law in New York State set strict mandatory sentences for various drug offenses. For example, a second conviction for selling heroin meant life in prison. Nevertheless, this law failed to demonstrate any influence on the level of heroin use in the state (Meyers 1980).

Decriminalization and Treatment

A final set of issues centers on how decriminalization would affect drug treatment programs. Research to date shows that the track record for treatment is not strong. In fact, prospects for a successful treatment, one which leads to abstinence from an abused drug, are typically quite low. Consequently, assertions of success must be evaluated very skeptically. For instance, Alcoholics Anonymous claims a high success rate, but does not keep records or cite any data to support such claims. When pressed, AA speaks of members who have already been in treatment for one year, excluding all those leaving the program before this time. Similarly, residential treatment communities appear to work for some people, who give sensitive personal witness to how the program has changed their lives. But in fact, the success story touches only a small group of addicts (Retting, Torres, and Garrett 1977).

One explanation for the low prospects of treatment success is that both the reasons why people use drugs, and which kinds of treatment are likely to succeed or fail for which individuals are not fully understood. The resulting variety in available approaches, then, is not so much a testament to pluralism in treatment philosophies as it is a commitment to the search for something that works. In terms of societal resources, treatment, research, and drug education are all a distant second in priority to law enforcement. In fact, since the mid-1970s, treatment facilities for drug users have been increasingly eliminated and existing services dramatically curtailed.

Reorientation of drug policy would allow consideration of alternatives such as the British system of heroin maintenance for addicts. Though the lessons from this program are not all clear-cut or without limitations, Trebach (1982) argues that such a system could be a valuable addition to American treatment approaches. While careful evaluation of the British experience would be necessary first, and modifications incorporating more monitoring or regulation might be required, such an approach should not be automatically ignored.

Ideally decriminalization would also provide a different sort of motivation for the addict seeking treatment. This would only be the case, however, if treatment were given a higher priority in the overall scheme of drug policy. If treatment were viewed as less custodial, then perhaps different treatment strategies could be pursued. Under such circumstances, an addict or drug abuser might no longer be coerced into treatment to avoid prison or to look good before a judge or probation officer. Instead, more positive motivations for treatment might be evident, potentially yielding more successful outcomes.

Conclusion

The present discussion has examined U.S. policy toward illicit drugs. In so doing, the primary concern has dealt with two questions: (1) what are the major consequences resulting from the current policy of drug criminalization? (and more specifically, the negative social costs involved); and (2) what changes might be expected with the adoption of a decriminalization approach to drugs?

Current drug policy in this country dates from the prohibitionism of the early 1900s. This policy began with the criminalization of the opiates (and cocaine) in 1914 and later continued with legislation on alcohol (1919) and marijuana (1937). However, this law-enforcement policy has not solved America's drug problems. Indeed, in many ways, this approach has served to aggravate and compound these difficulties.

Beyond simply playing the role of critical "devil's advocate" on drug policy, however, this article has also discussed and examined one of the oft-mentioned alternatives available, decriminalization. As we have sought to indicate, decriminalization is not a panacea. Indeed, the major point of this article is that there probably cannot be any instant, perfect solutions to America's problems with illegal drugs. Decriminalization does, however, provides a focus for rethinking drug policy, its present problems, and the goals it should strive toward.

Using the case of marijuana, where decriminalization has been tried and instituted in a fifth of the states in the United States, we have noted that this policy has not led to the "epidemic" of increased use and new users feared by its opponents. At the same time, considerable savings appear to have occurred for law enforcement regarding marijuana, without any strong evidence that public safety has been increasingly endangered. Presumably some reduction in stigma for marijuana use, and perhaps improved set, setting, and additional subcultural aspects have also taken place.

Marijuana decriminalization, however, has not been an unqualified success. Research in the area has had its share of methodological and statistical problems. In addition, there is some evidence to suggest that decriminalization has led to an increase in driving while under the influence of marijuana (Petersen 1981), and perhaps some increased conflict in police-offender interactions where possession of marijuana is involved.

More importantly for the perspective offered here, decriminalization of marijuana or other drugs does not provide a legitimate supply source, nor does it regulate the quality of the drug purchased. As a result, health problems for the drug user are quite likely to remain after decriminalization. Likewise, users will still be forced to obtain their drugs from illicit suppliers. In this situation, it is doubtful that decriminalization would have much effect on income-generating crimes committed by users to support their drug habits. Thus, to the extent that association with illegal suppliers is seen as socially unacceptable and perhaps risky in terms of exposure to other drugs and criminal activities, shifting to a policy of decriminalization would produce little real change.

For society, decriminalization may help remove some of the stigma associated with illegal drug use. To the degree that this means less formal (i.e., arrest, conviction, punishment, and establishment of a criminal record) and informal (stereotype and prejudiced attitude) negative consequences and fears for otherwise law-abiding citizens, decriminalization may have a quite beneficial impact on society. Indeed, such a policy might lead to specific settings that would make possible enjoyment of the more positive effects of given drugs (analogous to drinking alcohol at the corner bar) while emphasizing norms of moderate use and appropriate conduct when under the influence (Becker 1967; Cavan 1966; MacAndrew and Edgerton 1969; Rubin and Comitas 1976).

For addicts or those individuals interested in quitting or limiting their drug use, decriminalization might invigorate treatment efforts, both through: (1) broader social support and less stigma of drug use and the moral character of drug users, thus placing more emphasis on treatment rather than prison as a potential solution; and (2) the creation of supportive subcultural ties which informally advocate responsible drug use and a reputable life as social citizen, above and beyond one's drug use.

More generally, decriminalization would help get the government out of the business of legislating morality for private, victimless acts, and away from the philosophy of deterrence which has been so unsuccessful in this area.

As Petersen (1981) has noted, society needs to develop more rational approaches to drug policy. However, we should not and probably cannot be entirely consistent and uniform. For some drug issues and problems, decriminalization may be both useful and successful, as seems to be the case for marijuana from the information available so far. For other problems, however, such an approach may be quite unsound and inadequate. For example, in a case such as PCP ("angel dust") it would probably be unwise to decriminalize and lift any sanctions, indeep perhaps even stiffer penalties are warranted given this drug's negative effects (Graevan et al. 1981). In a similar fashion, the imposition of penalties for tobacco might be urged based on this substance's negative health effects and addictive properties. Alternatively, for heroin, decriminalization may be a step in the right direction, but simply not go far enough.

Decriminalization of small amounts of heroin for personal use would probably do little to affect the life-style of the user, usage of the drug, or the link to organized crime. Decriminalizing heroin will not reduce the costs of the drug to the addict, nor guarantee the purity of the drug, nor provide the money to obtain it. In this sense, we would expect decriminalization to dismally fail at reducing: (1) heroin-related crime, (2) the problems of the user's life-style and addiction, (3) the black market and strength of organized crime, and (4) health problems related to heroin use. Thus, heroin decriminalization would provide a negligible improvement over our current approach. In this case, a more radical approach toward controlled regulation and legalization (similar to the British approach) might be more adequate at producing changes and reducing heroin problems for this society.

Finally, decriminalization is only one option among a host of alternatives to present drug prohibition. Other available approaches might involve: over-the-counter regulation, drug maintenance and long-term treatment, a public health model, or a pure food and drug model. This article has focused on decriminalization as a vehicle for beginning to rethink current drug policy in America. As has been suggested, decriminalization has the potential to positively change some problems with drug use, but will undoubtedly also create new ones and fail to do anything about others.

Decriminalization offers a relatively imperfect policy and not a magical solution. In order to formulate an improved policy toward drugs much more discussion, experimentation, and research is necessary. Thus, we must move beyond the recognition that present policy is a dismal failure and move to the consideration, critical evaluation and eventual implementation of other options. What this discussion has emphasized is that the user and society, directly and indirectly, bear the brunt of present policy failures. Decriminalization would be a large step toward recognizing and addressing this situation. We cannot and must not simply accept the status quo.

References

Akers, Ronald L., and Richard Hawkins. 1975. *Law and Control in Society.* Englewood Cliffs, N.J.: Prentice-Hall.

Ball, John C., Lawrence Rosen, John A. Flueck, and David N. Nurco. 1982. "Lifetime Criminality of Heroin Addicts in the United States." *Journal of Drug Issues,* Summer 1982: 225–38.

Becker, Howard S. 1966. *Outsiders: Studies in the Sociology of Deviance.* New York: The Free Press.

———. 1967. "History, Culture and Subjective Experience." *Journal of Health and Social Behavior* 8: 163–76.

Brecher, Edward M., and the Editors of Consumer Reports. 1972. *Licit and Illicit Drugs.* Boston: Little, Brown and Co.

Bonnie, Richard J., and Charles H. Whitebread II. 1974. *The Marihuana Conviction: A History of Prohibition of Marihuana in the United States.* Charlottesville, VA: University of Virginia Press.

Cavan, Sherri. 1966. *Liquor License: An Ethnography of Bar Behavior.* Chicago: Aldine Publishing Co.

Chesler, Phyllis. 1972. *Women in Madness.* New York: Avon Books.

Duster, Troy. 1970. *The Legislation of Morality: Law, Drugs and Moral Judgment.* New York: The Free Press.

Goode, Erich. 1972. *The Drug Phenomenon: Social Aspects of Drug Taking.* New York: Newsday. Inc.

———. 1984. *Drugs in American Society* (2nd edition). New York: Alfred A. Knopf.

Graeven, David B., Jeffrey G. Sharp, and Stephen Glatt. 1981. "Acute Effects of Phencyclidine (PCP) on Chronic and Recreational Users." *Journal of Drug and Alcohol Abuse* 8: 39–50.

Graham, James. 1972. "Amphetamine Politics on Capitol Hill." *Transaction* 9: 14–22, 53.

Gusfield, Joseph R. 1963. *Symbolic Crusade: Status Politics and the American Temperance Movement.* Champaign, Ill: University of Illinois Press.

Hellman, A. D. 1975. *Laws Against Marijuana.* Champaign, Ill.: University of Illinois Press.

Heimer, John. 1975. *Drugs and Minority Oppression.* New York: Seabury Press.

Hughes, Richard, and Robert Brewin. 1979. *The Tranquilizing of America: Pill Popping and the American Way of Life.* New York: Warner Books.

Kelleher, Maureen E., Bruce K. Mac Murray, and Thomas M. Shapiro. 1983. *Drugs and Society: A Critical Reader.* Dubuque, Iowa: Kendall-Hunt Publishing.

Lemert, Edwin. 1966. *Social Pathology: A Systematic Approach to the Theory of Sociopathic Behavior.* New York: McGraw-Hill Book Co.

Maloff, Deborah. 1981. "A Review of the Effects of the Decriminalization of Marijuana." *Contemporary Drug Problems* 10: 307–22.

MacAndrew, Craig, and Robert B. Edgerton. 1969. *Drunken Comportment: A Social Explanation.* Hawthorne, N.Y.: Aldine Publishing Co.

Merton, Robert. 1968. *Social Theory and Social Structure.* New York: Macmillan Publishing Co.

Meyers, Eric. 1980. "American Heroin Policy: Some Alternatives." In *The Facts About Drug Abuse* (by The Drug Abuse Council). New York: The Free Press.

Morris, Norvil, and Gordon Hawkins. 1969. *The Honest Politician's Guide to Crime Control.* Chicago: University of Chicago Press.

Musto, David F. 1973. *The American Disease.* New Haven, Yale University Press.

Petersen, Robert C. 1981. "Decriminalization of Marijuana: A Brief Overview of Research-Relevant Policy Issues." *Contemporary Drug Problems* 10: 265–76.

Ray, Marsh. 1961. "Abstinence Cycles and Heroin Addicts." *Social Problems* 9: 132–40.

Retting, Richard, Manual J. Torres, and Gerald R. Garrett. 1977. *Manny: A Criminal-Addict's Story.* Boston: Houghton-Mifflin Co.

Rubin, Vera, and Lambros Comitas. 1976. *Ganja in Jamaica: The Effects of Marijuana Use.* Garden City, N.Y.: Anchor Press/Doubleday.

Ryan, William. 1971. *Blaming the Victim.* New York: Vintage Books.

Salerno, Ralph. 1979. "Organized Crime and Justice, Beyond 1984." In *Crime and Justice in America: Critical Issues for the Future,* edited by John T. O'Brien and Marvin Marcus. New York: Pergamon Press.

Schur, Edwin M. 1965. *Crimes Without Victims: Deviant Behavior and Public Policy.* Englewood Cliffs, N.J.: Prentice-Hall.

Silverman, Milton, Philip R. Lee, and Mia Lydecker. 1981. *Pills and the Public Purse.* Berkeley, CA: University of California Press.

Skolnick, Jerome. 1969. *Justice Without Trial.* New York: John Wiley and Sons, Inc.

Szasz, Thomas S. 1972. "The Ethics of Addition." *Harper's Magazine.* April: 74–79.

Trebach, Arnold S. 1982. *The Heroin Solution.* New Haven: Yale University Press.

Trice, Harrison, and Paul Roman. 1970. "Delabeling. Relabeling and Alcoholics Anonymous." *Social Problems* 17: 536–48.

Wilson, James Q. 1975. *Thinking About Crime.* New York: Basic Books.

Zinberg, Norman E., and Wayne M. Harding, 1979. "Control and Intoxicant Use: A Theoretical and Practical Overview." *Journal of Drug Issues,* Spring: 121–43.

Drug Issues in the Future

The history of societal attitudes toward drugs in America can be tracked in part through legislative action. This action is primarily characterized by a criminal justice approach which has either outlawed or attempted to contain certain types of drug use.

For example, The Harrison Narcotics Act (1914) was primarily a labeling and registration act which restricted the distribution of narcotic drugs only to physicians and pharmacists. Prior to that time, access to opium derivatives was not restricted in any formal way. Beginning with the passage of this Act, distributors had to be registered with the Bureau of the Treasury.

The passage of the Harrison Tax Act was quickly followed by the passage of Prohibition (1919–33). Prohibition was an attempt to control the use of alcohol by immigrant groups new to the United States, particularly the Irish and Germans. The "old guard", in this case primarily native-born, rural, Protestant Americans, used Prohibition as an attempt to stem the inevitable tide of industrialization and urbanization and the resulting change in social values and attitudes. The symbolic value of Prohibition was so significant that it resulted in the ratification of a constitutional amendment.

The Marijuana Tax Act (1937) was an explicit attempt to generally control the use of marijuana and, at least partially, to also control use of marijuana by migrant laborers in the Southwest, specifically Mexicans. This act was passed during the Depression and was one type of response to shortages in the labor market. In the Southwest, Mexicans were viewed as taking farm jobs that should go to Americans. Passage of this Act was a way to put an official *deviant* stamp on marijuana users as well as a way to legitimize formal bureaucratic groups as agents for controlling drug use.

A more recent piece of legislation, the Comprehensive Drug Abuse Prevention and Control Act (1970) was an attempt to establish a medical model as a guide for evaluating a drug's legal and social status by assessing its medical potential and utility against "side effects" and potential risks for abuse.

Such legislation reflects the contradictions and confusion surrounding the appropriate response to drug use in America and illustrates how models for response are imposed, often ineffectually, by such legislative action. This legislation also reflects the power of special interest groups to shape a national response to drug use based on their own particular agenda. National level legislative activity is not the only method by which attitudes and control over the use of drugs is shaped. The text has also illustrated a number of other vehicles including advertising, selective law enforcement, social movements and religion—but legislation does illustrate some of the inconsistencies and struggles that have been played out in America's response to drugs.

No drug is completely risk free, no drug is safe for everyone. Judgments, even scientific judgments, are not objective decisions reached in a social vacuum. At the very least, it is naive to believe that somehow we can manage to legalize only the "good" drugs and effectively prohibit only the "bad" drugs. Nonetheless, such judgments are attempted. Someone ultimately decides what kinds of risks are acceptable for what kinds of gains. As sociologists, we are concerned about the criteria that guide these decisions and the "special interest baggage" that decisionmakers carry with them.

The Drug Puzzle

Some drugs with high risk levels and minimal benefits are legal in the United States while others that have comparatively safe risk levels are illegal. What, then, accounts for a drug's legal and social status when that status is inconsistent with the scientific data?

The political power of the drug industry plays a significant role in determining which drugs get on the market and how widely they are used or misused. This power is true for social drugs—witness how the industry protects the tobacco and alcohol market—as well as for medicinal ones. The pharmaceutical industry spends about 20 cents of each sales dollar promoting drugs, while only 8 cents is spent on research. Furthermore, most of this research is conducted to improve upon moneymaking drugs—as evidenced by the creation of the "me-too" drugs—already on the market. In contrast, companies currently receive Federal tax subsidies to research and/or produce "orphan" drugs, that is, drugs needed by small numbers of people with rare diseases. Without this Federal help, following usual market criteria, drug companies would not make these needed drugs available.

Drugs banned in the U.S. by the Food and Drug Administration because they are too dangerous are often "dumped" onto unsuspecting international consumers, usually in the Third World. Drug companies also take advantage of weak regulatory structures to promote drug use for a wide variety of ailments while minimizing restrictions and counterindications. For example, Winstrol, restricted in the U.S. because it can cause irreversible sex changes in young children, is marketed in some countries as an appetite stimulant. Strict controls need to be implemented to severely limit or prohibit such corporate procedures.

A drug's status may also be the symbolic outcome of social conflicts between racial, ethnic, age or status groups. For example, cocaine was originally outlawed because it was seen as a way to exert social control over blacks. Similarly, the first opium laws were part of a racist campaign aimed at Chinese immigrants. Another example is the passage of anti-marijuana legislation in the Southwest, which was seen as a way to force Mexican-Americans to return to Mexico during the Depression. A drug's social and legal status can depend more upon the profile of its potential users than a scientific determination.

Conflicting conceptions of morality can become battlegrounds for status and prestige in a heterogeneous society. The label of acceptability placed on a specific drug is a means to reconfirm or challenge the status quo. These social definitions reflect a group's ability to translate its specific customs into broader societal values. During Prohibition the battle was not over alcohol but over whose values and cultural traditions would dominate in America. Prohibition was repealed during the Depression when battlegrounds shifted from value domination to economic survival. We are currently seeing a similar battle emerge over tobacco use.

The 1980s and Beyond

There are a number of struggles emerging over drug patterns that are likely to dominate the near future. Probably the most obvious and critical of these is the need for a social policy response to heroin that includes both treatment and enforcement components. Heroin historically and co-\ine more recently have played a critical role in the deterioration of urban life in America. For ·oin the link to AIDS has finally caused policy-makers to understand the vast (and now clearly ·l) ripple-effect of a drug's pattern of use. Better conceived methodone clinics and needle ex-·e programs will only begin to make a dent in this potentially explosive problem. Drug and sex education, job skills and more importantly job opportunities are also needed. Effective mobilization to this crisis however, is quickly being mired in a morality play over needle programs and treatment facilities.

For the inner city, "crack" has become the glue that is bonding together a new elaborate crime structure, beginning with gangs who terrorize city streets. The huge profits, the guns and the deaths associated with "crack", in many ways mimic the rum-running days of Prohibition. The current policy of benign neglect is a death sentence borne by many urban men, women and children.

On a more sanguine note, our lives in the everyday workplace may be permanently altered if the push for urine analysis gains legitimacy as an appropriate response to drug use. At the present time some high school districts, college sports teams and certain high risk occupations see urine analysis as an effective mechanism for screening out potential "problems". But such drug testing also raises serious civil liberties issues and is an improbable panacea to the pervasive problem of drug use in our society. While such testing might keep a given high school senior from playing in the "big game", it is questionable whether corporate America is ready to provide appropriate treatment services for all employees found *guilty* of drug use.

On the international front, besides concern with drug dumping, Americans have also become more aware of the "blind eye" used by some elements in our government toward international trafficking in drugs. Our domestic policy of "just say no" to drugs is certainly at odds with our support of foreign governments and officials deeply implicated in the trafficking of cocaine and heroin. The official "blind eye" exists because these governments are our "allies" and serve our professed international security interests.

These few examples point out that there are a number of lessons for policy consideration. One conclusion from the readings of this text points to the wisdom of a long-range comprehensive examination of all drugs. Drug problems cannot be isolated to those drugs that are currently illegal. One long-term goal of such an evaluation should be a more consistent national drug policy. To illustrate this point, how can society expect observance of marijuana laws when alcohol is widely available? Such consistency in values and policy may be impossible to attain because it requires the rethinking of the legal and social acceptance of many drugs.

Policy tools available to work toward these goals range from education and research, to taxes, law enforcement, distribution, and FTC and FCC advertising regulations to name but a few. In all likelihood, dramatic societal change will have to include a radical restructuring of the drug industry, or at least a major shift in the industry-doctor-government-consumer balance. Such a restructuring, together with a reformulated criminal justice response to drug use is a mamouth task. The vision, commitment and support necessary for this undertaking currently does not exist in this country.

Immediate Remedies

If long-term answers concerning drug values and the drug industry are too utopian or impractical, and if alternative policies are too morally abhorrent or politically unrealistic, short-term palliatives are still possible. Research, education, and treatment are examples of areas where increased commitments of time and resources can produce more knowledge, a better informed population and the availability of better treatment programs. Resources for these areas shift in the political winds—perhaps the spectre of AIDS will add a critical component to one aspect of this discussion.

Conclusion

This reader has introduced you to a variety of issues related to the use of drugs in America. Our primary goal has been to present a sociological perspective. As a result, we have introduced you to the worlds of crime and social deviance, social movements and social conflicts, law making and enforcement, the role of the mass media, and big business among others.

We have introduced authors who illustrate sociological concepts such as *symbolic crusade, medicalization of deviance, instrumental and symbolic functions of law,* and *set and setting.* We hope that you have found these sociological "hooks" helpful in understanding some of the issues discussed in this reader and encourage you to use them in order to better understand other social issues and problems in society.